# VIOLENT NON-STATE ACTORS
# IN WORLD POLITICS

# Violent Non-State Actors in World Politics

*Edited by*
Klejda Mulaj

Columbia University Press
New York

Columbia University Press
*Publishers Since 1893*
New York    Chichester, West Sussex
Copyright © Gulf Research Centre, 2010
All rights reserved
Printed in India

Library of Congress Cataloging-in-Publication Data

Violent non-state actors in world politics / edited by Klejda Mulaj.
    p. cm.
  ISBN 978-0-231-70120-4 (alk. paper)
  1. Political violence.  2. Non-state actors (International relations)  3. Terrorism.
  I. Mulaj, Kledja, 1969–

  JC328.6.V585 2009
  327.1'17—dc22

                        2009033081

References to Internet Web sites (URLs) were accurate at the time of writing.
Neither the author nor Columbia University Press is responsible for URLs
that may have expired or changed since the manuscript was prepared.

# Contents

CONTENTS

# Foreword

That states are not the only preponderant actors in world politics is nowadays a foregone conclusion. The intensification of globalization and the empowerment of non-governmental organizations (NGOs)—as well as individuals —have broadened the range of actors which impact—daily—on the events of international and national politics. This book grapples with a specific category within the myriad of non-state actors, namely the violent ones. Its inception dates back to the summer of 2006 when Hizbullah's rocket attacks on Jewish towns bordering Lebanon and the ensuing Israeli military response threatened to drag the region into a prolonged and deadly war. This unfortunate event provided the spark of the idea that a volume treating contemporary violent non-state actors (VNSAs) is much needed given that our century is being marked by dreadful attacks carried out by organized armed groups with worrying intensity and geographical reach. We are all witnesses of recent terrible terrorist attacks in New York and the Pentagon (2001), Istanbul (2003), Riyadh (2003, 2004), Madrid (2004), London (2005), Amman (2005), Bali (2005), Mumbai (2008) and Jakarta (2003, 2009); having fresh memories also of violent engagements of IRA, ETA, KLA, SPLA/M and other armed groups which justify their actions as liberation/freedom-seeking movements. In addition, we cannot help but notice the increasing number of private security firms currently used by states and NGOs alike to mitigate ongoing conflicts and to support peacekeeping efforts and humanitarian relief operations, especially in Africa and the Middle East.

The category of violent non-state actors is therefore very broad. Despite similarities between many armed groups, a solid understanding of any one of them requires an in-depth analysis of the specific environment, and political and socio-economic circumstances in which a given violent actor emerges, grows, adapts, falls or otherwise transforms itself into a political actor following a peace deal. Considering the impact and influence of a wide range of armed groups on the national and international security environment, this volume explores the relationships between VNSAs and the state and the ways in which the use of violence can alter such relationships, which impacts in turn on definitions of legitimacy in a given situation and the justification of the use of force itself.

Each of the contributors knows their subject intimately, providing a lucid and comprehensive analysis which does not fail to convey the complexity of the issues involved. Because violent non-state actors of many sorts are likely to continue impacting on the security environment of the twenty-first century, this volume offers an important contribution which will be relevant for a considerable time.

Abdulaziz O. Sager
Chairman
Gulf Research Centre
Dubai
U.A.E.

# Acknowledgements

Working on this collaborative project has been a unique learning experience, through which I have come across many new ideas and new people. The wide scope of our research topic provided a rare opportunity to engage—at once—with some of the most challenging cases of contemporary conflict involving violent non-state actors in various regions of the world. The solid analysis supplied by our contributors offers a range of ideas and interpretations which—as a scholar of conflict analysis—I found enlightening and stimulating. I owe a great debt of gratitude to the contributors in this volume for their dedicated and professional work.

I am also very grateful to the Gulf Research Centre in Dubai for lending their professional and financial assistance. The encouragement of Abdulaziz Sager and Christian Koch has been essential to overcome some stumbling blocks along the way.

At the University of Exeter, where this project was concluded, I have benefitted from the support and encouragement of Tim Niblock, Gerd Nonneman, Gareth Stansfield, and Rob Gleave. I am indebted to them for facilitating my work in completing this project.

Last but not least, I wish to express my gratitude to Michael Dwyer for taking an interest in this book and steering it to publication with care and professionalism.

Klejda Mulaj
University of Exeter
United Kingdom

# About the Contributors

**Kwesi Aning** currently serves as Head of the Conflict Prevention Management and Resolution Department (CPMRD) at the Kofi Annan International Peacekeeping Training Centre (KAIPTC) in Accra, Ghana. He writes reviews for several scholarly journals and serves on diverse boards. Dr. Aning holds a doctorate from the University of Copenhagen, Denmark, and has taught in several universities in Europe and Africa. His primary research interests deal with African security issues broadly defined, comparative politics, terrorism and conflict. His articles have recently appeared in *Review of African Political Economy*, *Journal of Contemporary African Studies*, *Journal of Asian and African Studies*, *African Security Review*, and *Encyclopedia of African History*.

**Omar Ashour** is Lecturer in Politics at the Institute of Arab and Islamic Studies, University of Exeter, United Kingdom. His research focuses on Islamist movements, conflict resolution, international security, and democratization. Dr Ashour has written extensively on the subject of Islamist radicalization and de-radicalization in the Middle East and Central Asia. He is the author of *The Deradicalization of Jihadists: Transforming Armed Islamist Movements*, (Routledge, 2009). Dr Ashour's work has appeared in *The Middle East Journal*, *Studies in Conflict and Terrorism*, *Journal of Conflict Studies*, *Canadian Journal of Political Science*, *McGill Journal of Middle Eastern Studies*, *Middle East Institute's Policy Papers*, among other academic and policy outlets.

**Alyson Bailes** spent more than thirty years in the British Diplomatic Service, including several security-policy assignments and academic sabbaticals, culminating in the Ambassador's post at Helsinki. She left the service in 2002 for a five-year stint as Director of the Stockholm International Peace Research Institute, SIPRI. In 2007 she moved to the University of Iceland in Reykjavik to teach security studies. She currently researches mainly on topics of European and Nordic defence, business roles and other non-state actors in security.

**Morten Bøås** is a Senior Researcher at Fafo—Institute for Applied International Studies, Oslo. He has published extensively on African politics and development. Bøås' latest book is *African Guerrillas: Raging against the Machine* (Lynne Rienner, 2007; edited with Kevin Dunn), and his articles have been published in journals such as *Journal of Modern African Studies*, *Journal of Contemporary African Studies*, *Global Governance* and *Third World Quarterly*.

**Judith Palmer Harik** is the author of *Hezbollah: The Changing Face of Terrorism* (I.B. Tauris, 2004) and numerous other publications on the Party of God and Lebanese politics. As professor of political science at the American University of Beirut from 1981 until 2003 when she joined Matn University as its president, Harik has had a front row seat on events taking place in Lebanon and is today considered one of the foremost experts on Hezbollah.

**Eric Herring** is Reader in International Politics at the University of Bristol, United Kingdom. His books include: *Iraq in Fragments: The Occupation and its Legacy* (Hurst / Columbia University Press, 2006, co-authored with Glen Rangwala); *The Arms Dynamic in World Politics* (Lynne Rienner, 1998, co-authored with Barry Buzan); and *Danger and Opportunity: Explaining International Crisis Outcomes* (Manchester University Press, 1995). He has published articles in journals such as *Review of International Studies*, *Millennium*, *Critical Studies on Terrorism*, *International Journal of Human Rights*, *Journal of Strategic Studies*, and *Third World Quarterly*.

**Syed Rifaat Hussain** is Professor and Chairman of the Department of Defence and Strategic Studies at Quaid-i-Azam University in Islamabad, Pakistan. Previously he was Executive Director of the Regional Centre for Strategic Studies (RCSS), Colombo, Sri Lanka (2005–2008). Dr Hussain was a visiting Professor of Political Science at Stanford University during the 2002–2003 academic year. He holds a PhD in international studies from University of Denver, Colorado, USA, and has published widely on Asian security issues.

**Hassanein Tawfik Ibrahim** is Professor of Political Science at Cairo University and Zayed University. His research interests include civil society, democratization and Islamic movements in the Arab world. Dr. Ibrahim received the Egyptian State Award in political science in 2006/2007 for his book *New Trends in Studying Arab Political Systems* (Centre for Arab Unity Studies, 2005). He is author of ten other books published in Egypt, Lebanon, and U.A.E. which explore violence in the Arab political systems; the state, civil society and development in Egypt; and political reform as well as the role of civil society in the GCC States.

**Assis Malaquias** is Professor of Defense Economics at the National Defense University in Washington, DC. His areas of specialization include International Relations, International Security, International Political Economy, and African Politics. Dr. Malaquias' current research focuses on the political economy security in central and southern Africa. His most recent publications include *Rebels and Robbers: Violence in Post-Colonial Angola* (Nordic Africa Institute, 2006); 'Angola: How to Lose a Guerrilla War,' in Morten Bøås and Kevin Dunn, eds, *African Guerrillas: Raging Against the Machine* (Lynne Rienner, 2007); 'Thirsty Powers: The United States, China and Africa's Energy Resources,' in Manuela Franco, ed., *Portugal, os Estados Unidos e a Africa Austral* (Instituto Portugues de Relacoes Internacionais, 2006).

**Ken Menkhaus** is professor of Political Science at Davidson College, where he has taught since 1991. He specializes on the Horn of Africa, focusing primarily on development, conflict analysis, peacebuilding, and political Islam. He has published over 50 articles and chapters on Somalia and the Horn of Africa, including the monograph *Somalia: State Collapse and the Threat of Terrorism* (Routledge, 2004) and 'Governance without Government in Somalia' in *International Security* (2007).

**Mohammad-Mahmoud Ould Mohamedou** is a former Associate Director of the Harvard Program on Humanitarian Policy and Conflict Research, and previously served as Research Director with the International Council on Human Rights Policy, based in Geneva, where he helped found and direct the research and policy program. He was a post-doctoral Scholar-in-Residence at the Center for Middle Eastern Studies at Harvard University, and Research Associate at the Ralph Bunche Institute on the United Nations in New York. He is the author of *Iraq and the Second Gulf War: State-Building and Regime Security* (Austin & Winfield, 2001); *Contre-Croisade: Origines et Conséquences du 11 Septembre* (L'Harmattan, 2004); and *Understanding Al Qaeda: The*

*Transformation of Warfare* (Pluto, 2007). He is currently the Foreign Minister of Mauritania.

**Klejda Mulaj** is Lecturer in International Relations and Leverhulme Fellow in Ethno-National Politics at the University of Exeter, United Kingdom. A specialist in conflict and security studies she previously taught at the London School of Economics and Political Sciences (LSE) and Goldsmiths College both of the University of London, as well as at the University of Malta. She is author of *Politics of Ethnic Cleansing: Nation-State Building and Provision of In/Security in Twentieth Century Balkans* (Lexington Books, 2008) and a contributor to *Nationalism and Ethnic Politics, Nationalities Papers, Security Dialogue, International Migration*, and *Studies in Conflict and Terrorism*.

**Daniel Nord** is the Deputy Director at the Stockholm International Peace Research Institute, SIPRI. Before joining SIPRI in 2005, Mr Nord worked at the Secretariat of the Weapons of Mass Destruction Commission (WMDC), an international commission headed by Dr Hans Blix. He has also worked at the Swedish Ministry for Foreign Affairs on issues related to disarmament and non-proliferation as well as UN sanctions, and with the Swedish National Defence College and the Swedish Red Cross as legal adviser and lecturer in international law.

**William Reno** is Associate Professor of Political Science at Northwestern University where he is the Director of Graduate Studies for his department. He is the author of *Corruption and State Politics in Sierra Leone* (Cambridge University Press, 1995) and *Warlord Politics and African States* (Lynne Rienner, 1999). His research focuses on the politics of conflict and on the organization and behaviour of armed groups in sub-Saharan Africa. He is currently completing a volume entitled *The Evolution of Warfare in Independent Africa* that describes and analyzes the causes and consequences of the changing nature of conflict on the continent.

**Nazih Richani** is Associate Professor and Director of Latin American Studies Program at Kean University. Author of several academic books and articles including *Dilemmas of Democracy in Sectarian Societies: The case of the PSP in Lebanon* (Palgrave, 1998); and *Systems of Violence: The Political Economy of War and Peace in Colombia* (State University of New York Press, 2002). He is a recipient of several awards including six Fulbright grants, two in the traditional Scholar program and four as Senior Specialist. Currently he is working on two manuscripts; one entitled *The Political Economy of Crime in Latin America* and another *Revisiting the State Making Process in Colombia*.

**Amin Saikal** is Professor of Political Science and Director of the Centre for Arab and Islamic Studies (the Middle East and Central Asia) at the Australian National University. His latest books include *The Rise and Fall of the Shah: Iran—from autocracy to religious rule* (Princeton University Press, 2009); *Modern Afghanistan: A History of Struggle and Survival* (I.B. Tauris, 2006); *Islam and the West: Conflict or Cooperation?* (Palgrave/Macmillan, 2003).

**Ignacio Sánchez-Cuenca** is the Research Director of the Centre for Advanced Study in the Social Sciences of the Juan March Institute (Madrid) and Associate Professor of Sociology at Complutense University (Madrid). He has held positions at Pompeu Fabra University (Barcelona) and University of Salamanca. He was the Rice Visiting Associate Professor at Yale University in 2004/05. His research areas are terrorism and comparative politics. Professor Sánchez-Cuenca is author of two books on ETA (in Spanish). His latest articles have appeared in *Journal of Peace Research, Annual Review of Political Science*, and *Terrorism and Political Violence*.

**P.W. Singer** is Director of the 21st Century Defense Initiative at Brookings, a public policy research institute in Washington, DC. He is the author of *Corporate Warriors: The Rise of the Privatized Military Industry* (Cornell University Press 2003; Iraq update 2007), *Children at War* (Pantheon, 2005), and *Wired for War: The Robotics Revolution and Conflict in the 21st Century* (Penguin, 2009). Dr Singer has previously worked for Harvard University, the International Peace Academy, and the US Department of Defense.

**Jonathan Tonge** is Professor of Politics at the School of Politics and Communication Studies at the University of Liverpool and President of the Political Studies Association of the United Kingdom. Recent books include *Irish Protestant Identities* (Manchester University Press, 2008, eds, with Mervyn Busteed and Frank Neal); *Northern Ireland* (Polity, 2006); *The New Northern Irish Politics* (Palgrave, 2005); *Sinn Fein and the SDLP* (Hurst/O'Brien 2005, with Gerard Murray); and *Britain Decides: the UK General Election 2005* (Palgrave 2005, eds. with Andrew Geddes). Recent articles include items in *Political Psychology, Political Studies, Electoral Studies, Party Politics* and *Terrorism and Political Violence*.

# List of Acronyms

| | |
|---|---|
| AAK | Aleanca për Ardhmërinë e Kosovës (Alliance for the Future of Kosovo) |
| ABSP | Arab Ba'th Socialist Party |
| ACRM | Anti-Corruption Revolutionary Movement |
| ACTC | All Ceylon Tamil Congress |
| AFL | Armed Forces of Liberia |
| AFRC | Armed Forces Revolutionary Council |
| AIS | Armée Islamique du Salut (Islamic Salvation Front) |
| ALCOP | All Liberian Coalition |
| AMIS | African Union Mission in Sudan |
| ANANGOLA | Associação dos Naturais de Angola (Association of Natives of Angola) |
| ANC | African National Congress |
| APC | All People's Congress |
| APM | Anti Personnel Mines |
| APP | All People's Party |
| AQI | Al Qaeda in Iraq |
| ARPCT | Alliance for the Restoration of Peace and Counter-Terrorism |
| ARS | Alliance for the Re-Liberation of Somalia |
| ASEAN | Association of Southeast Asian Nations |
| ATT | Arms Trade Treaty |
| AU | African Union |
| AUC | Autodefensas Unidas de Colombia (United Defence Forces of Colombia) |

| | |
|---|---|
| BAC | Basque Autonomous Community |
| BBC | British Broadcasting Corporation |
| CAA | Autonomous Anticapitalist Commandos (a faction of ETApm) |
| CCW | Convention on Conventional Weapons |
| CENTCOM | Central Command |
| CEO | Chief Executive Officer |
| CFA | Cease-fire Agreement |
| CIA | Central Intelligence Agency |
| CIC | Council of Islamic Courts |
| CIRA | Continuity Irish Republican Army |
| CNN | Cable News Network |
| CNT | Concorde nationale tchadienne (Chadian National Agreeement) |
| CPA | Comprehensive Peace Agreement (Chapters 12, 15, 17) |
| CPA | Coalition Provisional Authority (Chapter 18) |
| DCAF | Democratic Control of Armed Forces |
| DDR | Disarmament, Demobilization and Reintegration |
| DFLP | Democratic Front for the Liberation of Palestine |
| DIF | Darfur Independence Front |
| DST | Direction de la Surveillance du Territoire (Directorate of Territorial Surveillance) |
| DUP | Democratic Unionist Party |
| EAAQ | East African al Qaeda |
| EAJ | Euzko Alderdi Jeltzalea (Basque Nationalist Party) |
| ECOMOG | ECOWAS Ceasefire Monitoring Group |
| ECOWAS | Economic Community of West African States |
| EDF | Equatoria Defence Forces |
| EEC | European Economic Community |
| ELN | Ejercito de Liberacion Nacional (National Liberation Army of Columbia) |
| ELO | Eelam Liberation Organization |
| ENDF | Ethiopian National Defence Forces |
| EPRLF | Eelam People's Revolutionary Front |

| | |
|---|---|
| EROS | Eelam Revolutionary Organization |
| EU | European Union |
| EUFOR TCHAD / RCA | European Force Chad/Central African Republic |
| ETA | Euskadi ta Askatasuna (Basque Fatherland and Liberty party) |
| ETAm | military ETA |
| ETApm | political-military ETA |
| FAA | Forças Armadas de Angola (Armed Forces of Angola) |
| FARC | Fuerzas Armadas Revolucionarias de Colombia (Revolutionary Armed Forces of Colombia) |
| FBC | Fourah Bay College |
| FIG | Fighting Islamic Group |
| FIS | Front Islamique du Salut (Islamist Salvation Front) |
| FLGO | Forces de Libération du Grand Ouest (Liberation front of the Great West) |
| FLN | National Liberation Front |
| FNLA | Frente Nacional de Libertação de Angola (National Front for the Liberation of Angola) |
| FNLC | Front Nationale pour la Liberation du Congo (National Front for the Liberation of Congo) |
| FP | Federal Party |
| FPI | Front Populaire Ivorien (Ivorian Popular Front) |
| FUCD | Front Uni pour le Changement Démocratique (United Front for Democratic Change) |
| GAL | Antiterroristas de Liberación (Antiterrorist Liberation Groups) |
| GAO | Government Accountability Office |
| GDP | Gross Domestic Product |
| GIA | Groupe Islamique Armé (The Armed Islamic Group) |
| GoL | Government of Liberia |
| GPLF | People's Liberation Front |
| GRAE | Governo Revolucionário de Angola no Exilio (Angola's Revolutionary Government in Exile) |
| GRAPO | Antifascist First of October Revolutionary Group |

| | |
|---|---|
| GSPC | Groupe Salafiste pour la Prédication et le Combat (Salafist Group for Preaching and Combat) |
| HCP | Hamas Cabinet Platform |
| HSZs | High Security Zones |
| ICC | International Criminal Court |
| ICRC | International Committee of the Red Cross |
| ICTY | International Criminal Tribunal for the former Yugoslavia |
| ICU | Islamic Courts Union |
| IDF | Israeli Defence Forces |
| IDPs | Internally Displaced Persons |
| IEDs | Improvised Explosive Devices |
| IG | Islamic Group |
| IGAD | Intergovernmental Authority on Development |
| IHL | International Humanitarian Law |
| IPKF | Indian Peacekeeping Forces |
| IRA | Irish Republican Army |
| IRP | Islamic Renaissance Party |
| ISAF | International Security Assistance Force |
| ISCI | Islamic Supreme Council of Iraq |
| ISGA | Interim Self-Governing Authority |
| ISI | Islamic State of Iraq (Chapter 9) |
| ISI | Pakistan's Military Intelligence (Chapter 11) |
| ISPA | Indo-Sri Lanka Peace Agreement |
| JEM | Justice and Equality Movement |
| JVA | Jubba Valley Authority |
| JVP | Janatha Vimukti Peramuna (People's Liberation Front) |
| KAD | Kordofan Association for Development |
| KAR | Kurdish Autonomous Region |
| KAS | Koordinadora Abertzale Sozialista (Patriotic Socialist Coordination) |
| KBR | Kellogg Brown and Root |
| KDP | Kurdistan Democratic Party |
| KFOR | Kosovo Force |
| KLA | Kosovo Liberation Army |
| KPC | Kosovo Protection Corps |
| KPS | Kosovo Police Service |

| | |
|---|---|
| KRG | Kurdish Regional Government |
| KSF | Kosovo Security Force |
| LDF | Lofa Defence Force |
| LDK | Lidhja Demokratike e Kosovës (Democratic League of Kosovo) |
| LFF | Liberian Frontier Force |
| LNA | Liga Nacional Africana (African National League) |
| LOGCAP | Logistics Civilian Augmentation Program |
| LPC | Liberian Peace Council |
| LPK | Lëvizja Popullore e Kosovës (Popular Movement for Kosovo) |
| LPRK | Lëvizja Popullore për Republikën e Kosovës (Popular Movement for the Republic of Kosovo) |
| LRSHJ | Movement for the National Liberation of Kosovo |
| LTTE | Liberation Tigers of Tamil Eelam |
| LURD | Liberians United for Reconciliation and Democracy |
| MAP | Mass Awareness and Participation |
| MB | Muslim Brothers |
| MBP | Muslim Brothers in Palestine |
| MEJA | Military Extra-territorial Jurisdiction Act |
| MIGs | Islamic Militant Groups |
| MINURCAT | Mission des Nations Unies en République Centrafricaine et au Tchad (United Nations Mission to the Central African Republic and Chad) |
| MNLK | Movement for the National Liberation of Kosovo |
| MODEL | Movement for Democracy in Liberia |
| MONUC | Mission de l'Organisation des Nations Unies en République démocratique du Congo (United Nations Organization Mission to the Democratic Republic of the Congo) |
| MPCI | Mouvement Patriotique de la Côte d'Ivoire (The Ivory Coast Patriotic Movement) |

| | |
|---|---|
| MPIGO | Mouvement Populaire du Grand Ouest (The Ivorian Popular Movement of the Great West) |
| MPJ | Mouvement Pour la Justice et la Paix (Peace and Justice Movement) |
| MPLA | Movimento Popular para Libertação de Angola (Popular Movement for the Liberation of Angola) |
| NAR | Revolutionary Armed Groups |
| NATO | North Atlantic Treaty Organization |
| NCO | Non-Commissioned Officer |
| NCP | National Congress Party |
| NDA | National Democratic Alliance |
| NFZ | No Firing Zone |
| NGOs | Non-Governmental Organizations |
| NMRD | National Movement for Reform and Development |
| NPFL | National Patriotic Front of Liberia |
| NRC | National Reformation Council |
| NSAs | Non-State Actors |
| NTGL | National Transitional Government of Liberia |
| NUGP | National Unity Government Program |
| OAU | Organization of African Unity |
| OLF | Oromo Liberation Front |
| PA | Palestinian Authority |
| PANAFU | Pan-Africa Union |
| PCTV | Communist Party of the Basqueland |
| PDA | Partido Democrático de Angola (Democratic Party of Angola) |
| PDF | Popular Defense Forces |
| PDK | Partia Demokratike e Kosovës (Democratic Party of Kosovo) |
| PDPA | People's Democratic Party of Afghanistan |
| PEJAK | Kurdistan Free Life Party |
| PFLP | Popular Front for the Liberation of Palestine |
| PIRA | Provisional Irish Republican Army |
| PKK | Kurdish Workers Party |
| PLO | Palestinian Liberation Organization |
| PLOTE | People's Liberation Organization of Tamil Eelam |

| | |
|---|---|
| PMFs | Private Military Firms |
| POWs | Prisoners of War |
| PRC | People's Redemption Council |
| PRMSS | Patriotic Resistance Movement of South Sudan |
| PRTs | Provincial Reconstruction Teams |
| PSCs | Private Security Companies |
| PSI | Proliferation Security Initiative |
| PUK | Patriotic Union of Kurdistan |
| QB | al-Qassam Brigades |
| QBIO | al-Qassam Brigades Information Office |
| RAFD | Rassemblement des forces démocratiques (Rally of Democratic Forces) |
| RDFF | Revolutionary Democratic Forces Front |
| RDL | Rassemblement pour la démocratie et la Libertés (The Organization for Democracy and Liberty) |
| RFC | Rassemblement des forces pour le changement (Rally of Forces for Change) |
| RIRA | Real Irish Republican Army |
| RJF | Reform and Jihad Front |
| RUF | Revolutionary United Front |
| SA | Special Apparatus |
| SADF | South African Defense Force |
| SCIRI | Supreme Council for the Islamic Revolution in Iraq |
| SCUD | Socle pour le changement, l'unité et la démocratie (Platform for Change, Unity and Democracy) |
| SDLP | Social Democratic and Labour Party |
| SFDA | Sudan Federal Democratic Alliance |
| SHIK | Shërbimi Informativ i Kosovës (Information Service of Kosovo) |
| SIGIR | Special Inspector General for Iraq Reconstruction |
| SIPRI | Stockholm International Peace Research Institute |
| SLA | Sudan Liberation Army |
| SLAF | Sri Lanka Air Force |

| | |
|---|---|
| SLBA | Sierra Leone Bar Association |
| SLDFM | Sierra Leone Democratic Front/Movement |
| SLFP | Sri Lankan Freedom Party |
| SLM | Sudan Liberation Movement |
| SLMM | Sri Lanka Monitoring Mission |
| SLPP | Sierra Leone People's Party |
| SNA | Somali National Alliance |
| SNF | Somali National Front |
| SNM | Somali National Movement |
| SO | Special Organization |
| SOFA | Status of Forces Agreement |
| SPLA | Sudan People's Liberation Army |
| SPLM | Sudan People's Liberation Movement |
| SPM | Somali Patriotic Movement |
| SSDF | Somali Salvation Democratic Front |
| SSFF | South Sudan Freedom Front |
| SSIM | Southern Sudan Independence Movement |
| SSMA | Salah Shahade Military Academy |
| SSR | Security Sector Reform |
| SWAPO | South West Africa People's Organization |
| TELA | Tamil Eelam Liberation Army |
| TELO | Tamil Eelam Liberation Organization |
| TFG | Transitional Federal Government |
| TLO | Tamil Liberation Organization |
| TNT | Tamil New Tigers |
| TSL | Tamil Students League |
| TUF | Tamil United Front |
| TULF | Tamil United Liberation Front |
| TWP | True Whig Party |
| TYL | Tamil Youth League |
| UAE | United Arab Emirates |
| UCLAT | Unité de Coordination de la Lutte Antiterroriste (Anti-Terrorist Struggle Coordination Unit) |
| UCMJ | Uniform Code of Military Justice |
| UDR | Ulster Defence Regiment |
| UFDD | Union des forces pour le développement et la démocratie (Union of Forces for Development and Democracy) |

| | |
|---|---|
| UFDD-F | Union des forces pour le développement et la démocratie fondamentale (Union of Forces for Development and Fundamental Democracy) |
| UIA | Shi'a United Iraqi Alliance |
| ULIMO | United Liberian Movement for Democracy |
| UMAMID | Joint African Union / United Nations Hybrid Operation in Darfur |
| UN | United Nations |
| UNITA | União Nacional para Independência Total de Angola (National Union for the Total Independence of Angola) |
| UNMIK | United Nation's Mission in Kosovo |
| UNMIL | United Nation's Mission in Liberia |
| UNMIS | United Nations Mission in Sudan |
| UNMISET | United Nations Mission of Support in East Timor |
| UNOSOM | UN intervention mission in Somalia |
| UNP | United National Party |
| UNSC | United Nations Security Council |
| UNSCR | United Nations Security Council Resolution |
| UPA | União dos Povos de Angola (Union of the Peoples of Angola) |
| URFF | United Revolutionary Force Front |
| USAID | United States Agency for International Development |
| USC | United Somali Congress |
| USSR | Union of Soviet Socialist Republics |
| UUP | Ulster Unionist Party |
| VNSAs | Violent Non-State Actors |
| WMD | Weapons of Mass Destruction |
| WSB | West Side Boys |
| WTO | World Trade Organization |

1

# Introduction

## Violent Non-State Actors: Exploring Their State Relations, Legitimation, and Operationality

*Klejda Mulaj**

Violent non-state actors (VNSAs) are not a new phenomenon in world politics. The operations of some such actors already posed a threat to Western interests before the fateful day of 11 September 2001. Yet, although non-state actors—primarily economic—have received extensive coverage in political science literature, VNSAs have only recently received sustained interest amongst academic and policy circles.[1] Given that our era is being defined by a US-led war on terrorism, understanding violent non-state actors (some of

---

* For constructive comments on earlier drafts of this Chapter I am grateful to Yezid Sayigh, Christian Koch, Alyson Bailes, Gerd Nonneman, and the two anonymous reviewers for Hurst and Columbia University Press.

[1] A noticeable contribution is Troy S. Thomas, Stephen D. Kiser and William D. Casebeer, *Warlord Rising: Confronting Violent Non-State Actors*: Lanham, MD: Lexington Books/ Rowman & Littlefield, 2005. Starting from the premise that all VNSAs are bad—an assumption which is not endorsed unconditionally in the contributing chapters of the present volume—Thomas et al. have sought to offer a theory for defeating VNSAs. By contrast, the underlying assumption of the ensuing chapters is that whereas many violent non-state actors bear significant similarities, they are by no means uniform and hence it is best to analyze—and respond to—these actors on a case by case basis. The Daphné Josselin and William Wallace edited volume, *Non-State Actors in World Politics*, London: Palgrave, 2001, is another pioneering work which analyzes non-state actors—*mostly* non-violent.

1

which are targets of the said war) is crucial in order to ensure that sound policy responses are devised and implemented. Moreover, bearing in mind that in many cases (not least Afghanistan, Lebanon, Iraq, Somalia, and Sudan) violent non-state organizations conduct their activities in the context of state weakness, failure or fragmentation, it is necessary to explore the relations between these phenomena—state fragility, on the one hand, and operationality of VNSAs, on the other—in order to better understand the ways in which they impact upon each other, and comprehend strategies for dealing with their devastating effects.[2]

If operations of violent non-state actors are not new, their intensity is. In earlier, less interconnected eras the impact of VNSAs in distant lands could be isolated and kept apart from the developed world. Now, however, it is not only people living within the areas of VNSAs' conduct who are affected; the impact of their violence is felt across the globe both indirectly—in so far as knowledge of bloodshed can be virtually instant thanks to giant news networks like BBC, CNN, and Al-Jazeera—and directly, as demonstrated by the terrorist attacks such as those in New York, the Pentagon, Istanbul, Riyadh, Madrid, Amman, London, Bali, and most recently Mumbai.

Despite being small groups—and inferior to their adversaries in terms of equipment, training, and often doctrine—VNSAs are likely to continue, and even increase, their asymmetric operations with a view to achieving political objectives and influence. Because the security environment of the 21st century is set to be characterized by the influence and power of non-state armed groups, and because the latter are central to the understanding of regional and world politics, analysis of the nature of these actors ought to be taken more seriously. VNSAs' growing impact in world politics raises crucial questions for policy and academic circles alike: What are the conditions that produce and nurture VNSAs' activities? How does the state impact on the emergence of VNSAs? At what stage do non-state actors consider violence to be useful for their purposes? How does employment of violence alter the nature and purpose of relations between VNSAs and the state? Does the increasing operationality of violent non-state actors challenge the concept of legitimate use of

---

[2] This is not to suggest that the connection between VNSAs and weak states is all-encompassing. Sometimes violent non-state actors afflict 'strong' and rich states from the inside as in the cases of the IRA and ETA. Moreover, Al Qaeda has been able to recruit within *relatively* stable states like Saudi Arabia and Egypt, and on a smaller scale also in the West. Nonetheless, when VNSAs afflict strong states, they do so in the context of terrorist campaigns and criminal/trafficking networks associated with—rather—sporadic and, usually, low-level violence.

force vested—so far—solely in sovereign states? What are the tactics and strategies employed by VNSAs? How do external parties impact on the evolution and operationality of various violent non-state actors? And, how should VNSAs be dealt with? Contemplating answers to these questions is a critical task of the present volume.

## What are violent non-state actors?

Violent non-state actors are non-state armed groups that resort to organized violence as a tool to achieve their goals. 'Non-state' is understood here at least in nominal terms. This implies that the 'state'/'non-state' divide is not necessarily clear cut, given that VNSAs not only operate in opposition to, or co-optation by, a state or states, but often also exist in a dependent relation to the state/s in terms of support, benefits, and recognition.

Non-state organizations/movements which use violence to advance their political and other aims include:

1. National liberation movements confronting an occupying force, and/or separatist movements seeking to secede from a state with the view to either establish a new state or join an adjacent mother country: for example, the Basque Fatherland and Liberty party (ETA), the Irish Republican Army (IRA), the Kosovo Liberation Army (KLA) and the Sudan People's Liberation Army (SPLA).
2. Insurgent guerrilla bands which are engaged in a protracted political and military struggle aimed at weakening or destroying the power and legitimacy of a ruling government: such as the Palestine Liberation Organization (PLO), Hizbullah, Hamas, the Taliban, the National Union for the Total Independence of Angola (UNITA), and Islamic armed groups which operate currently in Iraq under the umbrella of various organizations such as the Islamic State of Iraq, Awakening (Sahwa), the Reform and Jihad Front, etc.
3. Terrorist groups who spread fear through the threat or use of violence—mainly against civilians—for political purposes, for instance Al Qaeda.
4. Militants made up of irregular but recognizable armed forces—including warlords[3] and paramilitary adjuncts—operating within an ungov-

---

[3] Warlords are armed groups based on local and particularistic appeals often centred on trusted local strongmen who deliver benefits and advantages to their followers. For authoritative contributions on warlords see Paul B. Rich (ed.), *Warlords in International Relations*, Basingstoke: Macmillan, 1999; William Reno, *Warlord Politics and African*

erned area or a weak, fragmented or failing state, such as various armed groups in Somalia.

5. Mercenary militias (such as private military firms).

This typology, nonetheless, does not have clear-cut boundaries. Indeed VNSAs frequently represent hybrid forms in which the above mentioned categories overlap. National liberation movements and separatist forces seeking to secede from a given state adopt military tactics similar to those of insurgent guerrilla bands engaged in a war[4] of attrition aimed at destroying the legitimacy of a ruling government. Insurgency can be defined as 'a technology of military conflict characterized by small, lightly armed bands practicing guerrilla warfare from rural base areas'.[5] As a specific form of warfare, insurgency can be used to serve diverse political agendas, motivations and grievances. Whilst the term has been often associated with communist insurgency, insurgent tactics serve equally Islamic fundamentalists, ethnic nationalists, and those who focus mainly on traffic in coca or diamonds.[6]

Terrorism can be broadly defined as the 'the deliberate creation and exploitation of fear through violence or the threat of violence in the pursuit of political change'.[7] Terrorist organizations tend to be smaller than guerrilla insurgencies. But just like insurgency, terrorism is a strategy of the weak against the strong. Indeed, both terrorism and insurgency are asymmetrical strategies available to weak actors who seek to level the strategic playing field through dramatic and shocking political events.[8] Whilst—in general—terror-

---

*States*, Boulder: Lynne Rienner, 1998; John Mackinlay, 'Defining Warlords', *Monograph 46, Building Stability in Africa: Challenges for the New Millennium*, Pretoria, South Africa: Institute for Security Studies, February 2000; in addition to Troy S. Thomas *et al.*, *Warlord Rising* (note 1). We have not replicated this existing literature by dedicating a specific chapter to warlords, although they are referred to in the analysis of many of the following chapters.

[4] A distinction can be made between 'war' and 'warfare'. As Colin Gray suggests, war is a relationship between belligerents. Warfare is the conduct of war, primarily, though not exclusively, by military means. Colin S. Gray, *Another Bloody Century: Future Warfare*, London: Weidenfeld & Nicolson, 2005, p. 37. War is here understood as an armed conflict with more than 1,000 battle-related deaths in any given year.

[5] James D. Fearon and David D. Laitin, 'Ethnicity, Insurgency, and Civil War', *American Political Science Review*, Vol. 97, No. 1, February 2003, pp. 75–90, at p. 75.

[6] Ibid.

[7] Bruce Hoffman, *Inside Terrorism*, New York: Columbia University Press, 1998, p. 43.

[8] Sean Kay, *Global Security in the Twenty-First Century: The Quest for Power and the Search for Peace*, Lanham, MD: Rowman & Littlefield, 2006, p. 227.

ism targets innocent civilians, insurgency is a tool used by clandestine fighters, normally, to attack military targets during an occupation. Insurgents, therefore, are often differentiated from terrorists in that they generally confine their attacks to military targets, rather than killing civilians. Nevertheless, insurgents have, increasingly, adopted asymmetrical tactics of terrorism as a tool of attrition for accomplishing their objective, which often seeks to prevent a local government—or an external power—from exerting effective control over a tract of territory, or even a whole country. As a consequence, civilians have been directly affected by the activities of insurgent movements.[9]

Private Military Firms (PMFs)—as defined by Peter Singer in this volume—are 'business providers of professional services linked to warfare, offering a wide range of services, ranging from conducting tactical combat operations and strategic planning to logistics support and technical assistance'.[10] Whilst some PMFs have served governments and their armed forces, or worked for the United Nations (UN) or Non-Governmental Organizations (NGOs), others have prospered at the other end of the marketplace, working for dictators, regimes of failing states, organized crime, drug cartels, and terrorist-linked groups.[11] It is when they are engaged in these kinds of activities that PMFs are likely to adopt tactics that are not very different from those of terrorists and/or insurgents.

Whereas, in principle, VNSAs may operate in the context of interstate conflict, in recent times they have been—more often than not—a central feature of civil war and intrastate conflict which reflect the non-Westphalian features of contemporary armed conflict. Whilst wars between states are characterized as formal wars, VNSAs are involved in 'informal wars ... where at least one of the antagonists is a non-state entity'.[12] VNSAs' involvement in informal wars is also an example of what K.J. Holsti has termed wars of the third kind, characterized by absence of fixed territorial boundaries, elaborate institutionalized military rituals, major fronts and (open) military

---

[9] Ibid., pp. 227–9.

[10] See Peter Singer's chapter 18 in this volume.

[11] Fred Schreier and Marina Caparini, 'Privatizing Security: Law, Practice and Governance of Private Military and Security Companies', Geneva: Geneva Centre for the Democratic Control of Armed Forces, *Occasional Paper No. 6*, March 2005, p. 2.

[12] The terminology of formal and informal wars comes from Steven Metz, *Armed Conflict in the 21ˢᵗ Century: The Information Revolution and Post-Modern Warfare*, Carlisle, PA: Strategic Studies Institute, 2000, p. 48, and resonates with more commonly used terms conventional/unconventional war.

campaigns.[13] As will be emphasized below, asymmetric tactics and strategy (vis-à-vis the state) are the key features of VNSA fighting.

Violent non-state actors may be characterized in multiple ways, for instance, in terms of seeking to change or maintain the status quo, or in terms of their primary or secondary relation to profit motivations.[14] Moreover, VNSAs may be characterized in terms of organization, identity, type of violence, goals, purpose, region, and recruitment methods. Troy Thomas and his collaborators have depicted three categories of the existing literature on VNSAs, namely: (1) environment, (2) organization, and (3) individual.[15] The first category seeks to provide contextual explanation, analyzing the political, economic and social landscape to find empirical commonalities or a theoretical basis for violent organizations to emerge. The second category of literature looks at the violent organization itself, searching for internal dynamics that help explain why a group turns to violence in pursuit of its goals. The third category, leaning more towards psychology, examines the individual. It looks for common traits or beliefs among the individual purveyors of violence. However, the boundaries between the latter approaches to the study of VNSAs are not mutually exclusive. Consequently, it is best to analyze VNSAs by examining the links between their environment (including relations to the status quo), their organization, and their leaderships.

## VNSAs and the state

The wide range of contemporary VNSAs renders it impossible to offer a general conclusion that VNSAs are either 'good' or 'evil'. Indeed, just like states, VNSAs are not inherently either 'good' or 'bad'. Furthermore, they are neither monolithic nor necessarily ideology driven. Evaluation of any given VNSA requires a careful analysis of the context and environment in which it operates, but also of its mission, strategy and tactics, as well as its leaders' agendas.

A key proposition advanced in this book is that VNSAs' relations to the state are crucial in comprehending their actions. VNSAs' operations can be understood as responses to state policies or as reflections of a state's efforts to co-opt these actors in its policies. As we shall see VNSAs often seek a state of

[13] K.J. Holsti, *The State, War and the State of War*, Cambridge University Press, 1996, p. 36.
[14] See figure 19.1, in Chapter 19 by Alyson Bailes and Daniel Nord in this volume , p. 446.
[15] Thomas et al., *Warlords Rising*, 2005.

their own whilst opposing a given state. Even when they operate in a context of state failure, fragmentation, and/or collapse, VNSAs' political power is closely linked to their ability to use, or threaten the use of, violence. They frequently manifest strategies that seek to provide themselves and their communities with some degree of order and security, which in conditions of mitigated conflict or post-conflict setting are likely to produce 'mediated states' where a feeble government shares power and sovereignty with VNSAs.

VNSAs frequently operate in states confronting crises, which are incapable of providing services and delivering public goods—including security—in all their territory.[16] In Afghanistan, Colombia, Sudan, Lebanon and Sri Lanka, although the government provides basic services and delivers public goods in the main cities, it is ineffective in the periphery of the country. In the latter areas, as Nazih Richani notes in his chapter in this book, the government shares its sovereignty with VNSAs—a condition known also as 'fragmented sovereignty' that is complemented by a 'system of violence' in which state and non-state actors interact, coexist, cooperate, or conflict tacitly and implicitly. When such a system of violence is consolidated, it acquires its own dynamic and political economy which allow its prolongation. The latter impairs the state's distributive and coercive capabilities, as well as the performance of state institutions, enabling VNSAs to penetrate such institutions and find safe havens and launching grounds.[17]

The blurring of lines between VNSAs and the state is apparent also in present-day Iraq. Eric Herring argues that armed groups in Iraq are both responding and contributing to the fragmentation and globalization of the Iraqi state. He makes the case for conceiving of the Iraqi state as a fragmented state, that is, 'one in which there is some state authority but a great deal of dispute over the location of that authority and over means of resolving such disputes'. Herring insists that the concept of state fragmentation goes beyond

---

[16] This is not to suggest that violent non-state actors always operate in conditions of anarchy where the government has either collapsed or cannot control unruly subjects. Sometimes, VNSAs operate in environments where the government continues to exercise (some degree of) control, as in the case of Serbia in Kosovo in the 1990s, or currently in the case of Iraq, for instance. The strengthening of central authority tends to become a permissive cause of violence for anti-government forces. See the contributions of Eric Herring, Syed Rifaat Hussain and Klejda Mulaj in this volume. ETA is a classic example of a VNSA which operates in a country—Spain—that does not experience problems of public order or social welfare, as the chapter of Ignacio Sánchez-Cuenca makes clear.

[17] In addition to Nazih Richani's chapter, on this point see also contributions of Amin Saikal and William Reno.

the failed or fragile states terminology, thus rejecting an ontology of VNSAs and the state as separate entities which might sometimes interact. Moreover, he argues that the concept of state fragmentation exposes the mutual constitution and varying degrees of overlap between VNSAs and the state as well as the international situation, and facilitates an understanding of such mutual constitution vis-à-vis globalization.

Yet, some of the VNSAs analyzed in this volume such as the Liberation Tigers of Tamil Eelam (LTTE), the IRA, the KLA, and Hizbullah are organized distinct from the state and in opposition to it, and they often demand a state of their own. They are actively engaged in a process of state-building through setting up parallel civil administrations within the territory under their control, and/or through military means—their armed struggle. It deserves emphasizing, nonetheless, that violence used by VNSAs to oppose the state and win legitimacy for their political cause imposes costs on the state. Indeed, VNSAs seek to impose as large a cost as possible on the state in order to break its resistance threshold. The repercussions of VNSAs' violence on the state are not only physical, but also economic, political and psychological. The more protracted the violence, the larger the cost it imposes on the state. ETA and the IRA are examples of VNSAs that have been engaged in a war of attrition against the state, with the aim of outlasting it. The violence of the IRA and ETA—but also the KLA—was intended to alert the masses to the existence of hard-core activists willing to fight the state. The hope of such VNSAs was that violence would escalate through the overreaction of the state. In addition, indiscriminate and disproportionate state repression would induce people to join VNSA ranks and overturn the correlation of forces against the state.[18]

VNSA–state relations, nevertheless, are not uniform. Just as some VNSAs exist as distinct from and in violent opposition to the state, others exist in a dynamic relationship with the state. In Afghanistan, for instance, a weak state exists in juxtaposition to powerful sub-national actors of which the Taliban are one of the most prominent. Amin Saikal emphasizes in his contribution to this book that while the state in Afghanistan may have a central authority, that authority, and the functioning of the state, can be at the mercy of numerous internal sub-actors, and external actors that can manipulate various sub-actors (tribes) for their purposes.

Some VNSAs not only coexist with the state, but are co-opted by it. They are integral to the exercise of state power in so far as they form part of state

---

[18] Refer to the chapters by Ignacio Sánchez-Cuenca, Jonathan Tonge, Syed Rifaat Hussain, Judith Palmer Harik, Omar Ashour and Klejda Mulaj in this volume.

efforts to exercise power at a distance—a strategy which, of course, reflects the state's administrative weakness. William Reno asserts in his chapter that this is the present picture in many countries in Africa, most notably Sudan. The central government in Khartoum cannot control distant parts of the country directly through security services or local administrative apparatuses, not only because it lacks the financial means but also because government control is controversial among local people who resent external interference in their local communities. In these circumstances the government uses non-state actors as proxies in order to exercise control over the periphery of the country. It is in this respect that VNSAs in Sudan have become central to the exercise of state power. Indeed, given its administrative weakness, the state projects power through flexible alliances with VNSAs. Reno notes that localized line-age disputes are brought into politics through shifting alliances that the state constructs with VNSAs. This is because groups of individuals who are margin-alized in local politics look to the capital for resources and political support. Governments in Sudan, Chad, Libya, Uganda, Ethiopia, Eritrea and Nigeria have shown themselves willing to patronize selective local armed groups which in turn accomplish political and military goals beneficial to the govern-ments—at a low cost. At the same time these governments have been keen to manipulate the formation of local political organizations and make sure that supported groups do not become effective or popular enough to form a broad-based political opposition to the state.

The relocation of authority from state to non-state actors is also acute in Somalia. Here, the prolonged collapse of the central government has resulted in a context where non-state actors have been the most significant form of political organization, with violence, or the threat of violence, the main cur-rency of power. Ken Menkhaus explains that during two and a half years of UN intervention in Somalia (UNOSOM), fortunes were made in conducting business with the UN operation. As a result, more enterprising militia leaders switched into legitimate, or semi-legitimate, businesses, contributing to the rise of an elite which helped to fund local governance and security arrange-ments in the aftermath of UNOSOM's departure in 1995. Subsequently, sizeable private security firms have emerged, which have offered growing political and military clout to their business owners. The local sources of informal authority have been able to provide a degree of local governance which, though not resembling a modern state, has offered a modicum of pub-lic security, order, and modest services to the community—a phenomenon which Menkhaus terms 'governance without government'. Given that no emerging Somali state is likely to secure a monopoly on the legitimate use of violence in the near future, he predicts that a likely scenario might be the emergence of a 'mediated state' in which a weak central government must broker arrangements with local VNSAs—including private security firms—to extend indirect control in distant parts of the country, not unlike the case of Sudan.

The utilitarian relationship between VNSAs and the state is present also in the case of Western private military firms.[19] As Peter Singer notes in this volume, given that in our times regular armies are operating in reduced capacities—the US military, for instance, is 35 per cent smaller than it was at the height of the Cold War, whereas the British military is as small as it has been since the Napoleonic wars—PMFs are usefully filling a gap in the force structure of Western militaries. PMFs offer the possibility of accomplishing policy ends through non-state, military means. Furthermore, they allow governments to carry out actions that risk not receiving public support and legislative approval. Given that losses incurred by PMFs have fewer negative impacts on governments and their approval ratings than losses of regular armies, operational symbiosis between governments and PMFs is likely to continue—if not increase.[20] The term 'private military firms' conceals, nonetheless, a crucial relation between the entities it inscribes and the institution of state, on the one hand, and PMFs' direct involvement in the conduct of state violence, on the other hand. This, once again, underscores the fact that the 'state'/'non-state' distinction is not clear-cut but rather nominal.

## Causal and environmental considerations

In his hugely influential treatise *On War*, Carl von Clausewitz argued that the political and social circumstances from which conflict arises also determine its conduct. This is popularly rendered in the aphorism: 'War is the continuation of policy by other means',[21] that is, war is indistinguishable from political and social structures and should thus be conceived in terms of them.[22] Hence, war

---

[19] See Christopher Coker, 'Outsourcing War', in Josselin and Wallace (eds), *Non-State Actors in World Politics*, pp. 189–202.

[20] See Peter Singer's chapter 18 below.

[21] Carl Von Clausewitz, *On War*, edited and translated by Michael Howard and Peter Paret, Princeton University Press, 1976, p. 605.

[22] Ibid., p. 607.

should not be thought of as something autonomous but always as an instrument of policy.

The historical record supports the Clausewitz thesis that warfare is primarily a political activity. Although VNSAs differ along social, cultural, and economic lines, they all seek to obtain some form of political power. The IRA, ETA, and the KLA sought political autonomy from London, Madrid, and Belgrade respectively; Somali warlords seek to gain power, protection and influence for their clans; Al Qaeda's terrorist attacks aim to influence US foreign policy in the Middle East, particularly towards Palestine, influence decision making in key regional powers such as Saudi Arabia, and mobilize and politicize Muslim public opinion worldwide; Hamas in Palestine and Hizbullah in Lebanon both endeavour to secure control of respective state's structures; whereas armed groups in present-day Iraq strive to oust the Americans from the country and assume its control. In a word, the rationale for the use of violence by non-state actors is the achievement of broadly conceived political goals.

Politics, however, is not the only factor influencing VNSAs' operations. Surely, historical animosities and long-term oppression—with concomitant perceptions of injustices and denial of rights—have played a role in the emergence and maintenance of armed resistance (This is stressed in Morten Bøås' chapter on Liberia, and also, in one way or another, in the other contributions in this volume). In addition, some analysts have suggested that the violence of non-state actors is a function of culture in so far as warrior culture dictates warrior goals.[23] Others stress grievance and greed as a motivating force.[24] Yet others emphasize religious beliefs or spiritual factors, given that violence is seen by many religious members of violent non-state organizations as a moral act that brings them closer to salvation.[25] Surely, some VNSAs seem to be more influenced by religion than others. This certainly appears to be the case

---

[23] See Martin van Creveld, *The Transformation of War*, New York: Free Press, 1991; and Ralph Peters, 'The New Warrior Class', *Parameters*, Vol. 24, No. 2, Summer 1994, pp. 16–26.

[24] Grievances of politically and militarily sidelined chiefs appear to have played a role in the operations of VNSAs in Sierra Leone and currently in Iraq. See David Keen, *Endless War? Hidden Functions of the 'War on Terror'*, London: Pluto Press, 2006, pp. 54–6; and Eric Herring and Glen Rangwala, *Iraq in Fragments: The Occupation and its Legacy*, London: Hurst, 2006. On greed, see also Mats Berdal and David Malone (eds), *Greed and Grievance: Economic Agendas in Civil Wars*, Boulder: Lynne Rienner, 2000.

[25] Hoffman, *Inside Terrorism*, p. 94; Raymond L. Bingham, 'Bridging the Religious Divide', *Parameters*, Vol. 36, No. 3, Autumn 2006, pp. 50–66.

of Al Qaeda and Militant Islamic Groups (MIGs), although Islamist fighters seem to want first and foremost to challenge the state/s with the aim of over-throwing the ruling regime/s.[26] It should be remembered, nevertheless, that religious rhetoric is often a cover for other significant factors of conflict, including political, economic, and social ones. Violence may well need religion in order to enable those who use violence for political goals to secure emotional commitments needed to incite and maintain the use of force.[27] An emphasis on the cultural—including religious—dimensions of VNSA violence should not obscure the political purpose behind fighting. Our contributing chapters show that the ultimate rationale of contemporary VNSAs is political. This is made abundantly clear, amongst other things, by the fact that VNSAs operate in relation, or response, to state power, and seek power—broadly defined—as their ultimate end.

The correlation of forces between VNSAs and states, however, involves a complex dynamic. The decline of state capacity to meet basic human needs and enforce the rule of law can be conducive to the operations of VNSAs. Weak or failed states, for instance, can serve as fertile recruiting grounds and/or training areas for VNSA sympathizers.[28] Al Qaeda operations in Yemen included using Yemeni ports for arms smuggling.[29] Somalia is another country that has suffered a prolonged crisis of state capacity and a significant rise in criminality. As pointed out by Ken Menkhaus elsewhere, a growing Islamic movement in Somalia, from which have stemmed terrorist actions such as those carried out by Al-Ittihadal Islami, is reported to have facilitated financial transfers to training camps where Al Qaeda members have been based.[30]

---

[26] See chapters by Mohammad-Mahmoud Ould Mohamedou and Hassanein Tawfik Ibrahim in this volume.

[27] See Mark Juergensmeyer, 'The Logic of Religious Violence', in David Rapoport (ed.), *Inside Terrorist Organizations*, London: Frank Cass, 2001.

[28] Refer to Robert Rotberg, 'The Failure and Collapse of Nation-States', in Robert I. Rotberg (ed.), *When States Fail: Causes and Consequences*, Princeton University Press, 2004, pp. 8–10. Also, Kwesi Aning's chapter in this volume.

[29] Anthony H. Cordesman and Khalid R. Al-Rodham, *The Gulf Military Forces in an Era of Asymmetric War*, Greenwood in cooperation with the Centre for Strategic Studies, Washington DC, 2006, Chapter on Yemen, available also at http://www.csis.org/media/csis/pubs/060728_gulf_yemen.pdf.

[30] Ken Menkhaus, 'Somalia: State Collapse and the Threat of Terrorism', *Adelphi Paper 364*, Oxford University Press for the International Institute for Strategic Studies, 2004, pp. 54–6.

Financially, organizationally, and politically weak central governments provide incentives to VNSAs. For one, a government which cannot provide protection against armed attack may be inclined to hire private security firms. Indeed, such firms are among the fastest growing economic endeavours especially in Africa, Central America, and the former Soviet Union. For another, a propensity for brutal and indiscriminate retaliation on the part of the government can help drive non-combatant locals into rebel forces. Furthermore, low per capita income favours VNSAs: recruiting young men in their ranks is easier when economic alternatives are poor. James Fearon and David Laitin have argued that state weakness marked by poverty, a large population, and instability, as well as a rough terrain, are key conditions that favour insurgency. Their data shows that cultural diversity and grievances fail to predict the onset of insurgency, although cultural differences are enhanced, and intense grievances are produced, in the course of conduct of violence.[31]

Structural factors have also had an impact on VNSAs. Weak or failed states provide conducive grounds for VNSAs' operations, and decolonization, for instance, led to an international system numerically dominated by fragile states with limited administrative control of their peripheries, especially in the Middle East and Africa.[32] Since the end of the Cold War and the demise of superpower policies which provided support to their proxy forces, militants have had to turn to other means to raise funds, such as local sources of revenue.[33] The presence of precious resources—but also cultivation of poppies, extraction of protection rents and/or taxes from local populations, and trading in drugs as well as precious minerals—have both financed (and prolonged) war efforts and driven warlords' motivation for personal gain.[34]

The end of the Cold War has also facilitated the global diffusion of small arms, and created surplus stocks of such weapons. Although the availability of small arms does not in itself cause VNSA violence, such weapons are significant contributing factors. Small weapons—assault rifles, submachine guns, rocket-propelled grenades, light mortars, land mines, and so on—have become

[31] Fearon and Laitin, 'Ethnicity, Insurgency, and Civil War', especially pp. 75–76, 80.

[32] Ibid., p. 88. See also Jeffrey Herbst, 'Let Them Fail: State Failure in Theory and Practice: Implications for Policy', in Rotberg (ed.), *When States Fail*, p. 302.

[33] See, for instance, Nazih Richani's chapter 2 in this book.

[34] Refer to Paul Collier 'Doing Well Out of War', in Berdal and Malone (eds), *Greed and Grievance*, pp. 91–111. Opium production has been a vital source of income for the Taliban in Afghanistan and armed groups in Colombia. Collection of taxes has played a key role in securing income for the LTTE and the KLA.

the standard equipment of VNSAs, since such weapons are inexpensive and easy to use, and are readily available from black-market sources.[35]

Amongst structural factors affecting the operationality of VNSAs, globalization has acquired crucial importance. As John Mackinlay has argued, the effects of globalization have gradually changed the relationship between weak governments and the insurgent forces that seek to oppose them, weakening governments and enriching insurgent leaders.[36] Globalization, therefore, may be empowering VNSAs. Al Qaeda appears to provide an example of a global violent non-state actor, given that members of this military network span several regions, launch attacks in varied countries, and draw support from a huge diaspora that shares the same religion.

Globalization has expanded the ambit of VNSAs. It has also entailed shifts in the practices by which states monopolize the use of legitimate force. In particular, globalization has reinforced the drive towards privatization and informalization of military force and security.[37] Indeed, the extent of PMFs' involvement that is found acceptable has increased significantly.[38] Moreover, the development of 'global' communications and media coverage does much to amplify and communicate the impact of VNSAs' actions— and not only to their supporters. By spreading information about VNSAs' causes, tactics and strategy, globalization may also be affecting the process of confinement of legitimacy—that is, legitimation—a theme which the next section explores.[39]

---

[35] Michael T. Klare, 'The Deadly Connection: Paramilitary Bands, Small Arms Diffusion, and State Failure', in Rotberg (ed.), *When States Fail*, especially pp. 116–17, 124.

[36] John Mackinlay, 'Globalization and Insurgency', *Adelphi Paper 352*, Oxford University Press for the International Institute for Strategic Studies, 2002, p. 11.

[37] See, for instance, Thomas K. Adams, 'The New Mercenaries and the Privatization of Conflict', *Parameters*, Vol. XXIV, No. 2, Summer 1999, pp. 103–16.

[38] Coker, 'Outsourcing War'.

[39] Legitimacy is normally used to imply justification or validation of a practical activity. Crucial moments for legitimacy are times of change—especially times of conflict and war—when criteria of legitimacy are challenged and contested. Whilst 'legitimacy' may be conceived as an abstract, ascribed quality, 'legitimation' refers to an activity, the making of claims. If legitimacy is a fiction, a metaphor employed to describe circumstances where people accept claims made by the rulers, legitimation is an observable activity, a contested political process that involves creation, modification, innovation, and transformation. See Rodney Barker, *Legitimating Identities: The Self-Presentations of Rulers and Subjects*, Cambridge University Press, 2001, Chapter 1.

## VNSAs and the puzzle of legitimation

A commonly held assumption in world politics is that states monopolize the legitimate use of force. Ever since the 1648 treaty of Westphalia, a sharp distinction between 'internal legitimacy' and 'external legitimacy' has been implied in international affairs. Such a distinction reflects adherence to sovereignty as a fundamental principle of the society of states, and until recently a rather widely held assumption that a state has authority to control—and sometimes subordinate—its population with little regard for, or fear of, external intervention. In this view, the state is considered the (sole) legitimate deployer of force. Conversely, violent non-state actors—normally—are not viewed as legitimate deployers of coercion.

The sharp distinction between 'internal legitimacy' and 'external legitimacy' has not gone uncontested, however. The dilemmas of such distinction are shown when various factions have competing claims over territory. As Anna Leander has pointed out, in wars of secession as well as in civil wars or revolutions, in general, there is no clear way of deciding which authority makes the most legitimate claim.[40] Furthermore, the problem of legitimacy confinement becomes complicated when the government uses disproportionate and indiscriminate force in counterinsurgency tactics. By alienating the civilian population such tactics may backfire and broaden the basis of, and support for, the rebels, thus sharpening the contest for legitimacy at the internal level.

Globalization, nonetheless, has rendered it easier for internal legitimacy to make its way into international politics. Indeed, the globalization of media contributes to placing legitimacy of 'internal' state uses of force on a transnational public agenda.[41] Moreover, people on the move (migrants, journalists, academics, law enforcers, tourists) play an important role in creating a transnational political space where the legitimacy of use of force at the internal level—by states and VNSAs alike—is contested. This blurring of the distinction between 'internal' and 'external' legitimacy is important because, by giving visibility to VNSAs and their causes, it makes possible to question the proposition that the state is the only legitimate deployer of coercion at the national level. The history of the IRA and the KLA, for instance, supports this latter claim.

The acquisition, or otherwise, of legitimacy by VNSAs is a widely debated issue. Given that the current international system is dominated by states, one

---

[40] Anna Leander, 'Globalization and the State Monopoly on the Legitimate Use of Force', University of Southern Denmark, *Political Science Publications No. 7/2004*, p. 8.
[41] Ibid., p. 10.

can argue that the non-state status of VNSAs determines their (lack of) legitimacy. Again, this stems from the widely held assumption that only states possess the legitimate monopoly of the use of force. But the fact that some VNSAs have challenged that monopoly, sometimes successfully, and have acquired domestic and international support may suggest that status alone is insufficient to determine a VNSA's legitimacy.

So far as military operations are concerned, irregular fighters (especially those linked with national liberation movements, but also insurgencies) seek to legitimize their use of violence, and translate this into meaningful support for their cause, by demonstrating moral superiority over their opponents—the state or states. For instance, a VNSA can demonstrate legitimacy by becoming the *de facto* government in areas under its control. This can include establishment of public and social service networks (such as schools and hospitals) as done by Hizbullah and Hamas, or setting up of parallel court and police services, and collection of taxes as done by the LTTE, the KLA, and armed groups in Colombia. These examples suggest that a VNSA's legitimacy is often contingent on the provision of order and security—real or perceived. Armed groups which are associated with efforts to provide security and governance can claim legitimacy and therefore the allegiance of their constituencies.

Furthermore, the success VNSAs have in challenging a given state is a function of their political causes. Indeed, a powerful method of legitimizing a struggle is to link military operations with a justifiable political end.[42] Self-determination and (perceived or real) injustices have been pervasive rallying cries. In general, VNSAs make strenuous efforts to justify their use of force within the discursive contours of the international community, suggesting that they are not indifferent to international practices and norms, although the international community does not always appear to realize how far its preferences impact on VNSAs' behaviour and policies. As shown in the chapters on Somalia, Sudan and the KLA, militia leaders are acutely aware that adapting their organizations to suit international preferences is crucial to secure international recognition.

In addition to substantial popular support at domestic level, in order to succeed VNSAs need external backing, whether moral—in the form of political recognition and lobbying—or in the form of resources or cross-border sanctuaries. Support from a big power can be indispensable in conferring

---

[42] James D. Kiras, 'Terrorism and Irregular Warfare', in John Baylis, James Wirtz, Eliot Cohen, and Colin S. Gray (eds), *Strategy in the Contemporary World: An Introduction to Strategic Studies*, Oxford University Press, 2006, pp. 208–32, at p. 219.

external legitimacy. During the Cold War, for instance, the United States and the Soviet Union supported insurgent and guerrilla movements in the Third World to advance their competing strategic and ideological agendas.[43] This, in turn, ensured the survival of movements receiving superpower support. Conversely, lack of great power support can seriously undermine a VNSA's existence. The existence of the National Union for Total Independence of Angola (UNITA) in the 1980s owed much to both covert and overt US assistance, the waning of which in the post-Cold War years was one of the important factors that precipitated UNITA's downfall.[44]

These examples suggest that circumstances under which VNSAs operate can evolve in ways which condition the definition of legitimacy. The difficulties inherent in assessing legitimacy become apparent also in relation to other VNSAs. For example, the KLA was initially branded a terrorist organization but was subsequently rehabilitated and collaborated with NATO in the course of the latter's bombing campaign against Serbia in spring 1999.[45] Another example concerns Hizbullah, which early in its history was held responsible for terrorist activities, including several high-profile kidnappings and the suicide bombings of the US Marines' and French forces' compounds in 1983. Members of Hizbullah, however, fought a protracted guerrilla campaign against Israeli forces, compelling the latter to withdraw from southern Lebanon after 18 years of sporadic conflict. Hizbullah also manages a substantial number of public service operations (reportedly funded by Syria and Iran) which have contributed to increased internal support for the organization.[46]

Intricacies of legitimacy do not spare PMFs, either. Their non-state status is not a totally determining factor when PMFs' legitimacy is concerned. Whereas PMFs are not considered to be as legitimate as the professional, civilian-controlled military of a democratic government, they should not be considered less legitimate than an unprofessional military operating on behalf of an authoritarian regime. This, however, may appear to render the PMFs' legitimacy a function of the hiring agent. In other words, the agent who directs PMFs' operations may condition the latter's legitimacy more than the PMFs themselves. But this still leads to some unsettled questions. For instance,

[43] Kay, *Global Security in the Twenty-First Century*, p. 229.
[44] Refer to Assis Malaquias' chapter in this book.
[45] The branding of the KLA as 'a terrorist group' came from the US special representative for the implementation of the Dayton Agreement, Robert S. Gelbard, when visiting Belgrade on 23 February 1998. For the KLA see chapter 4 in this volume.
[46] For Hizbullah see Judith Palmer Harik's chapter in this book.

is it more legitimate for a UN member state with a poor record of protection of its people's human rights to hire a PMF that in turn serves the state's policies, or is it more legitimate for a humanitarian group to hire the same PMF to protect the people? Answers to these questions go beyond PMF-related factors. While no one PMF/VNSA may be judged as inherently 'legitimate' or not, their conduct in the field, contracting processes, and systems of accountability may be used to form a judgment of its legitimacy in a given moment in time.[47]

Not infrequently, operational circumstances of VNSAs condition permutation of their legitimacy. This provides a challenge both to policy makers and political scientists. It also ensures that legitimation of VNSAs is ridden with complex puzzles, given that violent organizations illegitimate at some times seem to acquire legitimacy at other times. The political cause, however, appears to be crucial in mobilizing support domestically, as well as in determining the degree of external support, and therefore external legitimacy, granted to VNSAs by powerful members of the international community.[48] When the VNSAs' political cause receives the sympathy of both local population and the international community, the conferment of legitimacy—to a large extent—is likely to be a function of VNSAs' strategy and tactics.

## Strategy and tactics

Originating from the ancient Greek term for generalship, *strategos*, 'strategy' refers to the application of military power to achieve political objectives. Strategy implies the relationship between means and ends in warfare, and deals with the difficult problems of policy—the areas where political, economic, psychological, and military factors overlap. Strategy and policy are therefore closely interlinked.[49]

---

[47] I thank Peter Singer for pointing out controversies relating to the legitimacy of PMFs. E-mail exchange dated 30 July 2008.

[48] In the absence of an attractive political cause which is persuasively conveyed in connection with the interests of the international community, VNSAs will surely fail. Characteristics of a good cause—as Robert Tomes has pointed out—include: a large part of the population must be able to identify with the cause; the counterinsurgents cannot use the same cause or espouse it; and the essential social mobilization base remains the same while the cause changes over time as the insurgency adapts. See Robert R. Tomes, 'Relearning Counterinsurgency Warfare', *Parameters*, Spring 2004, pp. 16–28 at p. 21.

[49] John Baylis and James J. Wirtz, 'Introduction', in John Baylis *et al.* (eds), *Strategy in the Contemporary World*, p. 3.

More often than not, violent non-state actors are engaged in asymmetrical, dialectical, struggles. If conventional war involves adversaries more or less symmetrical in equipment, training and doctrine, in asymmetrical conflicts adversaries are characterized by huge disparities in capabilities. VNSAs seek to effect political change by organizing and fighting more effectively than their adversaries. They aim to use their strengths, such as mobility, organization, anonymity or stealth, against the weaknesses of their more powerful foes.[50] When the goal of insurgents is to prevent an external power or a local government from exerting effective control over a demarcated territory, their tactics include creation of confusion, chaos and fear to show that those in power cannot govern effectively.[51] The IRA, the PLO, the ETA Basque separatists, the LTTE and Al Qaeda are examples of VNSAs which have used terrorist methods to bring attention to their causes with a view to advancing claims of independence for specific territories, or to protest against the actions of particular governments and their policies. In general, violence applied by non-state actors—as in the case of Al Qaeda, PLO, ETA, or the IRA—has sought to inspire fear, draw wide attention to a political grievance, and/or provoke a brutal response, which will secure additional recruits, as well as support for the insurgents' propaganda against their enemies.

Camouflage, protraction, and attrition are key features of VNSAs operations.[52] Such asymmetrical tactics are intended to act as force multipliers for VNSAs. In making a weak actor strong in pursuit of its strategic goal, asymmetrical tactics aim to level a major imbalance of power.[53] Camouflage, or the capacity to dissolve into the local population and terrain, shields VNSAs from an enemy's superior firepower and compels the enemy to inflict politically self-defeating collateral damage on the civilian population. Protraction and attrition are also conditioned by the conventional military superiority of the enemy. Because most VNSAs—at least initially—have no hope of quick and decisive victory, they employ time and the steady inflicting of casualties to subvert the enemy's political will to continue fighting.[54] VNSAs—normally—

---

[50] See Kiras, 'Terrorism and Irregular Warfare', p. 212.

[51] Some VNSAs are reported to use terror against opponents in their own communities also, with a view to setting examples and induce compliance with VNSAs objectives.

[52] For background discussion refer to Jeffrey Record, 'Why the Strong Lose', *Parameters*, Vol. 35, No. 4, 2005–06, pp 16–31 at p. 20.

[53] Kay, *Global Security in the Twenty-First Century*, pp. 218–19.

[54] It could be thought that unlike the case of guerrilla bands, insurgents and terrorists, prolongation of the conflict may not be characteristic of PMFs since they are employed to

see conflicts as being fought over many years, even decades. With sufficient time a VNSA can organize, undermine the resolve of its adversary, and grow and strengthen the body of its militants.[55] Certain virtues can enhance the value of the time factor. For instance, patience and the will to persist and fight on against overwhelming odds can often be more effective than the will of a state to bear the human and financial costs of certain policies.[56]

In addition to seeking advantage over their adversaries in terms of time, VNSAs aim also to gain an advantage in terms of space. Space allows them to decide where and when to fight. If the adversary appears in overwhelming numbers, the VNSAs can make use of space to withdraw and fight again when the odds are in their favour.[57] Moreover, terrain is important to offset VNSAs' weaknesses and help them gain tactical advantages. Rather than fight against large armies, VNSAs tend to draw their enemy into isolated conflict where the advantages of heavy armour, artillery, air power, and technology are substantially affected. In such settings, VNSAs have an advantage as they know the terrain and have mobility within it.[58] Indeed, the exploitation of rough terrain, poorly served by roads, which limits the manoeuvres of enemy forces is a crucial way in which VNSAs offset their relative weakness in technology, organization, and numbers. Furthermore, difficult terrain provides insurgent forces with the opportunity to establish safe areas or bases from which to expand the struggle.[59]

VNSAs' operations include a target audience to be influenced by the visual consequences of asymmetrical attacks. News media, the Internet, and other forms of mass communication can help movements draw attention to their cause.[60] Media visibility is crucial in projecting VNSAs' power. Asymmetrical attacks might be limited in their physical effects, but various media dramatically multiply VNSAs' intended political impact.[61]

---

terminate fighting. Yet some have argued that since PMFs are paid to deal with conflict situations, they have little interest in bringing conflict to a rapid end. See Schreier and Caparini, 'Privatizing Security', p. 77.

[55] See Kiras, 'Terrorism and Irregular Warfare', p. 213.

[56] Kay, *Global Security in the Twenty-First Century*, p. 227.

[57] Kiras, 'Terrorism and Irregular Warfare', p. 214.

[58] See Kay, *Global Security in the Twenty-First Century*, p. 220.

[59] Kiras, 'Terrorism and Irregular Warfare', p. 215.

[60] As contributions in this volume show, many VNSAs operate their own radio stations, and Internet sites as well as newspapers.

[61] See Kenneth Payne, 'The Media as an Instrument of War', *Parameters*, Vol. 35, No. 1, 2005.

VNSAs' strategies are aided by the dynamics of the global security environment. The proliferation of inexpensive weaponry in the global market has strengthened the tendency for factions to be numerous and for chains of command to be weak.[62] Moreover, transport technology accelerates the pace and capacity for VNSAs to organize and act. Communication technology enables speedy interaction amongst members of VNSAs, in addition to publicity via the media and the Internet.[63] The deregulation of the international economy and the means of global trade help to facilitate the flow of money and weapons. The rise of global finance, the ability to hide financial resources in safe havens, the ability to trade in illicit items, the ability to encode communications with advanced technology, and the growth of transnational ethno-religious communities are manifestations of the global networks where VNSAs can work.[64]

In order to finance the acquisition of arms and other military commodities, some VNSAs have been involved in predatory and criminal activities. (This theme is treated in many of the following chapters. However, we have not looked exclusively at criminal violent actors, given that the focus of this volume is solely on non-state organizations that employ large-scale violence in pursuit of their goals). Because most VNSAs are usually unable to engage in legitimate business, they tend to turn to illicit commerce including drug trafficking, diamond smuggling, kidnapping for ransom, prostitution, and extortion.[65] Whereas the revenue from these endeavours is likely to widen and prolong the conflict, they also bring with them the risk that VNSAs' leaders are affected by the opportunities for personal enrichment through illegal means.[66]

Violent non-state actors adopt various tactics in pursuit of their strategies. The value ascribed by analysts to, and the perceived relationship between, different tactics for a given VNSA vary. This is because each and every VNSA operates within a set of circumstances that is unique to a specific conflict. The fact that VNSAs adopt a variety of tactics in pursuit of their strategies conditioned by unique circumstances seriously compounds difficulties in dealing with such actors.

[62] Keen, *Endless War?*, pp. 54; Klare, 'The Deadly Connection'.

[63] See Mackinlay, 'Globalization and Insurgency', Chapter 1.

[64] Refer to Kay, *Global Security in the Twenty-First Century*, pp. 229, 232.

[65] For background, see R.T. Naylor, 'The Insurgent Economy: Black Market Operations of Guerrilla Organizations', *Crime, Law and Social Change*, Vol. 20, 1993, pp. 13–51.

[66] See David Keen, 'The Economic Functions of Violence in Civil Wars', *Adelphi Paper 320*, Oxford University Press for the International Institute for Strategic Studies, 1998.

## Responding to VNSAs

A reasoned response to the operations of a given VNSA is bound to be a function of the 'cause/s' for which that actor fights. It is crucial, therefore, that the political, economic, and social intricacies of the 'cause/s' are comprehensively understood. In any conflict, the way the conflicting—and external—parties perceive what is at stake for them impacts directly on how they carry out the conflict and bring it to an end.

When asymmetries of values and interests do not allow for accommodation, as appears at present to be the case of Al Qaeda on the one hand and the West (especially the US) on the other, the counterinsurgency aims to defeat its foes. Coercion, primarily military force, is used to this end. The cases of Iraq and Afghanistan show, nonetheless, that combating terrorists and insurgents is very different from fighting a conventional war against a state and its military assets.[67] Engaging in unconventional warfare requires both conventional and unconventional methods. Surely, fighting a war against a tactic, rather than developing a clear plan to defeat a strategy, can play into the hands of one's adversaries.[68] Hence, understanding dynamics between strategy and tactics of VNSAs is essential for a successful encounter with them.

In discussing success criteria, Robert Tomes has suggested that counterinsurgents need success as early as possible in order to demonstrate the will, the means, and the ability to defeat the insurgency. Early, swift action to crash the rebels is thus crucial. In addition counterinsurgents, in Tomes' view, should avoid negotiations until they are in a position of strength.[69] Moreover, as Robert Cassidy asserts in the context of present conflicts in Afghanistan and Iraq, the early employment of indigenous forces in a counterinsurgent role can be an effective method in helping to defeat the rebels, given that such forces can provide a significant increase in the quantity of troops on the ground and contribute intelligence about the insurgency and its infrastructure.[70] Counterinsurgency theorists recognize that guerrilla insurgents and terrorists must be denied popular support, and this needs to be done through credible and efficient action that does not alienate the civilian population, so that their 'hearts

---

[67] Herring and Rangwala, *Iraq in Fragments*, p. 162.

[68] Refer to Kay, *Global Security in the Twenty-First Century*, pp. 220–1.

[69] Tomes, 'Relearning Counterinsurgency Warfare', p. 27. See also Klare, 'The Deadly Connection', in Rotberg (ed.), *When States Fail*, p. 117.

[70] Robert M. Cassidy, 'The Long Small War: Indigenous Forces for Counterinsurgency', *Parameters*, Vol. 36, No. 2, 2006, pp. 48, 60.

and minds' can be won.[71] Furthermore, given the strong correlation between external assistance and insurgent success, when the aim is to defeat insurgents, it is vital that they are deprived of external support.[72]

Responses to VNSAs have as the central aim of minimizing the risks emanating from the armed groups concerned, and transformation of habitats conducive to their violence. When violent conflict ceases without defeat of insurgents—as in the case of the IRA, the KLA and the SPLA—it is advocated that ex-combatants should be demobilized so that they avoid becoming serious security threats. Militias have been transformed into political parties and have participated in electoral processes, to help establish the fledgling institutions of a democratic political order. In this context, VNSAs may 'progress' out of their VNSA mode through programmes for the Disarmament, Demobilization and Reintegration (DDR) of units and combatants involved in conflicts.[73] Demobilization and reintegration programmes for combatants constitute a vital part of demilitarization and transitions from war to peace. Rebuilding social capital and the trust that could bridge social fault lines of a post-conflict society is critical to the strengthening of social cohesion in the aftermath of divisive violent conflict.[74]

As noted, privatization and commercialization of conflict have brought about particular types of VNSAs, most notably PMFs. Dealing with these actors has proved to be controversial as opinion about their utility appears to be divided between those who advocate outlawing involvement of PMFs in all

[71] Kiras, 'Terrorism and Irregular Warfare', p. 223.

[72] See Jeffrey Record, 'External Assistance: Enabler of Insurgent Success', *Parameters*, Vol. 36, No. 1, 2006. See also Hassanein Tawfik Ibrahim's chapter 6 in this volume.

[73] Disarmament refers to the voluntary or coerced turning-in of weapons by combatants but also by civilians. Demobilization refers to the elimination of military structures and units and, on an individual basis, the discharge of combatants from these units and the beginning of their transition into civilian life. Reintegration is a process intended to allow the demobilized ex-combatants to (re)integrate themselves into family and society and to earn their living by productive work. Whilst demobilization and disarmament lie within the responsibility of the military and have short-term security goals, reintegration lies within the responsibility of civilian actors and their time-frame and objectives are longer and more vague. See Reto Rufer, 'Disarmament, Demobilization and Reintegration (DDR): Conceptual Approaches, Specific Settings, Practical Experiences', Geneva: Geneva Centre for Democratic Control of Armed Forces (DCAF), Working Paper, 2005; and also the concluding chapter in this book.

[74] Nat J. Colletta, Markus Kostner, and Ingo Wiederhofer, 'Disarmament, Demobilization, and Reintegration: Lessons and Liabilities in Reconstruction', in Rotberg (ed.), *When States Fail*, pp. 170–81.

forms of direct combat and combat support and those who propagate the opposite.[75] Yet, the role of PMFs in contemporary warfare is becoming increasingly significant and the activities of the private military industry seem to have grown beyond the point of no return. Nevertheless, the absence of regulation in the private provision of military and security services, and the inadequacy of measures to hold their companies and their employees to account for their actions, are of particular concern. Indeed PMFs are not controversy-free. Whilst they are integral parts of military operations, they are not clearly part of the military. This indicates the blurring of lines between civilians and soldiers. As Peter Singer highlights in this volume, private military contractors are not exactly civilians, given that they often carry arms and fulfil military roles, but they are not clearly soldiers either, as they are not part of the service or in the chain of military command. Like other VNSAs—notably in Africa—PMFs have introduced dilemmas both on the legal side, since the law is state-centred, and on the accountability side, since it is frequently unclear who should investigate, prosecute and punish crimes committed by PMFs and/or their employees.[76] Hence the need for states to control the private provision of military and security services and develop standard contracting policies, establish monitoring systems, and ensure accountability and legislative oversight.[77] Legal responses relating not just to PMFs but to VNSAs generally are much needed, and this is a theme to which the concluding chapter of this book returns.[78]

## Concluding remarks

A wide gamut of violent non-state actors have acquired significant importance in contemporary world politics, in so far as such actors contest the legitimacy of state monopolization of organized violence more than ever before. The purpose of this Introduction has been to provide an overall context for the

---

[75] For the latter view see Steven Brayton, 'Outsourcing War: Mercenaries and the Privatization of Peacekeeping', *Journal of International Affairs*, Vol. 55, No. 2, Spring 2002, pp. 303–29. For the former view see Fabien Mathieu and Nick Dearden, 'Corporate Mercenaries: The Threat of Private Military and Security Companies', London: War on Want, November 2006 [www.waronwant.org].

[76] Refer to Peter Singer's chapter in this volume.

[77] Schreier and Caparini, 'Privatizing Security'.

[78] Alyson J.K. Bailes and Daniel Nord, 'Non-State Actors in Conflict: A Challenge for Policy and for Law', chapter 19 below.

contributions in this volume, by integrating their main arguments with those of the existing literature with a view to highlighting some key themes and laying out a framework for analyzing origins, evolution, operations, and responses to contemporary VNSAs, primarily from a political science perspective. Just like states, VNSAs are not inherently 'good' or 'evil'. Nor are they inherently 'legitimate' or 'illegitimate'. They are neither monolithic nor necessarily ideology driven. VNSAs are too diverse a phenomenon to lend themselves to parsimonious theory. Hence the search for generalizations that purport to explain all VNSAs might not be terribly useful. It is better instead to concentrate on the study of VNSAs on a case by case basis, whilst employing a compare and contrast analysis which may lead to contingent generalizations. In this spirit the contributions in this volume offer an in-depth treatment of the themes laid out above in the context of specific case studies.

# 2

# Fragmentation of Sovereignty and Violent Non-State Actors in Colombia

*Nazih Richani*

This chapter has three main objectives. One is to illustrate briefly key histori-cal differences between European and Latin American state formations; this is discussed in the first part. The second is to contextualize the crisis of the Colombian state within the changing global environment in which a state's sovereignty and functions are redefined by the imperatives of global capitalism while its power is contested by violent non-state actors (VNSAs)—guerrillas, regional political bosses, drug traffickers and their paramilitaries. Finally, this research concludes with a possible scenario under which state sovereignty may be reconstituted and the role of VNSAs mitigated.

## State weakness in historical perspective

The Treaty of Westphalia in 1648 inaugurated a new era in Europe where states were recognized as sovereign, a model that evolved and was replicated on a glo-bal scale. Nonetheless, the national state building process was never uniform even in the European context. European state building followed different paths that were determined by the dialectics between violence and capital, along with their respective institutional, organizational, and class embodiments.[1]

[1] Charles Tilly, *Coercion, Capital, and European States AD 990–1992*, Cambridge, Mass.:

Where coercive power was harnessed to facilitate the advancement of capital, the outcome was development and prosperity.[2] That was because institutional and class relations prevented those who controlled the instruments of violence from using them for their personal welfare. This explains why some states in Europe, for example England and France, were more successful in attaining progress than others, such as Poland, Italy, and Spain.

Greif attributed Europe's initial economic and political success to the weakness of the centralized state and the large kin-based social units, coupled with the distribution of military ability among economic agents;[3] as a consequence, in Greif's view, political actors and judges had limited power to structure the market and the polity for their exclusive interests.[4] The main countervailing powers were merchants and their respective guilds and institutions that represented their rules, beliefs, norms, and class interests, alongside peasant resistance which mitigated the rulers' predatory behaviour.[5]

Institutional arrangements also were shaped by external military threats and economic competition among states and corporations. The effectiveness of these arrangements determined the survival of the state or its disappearance, as in the case of several states that were absorbed or combined into larger national states.[6]

In contrast, the experiences of Third World countries differed markedly. One reason was that their independence was obtained under substantially different global conditions in which, for the most part, local political leaders did not have to contend with external threats or depend on local economic elites to raise capital. They could borrow from international institutions and/ or sell cash crops and minerals.[7] Consequently, the institutional arrangements

---

Blackwell Publishing, 1992; Avener Greif, *Institutions and the Path to the Modern Economy: Lessons from Medieval Trade*, New York and Cambridge: Cambridge University Press, 2006; Robert Bates, *Prosperity and Violence: The Political Economy of Development*. New York: WW Norton, 2001.

[2] Bates, *Prosperity and Violence*.

[3] Greif, *Institutions and the Path to the Modern Economy*, p. 401.

[4] Ibid.

[5] Tilly, *Coercion, Capital, and European States AD 990–1992*.

[6] Ibid., p. 190.

[7] During the 19th century Latin American countries borrowed heavily from Britain's banks and others to fund their wars of independence and their consequent internal wars. In 1824–25, for example, Colombia's foreign debt was the highest in the region, amounting to 6.75 million English pounds. See Roberto Junguito Bonnet, *La Deuda Externa en el Siglo 19: Cien Anos de Incumplimiento* (Bogotá: Banco de La República, 1995), p. 56.

that governed their relations with their respective constituencies gave those political rulers the upper hand in negotiating the state's relationship with the dominant and dominated classes. Consequently, a key component of democratic governance (defined as a set of institutional arrangements reflecting differentiated class and political interests) was weak or not present in states formed in the 19th and 20th centuries.

In the developing world, the state was formed top-down rather than by the bottom-up historical process characteristic of the European case after Westphalia. Local elites inherited the colonial states institutions. These largely superimposed political, organizational, economic and constitutional models of their colonizers were met with local resistance, as the Latin American experience demonstrates. After the collapse of Spanish colonial rule, a long period of civil war ensued, largely to determine who controlled the state, its resources, and the forms of government.[8]

These civil wars produced different state structures and capacities in Latin America. Consequently, the strength of state capacities depended on the type of political and class compromises between the main competing forces, political alliances, and civil-military relations. Thus some states graduated from the process stronger than others in terms of their control over the use of violence. Colombia, for one, emerged from its war of independence (1811–22) and its internal wars that characterized its post-independence period with a weak central government, a reduced national army of about 6,000 men by the turn of the 20th century, and strong regional *caudillos* who controlled their respective regions. It is not surprising that as late as 1876, Antioquia, one of the most industrious regions in Colombia, was able to amass an army of 14,000 men much better equipped than the central army, and defeat it.[9] As I have discussed elsewhere,[10] Colombia's state builders, for better or worse, had the

---

This borrowing from a foreign source weakened the institutional process of state making in Latin America then. And in the 20th century this pattern continues to affect the development of the instruments of good governance.

[8] Frank Safford, 'Politics, Ideology, and Society', in Leslie Betnel (ed.), *Spanish America after Independence, 1820–1870*, New York: Cambridge University Press, p. 84; Douglass North, William Summerhill and Barry Weingast, 'Order, Disorder and Economic Change in Latin America versus North America', in Bruce Bueno De Mesquita and Hilton Root, eds, *Governing For Prosperity*. New Haven: Yale University Press, 2000.

[9] Fernando Lopez-Alves, *State Formation and Democracy in Latin America 1800-1900*, Durham, NC: Duke University Press, 2000, p. 136.

[10] Nazih Richani, 'Caudillos and the Crisis of the Colombian State: Fragmented Sovereignty, the War System and the Privatization of the Counterinsurgency.' *Third World Quarterly*, Vol. 28. No 2, 2007, pp. 407–17.

daunting task of confronting the most inhospitable and scarcely populated terrain in Latin America with a weak army and limited extractive capacity.[11] These factors helped the challengers of the central government, thereby shaping Colombia's state formation in the 20th century and beyond.

In an analysis of non-violent actors it is imperative to contextualize the 'grey areas' in the international system where the Westphalian state model was deformed, or state formation was never completed or else was interrupted. The Colombian case represents a case of incomplete state formation in which the state-making process produced a loose federation in which the regions and their respective class and political elites occupied a privileged position at the expense of the central government—a situation that contributed to its inherent weakness and inability to expand its authority, marking the country's history ever since. Colombia approximates Charles Tilly's 'capital intensive mode' of state building in which rulers relied on pacts with capitalists (landowners, merchants and bourgeoisie) who in turn effectively refused to finance strong and permanent state structures, so that a condition of 'fragmented sovereignty' emerged. In such conditions, regional *caudillos* and their contemporary mutations (the narcobourgeoisie)[12] have continued to wield considerable power in determining state policies on a range of issues, including taxation, land reform and distribution, credit, and national security.

Thus it is no surprise that in the 20th century the country witnessed a protracted civil war, from 1948 to 1958, championed by the two rival political parties vying for political power, the Liberal and Conservative Parties. The state and its armed forces were caught between being observers and partici-

---

[11] Colombia is the least densely populated in Latin America, with a population density index of 0.42; the second and third lowest are Brazil with 0.49 and Venezuela with 0.54. Its terrain was classified as the third most inhospitable among 155 countries. See 'Vision Colombia' in *Centenario 2019*, Bogotá: Planeta, DNP, and Presidencia de la República, 2005, pp. 110–1.

[12] The term narcobourgeoisie is used to differentiate this faction from the rest of its class. This differentiation is based on the following criteria: a) its mode of extraction of surplus value from coca growers and the labour that is involved in the processing of coca into cocaine; b) profits that it draws from the marketing of its commodity; c) its peculiar position between legality and illegality; and finally d) the centrality of violence to organizing its business, from the surplus value extraction to enforcing of contracts. Notwithstanding these differences from the rest of the Colombian bourgeoisie, the narcobourgeoisie shares with some of its class counterparts a common interest in reinforcing a rentier-based capitalist economy in which services, speculation (including speculation in land rents and real estate), and some exports such coal, oil, gold, coffee and flowers play a dominant role.

pant observers in this conflict in which local *caudillos* (political bosses of both warring parties) commanded their partisans and also their followers in the police and the army. One of the main outcomes of this war was restoration of the political power of large landowners and the commercial bourgeoisie in determining land ownership and distribution, weakening the state's institutional capacities as an adjudicator or mediator of land conflict; this is key to our understanding of the underlying causes of a second civil war, led this time by anti-establishment insurgency in Colombia.

Two Marxist groups, the Fuerzas Armadas Revolucionarias de Colombia (FARC, Revolutionary Armed Forces of Colombia), and the smaller group of Ejército de Liberación Nacional (ELN, National Liberation Army), are the two principal violent non-state actors. Each insurgent group has been based in the country's peripheral regions where the state has scant presence in terms of services and institutions. Moreover, the most impoverished peasants, constituting around 30 per cent of the population, currently reside in these areas.[13]

The inherent weakness of the Colombian state since its independence was only compounded by intra-elite conflict and then by an armed opposition led by rebel groups. The following section underscores how the state's weakness manifested itself in the era of globalization.

## State redefinition and systems of violence

*Grey and dark in the global system.* At the outset, a clarifying note is in order. It is very important to differentiate among a host of states that are currently confronting crises. Roughly, these states can be divided into two broad categories. In one category are those states that have fragmented sovereignty but possess a functioning central government providing basic services (such as water, electricity, health, sanitation, education) and delivering public goods, including security in its main cities, and also have a working economy where the enforceability of contracts is viable. The second category comprises the collapsed states which lack functioning governments, as well as other characteristics mentioned above; quintessential examples are Somalia, Iraq and Afghanistan.

In the first category there are states which share their sovereignty with violent actors who largely operate in the peripheral areas of the countryside and/ or in the poor sections of main urban centres. In this category, alongside

[13] Nazih Richani, *Systems of Violence: The Political Economy of War and Peace in Colombia*, New York: SUNY Press, 2002.

Colombia, there are states such as Sri Lanka, India, Pakistan, Yemen, Sudan, Lebanon, Guatemala, El Salvador, and Honduras. In these states there is a condition of fragmented sovereignty, complemented by a 'system of violence', defined as a pattern of interaction among state and non-state violent actors (such as army, police, private security, organized criminal groups, gangs, warlords, and rebel groups). In this system state and non-state actors coexist, conflict, and cooperate tacitly and implicitly. Consequently, this system of violence, if consolidated, acquires its own dynamic and political economy which allow its perpetuation over a long period of time. This explains why some states are in a condition of perpetual, endless violence. Together these states constitute the 'grey areas' in which states partially control their territories but there are 'dark areas' where state authority has totally collapsed. In these two areas rebel groups, criminal organizations, and terrorists find safe havens and launching grounds.

It is not a novelty to claim that where there is a vacuum in a state's institutions the most likely outcome is that violent entrepreneurs will exploit it. We have witnessed this phenomenon not only in the cases I mentioned above but also in Eastern Europe and in the former Soviet Union during and after the period of transition. Questions could be asked about situations where the state is consolidated yet criminal groups still operate freely. The answer is that social control is a matter of degree, largely depending on the progression of the state's distributive and coercive capabilities on one hand and, on the other, violent actors' adaptability and ability to penetrate state institutions. The quintessential case is Italy where organized crime's sophistication, alongside the complicity of the state and the dominant classes, allowed the crime economy to reach around 7 per cent of Italy's GDP in 2006.[14]

Hence, VNSAs' success or failure does not depend only on states' control capabilities, but also on the VNSAs' co-opting power and the availability of political entrepreneurs that lend tacit or implicit support to these groups for political and economic returns.[15] Such conditions make the question in hand more complex, and answering it requires a multifaceted approach that takes into account the interests of the different actors involved in the political economy of violence.

---

[14] *New York Times*, 22 October 2007.

[15] It is interesting to note the role of criminal gangs in local elections in cases such as Nigeria's Delta region and India. See *New York Times*, 9 November 2007, p. 16; see also Charles Tilly, *The Politics of Collective Violence*, New York: Cambridge University Press, 2003.

*Colombia's state redefined by global trends and US security imperatives.* In the international system, states' social, economic, and policing functions are constantly being redefined. One can argue that from this system's inception the structures, functions, and institutions of states had to adapt continuously to their changing economic and political environment. But since the mid-20<sup>th</sup> century, and more so in the post-Cold War era, a new impetus has accelerated this process, bringing about fundamental changes whose full magnitude is yet to be appreciated.

The emergence and continuous consolidation of economic blocs such as the EEC and international trade organizations such as the WTO, accelerated internationalization of capital, growth of multinational corporations, increasing privatization of security, the enhanced norms of international human rights and their instruments such as the International Criminal Court (ICC)—these developments combined are undermining state sovereignty and reorienting control capacities. Such transformations are invariably catching states of the 'grey areas' like Colombia off guard. These transformations, however, take various forms depending on the degree of state consolidation, position in the global division of 'labour and security', local resistances to such transformations (including resistance by rebel groups), and international pressures on each of these cases to integrate into the international system.

Consequently, Colombia is currently facing three challenges upon which the outcome of its state building process and the future of its violent actors will depend. Two of these challenges are discussed in this section and the third, stemming from the armed contestation of power, is discussed in the following section.

The first challenge stems from the above-mentioned trend, coupled with the 'neo-liberal economic model' which the country adopted in the late 1980s. Colombia, however, stands out in the fragmented sovereignty pack of countries because of its security importance in the US-designated 'Drug War'. This led to a dual and seemingly contradictory process. On the one hand there is downsizing of the public sector's economic role by privatizing of telecommunications, electricity, banks, water, parts of the state oil company.[16] On the other

---

[16] It is important to mention that the central government's tax income amounted to only 14 per cent of GNP in 2003. This represented a significant increase from the 7 per cent level that began during the coffee boom period until the late 1980s. Tax income is composed of 57 per cent indirect tax and 43 per cent direct. In regional and international comparative terms, Colombia is about the level of Mexico in this respect and behind

hand, the state's instruments of social control have been strengthened. To accomplish this, since 2000 Colombia has received more than $5.4 billion in foreign aid—mostly military—from the United States under 'Plan Colombia'.

This aid contributed to the sharp increase in the country's military force from about 160,000 in 2000 to 380,000 in 2007. One would have expected such an increase in the state's war making capability to lead to an institutional change redefining civil-military relations, the state's relationship with its citizens—dominant and dominated groups. But this did not happen. US aid carried with it some important unintended consequences related to the balance of power among the branches of government. For example, it strengthened the executive at the expense of the legislature and the judiciary. The president gained more latitude in budget allocation and in war and peace decisions, thereby allowing him to avoid addressing competing interests that Congress would otherwise have brought to bear. Uribe's aggressive war agenda required an unprecedented increase in the defence budget (about 4.5 per cent of GDP), implemented with little resistance from the legislature or judiciary.[17] Consequently, during Alvaro Uribe's government, the legislature witnessed diminishing power in these crucial areas. This is compounded by the '*parapolítica*' scandal which implicated about 60 members of parliament in links with right-wing paramilitaries, thereby tarnishing the institutions' legitimacy, and consequently increasing the president's leverage in passing bills.[18] Last but not least, the military institution continues allocating its budget without civilian oversight and accountability.

The dominant economic groups on their part agreed to pay a 'war tax' of 1.2 per cent on capital that exceeds 1.3 million dollars, from January 2006 until 2010, thereby reinforcing a diminishing foreign aid commitment on the part of the US. The 'war tax' contribution, however, constitutes only a fraction of US aid, alongside what the government collects in indirect taxes, which undercut the bargaining power of the dominant classes vis-à-vis the executive.[19]

---

Chile (18 per cent), the USA (20.4 per cent), the UK (36.3 per cent), South Africa (24 per cent), and Turkey (19.1 per cent).

[17] Mauricio Cardenas, Ximena Cadena and Carlos Caballero, 'El Incremento en el Gasto en Defensa Y Seguridad: Resultados Y Sostenibilidad de la Estrategia', in Alfredo Rangel (ed.), *Sostenibilidad de la Seguridad Democrática*. Bogotá: Fundación Seguridad y Democracia, 2005. The military budget may have increased to 6 per cent of the GDP in 2007 from 4.5per cent that was recorded in 2002.

[18] Cristina Vélez, 'El Congreso de la Para-Política', *Semana*, 15 December 2007, no 1337.

[19] The government estimated that it would raise around $4 billion between 2006 and 2010

Another factor may have weakened the role of this social group, and that lies in its inherent dependence on the executive to promote economic policies that favour it. This is in spite of attempts during the last ten years to articulate and chart an independent path from the state (particularly the executive). This group has yet to articulate a vision and chart a distinct path and hence has exercised no leadership in the Gramscian sense.[20] The dominated groups' resistance to indirect taxation, which constitutes about 57 per cent of government revenue, has been minimal.[21]

Hence the state's ability to raise capital from an international source has made it less accountable domestically and has not contributed to consolidation of the democratic instruments of good governance. More important, this international subsidy allowed decision makers to choose 'guns rather butter' by minimizing the socioeconomic costs that their war decision may have entailed, thereby undermining the peace negotiation option.[22]

In conclusion, the emerging state in Colombia resulting from its civil war is deficient in the instruments of good governance and distributive capacities as evidenced in its 58.6 GINI index, which has not improved since the late 1990s, and is one of the highest in the world. More important, despite significant improvements in its military capabilities and its instruments of social control the state continues to share sovereignty with rebel groups and rightwing paramilitaries allied with narcotraffickers. These latter have penetrated state institutions, including the judiciary and military, which makes the notion of fragmentation more complicated, and makes the relationship

---

from the 1.2 per cent tax rate imposed on capital that exceeds $1.3 million; that is, an average of almost $1 billion a year to upgrade its military. US aid amounts to $700.000 per year. That is to say, the US is paying for almost 70 per cent of the war effort. I am considering that although the US aid is not only for military purpose, nonetheless it will allow the Colombian government to reallocate funds from social and judicial reform: *El Tiempo*, 22 October 2006. According to *El Tiempo*, the tax revenue on capital has only given the government 1.2 billion pesos in 2007: about $600 million, which is less than what the US aid was for this year: *El Tiempo*, 19 December 2007. Available at http://www.eltiempo.com/economia/2007-12-20/-3867211.html.

[20] Richani, *Systems of Violence*; Antonio Gramsci, *Prison Notebook*, vol. 2, New York: Columbia University Press, 1996.

[21] James Robinson and Miguel Urrutia, *Economia Colombiana del Siglo XX: Un Análisis Cuantitativo*, Bogotá: Banco de la República, 2007, p. 279.

[22] Nazih Richani, 'Third Parties, War System Inertia, and Conflict Termination: The Doomed Peace Process in Colombia 1998–2002', *Journal of Conflict Studies*, vol. 25 no. 2, Winter 2005, pp. 75–103.

between actors of the system of violence (state-paramilitaries-narcobourgeoisie) more intertwined and interdependent.

The following section discusses the contesting role of the two active rebel groups, the FARC and the ELN, and their impact on state sovereignty. Although the role of organized crime and their militias is as important as that of rebel groups in any comprehensive analysis of Colombia's political economy, the following section refers to these groups only when necessary to illustrate the narrative.

## FARC and ELN

The FARC, with an army of about 15,000 fighters, and the ELN, with about 3,000 rebels, have been active since the early 1960s and have succeeded in establishing areas of control since the 1970s and 1980s; the FARC operate mainly in the southeast of the country and the ELN's main areas of concentration are in the northeast. These two groups largely draw more than 70 per cent of their fighting force from the peasantry, especially landless and small peasants.[23]

Ideologically, the two groups differ in terms of their interpretation of revolutionary war and Marxism. The FARC believes that its people's army is the one carrying the revolution from rural to urban centres, drawing its inspiration from the Chinese and Vietnamese experiences. In contrast, the ELN was influenced by Che Guevara's theory of 'el foco' or a small vanguard armed group in rural areas that would promote insurrection in the cities. The FARC's interpretation and translation of Marxism were fused with nationalism as manifested in its Bolivarian ideological undercurrent. The ELN's Marxism is coloured with Liberation Theology doctrines in which the rebel emulates Jesus in his rebellion for the promotion of justice for the poor.

The relationship between these two groups has oscillated between an uneasy alliance in the 1980s and a conflictive one in this century. The causes stem from their political differences and their power struggle in some strategic areas, particularly in the oil-rich departments of Arauca and Casanare. And since the ELN started peace talks with Uribe's government in 2005, the FARC has attempted to co-opt some of the ELN's fighting force, preempting any peace deal with the Uribe government. As of this writing, there is no sign of an imminent deal between the ELN and the Colombian government, nor is there any abatement of tension between the FARC and ELN.

[23] Nazih Richani, *Systems of Violence*.

These two rebel groups have supported their war-making capabilities by extracting rents from multiple sources, including tapping local governments' budgets, ransoms, taxing narcotraffickers, investments in front companies and money laundering.

FARC and ELN Rent-Extraction (1998–99)[24]
($US million)

|  | FARC | ELN |
|---|---|---|
| Tax on narcotraffickers | 180 | 30 |
| Ransom-kidnapping and war tax | 198 | 40 |
| Assaults on financial institutions and banks | 30 | 20 |
| Diversion of government resources and investments | 40 | 60 |
| TOTALS | 448 | 150 |

In this mode, the Colombian rebels share a common characteristic with other movements in the post-Cold War era; they have become more independent in raising funds to finance their wars. The Colombian insurgency may have received assistance and training in the Soviet Union, Vietnam or Cuba during the 1970s and 1980s, but for the most part it has relied on its capacities to extract protection rents from local sources. This may explain that after the collapse of the Soviet Union and the weakening of Cuba's position, the two movements did not suffer from a reduction in resources. On the contrary, they both witnessed significant military growth during the 1990s.

With these war-making capacities, the rebel groups succeeded in establishing control over extensive rural areas. Considering its limited military capacities, the state adopted a military doctrine of containment which led to a condition of uneasy coexistence with the rebels.[25] Consequently, the elements of a war system were sown against the background of the state's weak institutional ability to mediate, arbitrate or adjudicate social conflicts, particularly land property disputes. Again, this weakness is reflected not only in the past military and political impasse with regional *caudillos* and in more recent times with guerrillas, but also in the state's inability to solve the agrarian question,

[24] Source: Richani, *Systems of Violence*, p. 64. In 2005, the Ministry of Finance (Unidad Administrativa Especial de Informacion y Análisis Financiero (UAIF) 2005) presented some estimates that put FARC's income close to $120 million, but these estimates omit some categories, such as returns from investments. This could explain the significant difference between the two estimates.

[25] Nazih Richani, *Systems of Violence*.

in spite of some attempts that were resisted by the large landowners and their allies. This institutional weakness reached a crisis point with the advent of the narcobourgeoisie, which increased the concentration of land in the hands of a few at the expense of the overwhelming majority of the rural population. This crisis can be solved either by introducing structural economic changes, which could allow for a more democratic distribution of land and income, or by the indefinite continuation of warfare until a decisive winner emerges. But even winning the war does not necessarily mean winning the peace, as is shown by the experiences of El Salvador, Guatemala, Nicaragua and South Africa, where criminal violence became new expressions of malaise in a context of intact social structures.

In Colombia, the resistance of the dominant classes—including the narcobourgeoisie—to structural economic changes contributed to the consolidation of a war system. A condition of perpetual violence ensued, maintained by a military balance that did not allow the emergence of a decisive winner, and was reinforced by the warring parties' perception that the costs (including the risks) of peace exceeded the costs of war. I think that this condition prevailed between the 1970s and the mid-1990s when a new force emerged, the narcobourgeoisie and its paramilitary militias; these generated a new dynamic that destabilized the war system, which until then consisted mainly of a bi-polar system (state versus guerrillas).

In the mid-1990s, a number of right-wing paramilitary groups formed a national confederation under the name of the Autodefensas Unidas de Colombia (AUC, the 'united self-defence forces of Colombia'). Its purpose was to combat the leftist insurgency and also to enhance its negotiating power with the central government; its leaders became some of the largest landowners in the country, with estimated landholdings ranging between 3 million and 5 million hectares with an estimated value of $US 2.4 billion.[26] These landholdings constitute about 4.4 per cent of the total land area of 114 million hectares.[27]

The AUC leadership, alongside the narcobourgeoisie, is the modern mutation of the traditional landowning class and regional *caudillos*. However, while the narcobourgeoisie shares with the traditional *caudillos* a mistrust of strong central government that may compromise their class interests, it differs from

---

[26] Ricardo Rocha, *La Economía Colombiana tras 25 años de Narcotráfico*, Bogotá: UNDCP, 2000, p. 121.

[27] Marcelo Giugale, Olivier Lafourcade and Connie Luff, *Colombia: The Economic Foundation of Peace*, Washington DC: The World Bank, 2003, p. 563.

the old landowning class in two crucial characteristics: it uses land as a money laundering mechanism, and the class origins of its members are middle and lower class, from small and intermediate sized cities.[28] In this mode, this force emerged with an articulated political goal: preventing a political settlement that would undermine its class interests, which touched on a fundamental issue in the search for a negotiated settlement with the FARC.

In alliance with cattle ranchers, agribusinesses, large landowners, and conservative political entrepreneurs, the AUC made it difficult for the Andrés Pastrana government (1998–2002) to compromise on land redistribution, which in part might explain the failure of the peace talks with the FARC.[29] More important, the AUC and its allies facilitated the consolidation of regional *caudillos'* political power, creating a 'reactionary configuration' in which labour-repressive practices are applied in agribusinesses and other businesses that operate in their areas of influence. With blood and fire, the AUC made this labour repression possible, leading to the assassination of hundreds of trade union leaders, human right activists, members of leftist organizations, and teachers. This has reduced considerably the negotiating power of labour vis-à-vis capital, which has been increasing the extraction of surplus value of labour by decreasing wages.

Now, in spite of the demobilization of some of the AUC's military structures under an amnesty deal negotiated with government, several military structures are still operating in different departments and new ones have emerged as well. This indicates that the state is yet to implement the rule of law throughout its territory. Moreover, at the municipal level there is no evidence that the AUC's influence has diminished after the demobilization of some of its armed structures. Informants in the Middle Magdalena region reiterated that the AUC command and control structure and its coercive capacities are still imposing its political will on the citizens of these areas.[30] These findings are consistent with the new political strategy articulated by Mancuso, one of the principal AUC leaders, now in a US prison. This strategy consists of three basic elements, two of which are relevant here: first, that the AUC's functions will not cease to exist with the demobilization; second, that

---

[28] Nazih Richani, 'Caudillos and the Crisis of the Colombian State'.

[29] Richani, 'Third Parties, War System Inertia, and Conflict Termination'.

[30] Author's interviews, 2005. Richani, 'Caudillos and the Crisis of the Colombian State'. For obvious security reasons the names of the informants interviewed by the author cannot be revealed. The interviews were carried out in August 2005 in Barancabermeja, Puerto Wilches and San Pablo, all in the Middle Magdalena region.

the AUC will not cede the territories under its control to the insurgency, but will rather continue protecting these regions within an integrated defence strategy that will safeguard the established socio-economic order, including the new political and economic power holders associated with the AUC.[31] This political strategy could explain why little has changed on the ground in the wake of the ostensible demobilization of 31,000 AUC fighters and members of logistical support units.

## The war system's dynamics 1998–2007[32]

The AUC targeted the guerrillas' support base by committing hundreds of massacres, destroying villages, and forcing people to move. Initially the ELN's base area was subjected to such a scorched earth approach because it was considered a softer target than the FARC, and because its forces and popular bases were in oil, coal, and gold rich areas in the north of the country which were considered strategic to all warring actors, including the state. As a result, the ELN's military and extractive capacities were considerably downgraded between 1998 and 2007, particularly in Middle Magdalena and South Bolivar and in the departments of Arauca, Casanare, Santander and North Santander. Consequently, the ELN was forced to retreat from its historic areas of influence.[33] The FARC, for their part, suffered important blows at the hands of an

---

[31] *Desmovilizar a los Paramilitares en Colombia: Una Meta Viable?*, Bogotá: International Crisis Group, 5 August 2004, p. 9.

[32] After the writing of this paper significant events took place that could further affect FARC's strategies as well as the correlation of forces between the warring parties. One was the killing of Raul Reyes and Ivan Rios, both members of the Secretariat, which is the highest authority in the FARC; then there was the death due to heart failure of the founder and supreme commander of the FARC, Manuel Marulanda. Alongside these losses, the FARC suffered a moral blow when military intelligence, with the instrumental help of the US military including its Special Forces (about 900 US personnel may have participated in this operation), carried out a successful operation in which the French hostage Ingrid Betancourt, three US military contractors, and 11 Colombian soldiers were rescued from the FARC. These events must be seen in the context of a series of other setbacks which make clear that the FARC are at a crossroads where their 44–year-long struggle could depend on their ability to regain the political and military initiative. The number of US personnel was quoted from the Simon Romero, 'US Aid Was a Key to the Hostage Rescue', 13 July 2008, p. 10. The US may have participated in the operation that led to the killing of Raul Reyes.

[33] For a discussion of the political economy of massacres and the strategies deployed by the right-wing paramilitaries since the mid-1990s see Richani, *Systems of Violence*,

empowered military with the technical, intelligence, and surveillance assistance of the US, forcing it to retreat in its military strategy from a 'war of positions' to a 'guerrilla war'. This tactical shift in military strategy demonstrates the FARC's ability to adapt to a changing confrontation. Now their forces are dispersed into smaller units making them less susceptible to detection from the air.

In military terms, then, since the second half of this decade there is a new correlation of forces emerging in which the military and its right-wing paramilitary allies have the edge, but this does not yet represent a qualitative leap, nor does it mean that the state's victory is imminent. The FARC still have some important cards to play including a favourable regional environment that could alter the war system balance. The two left-wing governments of Venezuela and Ecuador are providing 'tacit or implicit' logistical support that could help the guerrillas fortify their strategic depth by allowing them to regroup, train, rearm, and retreat. Finally, it is important to note, that the FARC's rent extraction capability may have been affected by the sustained military offensive in parts of the south, which would affect its recruitment and armament; but there is no evidence to assess the significance or magnitude of this.

What is evident, however, is that the FARC are dodging bullets and waiting out the offensive, while the state is attempting to consolidate its gains by positioning police forces in almost all municipalities that were under guerrilla control in the 1990s and early 2000s. These military gains, however, are falling short in terms of establishing the rule of law and have yet to address the economic plight of the country's rural population where the incidence of poverty is around 80 per cent, including 42 per cent within the range of extreme poverty.[34]

Colombia's future looks bleak because the core issues remain unresolved, namely, a more equitable land distribution supported by a long term plan for sustainable economic development. These issues are not on the agenda of the neo-liberal economic model adopted by the state. Consequently, the war system may remain as a default mechanism for conflict resolution, re-distribution of income, and an avenue for employment.

---

pp. 119–22. It is estimated by the UNHCR (Office of the UN High Commissioner for Refugees) that Colombia has about 3 million displaced people, a figure exceeded only by Sudan.

[34] Figures available at http://www.usaid.gov/policy/budget/cbj2006/lac/co.html.

It is not surprising, then, that the narcobourgeoisie and other large land-owners are finding it easy to rebuild their militias that were demobilized during the last two years. And one of the main causes of easy recruitment is the lack of economic and social opportunities in the rural areas as well as the medium-sized and large cities. It is estimated that more than 10,000 paramilitaries are currently active, who include former and new recruits.[35] The insurgents, on the other hand, continue to present a diametrically opposed avenue for the unemployed, underemployed, adventurers, and the politically motivated. Even before the full impact of the global economic crisis is felt in the rural economy, the insurgency has been able to continue its recruitment in at least 62 municipalities, allowing it to replace every 100 men lost in combat or through desertion between 2002 and 2007 by 84 new recruits.[36] Criminal groups, including gangs, also are important recruiting grounds in the main cities. In this regard, Bogotá alone has more than 12,000 gang members.[37] The same phenomenon exists in the cities of Medellín, Cali, Bucaramanga, Barranquilla, and Cartagena where 80 gangs and criminal groups with an estimated membership of 15,000 young people are operating.[38] It is plausible to argue that if the civil war ends tomorrow and the country does not address its economic ills, the most likely outcome is a new system of violence with a different set of actors (including some former combatants), dynamics and political economy.

## Concluding remarks

The state's commitment to the neo-liberal economic model and the Uribe government's push to sign a Free Trade Agreement with the US demonstrate that decisions-makers are not weighing the possible consequences of such policies and agreements on the Colombian conflict, the coca economy and the rural sector generally. Poor, small, and medium peasants are not expected to be able to compete with the influx of cheaper subsidized products from the US and elsewhere, which include traditional staples such as maize, rice,

---

[35] Comisión Colombiana de Juristas, Boletin N. 29, Bogotá, p. 3.
[36] José Fernando Isaza Delgado y Diogenes Campos Romero, 'Algunas Consideraciones Cuenatitativas Sobre la Evolución Recente del Conflicto en Colombia', unpublished paper, Bogotá, December 2007.
[37] Leandro Ramos, *Características, dinámicas y condiciones de emergencia de las pandillas en Bogotá*, Bogotá: Alcaldia Mayor de Bogotá DC, 2004.
[38] See Jorge Márquez Barbosa Sicarieos y pandilleros 'ponen' los muertos en Cartagena', *El Espectador*, 9 April 2009.

chicken, meat, dairy products and potatoes. This will force producers either to abandon their lands and migrate to the cities where jobs are already scarce or shift to alternative cash crops. The most likely cash crop substitute is coca plantations with three crops a year, minimal transport costs—since coca traders pick up the crops from centres not far from areas of production—and prices that are superior to any of the traditional crops. Obviously, then, it is plausible that if free market dogma persists as a policy coca production might increase, as evidently has been the case during this decade. According to the State Department's International Narcotics Control Strategy Report (2007 and 2008) the areas of coca cultivation increased from 113,850 hectares in 2004 to 144,000 and 157,200 in 2005 and 2006 respectively. This was the highest increase since 1997 when only 79,500 hectares were covered, except for 2001 when the acreage reached 169,800 hectares.

It is difficult to envisage a sustainable peace and viable state without the resolution of two intertwined undercurrents of the country's protracted conflicts: land distribution and a viable substitute for coca plantations, one of the main fuels of the civil war and crime. Both issues, alongside a rethinking of prevailing economic policies, will determine the nature of the state and of good governance. A core question can be posed here: will the state be able to reconstitute its sovereignty?

Given the new international political economy, Colombia, as well as other 'grey area' states, is constantly negotiating its sovereignty with international and national forces. These negotiations produce multiple outcomes depending on a number of variables, including the correlation of forces between a hegemonic class alliance that dominates the state at a given moment and its armed opposition. In Colombia, an educated guess is that the state will continue to share its power on one hand with regional *caudillos*, including the narcobourgeoisie and its right-wing militias, and on the other hand with the armed insurgency.

This condition could change if the state and its armed opposition succeed in reaching a 'historic compromise' that would permit formulation of a development strategy for the agrarian economy in which the economic interests of the landless, subsistence peasants, small peasants, and medium peasants are given as much consideration as those of agribusiness. Such a solution might contain elements of a long-term solution for coca plantations and narcotrafficking, and consequently might mitigate the 'fragmentation of sovereignty' and its corollary war system. Until then, the war system with its violent actors and political economy will continue to operate.

In conclusion, from the 19th century violent actors successfully challenged the state, which struggled to overcome its inherent weakness, particularly its ineffectiveness to extract rent. The dominant classes and regional *caudillos* constantly resisted paying taxes and perfected the art of evasion, while the state was unable to enforce the law. The repercussions were multiple, including restriction of the state's distribution and coercive capacities. This in turn reduced significantly the opportunity costs of rebellion. Rebellion became cheaper given the dismal social conditions of the bulk of the country's population, while the state's coercive capacity has remained limited.

From 2000 this dilemma of the state was exacerbated by the United States aid, which relieved the state and the dominant classes from assuming their responsibilities of good governance. While this aid contributed to the strengthening of coercive capacity it did not consolidate the other important instruments of good governance such as alleviating the condition of poverty, reducing the income and land distribution gap, respect for human rights and the rule of law, sustainable economic development, and a negotiated peace agreement with the guerrilla groups.

3

# From VNSAs to Constitutional Politicians

## Militarism and Politics in the Irish Republican Army

*Jonathan Tonge*

## Introduction

Northern Ireland has been the site of the worst ethnic conflict in Western Europe since the Second World War. Between 1970 and 2005, more than 3,700 people were killed through political violence, in a country of only 1.6 million citizens. The organization responsible for over 1,800 of those deaths was the Irish Republican Army (IRA), the largest and most destructive irregular army in Europe during much of this period. Its demands appeared clear: the withdrawal of the British government's sovereign claim to Northern Ireland and the establishment of a united, independent Ireland. The IRA argued that it was fighting an anti-colonial war against the British government's illegitimate 'occupation' of Northern Ireland. The British government had withdrawn from the remainder of Ireland early in the 20th century, partly because of the force displayed by Irish Republicans, and the IRA believed it could completely end Britain's foothold on the island. Yet by 2005, when the IRA formally abandoned its armed campaign to pursue exclusively political means, the organization and its 'political wing', Sinn Fein, had reached a political agreement with the British which fell far short of declared objectives. This chapter traces the evolution of the IRA, examines the conduct of its violent campaign and explores the reasons why politics and (an imperfect) peace eventually displaced its armed struggle.

## A convoluted IRA history

Assessing the development of the IRA is not an easy task, given the organization's tendencies towards fragmentation and schism. The IRA's antecedents can be found in rebellions against British rule in Ireland from the 1600s onwards. The formation of the Irish Republican Brotherhood in the 1850s, a secret group committed to violence against British rule in Ireland, was followed by the creation of the Irish Volunteers, who with other groups rose against British forces at Easter in 1916. Sympathy for the rebellion increased markedly after the British executed its leaders. The political wing of Irish Republicanism, Sinn Fein, won 73 of the 105 Westminster seats in the 1918 all-Ireland election, with the party refusing to recognize the authority of the British parliament. Sinn Fein demanded full independence for Ireland and a government of the Irish Republic was declared the legitimate government. It remained diehard Republican orthodoxy for generations afterwards, influencing 'successor' IRAs, to claim loyalty to the true Irish Republic proclaimed in 1916.

The Republican demand for full independence was, however, not to be met. Under pressure from Protestant British Unionists based predominantly in the north-east corner of Ireland, the British government compromised between the rival forces of Irish nationalism, whose armed Volunteers became the IRA, and Ulster Unionism by partitioning Ireland. A 26–county state was formed in the South of Ireland, with its parliament based in Dublin, eventually becoming the fully independent Republic of Ireland by 1949. The new six-county state of Northern Ireland remained, however, a resolutely British province. Governed at arms' length from the British parliament at Westminster, the devolved regional government and parliament in Belfast were controlled permanently by pro-British Unionists, perceived by the Irish nationalist minority 'trapped' within British Northern Ireland as sectarian, anti-nationalist and anti-Catholic.[1]

For the IRA of the early 1920s, partial progress towards Irish independence was highly divisive. Many within the organization accepted the 1921 Anglo-

[1] Michael Farrell, *Northern Ireland: The Orange State*, London: Pluto, 1980.

Irish Treaty, which offered limited autonomy and partition, as the best deal on offer at the time. Others fought on for a fully independent, united Ireland, leading to the Irish Civil War of 1922. The anti-Treaty wing of the IRA was defeated by its former comrades within the pro-Treaty forces. Although the vast bulk of the anti-Treaty IRA soon entered constitutional politics, via the Fianna Fail party, a small rump remained committed to violence as a tool to end Britain's sovereign claim to Northern Ireland. For this group, British interference in the 'indivisible island' was unacceptable. Acceptance of British rule and the partition of Ireland was a betrayal of the previous generations of 'blood sacrificers' who had given their lives in the cause of Irish freedom: a mandate from the dead rather than the living.[2]

Utterly marginalized from the 1920s until the beginning of the 1970s, the IRA struggled merely to exist. The lack of impact was emphasized by its campaign of violence along the Irish border from 1956 until 1962. 'Operation Harvest' led to 17 deaths, the majority (11) of whom were IRA members, and attracted little backing from 'oppressed' Irish nationalists in Northern Ireland, from whom the IRA might have expected support. As obituaries were issued for the IRA, the organization called off its campaign, claiming that the Irish population had been distracted from the issue of national, indivisible Irish sovereignty.[3]

## Understanding the rebirth of the IRA in 1970

Given the marginalization of the organization from the early 1920s until the late 1960s, the rise of the IRA at the beginning of the 1970s, from an irrelevance into the most formidable violent non-state actor in Europe, was a remarkable achievement. Formed in January 1970 after a split in the Republican movement, the Provisional IRA (the term 'Provisional' was used to demonstrate allegiance to the Provisional government established in Ireland earlier in the century, usurped by the British government) quickly displaced the more Marxist-leaning 'Official' IRA in terms of its level of violence. The Republican traditionalists of the Provisionals split because of the IRA's willingness, by the end of the 1960s, to recognize 'partitionist' parliaments in Northern Ireland and the Irish Republic, which remained illegitimate in Republican

---

[2] J. Bowyer Bell, *The Secret Army: The IRA*, Dublin: Poolbeg, 1997; Tim Pat Coogan, *The IRA*, London: HarperCollins, 2000.

[3] Patrick Bishop and Eamonn Mallie, *The Provisional IRA*, London: Heinemann, 1987.

orthodoxy.[4] Moreover, the Provisionals wished to defend nationalist areas from pro-British loyalist attacks, a measure seen as sectarian within the IRA of the late 1960s, which was anxious to promote working-class unity across Northern Ireland's traditional faultline.

Provisional IRA leaders had become disenchanted with the leftward drift of the IRA during the 1960s and the movement away from physical force. The fracture within a moribund IRA might have passed largely unnoticed had it not been for the conjunction of that event with political deterioration in Northern Ireland. The physical force traditionalists, uninterested in reforming Northern Ireland as part of a 'stageist' approach to political change, argued that the state could not be reformed, an argument strengthened by the mistreatment of civil rights protests by the authorities. Such a claim appealed to a section of the working-class Catholic population suffering disadvantage in an Orange state. For some within this grouping, a campaign to overthrow British oppressors, whether based in Northern Ireland in the local security services or 'imported' from Britain via the Army, was an appealing proposition.

The IRA's rebirth needs to be understood in the context of the failings of the one-party Unionist government presiding over the Northern Ireland state from 1920 onwards, exemplified by its unwillingness to incorporate Catholic nationalists within structures of government and the physical force displayed by its police service in response to civil rights protests during the late 1960s. The sectarian excesses of the Unionist government and authorities were more influential than long-held Irish Republican ideological principles in reviving the IRA. Situational factors were thus more important than ideational principles in explaining the rebirth of the IRA.[5]

As the Unionist government struggled to reform Northern Ireland during the 1960s, civil rights campaigners, mainly but not exclusively nationalist, demanded changes to policing, housing, employment and the local government election franchise. The government found its willingness to improve the plight of Catholic nationalists compromised by hard-line resisters within and beyond its ranks. Based on the black civil rights protests of the United States,

[4] John Horgan and Max Taylor, 'Proceedings of the Irish Republican Army General Convention 1969', *Terrorism and Political Violence*, Vol. 9, No. 4, 1997, pp. 151–8.

[5] Anthony McIntyre, 'Modern Irish Republicanism: The Product of British State Strategies', *Irish Political Studies*, 10, 1995, 97–121; A. McIntyre, 'Modern Irish Republicanism and the Belfast Agreement: Chickens Coming Home to Roost, or Turkeys Celebrating Christmas?' in Rick Wilford (ed.) *Aspects of the Belfast Agreement*, Oxford University Press, 2001, pp. 202–22.

demonstrations for civil rights were met by violence from the police, with the exclusively Protestant 'B' Special reserve force acting in a particularly robust manner. As sectarian violence spread throughout urban areas of Northern Ireland, the British Army arrived to provide a physical barrier between the Protestant and Catholic communities. Although a brief honeymoon period of cordial relations between nationalists and the British Army ensued, deterioration commenced early in 1970. This souring of relations was fuelled partly by IRA attempts to persuade the community not to 'fraternize', but was created mainly by political inertia and Army mistakes. Amid a political vacuum, the British Army came to be viewed as an oppressor of the nationalist population it had initially protected from Unionist and loyalist attacks, a problem exacerbated by the security operations that it conducted, and most notably by internment without trial from 1971. British Army blunders reached their nadir with the killing of fourteen civilians on 'Bloody Sunday' in January 1972; shortly after that the devolved Unionist government was suspended and replaced by direct rule by the British government.

It is thus within the context of local resentments towards the rival loyalist population, the Unionist government, a partisan police force and the perceived oppression of the British Army that the rise of the Provisional IRA is best understood. For many IRA volunteers, there was little ideological commitment to the Republican shibboleths of an indivisible Ireland, the need for unity of Catholic, Protestant and dissenter and severance of the British connection, as espoused by the supposed 'father' of Irish Republicanism, Wolfe Tone, in 1798. The 1916 proclamation of Irish freedom meant far less to many joiners than a desire to 'hit back' at their perceived oppressors, although a united Ireland was seen as a useful final goal in ending repression. English summarizes this neatly: The IRA's appeal 'lay in the manner of its seeming to satisfy so many demands at one. It offered a large-scale promise of defence of person, property and interests, as well as the ultimate reward of sharing in sovereignty as part of a national majority'.[6] In its early years, the Provisional IRA, as a fusion of defensive Catholic nationalism and ambitious Irish Republicanism, enjoyed a short-lived modicum of sympathy from elements within the Fianna Fail government in the Republic of Ireland, which still regarded the Unionist-British control of Northern Ireland as 'unfinished business' to be settled by the British government's withdrawal of its claim to sovereignty.[7]

---

[6] Richard English, *Irish Freedom: The History of Nationalism in Ireland*, London: Macmillan, 2006, p. 400.

[7] Tom Hennessey, *The Origins of the Troubles*, Dublin: Gill and Macmillan, 2005. Henry

What mattered to IRA 'foot-soldiers' was less the principles of Irish Republicanism and more the actuality of local conditions and alienation from the state; ideological development occurred after imprisonment.[8] Despite this, the leadership of the Provisional IRA claimed fidelity to traditional Republican principles. Within this scenario, the Provisional IRA rapidly gained in strength. Middle-class elements within the civil rights movement gravitated towards the moderate constitutional nationalism of the Social Democratic and Labour Party (SDLP) formed in 1970, but working-class militants gravitated towards the IRA.[9]

## From 'quick victory' to 'long war': IRA tactics and strategy

As its violence soared from 1970 until 1972, the IRA believed in a short, sharp victory, leading to rapid British disengagement from Northern Ireland. The death toll was at its highest in 1972, with 497 killed, the majority of deaths arising from IRA bombings and shootings. With Northern Ireland ungovernable, the British government suspended the devolved Unionist government and imposed direct rule from Westminster. In the summer of 1972, the British government invited the IRA leadership for secret talks in London. It appeared that fifty years of marginalization might have ended on the basis of a remarkable rise in Republican fortunes. However, the IRA leadership was not interested in compromise, and overplayed its hand in rejecting anything short of an unambiguous commitment from the British government to withdraw from Northern Ireland. The Senior British Intelligence Officer present, Frank Steele, commented that the IRA Chief of Staff, Sean Mac Stiofain, 'behaved like the representative of an army that had fought the British to a standstill'.[10]

Following the breakdown of the talks, the IRA attempted to step up its campaign. Its core targets were members of the British security forces comprising the British Army, the Ulster Defence Regiment (UDR, the local Army and police support) and police officers in the Royal Ulster Constabulary. These forces suffered 470 (Army), 229 (UDR) and 296 (police) deaths due to

---

Patterson, *The Politics of Illusion*, London: Serif, 1997; Henry Patterson, *Ireland since 1939*, Oxford University Press, 2002.

[8] Richard English, *Armed Struggle: A History of the IRA*, London: Macmillan, 2003.

[9] Gerard Murray and Jonathan Tonge, *Sinn Fein and the SDLP: From Alienation to Participation*, London: Hurst, 2005.

[10] Peter Taylor, *Provos: The IRA and Sinn Fein*, London: Bloomsbury, 1997, p. 123.

IRA actions from 1970 until 1997.[11] However, the deaths of innocent civilians, as on Bloody Friday in July 1972, when the IRA killed nine, alienated those beyond the IRA's core support base. A backlash was already under way, with loyalist paramilitaries killing Catholics (mainly non-IRA members) in an attempt to deter the nationalist community from supporting the IRA. The no-go areas in Belfast and Derry in which the IRA operated with impunity were overrun by the British Army, making it more difficulty for the IRA to operate. A ceasefire in 1974–75 led to the running down of the IRA, although, in border areas in particular, the truce was ignored, leading to a cycle of sectarian killings, belying the IRA's claim to be 'non-sectarian'. More generally, the claim that the IRA was motivated largely by religious sectarianism is unpersuasive.[12] Although the IRA's recruitment base was the Catholic community, the organization was more interested in a victim's membership of the security forces than in their religious denomination, notwithstanding the large number of Protestant civilians killed. Moreover, the IRA was obliged to contend with persistent criticism from the Roman Catholic Church hierarchy, which made clear its view that the IRA was certainly not fighting a 'just war' according to Catholic teaching.[13] This criticism may have impacted adversely upon Sinn Fein's support; practising Catholics are more likely to support the SDLP, subject to variations in social class, for example.[14]

By the mid-1970s, the IRA leadership recognized privately that it could not achieve outright military victory, although the organization could veto any attempt at an internal settlement within Northern Ireland. The IRA needed to restructure its organization into tighter cell units; widen its tiny support base in the Irish Republic; deepen the ideological and political commitment of its members beyond mere 'hitting back' at immediate 'oppressors'; and condition volunteers for a prolonged struggle. The new thinking was outlined by a member of the Republican leadership, Jimmy Drumm, at the Wolfe Tone commemoration in 1977:

...a successful war of liberation cannot be fought exclusively on the backs of the oppressed in the six counties, nor around the physical presence of the British Army.

---

[11] Malcolm Sutton, *An Index of Deaths from the Conflict in Ireland*, Belfast: Beyond the Pale, 2002.

[12] English, *Armed Struggle*, 2003: Robert White, 'The Irish Republican Army and Sectarianism: Moving Beyond the Anecdote', *Terrorism and Political Violence*, Vol. 9, No. 2, 1997, pp. 120–31.

[13] Claire Mitchell, *Religion, Identity and Politics in Northern Ireland*, Aldershot: Ashgate, 2006.

[14] Ian McAllister, 'The Armalite and the ballot box: Sinn Fein's electoral strategy in Northern Ireland', *Electoral Studies*, Vol. 31, No. 1, 2004, pp. 123–42.

Hatred and resentment of this army cannot sustain the war and the isolation of socialist republicans around the armed struggle is dangerous and has produced, at least in some circles, the reformist notion that 'Ulster' is the issue, which can somehow be resolved without the mobilization of the working-class in the twenty-six counties.[15]

Following Drumm's speech, the IRA settled down to a long war, designed to 'sicken the British' into eventual withdrawal. The IRA was confronted by a tough British security policy, with the Secretary of State for Northern Ireland, Roy Mason, promising to 'squeeze the IRA like a tube of toothpaste'.[16] By 1979, however, the IRA had reorganized sufficiently effectively for its ability to continue its campaign to be apparent. Indeed, during that year, the IRA carried out its most destructive attack on British forces, killing 18 soldiers at Warrenpoint.

## Electoral politics and armed struggle

With its military campaign incapable of achieving much in isolation, the IRA opened a second front in the early 1980s, conducting electoral politics via Sinn Fein. The new tactic was developed despite misgivings. The IRA insisted that 'there is no such thing as constitutional politics' in a partitioned Ireland.[17] Sinn Fein's President, Gerry Adams, claimed that 'the terms constitutional nationalism are in fact a contradiction. What we are talking about is British constitutionality'.[18]

Electoralism was to redevelop the link between the IRA and Sinn Fein, reviving the latter. Since the 1930s, the IRA had controlled Sinn Fein.[19] In the 1950s, IRA prisoners stood successfully as Sinn Fein candidates. Throughout the 1970s, Sinn Fein was moribund, subservient to the militarism of the IRA. During the 1980s, this relationship between the two wings of the movement shifted towards parity, before Sinn Fein assumed ascendancy during the peace process of the 1990s, prior to the eventual disappearance of the IRA. This was not a simplistic militarist IRA 'bad cop' versus 'softer' political Sinn Fein 'good cop' relationship. The importance of the IRA meant that for years it 'licensed' political change and promoted a peace process via Sinn Fein. As

---

[15] *Republican News*, 18 June 1977, p. 6.
[16] Mark Urban, *Big Boy's Rules: the SAS and the Secret Struggle against the IRA*, London: Faber and Faber, 1992, p. 111.
[17] *An Phoblacht/Republican News*, 5 September 1981, p. 1; *Iris*, November 1981, p. 98.
[18] *An Phoblacht/Republican News*, 8 August 1985, p. 8.
[19] Brian Feeney, *Sinn Fein: A Hundred Turbulent Years*, Dublin: O'Brien, 2002.

Coakley observes: 'there were important respects in which the IRA 'tail' wagged the Sinn Fein 'dog': there is evidence that significant ideological shifts in Sinn Fein have been preceded—and sanctioned in advance—by fundamental policy re-orientation within the IRA army council'.[20]

At the start of the 1980s, the move into electoral politics and the 'seemingly meteoric political rise' of Sinn Fein were more accident than grand Republican strategic design.[21] They arose from the campaign by Republican prisoners for recognition of their political status, using the tactic of hunger strikes. A Westminster parliamentary by-election was contested by the imprisoned hunger striker Bobby Sands in 1981. Sands rode a rising tide of emotional nationalist sentiment and monopolized the nationalist vote through the decision of the SDLP not to contest the election. These factors led to Sands' victory, a triumph repeated after his death on the hunger strike by his election agent. In the Irish Republic, hunger strikers also enjoyed election victories.

In terms of its immediate demands, the hunger strike failed, having been unnecessarily prolonged despite diminishing propaganda value.[22] However, the political impact of election successes upon a hitherto cautious IRA leadership was seismic. The hunger strikes were instrumental in the 're-interpretation and reconstruction of a dynamic Irish republicanism', one in which fixed ideological positions and campaigning tactics were eventually replaced with much greater flexibility.[23]

Within six months of Sands' death, the Sinn Fein leadership voted to contest elections throughout Britain and Ireland, whilst declining to take seats in any institutions except local councils. This 'armalite and ballot box' strategy was designed to complement the IRA's militarism with regular demonstrations of popular support. With Sinn Fein's electoral candidates mandated to offer unambiguous backing for the IRA's campaign, a vote for the party could indeed be interpreted as support for 'armed struggle', notwithstanding Sinn Fein's movement into community and welfare politics during the 1980s. At the first elections contested by the party under the dual strategy, the 1982

---

[20] John Coakley, 'Constitutional Innovation and Political Change in Twentieth-century Ireland', in John Coakley (ed.) *Changing Shades of Orange and Green: Redefining the Union and the Nation in Contemporary Ireland*, Dublin: University College Dublin Press, 2002, pp. 1–29.

[21] Peter Taylor, *Provos: the IRA and Sinn Fein*, p. 284.

[22] Richard O'Rawe, *Blanketmen: An Untold Story of the H Block Hunger Strike*, Dublin: New Island, 2005

[23] Lawrence McKeown, *Out of Time: Irish Republican Prisoners in Long Kesh 1972–2000*, Belfast: Beyond the Pale, 2001.

Northern Ireland Assembly elections, Sinn Fein performed respectably, gaining one-third of the nationalist vote, a success followed by Gerry Adams' capture of the West Belfast Westminster parliament seat at the following year's British general election.

However, following a promising beginning, Sinn Fein's baseline vote proved also to be a ceiling. The 1985 Anglo-Irish Agreement, prompted by the SDLP and offering the Irish government a voice in Northern Ireland affairs, checked the growth of Sinn Fein support. Atrocities such as the 1987 Enniskillen bombing, in which 11 people were killed while attending a British war commemoration, were viewed with revulsion, the IRA being obliged to acknowledge the 'catastrophic consequences' of its action.[24] Outright condemnation of IRA violence was unthinkable for Sinn Fein's elected representatives, but, aware of the negative impact upon popular opinion of such disasters, Adams warned the IRA at Sinn Fein's *ard fheis* (annual conference) after the Enniskillen bombing to be 'careful and careful again'.

Among Republicans, there were tensions between those wishing to concentrate resources on the armed campaign and others who looked to the eventual supplanting of IRA violence by political activity. Internal critics of the promotion of Sinn Fein activity at the expense of the IRA were removed by the leadership. Meanwhile, Sinn Fein's elected representatives came into ever closer contact with the northern state through their work on local councils. This normal local ward work and entry into local state structures, demanding greater resources for constituents, was set against an IRA campaign attempting to deter inward investment, a contradiction which eventually created pressure for an IRA ceasefire. The IRA's claim that Northern Ireland could not be reformed was set against amelioration of the worst effects of poverty through progressive British social policy.[25]

As Sinn Fein developed as an electoral force, the Republican vision of a united Ireland altered. Federalism was abandoned as policy in favour of a unitary state bereft of concessions to loyalists. This change reflected the gravitation of power to a Northern leadership, centred on Gerry Adams, offering populist polices which rejected political structures in which Unionists could be a majority in a federal Ulster parliament. Concurrently, however, Adams initiated moves which would eventually create the IRA ceasefires and peace process of the 1990s. Via an intermediary reporting to the British govern-

---

[24] *An Phoblacht/Republican News*, 12 November 1987, p. 1.
[25] Michael Cunningham, *British Government Policy in Northern Ireland 1969–2000*, Manchester University Press, 2001.

ment, Adams explored the possibility of a formula for the exercise of Irish self-determination which might end the IRA's campaign, even if its outcome did not automatically produce Irish unity.[26] The public face of the deliberations over Irish self-determination was 'Hume-Adams', the dialogue between the Sinn Fein leadership and that of the SDLP, under John Hume. By 1993, the two leaders had produced a formula under which Sinn Fein had moved closer to the SDLP's position that an 'agreed Ireland' was of greater importance, at least in the short term, than a united Ireland.

Meanwhile, the Adams leadership of the Republican movement shifted the IRA and Sinn Fein towards greater pragmatism, beginning a process of ditching Republican shibboleths. The first aspect of Republican dogma to be swept aside was the boycott of Dail Eireann, the Irish Parliament, hitherto dismissed as a 'partitionist' entity. Pragmatists within the IRA and Sinn Fein argued that Republicans must accept the reality that, whatever the inadequacies of an institution with jurisdiction over only 26 of the 32 counties on the island, Dail Eireann was viewed by the vast majority of Irish people as their legitimate parliament. Backed by correspondence from IRA prisoners to the Republican newspaper *An Phoblacht/Republican News* supporting change, abstention was dropped by a 429–161 vote at the 1986 Sinn Fein *ard fheis*. Critics of the change, some of whom left the party to form Republican Sinn Fein, argued that abandoning the prohibition on entry to 'partitionist' institutions was a fundamental breach of Republican principle, which would eventually be followed by entry into a Northern Ireland parliament.[27]

Republican changes were juxtaposed with a determination to strengthen the IRA's military capability, allowing the IRA and Sinn Fein leaderships to insist that change did not represent compromise or 'sell-out'. Central to this argument was the import of large quantities of large weapons from Libya, the deployment of which was intended to make border areas inoperable for British security forces. It is questionable whether the IRA had sufficient volunteers to execute such a plan, although the interception of the largest consignment of arms by the Irish police rendered any such ambition academic.[28] Whilst the IRA remained a threat, its containment and penetration by agents run by the security forces undermined the organization's effectiveness. Moreover, loyalist paramilitaries, benefiting in some cases from collusion with elements within

[26] Ed Moloney, *A Secret History of the IRA*, London: Allen Lane, 2002.
[27] Robert White, *Ruairi O'Bradaigh: The Life and Politics of an Irish Revolutionary*, Bloomington: Indiana University Press, 2006.
[28] Moloney, *A Secret History of the IRA*.

the police Special Branch and covert units of the British Army, began to target Republicans to an unprecedented extent.[29] Efforts by the IRA to 'remove' loyalist paramilitaries precipitated more sectarian violence. In attempting to target loyalist paramilitary leaders in Belfast in October 1993, the IRA instead killed nine innocent civilians (one of the bombers also died) by detonating a bomb in a fish shop; it had been reported that loyalist paramilitary leaders held a meeting earlier above the shop.

## Developing a peace process

With its military campaign apparently stalled and the political outlet of Sinn Fein having peaked electorally, the initiation of peace was logical for the IRA. However, the process contained several risks. First, it would involve an inevitable dilution of immediate goals and risked splitting a movement far from immune to schism and fracture. Secondly, the commitment of the British government to conflict transformation was unclear. Thirdly, the IRA and Sinn Fein's inexperience in terms of negotiation and their representative position as a minority of the nationalist minority meant that Republicans were reliant upon nationalist allies to back at least some of their stances. Traditionally, Northern Irish nationalists had themselves been beset by division.[30] Given this, the identification of a pan-nationalism which was supposed to allow the IRA, Sinn Fein, the SDLP, the Irish government and Irish America to 'row in the same direction' for the first time, according to a document circulated among IRA members in 1994, seemed ambitious.[31] Whilst there was a cross-nationalist unity desire to see the IRA end its campaign, the political outcome of a pan-nationalist project was not necessarily the same as the IRA's earlier desired direction of a united sovereign Ireland. That document was entitled the TUAS document; it was unclear whether the acronym represented 'Tactical Use of Armed Struggle' or 'Totally Unarmed Strategy'.[32] Such obfuscation formed part of the constructive ambiguity upon which the peace process was constructed, with IRA volunteers regularly being informed by their leadership that a return to violence remained an option, whilst the same leadership gradually placed ever greater distance from the prospect.

[29] Peter Taylor, *Brits: The War Against the IRA*, London: Bloomsbury, 2001.
[30] Enda Staunton, *The Nationalists of Northern Ireland 1918–1973*, Dublin: Columbia, 2001.
[31] Eamonn Mallie and David McKittrick, *The Fight for Peace: The Secret Story of the Irish Peace Process*, London: Heinemann, 1996.
[32] Patterson, *Ireland since 1939*.

The TUAS document followed Sinn Fein's 1992 political offering, *Towards a Lasting Peace in Ireland*, which, whilst restating traditional Republican objectives, removed the timescale for their achievement.[33] The document indicated that the consent and allegiance of loyalists would be required for a united Ireland, although the question of whether this was a prerequisite for the creation of a unitary state was fudged. Throughout the previous decade, Republicans had preached 'unflinching opposition' to the 'reactionary, pro-imperialist philosophy of loyalism'.[34]

Meanwhile other Republican baggage was ditched, most notably at the 1992 Wolfe Tone commemoration at Bodenstown, when the senior Republican Jim Gibney informed the audience that the IRA did not constitute 'a government in waiting'—a repudiation of the position to which the irregular army had clung, however unrealistically, since 1919. Gibney's sub-text was clear: the IRA would have to be included in negotiations, but it could not determine the outcome of such brokering. This softening of position indicated the movement of the IRA and Sinn Fein into a pluralist political marketplace in which they would merely be one actor, rather than the ultimate interpreter and embodiment of the wishes of the Irish people.[35]

Arriving in August 1994, the IRA's ceasefire was widely predicted, even if some members were not informed in advance. The term 'cessation' was used rather than ceasefire, as the latter would have required a full IRA convention, the deliberations of which could not be predicted with certainty. Having assumed that its political representatives in Sinn Fein would quickly be admitted to talks with the British government, the IRA grew impatient as Republicans were forced to undergo an indefinite 'quarantine' period. Delicate parliamentary arithmetic at Westminster meant that the Conservative government was reliant upon Unionist support, a condition hardly conducive to brokering a deal with Sinn Fein. At a Republican rally in 1995, Gerry Adams warned that the IRA had 'not gone away you know', a point conclusively demonstrated early in 1996, when the organization bombed Canary Wharf in London. In June that year, the IRA detonated the largest bomb of the entire campaign, in Manchester. These bombs emphasized the potential economic cost to the British government of a renewed IRA campaign.

[33] Sinn Fein, *Towards a Lasting Peace in Ireland*, Dublin: Sinn Fein, 1992; Kevin Bean, 'The New Departure? Recent Developments in Republican Strategy and Ideology', *Irish Studies Review*, Vol. 10, 1995, pp. 2–6.

[34] *An Phoblacht/Republican News*, 17 October 1981, p. 1.

[35] Jonathan Tonge, *The New Northern Irish Politics?* Basingstoke: Palgrave, 2005; Jonathan Tonge, *Northern Ireland*, Cambridge: Polity, 2006.

Despite the fracturing of the IRA's ceasefire, there was relatively little activity in Northern Ireland, partly because of the IRA's anxiety to avoid another loyalist backlash. The IRA wished to demonstrate the need to include Sinn Fein in talks, rather than generate a return to full-scale violence. The election of a Labour government in 1997, enjoying the luxury of a huge parliamentary majority and prepared to downgrade weapons decommissioning as an issue until after a deal, led the IRA to revive its ceasefire, clearing the path towards inclusive political agreement.

## The IRA and the 1998 Good Friday Agreement

In its 1972 talks with the British government, the first demand lodged by the IRA leadership was that Britain 'make a public declaration that it was for the whole people of Ireland acting and voting as a unit to decide the future of Ireland', while the second 'request' being for the British government to complete withdrawal within three years.[36] It was a measure of the IRA's retreat from absolutism that in 1998 it accepted a deal which offered no guarantee of the second demand and a heavily qualified implementation of the first requirement. The Irish people voted as a whole on the Good Friday Agreement, but on a separate North and South basis. The Agreement kept Northern Ireland in the United Kingdom for as long as the majority of Northern Ireland's citizens so decided. The sophistry of language, the apparent impermanence of constitutional decisions, and the genuflection to Irish self-determination embodied in having referenda north and south of the border could not disguise the legitimacy conferred upon the entity of Northern Ireland evident throughout the Agreement. A united, independent Ireland was not an option which appeared on any Irish citizen's ballot paper in the subsequent all-island vote on the deal. Instead, the Agreement was the 'only show in town', restating the principle of consent within Northern Ireland, establishing an Assembly and Executive to govern the region within the United Kingdom, and creating, via modest cross-border bodies, what Republicans had previously dismissed as 'that sickening English term, the Irish dimension'.[37]

For the IRA, the Good Friday Agreement represented compromise, but facilitated the entry of its political wing into coalition government in Northern Ireland, without the IRA having initially to shed a single weapon. Accept-

[36] Tim Pat Coogan, *The Troubles: Ireland's Ordeal 1966–1995 and the Search for Peace*, London: Hutchinson, 1995, p. 148.
[37] *An Phoblacht*, 20 September 1974, p. 7.

ance of the deal highlighted the recasting of the IRA strategy towards displacement of militarism and fundamentalism by politics and pragmatism. Such change meant temporary embarrassment, epitomised by the sudden switch from 'No return to Stormont' (Northern Ireland's Assembly) in 1997 to support for entry to Stormont in 1998. In this respect, the IRA and Sinn Fein were assisted by the essential teleology of Irish Republicanism: Irish unity is inevitable and therefore reshaped strategies are mere adjustments towards this end of history.

In selling the Good Friday Agreement as progress, Republicans were assisted by the internal wrangling among Unionists, between the then anti-Agreement Democratic Unionist Party (DUP) and the pro-Agreement Ulster Unionist Party (UUP). Although the leader of the UUP at the time of the deal, David Trimble, asserted that the IRA's campaign had 'gone because it was beaten',[38] the DUP, expressing genuine belief but also for tactical advantage, continued to publicly disbelieve for some years afterwards that the IRA's war was over and demanded more from Republicans. The DUP required full decommissioning of IRA weaponry and commitment to the state's police force. Without delivery of these gestures of *bona fides*, it saw Sinn Fein's policy changes as inadmissible.[39]

Decommissioning of IRA weapons was not required under a literal reading of the Good Friday Agreement. Instead, the Agreement placed the issue under the remit of the International Commission on Decommissioning, beyond political parties. Although Sinn Fein had committed to Six Principles of Non-Violence devised by the negotiations broker, Senator George Mitchell, in 1996, the IRA was not a signatory to the Mitchell Principles. Meanwhile, the IRA benefited from the key concession in the Good Friday Agreement: the release of its prisoners within two years of the deal, provided that the IRA's ceasefire remained intact. Other paramilitary groups received the same benefit, but the IRA prisoners formed by far the largest group. Effectively, the British and Irish governments recognised IRA volunteers as political

---

[38] Peter Shirlow and Brendan Murtagh, *Belfast: Segregation, Violence and the City*, London: Pluto, 2006, p. 45.

[39] Peter Shirlow, 'Sinn Fein: Beyond and within Containment', in Jorg Neuheiser and StefanWolff (eds) *Peace at Last? The Impact of the Good Friday Agreement on Northern Ireland*, London: Berghahn, 2002, pp. 60–73; Jonathan Tonge, 'Nationalism and Republicanism', in Paul Carmichael, Colin Knox and Robert Osborne (eds) *Devolution and Constitutional Change in Northern Ireland*, Manchester University Press, 2007. pp. 96–109.

prisoners, with their release at the end of conflict appearing tantamount to treatment as prisoners-of-war. For the IRA, such releases were the 'bottom line' in terms of Sinn Fein's negotiating position.

Constructive ambiguity assisted the construction of the Good Friday Agreement, but could not be sustained in perpetuity. The UUP, which had negotiated the deal on behalf of Unionists, was overtaken by the ostensibly more hard-line DUP, which objected to 'terrorists in government' in advance of full decommissioning of weapons and support for the state's police force. It was not merely DUP pressure that eventually led the IRA to abandon its weapons in 2005, as external factors, notably 9/11, made a return to terrorism a remote prospect, given that fund-raising in the USA would have been exceptionally difficult. Nonetheless, when the Northern Ireland Assembly collapsed in 2002, amid allegations of an IRA spy ring in its midst, the newly ascendant DUP made it abundantly clear that the re-formation of a government which included Sinn Fein would be conditional upon the IRA decommissioning and dissolving and Sinn Fein supporting the police. The IRA's oscillation between continued activity and a place in the government of a state it opposed was no longer an option.

Between the Good Friday Agreement and its announcement in 2005 that the armed campaign was over, the IRA continued to operate. Its members were involved in several killings for personal or political reasons, recruitment and targeting continued; a spy ring was alleged within the Assembly, and the IRA was blamed for the largest bank robbery in British history. After the abandonment of the armed campaign, the IRA Army Council remained intact, but this was mainly to oversee the organization's dismantling.

## Necessary compromise, sell-out, or both? Assessing the IRA's move from violence

As the British Army's longest counter-insurgency operation, Operation Banner, closed after 37 years in 2007, Republicans noted the Army's acknowledgement that the IRA had been professional, dedicated, highly skilled and resilient.[40] For Republicans, Northern Ireland had been reshaped, Britain's constitutional claim to it diminished, and embryonic structures of Irish unity put in place. This made the sacrifices of its volunteers and the killings undertaken by the IRA worthwhile. Although the IRA apologized for 'non-combatant' victims, there was no apology to British security forces

[40] *An Phoblacht*, 12 July 2007.

victims. According to critics, however, the IRA's campaign of violence was unnecessary, unjust and sectarian, and its armed struggle required 'categorical de-legitimization'.[41]

There is no single explanation why the IRA abandoned its campaign of violence and a diverse range of causes are emphasised in the literature. Perhaps most striking is that only English's account highlights ideological change among Republicans as a partial harbinger of change, as distinct from pragmatic adjustment.[42] His account demonstrates how debates among IRA prisoners promoted some doubts about the righteousness of their cause. Some prisoners would adopt loyalist viewpoints in the jail and argue with their Republican colleagues. The debates forced a limited reappraisal of what constituted the real barrier to Irish unity.

In attacking the 'British presence' in Northern Ireland, Republicans appeared to regard merely its uniformed security personnel (who were regarded as legitimate targets) as 'the British', ignoring the political and cultural identity of one million Protestant British Unionists. A more nuanced view of what constitutes the British presence in Ireland has emerged among Republicans, although there remains doubt over the extent of ideological change among rival paramilitaries. But among many IRA former prisoners there remain negative perceptions of loyalism: first, that it is still a non-autonomous construct, wholly dependent upon Britain; secondly, that it is predominantly sectarian and anti-Catholic; thirdly, that it is non-progressive, with Republicans echoing the insistence of their leader that one 'cannot be a socialist without being a separatist';[43] and fourthly, that loyalism is inextricably linked to crime and gangsterism. Given these continued negative perceptions, the standing down of the IRA can be seen less as ideological change and instead much more as a product of leadership compromise, in order to enter an elite-level consociational government.

Indeed the IRA's tactical and strategic somersaults were eased by the absence of deep ideological commitment among its members. The Republican leadership promoted the idea that all that was principle (such as abstention) was actually tactical, a claim easy for many IRA personnel to accept, given that few had joined the movement out of deep-seated ideological fervour. Whether because they were ideologically confused individuals,[44] prisoners of British

[41] Rogelio Alonso, *The IRA and Armed Struggle*, London: Routledge, 2007, p. 194.
[42] English, *Armed Struggle*.
[43] Gerry Adams, *Free Ireland: Towards a Lasting Peace*, Dingle: Brandon, 1995, p. 127.
[44] Alonso, *The IRA and Armed Struggle*.

state strategies,[45] or members of a Republican movement which had never been overly specific about its tactics,[46] IRA volunteers found it easy to adapt to changed thinking by their leaders, as few fixed principles had led to their arrival in the IRA. Insofar as the Republican leadership had difficulty in selling the peace process, it lay more in convincing those who had endured most that their sacrifices were fully recognized within the movement. The IRA leadership thus embarked on a series of commemorations during the peace process, in which Republican leaders praised the IRA and its volunteers, whilst preparing the final burial of armed struggle. As Gormley-Heenan argues, 'chameleonic leadership' was a requirement of the peace process: tactical shifts had to be managed carefully by a cautious IRA command, conscious of the need to keep Republicans onside.[47]

A global perspective on the IRA's new *modus operandi* is offered by some. Adrian Guelke highlights the influence of other 'national liberation' movements, notably the African National Congress (ANC), in selling the idea of peace to the IRA.[48] ANC leaders found a convivial reception from a Republican leadership anxious to end the conflict on terms which would not appear to constitute surrender. In constructing a peace process vernacular of conflict transformation, transition and 'historic rapprochement' (as in the de Klerk-Mandela deal) the ANC encouraged the IRA to move away from conflict. This provided useful political cover for Irish Republicans, given the dissimilarities of the South African model (where the ANC, broadly, won) and the Northern Ireland one (where the IRA didn't). Indeed the IRA began to export its peace process approach to other conflicts, most notably, if somewhat unsuccessfully, to the Basque region, where the IRA supported ETA ceasefires and offered advice to ETA's political wing, Batasuna.

Michael Cox's international perspective is rather different.[49] He places the IRA ceasefire within the context of the abandonment of United States-Soviet

[45] McIntyre, *Modern Irish Republicanism*; McIntyre, *Modern Irish Republicanism and the Belfast Agreement*.

[46] Agnes Maillot, *New Sinn Fein. Irish Republicanism in the Twenty-First Century*, London: Routledge, 2004.

[47] Cathy Gormley-Heenan, *Political Leadership and the Northern Ireland Peace Process*, Basingstoke: Palgrave Macmillan, 2007, p. 3.

[48] Adrian Guelke, 'Political Comparisons: from Johannesburg to Jerusalem', in Michael Cox, Adrian Guelke and Fiona Stephen (eds) *A Farewell to Arms? Beyond the Good Friday Agreement*, Manchester University Press, 2006, pp. 367–76.

[49] Michael Cox, 'Rethinking the International and Northern Ireland: a defence', in Michael Cox, Adrian Guelke and Fiona Stephen (eds) *A Farewell to Arms?*, pp. 427–42.

Union bi-polarity and the consequent diminished strategic importance of Northern Ireland as an Atlantic base. This allowed the British government to deal more flexibly with the IRA, heralding an approach based upon inclusion rather than exclusion and an unrealistic search for military victory. The collapse of communism also aided the IRA in moving from its leftist rhetoric of the 1980s, in which the organization appeared to be sufficiently revolutionary to prompt fears that it would turn Ireland into an 'offshore Cuba' if successful. Nonetheless, Marxism was only ever one ideological input among many others within the eclectic mix that constituted the IRA. Its members included right-wing Catholic conservatives, socialists, communists and many of no strong ideological bent. Moreover, the IRA was beginning the dilution of its fundamentalism before the end of the Cold War.

In separate accounts, Smith and McGladdery analyse the military prowess of the IRA.[50] McGladdery offers the more sceptical view, arguing that the IRA's attempt to take the war to England by bombing large cities was a failure, making scant impact on British policy. Writing before the IRA's big 1996 bombings, Smith suggests that the IRA's failings owed much to an inability to recognize the brief periods when it held sufficient military clout to bargain for a reasonable deal, notably in 1921 and 1972; instead the IRA allowed its ideological fundamentals to cloud more rational-strategic decision-making. Applying this analysis to the IRA's 1990s bombing campaign, it is evident that much of the latter stage of IRA activity was designed to force Sinn Fein into negotiations with the British. The IRA's huge bombs of the 1990s, mainly in London with one in Manchester, produced economic damage exceeding that of the entire campaign during the previous two decades. In greatly increasing security costs, for example by forcing the creation of 'Ring of Steel' security protection around the financial centre of London, the IRA arguably increased the bargaining power of its political voice in Sinn Fein and demonstrated that, undefeated, the organization's capacity for destruction remained.

Throughout its bombing campaign, the IRA was obliged to contend with an evident asymmetry of might: a British government with near-infinite military and financial resources ranged against a paramilitary organization with no realistic hope of military victory. As Smith notes, strategic theory indicates how in such circumstances, 'another alternative military objective might be adopted that will serve the political purpose and symbolize it in peace

[50] Michael Smith, *Fighting for Ireland? The Military Strategy of the Irish Republican Movement*, London: Routledge, 1995; Gary McGladdery, *The Provisional IRA in England: The Bombing Campaign 1973–1997*, Dublin: Irish Academic Press, 2006.

negotiations'.[51] For Irish Republicans, this alternative military objective was to force Sinn Finn into negotiations with the British government. Whether the IRA's move was strategic or merely a salvage operation is the moot point here. Effectively, the IRA did force Sinn Fein into negotiations, but the bargain eventually struck merely allowed the IRA, at best, to achieve 'undefeated' status, without coming closer to achieving its overarching political goals. Much of what was obtained in the Good Friday Agreement, in terms of its consociational elements and its constitutional and institutional architecture of a Northern Ireland Assembly, all-Ireland links and British-Irish intergovernmental arrangements, had been offered by the British state in the 1973 Sunningdale Agreement, a deal regarded with utter contempt by the IRA at the time. As the initial Deputy First Minister in the post-1998 Northern Ireland Assembly, Seamus Mallon, pithily commented, the Good Friday Agreement amounted merely to 'Sunningdale for slow learners'.[52]

A final category of explanation lies in the changing roles of other political actors in facilitating a peace process. Within this category lie accounts stressing the symmetry of changes among protagonists or the consequential nature of tactical shift. Thus for Ruane and Todd, the repositioning of the relationship between Britain and Ireland and the growth of nationalist resources allowed movement away from military stalemate.[53] O'Kane also stresses the importance of increasingly cooperative relations between Britain and Ireland, which gradually permitted a common front to be formed in dealing with the IRA.[54] Paul Dixon highlights the choreography of movement among the British, Irish and American governments, in which even supposed public differences were accompanied by private reconciliation.[55] Other accounts emphasize the importance of new negotiating styles from the British government, based on the inclusion rather than the exclusion of paramilitary groups.[56]

---

[51] Smith, *Fighting for Ireland?*, p. 3.

[52] Jonathan Tonge, 'From Sunningdale to the Good Friday Agreement: Creating Devolved Government in Northern Ireland', *Contemporary British History*, Vol. 14, No. 3, 2000, pp. 39–60.

[53] Joseph Ruane, and Jennifer Todd, 'Path Dependence in Settlement Processes: Explaining Settlement in Northern Ireland', *Political Studies*, Vol. 55, 2007, pp. 442–58.

[54] Eamonn O'Kane, *Britain, Ireland and Northern Ireland since 1980*, London: Routledge, 2007.

[55] Paul Dixon, *Northern Ireland: The Politics of War and Peace*, Basingstoke: Palgrave Macmillan, 2002.

[56] Tonge, *The New Northern Irish Politics*; Tonge, *Northern Ireland*.

## The new violent non-state ultras? The Continuity and Real IRAs

As the Provisional IRA formally called off its armed campaign and disarmed in 2005, two ultra-IRAs attempted to maintain the violent aspect of Irish Republicanism. The Continuity IRA (CIRA) emerged during the 1990s as a small armed group, associated with the fundamentalist positions adopted by the political grouping Republican Sinn Fein (RSF), which parted company with Provisional Sinn Fein in 1986 over the latter's recognition of the 26–county Irish Parliament, Dail Eireann.[57] The CIRA's first claimed bombing was that of a hotel in Fermanagh, a curious target, and its campaign remained on a very small scale until the organization killed a Police Service of Northern Ireland officer in 2009. A more serious dissident threat has been posed by the Real IRA (RIRA), which emerged from a split in the IRA and Sinn Fein in 1997. The political associates of the RIRA, the 32 County Sovereignty Committee, were expelled from Sinn Fein in 1997 for attempting to mobilise opposition to the party's peace strategy. When the IRA reinstated its ceasefire in 1997, following the election of a Labour government under Tony Blair, a number of Provisionals, mainly in the border counties, left to form the RIRA. Although tiny, the RIRA contained members capable of delivering a campaign of violence in an attempt to thwart the peace and political process. This was made graphically clear when the organization killed 29 civilians in its bombing of Omagh in August 1998.

Outrage over the Omagh bombing led to the RIRA declaring a ceasefire, though this was more cosmetic than actual. The organization attacked targets in London, including the headquarters of the security services and the BBC, and also killed a Territorial Army volunteer. Its capability was of sufficient concern for the Irish Taoiseach (Prime Minister) to send an envoy to secret meetings with the RIRA leadership, in a futile attempt to produce a permanent ceasefire. Penetration by the security services, lack of finance and weaponry, internal divisions and the absence of popular support have nonetheless made it difficult for the RIRA to produce anything beyond episodic activity. In 2007, it shot two police officers in an attempt to deter recruits to the Police Service of Northern Ireland and to highlight its opposition to Sinn Fein's acceptance of policing. In 2009, the RIRA killed two British Army soldiers at an Army base in Antrim. This, combined with the CIRA's killing of a police officer immediately afterwards, showed that the 'dissident' armed Republican

---

[57] Jonathan Tonge, "'They haven't gone away you know": Irish Republican "Dissidents" and "Armed Struggle'", *Terrorism and Political Violence*, Vol. 16, No. 3, 2004, pp. 671–93.

groups remained determined to continue a 'military campaign', however limited, for as long as the British sovereign claim to Northern Ireland remained. Most former Provisional IRA members eschewed the revival of violence. Sinn Fein's Martin McGuinness described the Republican extremists as 'traitors to Ireland' for ignoring the consensus for peace. The issue of a mandate for violence is awkward, in that the Provisional IRA enjoyed far more community support than 'dissident' IRAs, but never an electoral mandate for their actions, if measured in terms of majority nationalist support for Sinn Fein.

Aside from the logistical difficulties of prosecuting a war with little weaponry, the main problem for diehard Republicans was the lack of support for absolutist political positions. The 2009 killings emphasized that the Northern Ireland problem was not entirely solved, but the response of Unionist and nationalist leaders was to re-emphasize their support for power-sharing within Northern Ireland. Successive surveys have indicated that a united Ireland is the majority choice of Catholics in Northern Ireland.[58] Moreover, a unitary state remains the aspiration of the population of the Irish Republic.[59] Nonetheless, few Irish citizens feel very strongly in favour of a united Ireland.[60] The overwhelming willingness of Irish citizens to downgrade the constitutional claim to Northern Ireland to a mere aspiration in the Good Friday Agreement referendum indicates their preference for an agreed Ireland over enforced territorial unity. Moreover, whilst the IRA was reborn in 1970 because of the seeming irreformability of the Northern state, no such adverse structural conditions existed by the 21st century to motivate nationalists for an armed campaign.

## Conclusion

Militarily, the IRA was unable to realize its goal of an independent sovereign and united Ireland, and much of the Irish peace process concerned involved a retreat from cherished Republican fixed positions. The IRA concluded its

---

[58] www.ark.ac.uk/nilt.

[59] Tony Fahey, Bernadette Hayes and Richard Sinnott, *Conflict and Consensus: A Study of Values in the Republic of Ireland and Northern Ireland*, Dublin: Institute of Public Administration, 2005.

[60] Maurice Bric and John Coakley, 'The Roots of Militant Politics in Ireland', in Maurice Bric and John Coakley (eds), *From Political Violence to Negotiated Settlement: The Winding Path to Peace in Twentieth Century Ireland*, Dublin: University College Dublin Press, 2004, pp. 1–12.

armed campaign and dispensed with its weapons. Instead of ending Britain's claim to Northern Ireland, the IRA supported its political wing, Sinn Fein, in entering devolved power-sharing in a hitherto 'illegitimate' state and then supported the reformed police service of a country the IRA had attempted to destroy. The startling extent of the IRA's U-turns was, for years, overshadowed by a non-realization among some Unionists that the (Provisional) IRA's war was over, when that was evidently the case from 1997 onwards. The route to a united Ireland remains far from clear. Republicans have tried abstentionist and violent routes in previous generations; now they have (mostly) adopted participatory tactics. A united Ireland is only likely to be achieved via a remarkable change in attitude among the Protestant-Unionist-British population towards the prospect, or an unlikely rapid growth in the Catholic-nationalist population in Northern Ireland, prepared to outvote its Protestant-Unionist-British counterpart into a united Irish state.

Skilful management of transition by the Republican leadership averted a major split in the movement, a process of change abetted by a lack of ideological depth among many IRA members and local respect for those volunteers who had made sacrifices during the conflict. Conspiratorialism, central control and loyalty, evident in the military campaign, were more important than traditional Republican principles, which were relegated to mere tactics. As former IRA prisoners moved into political work with Sinn Fein, Republicanism was redefined to become merely synonymous with whatever constituted Sinn Fein policy. Former IRA volunteers buried any doubts about the new Republican departure by insisting that the decision to end violence was a 'purely pragmatic, not moral' decision, which did not diminish their Republicanism.[61] The transfer of IRA volunteers into senior positions within Sinn Fein was an attempt to win the peace and utilize the resourcefulness that characterised the Republican military campaign in a political setting.

Politically, the IRA has been obliged to dilute the territorial basis of its claim to Irish national self-determination amid a new paradigm of identity politics.[62] The traditional IRA ethno-geographical determinism of Ireland constituting a single island populated by a single Irish people has been displaced by a more nuanced, if blurred, approach in which self-ascribed identity is seen as legitimate. The IRA's former members now talk of reaching out to

---

[61] Jim McVeigh, Speech to Republican Hunger Strike Commemoration, Irish World Heritage Centre, 14 June 2006.

[62] Chris Gilligan, 'The Irish Question and the Concept 'Identity' in the 1980s', *Nations and Nationalism*, Vol. 13, No. 4, 2007, pp. 599–617.

the Unionist-British population on the island of Ireland. As identity politics have displaced issues of contested sovereignty, Sinn Fein argues for an 'Ireland of Equals', a slogan which means everything and nothing. Revolutionary, anti-imperialist rhetoric has been replaced by neo-liberal policies and the introduction of Private Finance Initiatives by Sinn Fein ministers.

Whilst premature death notifications for the IRA have been issued in previous eras and some circumspection is thus prudent, it is difficult to conceive of circumstances in which the modern splinter IRAs—the Real and Continuity versions still favouring violent attempts to create a united Ireland—could mount a serious, sustained campaign, akin to that waged by the Provisional IRA for three decades, given their lack of support and weaponry. With nearly 50 members imprisoned North and South of the border and episodic, if low-key, activity, these 'ultra'-IRAs are nonetheless a flickering reminder of the role played by armed groups in attempting to shape Irish-British political questions. Since the 'agreed' Ireland of the post-Good Friday Agreement era, violence has largely disappeared, replaced eventually by a far-reaching elite consociation of nationalist and Unionist former adversaries. The assumption, albeit one as yet unproven, is that the cordiality of top-level consociation might eventually permeate a communally divided Northern Ireland society, removing any remaining violent non-state actors.

# 4

# The Persistence of Nationalist Terrorism

## The Case of ETA

*Ignacio Sánchez-Cuenca*

## Introduction

ETA (*Euskadi ta Askatasuna*, Basque Homeland and Freedom) is one of the oldest terrorist organizations in the world. It was born in 1959, it claimed its first victim in 1968 and it is still active today, having killed 777 people (until the end of 2007) and wounded thousands of others. It is a nationalist group that fights for the independence of the Basque Country. It has survived regime change, a process of devolution, several internal splits, changes of strategy, negotiations with almost every democratic Spanish government, several cease-fires, and numerous blows by security forces that have made it much weaker than in the past.

ETA is the only remaining terrorist organization in Western Europe among those that emerged in the wave of political violence of the late 1960s and early 1970s. Many countries in the developed world witnessed the emergence of terrorist groups of very different ideologies: revolutionary groups such as the Red Brigades (Italy), the Red Army Faction (Germany) and the GRAPO (Antifascist First of October Revolutionary Group, Spain); fascist groups such as the NAR (Revolutionary Armed Groups, Italy) and the Spanish Basque Battalion (Spain); vigilante groups such as the Ulster Volunteer Force and the Ulster Defence Association (both in Northern Ireland); and national-ist groups such as ETA itself and the PIRA (Provisional Irish Republican Army, Northern Ireland). In comparative terms, only the PIRA has a bloodier record than ETA. The PIRA killed around 1,650 people, more than twice the number of fatalities by ETA in a similar time span.

Despite its resilience and its bloody trajectory, there is still very little writ-ten in English about ETA and Basque nationalist violence.[1] Indeed, the Eng-lish literature on ETA is not comparable in quantity to the enormous body of literature on terrorism in Northern Ireland and in Italy. Moreover, this litera-ture has tended to focus on the nationalist conflict and the social movements rather than on ETA itself.[2]

In this chapter I provide an overview of ETA regarding the following aspects: (i) origins and history, (ii) organization, recruits, and social base, (iii) strategic evolution, and (iv) target selection.

---

[1] See Jan Mansvelt Beck, *Territory and Terror: Conflicting Nationalisms in the Basque Coun-try*. London: Routledge, 2005; Luis de la Calle, 'Fighting for Local Control: Street Vio-lence in the Basque Country', *International Studies Quarterly*, Vol. 51, 2007, pp. 431–55; Robert P. Clark, *The Basque Insurgents. ETA, 1952–1980*, Madison: University of Wis-consin Press, 1984 and *Negotiating with ETA: Obstacles to Peace in the Basque Country, 1975–1988*, Reno: University of Nevada Press, 1990; Marianne Heiberg, 'ETA: Euskadi 'ta Askatasuna', in Marianne Heiberg, Brendan O'Leary and John Tirman (eds), *Terror, Insurgency, and the State: Ending Protracted Conflicts*, Philadelphia: University of Penn-sylvania Press, pp. 18–49; Cynthia L. Irvin, *Militant Nationalism: Between Movement and Party in Ireland and the Basque Country*, Minneapolis: University of Minnesota Press, 1999; David Laitin, 'National Revivals and Violence', *Archives Européennes de Soci-ologie*, Vol. 36, 1995, pp. 3–43; Enric Martínez-Herrera, 'Nationalist Extremism and Outcomes of State Policies in the Basque Country, 1979–2001', *International Journal of Multicultural Societies*, Vol. 4, 2002, pp. 16–40; Ludger Mees, 'Between Votes and Bul-lets: Conflicting Ethnic Identities in the Basque Country', *Ethnic and Racial Studies*, 24, 2001, pp. 798–827; Ignacio Sánchez-Cuenca, 'The Dynamics of Nationalist Terrorism: ETA and the IRA', *Terrorism and Political Violence*, Vol. 19, 2007, pp. 289–306; Goldie Shabad and Francisco Llera, 'Political Violence in a Democratic State: Basque Terrorism in Spain', in Martha Crenshaw (ed.), *Terrorism in Context*, University Park: The Pennsyl-vania State University Press, 1995, pp. 410–69; John Sullivan, *ETA and Basque National-ism: The Fight for Euskadi, 1890–1986*, London: Routledge, 1988; Benjamín Tejerina, 'Protest Cycle, Political Violence and Social Movements in the Basque Country', *Nations and Nationalism*, Vol. 7, 2001, pp. 39–57; Paddy Woodworth, *Dirty War, Clean Hands: ETA, the GAL and Spanish Democracy*, Cork University Press, 2001.

[2] For a review of the Spanish literature on ETA, see Ignacio Sánchez-Cuenca, Ignacio, 'Vio-lencia política, orden y seguridad', in Manuel Pérez Yruela (ed.), *La sociología en España*, Madrid: Centro de Investigaciones Sociológicas, 2007, pp. 289–303.

## History and background

The Basque Autonomous Community (BAC) is made up of three provinces in the North of Spain (Álava, Guipúzcoa, and Vizcaya). It is a relatively small territory with a population of around 2.1 million people (as of 2006). Vizcaya is by far the most populated province (around 1,100,000 inhabitants) and also the most industrialized one. The BAC was constituted after the death of Franco in 1975. It is regulated by the so-called Gernika Statute, approved in 1979, which specifies the powers of the Basque institutions. The BAC is a wealthy region, with a GDP per capita well above the Spanish average.

There is a Basque parliament and a Basque government. The BAC has its own fiscal regime (it does not participate in the flows of redistribution between the other Spanish regions). It has extensive legislative powers, its own police force (the Ertzaintza), its own education system, mostly run in Basque, its own health system, and a public TV channel (see articles 10–24 of the Gernika Statute for a full list of powers). The only areas excluded from autonomy are social security, defence and foreign policy.

Whereas the BAC is the administrative reality, Basque nationalists usually employ the term 'Basque Country' (*Euskal Herria*) to refer to a much larger territory. They claim that the Basque Country is made up of the BAC, Navarre, and the three Basque provinces of the South of France (the French Basque Country, or *Iparralde*). Among radical nationalists, one of the central claims is precisely what they call 'territoriality', that is, the unification of the seven provinces in a single Basque state.

As a matter of fact, nationalism is very unevenly distributed in these territories. In Iparralde, it is clearly marginal. France has been successful in the national assimilation of its Basque population: voting for Basque nationalist parties or the use of the Basque language is almost negligible in this territory. In the south of Navarre and in Álava, the southern province of the BAC, Basque nationalism is also rather weak. During the transition to democracy, the possibility of incorporating Navarre in the BAC was discussed, but eventually rejected. Nonetheless, the Autonomy Statute of Navarre contemplates unification with the BAC if a majority of people in Navarre is in favour. Today, Navarre is definitely more pro-Spain than pro-Basque Country. Nationalism is stronger in Vizcaya, Guipúzcoa and the north of Navarre. These are also the areas where violence has been more intense.

Basque nationalism emerged as a reaction to two dramatic changes. On the one hand there was the early wave of industrialization in the late 19th century, which provoked a massive flow of immigration to the Basque provinces from other regions of Spain. On the other, there was the defeat of the Basque traditionalists (also called the Carlistas, because of a dynastic dispute about the monarchy) in the third Carlist civil war (1872–76), which brought about the abolition of the Basque *fueros*. The *fueros* were the local civic and economic rights that had survived from medieval times in the Basque provinces and Navarre. They represented a sort of exceptionalism within Spain; their elimination was part of the process of Spanish nation building.[3]

Basque nationalism was anti-liberal from the beginning, based on an idealization of rural life and ancestral traditions, with a strong influence of the Church. Unlike Catalan nationalism, which was more civic-oriented, Basque nationalism was ethnic-oriented. This difference is still visible.[4] There was a clear element of racism against Spaniards in the writings of the founder of the Basque Nationalist Party (Euzko Alderdi Jeltzalea—EAJ), Sabino Arana (1865–1903).

The EAJ has been the hegemonic political force in the Basque Country at least since 1917, when it became a mass party. It has always been internally divided into two factions, the moderates, who seek autonomy within Spain, and the radicals, who seek full independence.[5]

The first Basque government was created during the civil war (1936–39). The Autonomy Statute was approved on 1 October 1936. A grand coalition between the EAJ and the socialists was created, under the leadership of José Antonio Aguirre (from the EAJ). This experience, however, was short-lived. Whereas Navarre and Álava supported Franco, Vizcaya and Guipúzcoa were against him. These two provinces were particularly repressed after the victory of Franco, who immediately suppressed Basque autonomy.

ETA emerged in the context of the long dictatorship period under Franco, coinciding with a second wave of industrialization and a second massive flow of immigrants from other parts of Spain. A group of young people, mainly

---

[3] The *fueros* of other regions, Aragon, Catalonia, Mallorca and Valencia, had already been abolished by Philip V at the beginning of the 18th century.

[4] See Paloma Aguilar and Ignacio Sánchez-Cuenca, 'Performance or Representation? The Determinants of Voting in Complex Political Contexts', in José María Maravall and Ignacio Sánchez-Cuenca (eds), *Controlling Governments: Voters, Institutions and Accountability*, Cambridge University Press, 2008, pp. 105–30; and Araceli Serrano, 'Manifestaciones étnicas y cívico-territoriales de los nacionalismos', *Revista Española de Investigaciones Sociológicas*, Vol. 82, 1998, pp. 97–125.

[5] See the two volumes of de Pablo, Santiago, Ludger Mees and José Antonio Rodríguez, *El péndulo patriótico: Historia del Partido Nacionalista Vasco*, Barcelona, Crítica, 1999 and 2001.

students, acting under the name of Ekin ('doing' in Basque), were dissatisfied with the passive stance of the EAJ towards the authoritarian regime. In the 1950s, Ekin merged with the youth organization of the EAJ, EGI. The critical attitude of this group led to expulsions and eventually to the first split in the ranks of the EAJ in 25 years.

The splinter group chose the name Euskadi ta Askatasuna (ETA) and wrote its founding charter in July 1959.[6] It is a brief document in which the organization defines itself as a patriotic, non-religious, non-political group with the goal of 'saving the Basque soul' and 'the self-determination of our homeland's destiny'. At that time it was hard, if not inconceivable, to expect that ETA would end up as an organization engaged in full terrorist violence.

ETA's first actions were rather naïve: graffiti, the hoisting of Basque flags (which were forbidden), and the destruction of Francoist symbols. The first serious attack was the explosion of a bomb on 18 July 1961 to derail a train full of Franco's volunteers going to a remembrance service (the fascist rebellion against the Republic had started on 18 July 1936).[7] The regime overreacted to these acts; many activists were arrested and many others had to move to the French Basque Country.

ETA organized several assemblies to design a strategy for fighting against the dictatorship. There were basically two alternatives. On the one hand, if the fight was aimed against the regime, it could be understood in terms of class struggle, as part of a wider revolutionary movement in the whole of Spain against the dictator. On the other hand, if the fight was against Spain rather than against Franco, then it could be framed in terms of a national liberation campaign.

During the 1960s ETA was badly divided between those who stressed class struggle and those who stressed national liberation.[8] There were various attempts to reach a compromise: ETA's ideology was defined in the socialist or Marxist jargon of the time as a national liberation movement inspired by anti-colonial experiences (Algeria, Cyprus and the Irgun were for ETA impor-

---

[6] Reproduced in de Pablo, Mees and Rodríguez, Vol. II, p. 236 (see fn. 5).

[7] On 28 June 1960, a bomb exploded in a train station in San Sebastián (Guipúzcoa). A baby girl (Begoña Urroz) died as a consequence of the wounds. The attack was never claimed. Although some people think that this act was the work of some anarchist group, there is some consensus in imputing the killing to ETA (though there is no hard evidence on that).

[8] For a history of ETA in the 1960s, see José M. Garmendia, *Historia de ETA*, San Sebastián: Aramburu, 1996, and Gurutz Jáuregui, *Ideología y estrategia política de ETA: Análisis de su evolución entre 1959 y 1968*, Madrid: Siglo XXI, 1981.

tant models to emulate). If no equilibrium was reached it was, among other reasons, because the Basque Country did not fit either a national liberation story (the Basque Country has never been, by any means, a Spanish colony) or a revolutionary situation (the working class was not prepared for a revolution).

There were numerous splits in those years. The winners were always the nationalists. In the V Assembly, held in 1966–67, the orthodox Communists were expelled (they formed the short-lived ETA *berri*, or new ETA). This internal dynamic of ideological clarification was precipitated by an unexpected event. By pure chance, Javier Echebarrieta, one of the leaders of ETA, was stopped by the Civil Guard (militarized police) on 7 June 1968. He killed Civil Guard José Pardines and escaped. But some hours later he was found and shot by security forces. Echebarrieta became the first killer and the first martyr of ETA. That episode sparked the spiral of violence that has lasted for almost forty years. ETA decided to take revenge by killing on 2 August 1968 Melitón Manzanas, a police commissioner with a notorious reputation as a torturer of political prisoners. The reaction of the regime was indeed tough. There were mass arrests and a state of emergency was declared in the Basque provinces and later on in the whole of Spain.

Regime repression created a cleavage between those who remained in the Basque Country and those who left for France. The veterans, who were in France, considered that the new leadership was not sufficiently nationalist. They were extremely worried about a new Marxist deviation. During the VI Assembly there was a new split. The organization was by then decimated by arrests and internal divisions. But the nationalists recovered full control of the organization.

ETA survived thanks to the mistake made by Franco, who organized a spectacular trial of several activists accused of the killing of the torturer Manzanas. The so-called Burgos trial (called after the city in which it took place) was used by ETA activists to gain publicity, to reach audiences beyond Spain and to trigger an international solidarity campaign. ETA gained wide popularity from the repressive excesses of the regime.[9] Its popularity augmented still more with the assassination of the Prime Minister, Admiral Luis Carrero Blanco, who was second to Franco, in Madrid on 20 December 1973. This sent a signal both to the state and to the opposition forces that ETA was indeed a powerful organization.

[9] On the Burgos trial, see the first hand report in the memoirs of Mario Onaindía, *El precio de la libertad: Memorias (1948–1977)*, Madrid: Espasa-Calpe, 2001.

Franco fell ill in 1974. Expectations of his death set in motion another internal rift within ETA about the strategy to be followed after the end of the dictatorship. The majority opted for some combination of armed struggle and political participation. The minority, on the other hand, considered that armed struggle should be the only activity for ETA. This disagreement led to the most important split in the history of the organization. The split was precipitated by another attack in Madrid on 13 September 1974. The terrorists exploded a bomb in a restaurant attached to the central police headquarters, assuming that most customers would be police officers. Thirteen people died as a consequence of the explosion and only one was a policeman.

There was a bitter argument within ETA on whether the attack should be claimed or not. The majority imposed its position: it decided to deny any involvement in the attack, saying that acknowledging it would undermine popular support. At the end of 1974, ETA split into two different organizations: the majority, political-military ETA (ETApm), and the minority, military ETA (ETAm). The military branch considered that political participation in the process of transition would imply a diversion of resources and that the organization would ultimately succumb to electoral politics.

In a sense, ETAm was right. ETApm, despite being more numerous, was unable to sustain armed struggle for long. Within ETApm, those more involved in politics (after Franco eventually died in November 1975) concluded that armed struggle was a deadweight loss for the movement. In 1977, the military commandos of ETApm, increasingly dissatisfied with the political evolution of the organization, left for ETAm. The flow of activists and weapons into ETAm made it much more powerful. One year later, its violence skyrocketed and it became the dominant group in terms of armed struggle.

ETApm abandoned armed struggle in 1982. Its violence was subordinated to the strategies of the political party associated with ETApm, the Basque Revolutionary Party (*Euskal Iraultzarako Alderdia*). In fact, the aim of its attacks was mainly to gain support and followers. In that sense, the kind of violence that ETApm carried out was more similar to the typical revolutionary type (as exemplified by the Red Brigades or the GRAPO) than to the typical nationalist type (as exemplified by ETAm or the PIRA). The same can be said of the CAA (Autonomous Anticapitalist Commandos), an armed group formed by those military activists who left ETApm in 1977 but refused to enter ETAm. Heavily influenced by the anarchist experiences of the Autonomia movement in Italy, Germany and France, they conceived violence as an instrument for the development of class-consciousness and the advancement of anti-system social movements. The CAA were active between 1978 and 1984.

After 1984, ETAm was the only terrorist group operating in the Basque Country. Given the continuity between the pre-1974 ETA and ETAm, I will refer indistinctly to either of the two organizations as ETA. Only when the context makes it necessary shall I distinguish between ETAm and ETApm.

## Organization, recruits and popular support

Terrorist organizations tend to be rather small compared with guerrilla insurgencies. To estimate the size of ETA, it is necessary to make a distinction between the hard core of the organization, made up of the leadership and the people who take up arms in the commandos, and a wider circle of those who are somehow related to the organization and help it in different tasks such as intelligence, housing, and border-crossing. In the case of ETA, all estimates coincide in giving figures of below 500 people for the hard core. According to some estimates, there were 300/350 activists in the hard core in 1978, the year in which ETA launched its offensive against the state and the number of killings skyrocketed.[10] In the early 1980s the number of activists gradually started to decline, meaning that the organization was unable to find new recruits to replace all the activists who were being arrested. The reduction in ETA's activity, particularly after the arrest of the entire leadership in Bidart (in the south of France) on 29 March 1992, was probably caused by the shrinking of the organization. In recent years the hard core has most likely numbered less than one hundred people.

Its capacity to attract recruits to the hard core explains the resilience of ETA's violence. ETA has seen itself as the vanguard of a much wider movement which is subordinated to the needs of armed struggle. The dense network of organizations, associations and firms was called KAS (*Koordinadora Abertzale Sozialista*, Patriotic Socialist Coordination) during the period 1975/98, and Ekin afterwards. Sometimes it is also referred to in a more generic way as the Basque National Liberation Movement. The network includes newspapers and other publications, a political party (adopting various names over time, Herri Batasuna being the most enduring one), a trade union, a women's organization, a youth organization, associations in support

---

[10] Florencio Domínguez, *ETA: Estrategia organizativa y actuaciones. 1978–1992*, Bilbao: Universidad del País Vasco, 1998, p. 39.

of ETA's prisoners, organizations aimed at spreading the Basque language, and even firms (travel agencies, fish importers, etc.). The core of the movement is underground, the external belt is legal.

For many years, the courts were unable to establish the link between ETA and the rest of the movement. Thanks to various initiatives launched by Judge Baltasar Garzón since 1998, this link has been proved and many of the organizations and associations of the movement have been declared illegal and their members sent to prison.[11] The effect of these court initiatives has been the increasing isolation of ETA and greater difficulties in finding recruits and money. Moreover, the right-wing Popular Party government passed a law in 2002, with the support of the Socialists in the opposition, that makes parties connected to a terrorist organization illegal. This means that the political branch of ETA has not been able to run in the elections held since that year.

Nationalist terrorist organizations try to penetrate society in various ways. It is well known, for instance, that Hamas, apart from terrorist violence, spends part of its resources on welfare provision (schooling, health, and other services).[12] The PIRA, in Northern Ireland, was involved in public order in the Catholic strongholds, punishing petty criminals and joy riders through beatings and kneecapping.[13] In both cases, the terrorists tried to fill a gap left by a defective state. In the Basque Country there has not been a problem either of welfare (which is generously provided by the Basque and Spanish governments) or of public order (unlike Northern Ireland, there is no sectarian conflict in the BAC). In order to be present in society and gain popularity, ETA's strategy has been to penetrate and manipulate new social movements (environmentalist and, ironically enough, antimilitarist and pacifist ones).

The most important way of attracting new people into the organization is through personal networks.[14] The average militant is someone who has been socialized in the movement and has a relative or a friend in the organization (or in jail). If the person has experienced, personally or through someone close enough, an episode of state repression (arbitrary arrest, torture), it is much more likely that he or she will take the step of entering the organization. Since

[11] See Baltasar Garzón, *Un mundo sin miedo*, Barcelona: Plaza Janés, 2005, Chapter 4.
[12] Shaul Mishal and Avraham Sela, *The Palestinian Hamas: Vision, Violence, and Coexistence*, New York: Columbia University Press, 2000.
[13] Rachel Monaghan, "An Imperfect Peace': Paramilitary 'Punishments' in Northern Ireland', *Terrorism and Political Violence*, Vol. 16, 2004, pp. 439–61.
[14] Domínguez (fn. 10), pp. 22–6; Fernando Reinares, *Patriotas de la muerte: Quiénes han militado en ETA y por qué*, Madrid: Taurus, 2001.

the early 1990s, the most important recruit mechanism has been street violence.[15] Youngsters are trained in acts of street violence; some of them, to avoid arrest, go underground and end up in the ranks of ETA.

The internal structure of ETA is strongly hierarchical. At the top there is an Executive Committee that makes all the important decisions and establishes the goals and the strategic line to be followed. Members of the Executive Committee are selected through cooptation.[16] Formally, there is no leader of ETA, although in practice someone can play that role (for instance, Domingo Iturbe, aka Txomin, in the early 1980s). The Executive Committee is responsible for the different branches of the organization. These are the military, political, logistic, finance and border-crossing branches. The Executive Committee is not an accountable body within ETA. Owing to the constraints of being underground, there is very little interaction between the leadership and the militants. The assemblies that were held in the 1960s have not been repeated, although there have been some general meetings to discuss major decisions (such as a ceasefire).

Members of the executive committee are all in France. France has been for many years ETA's sanctuary. Things started to change because of the 'dirty war' against ETA in the 1983–87 period. A state-sponsored organization, the GAL (Grupos Antiterroristas de Liberación, Antiterrorist Liberation Groups), acted mainly in the South of France against ETA's members and sympathizers. The GAL killed 27 people in this period, though many of them had no relationship whatsoever with ETA.[17] In any case, France toughened its policy against ETA; extradition of terrorists, for instance, became a reality. Since then, there has been an ever-increasing degree of cooperation between France and Spain.[18]

Regarding finance, ETA has obtained money through bank robberies, kidnappings and extortion. Bank robberies occurred only in the early days. This is a risky operation for the terrorists and it often produces collateral victims; it is interesting to note that the PIRA did not resort to this tactic either, during the 'armed struggle' years. Kidnappings, by contrast, have been much more frequent in the history of ETA. Although some of them were carried out for political reasons, most of them had economic motivation. Almost eighty peo-

---

[15] On street violence in the Basque Country, see de la Calle (fn. 1).

[16] Domínguez (fn. 10), p. 84.

[17] About the GAL, see Woodworth (fn. 1).

[18] See Sagrario Morán, *ETA entre España y Francia*, Madrid: Universidad Complutense, 1997.

ple have been kidnapped by all the Basque terrorist groups.[19] However, kidnappings are not a stable source of money. The outcome of a kidnapping is always uncertain: the family may refuse to pay ransom, the police may foil the payment or find the place where the person is held prisoner. Moreover, kidnappings are highly visible in the media and may be unpopular among supporters because of the 'mafia' image. For all these reasons, ETA abandoned kidnapping in 1996.

Extortion is by far the most important source of finance. The terrorists regularly ask entrepreneurs and shopkeepers to pay the so-called 'revolutionary tax'. To make the threat of extortion credible, eight people have been killed for financial reasons.[20] The extortion system requires a dense network of people in charge of collecting the money. Only powerful organizations, with some degree of territorial control over the population, can put this method into practice. On a larger scale, guerrillas extract rents from peasants in the territories they liberate from the state; powerful terrorist organizations such as ETA or the PIRA emulate this behaviour. Systematic extortion is not found in groups without a definite territorial base and with less popular support. Organizations such as the Red Brigades, the GRAPO and the Red Army Faction have to finance themselves mainly through bank robberies.

It is difficult, nonetheless, to specify objectively the amount of popular support terrorist organizations have. Basically, we do not have reliable indicators of direct support, although it is possible to extract some information from surveys and electoral results. If we assume that voting for Herri Batasuna (HB) can be taken as an indicator of support for ETA, Table 4.1 shows that on average 10 per cent of the Basque adult population supports ETA. This amounts to around 172,000 people. In terms of votes, HB has a vote share of 15 per cent. If we calculate this as a percentage of the total nationalist vote, then HB represents 26 per cent (one in four nationalist voters vote for ETA's political branch). These figures are calculated on the basis of the eight Basque legislative elections run between 1980 and 2005.

Table 4.1 also shows that support is rather stable. Even when HB was not allowed to compete in the 2005 elections, a surrogate party, the PCTV (Communist Party of the Basqueland), obtained 150,000 votes. The most deviant elections are those of 1998 and 2001. In 1998 the elections took place one

---

[19] See the appendix in José María Calleja, *La diáspora vasca: Historia de los condenados a irse de Euskadi por culpa del terrorismo de ETA*, Madrid: El Pais-Aguilar, 1999.
[20] José María Calleja and Ignacio Sánchez-Cuenca, *La derrota de ETA: De la primera víctima a la última*, Madrid: Adhara, 2006, p. 97.

month after ETA declared a ceasefire. That year, HB obtained its best result ever, with 224,001 votes, showing that some people are willing to vote for an independentist party when ETA ends the violence. The breakdown of the ceasefire gave rise to a particularly cruel campaign by ETA against local non-nationalist politicians. As a consequence, in the following elections, in 2001, HB suffered a dramatic fall in its electoral support.

Table 4.1. Electoral support for the political branch of ETA
in Basque legislative elections, 1980–2005.

| | Votes | Percentage of the census | Percentage of total vote | Percentage of nationalist vote |
|---|---|---|---|---|
| 1980 | 151,636 | 9.75 | 16.55 | 25.67 |
| 1984 | 157,389 | 9.93 | 14.65 | 22.67 |
| 1986 | 199,900 | 12.04 | 17.47 | 25.74 |
| 1990 | 186,410 | 11.04 | 18.33 | 27.78 |
| 1994 | 166,147 | 9.50 | 16.29 | 28.86 |
| 1998[a] | 224,001 | 12.30 | 17.91 | 32.80 |
| 2001[a] | 143,139 | 7.89 | 10.12 | 19.15 |
| 2005[b] | 150,644 | 8.37 | 12.44 | 23.28 |
| Average | 172,408 | 10.10 | 15.47 | 25.74 |

[a] Herri Batasuna ran under the name of EH (Euskal Herritarrok)
[b] Herri Batasuna was banned, but Batasuna's voters voted for a marginal party, the PCTV (Communist Party Basqueland).
*Source*: Basque Government.

Survey information provides a similar picture. Although there are no systematic longitudinal data for the whole period, it is possible to calculate a mean of support on a scale 0–1 (where 1 is full support and 0 no support at all) for fifteen years on the basis of the Euskobarometro survey.[21] The mean is 0.18, which is consistent with the figures corresponding to electoral results.

Support for ETA is clearly a minority sentiment in the Basque Country, but it is large enough to sustain a terrorist organization. Around 10 per cent of the population is sympathetic to the goals and means of the terrorists. Thanks to this significant support, ETA has survived all these years and has been able to create an important physical and human infrastructure that makes possible the extortion network, infiltration into social movements, or

[21] At www.ehu.es/cpvweb. See Sánchez-Cuenca (fn. 1), pp. 300–2, for a full description of the rules followed to calculate mean support.

the creation of a parallel world in which youngsters are socialized in the values of armed struggle.

## Strategy[22]

Nationalist terrorism is about territory, whereas revolutionary terrorism is about mobilization. Nationalist terrorism aspires ultimately to the creation of a new state in the territory under dispute. Revolutionary terrorism, by contrast, seeks to ignite a mass uprising against the system. While the demands of the nationalists are negotiable (there is a continuum of possible agreements between no territorial concession and independence), revolutionaries cannot negotiate with the state, since they want its demise.

Mobilization is also important in the case of nationalist organizations, but it is purely instrumental with regard to the territorial goals. The terrorists are aware that the more people mobilize calling for greater autonomy or independence, the more bargaining power the terrorist organization has to negotiate with the state. Mobilization is then needed as a way of increasing the terrorists' bargaining power vis-à-vis the state.

In order to force the state to make concessions, nationalist terrorists use violence. Violence imposes a cost on the state. The terrorists' expectation is that if the cost is sufficiently high, the state will opt for abandoning the territory. Obviously, the terrorists do not know the resistance threshold of the state. They simply try to impose as high a cost as possible, for the purpose of breaking the state's resistance will.

This structure of interaction between a nationalist terrorist organization and the state fits the general model of war of attrition. In a military war of attrition, there is a protracted conflict and each further period of fighting reduces the military power of the parties. It is a matter of exhausting the capacity of the enemy. In the case of terrorism, the parameters of the problem are somewhat different. The exhaustion produced by terrorist violence is not physical, but economic, political and ultimately psychological. For instance, in economic terms, it has been estimated that the cost of ETA's violence has been around 10 per cent of the BAC's GDP.[23] Terrorism also puts serious

---

[22] This section draws heavily on Florencio Domínguez, *De la negociación a la tregua: ¿El final de ETA?*, Madrid: Taurus, 1998, and Ignacio Sánchez-Cuenca, *ETA contra el Estado: Las estrategias del terrorismo*, Barcelona: Tusquets, 2001.

[23] Alberto Abadie and Jon Gardeazabal, 'The Economic Costs of Conflict: A Case Study of the Basque Country', *American Economic Review*, Vol. 93, 2003, pp. 113–31.

political strain on the system. And, in the last instance, people are repulsed by terrorist killings. For all these reasons, protracted terrorist violence imposes a cost on the state. The state decides in each period whether this cost is worth paying or not. When the state concludes it is not, it yields to the terrorists.

Both ETA and the PIRA are paradigmatic examples of nationalist terrorist organizations involved in a war of attrition against the state. However, in the case of ETA, it was not obvious in the early period that war of attrition was the strategy to be followed. In fact, although the bulk of ETA activity corresponds to a war of attrition, it is necessary to distinguish three strategic periods since the first fatality in 1968.

Under Franco, ETA saw itself as the armed vanguard that would create the dynamics of a mass uprising of the Basques. Violence was supposed to send a signal to the masses about the existence of a hard core of activists willing to fight against the system. Inspired by episodes of anti-colonial struggle in other countries, the idea was that violence would escalate thanks to the overreaction of the state. Ruthless and indiscriminate state repression would move many to join the rebels, which would in turn lead to an increase in violence. This spiral of violence and repression would eventually bring about the collapse of the state.

The revolutionary hopes of the early ETA failed to materialize. When the end of the Franco regime was close, ETA had to rethink its strategy. If the masses had not made the revolution under dictatorship, it was clear that they were not going to make it under democracy either. Around 1975 we observe the first internal documents about the strategic shift towards war of attrition. But it was in 1978 when ETAm clearly adopted the new strategy: 'The function of the armed struggle is not to destroy the enemy, for that is utopian, but it is indeed to force him, through a prolonged war of psychological and physical attrition, to abandon our territory due to exhaustion and isolation.'[24]

It was also in that year, 1978, that ETAm announced a set of five conditions that, if met by the state, would lead to the cessation of violence. Basically, these conditions (the so-called KAS Alternative) covered the right of self-determination, amnesty for terrorists in prison, the constitution of an autonomous region comprising the three Spanish Basque provinces plus Navarre, and the withdrawal of Spanish security forces from the Basque Country. For the next twenty years, ETA killed in order to force the state to accept these demands.

---

[24] Quoted in Francisco Letamendía, *Historia del nacionalismo vasco y de ETA* (3 volumes), San Sebastián: R & B Ediciones, 1994, Vol. II, p. 114.

A statement made by an ETA spokesperson in 1988 showed that the strategy had not changed: ETA 'has opted for a prolonged war of attrition, the aim of which is to outlast the enemy. We know that ETA cannot destroy the Spanish state, and this is not our aim. (...) But the Spanish state cannot destroy us either.'[25]

Once the new strategy was clear, ETAm launched an extremely violent campaign to break the state's resistance. As can be seen in Figure 4.1, which represents the quarterly number of fatalities for the period 1968–2006, terrorism escalated dramatically in 1978. The bloodiest quarter in terms of fatalities in the whole history of ETAm was the fourth one in 1978. In December of that year the referendum on the new democratic constitution of Spain was held. It is plausible to consider that the terrorists wanted to prevent participation as much as possible.

ETA was able to sustain a high level of violence until the end of 1980. In 1981 a spectacular fall in the number of killings is observed (see Figure 4.1). A possible explanation is that the escalation of violence led to more arrests, to the point that in 1980 so many activists had been arrested that ETA was not able to replace all of them with new recruits. Violence was then reduced.

From 1981–82 onwards, there was a sort of stalemate between the terrorists and the state. Terrorism and counterterrorism reached some sort of equilibrium, so that the level of violence was contained. This period was characterized by intense dialogue and negotiation between the Socialist government and ETA.[26] Although there had been contacts already in November 1975 and in December 1976–January 1977 (two meetings were held in Geneva), contacts did not become frequent until 1983. Any approach by the government was interpreted by the terrorists as a sign of state weakness. Hence ETA became convinced that further pressure in the form of more lethal attacks would end up with the state sitting at the negotiating table and accepting secession. Some of the worst attacks in the history of ETA are related to the process of dialogue and negotiation. For instance, the car bomb that exploded in a building of the Guardia Civil that killed eleven people (five children among them) on 11 December 1987 was planned by ETA's leader-

---

[25] Quoted in Patxo Unzueta, *Los nietos de la ira: Nacionalismo y violencia en el País Vasco*, Madrid: El País-Aguilar, 1988, p. 251.

[26] For a fuller analysis of the contacts between ETA and the government, see Sánchez-Cuenca (fn. 22), Ch. 4. The Socialist Party won a majority in 1982 and remained in power until 1996. From 1996 to 2004, the Popular Party (conservative) was in government. In 2004, the Socialists gained power again.

Figure 4.1

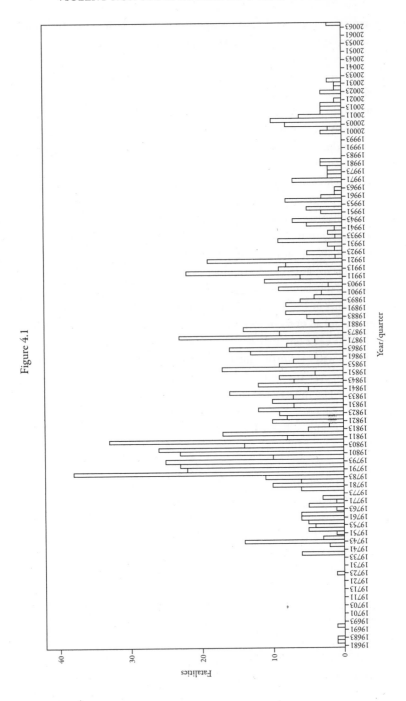

ship as a bargaining tool for the negotiations. The state, however, thought that contacts were useful to weaken the terrorist organization. Contacts, the state assumed, might provoke tensions and eventually a rift in the organization; internal division between 'moderates', willing to reach some agreement, and 'radicals', rigid supporters of continuation of armed struggle, could end up in a split.

After many preliminary contacts, ETA and the government agreed to hold formal negotiations in Algiers. On 8 January 1989 ETA announced a 15-day ceasefire that allowed the process to begin. The ceasefire was extended until 4 April. During this period six meetings were held, but no agreement was possible. The government did not want to engage seriously in political negotiations and the terrorists did not accept less than full satisfaction of the KAS Alternative (basically, self-determination). Despite this failure, there were numerous other contacts between 1990 and 1996. Yet, these contacts did not give rise to a new round of negotiations. When the Popular Party won elections in 1996, it made public its commitment not to negotiate with the terrorists.

The most important event in the war of attrition was the downfall of the entire ETA leadership in a police operation in Bidart on 29 March 1992. The blow to ETA was terrible. It led to a process of internal reflection among the terrorists that in turn led to the abandonment of their strategy. They understood that their violence would never surpass the resistance threshold of the state.

In 1995, ETA issued a new set of demands that replaced the old KAS Alternative. The new document, known as 'Democratic Alternative', was rather opaque. At first reading, it was not obvious whether there was any significant change with regard to the war of attrition model. However, a new emphasis was added on the necessity of achieving independence not in direct negotiations with the state, but rather through an agreement with all nationalist forces in the BAC. The idea was that the state would not be able to prevent secession if there was a broad consensus among parties, trade unions, social movements, and ETA about the necessity of exercising the right of self-determination. The Democratic Alternative was publicized after a failed attack against the leader of the Popular Party, José María Aznar, on 19 April.

The third strategic period, that of the nationalist front, was made visible through a radical change in the pattern of target selection (see next section). For the first time in its long history, ETA started to kill non-nationalist elected politicians, particularly at the local level. The calculation of ETA was the following: by killing non-nationalists, the BAC would be split into two non-reconcilable halves, nationalists and non-nationalists, and the moderate nationalists would have no other option but to reach a consensus with the radical ones. Thus a nationalist front would be constituted, according to the plan expressed in the Democratic Alternative.

The politics of the nationalist front crystallized in the so-called Lizarra Pact (Lizarra is a town in Navarre) on 12 September 1998. It was considerably inspired by the political front created by the PIRA with John Hume's SDLP, the Dublin government, and the Irish lobby in the United States. The contents of the Pact were based on a secret agreement between ETA and the EAJ signed in August of that year. The moderate nationalists agreed to fight for independence and to isolate the non-nationalist parties politically, in exchange for an indefinite truce by ETA. The truce was declared on 19 September.

The EAJ's pact with the terrorists created high political tension in Spain. Many thought at the time, nonetheless, that ETA would not resume violence. The conservative government under Aznar held a meeting with the terrorists in Switzerland, but ETA was not interested in this case in negotiating with the state. Its focus was on other Basque political forces.

When ETA found out that the moderate nationalists were not ready to provoke a constitutional crisis by issuing a unilateral declaration of independence, it broke the truce. The announcement was made on 28 November 1999. The truce had lasted almost fourteen months. The terrorist campaign after the truce (see Figure 4.1) was brutal—not so much in terms of the number of killings, but rather in terms of the impact that the killing of politicians had. The government, with the support of the Socialists in the opposition, passed a law banning the political branch of ETA. There was wide consensus that a party linked to a terrorist organization that killed politicians was not acceptable in a democratic system.

The new cycle of violence was quite short. In 2000 ETA killed 23 people. In 2003 the death toll was lowered to three. After the 2000–3 cycle of violence, ETA found itself without a strategy. Once the strategies of insurrection, war of attrition and the nationalist front had failed, ETA could not provide a political justification for armed struggle. The terrorists entered into a new phase of decadence and collapse. In fact, they did not kill anyone for three and a half years.

During this period, ETA asked for meetings with the government. The new Socialist Prime Minister, José Luis Rodríguez Zapatero, agreed to begin a peace process. On 22 March 2006, ETA announced 'a permanent ceasefire'.

There were some contacts between the government, the terrorists and international mediators, but the strong opposition of the Popular Party to a negotiated settlement prevented any progress in the peace process. The government was very cautious and did not make any concessions. ETA exploded a car bomb in the car park of the new terminal of the Madrid Airport on 30 December 2006, killing two immigrants from Ecuador. That was the end of that short-lived peace process.

## Patterns of target selection

An important difference between guerrilla insurgencies and terrorist conflicts is that in the latter the number of fatalities is much lower, so that counting and codifying all victims is time-consuming but ultimately feasible. Whereas in the case of civil wars target selection can only be analyzed through sampling (based on time, or on geographical space), in the case of terrorism we can have access to all the fatalities. I have collected a large dataset with all fatalities killed by ETA.[27] Thanks to this dataset, it is possible to provide some basic information about the main features of ETA's violence.

As Table 4.2 shows, ETA and all other Basque nationalist terrorist organizations killed 834 people between 1960 and 2006. This count does not include more diffuse political violence (such as street violence) in which it is impossible to attribute the crime to a particular organization. Almost 93 per cent of the killings were done by ETAm; ETApm and CAA represent only the remaining 7 per cent. Compared with Republican terrorism in Northern Ireland, fragmentation is much lower in the Basque Country.

As for the geographical distribution of the killings, 67 per cent of them took place in the BAC (561 fatalities). Within the BAC, Guipúzcoa, the most nationalist province, concentrates the highest number of fatalities (309, or 55 per cent of all fatalities in the BAC). By contrast, Álava, the least nationalist province, represents only 7.7 per cent. Outside the BAC, Madrid is the region with the highest death toll (121 fatalities, 14.5 per cent of the total), followed by Catalonia (54 fatalities, 6.5 per cent of the total).

The geographical pattern is revealing about ETA's strategy. For instance, ETA has carried out indiscriminate attacks with car bombs not in the BAC,

---

[27] The dataset is publicly available at www.march.es/dtv. For a more detailed analysis of ETA's target selection, see Luis de la Calle and Ignacio Sánchez-Cuenca, 'La selección de víctimas en ETA', *Revista Española de Ciencia Política*, 10, 2004, pp. 53–79; and Calleja and Sánchez-Cuenca (fn. 20).

Table 4.2

| Year | ETA/ETAm | ETApm | CAA | Others | Annual total |
|------|----------|-------|-----|--------|--------------|
| 1960 | 1 | – | – | – | 1 |
| 1968 | 2 | – | – | – | 2 |
| 1969 | 1 | – | – | – | 1 |
| 1972 | 1 | – | – | – | 1 |
| 1973 | 6 | – | – | – | 6 |
| 1974 | 19 | – | – | – | 19 |
| 1975 | 11 | 4 | – | – | 16 |
| 1976 | 16 | 2 | – | – | 18 |
| 1977 | 8 | 2 | – | – | 10 |
| 1978 | 60 | 1 | 4 | – | 65 |
| 1979 | 65 | 10 | 5 | – | 79 |
| 1980 | 82 | 5 | 9 | – | 94 |
| 1981 | 30 | – | 2 | – | 30 |
| 1982 | 36 | – | 3 | – | 39 |
| 1983 | 31 | – | 8 | 1 | 40 |
| 1984 | 31 | – | 1 | 1 | 33 |
| 1985 | 37 | – | – | – | 37 |
| 1986 | 40 | – | – | 1 | 41 |
| 1987 | 50 | – | – | – | 50 |
| 1988 | 19 | – | – | – | 20 |
| 1989 | 18 | – | – | – | 18 |
| 1990 | 25 | – | – | – | 25 |
| 1991 | 45 | – | – | – | 46 |
| 1992 | 26 | – | – | – | 26 |
| 1993 | 14 | – | – | – | 14 |
| 1994 | 13 | – | – | – | 13 |
| 1995 | 163 | – | – | – | 16 |
| 1996 | 53 | – | – | – | 5 |
| 1997 | 133 | – | – | – | 13 |
| 1998 | 63 | – | – | – | 6 |
| 1999 | 3 | – | – | – | 0 |
| 2000 | 233 | – | – | – | 23 |
| 2001 | 153 | – | – | – | 15 |
| 2002 | 53 | – | – | – | 5 |
| 2003 | 33 | – | – | – | 3 |
| 2004 | 3 | – | – | – | 0 |
| 2005 | 3 | – | – | – | 0 |
| 2006 | 23 | – | – | – | 2 |
| Total | 775 | 24 | 32 | 3 | 834 |
|  | (92.9%) | (2.9%) | (3.8%) | (0.4%) | (100%) |

*Source*: The ETA dataset (at www.march.es/dtv).

but in the rest of Spain. Of all fatalities killed by car bombs, only 16 per cent occurred in the BAC. It is obvious that the terrorists tried to prevent the killing of Basque civilians in order to preserve its support base.

Generally speaking, Basque terrorist organizations have been rather selective in their violence. There have been 596 lethal attacks, producing 834 fatalities. The average number of fatalities per lethal attack is 1.4.[28] Such a low average is due, as I have pointed out above, to support constraints. Supporters have more moderate preferences about violence than activists. They do not approve of indiscriminate killings or killings of civilians. These data are consistent with the fact that 64 per cent of the victims were killed by shootings; shootings are normally more selective than bombings.

If we look at the status of the victims in Table 4.3, we can see that security forces, including the army, represent 58 per cent of all fatalities. Most of them were police officers. It is important to bear in mind that in Spain counterterrorism is in the hands of the police forces, not the military. This explains why the military represent only 11 per cent of all fatalities.

Civilians amount to 42 per cent of all victims. It is indeed a considerable figure, but it contradicts the commonplace notion that terrorism is to be defined as violence against non-combatants or civilians. In fact, terrorist organizations usually kill fewer civilians than guerrilla insurgencies. Civilians, for instance, are around 80 per cent of all victims of killings in the case of the Peruvian Shining Path.

ETA claims that it does not approve of the killing of civilians, except if the person has done something contrary to ETA's interests. Informers, drug-dealers, entrepreneurs who do not succumb to the financial extortion, people with extreme right-wing ideology, or people involved in the 'dirty war' against ETA are exceptions to this general rule. These are normally selective killings and have more to do with issues of security for the organization than with issues of influence.[29] In other words, selective killings are rarely part of the campaign against the state. In ETA, 21.5 per cent of the killings were selective in the sense specified here.

[28] The equivalent figure for the PIRA is even lower, 1.3 fatalities per lethal attack. See Sánchez-Cuenca (fn. 1), p. 300.

[29] On the distinction between influence and security, see Gordon H. McCormick, 'Terrorist Decision Making', *Annual Review of Political Science*, Vol. 6, 2003, pp. 473–507. Security is related to the survival of the organization (avoidance of denunciations, financing, internal feuds, competition with other organizations); influence has to do with the capacity of the organization to achieve its goals.

Table 4.3

| Victim status | Fatalities | Percentage |
|---|---|---|
| Military | 96 | 11.5 |
| Spanish Police (National police and Civil Guard) | 350 | 42 |
| Basque police (*Ertzaintza*) | 13 | 1.6 |
| Local police | 25 | 3 |
| Politicians and public officials | 49 | 5.9 |
| Members and former members of ETA | 7 | 0.8 |
| Other civilians | 294 | 35.2 |
| Total | 834 | 100 |

*Source*: The ETA dataset (at www.march.es/dtv).

Yet there is an important gap between this 21.5 per cent of selective killings of civilians and the overall 42 per cent of civilians killed. This difference is largely explained by indiscriminate and collateral killings. For instance, on 19 June 1987, ETA exploded a car bomb in the car park of a megastore in Barcelona, killing 21 civilians. ETA made a call warning about the existence of a car bomb (with no further details about the exact location), but the police did not take the threat seriously and people were not evacuated. This is typical of an indiscriminate attack. Indiscriminate and collateral victims are around 16 per cent of all fatalities.

Finally, politicians and public officials merit some attention. During the war of attrition period ETAm did not target politicians, though it killed some non-elected mayors of the Franco period. By contrast, ETApm attacked elected politicians in the early years of democracy (there was a campaign against right-wing, non-nationalist Basque politicians who belonged to the incumbent party). If we limit ourselves to the case of ETAm, we observe that in the period 1968–92, which covers both the insurrection and the war of attrition strategies, politicians and public officials are only 2.7 per cent of the fatalities. Yet, in the period of the nationalist front, from 1993 onwards, the percentage goes up to 22 per cent.

The killing of politicians starting in 1995 has had a profound impact on Spanish society. Even if the number of fatalities per year had a clear declining trend in the 1990s (see Figure 4.1), the Spanish people became much more concerned with ETA's violence in this period than in the war of attrition phase. In the last 15 years, each killing has been in the newspaper headlines and terrorism has become a central issue in the political debate. ETA has been more present in public life despite the substantial reduction in fatalities.

As some authors have pointed out, the impact of violence is a complex function of both the quantity and the quality of violence.[30] By changing target selection, ETA has been able to maintain its presence in Spanish politics even with fewer fatalities. This change of targets, however, has been highly costly to ETA in terms of popular support. Its image has worsened considerably in the eyes of both radical and moderate Basque nationalists.

## Conclusions

ETA belongs to the wave of terrorist organizations that emerged in many developed countries at the end of the 1960s and during the 1970s. What is particularly puzzling is not its origin, but rather its extraordinary duration. ETA was born under an authoritarian regime, but its lethal activity escalated during the early years of the transition to democracy. Despite the introduction of democracy, and despite a process of devolution of fiscal, social, security, education, and health powers to the BAC, ETA has not renounced armed struggle.

ETA has been able to survive for such a long time because of the existence of a small but extremely cohesive base of supporters (around 10 per cent of the BAC's population). Moderate nationalists do not support ETA, but nonetheless have an indulgent attitude to violence. In order to keep this basis of support, the terrorist organization has created a vast and complex network of legal, semi-legal and illegal organizations around the hard-core armed group. ETA has a newspaper, a party, a trade union, associations and firms. Moreover, it has tried to capitalize on new social movements.

ETA's lethal activity is low compared with that of guerrilla insurgencies, but high compared with other terrorist organizations in the Western world. Today, ETA has caused the highest death toll after the PIRA's in Northern Ireland. ETA and its various splinters killed 834 people in the period 1960–2006. Basque nationalist terrorism is rather selective: 1.4 fatalities per lethal attack on average. Most of the victims are members of police forces and the military; civilians represent 42 per cent of all fatalities.

ETA has gone through three strategic periods: the insurrectionary one (until 1977), the war of attrition (1978–92), and the nationalist front (1993–

[30] Ethan Bueno de Mesquita, 'The Quality of Terror', *American Journal of Political Science*, Vol. 49, 2005, pp. 515–30, and Gordon H. McCormick and Guillermo Owen, 'Revolutionary Origins and Conditional Mobilization', *European Journal of Political Economy*, Vol. 12, 1996, pp. 377–402.

2003). After the failure of the nationalist front, no strategy is discernable. There are solid empirical grounds to argue that after 2003 ETA entered into its final phase of extinction. It did not kill anyone from June 2003 to December 2006. After a short, failed peace process, ETA has resumed violence, but it is much weaker than in the past, in terms both of public support and of offensive power.

# 5

# The Kosovo Liberation Army and the Intricacies of Legitimacy

*Klejda Mulaj*

The language of legitimacy has become a recurrent feature of contemporary world politics. One area in which this has been particularly vivid is that of debates surrounding warfare and the legitimacy of the use of force. This may be because our era has included very many transitional periods from an old to a new system, as well as times of conflict and war. And it is times of change—when criteria of legitimacy are challenged and contested—that are crucial moments for legitimacy.

The term does not have a clear and uncontested meaning. There is, though, a general agreement that it is a political notion in so far as 'legitimacy cannot be divorced from power': legitimacy constrains power whilst also being a constituent part of it. It is only within the context of power relations that legitimacy becomes relevant.[1] Indeed, legitimacy is inherent in power relations in so far as it justifies them and renders them acceptable.[2] Consequently, power and its distribution cannot be comprehensively understood outside conceptions of legitimacy. Moreover, the nature of state interests and their evolution, as well as the character of power-struggle conflicts—but also value conflicts—cannot be comprehended outside conceptions of legitimacy.

[1] Ian Clark, *Legitimacy in International Society*, Oxford: Oxford University Press, 2005, p. 20.
[2] Thomas Luckmann, 'Comments on Legitimation', *Current Sociology*, Vol. 35, No. 2, 1987, p. 111.

The law, and competing ideologies and morality, offer a framework in the context of which states and non-state actors question the legitimacy of the use of force in world politics. Key to such deliberations is providing persuasive and reasoned arguments that a course of action is justified and valid, and therefore legitimate. As Andrew Hurrell notes, reason-giving—that is, persuasion—is a crucial component of legitimacy. The politics of legitimacy are played out to multiple audiences (domestic, international and transnational) through a complex set of media, and successful claims to legitimacy require management of their divergent demands. What makes persuasion achievable is a shared language through which such claims can be articulated, addressed and received.[3] This shared language often stems from established patterns of argumentation about the use of force which exist in the law and diplomatic conventions. Furthermore, institutions such as the United Nations (UN), the North Atlantic Treaty Organization (NATO) and the European Union (EU) provide fora in which the fervent pursuit of legitimacy is practiced. The record of these institutions shows that 'legitimacy is the conceptual place where facts and norms merge',[4] and that a clear-cut distinction between a normative and a descriptive meaning of legitimacy cannot be reasonably made.

Most recently it is the Iraq War that has publicly exposed disagreements surrounding the legitimate use of force by state and non-state actors. Debates on this issue in the UN Security Council clearly show that states—and to some extent also non-state actors—use diplomacy and international organizations to debate whether deployment of organized violence is justified or not. Of course, this debate is not new. Indeed, it emerged with equal vigour in 1999 when NATO took the decision to use force in order to end the Serbian-led ethnic cleansing of Kosovo Albanians and in the process collaborated with Albanian guerrillas. As pointed out in several studies[5] the Kosovo case illustrated, perhaps more forcefully than the case of Iraq, the tension between law and legitimacy in the use of force, as well as revealing tensions between two

---

[3] Refer to Andrew Hurrell, 'Legitimacy and the Use of Force: can the Circle be Squared?' in David Armstrong, Theo Farrell and Bice Maiguashca (eds), *Force and Legitimacy in World Politics*, Cambridge: Cambridge University Press, 2005, pp. 16, 23–4.

[4] Ibid., p. 29.

[5] Independent International Commission on Kosovo, *Kosovo Report: Conflict, International Response, Lessons Learned*, Oxford University Press, 2000; Alex J. Bellamy, *Kosovo and International Society*, Basingstoke: Palgrave Macmillan 2002; Nicholas J. Wheeler, *Saving Strangers: Humanitarian Intervention in International Society*, Oxford University Press, 2000.

key international norms: non-intervention, on the one hand, and protection of human rights of repressed peoples, on the other. These tensions reflected in many ways dilemmas which the international community had faced in Bosnia in the early 1990s.

In addition to exposing how contested and contingent is the notion of legitimate use of force, contemporary conflicts reflect also the novel ways in which competition for influence and support is conducted. Prominent in this respect is the use of media, chiefly television, but also alternative means of image delivery. So pronounced has competition over images become that two writers have recently argued that images are the key weapons in contemporary warfare.[6] Indeed, images have become important not only as a support for strategy but also as an object of strategy itself.[7] By influencing understanding of the conflict, 'the battle for hearts and minds', and the dynamics of mobilization and popular support, as well as by influencing policy decision-making, images have an impact—direct or indirect—on the question of legitimacy of the conflict, its conceptualization and its interpretation. Television images of tortured people in Serbian-run camps in Bosnia were an important factor in shaping international policy and inducing Western military engagement, whilst simultaneously enhancing the cause of the government in Sarajevo and strengthening Bosnian resolve. Similarly, images of massacred Albanian civilians and their mass ethnic cleansing were crucial factors in securing support for NATO's air campaign and strengthening the legitimacy of both NATO action and the armed resistance of the Kosovo Albanians on the ground, while delivering a decisive blow to Belgrade's policies and military actions.

This chapter analyzes the question of legitimacy—and its permutation—in regard to the Kosovo Liberation Army (KLA) and its struggle against Serbian oppression in Kosovo. Given that the number of VNSAs receiving national and international support and recognition remains limited, the KLA is not necessarily the epitome of contemporary VNSAs. But what makes its analysis interesting from the point of view of both political practitioners and academics is the fact that it is frequently described as the most successful guerrilla movement in recent history. This chapter suggests that what accounts most for the KLA's success is the acquisition of legitimacy at national and international levels. The distinction between 'national' and 'international' legitimacy is employed here as an analytical device based upon the observation that they

---

[6] Milena Michalski and James Gow, *War, Image and Legitimacy: Viewing Contemporary Conflict*, London: Routledge, 2007.

[7] Ibid., p. 123.

involve distinct audiences. However, as stressed also in the introductory chapter in this volume, no clear-cut division between the two realms should be assumed, as the evolution of each one of them impacts on the other.

The KLA's achievement of its aims does not imply that its legitimacy is not contested—especially so on the Serbian side. But the above thesis—by and large—applies to the international community's and Albanian people's view of the KLA, as well as the KLA's perception of itself. This chapter will show that the very existence and legitimacy of the KLA have been a function of power relations and processes of war and peace in Kosovo. The point of departure of the unfolding analysis is that the historical origins and evolution of the KLA offer a crucial way for presenting an account of its claims and objectives, as well as the extent to which they were embraced nationally and internationally. Moreover, the following shows how the understanding and interpretation of KLA's legitimacy and success have been closely intertwined with its tactics and strategy, and, more important, with the changing security environment in Kosovo and the wider region—that is, management of insecurity and generation of security.

## Albanians and Serbs in Kosovo: dynamics of confrontation

A key starting point in the tense relationship between Kosovo Albanians and Serbs dates back to the annexation of Kosovo by Serbia in 1912. Noel Malcolm—a British academic who has studied the legality of that occupation—argues that Kosovo's annexation by Serbia was both unconstitutional and illegal: it was unconstitutional as it was not sanctioned by Serbia's Grand National Assembly; it was illegal as it was not the product of a bilateral treaty between the Ottoman Empire—under which Kosovo belonged prior to its annexation—and the Serbian state.[8] In the course of the occupation in 1912–13 cruel atrocities were committed by the Serbian military against Kosovo Albanians. Ruthless Serbian violence was reported vividly both by Leon Trotsky[9] and by the International Commission of Inquiry established by the Carnegie Endowment. The latter, for instance, considered that Serbian violence sought an 'entire transformation of the ethnic character of regions inhabited exclusively by Albanians'.[10]

[8] Noel Malcolm, *Kosovo: A Short History*, London: Papermac, 1998, p. 258.

[9] Leon Trotsky, *The Balkan Wars 1912–13*, New York: Monad Press, 1980.

[10] *The Other Balkan Wars: A 1913 Carnegie Endowment Inquiry in Retrospect with a New Introduction and Reflections on the Present Conflict*. Introduction by George F. Kennan. Washington, DC: Carnegie Endowment for International Peace, 1993, p. 151.

Serbian occupation brought with it very unfavourable conditions for Albanian livelihood, ranging from attempts at language and culture annihilation, imposition of atrocious living conditions and, worst of all, ethnic cleansing.[11] Consequently, Kosovo Albanians resisted Serbian rule in the province from the beginning, both passively by means of peaceful resistance, spontaneous as that might have been, and actively by means of armed rebellion. In the summer of 1913, in the Peja and Gjakova regions, small bands of Albanian fighters by the name of Kaçaks formed an armed opposition to Kosovo's annexation to Serbia. By 1919 Kaçak fighters numbered about 10,000. Constituting the first organized armed resistance movement against the legitimacy of Serbian/ Yugoslav rule in Kosovo, they set an example which was emulated by ensuing Albanian generations in their struggle against Serbian oppression. Yet the Kaçaks, poorly armed, could not match the military power of the Yugoslav army. Failing to generate wide national support and to secure international backing, the Kaçaks were eventually defeated by the Serbian forces. By the end of the Kaçak rebellion in 1924 more than 12,000 Albanians had been killed and about 22,000 were imprisoned, and roughly 6,000 houses had been burned.[12]

During the interwar period, Belgrade encouraged resettlement of Montenegrins and Serbs in Kosovo and negotiations were started with Ankara for the population 'transfer' of Kosovo Albanians to Turkey, which did not materialize because of the outbreak of World War II.[13] The Kosovo Albanians' fate continued to deteriorate after that war, when they were labelled by the Serbian officials as collaborators with the Axis powers. Consequently there were fresh massacres in Drenica in the winter of 1944–45, and a policy of Turkification of Kosovo Albanians was promoted by Belgrade.[14] Indeed, by the mid-1960s, following constant repression by the Serbian secret police, around 200,000 Albanians left Kosovo for Turkey.[15]

---

[11] Klejda Mulaj, *Politics of Ethnic Cleansing: Nation-State Building and Provision of In/Security in Twentieth Century Balkans*, Lanham, MD: Lexington Books/Roman & Littlefield, 2008, Chapters 2 and 3.

[12] Figures are cited in Malcolm, *Kosovo*, p. 278.

[13] Mulaj, *Politics of Ethnic Cleansing*, pp. 33–7.

[14] Anton Logoreci, 'A Clash Between Two Nationalisms in Kosova', in Arshi Pipa, and Sami Repishti (eds), *Studies on Kosova*, Boulder: East European Monographs/Columbia University Press, 1984, p. 188.

[15] Elez Biberaj in Stevan K. Pavlowitch and Elez Biberaj, *The Albanian Problem in Yugoslavia: Two Views*, London: Institute for the Study of Conflict, 1982, p. 29.

Following protests by Kosovo Albanians in 1968 and 1981, the Serbian police once again carried out a harsh attack on the Albanians. From March 1981 to November 1988 584,373 Kosovars—or half of the adult population—were arrested, interrogated, interned or reprimanded.[16] The worst repression against the Kosovo Albanians came with the rise to power of Slobodan Milošević.[17] It was he who revoked the constitutional autonomy of Kosovo gained in 1974, transferred to Belgrade the control of Kosovo's police, judicial system, civil defence, economic, social and educational policy, instituted a policy of 'Serbianization' of Kosovo institutions, raised the unemployment rate of Kosovo Albanians to record levels, and imposed upon them mandatory education in the Serbian language.[18]

Under Milošević's rule, the Kosovo Albanians embraced a policy of peaceful resistance against Serbian oppression, contesting the legitimacy of Belgrade imposed institutions. Kosovo Albanian leaders appealed to the international community for Kosovo's independence from Serbia, but their appeals were not heeded.[19] On 2 July 1990, nevertheless, the Albanian Assembly in Prishtina approved Kosovo's independence; but Serbia on that same day endorsed the imposition of direct rule on Kosovo, and subsequently dissolved its parliament and government. Undeterred, on 7 September 1990 the Kosovo Assembly proclaimed a new Constitution declaring Kosovo 'a sovereign and independent state' and appointed a new Albanian 'government'. Three weeks later, however, Serbia annulled Kosovo's autonomy. Nonetheless, following democratic elections in 1992 won by the Democratic League of Kosovo (Lidhja Demokratike e Kosovës, LDK), its leader, Ibrahim Rugova, was elected 'president of the republic of Kosovo'. These elections gave legitimacy to the LDK and to Rugova, at least in the eyes of the Albanian people. But despite Rugova's implementation of a peaceful resistance strategy against the Serbian

[16] This figure comes from Howard Clark, *Civil Resistance in Kosovo*, London: Pluto Press, 2000, p. 43.

[17] Slobodan Milošević assumed the presidency of Serbia in 1989. He served in this capacity till 1997 when he became President of the Federal Republic of Yugoslavia, a post which he kept until 2000, when he was forced out of power by popular dissent. For his role in the wars in Croatia, Bosnia and Kosovo, he was charged by the International Criminal Tribunal for the Former Yugoslavia with crimes against humanity, violation of the laws of war and grave breaches of the Geneva Conventions. He died in detention at The Hague on 11 March 2006.

[18] Mulaj, *Politics of Ethnic Cleansing*, p. 102.

[19] Refer to Clark, *Civil Resistance*. Albanians constitute 90 per cent of Kosovo's 2 million population.

rule, the latter was by no means inclined to cede any of its powers to the Kosovo Albanians. On the contrary, Belgrade continued persistently with human rights violations against the Kosovars.

## The KLA and its quest for legitimacy

Although all Albanian political factions had one common goal in Kosovo—self-determination—the way to achieve this was undetermined. In 1978, for instance, the Movement for the National Liberation of Kosovo (MNLK, Lëvizja për Çlirimin Kombëtar të Kosovës) was established in Prishtina with the aim of working towards organizing of armed resistance to achieve the independence of Kosovo. Forced to work in exile as a result of the Serbian regime's purges, the movement dissolved following the assassination of its leaders in January 1982 in Stuttgart in Germany—an act widely attributed to the Yugoslav secret service. A sister organization formed in 1982 in Prishtina—the Movement for an Albanian Republic in Yugoslavia (Lëvizja për Republikën e Shqipërisë në Jugosllavi, LRSHJ)—was similarly targeted by the Serbian regime when its principal leader was shot dead in Prishtina in 1984.[20] The latter movement, however, survived and was later renamed as the Popular Movement for the Republic of Kosovo (Lëvizja Popullore për Republikën e Kosovës, LPRK).

The Democratic League of Kosovo (LDK)—the largest Albanian political party in Kosovo—considered the chances of success for any Albanian armed resistance to Serbian rule as negligible, and declined to endorse violent resistance. Owing its popularity, largely, to its Gandhi-like leader Ibrahim Rugova, the LDK opted for an alternative to violence, namely peaceful resistance to Serbian rule, believing that this strategy had the advantage of attaining two objectives: uniting Kosovar Albanians towards a common aim and at the same time challenging the legitimacy of Serbian institutions. Rugova's strategy of peaceful resistance was premised on courting and securing international support. The latter, nevertheless, was not forthcoming as the international community viewed the Kosovo issue as an internal matter of Serbia, which did not threaten Western interests. Consequently, the LDK's strategy failed to deliver the desired results.

Belgrade's massive human rights violations and the atrocious living conditions meted out to Kosovo's population, as well as Rugova's lack of success in effectively challenging oppression in Kosovo, were crucial factors in planting

[20] Paulin Kola, *The Myth of Greater Albania*, London: Hurst, 2003, p. 317.

the seeds of a new armed resistance amongst Kosovo Albanians. As time passed and no concrete results were obtained by Rugova's party, armed resistance began to raise its head, with unclaimed attacks against the Serbian police in 1990–91 first, and then attacks on the Serbian army and intelligence forces. These attacks were carried out by members of the LPRK. Yet sporadic attacks by some 100 LPRK fighters who were trained in neighbouring Albania between 1990 and 1992 did not have a significant impact in Kosovo, as many of them were arrested or killed by Serbian forces. Not only was the LPRK challenged by persistent attacks from the Serbian regime, its activities were also derailed by the popularity of Rugova and his policy of peaceful resistance. Nevertheless, belief in the validity of resort to arms was alive and in 1993 LPRK held a meeting in Drenica, in Kosovo, with the view of forming an organized armed resistance. Subsequently, the majority of LPRK followers agreed on a name change, to the Popular Movement for Kosovo (Lëvizja Popullore e Kosovës, LPK). The new movement dropped its leftist leaning and agreed to form an armed force to oppose Serbian rule in Kosovo.[21] The name of the Kosovo Liberation Army was chosen in December 1993. Although recognizing that the Kosovo Albanians never had their own army, one of the KLA founders—Rexhep Selimi—states that the term 'Army' was used 'to reflect our aim of having one in the near future'. He further contends that in order to liberate Kosovo from Serbian occupation, the Kosovo Albanians needed to have their own armed forces as they could not rely on Albania: hence the term 'Kosovo Liberation Army'.[22]

The KLA had a difficult beginning. It faced severe constraints ranging from Kosovo Albanians' lack of knowledge about its existence to limited numbers of recruits, lack of finance, poor military training, meagre ammunition and scanty weapons. To make things worse for the KLA, its members had to contend militarily with a strong, well trained and well armoured Serbian force, and in addition the KLA fighters were continuously destabilized by their own fellow compatriots who were advocating a peaceful path to attainment of statehood. In this triangle of contest for legitimacy the KLA was in the worst corner, especially in the initial phase. Indeed, in the given circumstances—as Xhavit Haliti, one of the founders of the movement, admits—the KLA's leaders, warriors, and followers were prepared to continue their fight for a long time, a decade or perhaps longer.[23]

---

[21] Tim Judah, *Kosovo: War and Revenge*, New Haven: Yale University Press, 2000, p. 111.

[22] Conservation with the author, Prishtina, 26 October 2007.

[23] Conversation with the author, Prishtina, 12 June 2008.

However, the KLA's determination was rewarded, first through the failure of Rugova to attain international legitimacy, and secondly through the collapse of the fragile institutions of the Albanian state in 1997. As hinted earlier, the prevalent international perception between 1991 and 1998 was that Kosovo was a Serbian internal matter and hence there was no scope for any international intervention. The international acceptance of Serbia's claim over Kosovo was one key factor that delegitimized Rugova's strategy of peaceful resistance, while the conditions of life for the Albanians worsened rapidly. The Dayton Conference (November 1995) which ended the war in Bosnia made this failure evident, given that the Kosovo issue—and the suffering of its population—were not even considered there; this contributed to the radicalization of the Albanians and convinced them that violence paid, since the Republika Srpska—a creation of ethnic cleansing—was recognized at this Conference as an entity within Bosnia. Subsequently, the KLA intensified its guerrilla warfare. The collapse of state institutions in Albania proved to be a blessing in disguise for the KLA: the ransacking of army depots across the country enabled the guerrillas to purchase the much needed weapons with funds raised mainly in the West by members of the Albanian diaspora. These weapons made a difference: they helped transform the KLA into a guerrilla army, and hence enabled it to constitute a military menace to the Serbian regime and its forces.[24]

Once the KLA's presence began to be felt through increased anti-Serbian attacks, the movement gained growing admiration among Kosovo Albanians, thereby widening its organizational base and popular support. This, in turn, enabled the KLA to step up its guerrilla offensive and become a force to be reckoned with. By August 1998 it controlled around 40 per cent of Kosovo's territory.[25] Ironically, Milošević's regime—even if unintentionally—provided fuel for the KLA's fire through the international community's outrage following the killing of Adem Jashari and more than fifty of his relatives at his family compound on 5 March 1998.[26] With Serbian forces targeting civilians, the

---

[24] The KLA purchased weapons in the Western countries also. In addition, some weapons came from Serbian sources. International Crisis Group, Balkans Report No. 88, 'What Happened to the KLA?', 3 March 2000, p. 17.

[25] Philip Auerswald and David Auerswald (eds), *The Kosovo Conflict: A Diplomatic History Through Documents*, Cambridge, MA: Kluwer Law International, 2000, pp. 180, 210.

[26] An account of this event is provided in Bedri Tahiri, *Adem Jashari: Legjendë e Legjendave*, Prishtina: Rilindja, 2006. For his resistance to Serbian rule, Adem Jashari has become an Albanian legend. The Jasharis' response to fire with fire marked an important

Kosovo Albanians increasingly saw their only salvation in the KLA, especially since the outside powers were not inclined to provide security to the targeted civilian population—at least until 1999. Not surprisingly, the summer of 1998 (following the Jasharis killing) saw a phenomenal increase in the KLA's ranks and local support for it. Concomitant with the KLA's increased legitimacy at the national level there was increased interest among the international community in the KLA's mission and operationality. A number of meetings between high level American diplomats and KLA representatives were conducted in Drenica, a KLA stronghold, in the summer of 1998,[27] preparing the ground for the ultimate international recognition of the KLA which occurred in February-March 1999 at the Rambouillet and Paris diplomatic conferences.

## The KLA's strategy and tactics

Leading an armed insurrection against Serbian subjugation, the KLA did not fight the Serbs in Serbia. On the contrary, it opted for a guerrilla warfare localized on Kosovo's territory and restricted to combating Serbian repression. Initially, the KLA units were organized into small groups consisting of not more than five combatants each, who carried out hit-and-run attacks from short distances and occasional large-scale ambushes on the Serbian armed forces in Kosovo.[28] This strategy dented the self-confidence and prestige of the Serbian military, thereby breaking the myth of their invincibility. Nonetheless, although Kosovo's wooded hills helped the KLA hide from enemy detection, the small geographic size of Kosovo proved to be a disadvantage for the KLA. This drawback was however overcome by using territory in Albania where the KLA set up training camps. Albania also served as a transit link for the KLA to obtain weapons, money, and people both from Albania and from third countries such as Switzerland, Germany and the USA.

As the KLA originally did not have more than 150 active members, its rate of growth tended, initially, to be slow. McCormick and Giordano identify a

---

change in the popular mood in Kosovo setting a stark contrast with pacifist attitudes prevalent until then.

[27] Bellamy, *Kosovo and International Society*, p. 83. The first contacts between KLA representatives and US officials went back to 1996. They were gradually enhanced and came to include EU officials—especially UK diplomats—in 1997 and 1998. Hashim Thaçi in 'Opinion', TV Klan, Tirana, Albania, 7 June 2008, 18:30 GMT.

[28] Halil Katana, *Tri Dimensionet e Luftës Çlirimtare të Kosovës*, Tirana: ARGENTA-LMG, 2002, p. 41.

dilemma for insurgency movements generally: that 'until they are able to establish an effective base of support they cannot go on to win, but until they convince people that they are winning, it is very hard to mobilize a winning base of support'.[29] To counter this dilemma it is not uncommon for armed groups to utilize violent images and use their effects to enhance the mobilization process itself.

Guerrilla war is profoundly asymmetrical. This asymmetry is exploited by insurgents to provoke the state into striking out at targets it cannot see, such as insurgents hidden amongst civilians, thus alienating the latter and driving them into the arms of the guerrilla fighters. As Gordon McCormick notes, the state enters the war with a force advantage but with an information disadvantage. It has the strength to hit what it sees, but can see little of what it wishes to hit. On the contrary, guerrilla fighters start the war with a force disadvantage but with an information advantage. Although they can see what they wish to hit, they have limited capabilities to hit what they see.[30]

Manipulation of violent images for agitation and provocative effects is likely to reduce guerrillas' mobilization dilemma but not eradicate it altogether. This is because people's standing towards the guerrilla movement is conditioned by their belief in the guerrillas' chances of success. The latter depends on people's subjective perception of the rise of guerrillas and their level of support.[31] To overcome this barrier, guerrillas use violence to generate an exaggerated impression of insurgent strength and regime weakness. This demonstrative effect of violence is intended to alter the image in people's minds and their level of support, on the basis not necessarily of facts, but of perception of insurgents' capabilities. A sustained targeting campaign by KLA fighters may indeed have created the impression that it was stronger than it really was.

KLA actions not only gained local attention but were also transmitted by mass media, both inside Kosovo and Albania, as well as in the West.[32] Media attention amplified the impression of KLA strength and of the righteousness

---

[29] Gordon H. McCormick and Frank Giordano, 'Things Come Together: Symbolic Violence and Guerrilla Mobilization', *Third World Quarterly* Vol. 28, No. 2, 2007, p. 300.

[30] See Gordon H McCormick, 'Terrorist Decision Making', *Annual Review of Political Science* 4, Palo Alto, CA: Annual Reviews, 2003.

[31] McCormick and Giordano, 'Things Come Together', p. 309.

[32] The KLA operated one radio station 'Kosova e Lirë' as well as a news agency 'Kosova Press' inside Kosovo. The Albanian media in Albania proper regularly reported KLA activities, especially from 1998 onwards. Moreover, KLA communiqués were transmitted by the BBC Albanian services, and were printed in Albanian and foreign newspapers in Switzerland, Britain, Germany, etc.

of its liberation cause, thus enlarging the pool of KLA supporters. For instance, simultaneously with the increasing positive image and rising popularity of the KLA in the post-Dayton period, donations by the Albanian diaspora to the KLA's Homeland Calling Fund increased considerably, with up to US$ 30 million being raised by its US branch alone between 1997 and 1999.[33]

The spectacular rise in popularity and strength of the KLA challenged irreversibly the legitimacy of Serbian rule in the province. The irony is that the brutal Serbian counter-insurgency offensive sowed the seeds of Serbia's own defeat by strengthening the KLA's resolve and outraging the international community with appallingly large-scale violations of humanitarian and human rights law.

## The KLA's international *exequatur*

Until the late 1990s the international community's policy reflected an acceptance of Serbia's claim to sovereignty over Kosovo. The Kosovo question was marginalized and excluded from the agendas of diplomatic conferences convened in 1992 and 1995 to address the dissolution of the federation of Yugoslavia. By mid-1998, nonetheless, two-fifths of Kosovo's territory was seized by the KLA and the conflict had serious potential to escalate similarly to that of Bosnia.

The disproportionate Serbian response to the Albanian insurgency led by the KLA had the unintended consequence of alerting the international community to the interdependent relationship between international responses (and/or lack thereof) to the conflict and human rights abuses on the one hand, and Kosovo Albanians' demands for self-governance on the other. Belgrade's policy of large-scale ethnic cleansing prompted the UN Security Council to issue a number of resolutions which requested a prompt halt to

---

[33] This is due—in part—to the fact that the three per cent levy on all earnings abroad which was dedicated to the LDK was diverted to the KLA. The Homeland Calling Fund was established in 1995 by a group of Kosovar émigrés in Switzerland who had long advocated waging a liberation war against Serbian occupation of Kosovo. The fund expanded with branches in the US, Germany, Austria, Norway, Denmark, France, Sweden, Italy, Belgium, Canada, and Australia. See Stacy Sullivan, *Be not Afraid for You Have Sons in America*, New York: St. Martin's Press, 2004; Paul Hockenos, *Homeland Calling: Exile Patriotism and the Balkan Wars*, Ithaca: Cornell University Press, 2003, Chapter 11.

hostilities,[34] declaring the situation in Kosovo as a threat to international peace and security whilst putting the blame squarely on Serbia.

On 9 January 1999, a KLA ambush killed three Serb soldiers and took eight prisoners. On 15 January, 45 Albanian civilians were massacred by Serbian forces in the village of Raçak, most of them women, children and elderly. Images of executed bodies were revealed by the chief of the Kosovo Verification Mission (of the Organization for Security and Co-operation in Europe), William Walker, and viewed on TV screens by people across the world. These images contributed significantly to the KLA's cause, exposing the cruel nature of Serbian domination of Kosovo, whilst at the same time dealing a decisive blow to Belgrade's claims that Serbia had sovereign rights over Kosovo. Moreover, these images affected the understanding of the conflict throughout the world and granted legitimacy to international efforts to intervene—first diplomatically and then militarily.

Aiming to prevent the escalation of the conflict, the Contact Group—France, Germany, Russia, the UK and the US—convened two diplomatic conferences at Rambouillet and Paris in February and March 1999 respectively, thus providing Albanian and Serbian delegations with a forum to explore possibilities of accommodation. That the Albanian delegation was consensually headed by the political director of the KLA, Hashim Thaçi, strengthened further the legitimacy of the KLA's cause. It was in these diplomatic conferences that the guerrilla movement openly received international recognition as a political force, vital for any agreement regarding the future of Kosovo. Accounts of these diplomatic efforts already exist and it is not necessary to reproduce them here. It should be recalled, nevertheless, that the talks in Paris and Rambouillet reached an impasse since the Serbian delegation was not willing to reach an agreement which would end Serbian oppression in Kosovo.[35]

The failure of peace talks prompted the Western Alliance to resort to military action against Serbia on 24 March 1999. It continued till 8 June of the

---

[34] See, for instance, United Nations Security Council Resolution 1160 of 31 March 1998 and Resolution 1199 of 23 September 1998.

[35] Refer to Marc Weller, 'The Rambouillet Conference on Kosovo', *International Affairs*, Vol. 75, No. 2, 1999, especially p. 236. It does not appear that the Serbian President, Slobodan Milošević, intended to desist from his offensive even while the peace talks were convened in France. As many analysts have argued, the Serbian leader was instead using the negotiations to buy time in order to prepare for the next round of Serbian military attacks on Kosovar Albanians. See Independent International Commission on Kosovo, *Kosovo Report*, p. 152; and Nicholas J. Wheeler, *Saving Strangers*, p. 283.

same year, powerfully internationalizing the Kosovo problem.[36] NATO's intervention impacted on Serbian military tactics. To avoid the Alliance's air attacks Serbian forces were split up into small units, but this tactic favoured the guerrillas' strategy of attacks on the Serbian army.[37] The KLA co-operated with NATO forces, with the former providing on-the-ground intelligence for the latter to identify targets to strike. NATO's decision not to deploy ground troops in Kosovo enabled the KLA to provide a complementary ground force for NATO's tactical operations.[38] The epitome of NATO-KLA cooperation was the fight to secure Mount Pashtrik in May 1999, whilst facing heavy Serbian fire. NATO intervened with air attacks to ensure that the KLA, which was lightly armed and outnumbered by Serbian forces, would not be overrun by the latter. NATO's chief commanding officer of that time, General Wesley Clark, has written in his book *Waging Modern War* about this experience:

I was concerned that the Serb forces not be allowed to push the KLA back across the crest of Mount Pastrik. ... At the VTC I could not have been clearer with Mike Short and Jay Hendrix. "By one o'clock" I directed, "you're going to tell me what you are going to do to help the KLA hold the top of that mountain. That mountain is not going to be lost. We're not going to have Serbs on the top of that mountain. We'll have to pay for the top of that hill with American blood if we don't help the KLA hold it now. That's my number-one priority".[39]

In sum, NATO's intervention was indispensable for the KLA. The Alliance's air campaign shortened the time of fighting and minimized the casualties on the side of both the Albanians and the Serbs, as well as minimizing material damage. For the population of Kosovo, NATO's humanitarian intervention was a watershed, a historical event which drew the line between an oppressive past under foreign (Serbian) rule and a future which promised attainment of self-rule and democracy, under the supervision, and assistance, of the international community.

---

[36] I have dealt with the rationale of this intervention in *Politics of Ethnic Cleansing*, pp. 57–59, 104–7.

[37] Katana, *Tri Dimensionet*, p. 38.

[38] Kudusi Lama, *Kosova dhe Ushtria Çlirimtare*, Tirana, 2005, p. 373. See also Tony Mason, 'Kosovo: The Air Campaign' in Stephen Badsey and Paul Latawski (eds), *Britain, NATO and the Lessons of the Balkan Conflict 1991–1999*, London: Frank Cass, 2004, pp. 39–63, especially p. 62.

[39] General Wesley K. Clark, *Waging Modern War: Bosnia, Kosovo, and the Future of Combat*, Oxford: Public Affairs, 2001, pp. 336–7.

## Post-conflict transformation

As mentioned, the Rambouillet Conference was a decisive point so far as international recognition—and therefore acquisition of international legitimacy—for the KLA were concerned. In addition to this a crucial gain for the KLA at Rambouillet was the initiation of discussions on the post-conflict transformation of the guerrilla movement. Such transformation occurred on two planes, military and political.

*Military transformation of the KLA.* The military transformation of the KLA has been tied up with security sector reform in post-conflict Kosovo and the concomitant belief that disarmament, demobilization and reintegration of former combatants contribute to increased security and sustainable peacebuilding. Demilitarization of the KLA finds legal expression in paragraph 15 of UN Security Council Resolution 1244, which formalized the ending of NATO's intervention; this required that the KLA should bring to an end 'all offensive actions and comply with the requirements for demilitarization ...'.[40] Ten days after UN Security Council Resolution 1244, on 21 June 1999, the 'Undertaking of Demilitarization and Transformation' by the KLA was signed between the Kosovo Force (KFOR) and the KLA, under which the latter would cease to exist from 20 September 1999 when its demilitarization was to be completed.[41] The 'undertaking' mandates disengagement of the KLA from the zones of conflict, its demilitarization and its reintegration into civil society. It also provides for the inclusion of KLA fighters in the Kosovo Protection Corps (KPC) and the Kosovo Police Service (KPS). An unknown—but presumably small—number of KLA members were incorporated in Kosovo's Information Service (Shërbimi Informativ i Kosovës, SHIK), an intelligence organization affiliated with the Democratic Party of Kosovo (see below p. 110).[42] In particular, the formation of the KPC was intended by the

---

[40] UN Security Council Resolution S/RES/1244, 10 June 1999.
[41] The NATO-led force KFOR was deployed in Kosovo under UN Security Council Resolution 1244 and has been the main security provider in Kosovo since the ending of NATO's bombing.
[42] In the absence of a central state organization, intelligence services in Kosovo have been tied to the main political parties. The LDK, for instance, had also acquired intelligence capabilities through the Institute for Strategic Research of Public Opinion, which originated from the former 'Ministry of Defence' of Kosovo's Government in exile. See Lulzim Peci, 'How to Conduct Security Sector Reform in Kosovo in Order to Increase Internal and Regional Security', *Foreign Voices*, No. 2, April 2006.

KLA leadership to be an embryo of a future army of Kosovo, offering a compromise between the UN mandate to demilitarize Kosovo and the KLA leaders' determination to maintain some form of standing force.[43]

Whereas disarmament and demobilization of the KLA have been accomplished smoothly, reintegration of former fighters has proved a more challenging task. By November 1999 the number of registered KLA combatants was more than 25,000, of whom 16,229 were expected to acquire social and economic reintegration.[44] The KPC absorbed about 5,000 former KLA fighters (3,000 full members and 2,000 reservists) whilst the KPS absorbed about 3,000. Clearly, the vast majority of KLA warriors were expected to be reintegrated in the post-conflict society of Kosovo outside the KPC and KPS structures; this, given the dire economic situation of the country, has proved to be a daunting task.[45]

But whereas KPS has worked closely with KFOR to ensure provision of security in Kosovo, this has not been the case with the KPC whose mission was defined in rather strict civilian terms, namely: 1) to assist in rebuilding the infrastructure of Kosovo; 2) to respond to man-made or natural disasters; 3) to conduct search and rescue operations; 4) to offer support to KFOR and the UN Mission in Kosovo (UNMIK)—when required. The transformational experience of KPC seems to suggest more than inadequacies in terms of the quality of training and available facilities; more seriously, it seems to

[43] Nonetheless, the KPC did not live long, being dissolved in 2008. Although it was intended by the UN/KFOR to be a new organization, many viewed it as a continuation of the KLA, inheriting its leaders and loyalties. The latter view is associated especially with Kosovo Serb leaders. Moreover, the very term Kosovo Protection Corps contained an inherent ambiguity in its Albanian version: Trupat Mbrojtëse të Kosovës, where 'Mbrojtëse' refers both to 'protection' and 'defence'. Whilst internationals assigned the KPC a protection mission, the KLA leaders preferred to see it as a 'defence' corps. See ICG, 'What Happened to the KLA?', pp. 6–7.

[44] Alpaslan Özerdem, 'From a 'Terrorist' Group to a 'Civil Defence' Corps: The 'Transformation' of the Kosovo Liberation Army', *International Peacekeeping*, Vol. 10, No. 3, 2003, pp. 79–101, at p. 85. Özerdem estimates that 50 per cent of KLA combatants had 6–15 dependents each, 60 per cent had heavily damaged or destroyed houses, and 60 per cent were unskilled and therefore needed training.

[45] The World Bank's Poverty Assessment of 2007 classified 37 per cent of the population of Kosovo as 'poor', i.e., living on less than 1.42 euros per day, whereas 15 per cent of the population lived below the extreme poverty line of 0.93 euros per day. Cited in Nora Hasani and Zana Limani, 'Sharp Rise in Postwar Suicides Alarms Kosovo', *Balkan Investigative Reporting Network* (BIRN), 4 June 2007, http://kosovo.birn.eu.com/en/1/70/3152.

have been ridden with a perception on the side of KPC members that, far from being viewed as 'partners' or 'allies' in the international community's efforts to provide security in post-conflict Kosovo, they were treated like a 'source of cheap labour'.[46]

However, KPC members view themselves as 'victors'—with NATO's support—in the war against Serbia. They see themselves as Western—and especially British and US—allies, and take pride in having taken up arms and risked their lives to liberate their country. They like to see the KPC as the future army of Kosovo. Yet, contrary to KPC members' expectations, the Comprehensive Proposal for the Kosovo Status Settlement prepared by Marti Ahtisaari—which provides the blueprint for implementation of Kosovo's independence—considers that the KPC has 'accomplished its goals, including the facilitation of Kosovo's post-conflict recovery' and recommends its dissolution within one year of Kosovo's independence, a new professional organization, the Kosovo Security Force (KSF) being established instead.[47]

The KSF is intended to be multi-ethnic and lightly armed; not to possess heavy weapons such as tanks, heavy artillery or offensive air capability. Of its new 2,500 active members and 800 reservists only 500 originate from KPC personnel. The fate that waits KPC members forced into retirement is indeed a sensitive and controversial issue which could lead to tensions and disputes. As a think tank in Prishtina has noticed, 'the main dispute is the identity succession of the KLA to the new force on which Kosovo Albanians insist'.[48] The disbanding of the KPC is intended to address security concerns in Kosovo as well as the neighbouring region, and ensure that the new force, the KSF, attracts Serbs and other minorities in the new polity and thus distances itself from past baggage and the image of mono-ethnic composition of the KPC. Yet whilst there is need for a professional body without any past baggage and offensive capacity in order to dissipate fears of neighbouring states and display peaceful attitudes, there is also need to address the KLA tradition and utilize the capacities of KLA members and thus avoid their resentment which could become a security risk in Kosovo. Effective reintegration of former KLA combatants is of utmost importance.

[46] See Özerdem, 'From a 'Terrorist' Group to a 'Civil Defence' Corps', p. 98.
[47] See the Report of the Special Envoy of the UN Secretary-General Martti Ahtisaari 'Comprehensive Proposal for the Kosovo Status Settlement', 26 March 2007, S/2007/168/Add.1 at http://www.unosek.org/unosek/en/statusproposal.html. The Ahtisaari Plan has been incorporated in the Constitution of the Republic of Kosovo.
[48] Kosovar Institute for Policy Research and Development, 'Analysis of the Comprehensive Package for the Status of Kosovo', Policy Brief No. 5, Prishtina, February 2007.

*Political transformation of the KLA.* The political transformation of the KLA occurred concomitantly with its military transformation. At the end of the Rambouillet talks the three main Albanian negotiators—Hashim Thaçi (the political leader of the KLA), Ibrahim Rugova (the 'President' of Kosovo), and Rexhep Qosja (President of the United Democratic Movement, Lëvizja e Bashkuar Demokratike)—signed a document stating that a member of the KLA should hold the office of prime minister in a new Kosovo interim government. The three parties did not implement the agreement jointly. However, on 2 April 1999 Hashim Thaçi formed a provisional interim government of Kosovo with representatives of Qosja's movement joining but not Rugova's LDK. Thaçi's government quickly created administrations for 27 of 29 municipalities of Kosovo (where Albanians constituted a majority), in which KLA leaders were rewarded with portfolios and important posts. Although the provisional government expected to be recognized as a partner by the international community, Thaçi's interim government was not recognized by the UN. But as the International Crisis Group has pointed out, even though the provisional government lacked legitimacy in the absence of elected bodies and provisions of Security Council Resolution 1244, this government could be seen as a positive attempt to bring some order in Kosovo at a time when UNMIK did not have personnel or money to carry out its assigned duties.[49]

One key component of political transformation of the KLA is a new political party as the political successor of the guerrilla movement. The Democratic Party of Kosovo (PDK) led by Hashim Thaçi was formed on the eve of the first municipal elections in 2000. However, violent acts that crippled Kosovo in 1999–2000–targeting members of the Serb minority but also Albanians who did not endorse the KLA—tarnished the image of the new party.[50]

[49] ICG, 'What Happened to the KLA?', p. 4.

[50] It is impossible to argue that the KLA—as a movement—was behind the violence, although some KLA elements have been accused of association with violent acts. In an investigative report concerning the violence that followed ending of NATO's bombing of Serbian forces, the International Crisis Group has suggested that some opportunist or rogue KLA elements finding themselves somewhat redundant (not being recruited in the KPC or KPS) retained their arms to exploit the rich pickings in urban districts especially Prishtina. But this was not behaviour representative of the guerrilla movement, whose ranks were filled for the most part by devoted and responsible men and women. Indeed, the ICG identified Serbian paramilitaries and wanted criminals from Albania who had found a safe haven in Kosovo as being behind the violence. Radicalized Kosovo Albanians and KLA political rivals interested in tarnishing the KLA's image were also involved in violent acts. See International Crisis Group, Balkans Report No. 78, 'Violence in Kosovo: Who's Killing Whom?', 2 November 1999.

Moreover, the perception that KLA elements assisted the fighting by Albanians in the regions of Preševo, Medvedja and Bujanovac (2000), an area in southern Serbia known to the Albanians as 'Eastern Kosovo', and in other fighting by Albanians in the Republic of Macedonia (2001) was detrimental to the peace-loving image the KLA leaders were keen to embrace.[51]

The above factors might explain the temporary disenchantment of Kosovo Albanians with the KLA and voters' punishment of the PDK in elections where the LDK won a majority of votes until 2007. It was in this context that in 2000 the former KLA commander of the Dukagjini region, Ramush Haradinaj, established his own party—the Alliance for the Future of Kosovo (Aleanca për Ardhmërinë e Kosovës, AAK)—with the aim of providing an alternative by bridging the political divide between the 'party of war' and the 'party of non-violence'.[52] Following the 2004 general elections a governing coalition was formed between the LDK and AAK, with Haradinaj emerging as the Prime Minister of Kosovo and Rugova as Kosovo's President. In the post-war Kosovar politics dominated by a fierce contest between LDK and PDK, many members of the latter party regarded the AAK/LDK alliance as unprincipled and a betrayal of the PDK's and AAK's shared KLA heritage. Indeed, bitter and adverse reactions were exchanged between PDK and AAK supporters, including some in the respective party newspapers, following the formation of the LDK/AAK governing coalition.[53]

However, Ramush Haradinaj served only 100 days as Kosovo's premier. Indicted in March 2005 by the International Criminal Tribunal for the former Yugoslavia for war crimes in the Kosovo War, he resigned from his post and travelled to The Hague to face charges: an act praised by many world states-

---

[51] Whilst appreciating the rationale for their brethren's uprising and their quest for more rights, former KLA leaders have denied official connections with events in Macedonia and southern Serbia, and have been at pains to avoid any strains with the international community. Also, they have forcefully denied any connection with criminal activities and have interpreted acts of violence as isolated acts committed by persons who do not belong to political organizations or parties associated with the KLA.

[52] Haradinaj's decision to form his own party rather than join the PDK may have stemmed from his old independence as the KLA's Dukagjini commander and dissatisfaction with the paucity of Dukagjini representation first in the KLA general headquarters and then in Thaçi's provisional government. See International Crisis Group, 'Kosovo after Haradinaj', Europe Report No. 163, 26 May 2005, pp. 21–2.

[53] Ibid., p. 12. These tensions reflected also a conflict of interests brought about by the change of government. The PDK's loss of ministries to the LDK and AAK meant a loss of jobs and businesses for PDK followers—a serious issue in a country characterized by a poor economy and scarce jobs.

men—including the US Senator, now Vice-President, Joe Biden and the late British Foreign Secretary Robin Cook—for having prevented violence and civil unrest. Haradinaj has been also praised for his dynamic and committed leadership in running his government in Prishtina.[54] The trial chamber rendered its decision on 3 April 2008, finding Haradinaj not guilty.[55] Subsequently, he has returned to Prishtina where he continues to lead his party.

The LDK/AAK coalition survived Haradinaj's indictment, but in November 2007 general elections it was the PDK that emerged as the winner. Resuming the post of prime minister, Hashim Thaçi steered the process of coordinated declaration of independence of Kosovo in February 2008 and was received in the White House by President George W. Bush in July of the same year.

## Conclusion

The emergence, evolution, survival and transformation of the KLA have been contingent on historical, political, and security factors. In its beginnings the movement justified its use of force in terms of modern international norms and practices which prohibited massive violations of human rights and freedoms which Serbian rule in Kosovo was infringing deliberately. Facing a ruthless oppressor which was well armed, the KLA vied simultaneously for domestic and international support—among the Albanian communities in Kosovo and abroad, and among the international community. In the process of achieving national and international legitimacy, the KLA benefited from diplomacy and deliberations at the UN Security Council and NATO, whilst the Serbian military wreaked havoc in Albanian villages and towns. As Serbian forces targeted civilians indiscriminately, Kosovo Albanians increasingly saw their salvation in the KLA, so much so that Western powers were reluctant to provide security for targeted civilians, at least until 1999 when NATO decided to launch a bombing campaign against Serbia.

Arising from opposition to a common enemy and pursuit of the common aim of protecting human rights and freedoms of suppressed Kosovo Albani-

---

[54] In January 2005 the Special Representative of the UN Secretary General, Søren Jessen-Petersen of Denmark, confessed that 'every day of work with the new prime minister [Haradinaj] is a pleasure, and his indictment would be a colossal loss'. Cited in ICG, 'Kosovo after Haradinaj', p. 27.

[55] See ICTY judgment Prosecutor vs. Ramush Haradinaj, Idriz Balaj, and Lahi Brahimaj, IT-04-84-T, 3 April 2008 at http://www.un.org/icty/haradinaj/trialc/judgement/tcj080403e.pdf.

ans, the KLA's cooperation with NATO crucially enhanced the movement's legitimacy and its image as a security provider amongst the Albanians. The guerrilla movement possessed limited military capabilities. But NATO's intervention benefited the KLA greatly as it shortened the time of fighting and minimized casualties and material damage. Cooperation with NATO ensured also that the KLA would be recognized as a political force in the post-conflict setting.

Defying critics, the KLA has proved more resilient than many expected. Carefully transformed in the post-conflict setting, it has survived in different political and defence structures from the Kosovo Protection Corps to the Kosovo Police Service and the Kosovo Security Force, and two main political parties, the Democratic Party of Kosovo and the Alliance for the Future of Kosovo; these parties have, alternately, been part of the government in Prishtina since 1999, and—in coordination with the international community— have nurtured Kosovo's independence. That the movement—in its various permutated forms—remains a powerful and active element of Kosovo political life is a testimony both to its adaptability to change and to the need and potential capacity to provide security and civic services to Kosovo's population.

# 6

# The Rise and Fall of
# Militant Islamic Groups in Egypt

*Hassanein Tawfik Ibrahim*

## Introduction

Militant Islamic Groups (MIGs)—described variously as 'violent', 'radical', *'jihadiyaa'* or 'Qutbist' (in reference to Sayyid Qutb) groups—represented a major challenge to the Egyptian political regime from the mid-1970s until the mid-1990s. Although these groups fought against the regime for a long time, they could not bring it down, or present themselves as a real alternative. The regime succeeded to some extent in liquidating its opponents through its security forces' multiple armed confrontations with these groups. The regime's success can be attributed to a number of factors: Egypt is a centralized state, with cohesive society. Egypt does not have the vertical tribal, racial, sectarian or religious differences which are found in other societies. Besides, the MIGs were unable to come up with a persuasive political and intellectual agenda which could be presented to the public, and this reduced their capacity to expand their social base. In addition, the state possessed superior military power when dealing with militant Islamic groups[1].

---

[1] For more details on radical Islamic movements which appeared in Egypt from the 1970s, see: Hala Mustafa, *Political Islam in Egypt: From Reform Movement to Groups of Violence*, Cairo: General Egyptian Book Organization, 2nd ed., 2005, Chapter 3 (in Arabic); Saad Eddin Ibrahim, 'Islamic Activism in the 1980s', *Third World Quarterly*, Vol. 10, April

This study will discuss the MIGs in Egypt with the focus on the Jihad Organization and the Islamic Group (Al-Jama'a Al-Islamiyya), by analyzing and evaluating their intellectual sources, social roots, organizational structures, methods of recruitment, types of relations between leaders and members, and financial sources, as well as strategies towards the state and society. The study will examine conditions which have led to the emergence of these groups. It will also look at the state's strategy in dealing with these groups, which enabled it finally to put an end to their activities, as these groups have not committed any act of violence since the infamous Luxor incident in November 1997 in which about 58 tourists were killed.

## Reasons for the emergence of militant Islamic groups

Religious extremism as well as the rise of armed Islamic organizations in Egypt from 1970s onwards resulted from a structural societal crisis going back to the 1960s, particularly in the aftermath of the war of June 1967, where Israel occupied new land from three Arab states, Egypt, Jordan and Syria. Religious explanations were given for that defeat and a religious radical trend began to rise in prisons, following torture and physical and moral ill-treatment of arrested members of the Muslim Brotherhood, as explained below. While the radical religious trend was born in the prisons during the 1960s, the societal crisis that became more intense provided a fertile ground for the spread of that trend, especially with the influence of external factors.

In spite of the symbolic, historical and national importance of the victory in the 1973 October war against Israel, President Sadat's policy from the mid-1970s aggravated the crisis. The open economic policy intensified social and economic inequalities, led to spreading administrative and financial corruption, and increased poverty and unemployment rates. At the political level, despite the shift from a single party system to limited political pluralism, the regime restricted this new experience by issuing a number of laws limiting rights and freedoms of citizens. The regime also kept political participation channels narrow, monitored the activities of the opposition parties, rigged

---

1988, pp. 632–57; Saad Eddin Ibrahim, 'Islamic Militancy as a Social Movement: The Case of Two Groups in Egypt' in Ali E. Hillal Dessouki (ed.), *The Islamic Resurgence in Arab World*, New York: Praeger, 1982; Salwa Ismail, 'The Popular Movement Dimensions of Contemporary Militant Islamism: Socio-Spatial Determinants in the Cairo Urban Setting', *Comparative Studies in Society and History*, Vol. 42, No.2, April 2000, pp. 363–93.

elections and undermined the legitimacy of the two most important political tendencies of that time: the Nasserists and the moderate Islamic trends represented by the Muslim Brotherhood. Moreover, the judicial system became less independent and was affected negatively by the executive branch, particularly with the continuation of the state security and military courts as judicial organizations parallel to the natural justice system.[2]

Another factor that contributed to the worsening societal crisis and the divide between the regime and the opposition in Egypt was the visit of President Sadat to Jerusalem in 1977, which was followed by the Camp David agreements between Egypt and Israel and their peace treaty. This visit was strongly opposed by the key political forces and parties including the radical Islamic groups. Egypt under Sadat also became more subjected to the West, especially the US. This caused an additional factor of tension between the regime and political opposition forces. Besides, President Sadat's hosting of Iran's Shah after he was overthrown by his people and let down by his closest allies, especially the US, was another factor that widened the gap between the Egyptian people and the regime. In sum, the crisis in the country during President Sadat's era seriously affected the legitimacy of his political regime. This in turn pushed President Sadat to order widespread arrests in September 1981 including more than 1,500 persons from the various political and intellectual groups in the country. University professors and other intellectuals were not excluded from this action. It was one month after these arrests that President Sadat was assassinated by the Jihad Group.

The structural societal crisis the country experienced during the Sadat era provided a suitable setting for the emergence and growth of the militant Islamic groups. These groups began to highlight Islam as a framework for social and political rejection of Sadat's regime and endeavoured to attract categories of frustrated youth to their ranks. Other factors encouraged the growth of such groups. At the beginning of the 1970s President Sadat, directly and indirectly, encouraged the Islamic groups and used them to minimize the influence of those he considered his main opponents on the left. President Sadat also attempted to use Islam as a source of political legitimacy. Thus, he called himself 'the pious president', emphasizing that he 'follows the steps of the Muslims' Caliph Omar Bin Al-khattab'. He took 'Science and Faith' as the

---

[2] Raymond A. Hinnebusch. Jr., *Egyptian Politics under Sadat: The Post-Populist Development of an Authoritarian-Modernizing State*, Cambridge: Cambridge University Press, 1985; Hamied Ansri, *Egypt: The Stalled Society*, Albany: State University of New York Press, 1986.

slogan of the state and amended the constitution in 1980 so to make Islam 'the main source of legislation'. In addition, the role of the official religious institutions, represented in Al-Azhar and Dar Ifta'a (the office for delivering official Islamic legal opinions), supported the political regime in various ways such as the issuing of politicized legal opinions (*fatwa*s) to justify some of the regime's actions and decisions. This was made possible because religious institutions lacked autonomy and were under the domination of the state that had endeavoured to monopolize religion and subordinate it since the early 1960s. Although the regime tried to use Islam to gain political legitimacy, the radical Islamic organizations opposed this attempt. They wanted the state to follow 'true' Islamic religious principles according to their own interpretation, and described the scholars of Al Azhar as 'the Sultan's Jurists'.[3]

The success of the Islamic Revolution in Iran was one of the factors that fuelled the growing radical Islamic trends in Egypt and the rest of the Arab World. The Iranian case provided an example of people who could be mobilized to overthrow a secular regime and build an Islamic one.[4]

One question that may be raised here is that if the structural crisis provided a reason for the growing influence of radical Islamic groups, why were the leftist groups, which also called for social and economic change, unable to develop their social base? The answer may lie in the easy and clear religious discourse of the political Islamic organizations, whether they were peaceful and moderate or armed and radical. They had simple slogans such as 'Islam is the solution', 'Applying the Islamic law (Sharia)' and 'Building the Islamic state'. Such slogans, loaded with religious emotional feelings, were more effective in attracting supporters and followers. Also, the spread of the Islamic revival phenomenon in general since the early 1970s provided a suitable religious background which was exploited by the radical organizations to promote their ideas on establishing an Islamic state and society. Other organizations calling for change, such as the left-wing and nationalist organizations, had a weak social base as they lacked credibility in the eyes of the public, especially with their image marred by the regime and the Islamic forces. They were described as secular infidel organizations hostile to Islam

[3] See, for instance, Nazih N.M. Ayubi, 'The Political Revival of Islam: The Case of Egypt', *International Journal of Middle East Studies*, Vol. 12, Dec. 1981, pp. 488–96; Malika Zeghal, 'Religion and Politics in Egypt: The Ulema of al-Azhar, Radical Islam, and the State (1952–94)', *International Journal of Middle East Studies*, Vol. 31, Aug. 1999, pp. 371–99.

[4] Hala Mustafa, *Political Islam in Egypt*, p. 241.

and as followers and agents of the Soviet Union. As a result, the radical Islamic discourse of the militant Islamic organizations succeeded in attracting frustrated, unemployed youth who became supporters of radical change based on Islamic foundations, believing that this would give them salvation.[5]

When President Mubarak came to power in 1981, the regime adopted a dual policy in dealing with the political Islamic movements: he followed a strategy of compromise with the Muslim Brotherhood group and a security strategy with the organizations of radicalism and violence. Yet, the regime's policy failed in alleviating the social crisis. The economic difficulties in the country enabled the Islamic groups to re-emerge and challenge the authorities again. This situation lasted for about a decade (from the mid-1980s till the mid-1990s).

It is worth remembering that the economic reform policy adopted by the regime had a terrible social price paid mostly by the deprived and low-income people. The rates of inflation and unemployment went up. Poverty rates also went up, as did the gap between the rich and the poor. Corruption also spread in a way unprecedented in the modern history of Egypt. The middle class especially was affected badly by this situation.[6]

At the political level, the regime's political reform process seemed to take one step forward and two steps back. In fact, the reform process was a modification, a kind of modernization of the authoritarian regime rather than a process of real, gradual democratic change. Indeed, the domination of the National Democratic Party (the president's party) over political life continued unabated. Systematic rigging of elections, the failure of a large section of Egyptians to participate in the political life, the submissive attitude of the political elite, the insignificant role of civil society organizations, the increasing adoption of security methods to deal with political powers, and persisting human rights violations under the continuing emergency law were all characteristic features of the Egyptian regime. The intensifying internal crisis in Egypt was reflected in Cairo's external policy at both regional and international levels. Egypt no longer enjoys a prominent role commensurate with its cultural, demographic, civilizational and historical importance. Nor has the

---

[5] Saad Eddin Ibrahim, 'Egypt's Islamic Militants', *MERIP Reports*, No. 103, Feb. 1982, pp. 13–14.

[6] Cassandra, 'The Impending Crisis in Egypt', *Middle East Journal*, Vol. 49, Winter 1995, pp. 9–27; Ebehard Kienale, 'More Than Response to Islamism: The Political Deliberalization of Egypt in 1990s', *Middle East Journal*, Vol. 52, Spring 1998.

regime established a strategic vision to play an active or influential role at the international arena.[7]

So economic depression, social degradation, political repression and a diminishing external role for Egypt are the defining features of President Mubarak's era. While the optimistic figures of successive governments showed growth and development rates, the reality was very different. The rates of poverty, unemployment, corruption and crime went up; there were housing inadequacies and transport problems, pollution, lack of medical care, and a deterioration of education standards—clear examples of the deep crisis that permeates the country.

## Militant Islamic groups: emergence and evolution

*Beginning and development.* The year 1952 represented the begging of a new era in the Egyptian history. In that year, the Free Officers organization overthrew the monarchial regime and assumed power. Afterwards Islamic extremist thought in Egypt first appeared inside the prisons and detention camps during the 1950s and 1960s. The physical and moral torture to which the prisoners of the Muslim Brotherhood group were subjected reinforced the resolve of one of the Brotherhood's leaders, Sayyid Qutb, to publicize his thoughts concerning ignorance (*jahiliyya*), infidelity (*al-takfir*), Islamic rule (*al-hakimiyya*), armed struggle (*jihad*), and the Quranic generation, especially in his work *Signposts on the Road*. Sayyid Qutb went through a bitter experience, as he was sentenced to 15 years in prison in 1955, after the attempted assassination of President Abdul Nasser in Al-Manshiya, Alexandria. He was released in 1964, but returned soon to prison and was eventually sentenced to death in 1966 after being accused of conspiracy to change the ruling regime. The tortures inside the detention camps forced some youth groups of the Muslim Brotherhood to embrace the ideas of Sayyid Qutb. Some of them went even further to establish the armed Islamic groups and organizations which appeared in Egypt in the mid 1970s.[8]

When President Sadat assumed power in Egypt in 1970, his regime began to encourage politicized Islamic groups, directly and indirectly, in order to use them to restrict the influence of the Nasserite and left-wing forces that Sadat

[7] Michele Dunne, 'Evaluating Egyptian Reform', *Carnegie Papers-Middle East Series*, No. 66, Jan. 2006.

[8] Salem Albahnasawi, 'Behind Bars, they were born', *Al-arabi Magazine* (monthly magazine issued in Kuwait), issue 278, Jan. 1982 (in Arabic).

considered as his principal enemy. This gave some power to the Islamic groups and enabled them to extend their role, especially in Egyptian universities.[9]

By the mid-1970s, the Islamic movement in Egypt began to evolve around two main trends: the first was the moderate trend embodied by the Muslim Brotherhood, which rejected violence, accepted the politics of the current regime, and believed in gradual change through legal political channels, peaceful methods, and social work; however, the state's policy towards the Muslim Brotherhood continued to vary between conciliation and confrontation.[10] The second trend was the Jihadi militant, radical trend which adopted violence as the method to uproot the current regime and to build an Islamic state and an Islamic society in conformity with righteous Islamic teachings according to the perspective of the radical Islamic organizations.

The Technical Military Academy Group (Muhammad's Youth) is considered the first radical Islamic organization that accused the ruling regime of being infidel and endeavoured to oust it by force. This group carried out an armed attack on the Technical Military Academy in 1974 so as to use it as a base to achieve their goals. However, the attempt failed and dozens of people were killed and injured during the confrontation between the attackers and state security forces. The founder of this group was Salih Siriyya, a Palestinian with a PhD degree. He was previously a member of the Jordan branch of the Muslim Brotherhood, and then followed the Islamic Liberation Party. He settled in Cairo in the early 1970s and began to establish the Group of Muhammad's Youth which included mostly young people, especially university students and recent graduates. Most members were from Cairo, Alexandria and some Delta governorates. Following the failed attack on the Technical Military Academy, some of the group's leaders and members were arrested and put on trial. Salih Siriyya was executed in 1975.[11]

In 1977, the security forces uncovered Jama'at al—Muslimin (the Society of the Muslims), known in the Arab media as the Group of Repentance and Holy Migration (Al-Takfir Wa'l-Hijra). This group was founded by Shukry Mustafa, who had a degree in agricultural science and was a member of the

---

[9] Gilles Kepel, *Muslim Extremism in Egypt: The Prophet and Pharaoh*, Berkeley: University of California Press, 1986.

[10] Sana Abed-kotab, 'The Accommodationists Speak: Goals and Strategies of the Muslim Brotherhood of Egypt', *International Journal of Middle East Studies*, Vol. 27, Aug. 1995, pp. 321–39; Hesham Al-Awadi, 'Mubarak and the Islamists:Why Did the 'Honeymoon' End?' *Middle East Journal*, Vol. 59, Winter 2005, pp. 62–80.

[11] Saad Eddin Ibrahim, 'Egypt's Islamic Militants', *Islamic Activism in the 1980s*, pp. 5–14.

Muslim Brotherhood. He was arrested in 1965 but then released in 1971. While the Military Academy Group accused only the political system of being infidel, the Society of the Muslims accused both the political system and the Egyptian society of infidelity. This suggests that Shukry Mustafa was influenced, to a large extent, by the ideas of Sayyid Qutb, as will be shown below. The group isolated itself from the state and society in order to build itself up to be able, in the next stage, to confront both the 'infidel' regime and society. The group aimed at building up the Islamic society according to the righteous Islamic rules as they conceived them.

Many members of the Society of the Muslims went to the desert of the Minya governorate in Upper Egypt from 1973 to be trained in using arms. Although the group postponed any confrontation with the authorities until it possessed sufficient strength, the discovery of the group by the state's security forces forced it to resort to confrontation. Dr Husain Al-Dhabi, former minister of Awqaf (endowments), was kidnapped and then murdered by the group. Subsequently, many leaders and group members were arrested. Five of them were sentenced to death, including the group's founder, Shukry Mustafa.[12]

Around 1980, the unified Jihad Organization was established by the merger of three small militant Islamic groups in one organizational entity. These groups appeared during the second half of the 1970s and had a common ideological goal: to overthrow the ruling regime. The first group was headed by Kamal Saeed Habeeb, a graduate of Cairo University who took over from the founder of this organization, Salem Rahhal, a Jordanian who had been a member of the Technical Military Academy Group. The second group, named the Al Jihad Organization, was founded by Mohammad Abd al-Salam Farag, an electrical engineer working in Cairo University; Abboud Al-Zumur, a military intelligence officer, joined this group. The third group was the Islamic Group (al Jama'a al-Islamiyya), which was established and became active in the universities of Upper Egypt. Karam Zohdy and Nageh Ibrahim were among its top leaders.

Mohammed Abd al-Salam Farag oversaw the merger of the Islamic Group with the Jihad Organization. Then, a consultative council for the organization was formed in 1980, and the blind religious scholar Dr Omar Abd al-Rahman,

---

[12] Hala Mustafa, *Political Islam in Egypt*, pp. 197–9; Saad Eddin Ibrahim, 'Anatomy of Egypt's Militant Islamic Groups: Methodological Note and Preliminary Findings', *International Journal of Middle East Studies*, Vol. 12, Dec. 1980, p. 442.

a professor of exegesis and Hadith in the Asyut branch of al-Azhar University, was selected as the organization's expounder of Islamic law[13].

After the assassination of President Sadat by the unified Jihad Organization in October 1981, disagreements began inside the prisons between the leadership of the Islamic Group on the one hand and that of Al Jihad on the other hand. The disagreements were focused on many issues including the method of operation: should it be secret as Al Jihad leaders wanted? Or should it be a mix of secret and public work as the Islamic Group leaders wanted?

The two parties also disagreed over operational methods. While Al Jihad wanted to focus on big and effective targets, working on penetration of key state institutions and preparation for a coup, the leaders of the Islamic Group preferred to expand the circle of those targeted by violence (armed attacks), along with their peaceful social and religious work. The two parties disagreed also over the leadership of the organization after the execution of the leader Mohammed Abd al-Salam Farag; the Islamic Group leaders wanted Omar Abd al-Rahman, the blind preacher of al-Azhar University, to be the Amir, while Al Jihad leaders preferred Al-Zumur, a former military intelligence officer, as the head. As a result, a dispute over religious interpretation occurred between the two parties: the Islamic Group leaders insisted that 'No prisoner can be a leader', while Al Jihad leaders responded by stating 'No blind man can be leader'. By 1984, the Islamic Group was separated from the Jihad Organization, and the two organizations began to act independently.[14]

Many attempts were made to revive the Jihad Organization and strengthen its military wing embodied in Talai' al-fath (Vanguard of Conquest). The most important attempt was that of Ayman Al-Zawahiri, the leader of the organization in the early 1990s. Al-Zawahiri joined the Al Jihad Group in 1981, and was arrested among more than 300 people after the assassination of Sadat and accused of attempting to overthrow the regime. He was sentenced to imprisonment for three years. Released in 1984, he moved to Afghanistan.

Under the leadership of Al-Zawahiri, the organization conducted a limited number of major violent operations inside and outside Egypt, as will be shown.

---

[13] Omar Abd al-Rahman was sentenced for life imprisonment in the US after being convicted of the attack on the World Trade Center in 1993. For more details about the Jihad Organization, see Hamied N. Ansari, 'The Islamic Militants in Egyptian Politics', *International Journal of Middle East Studies*, Vol. 16, March 1984, pp. 125–6.

[14] Dia'a Rashwan, *Guide of Islamic Movements in the World, first issue*, 2nd edition, Cairo: al-Ahram Center for Strategic and Political Studies, 2006, pp. 136–7 (in Arabic); ICG Middle East and North Africa Briefing, 'Islamism in North Africa II: Egypt's Opportunity', Cairo/Brussels, 20 April 2004, p. 5.

In February 1998, an important development took place in the Jihad Organization when Al-Zawahiri signed a statement on the Foundation of the 'World Islamic Front for Jihad against the Jews and the Crusaders' with Osama bin Laden (the leader of the Al Qaeda network) and leaders of other militant organizations.[15]

This development reflected a noticeable change in the ideology and strategy of the Jihad Organization. In the past, it had adopted the views of its leader Mohammed Abd al-Salam Farag as described in his book entitled *Al-Jihad: al-Farida al-Ghaiba* (*'Jihad: The Forgotten Obligation'*), indicating that 'the nearer enemy is worthier to be fought than the distant one'—the nearer enemy being the 'infidel' Egyptian regime. However, after the alliance with the Al Qaeda organization, the distant enemy, embodied by the United States, Israel and all Western countries, was seen as the worthiest to be fought. The alliance of the Jihad Organization with Al Qaeda led to many disagreements within Al Jihad because many of its leaders and members in Egypt, both inside and outside prison, rejected this arrangement. Thus Al-Zawahiri gave up the leadership of the organization by the end of 1999 and took many of its members with him to the external Jihad Group which became connected to the Al Qaeda network. On the other hand, after the Islamic Group was separated from the Jihad Group in 1984, it reorganized itself and resorted to violence against the state and society until 1997. In July 1997, the Islamic Group issued a first statement calling for a stopping violence, known as the Initiative, which was confirmed by another statement of the Group's consultative council in March 1999. Since then, the Islamic Group has not been involved in any violent act. On the contrary, it adjusted its ideas and turned itself into a peaceful Islamic social group, as will be explained below.

After the Islamic Group announced its initiative to stop violence, a number of the leaders and members of Al Jihad inside Egypt welcomed the initiative, and some of them declared that they would take a similar step so as to stop all violent acts. Al-Zawahiri and those who accompanied him in Afghanistan and Pakistan remained part of Al Qaeda. After the events of September 11 and their fallout, Al-Zawahiri was described as the second man in the Al Qaeda organization.[16]

*Ideology.* In spite of the existence of some ideological differences among the MIGs which emerged in Egypt from the 1970s, most of the disagreement

---

[15] Dia'a Rashwan, *Guide of Islamic Movements*, pp. 138–9.

[16] Ibid., pp. 142–3; ICG Middle East and North Africa Briefing, 'Islamism in North Africa II...', pp. 4–6.

remained superficial because these organizations drew their views and opinions from common ideological and intellectual sources as mentioned below.

Generally, the most essential elements of the ideology of these groups can be described as follows:[17]

1. Accusing the ruling regimes of being infidels. The MIGs consider the ruling regime in Egypt and other regimes in the Muslim countries to be infidel regimes because they do not rule according to the Shari'a. There are some groups, such as the Society of the Muslims, which accuse not only the regime but also the whole Muslim society of being infidel.

2. Belief in *jihad* as the way to change infidel regimes. For the MIGs, this means the use of force and violence to overthrow regimes in order to pave the way for building of an Islamic state and society in conformity with the Islamic teachings and according to the perspective of the concerned groups.

3. Rejection of secularism. These organizations argue that secularism emerged and developed as part of the historical experience of Western societies; at later stages, secularism was imposed on the Islamic world to produce infidel regimes which replaced the divine regulations and rules with those made by human beings. In addition, the MIGs reject political pluralism and democracy as well as systems based on them because Islam, in their view, recognizes only two parties: 'the Party of Allah' and 'the Party of Satan'. Democracy grants sovereignty to people, and thus violates the concept of rule which belongs only to God. According to the MIGs, democracy gives people, through parliaments, the right to legislate which belongs only to God, and therefore Muslims do not need Western-style democracy.

4. Rejection of the ideologies of capitalism and socialism and any economic, social and political systems based on them. These ideologies are manifestations of infidelity and delusion, and violate and contradict Islam. The MIGs present their own ideology as an alternative.

5. Rejection of Western civilization because it is founded on materialism and atheism. The MIGs argue that the principles of Western civilization relating to freedom, world peace, human rights and other slogans are all false, and aim at deceiving the peoples of the world in order for the West to dominate and govern them.

---

[17] Hala Mustafa, *Political Islam in Egypt*, third chapter; Saad Eddin Ibrahim, 'Anatomy of Egypt's Militant Islamic Groups: Methodological Note and Preliminary Findings', pp. 429–35; John L. Esposito, *Islam and Politics*, Fourth Edition, Syracuse: Syracuse University Press, 1998, pp. 240–1.

6. Emphasis on the religious dimension in the Arab-Israeli conflict, by stressing that it is an Islamic-Jewish struggle, hence a crucial battle that will end only by declaring *jihad*. This will not be accomplished until the establishment of an Islamic state and the application of the Islamic Shari'a.

Most militant Islamic organizations were influenced in different ways by the ideas of Ibn Taymiyya, Abu al-A'la Al-Mawdudi, Ali Shari'ati, Sayyid Qutb and others. Some of the works that Qutb wrote in prison, particularly his book *Signposts on the Road*, are considered major intellectual sources for many modern radical Islamic organizations in Egypt and the Arab World in general. This book contains a juristic and intellectual correction regarding the root and origin of the concepts of God's sovereignty (*al-Hakimiyya li-Llah*), infidelity, Jihad and the Quranic generation, which many radical organizations relied upon to justify their juristic stands and strategy.

Sayyid Qutb had no respect for contemporary societies, since he saw them as following a lifestyle similar to that which prevailed among the unbelievers in the pre-Islam Arabian peninsula. In the pre-Islam era, command and sovereignty were not only held by Allah; that is, they rested with human beings who had the right to legislate and set regulations and rules other than those taught by God.

On the basis of his view of the two concepts of God's sovereignty (*al-hakimiyya*) and ignorance (*jahiliyya*), Qutb called for an absolute and complete change in all existing societies and their ruling regimes, considering the latter infidel. For him, the tool of such change was the Quranic generation or the Muslim group which believes that Allah is the sole sovereign and commander. Qutb believed that this group would realize its mission of changing the infidel order and building a true Muslim society, relying on force and *jihad* to overthrow the existing regimes.[18]

It appears that the great majority of the MIGs emerging since the 1970s in Egypt and other Arab world countries have, at different levels, adopted the ideas of Sayyid Qutb and endeavoured to apply them. Hence, some analysts describe them as 'the Qutbia movements' and call their members the 'Qutbists'.[19]

---

[18] Sayyid Qutb, *Signposts on the Road*, 16th edition, Cairo: Dar al-Shorok, 1993 (in Arabic); Adnan A. Musallam, *From Secularism to Jihad: Sayyid Qutb and the Foundations of Radical Islamism*, London: Greenwood Press 2005; Ahmad S. Moussalli, *Radical Islamic Fundamentalism: The Ideological and Political Discourse of Sayyid Qutub*, Beirut: American University of Beirut Press 1992.

[19] ICG Middle East and North Africa Briefing, *Islamism in North Africa I: The Legacies of History*, Cairo/Brussels, 20 April 2004.

*Social background.* Some of the studies dealing with the MIGs in Egypt conclude that most of their members were young people, mainly university students and recent graduates whose ages varied between 21 and 35. Most of them had rural roots and went to cities such as Cairo, Alexandria and Asyut to complete their higher education. Most of them also belonged to the middle and lower middle classes. The Egyptian middle class came under pressure with the application of the economic openness policy during the mid 1970s. Such pressure increased in the era of President Mubarak through implementation of economic reform policy known as the 'Economic Stabilization and Structural Adjustment' policy, which contributed to the deteriorating status of the middle class. The people most affected by this policy, particularly young people, became a ready audience for the radical and violent organizations.[20]

As for the regional background of the MIGs' members, it has been noted that members of organizations such as the Technical Military Academy Group and the Jihad Organization were mostly based in Cairo, Alexandria and some Delta provinces. Other organizations such as the Society of the Muslims and the Jihadi Islamic Group were concentrated in the Upper Egypt governorates. Although the latter emerged and was concentrated in Upper Egypt, it began from the mid-1980s to make its presence felt in some of the quarters of Cairo and Giza, particularly in the poorer districts and peripheral areas which have grown quickly owing to the wave of immigration from rural areas.[21]

*Organizational structure and recruitment methods.* The fact that the MIGs resorted to violence against the state and society was reflected in the nature of their organizational structures and internal relations. Their activities were mostly secret. Even in the case of those organizations that called for the Islamic values publicly and carried out some social works, like the Islamic Group, their armed wings and activities remained secret. Thus, in spite of the differences in the MIGs' organizational structures, they had some common features such as grouping members in cells and small groups, because this was the most suitable for secret work; it made geographical deployment easier, and enabled the organization to avoid government repressive action.[22]

[20] Saad Eddin Ibrahim, 'Egypt's Islamic Militants', p. 11.
[21] Saad Eddin Ibrahim, 'Anatomy of Egypt's Militant Islamic Groups: Methodological Note and Preliminary Findings', pp. 438–9; Salwa Ismail, 'The Popular Movement Dimensions of Contemporary Militant Islamism', pp. 372–82.
[22] Hala Mustafa, *Political Islam in Egypt*, chapter 3.

As for recruiting methods, the MIGs recruited members from relatives, friends, and mosques, particularly the private ones. These organizations focused on recruiting the youth, especially university students and recent graduates. The Islamic Group was the most powerful radical organization in recruiting. The group benefited a great deal from the mosques in its recruiting operation, making use of a number of private mosques, which were out of the control of the Ministry of Endowments. It was helped by the huge rise in the number of private mosques, especially in the poorer areas of the capital and major cities, during the 1970s. According to a study, in 1962 the number of private mosques was 14,212; this number increased to 26,622 in 1982, representing about 81 per cent of the total number of mosques in the state, while the mosques under the control of the ministry of Endowments in 1982 was 6,071, or about 19 per cent[23].

## Militant Islamic Groups challenging the state

Although the MIGs chose violence in their bid to overthrow the regime and build an Islamic state and society according to their view of Islamic laws, there were differences among them regarding the timing of the confrontation with the regime, methods of operation, and the targets. The Society of the Muslims (Al-Takfir Wa'l Hijra) wanted to postpone the confrontation with the authorities until it became powerful enough to be able to change both the 'infidel' regime and the society. However, it was forced into confrontation at an early stage after being discovered by state's security forces, as mentioned earlier. The other groups such as the Technical Military Academy group, the Jihad Organization and the Islamic Group believed in immediate and direct action against the regime. Thus, the Military Academy group and the Jihad Organization worked for a coup to overthrow the regime so as to enforce Islamicization in the state and society from the top. Hence the first group carried out the Technical Military Academy operation in 1974, while the Jihad Organization carried out the assassination of President Sadat and the armed rebellion in Asyut in Upper Egypt in 1981. The Islamic Group, which was a part of the Jihad Organization at that time, played a key role in the rebellion that followed the assassination because of its widespread presence in the Upper Egypt governorates.

[23] Saad Eddin Ibrahim, 'Egypt's Islamic Militants', pp. 10–11; Tamir Moustafa, 'Conflict and Cooperation between the State and Religious Institutions in Contemporary Egypt', *International Journal of Middle East Studies*, Vol. 32, Feb. 2000, pp. 7–8.

After the Jihad Organization and the Islamic Group parted ways in 1984, the former began to focus further on specific terrorist and violent acts, targeting senior state politicians and officers in order to exert maximum pressure. Accordingly, the organization carried out three failed operations during April, August and November 1993. Those operations targeted former ministers of Information (Safwat Al-Sherif) and the Interior (Hasan Al-Alfi) and a former Prime Minister (Dr Atef Sedqi). The organization also attempted the assassination of President Mubarak in Addis Ababa in Ethiopia in June 1995, and caused an explosion at the Egyptian embassy in Pakistan in November of the same year. Consequently, the Egyptian authorities launched strong military strikes against the organization, especially its military wing represented by Talai' al-Fath, thus crippling the organization and hindering it from any further operations inside and outside Egypt.

As for the Islamic Group, after its separation from the Jihad Organization it engaged in acts of violence for about a decade, from the mid-1980s to the mid-1990s. What expanded the violent operations of the Islamic Group and the Jihad Organization from the early 1990s was the return of hundreds of 'Egyptian Afghans' who had been fighting in the Afghan war, following the withdrawal of Soviet forces from Afghanistan. Many of them joined radical organizations, their high-level training helping to strengthen the radical Islamists' power, thus aggravating the confrontation with the Egyptian regime[24].

Given that the Islamic Group was the main militant Islamic organization that represented a real challenge to the political regime from the mid 1980s, it is important to shed light on the dimensions of the group's strategy. Its violent acts against the state and society from the early 1990s were characterized by several features including specific geographical distribution. Violence spread to include many governorates, with a higher concentration in Upper Egypt. In addition, armed confrontations between the group and the security forces became more intense. In such confrontations government security forces deployed armoured vehicles and artillery while the Islamic Group activists used automatic guns with a wide range. This caused more dead and injured on both sides and among ordinary citizens[25].

[24] Dia'a Rashwan, p. 140; ICG Middle East and North Africa Briefing, *Islamism in North Africa II...*, pp. 7–8.
[25] Hasanein Tawfik Ibrahim, 'Political Violence in Egypt' in Neveen Musaad (ed.), *Political Violence Phenomenon from a Comparative Perspective*, Cairo: Centre for Political Studies and Research, 1995), pp. 392–95 (in Arabic).

In addition, the Islamic Group endeavoured to expand the circle of its targets. It began to target senior politicians, intellectuals and various elements of the security apparatus including officers, soldiers and intelligence agents. It also targeted tourists, carrying out many operations against tourist buses and Nile cruises in order to hit Egypt's vital tourist income. Between 1991 and 1997, about 25 operations targeted tourism, causing the death of 93 tourists. The most remarkable one was the Luxor operation in November 1997. Some of the Islamic Group's violent acts were aimed at Christians in Egypt, including burglaries at some gold stores owned by Christians, killings of the guards of some churches, and attacks against Christians in different areas.

Violence practiced by both the Jihad Organization and the Islamic Group aroused many questions about their financial sources. Although it is difficult to find documented information on this issue, the Egyptian authorities routinely accused the Sudanese and Iranian regimes of providing financial and military support to the radical Islamists. In any case attacks carried out by the Islamic Group on gold shops owned by Christians provided them with some funds. Some reports pointed to financial transfers made by some members of organizations working outside Egypt or their advocates. Moreover, the poor regulation of the arms trade in Egypt allowed such organizations easy access to automatic weapons and explosives.[26]

From the early 1970s there was a large increase in the number of private mosques not subject to state supervision represented by the Ministry of Endowments. The militant Islamic organizations, particularly the Islamic Group, controlled many of these mosques and used them as channels to promote their ideas on the one hand and to attract and recruit new members on the other.[27]

Because of the importance of educational institutions, the Islamic Group sought to infiltrate them, particularly the faculties of education and arts whose graduates would be educators in the primary, preparatory and secondary schools. Hence the group's members would be able to promote their radical ideas among schoolchildren, who would grow up to form a base for the group and pehaps also be recruited to its organizational staff. Therefore the Ministry of Education, during the first half of 1990s, launched a warlike campaign and

[26] Mahmud A. Faksh, *The Future of Islam in the Middle East*, London: Greenwood Press, 1997, chapter 3.

[27] Tamir Moustafa, 'Conflict and Cooperation', p. 8.

reassigned more than 1,000 teachers with radical ideas to administrative positions, to keep them away from the educational process.[28]

*The state and its confrontation with MIGs.* The political regime followed a strict security strategy in dealing with the militant Islamic organizations during the years that followed the assassination of President Sadat. As a consequence, these organizations' acts of violence decreased during the first half of the 1980s. However, after the separation between the Islamic Group and the Jihad Organization, the groups revived and began to practice violence against the state and society once again. Their violence peaked during the first years of the 1990s, as noted earlier. Then the regime began to develop a strategy—as . explained below—to confront the Jihad Organization and its military wing Talai' al-Fath, and the Islamic Group. This strategy led to positive results. In addition, it should be pointed out that the weak and fragile ideological base of the Jihad Organization and the Islamic Group prevented them from gaining real popular support.

The most important features of the regime's strategy that enabled it to defeat the MIGs can be summed up as follows:[29]

*Developing a security confrontation strategy.* After years of confusion in confronting the Jihad Organization and the Islamic Group, leading to a loss of confidence on the part of the security forces in their capability to win the battle, the state shifted its security strategy of confronting the MIGs, beginning in 1993. The new plan aimed at developing and modernizing the police and security sectors, especially those concerned with combating terrorism. The modernization process included both material and human elements. Databases were established to collect information on the members and cells of the Jihad Organization and the Islamic Group. The state then launched powerful security strikes against the two organizations, leading to the destruction of their organizational structures and the killing or arrest of a number of their leaders and members. Meanwhile, the two groups' potential funding sources were identified. The security authorities were helped by the amendment of the penal code which stipulated stricter penalties on those who plan, execute or

---

[28] A talk with Dr Hussen Kamel Bahaa'Eddin—former Egyptian Minister of Education, *Alhawadeth* [Lebanese magazine] (3/11/1995).

[29] Nachman Tal, *Radical Islam in Egypt and Jordan*, Brighton: Sussex Academic Press, 2005; Fawaz A. Gerges, 'The End of the Islamist Insurgency in Egypt: Coasts and Prospects', *Middle East Journal*, Vol. 54, Autumn 2000.

finance terrorist crimes, and referred those accused of terrorism to military courts known for their rapid procedures. Such courts have passed sentences of death and imprisonment on many of those belonging to the militant Islamic organizations.

*Restricting the activities of the MIGs.* From the early 1990s, it was clear that confronting the challenge of militant Islamic organizations at the security level was not enough. The state institutions needed to restrict the influence of radical Islamic organizations. Thus, the Ministry of Education removed hundreds of teachers with raical ideas who were trying to spread their views among schoolchildren. The Ministry of Endowments (*Awqaf*) proceeded to bring thousands of mosques under its control and supervision. As mentioned earlier, the Islamic Group and other radical organizations dominated very many mosques and used them as channels to promote their thoughts and recruit members. Moreover, fighting terrorism became part of the duties of the Ministry of Foreign Affairs through coordination and agreements with other countries to ban the activities of militant Islamic groups.

Furthermore, the state organized intensive information campaigns to criticize the MIGs' ideas, to explain how they deviated from tolerant Islamic teachings, and to emphasize that such groups are nothing but criminal terrorist organizations threatening the security, stability and way of life of innocent citizens. Al Azhar played a prominent role in this respect. It issued numerous books and statements to expose the organizations' ideas on extremism and violence. Furthermore, the state authorities moved to develop and improve the conditions of the peripheral areas and poorer districts which were the bases of these organizations. The state worked under the slogan of 'developing Upper Egypt' which had for a long time been neglected and impoverished.

*Strict control of Egypt's borders.* Egyptian officials believed that the MIGs received outside support. So during the first half of the 1990s they began to strengthen the control of the borders to stop any external aid sent to these organizations, whether money, weapons or explosives. Tension in relations with the regimes of Sudan and Iran escalated as the Egyptian authorities accused them of providing financial and military support to the radical organizations. In this context, Egypt worked to block the sources of financing for those militant organizations. The Egyptian authorities cooperated with many Arab and non-Arab countries and concluded agreements with many of them, such as Pakistan, in order to arrest members of the Egyptian radical organizations based in those countries. The regime also worked on increasing the control of money transfers from those states to the militant groups in Egypt. All those measures led finally to cutting off or, at least, restriction of the militant Islamic organizations' external communications.[30]

In addition, the unsound intellectual foundation of the militant Islamic organizations was one of the main factors that enabled the state to put an end to their activities. They adopted a radical, strict and introverted ideology based on notions of association (with God), infidelity and violence, and uttered general slogans relating to the application of the Sharia and the building of an Islamic state and society; yet they did not present any concrete intellectual or political programme, or actual plans for reform and change. Hence, they could not establish a real popular base in Egyptian society.[31]

In view of this one can say that the militant Islamic organizations' success in attracting young people to their fold was not due to the value or importance of the ideology they adopted, but was rather the result of the state institutions' failure in understanding the youth or providing them the chance to participate effectively in public affairs and giving them hope for the future. Young unemployed people who lacked enlightening religious education and had no role models grew increasingly frustrated and thus became a reservoir for the militant Islamic groups, which began to reeducate some of them intellectually and psychologically in the hope of recruiting them.

Proof of the weakness of the militant Islamic organizations' ideology came with the initiative to cease all acts of violence announced in July 1997 by the Islamic Group which had challenged the ruling regime until the mid-1990s. The initiative was announced in a statement read out by one of its members during his trial (with others) before a military court. The statement was signed by the leaders of the group. In March 1999, the consultative council of the group issued a statement re-emphasizing the decision to cease all violent activity. Moreover, the group's jailed leaders reconsidered their ideology and activities. The outcome was the issuing of four books in 2002 in a 'Correction Series' indicating clearly revised content and objectives. The books were entitled *The Initiative of Ceasing Violence: Actual Vision and Legal View*; *Forbidding Religious Extremism and Accusing Muslims of Disbelief*; *Shedding Light*

---

[30] Mahmud A. Faksh, *The Future of Islam in the Middle East*, p. 51.

[31] Mohammed Amara, 'Features of Disorder in the Contemporary Islamic Movements', in Abdullah al-Nafissy (ed.), *Islamic Movement: Future View—Papers of Self-Criticism*, Cairo: Madboli, 1st ed., 1989 (in Arabic).

*on the Mistakes Committed by Jihad*; and *An Advice in Clarifying the Correction of the Concepts of Tellers*. They were accompanied by a web campaign.[32]

The titles of the books obviously suggest the Islamic Group made certain mistakes, especially concerning their accusations of "unbelief" on the part of the political regime which was a deviation from established Islamic principles in this regard. It also admits the ill-judged acts of violence and terrorism committed by the group which brought absolutely no benefits. Thus, the group admitted its mistaken view of *jihad*, its methods and conditions of application. It also revisited ideology that violated and misinterpreted the principle of calling for good deeds and rejecting evil acts. The group also admitted its mistakes and violations when targeting some categories of the society such as policemen, Christians and tourists, which were all acts violating established and settled legitimate Islamic regulations. Violence led to more corruption, injustice and killing of innocent people. In the aftermath the group shifted from being an armed Jihadi organization and became a socio-political Islamic group that now encourages its ideas peacefully and has a role in society. The group has not been involved in any acts of violence since the Luxor events in November 1997. During the second half of 2007, the Jihad Organization announced an initiative similar to that of the Islamic Group concerning ideological correction, accepting that the organization had committed violations of the law and misdeeds, while totally abandoning the strategy of violence.

## Conclusion

Egypt represents the case of a state able to successfully confront the militant Islamic organizations that had challenged it over two decades. It differs therefore from other cases where the state failed to meet the challenge of armed groups, such as Somalia, post-Saddam Iraq, Lebanon and Afghanistan.

The reasons for Egypt's success are related to the inability of the militant Islamic organizations to strengthen their social base and gain popular legitimacy. This was due in part to the ideology they adopted and their anti-social activities in a strong centralized state in Egypt, and to the cohesiveness of Egyptian society.

These factors ruled out the kind of disunity experienced elsewhere. In Iraq, for example, the state appears to have lost one of its most important charac-

---

[32] Dia'a Rashwan, *Guide of Islamic Movements*, p. 275; ICG Middle East and North Africa Briefing, *Islamism in North Africa II...*, pp. 8–9.

teristics, namely, its monopoly over the legal use of violence, which indicates that its legitimacy is not deep-rooted; this is reinforced by the presence of deficient institutions and ineffective politics.[33]

What is more, militant Islamic movements in Egypt benefitted from only limited external aid. In spite of the statements of Egyptian officials about the alleged support militant Islamic groups received from external parties, especially Sudan and Iran, this support does not compare with—for example—the massive external aid delivered to the Lebanese parties during the civil war. The rebel movement in southern Sudan also relied on significant support from external forces during its twenty one years of confrontation with the Sudanese regime. Similarly, Hizbullah could not have built its military power without Iran's powerful support.

External parties' aid to the militant Islamic groups in Egypt was not as sizeable or intensive as in above mentioned cases. The Egyptian government succeeded in blocking such aid by effective control of Egypt's borders, the escalatory policy against the two MIG-friendly regimes of Sudan and Iran, and coordination with other countries to keep tabs on the activities of the latter groups outside Egypt. Eventually, the Egyptian state succeeded in preventing the delivery of any external aid to the Islamic armed groups, which made it easier for it to rein in their activities.

[33] For example, the events of 2006 and 2007 might suggest that Hizbullah in Lebanon is stronger than the Lebanese state itself. In a fierce 33–day war against Israel, which owns the most powerful air force in the Middle East, for the first time in the history of the Arab-Israeli conflict Hizbullah took the struggle inside Israel. In the end, Israel could not achieve its announced goals in the war with Lebanon; this opened the way for investigations and inquiries on the poor performance of Israel's army during the war. As for Iraq, the government is weak and fragile because neither itself, nor the coalition forces, have been able to impose security and order in Iraq, and the country thus came under the control of armed militias. Refer to chapters 7 and 9 in this book.

# 7

# Force of Arms and Hizbullah's Staying Power in Precarious Lebanon

*Judith Palmer Harik*

In the summer of 2006, a VNSA—Hizbullah (the Party of God)—delivered a punch to the Israeli political and military establishment that knocked America's 'road map' for Lebanon off course. The struggle to disarm Hizbullah and thus neutralize Syria's most important card in the Arab-Israeli conflict then entered the political domain, where a politically ascendant Party of God began to spearhead a coalition of Lebanese opposition forces bent on ousting the pro-American authorities and restoring Syrian influence. Two years later, on the heels of violent clashes with Lebanese factions, Hizbullah appears to have achieved the political goals that make that possible. Despite all efforts by the Lebanese authorities and supporters to clip the Party of God's wings, the Shiite organization calls the political shots as never before.

This chapter explains how Hizbullah became a key actor in the Middle East peace/war equation and how it was able to gain the formidable political power it now wields in the Lebanese arena. The chapter's major premise is that the precariousness of the Lebanese Republic played a major role in this phenomenon and is central to the crisis Hizbullah is exploiting today.

Lebanon's fragility and Hizbullah's political and military ascendancy there underline the increasingly potent roles of violent non-state actors (VNSAs) in the political turmoil engulfing some Middle Eastern states.[1] Yet research on

[1] John Mackinlay's important work *'Globalization and Insurgency'*, Adelphi Paper 352,

the environmental conditions that cause state weakness and failure and are exploited by VNSAs to assist and sustain themselves still leaves much to be desired. Specific, in-depth information is still lacking about the evolution and dynamics of state/VNSA relations and about the legitimating process that nurtures and protects some armed groups, but not others, at the expense of the governing authorities.

This chapter addresses these issues by determining the extent to which Lebanon's shaky sovereignty influenced the emergence and evolution of an organization that is arguably the Middle East's strongest and most solidly based VNSA today. By inquiring into the relationships, characteristics and actions that have allowed this organization to adapt itself to fluctuating military and political conditions within the country, the author hopes to shed stronger light on the dynamics driving the troubled state/resistance relationship today, and also on how the power resources Hizbullah accumulated over the years are currently being marshalled to retain its weapons and deny the United States and its Lebanese allies their goals. At the end of the chapter some ideas about the implications of Hizbullah's present trajectory for domestic and foreign stakeholders will be presented, and finally, the issue of how Hizbullah might be reined will be addressed.

A brief look at how Lebanon's institutions, its demography and its location at the front line of the Arab-Israeli crisis affected its sovereignty and set the stage for Hizbullah's emergence is now in order.

## The precarious republic revisited

The modern state of Lebanon was cobbled together from parts of Greater Syria by the French Mandate authorities during the 1920s and 30s. The multi-sect nation came into being as an independent state in 1943 through a compromise worked out by the politicians Riyad Soleh, a Muslim, and Bishara al-Khouri, a Maronite Christian, who agreed that the fledgling state would be neither fully Western, as the Christians would have liked, nor Eastern or Arab as Lebanon's Muslim population desired.

---

London: Oxford University Press for the International Institute for Strategic Studies, 2002 underlines this problem, while Troy S. Thomas, Stephen D. Kiser and William D. Casebeer's, *Warlords: Confronting Violent Non-State Actors*, Lanham: Lexington Books, 2005, points up the difficulties involved in combating such groups and offers advice on how to do so.

Unfortunately, the historic agreement only allayed but did not erase Christian fears of absorption into the Muslim-dominated region, while at the same time it angered many Muslims and others who found dilution of Lebanon's ties to the Arab region objectionable.

The political structure that was established to govern independent Lebanon attempted to provide the Maronite Christians with the political security they craved in the pluralistic nation. As a 1932 census revealed that this community was more numerous than others, Maronites were awarded the presidency, command of the army and security forces and the headship of the central bank, while the premiership went to the Sunnis and the Shiites received the post of Speaker of parliament. Other roles were distributed among the other sects. Christians also received the lion's share of the seats in parliament.

Major bones of contention as the years passed were the unyielding grip on the political system of conservative figures of all sects, and the fact that although the Muslim population was suspected to have multiplied more rapidly than the Christian, no census was taken through which political imbalance could be addressed.

The birth of Israel several years after Lebanese independence ultimately exacerbated tensions over Lebanon's identity and threatened the country's delicate confessional balance as thousands of displaced, mainly Muslim Palestinian families entered Lebanon and were established in refugee camps there. When armed Palestinian resistance groups arose in the camps and the Cairo Accord was enacted by the Arab League on 3 December 1969 the Maronite Christians' nightmare seemed to be on its way. That accord endorsed the right of the newly formed Palestine Liberation Organization (PLO) to carry on an armed struggle against Israel from Lebanese territory. Thus Lebanese sovereignty was undermined.

Syria's President Hafiz al-Asad played a leading role in the Accord as he planned to manipulate the PLO in his bid to regain the water-rich Golan Heights, which had been annexed and then settled by Israel in the aftermath of the 1967 Arab-Israeli conflict. Cross-border attacks on Israel by commandos during the 1970s were meant to remind Israel of Syria's claim, much as Hizbullah's actions do today. Retaliatory attacks severely punished Southern Lebanon's mostly Shiite population and began its displacement to Beirut's southern suburbs and its political mobilization. The dislocation and suffering of this backward community was a major factor in its political mobilization and the militancy of those who would later form and lead Hizbullah.

The story of how the PLO's presence, and the Syrian-Israeli struggle for Lebanon, helped to ignite the 17–year civil war is well known. During the lengthy struggle between contending militias armed and assisted by Lebanon's powerful neighbours, the country broke up into confessional cantons, and the army disintegrated. During this crisis, the southern part of the country was wracked by a war fought by foreigners until 1982 when the Israeli Army drove into Lebanon as far as the capital to remove the PLO fighters and try to negotiate a peace treaty with Beirut. The chaos that resulted from the invasion and its subsequent disastrous effect on American and French peacekeeping forces sent to Lebanon is a well known story that does not need repetition here. The salient point is that Lebanon's catastrophic collapse not only facilitated Israel's destructive 'Operation Peace for Galilee' but inadvertently brought about the birth of Hizbullah and later legitimated its role as a national resistance.

## The design and development of Hizbullah

Hizbullah was born to further the shared foreign policy goals that President Hafiz al-Asad and Iran's Ayotallah Ruhallah Khomeini had formulated in 1980. Those goals were denial of US hegemony in the region and termination of Israeli occupation of Arab land. To achieve these goals a long-term strategy was formulated, part of which began to take shape in Lebanon in 1982. With the PLO routed from the border area by the Israeli invasion that year, Asad needed another surrogate force to replace them. For his part, Khomeini saw in Asad's predicament a chance to influence the Middle East conflict from the front lines by cooperating with him in fielding a Lebanese fighting force whose allegiance to Iran could be assured. Recruitment for this force from among members of Lebanon's Shiite community were calculated to ensure solidarity with Iranian interests for a number of reasons. These included the community's close cultural ties to Iran, its excitement over Khomeini's feat in dislodging the American-backed Shah and establishing the Islamic Republic, and the fact that many Shiites had fought on the side of the PLO in South Lebanon and were available for recruitment. Khomeini calculated that such a force would not only allow the export of his revolution but would advertise Iran's power. The militant Islamic trend already present within the Shiite community was thus tapped to provide strong and committed lay and clerical leaders for the fledgling organization.

Iran's further role in the deal made with Syria was to organize and bankroll the new group and to equip and train its officers and recruits. For the latter purpose Iranian Revolutionary Guards were dispatched to the Bekaa Valley, where it was estimated by various sources that by 1984 some 7,000 troops had been trained. For its part, Syria would provide security in the Bekaa Valley where its army was in control. Damascus would also take arms deliveries from Iran and move them across the Syrian border to the Bekaa. Asad would control the timing, type and extent of Hizbullah's clashes with the enemy so as to most effectively deliver his message to the Israeli leadership regarding return of the Golan Heights. On the other hand, most field operations and the development of tactics suitable to the rough terrain of South Lebanon would be left to the field commanders of the organization that came to be known as Hizbullah. The grand strategy, operational framework and division of labour described above have never been altered.

## Winning legitimacy through arms

Fighting the Israelis, threatening to do so or even railing against them from podiums has, over the years, never failed to win support for Arab politicians. It can thus be said that Hizbullah's legitimacy was determined by its very purpose. However, the fact that the Islamist organization was the brainchild of external powers whose interests seemed to override Lebanon's in the fielding of this force was bound to create an uneasy relationship between Hizbullah, the state authorities and parts of the Lebanese population, the Christians in particular. Ironically, most of this problem was solved for Hizbullah leaders when Israeli troops withdrew to South Lebanon in 1985 and created a fortified 'Security Zone' on the Lebanese side of the border. At one stroke the Jewish state's army became an illegal occupying force and Hizbullah's war to dislodge it became a national resistance. As a result it was incumbent upon all Lebanese to support the patriotic struggle, or at least keep their reservations to themselves.

Much has been written about the occupation and the long-term, low intensity war that eventually turned South Lebanon into Israel's Vietnam. Israeli casualties in the 'Security Zone' elicited full-scale invasions including aerial attacks on Lebanese infrastructure in 1993 and 1996 to cripple Hizbullah and force the Lebanese government to rein in the Islamic guerrillas. During each struggle, Hizbullah's unceasing rocket attacks on the Galilee panhandle could be stopped only by US Secretary of State Warren Christopher's visits to Damascus to request Asad's intervention with Hizbullah.

By 2000 Hizbullah, mounting as many as 40 attacks a day against Israel, had worn out Israeli patience with the occupation and caused the Ehud Barak administration to finally withdraw its troops from Lebanon—or most of Lebanon, as the Israelis still occupy the Shebaa Farms area that is asserted to be part of Lebanese territory. The unprecedented scenes of Israel's retreat under duress from captured Arab territory that were presented on Hizbullah's *al-Manar* (The Beacon) television channel during the last week of May 2000 brought the party euphoric acclaim in Lebanon, which overshadowed the tensions engendered by Syria and Iran's role in the victory.

The vacuum left by Israeli troops at the frontier was immediately filled by Hizbullah fighters whose arms would now be able to strike far deeper into Israeli territory.[2] These feats of arms between 1993 and 2000 catapulted the Hizbullah Secretary General Hasan Nasrallah, a charismatic cleric educated in Iraqi theological seminaries, to a level of popularity in the Arab world probably matched only by Egypt's Gamal Abdul Nasser. Within Lebanon, it can now be seen how difficult it was for Lebanese of all political persuasions *not* to give Nasrallah and the Party of God credit for their efforts to liberate national territory. Although the party had usurped the prerogatives of the state by replacing the army at the frontier, it was clearly understood that the army's lack of training and equipment prevented any role in the liberation of national territory by conventional means.

Nevertheless, Hizbullah's patriotic intents had been viewed with suspicion from the outset by those Lebanese who feared that the organization pursued Islamic, Syrian or Iranian agendas. The Party of God needed to soothe these fears in order to generate a level of support that would protect it from further threats by Israel and from America's campaign to punish it for the Beirut attacks against US citizens and military personnel in 1983, which were attributed to Hizbullah operatives. What actions, relations and characteristics were thus drawn upon to enable Hizbullah to rebut accusations that it was an agent of Syria or a puppet of Iran, and that its political agenda did not include an Islamic Republic for Lebanon? One answer to this problem was for Hizbullah leaders to achieve a healthy relationship with the post-war Lebanese authorities.

---

[2] The strategic value of Hizbullah's achievement in 2000 was realized in the 2006 Hizbullah-Israel war as rockets began to reach Haifa, some 120 kilometres south of their launching point, in August.

## Hizbullah's relationship with the state and its legitimation as a political party

As we have seen, there was little state in Lebanon to have relations with from 1982 until 1989. At that time Syria received a green light to disarm the warring militias and restructure the Lebanese army and security apparatus. Damascus received this mandate under an accord brokered by representatives of Morocco and Saudi Arabia that was signed by Lebanese parliamentarians in Taif, Saudi Arabia. There was no objection to formalizing the presence of Syrian troops on Lebanese soil by America and the international community, since Syria was considered to be the only power that could tie down the region's loose cannon. Moreover, a timetable had been established for the Syrian army's partial withdrawal from Lebanon and final departure arrangements were to be decided by the Lebanese and Syrian governments. The weaker partner then agreed to the continued presence of Syrian troops on Lebanese soil for 'security reasons'.

As Hizbullah's resistance credentials excluded it from being considered a militia, its weapons were not collected when the arms collection began. The party then decided to field candidates in the first post-war parliamentary elections as a means of solidly integrating itself into the political system. By the time this happened Hizbullah leaders had faced the realities of the Lebanese system where no confessional group in the pluralist state could impose its will on others without opposition. They therefore opted for political pragmatism and ideological flexibility and toned down Islamic rhetoric. The ideal of an Islamic state for Lebanon was shelved as it was a sure way of alienating Christians, Sunnis and secular Shiites and dooming the party's electoral chances.

In the first post-war parliamentary election and in all subsequent ones, including the most recent held after Syrian troops had left Lebanon, Hizbullah's successful candidates formed the largest single party bloc in the National Assembly, with 12 or 13 deputies out of 128. Until the establishment of a pro-American cabinet in 2005, Hizbullah's political policy was therefore one of coexistence and cooperation with the Syrian-backed Lebanese authorities whose formal endorsement was a necessary condition for the party's national resistance status.

However, this unique relationship with the government was not without its tensions. For instance, after the 1993 Israeli-Hizbullah war, Hizbullah leaders were taken to task by government leaders, who had not been consulted about the party's plans and resented the usurpation of state prerogatives by a

VNSA. Since this friction could negatively affect the cooperative relationship that Syria had fostered between the Lebanese authorities and Hizbullah, Damascus took steps to control it. State/resistance behaviour during the next major round of fighting between Hizbullah and Israel in 1996 seemed to indicate that 'rules of behaviour' had been established by Damascus to keep incipient tensions between the two actors in check.[3] The 'rules' required that each party must perform its own role without criticism or interference in the tasks allotted the other. Hizbullah would fight the enemy and the government would support its struggle by manning the diplomatic track. Any argument between the two parties would be settled by Syria in the resistance's favour, as was seen after the cease-fire in 1996 and several times thereafter.[4] Of course these 'rules' vanished when Syria could no longer enforce them after 2005. At that time Hizbullah's relationship with the state and its supporters drastically altered, as shall be seen later in this chapter.

## Social and public services and popular support

Of particular importance to Hizbullah's efforts to marshal the public support that would sustain its resistance activities were the public and social service networks established in 1985 and thereafter. These services were designed to assist Shiites who had suffered government neglect for decades, borne the brunt of Hizbullah-Israeli clashes, and supplied the cadres needed for the party's continuing *jihad*. As pointed out above, Shiites had fled to Beirut's overcrowded southern suburb during Israeli incursions and years of fighting in southern Lebanon. There they found, among other disagreeable features, polluted water networks, piled-up garbage, and lack of electricity. Their brethren in the Bekaa Valley and the South endured similar but not as critical disadvantages. With assistance from Iran and the formation of a corps of professional managers, engineers and volunteers employed in Hizbullah's *Jihad al Binaa* (Reconstruction Campaign)—a carefully organized and professionally managed organization[5]—these problems were soon addressed. Hizbullah then went on to find other means to meet communal needs. In fact,

[3] Judith Palmer Harik, *Hezbollah: The Changing Face of Terrorism*, London: I.B. Tauris, 2004, 'The Mechanics of Military Jihad, pp. 113–15.

[4] Ibid, 123–4.

[5] Lamia el-Moubayed, *Strengthening Institutional Capacity for Rural Community Development: Two Case Studies from Lebanon*, Beirut: Economic and Social Commission for Western Asia, 1999, pp. 23–4.

in a country whose socio-political foundations rest on patron/client relationships, ever expanding programmes of assistance such as the extension of micro credit in 1984, construction of low cost housing, vocational training centres, hospitals and clinics, etc. made Hizbullah Lebanon's largest patron. Allegiance in the form of votes and fighters followed.

It should also be pointed out here that in addition to fostering community dependence on Hizbullah, the micro credit programme and others may have produced an even greater payoff for the Party of God by boosting its capacity to generate funds from internal sources and thus reducing its reliance on Iran for financial support. According to Shaykh Hussein Shami, director of social services and head of Hizbullah's micro credit bureau, as of December 2006 the popular organization he heads had accumulated a loan fund in excess of a billion US dollars, which is available for micro credit purposes that are not limited to the Shiite community.[6]

The above discussion has pointed out the confessional, ideological and material dynamics that fuel Hizbullah's vital relationship with the Shiite community, a community that it counts on to assist and defend its struggle with Israel. It also pointed out the state/resistance dynamic that was carefully orchestrated and controlled by Syria until its political setback in 2005. At that time the question arose of whether the Party of God had mustered enough assets to be able to protect its arms under adverse political circumstances.

## New challenges For Hizbullah—the Cedar Revolution and the Summer War of 2006

*The Cedar Revolution.* Between May 2005 and 11 July 2006 there was a brief moment of hope among anti-Syrian groups in Lebanon that a closing of ranks, American support and French assistance might finish Damascus' influence in Lebanon for good. The achievement of that goal, of course, depended on disarmament of Hizbullah. Crystallized by the assassination of Prime Minister Rafiq Hariri on 14 February 2005, a deed immediately attributed to Syria by his mourners, a movement led by Hariri's son Saadeddin was formed a month later to direct what became known as the 'Cedar Revolution'. The extent of the popular outcry over Hariri's death and America's willingness to assist the spearhead of the revolution, dubbed the 14 March Movement, were among the reasons why Bashar al-Asad withdrew his country's troops a few months

---

[6] Interview with Shaykh Hussein Shami, Haret Herayk, Beirut, 12 January 2007.

later. However, the major reason for the Syrian President's abrupt decision was the possibility of a military confrontation with the United States from neighbouring Iraq. Hariri's coalition of Christian, Sunnis and Druze notables celebrated the withdrawal as the Cedar Revolution's first victory and a bevy of Christian leaders who had sat out the Syrian regency abroad or in jail immediately returned to the political arena. A majority of seats was won by these personalities in the parliamentary elections that followed.

This outcome proved to be highly contentious. Pointing to real shortcomings in the electoral system, the opposition coalition claimed that the election results were unfair and that the new government led by Prime Minister Fouad Siniora was therefore illegal. One of the losers in the election was Michel Aoun, former army commander and interim president from 1988 to 1990, who is arguably the most popular Christian political figure in Lebanon. Following the defeat of his candidates, Aoun, whose army units had adamantly fought Syrian-sponsored militias until his forced exile in France, then signed a document of understanding with Hizbullah that made him an opposition partner. The former general's inclusion in opposition ranks was a major coup for Hizbullah as the party's coalition gained many more enthusiastic supporters whose confessional identity gave it a less Shiite coloration and a more balanced appeal.

Spearheading the opposition coalition, Hizbullah demanded an expanded cabinet and redistribution of ministerial posts that would fairly represent Aoun's political weight and that of a few other leaders. The cabinet already included three Hizbullah ministers, who of course joined in arguing the critical importance of a national unity cabinet that would adequately represent all of the country's major political forces.

It is easy to see why the Siniora government rejected this demand, as such a cabinet would have been able to stymie any government initiative that ran counter to opposition interests. In particular, any efforts to disarm Hizbullah and otherwise neutralize Syrian influence in Lebanon would have been nipped in the bud. The Siniora government therefore flatly rejected the national unity cabinet Trojan Horse, and in turn began attacking the pro-Syrian President Emile Lahoud, whose term of office had been illegally extended shortly before the Syrian army pulled up stakes. By July 2006 the political battle for Beirut was gaining force.

*The Summer War and its results.* On 12 July, after Hizbullah fighters had captured three Israeli soldiers and killed seven, Israel's Prime Minister Olmert announced a lightning thrust into Lebanon to destroy Hizbullah and prevent further attacks on the settlers of northern Israel. Although Party of God leaders were surprised by the onslaught, they were not unprepared, as another Israeli incursion to crush Hizbullah had been expected as part of the Bush Administration's war on global terrorism. Between 2000 and 2006 ritual shelling of an Israeli outpost in the Shebaa Farms area of South Lebanon and continual Israeli over flights of Lebanese territory had been common fare. In addition, two prisoner exchanges had taken place between Hizbullah and the Jewish state. There had been relative calm along the frontier, but it was deceptive. We now know that during that period Hizbullah engineers were hard at work digging tunnels and distributing weapons, while elite fighters were being trained to confront Israeli troops and cavalry with the sophisticated weapons systems they had been receiving from Iran and Syria.

When Israel attacked, there was a massive mobilization of Hizbullah village fighters to assist elite cadres. Classic guerrilla tactics were used by the latter to slow and confuse advancing Israeli troops. Their destruction of Israeli tanks and helicopters and the shelling of Israeli warships off the coast were among the surprises Hasan Nasrallah had promised a week after the outset of the war.[7]

While the ground war was in process, highly mobile artillery teams sent an almost continuous rocket barrage into Israel, which by the end of the war had reached beyond the port city of Haifa. Although the US Ambassador to the United Nations, John Bolton, did all he could to produce resolutions condemning Hizbullah and its allies and to help Secretary of State Rice's efforts to delay a cease-fire so that Israel might still achieve its goals, after 33 days the campaign to destroy the Islamic guerrillas once and for all had been lost. In Bolton's words, 'the battle ended in just another Middle East cease fire.'[8]

The price paid for the war by the Shiite community and the Lebanese state was horrendous. Israel's aerial bombardments caused more than a thousand civilian casualties and destroyed whole blocks of the capital's southern suburbs, all bridges and most major highways, while also erasing or severely damaging many Shiite villages in the south, punishing Baalbek and hitting other

---

[7] See *An Nahar* daily newspaper 21 August 2006, p. 1 for the complete text of this speech.

[8] John Bolton *Surrender is not an Option: Defending America at the U.N. and Abroad*, New York: Threshold Editions, 2007, p. 411. The Olmert government faced severe criticism for its incompetent performance during the war and soon after military Chief of Staff Dan Halutz resigned his post under pressure.

locations in the Bekaa. The Siniora government and the 14 March Movement placed the blame for this destruction squarely on Hizbullah and its foreign supporters. During the hostilities Beirut had tried hard to answer Secretary Rice's demands for more action against Hizbullah, but as before, the authorities were unable to rise to the occasion.

One result of the fighting was a beefed up international peacekeeping force and the deployment of 15,000 Lebanese army troops along the Israeli-Lebanese frontier. They were to arrest anyone bearing arms in that area. To date there have been no signs of armed men and no arrests in the border area, although it is common knowledge that the Party of God is not only rearming but fortifying areas both south and north of the Litani River. Another result of the Summer War of 2006 was recognition of Hizbullah as a full-fledged Arab army that, according to Israeli field commanders and intelligence officers, had confronted the Israeli war machine with no battlefield assistance from either Iranian Revolutionary Guards or Syrian officers.[9]

On 6 September 2006 Hizbullah celebrated its 'divine and historic' victory over Israel with a massive rally in south Beirut. All the leaders of opposition factions, religious and social notables, and more than a million euphoric individuals (according to estimates by local and international press and wire services) were present. Ironically, although no representative of the government attended the rally, commanders of the Lebanese Army whose troops had worked beside the resistance during the war had front row seats.

Beirut's lack of efficiency and transparency in handling the material and cash donations that poured in for reconstruction purposes after the war were in striking contrast to Hizbullah's well-oiled emergency relief operation. The programme began immediately after the cease-fire took place, when stacks of cash provided by Iran began to be distributed to families, $12,000 to each, who had lost homes during Israel's aerial bombardments. This cash was to provide a year's rental costs while reconstruction of Beirut's flattened southern suburbs was being carried out by *Jihad al-Binaa*. Fourteen months later, in November 2007, a tour of the construction sites indicated that work was well under way on 220 multi-storied blocks of flats, scheduled for completion in 2009.[10]

---

[9] Anthony Cordesman, 'Preliminary Lessons of Israeli-Hezbollah War', Washington, DC: Center for Strategic and International Studies, 18 August 2006, p. 9.

[10] Part of *Al-Manar* Television's programme 'Hizbullah's works in progress', 15 December 2007, presented detailed information on this project.

## Hizbullah's impact in the post-war political arena

Having failed to bring about Hizbullah's demise in combat, and understanding that Beirut could not implement Security Council Resolution 1559 calling for the disarmament of all militias (a reference to Hizbullah) and the end of foreign (meaning Syrian) interference in Lebanon, the Bush administration chose another course: active support of its Lebanese allies' efforts to outsmart or ride out any opposition tactics aimed at achieving the national unity cabinet previously demanded.

Hizbullah's relationship with the authorities therefore went from uneasy, between May 2005 and July 2006, to highly acrimonious after the Summer War. Each side accused the other of treachery, Hizbullah pointing to Siniora's order to seize a truckload of arms meant for the resistance while the fighting was in progress, and the government questioning the party's allegiance to Lebanon.

After weeks of futile wrangling over an expanded cabinet, on 11 November Hizbullah leaders implemented the first stage of a carefully planned protest campaign by having the party's three cabinet members tender their resignations. By removing representation of the country's largest sect, Hizbullah sought to cripple the government's legitimacy. President Emile Lahoud and the Shiite Speaker of the Assembly, Nabih Berri, whose Amal Movement is a resistance partner, immediately fell in line with Hizbullah's initiative by refusing to recognize the Siniora cabinet's competence and renouncing any further participation in the decision-making process as prescribed in the constitution. Since the Speaker no longer called the parliament into session, it shut down. To all intents and purposes the political process had been derailed more completely than it had been during the civil war—then, at least, deputies and cabinet members had met fairly regularly.

Hizbullah's political resistance programme then continued with threats of civil disobedience. The fragility of Lebanon's security situation was again demonstrated on 20 November when the Minister of Industry Pierre Amin Gemayel, son of a former president, joined the list of anti-Syrian politicians who had been assassinated since 2005 as number five. Fearing for their lives, cabinet members then confined themselves within the fortress-like government house in central Beirut and stayed put until December 2007 when they moved to a heavily guarded sea front hotel.

Ten days later, on 30 November, Hasan Nasrallah declared, 'All attempts at dialogue (with the government) have failed and that is why, taking into account constitutional provisions as well as democratic principles, we have no other recourse but to resort to public pressure.'[11] On 1 December a huge crowd flocked to a protest rally held directly below the ramparts of Government House. Ten days later the protest had assumed a permanent nature with the erection of some 100 tents to house the demonstrators. The 'camp-in' continued for 18 months.

In January 2007 further pressure was exerted by Hizbullah and its local partners through a series of strikes and sit-ins. When there were no results, a one-day nationwide wildcat strike called on 23 January was the next move to try to shake the government off centre. The number of people who immediately responded to the summons by blocking highways and staging demonstrations was another reminder of the political clout enjoyed by Hizbullah and its coalition. Unfortunately, however, clashes erupted between Aoun's supporters and the Lebanese Forces, a former Christian militia. Four Aounists were killed and more than 150 people were injured.

This incident was followed two days later by clashes between Hizbullah and Amal supporters on one side and Hariri Future Current supporters on the other, on and near the campus of Beirut Arab University. The toll this time was four Shiite youths killed and more than 200 people wounded. Fears of confession-based violence rose and loyalist figures claimed a coup d'etat was being prepared by the opposition. Hasan Nasrallah responded to this charge by saying 'If we had wanted a coup we could have made one from day one.'[12] His organization's capacity to do so was beyond doubt.

## Crisis within a crisis: the 2007–8 presidential non-elections

After the actions described above, opposition leaders apparently agreed that it was time to simply sit back and let the confrontation 'mature'. In a speech on 8 April Nasrallah said, '... only a national poll on what the people want or early parliamentary elections can end the impasse. The idea of a national unity cabinet is finished.'[13]

The assassination of the 14 March deputy Walid Eido, who was leaving a Beirut swimming club when a car bomb exploded nearby, now left Hariri and his colleagues with a parliamentary majority of only one. Then, in May, violence erupted in northern Lebanon and continued for three months as the

[11] *Al-Manar* Television, Hasan Nasrallah address, 30 November 2006.
[12] *The Daily Star*, 25 January 2007, p. 3.
[13] Address. *al-Manar* Television, 8 April 2007.

army sought to evict an Al Qaeda-linked Palestinian organization, Fatah al-Islam, that had infiltrated the Nahr al-Barid refugee camp.[14]

As if this was not enough for the floundering state to bear, a political battle royal over the presidential election scheduled for the autumn of 2007 then began. Simply put, the 14 March Movement sought a means to hold the election and elect an anti-Syrian president, while its opposition manoeuvred to prevent this from happening in any way possible. Unfortunately for the 14 March coalition, Article 49 section 2 of the Lebanese Constitution provided an easy way to derail the election. This article states that 'The president of the republic shall be elected by secret ballot by a two thirds majority of the Chamber of Deputies. After a first ballot an absolute majority shall be sufficient.' The 57 opposition deputies had therefore only to continue their boycott of parliament when Speaker Berri summoned them to vote; this they did 19 times.

Lacking an elected successor when he left office, President Emile Lahoud placed responsibility for the country's security in the hands of Michel Suleiman, Commanding Officer of the Lebanese Army. In his address to the nation at that time, Lahoud explained the reasons behind his act as follows:

As the government lost its legitimacy and cannot therefore execute executive power, the functions of the High Committee of National Defense are affected with regard to its capacity to meet the dangers presently weighing on the country. This being the case, the President (Lahoud speaking in the third person) believes that the conditions necessary for declaration of a state of emergency are present and he charges the armed forces under the army's command, to preserve security. The army should thus account for the measures it takes before the next constitutional cabinet.[15]

Before his departure from the presidential palace Lahoud also paid homage to 'the resistance that stood up to Israel' and asserted that in his opinion the essential requirement of a new president was that '...he must believe in the role of the army and the resistance.'[16]

The next proposal to resolve the crisis was the election of Michel Suleiman, a professional soldier of relative neutrality, as President. The Siniora cabinet would then resign and formation of a new government would take place. If

---

[14] The introduction of the Sunni fighters may have been part of a plan by some regional governments to try to counter growing Shiite influence in Lebanon.

[15] *L'Orient—le Jour*, 24 November 2007, p. 2. The Siniora government immediately denied Lahoud's capacity to call a state of emergency citing Article 56 of the Constitution which gave the cabinet that privilege.

[16] Ibid.

that were to happen Article 49 (1) of the constitution that prohibits a public servant currently holding office from assuming the presidency would have to be amended. However, Michel Aoun, Hizbullah's choice for president, put a spanner in that idea by declaring that there could be no election without the prior achievement of political consensus between the contending sides.[17] In other words, before Suleiman could take office critical issues such as the political balance of the new cabinet and the distribution of key ministerial portfolios would have to be agreed. Unwilling to compromise the position it had taken, the 14 March Movement rejected this demand and stuck to its guns until a far more dangerous political crisis that occurred at the end of April 2008 caused a review of its position.

This crisis was precipitated by the Siniora government's launch of an investigation into Hizbullah's private and secure telecommunications network, plus the reassignment of the head of airport security purported to be close to the Party of God. These two actions triggered an immediate response from Hizbullah and opposition allies who considered them as a direct challenge to the resistance. A programmed campaign to scuttle the government's actions began with blocking of major roads including the highway leading to Rafik Hariri International Airport, closing it to commercial flights for more than a week. Civil disobedience turned to armed conflict on 7 May, when Hizbullah and its allies took over wide swathes of Sunni territory in West Beirut, closing down Hariri media and political offices and disarming Hariri militiamen. At the same time Government House in downtown Beirut was surrounded. In the mountains south-east of Beirut, Druze militiamen loyal to Walid Jumblat were also pursued and disarmed. Sixty-two people were killed in the clashes that occurred during this operation and more than 200 were wounded.

Although other organizations and factions of various religious affiliations participated, the battle was viewed as one mainly between Shiites and Sunnis, and many asked whether the enfeebled state was again lurching towards a civil war. For its part, the Lebanese army made no move to interfere in the rounding up of pro-government militias, but rather coordinated action with Hizbullah and its allies by taking control of evacuated offices and positions of 14 March militiamen. On 14 May the Siniora government was forced to rescind the decisions it had been unable to enforce.

This tense situation was defused by a joint Arab League-Qatari initiative which brought all Lebanese factions together in Doha to push through a com-

---

[17] Address carried by Aoun's Orange Television channel, 3 December 2007. Aoun's symbolic colour in Hizbullah's 'Rainbow coalition' is orange, Hizbullah's is yellow, etc.

promise solution to this long festering political crisis. During the Doha conference, from 16 to 21 May, a memorandum of understanding that had been announced in Beirut on 15 May under the aegis of the Arab Ministerial Commission was formalized. The results of the agreement reflected the weak state/ strong party conundrum, as every opposition demand was finally agreed. A national unity cabinet with a distribution of ministerial seats that permitted blocking of any decision or action considered detrimental to Hizbullah's resistance agenda was finally established. Furthermore, a presidential candidate acceptable to Hizbullah, Michel Suleiman, would be elected by consensus and electoral reforms that favoured Michel Aoun's Free Patriot Movement were to be enacted. Fouad Siniora retained his post as Prime Minister and Nabih Berri continued in his role as Speaker of the National Assembly. The new President took office on 25 May, calling for coordination between the army and the resistance in his inaugural speech.

The two-year standoff between Syria and the United States over Lebanon's direction was resolved in Syria's favour. Moreover, through the UN initiative and German mediation, Hizbullah's prisoner exchange agenda that had precipitated the 2006 Summer War was finally agreed. Hasan Nasrallah was thus able to announce on al-Manar TV on 3 July 2008, 'We have completed the whole mission.' More solidly entrenched in Lebanese society and more dominant in the political arena, Hizbullah appears to be more determined than ever to continue its struggle with Israel—with or without the state's approval.

## Conclusions and implications

This chapter has shown how Lebanon, fell to pieces in the 1960s and has yet to put itself back together. The contemporary history of this shattered country is one of almost unceasing conflict in which transnational actors played major roles. With encouragement from Israel and Syria, Lebanon's sectarian militias first fought each other in and around the capital for almost two decades while Palestinian commandos ruled the southern part of the country. Then the South Lebanon Army and Israeli troops faced off with Hizbullah in a battle zone inside Lebanon for 17 years. Sporadic clashes between the Islamic guerrillas and the Israeli military continued from 2000 to 2006 when an all-out war broke out between these forces. This turmoil put the frontier region off limits to the Lebanese army for more than 40 years, and it is well known that the troops deployed there now are no match for Hizbullah's seasoned and well equipped fighters.

153

After the civil war was concluded in 1990, Lebanon was pieced back together to further serve the foreign policy interests of Syria and its allies. The feeble state then became a partner of the very VNSA that had monopolized force within the country. This state/resistance relationship so carefully managed by Syria helped ward off American and Israeli threats and attacks between 1992 and 2005 that were aimed at forcing Beirut to rein in the 'terrorist' group.

This chapter looked at how this VNSA was able to build a formidable army and what some have called a state within a state in the relatively short period of its existence. While it found that Lebanon's weakness was a major factor in Hizbullah's capacity to field an effective fighting force and transform itself into a national resistance and mainstream political party in the Lebanese arena, and that the Party of God had a great deal of help from its foreign mentors in accomplishing these feats, it presented the actions taken by Party of God leaders to popularize and fortify their organization as indispensable to its staying power. These actions included military, political and social strategies and tactics that legitimated the Islamic organization and deepened its niche within society.

Military successes in combating the Israeli occupation, it was suggested, had a key role in popularizing the resistance and thus paving the way for Hizbullah's deep integration into the socio-political fabric of the nation. The extension of broad social and public services to the deprived Shiite community, with help from Iran, and the personal qualities of Hizbullah's pragmatic leaders were also cited as creating the relationships that fortify the Islamist group's political stand today.

The backlog of goodwill that these characteristics and programmes created for Hizbullah, and its stunning performance during the Summer 2006 War, created a surge of popularity that strengthened the Islamic organization's ability to meet challenges posed by an unfriendly government and its superpower ally in the post-war period. Relying heavily on its charismatic leader's ability to quickly mobilize extensive public support, Hizbullah was thus able to formulate and lead a campaign of civil disobedience that successfully checked all moves by the Siniora government and the 14 March Movement to impose a pro-American, anti-Syrian president on Lebanon. By the summer of 2008 Hizbullah and its allies had prevailed, but not without force of arms; this time the arms were used against armed Lebanese opponents who were part of the 14 March Movement and who opposed the Party of God's political ascendancy.

More than anything else, the Doha agreement pointed up the extent of Hizbullah's dominance in Lebanon's political arena. Quite simply, what Hizbullah wanted Hizbullah obtained, whether by its capacity to block any initiative by weight of numbers or by military strength that greatly exceeds that of any other Lebanese group including the Lebanese Army.

The implications of a continuing trend in this direction are not positive for America's Lebanon agenda or Israel's interest in sidelining Hizbullah. It thus seems fair to say that only Syria may be able to make this VNSA go away should a land-for-peace deal with Israel eventually be negotiated. However, even if such a deal could be worked out between Syria and Israel there is now some doubt whether the Party of God would follow orders to disband its fighting force. Hizbullah's performance in the 2006 war raised doubts about the assumption that the Shiite organization is a mere surrogate of Syria and Iran rather than a partner with its own agenda. It can no longer be assumed that Party of God leaders would automatically carry out the wishes of either of its allies if they conflict with what those leaders consider to be in Lebanon's or their organization's best interests. Hizbullah will thus continue to make all efforts to retain its arms, whether by defence on the battlefield or by continuing to call the shots in the political arena it now dominates. If this scenario prevails, the Lebanese state will, as usual, be more witness to the events unfolding within its borders than actor.

# 8

# Hamas and the Prospects of De-Radicalization

*Omar Ashour*

## Hamas and the phenomenon of armed Islamist de-radicalization

Since the mid-1990s, there have been several transformations in the behaviour, ideology, and rhetoric of Harakat al-Muqawama al-Islamiyya (Islamic Resistance Movement, Hamas). Although the 1988 Charter of the movement clearly calls for the liberation of all mandated Palestine *min al-bahr ila al-nahr* (from the Mediterranean Sea to the Jordan River) via *jihad*,[1] the founder of Hamas, Sheikh Ahmad Yassin, declared in 1999 that the Movement is willing to offer a ten-year truce in exchange for an Israeli withdrawal to the 1967 borders.[2] Since then, the leaders of Hamas appear to have recognized that a compromise regarding Israel's existence is a necessity for the establishment of a Palestinian State. That compromise will probably translate into a de-radicalization process,[3] putting an end to political violence perpetrated by the move-

---

[1] *Jihad* should be understood here as armed struggle, despite the existence of other peaceful forms of the concept in Islamic theology and jurisprudence.
[2] Ahmad Yassin, '*Hamas Kama Yaraha al-Sheikh Ahmad Yassin* (Hamas as perceived by Sheikh Ahmad Yassin).' Interview by Ahmad Mansur in *Shahid 'ala al-'Asr*, Al-Jazeera Satellite Channel, nine episodes. 17 April 1999 to 9 June 1999, episode 9.
[3] The process and its types will be elaborated upon later in the chapter.

ment. Indeed, as Ismail Abu Shanab—a high ranking leader in Hamas—has pointed out: 'the practical solution for us is to have a state alongside Israel... When we build a Palestinian state, we will not need these militias; all the needs for attack will stop.'[4]

The idea of abandoning, and even de-legitimizing, political violence is not new to armed Islamist movements in general, and to branches and offshoots of the Muslim Brothers (like Hamas) in particular. In late 1951, Hassan al-Hudaybi, the new General Guide of the Jam'iyyat al-Ikhwan al-Muslimin (Society of the Muslim Brothers, MB) in Egypt attempted the first de-radicalization process of an urban, armed Islamist movement in the 20th century. Al-Hudaybi decided to dismantle the main armed wing of the Society that was known at the time as *al-Nizam al-Khass* (the Special Apparatus, SA). This is despite the British military presence in Egypt and the existence of the State of Israel, the two official raisons d'être of the SA.[5] However, al-Hudaybi's leadership was already being challenged, and the decision was controversial. It thus led to further factionalization and even internal violence within the Society. Ultimately, it took approximately two decades for the MB leadership to dismantle the SA completely. Since the early 1970s, the Egyptian Muslim Brotherhood has abandoned violence against national regimes, and has de-legitimized and prohibited that type of violence with ideological and theological arguments. Additionally, the leadership of the MB in Egypt has also dismantled all of its armed units. These conditions indicate a successful, comprehensive de-radicalization process that took place on the behavioral, ideological and organizational levels.

The phenomenon of 'de-radicalization' is not only confined to the MB and its branches. A few decades later, Egyptian armed Islamist organizations which had been vehemently critical of the MB's non-violent behaviour followed onto the path of de-radicalization. Al-Gama'a al-Islamiyya (Islamic

---

[4] Matthew Gutman, Nina Gilbert and Herb Keinon, 'Hamas official has a vision of living next to Israel', *Jerusalem Post*, 25 June 2003, p. 1.

[5] Omar Ashour, *The Deradicalization of Jihadists: Transforming Armed Islamist Movements*, New York, London: Routledge, 2009, pp. 63–90; Abdul Azim Ramadan, *Al-Ikhwan al-Muslimun wa al-Tanzim al-Sirri* (The Muslim Brothers and the Secret Organization), Cairo: al-Hay'a al-'amma lil Kitab, 1993, p. 94; Ahmad Kamal, *Al-Nuqat Fawq al-Huruf: al-Ikhwan al-Muslimun wa al-Nizam al-Khas* (Dots on letters: the Muslim Brothers and the Special Regime), Cairo: al-Zahraa, 1987, p. 242; Richard Mitchell, *The Society of the Muslim Brothers*. Cambridge University Press, 1969; Brynjar Lia. *The Society of the Muslim Brothers in Egypt: The Rise of an Islamic Mass Movement 1928–1942*, Reading, UK: Garnet, 1998.

Group, IG) successfully dismantled its armed wings and abandoned its *fiqh al-'unf* (Islamic jurisprudence justifying violence) literature between 1997 and 2002.[6] In 2007, the al-Jihad Organization initiated a similar de-radicalization process following the lead of the MB and the IG.[7] Outside Egypt, Islamist de-radicalization took place in several other states in the late 1990s and the 2000s.[8] These de-radicalization cases include Algerian, Libyan, Jordanian, Iraqi, Saudi, Yemeni, Afghan, Tajik, Malaysian, Singaporean, and Indonesian armed Islamist groups, factions, and individuals.[9] Additionally, the de-radicalization processes in Egypt have influenced several British and other European Islamist leaders who revised their views on violence and democracy.[10] Moreover, some of the de-radicalized Islamist groups and figures have been criticizing the violent behaviour and policies of Hamas. The most recent of those is the former ideologue of Al Qaeda, Dr Sayyid Imam al-Sharif (alias Dr Fadl and Abd al-Qadir Ibn Abd al-'Aziz). This is in addition to the ideologue and *de facto* leader of the Egyptian IG, Dr Nagih Ibrahim, and several other formerly Salafi-Jihadi figures from Saudi Arabia.[11]

Hamas, therefore, is not likely to be an exception to the phenomenon of de-radicalization, especially as other Palestine groups, like Fatah, underwent similar processes. This chapter will be investigating the prospects of de-radicalization for Hamas in the light of similar cases, particularly that of the Egyptian Muslim Brothers. The analysis will overview the historical background of

---

[6] Omar Ashour, 'Lions Tamed? An Inquiry into the Causes of De-Radicalization of the Egyptian Islamic Group', *Middle East Journal* Vol. 61, No. 4 (Autumn 2007), pp. 596–627. In 2002, the leadership of the IG replaced its curricula with those of the MB: see Abdu Zinah '*al-Jama'a al-Islammiya Fi Misr Tulghi Manahijiha Wa Tastabdil Kutub al-Ikhwan Biha* (The Islamic Group in Egypt rescinds its curricula and replaces them with the Brothers' books).' *Al-Sharq al-Awsat*, 8 June 2003, p. 16.

[7] Omar Ashour, 'De-Radicalization of Jihad? The Impact of Egyptian Islamist Revisionists on Al Qaeda', *Perspectives on Terrorism* Vol. 2, No. 5 (Spring 2008), pp. 1–14.

[8] The scale of these processes was relatively small, except for the two cases of de-radicalization in Algeria (Islamic Salvation Army and affiliated militias) and Tajikistan (armed militias of the Islamic Renaissance Party).

[9] Ashour, 'Lions Tamed'; Omar Ashour, 'De-Radicalization of Jihad? The Impact of Egyptian Islamist Revisionists on al Qaeda', *Perspectives on Terrorism* Vol. 2, No. 5 (Spring 2008), pp. 1–14; International Crisis Group, 'Deradicalization and Indonesian Prisons', 19 November 2007.

[10] Majid Nawaz, '*Muffakir Hizb al-Tahrir Yutalliq al-Usuliyya* (The ideologue of the Liberation Party divorces fundamentalism). Interview by Muhammad al-Shaf'i. *al-Sharq al-Awsat*, 17 September 2005, pp. 1, 5.

[11] Muhammad Abu Shama, '*Munazir al-Jihad al-Masry* (The ideologue of Egyptian Jihad)', *Al-Sharq al-Awsat*, 23 April 2009, 1.

Hamas and its armed wings, its rise in Palestinian and Arab politics, the process of violent radicalization that it underwent during the late 1980s, and the transformations and the nuances in its ideology and behaviour since then. The analysis is grounded on a specific definition of 'Islamist de-radicalization', a related typology and a theoretical framework to explain the causes behind that process—as explained below.

## The processes of de-radicalization of armed Islamist movements

Despite the fact that many armed Islamist movements which used to engage in terrorist acts have shown remarkable behavioral and ideological transformations towards non-violence, and the 'de-radicalization' processes of these movements have removed tens of thousands of former militants from the ranks of Al Qaeda's supporters and acted as disincentives for would-be militants, the subject is still understudied in the literature—in spite of the great interest in explaining Islamism and the huge volume of literature produced after the 9/11 attacks.

As I have explained elsewhere, Islamist movements are 'sociopolitical movements which base and justify their political principles, ideologies, behaviors, and objectives on their understanding of Islam or on their understanding of a certain past interpretation of Islam.'[12] De-radicalization is a process of relative change within Islamist movements, one in which a radical group reverses its ideology and de-legitimizes the use of violent methods to achieve political goals, while also moving towards acceptance of gradual social, political and economic changes within a pluralist context. A group undergoing a de-radicalization process does not have to abide ideologically by democratic principles, whether electoral or liberal.[13] Many de-radicalized Islamist groups still uphold anti-democratic, misogynist, homophobic, xenophobic, and unprogressive views.[14] However, the new development is abandoning and de-legitimizing the idea of using violence to impose such views.

[12] Ashour, 'Lions Tamed', p. 599.

[13] The main example is the Egyptian Islamic Group which—on the basis of its interpretation of Islam—still rejects democracy. However, its newly developed ideology de-legitimizes violence and accepts 'the other', not necessarily as an 'enemy'. In general, de-radicalization is primarily concerned with changing the attitudes of armed Islamist movements towards violence, rather than towards democracy.

[14] Like the IG and al-Jihad in Egypt and the de-radicalized factions from the GIA and the GSPC in Algeria. Additionally, even relatively 'moderate' groups like the MB hold similar non-progressive views.

As distinct from the ideological dimension, de-radicalization can occur on the behavioral level only. On that level, it means practically abandoning the use of violence to achieve political goals without a concurrent process of ideological de-legitimization of violence. De-radicalization can occur in one of the two dimensions, behavioral and ideological.

There is, nevertheless, a third dimension. Following the declaration of ideological and/or behavioral de-radicalization by the leadership of an armed group, there is usually the challenge of organizational de-radicalization: the dismantling of the organization' armed units, which includes discharging/demobilizing their members without splits, mutiny, or internal violence.

Several types of de-radicalization correspond to the previously mentioned dimensions. Comprehensive de-radicalization refers to a successful de-radicalization process on the three dimensions: ideological, behavioral and organizational. Egypt well represents comprehensive de-radicalization cases as two large Egyptian organizations underwent that process successfully: the armed wings of the MB (1969–73) and the IG (1997–2002).[15]

Substantive de-radicalization entails a successful process of de-radicalization on both the ideological and behavioral levels, but not on the organizational level (usually a failure on that level is followed by splits, factionalization, and internal organizational conflict, and/or the marginalization of the de-radicalized leadership). Examples of substantive de-radicalization include the cases of the Egyptian al-Jihad Organization, factions from the Indonesian Jama'a Islamiyya (Islamic Group), and the Libyan Fighting Islamic Group (FIG). In the cases of al-Jihad and the FIG, significant internal conflicts remain, with some factions joining Al Qaeda instead of de-radicalizing.

A third type of de-radicalization is pragmatic de-radicalization. This is a successful behavioral and organizational de-radicalization process, but without an ideological de-legitimization of violence. The Algerian Islamic Salvation Army (AIS)[16] and the militias affiliated with the Tajik Islamic Renaissance Party (IRP) are examples of organizations that underwent that type of de-radicalization.

How does de-radicalization develop? In previous works, I have shown that a combination of charismatic leadership, state repression, interactions

---

[15] See also chapter 6 in this volume.

[16] In addition to the AIS, other affiliated militias like the Islamic League for Da'wa and Jihad (LIDD) and the Islamic Front for Armed Jihad (FIDA) as well as factions within the Armed Islamic Group (GIA) and the Salafi Group for Preaching and Combat (GSPC) pragmatically de-radicalized between 2000 and 2007.

with the 'other'[17] as well as within the organization, and selective inducements from the state and other actors are common causes of de-radicalization.[18] There is a pattern of interaction between these variables leading to
de-radicalization in many of the aforementioned cases. State repression and
interaction with the 'other' often affect the ideas and the behaviour of
an armed organization's leaders and probably lead them to initiate three
endogenous processes: strategic calculations, political learning, and *Weltan-
schauung* revision. The first process is based on rational-choice calculations
and cost-benefit analyses. The second is a product of socialization and interaction with the 'other'; the leadership will update its beliefs and reassess
its behaviour in view of the behaviour of their interaction partner(s). The
third process is mostly based on perceptional and psychological factors. In
this process the leadership of an armed Islamist movement modifies its
worldviews 'as a result of severe crises, frustration and dramatic changes in the
environment.'[19]

Following these processes, the leadership initiates a de-radicalization process that is bolstered by selective inducements from the state as well as by
internal interactions (lectures, discussions, and meetings between the leadership, mid-ranking commanders, and the grassroots in an effort to convince
them about the merits of de-radicalization). Also, de-radicalized groups
often interact with violent Islamist groups and, in some cases, the former
influence the latter (a domino effect).[20] In the particular case of Hamas, such
interaction was witnessed recently with the letters addressed to it by Dr Fadl,
the former ideologue of Al Qaeda and former Emir of the al-Jihad Organization (1987–93).[21]

Let us now proceed to discuss the history of Hamas, the transformation
within the organization, and the prospects of de-radicalization of movement
in the light of the above mentioned framework.

---

[17] The 'other' is defined here as any social actor or entity who/which is not Islamist or who/
which is not recognized by the movement(s) under study as 'Islamist'.

[18] Ashour, *The De-Radicalization of Jihadists*; Ashour 'Lions Tamed?'

[19] Nancy Bermeo, 'Democracy and the Lessons of Dictatorship.' *Comparative Politics*
Vol. 24 No. 3 (April 1992), p. 273.

[20] Most notably, the interactions between the Islamic Group and al-Jihad Organization in
Egypt and the Islamic Salvation Army (AIS) and other smaller Islamist militias as well
as factions from the GIA and the GSPC in Algeria.

[21] Muhammad Abu Shama, 'Munazir', p. 1.

## Hamas: a historical overview

*The foundation of the Islamic Resistance Movement (Hamas).*  In December 1987, Sheikh Ahmad Yassin publicly declared the foundation of an Islamist armed resistance movement. Hamas was officially established after a meeting between Yassin and six other leaders of the Palestinian branch of the Muslim Brothers in the Gaza Strip. Those leaders included Abdul Aziz al-Rantissi, the leader of Hamas after the assassination of its founder (Ahmad Yassin), and Salah Shahade, the founder and first commander of the armed wing of Hamas, the Brigades of Izz al-Din al-Qassam, or al-Qassam Brigades (QB).[22]

The declaration of foundation came out during the first Palestine Uprising, or *Intifada I* (1987–91), in which Hamas organized a wave of strikes, demonstrations, assassinations of alleged Palestinian 'collaborators', and armed attacks on Israeli soldiers and settlers in Gaza.[23] Sheikh Yassin claims that Hamas issued the first communiqué of the Intifada on 14 December 1987. Therefore it takes pride in being the first group to organize and support the uprising. However, that claim is contested by the leaders of Fatah and other PLO factions. During the Intifada, Sheikh Yassin and other Hamas leaders were arrested by the Israeli security forces in May 1989.[24] Yassin was accused of attempting to 'destroy the state of Israel and establishing an Islamic state' and he was sentenced to fifteen years in prison.[25]

*Political ideology and behaviour.*  The Charter of Hamas was published on 18 August 1988. It declared that the Movement is one of the branches of the Muslim Brothers' International Organization (al-Tanzim al-'alami).[26] At the beginning of the Charter, Hasan al-Banna, the founder of the Egyptian MB, is quoted as saying 'Israel will rise and will be established, until Islam dismantles her like it dismantled her predecessors.'[27]

Besides that quote, the thoughts of al-Banna are strongly present not only in the Charter but also in the general ideology and the political behaviour of Hamas. As early as the 1930s, al-Banna elaborated on his vision of the militarization of Islamist activism. In 1936, he argued in one of his letters under a

---

[22] The history and the development of the QB will be discussed later in the chapter.

[23] Yassin, 'Hamas Kama Yaraha', episode 6.

[24] Ibid.

[25] Ibid.

[26] Hamas, '*Mithaq Harakat al-Muqawama al-Islamiyya—Hamas*' (The Charter of the Islamic Resistance Movement—Hamas), article two.

[27] Ibid., p. 1.

section entitled 'soldierism in Islam' that *jihad*, defined here as armed struggle, is an Islamic obligation (*fard*) and that it should be carried out to attain 'Islamic objectives.'[28] Al-Banna thought that Islam had made military power 'sacred'.[29] In another letter entitled 'Letter of al-Jihad', he advances his theological evidence mainly to support the argument that *jihad* is *fard 'ain*[30] to defend 'Muslim lands' against foreign aggression and *fard kifaya*[31] when Muslim lands are not under threat. He concludes by saying that 'ultimate martyrdom' can be attained only through getting killed for the sake of God.[32] Al-Banna considered *jihad* as the fourth pillar of the MB *bay'a*.[33] The main slogan of the MB has five phrases. The fourth one is *al-jihad sabiluna* (*Jihad* is our way) and the fifth translates as 'the death in the way of God is our most sublime wish'.[34] Whereas these pillars and slogans apply to the MB members in general, they were strongly reflected in both the 1988 Charter and the religious-political rhetoric of Hamas. At a later stage, the armed wing of the movement, the Izz al-Din al-Qassam Brigades, was to represent the institutional embodiment of al-Banna's understanding of '*jihad*' and 'soldierism' in Islam.

More specifically, the 1988 Charter of Hamas covers the movement's political ideology, including both major and minor issues—from stances on the peace process, women's rights and citizenship to scope of action, and all the way to arts and music. Three issues in the Charter are quite salient and defined the behaviour of Hamas for the years to come: the stance on the peace process, the impact of Jihadism, and the international dimension. Regarding the peace process, like Fatah, the Popular Front for Liberation of Palestine (PFLP) and the Democratic Front for the Liberation of Palestine (DFLP) and other PLO factions, Hamas initially declared that its aim was the liberation of historical

---

[28] Al-Banna, Hasan. *Mujmu'at Ras'il al-Imam al-Shahid Hasan al-Banna* (The Complete Collection of Letters of the Martyr Imam Hasan al-Bana). Beirut: Dar al-Qalam, 1990, 176.

[29] Ibid., 176.

[30] Islamic obligation/duty required to be performed by every individual Muslim, like prayers.

[31] Islamic obligation/duty for the whole community of believers (*ummah*). The Muslim individual is not required to perform it as long as a sufficient number of community members fulfil it.

[32] Al-Banna, Hassan. *Muzakkarat al-Da'wah wa al-Da'iya* (The Memoirs of the Call and the Preacher). Cairo: Dar al-Tawzi' wa al-Nashr al-Isamiyya, 1986, 59.

[33] Ibid., pp. 7, 14. Al-Bay'a is the oath of allegiance given by an MB member to the MB leaders.

[34] Ibid., p. 14. The other three phrases are: God is our objective. The Messenger is our leader. The Quran is our constitution.

(mandated) Palestine.[35] The justification for that objective was different, nonetheless, from those secular organizations. Hamas considers Palestine an Islamic *Waqf*, a territory earmarked as a religious endowment entrusted to all generations of Muslims.[36] This means that there can be no religious legitimacy in giving up parts of this 'endowment' to Israel or to any non-Muslim power. Peace efforts are usually denounced as acts of treason by Hamas and the organization was partly responsible for undermining negotiations since the mid-1990s.

Another salient issue in the Charter is the blend of Jihadism and modern nationalism. For example, the charter restates the *fatwa*[37] of Dr Abdullah Azzam[38] about defensive *jihad* (defined here as armed struggle) being a *fard 'ain*, or a religious obligation on each and every individual Muslim, just like the daily five prayers.[39] The liberation of Palestine within the pre-1948 borders, a national objective par excellence, is reinstated in the Charter in religious terms to gather support across national boundaries.

A third and final issue that is well-emphasized in the Charter is the global nature of Hamas and the Islamic effort to liberate Palestine. For example, article seven is entitled the 'Global Islamic Resistance Movement' and stresses that the followers and the supporters of the Hamas are everywhere in the globe, that they adopt its policies, and support the movement's *jihad*.[40] Article fourteen in the Charter stresses the existence of the three supportive 'circles' in the struggle against Israel. The first is the Palestinian, the second is the Arab, and the third is the Islamic circle. The relationship of the movements with some of the Arab and Islamist regimes is legitimized by that ideological framework, especially in the case of Iran and Syria.

[35] Hamas, '*Mithaq*', article six.

[36] Hamas, '*Mithaq*', article eleven.

[37] That *fatwa* is recycled from older Islamic sources that date back as far as the 10th century.

[38] Azzam was a highly influential Palestinian theologian and a central figure in preaching and organizing defensive *jihad*, particularly in Afghanistan. He raised funds, recruited, and organized the Arab-Afghans throughout the 1980s. He is also famous as a teacher and mentor of Osama bin Laden who persuaded the latter to come to Afghanistan and help the *jihad*. Azzam's efforts in the foundation of Hamas and recruiting members to the movement are less known, however. He published his experience with Hamas and the Palestinian Muslim Brothers in *Hamas:al-Judhur al-Tarikhiyya wa al-Mithaq* (*Hamas: the historical roots and the Charter*), Peshawar: Markaz Shahid Azzam, 1989.

[39] Hamas, '*Mithaq*', article fifteen; Abdullah Azzam, *al-Difa' 'an 'aradi al-Muslimiyn* (*Defending the Muslim lands*), Peshawar: Markaz Shahid Azzam, 1988, p. 9.

[40] Hamas, '*Mithaq*', article seven.

Finally, it should be noted that several documents were issued after the 1988 Charter. Those documents can be seen as ideological and behavioral transformations and possibly departures from the Charter, if not modifications to it. The 2005 Electoral Platform of Hamas and the Cabinet Platform that was declared on 27 March 2006 are two examples of those documents.[41]

## International relations

Like other Palestinian organizations, Hamas has strong ties with the Arab-majority world. For example, many Hamas leaders were brought up and educated in the Gulf States, particularly in Kuwait. Khalid Mash'al, the head of the Political Bureau of Hamas, was raised and educated and worked in Kuwait. In one interview, Mash'al recalls that the 'Hamas project' was developed 'in three main arenas: Gaza Strip, West Bank, and Kuwait'.[42] Other leading figures from the 'Kuwaiti Arena' include Jamal Issa, the Hamas representative in Yemen; Munir Said, who has been the Hamas representative in both Sudan and Yemen; Muhammad Nazzal, a member of the Hamas political bureau; Izzat Rishq, another political bureau member; Sami Khatir, also a politicl bureau member; Usama Hamdan, Hamas' senior representative in Lebanon; and Ibrahim Ghosha, Hamas spokesperson between 1991 and 1999.[43] In addition, Hamas enjoyed financial support from the oil-rich Gulf during the late 1980s and 1990s, especially when the PLO under Yasser Arafat had supported Saddam's invasion of Kuwait.

In Jordan, Hamas has had a tumultuous relationship with the Hashemite regime. Ibrahim Ghosha, the former Hamas spokesperson, admits the close ties with the Jordanian branch of the Muslim Brothers, and an initial understanding was developed between the regime and Hamas in 1992–93. For the Hashemite regime, the main objective of dealing with Hamas was to avoid any armed activity or support for violent action from Jordanian territory.[44] However, the relationship was never stable. Several Hamas leaders were detained and removed from Jordanian territory in the second half of the 1990s, including Ghosha and Mash'al. However, King Hussein of Jordan was given credit for securing the release of Ahmad Yassin, the founder of Hamas, from an

[41] Khaled Hroub, 'A New Hamas Through Its New Documents', *Journal of Palestine Studies*, Vol. 35, No. 4 (Summer 2006), p. 6.

[42] Khalid Mish'al, 'The Making of a Palestinian Islamist Leader.' Interview by Mouin Rabbani, *Journal of Palestine Studies*, Vol. 37, No. 3 (Spring 2008), p. 68

[43] Ibid., p. 68; Ibrahim Ghosha, '*Muraja'at* (Revisions)' Interview by Azzam al-Tamimi, al-Hiwar Channel, episode three, March 2008.

Israeli jail and saving the life of Khalid Mash'al after a failed attempt on the latter's life in 1997.[45]

Hamas also enjoys official support and backing from two regional powers, the Islamic Republic of Iran and Ba'thist Syria. Ideological affinity and similar policies against Israel (or the 'Zionist Entity') form the basis of alliance with Iran, while pragmatism and mutual interests form the basis of alliance with Syria. The latter's Golan Heights are still occupied by Israel since 1967 and one way to exert pressure on the Israeli government is to support Hamas, Hizbullah and other anti-Israel organizations. This is despite the differences in ideology and sect between the Alawi-based, Ba'thist regime in Syria and the Sunni Islamist Hamas, an offshoot of the MB whose membership is punishable by death in Syria.

Finally, Hamas is at the core of a more recent intra-Arab division. Following the takeover of the Gaza Strip by Hamas in June 2007,[46] two opposing camps in Arab international relations were formed. The camps are known in the Arab media as the 'Axis of Resistance' and the 'Axis of Moderation'. The former is composed of Syria, Qatar, Hamas and Hizbullah. The latter is led by Egypt and Saudi Arabia, and includes Jordan and Palestinian Fatah within its ranks. As their titles suggest, the two camps have opposing perceptions regarding Israel and the peace process. The 'Axis of Resistance' does not exclude armed action against Israel as a mean for retaining lost territories; the 'Axis of Moderation' prefers peaceful negotiations. Another difference is over the relations between the Arab-majority states and Iran. Whereas most members of the 'Axis of Resistance' believe that Iran is a reliable ally and, for some members like Hizbullah, a source of inspiration and material support, the 'Axis of Moderation' believes that Iran has expansionist tendencies and is possibly more threatening than Israel. The rise and the behaviour of Hamas in 2006

---

[44] Ibid., episode 4; Ibrhaim Ghosha, *al-Mi'zana al-Hamra'* (The Red Mosque Tower), Beirut: Markaz al-Zaytuna, 2008.

[45] On 25 September 1997 Misha'al was the target of an assassination attempt by the Israeli Mossad. The attempt failed and immediately after the incident, Jordan's King Hussein demanded that Benjamin Netanyahu turn over the antidote for the nerve toxin. At first Netanyahu refused, but as the incident grew in political significance, American President Bill Clinton intervened and forced Netanyahu to turn over the antidote. Jordanian authorities later released the two Mossad agents in exchange for the release of Sheikh Ahmed Yassin.

[46] The Battle for Gaza was a military conflict between Hamas and Fatah. It resulted in Hamas remaining in control of the Gaza Strip after forcing Fatah out. The ICRC estimated that at least 118 people were killed and over 550 wounded during the fighting between 7 and 15 June 2007.

and 2007 can be seen as defining moments for the establishment of these two camps in Arab international relations.

*Movement building and violent radicalization process.* Hamas is an offshoot of the Muslim Brothers in Palestine (MBP), a movement whose branch in Gaza did not engage in armed activities[47] and focused instead on missionary work, Islamic education, charity, and social services until 1983.[48] Considering the strength of the occupier, that behaviour was tactical due to the lack of capacity. Additionally, Ahmad Yassin refused to join Fatah and the PLO as early as 1965. His reasons were both ideological and rational. The rational consideration was that Fatah's objective in the 1960s was to liberate Palestine 'from the outside' and that the Arab countries were not strong enough to do this.[49]

Between the early 1960s and until the late 1980s, the MBP focused on an indoctrination process that they refer to as the *tarbiyah* (bringing up). That involved different activities ranging from regular prayers at specific MBP mosques to monthly camping and weekly soccer games.[50] This was in addition to direct ideological lecturing and, for selected members, paramilitary training.

Small armed wings affiliated with the MBP existed at that time, most notably the Security Apparatus and the Military Apparatus.[51] They were both founded in 1980. The Security Apparatus had the task of collecting intelligence data in Gaza.[52] The Military Apparatus aimed at the protection of the MBP leadership and members against various security threats, including the Israeli Defence Forces (IDF) and rival Palestinian organizations. The two apparatuses merged in the mid-1980s to constitute the first united armed wing for the MBP, the predecessor of the Qassam Brigades which was known as the Palestinian Mujahidiyn (al-Mujahidun al-Falastiniyun).[53]

---

[47] There are a few exceptions, most notably between 1968 and 1970 where some members of the MBP operated from Jordan and attacked Israeli troops in the West Bank. Abdullah Azzam was one of the figures participating in these actions; see Abdullah Azzam, *Hamas:al-Judhur al-Tarikhiyya wa al-Mithaq* (Hamas: the historical roots and the Charter), Peshawar: Markaz Shahid Azzam, 1989.

[48] Jeroen Gunning, 'Peace with Hamas?' *International Affairs*, Vol. 80 No. 2 (2004), p. 246; Yassin, 'Hamas', episode 4.

[49] Ibid.

[50] Ibid., episode 6.

[51] Salah Shahade, '*Harakat Hamas..Shahada Tarikhiyya* (Hamas movement...A historical testimony)', anonymous Interviewer, Al-Jazeera Satellite Channel, 31 July 2002.

[52] Ibid.

[53] Ibid., Muhammad al-Daif, '*fi Diyafat al-Bunduqiyya* ...(In the Company of the Gun)', Interviewed by Iyad al-Dauod, *Al-Jazeera Satellite Channel*, 3 July, 2007.

By 1982, Ahmad Yassin and other leading figures in the MBP were convinced that armed action from the Occupied Territories was the only way to liberate Palestine.[54] Therefore, they started buying large amounts of arms in 1983. However, Israeli security strikes delayed the final decision for executing military operations until 17 November 1987.[55] A number of reasons were behind the turn to violent action. On one side, the MBP leadership decided in 1982 that there were enough indoctrinated men ready to fight and enough moral and material support from the outside. In other words, there were sufficient resources mobilized in the 1980s by comparison with the 1960s, when Ahmad Yassin and other leaders refused armed action. This was an addition to many other obvious factors facilitating mobilization and recruitment, including the Israeli occupation and the religious rhetoric. The socioeconomic factor was quite significant. Sheikh Yassin recalls how that factor caused mosque Imams to collaborate with Hamas: 'they were not scared of the Israelis because the salary that the latter gave them is not enough to buy lunch.'[56]

*Izz al-Din al-Qassam Brigades: the armed wing of Hamas (1992–2009).* On 1 January 1992, Hamas officially declared the existence of an armed wing that bore the name 'Izz al-Din al-Qassam Brigade'. Historically, Izz al-Din al-Qassam was a Sunni Muslim preacher and a leading figure in the campaign against the British Mandate and the Zionist migration to Palestine between 1921 and 1935. He founded the Black Hand movement, which was designated by the British as a terrorist organization. The organization fought the British and al-Qassam himself was killed in a firefight with the British authorities in November 1935. Abdullah Schleifer describes the circumstances surrounding his death and its symbolism to the Palestinians and the Arabs: '... surrounded he told his men to die as martyrs, and opened fire. His defiance and manner of his death (which stunned the traditional leadership) electrified the Palestinian people. Thousands forced their way past police lines at the funeral in Haifa, and the secular Arab nationalist parties invoked his memory as the symbol of resistance. It was the largest political gathering ever to assemble in mandatory Palestine.'[57] Naming the armed wing of Hamas after a

---

[54] Yassin, 'Hamas', episode 4.

[55] Ibid.

[56] Ibid., episode 6.

[57] Abdullah Schleifer, 'Izz al-Din al-Qassam: Preacher and *Mujahid*', in Edmund Burke (ed.), *Struggle and Survival in the Modern Middle East*, London and New York: I.B. Tauris, 1993, p. 164.

Syrian-born[58] Islamic theologian/fighter is full of symbolism—not the least aim of which is capturing the Arab, Islamic, and armed resistance dimensions of their mandate.

The founder of the Qassam Brigades was Salah Shahade. With family ties to Jaffa, Shahade was born in the Beach Refugee Camp in Gaza in 1952. A graduate of the Social Services Institute in Alexandria, he was recruited by the Egyptian Muslim Brothers during his studies. In 1980 Shahade founded two small armed apparatuses (security and military), and he was able to unite them at a later stage under the name of the Palestinian Mujahideen,[59] an organization which ultimately became the nucleus of the QB. The latter were declared officially in 1992 after Deir al-Balah operation, in which a group from the QB killed an Israeli settler[60] in south of Gaza.

Throughout the 1990s, the QB engaged in a series of suicide attacks that peaked in 1996 (59 operations). This peak in activities came after the assassination of a leading QB commander and chief bomb-maker, Yahya Ayyash, by the Israeli Shin Bet on 5 January 1996.[61] The QB operations between 1993 and 1996 were largely responsible for undermining peace talks between the Palestinian Authority (PA) and the Labour-led Israeli government. Towards the end of the 1990s, armed attacks dropped significantly. There was only one suicide bombing in 1998 and none in 1999. This was a result of coordination between Israeli, Palestinian and Jordanian security services, the death of several top bomb-makers and commanders within Hamas, and limited Palestinian public support for the movement.

However, Hamas and the QB survived the storm. The collapse of the peace process, Ariel Sharon's visit to Temple Mount/Noble Sanctuary, and the ensuing second Intifada gave a new role to the QB, a much more significant one by comparison with the first Intifada. According to the Qassam Brigades Information Office (QBIO), Hamas-affiliated predecessors of the QB carried out 53 operations during the first Intifada (between 1988 and 1991). During the second Intifada, the QB executed 80 operations in 2000 alone and a stagger-

---

[58] Al-Qassam was born in the City of Jableh, in the northern Latakia Governorate of Syria. When he was born, modern (initially mandated) Syria did not exist and the region was still under the Ottomans.

[59] Shahade, 'Harakat'

[60] In Communiqué No. 1 dated 1 January 1992, QB claims that the victim was an Israeli security official.

[61] Khalid Mash'al, 'Hamas Perspective on The Movement's Evolving Role.' Interview by Mouin Rabbani, *Journal of Palestine Studies*, Vol. 37, No. 4 (summer 2008), p. 62.

ing 707 operations between 2000 and 2004.[62] Overall, the QB and their predecessors carried out 1,237 violent operations between 1988 and 2007, killing 1,270 persons. The overwhelming majority of those operations were suicide attacks (617 operations), carried out mainly in 2001 (144 operations) and 2002 (155).[63]

Organizationally, the QB are currently led by Muhammad al-Daif, who has been on the top of the Israeli most wanted list since 1992.[64] Ahmad al-Ja'bari is second-in-command after al-Daif according to Israeli claims;[65] however, he refuses to give himself any official titles.[66] The organizational structure of the QB is secretive and constantly evolving.[67] However, al-Daif explains that the leading executive unit in the QB is the military council.[68] In addition, Al-Ja'bari asserts that the QB have multiple training units, including scientific development, cultural and educational, and 'counter-terrorism' ones. The training of QB members is provided by what is referred to as the Salah Shahade Military Academy (SSMA).[69] Also, there have been efforts to establish a 'military judicial system' within the QB.[70] The QB's leadership refuses to give the number of their members; Israel's estimate is in the range of 40,000.

Militarily, the QB constantly prove to be credible and resilient. Their Gaza branch was able to resist many IDF incursions in 2003 and 2004. After the electoral victory of Hamas in January 2006 and the kidnapping of the IDF soldier Gilad Shalit, mounting international pressures on the PA to disarm the QB and intense political rivalry between Fatah and Hamas resulted in the Battle of Gaza in June 2007. The QB were able to force Fatah out and control the Gaza strip. Finally, despite killing many of their members and some of their commanders, the IDF failed to dismantle or destroy the QB during the brief and brutal reinvasion of Gaza in December 2008 and January 2009.

---

[62] Qassam Brigades Information Office. *'Ihsa'iyat Tafsiliya lil Qatla al-Sahaina* (Detailed Statistics for Zionists Deaths)', report No. 7, 7 June 2008.

[63] Ibid.

[64] al-Dauod, 'fi Diyafat.'

[65] Ibid. Some Israeli repots claims that he was killed in the recent Israeli incursions in Gaza in December 2008 (see for example Yaakov Yatz, and Khaled Abu Toameh, 'Hamas chief of staff may be dead' *Jerusalem Post*, 29 December 2008, 1). There was no confirmation by Hamas.

[66] Al-Ja'bari, 'fi Diyafat.'

[67] Ibid.

[68] Ibid.

[69] Unnamed administrator in SSMA, 'fi Diyafat.'

[70] Al-Ja'bari, 'fi Diyafat.'

## Transformations within Hamas (1999–2009)

Since the mid-1990s, there have been several transformations in the behaviour, ideology and rhetoric of Hamas. Although the 1988 Charter clearly calls for the liberation of all the territory covered by the Mandated Territory of Palestine (from the Mediterranean Sea to the Jordan River), Sheikh Ahmad Yassin declared in 1999 that Hamas is willing to offer a ten-year *hudna*: a type of truce whose conditions are well developed and explained in Islamic jurisprudence and resonate well in Islamic culture. For Hamas, the main condition for a *hudna* was Israel's withdrawal to the 1967 borders.[71] Since 1999, the *hudna* proposal had several reinforcements from various leaders within Hamas. In Gaza, Yassin repeated the same proposal in 2002 and adopted a short truce in June 2003. Although that truce ended quickly, Yassin stated his willingness to renegotiate a ceasefire in October 2003, if a proposal was offered.[72] Ismail Abu Shanab, whose assassination sealed the end of the June 2003 ceasefire, stated clearly in an interview that 'the practical solution for us is to have a state alongside Israel... When we build a Palestinian state, we will not need these militias; all the needs for attack will stop. Everything will change into a civil life.'[73]

In 2007, after the takeover of Gaza by the QB and in the middle of the rivalry with Fatah, Ahmad Yusuf, the political adviser to Prime Minister Ismail Haniya, asserted that the ideology of Hamas might see some major changes because 'politics can achieve what armed action cannot...if it failed then we can go back to resistance.'[74] In the same interview, Yusuf strongly criticized al Qaeda's behaviour, asserted that Hamas accepted a Palestinian State within the 1967 borders, and restated the late Sheikh Yassin's ten-year truce offer, adding that the truce would be renewable.[75] In 2009 Hamas' Prime Minister Haniya declared during a joint press conference with the former US President Jimmy Carter that he supported the establishment of a Palestinian State within the Borders of 1967, with Jerusalem as its capital, and that he 'will push in the direction of fulfilling that dream.'[76] In Damascus, Khalid Mash'al

---

[71] Yassin. 'Harakat', episode 7.

[72] Ahmad Yassin, 'Sanabhath al-Hudna...(We will study the truce)', Interview by Mustafa al-Sawaf. *Islam online*, 27 October 2003.

[73] Gutman *et al.*, 'Hamas official has a vision of living next to Israel.'

[74] Ahmad Yusuf, '*Fikr Hamas qad Yashhad Yahawulat* (The ideology of Hamas might witness transformations)', *Dunya al-Watan*, 14 March 2007, p. 1.

[75] Ibid.

[76] Abdul Rahman Abu Hakma, 'Hamas...Wada'a lil Silah (Hamas...farewell to arms).' *Shihan*, 17 June 2009, p. 7.

declared in an interview that Hamas would be a part of any final solution to the Palestinian issue and the Palestinian state should be within the 1967 borders.[77] Overall, many Hamas leaders recognize that the compromise regarding Israel's existence may be a necessity in the interest of national unity and organizational survival.[78]

Beyond rhetoric, Hamas participated in the 2005 parliamentary elections, a remarkable shift from its 1996 position. The response of Hamas back in 1996 was that the parliamentary elections were unacceptable because they were based on an illegitimate process (the Oslo Agreements).[79] Hamas, therefore, boycotted the elections, harshly criticized them, and continued a spoiling violent campaign. But in 2005, Hamas decided to participate in the elections.[80] Additionally, Hamas issued an electoral platform that stressed building 'an advanced Palestinian civil society based on political pluralism and the rotation of power.' Throughout the platform there was not much reference to Islam. Khaled Hroub, for example, concludes that except for the 'Religious Guidance and Preaching Section' in the platform, 'Islamic references are overshadowed by clauses that would be standard in any secular document.'[81]

The electoral platform was not the only document contradicting and possibly overruling the 1988 Hamas Charter. Two other documents followed the same lines: the National Unity Government Programme (NUGP) and the Hamas Cabinet Platform (HCP). The first was a programme proposed by Hamas, following its electoral victory, for power sharing with other factions, most notably Fatah. The second document was declared on 27 March 2006, after the collapse of the national unity government in 2006. Both documents reflected Hamas' new stances. In addition to calling for pluralism and coalition government, the NUGP especially hovered around the concept of the two-state solution without any hint about the 'liberation of the entire land of Palestine' or the 'destruction of Israel' as found in the 1998 Charter.[82]

To recap, Hamas transformations and changing rhetoric between 1999 and 2009 were related to three issues: electoral democracy, peace process, and

---

[77] Masha'al, 'A Hamas Perspective', p. 76.

[78] Gunning, 'Peace with Hamas?' p. 249.

[79] For more on the Oslo agreements and Hamas behaviour regarding them see Shaul Mishal and Avraham Sela, *The Palestinian Hamas: Vision, Violence and Coexistence*, New York: Columbia University Press, 2000.

[80] The perception then changed after the Israeli withdrawal from Gaza and the practical collapse of the Oslo process.

[81] Hroub, 'The New Hamas', p. 8.

[82] Ibid., p. 17

political violence. On the first issue, there has been agreement to participate in the electoral process, and even acceptance of elements from constitutional liberalism like supporting a Christian female candidate until she became the mayor of Ramallah in 2005.[83] Regarding the peace process, Hamas also changed its demands, from liberating the whole of Palestine via armed action to accepting a Palestinian State within the 1967 borders. Hamas also transformed its methods of achieving goals by accepting that 'politics' is a means, if not necessarily the means, of achieving its objective. Political violence then becomes another means for achieving ends—not necessarily the only practical and legitimate means as implied in the 1988 Charter.

Finally, there are a few insignificant changes regarding the stance on terrorism and political violence. For example, some statements from the Hamas political leadership imply that there can be serious shifts in the organization's behaviour and ideology with regard to political violence. Ahmad Yusuf for instance stated that if Hamas can achieve its objectives[84] via peaceful politics then there will be no need for armed action.[85] In 2006, Ismail Haniya declared he would not order any terrorist operations in Israel and would never send any of his nine children on suicide bombing missions.[86] Despite those statements from the political leadership in Gaza,[87] most of the statements from other leaders imply a more radical, pro-violence stance. Additionally, the QB and the QBIO are more consistent in using escalatory language, more recently against the security services of the PA in the West Bank (which they refer to as 'criminal gangs of Abbas').[88]

## Comparative Islamist de-radicalization: Hamas and the Muslim Brothers

If there are real transformations within Hamas and if the movement may possibly be heading the way of Fatah and other PLO factions into compromise,

---

[83] Saad Eddine Ibrahim, 'Hamas wa Tariq al-Zaytun (Hamas and the way of the olives).' *Al-Masry al-Youm*, 29 April 2006, p. 5.

[84] He mentioned the objectives: a state within the 1967 borders, the release of prisoners, and the right of return.

[85] Yusuf, 'Fikr Hamas', p. 1.

[86] Abu Hakma, 'Hamas...Wada'an', p. 7.

[87] Sometimes the political leadership in Damascus has a different stance, a harder one when it comes to the issue of political violence.

[88] Qassam Brigades, '*Ightiyal al-Wakala al-Lahdiya lil Qa'id al-Qasami* (Qassam Leader assassinated by the Lahdist agency', Communiqué No. 0905–09. 31 May 2009, p. 1.

then two questions arise. The first is, why did Hamas contemplate that route? And the second is, what is hindering the path to comprehensive de-radicalization? Space does not permit detailed elaboration, and so this section will argue briefly that the model of de-radicalization that was introduced earlier in the chapter is applicable to Hamas. This means that external interactions with pro-peace and anti-violence international players, organizations and figures, combined with repression from Israel and other international powers, have led the leadership of Hamas to a process of strategic calculations, political learning, and reevaluation of its worldviews. As is evident from this chapter, and from the statements of the Hamas political leadership, some changes have already happened, but not to the extent of de-radicalization and abandonment of political violence. Inducements, in the form of addressing some of the socioeconomic and political grievances, as well as internal dialogue between the layers of Hamas, including primarily the QB, are essential for a comprehensive de-radicalization process.

To judge from previous cases of armed Islamist and non-Islamist de-radicalization, usually tensions, and sometimes outright conflict and internal organizational violence, take place between the armed wing(s) and the political leadership, when the latter decides to de-radicalize.[89] Whereas the political leadership usually glorifies its armed elements during the periods of violent struggle, that same leadership is most likely to abandon the armed wing(s) and blame it for 'faults', bloodshed, unpopularity and other negative aspects during the periods of de-radicalization and relative moderation. This is illustrated by the case-studies of the Muslim Brothers in Egypt and several others.

To assess the potential for a successful de-radicalization of Hamas, this section will provide an analytical overview of the attempts to dismantle the armed wings of the mother organization, the Muslim Brothers in Egypt. As previously mentioned, the attempts to dismantle the Special Apparatus (SA) of the MB in 1951 and 1964 were unsuccessful. However, a renewed effort between 1969 and 1973 not only ended the existence of armed wings within the Egyptian Muslim Brothers, but also took the very legitimacy for their existence away from them.

Several lessons can be learned from the Egyptian MB and can be applied to their Palestinian branch. However, to control for the foreign presence, an essential variable affecting de-radicalization and demobilization attempts, the analysis here will focus on the only de-radicalization attempt that took place

---

[89] Examples include the cases of the Egyptian Muslim Brothers, the Algerian Armed Islamic Group (GIA), and, among non-Islamists, the Irish Republican Army (IRA).

under a foreign (British) presence in Egypt. That was the attempt between 1951 and 1953. Although it was a failure, the reasons behind such a failure can be useful in assessing the prospects for de-radicalization of Hamas and dismantling of the QB. Finally, some references will be made to the other two attempts, especially the successful one in 1973.

Al-Banna had the idea of establishing an armed wing for the MB in the late 1930s. From the very beginning, the Palestinian issue was at the core of the idea. Most historical accounts show that the establishment of the SA in 1940 was a reaction to the failures of the MB to gather arms and militarily assist the Arab uprising in Palestine in 1936.[90] Starting in 1946, the SA conducted several operations against both national and colonial targets, culminating in the assassination of the Egyptian Prime Minister Mahmud Fahmy al-Nuqrashi in December 1948 and a series of attacks on Egyptian Jewish targets as a reaction to the first Arab-Israeli war.[91] The SA was also involved in the armed resistance against the British in the Suez Canal area in 1951.[92] Outside Egypt, the SA played a role in the Arab-Israeli conflict of 1948 with more than 2,000 MB volunteers and SA operatives fighting alongside the Palestinians.[93]

As noted, the leadership of the Egyptian Muslim Brothers attempted to de-radicalize the group three times: between 1951 and 1953, between 1964 and 1965 and between 1969 and 1973. As opposed to the de-radicalization attempts of 1951 and 1964, the third attempt (1969–73) was relatively successful. In 1951, the attempt failed disastrously. It led to deep divisions within the MB that culminated in the assassination of Sayyid Fayez, the SA commander in charge of the dismantling process, in November 1953.[94] It also led to a mutiny in which the supporters of the SA stormed al-Hudaybi's house to force his resignation and then occupied and staged a sit-in in the General

[90] Salah Shadi, *Safahat Min al-Tarikh* (Pages from History), Kuwait: al-Shu'a', 1981, p. 128; Richard Mitchell, *The Society of the Muslim Brothers*, Cambridge University Press, 1969, p. 171.

[91] Kamal, *al-Nuqat*, p. 189.

[92] Abdul Azim Ramadan, *Al-Ikhwan al-Muslimun wa al-Tanzim al-Sirri* (The Muslim Brothers and the Secret Organization), Cairo: al-Hay'a al-'amma lil Kitab, 1993, 50, 227. Kamal, *al-Nuqat*, p. 269.

[93] Ramadan, p. 75; Abbas Al-Sisi, *Fi Qafilat al-Ikhwan al-Muslimiyn* (In the caravan of the Muslim Brothers), Asyut, 1986, pp. 178–84.

[94] Mahmud Al-Sabbagh, *Al-Taswib al-Amin lima Katabahu Ba'du al-Qada al-Sabiqiyn 'an al-Tanzim al-Khaz lil Ikhwan al-Muslimiyn* (The honest correction for what some of the former commanders have written on the Special Organization of the Muslim Brothers), Cairo: Al-Turath al-Islami, 1998, p. 71.

Headquarters of the MB in Cairo.[95] In the end, the process of de-radicalization was cancelled by the MB leadership, which opted for a less ambitious restructuring process.

The third attempt, however, was relatively successful. Hasan al-Hudaybi took the decisions to permanently forgo any military or paramilitary activities and, in contrast to the 1950s and early 1960s, he did not face any organizational opposition from the leaders of the armed wings. The Egyptian MB issued the book *Preachers Not Judges* in 1969 to support the decision to de-radicalize theologically and ideologically.[96] The book represented a counterargument mostly against Takfiri ideologies and, to a lesser extent, Jihadi ones.[97]

The MB, however, still supports armed action against non-Muslim 'occupiers' in Muslim-majority states and territories, especially in Palestine. This stance, however, is not usually consistent. The first attempt by the MB to disarm and de-radicalize the group took place under the British military presence in Egypt. Al-Hudaybi clearly stated in an interview with the *al-Jumhur al-Masry* newspaper in 1951 that the MB was only interested in spiritual power, while material power was exclusively the domain of the government.[98] He also denied the involvement of the MB in fighting the British in the Canal Zone in 1951[99] and was quoted as saying that armed resistance would not

---

[95] Shadi, *Safahat*, pp. 104–6.

[96] Hasan al-Hudaybi, *Du'ah La Qudah* (Preachers Not Judges), Kuwait: al-Faysal al-Islami, 1985.

[97] The latter thought was not fully developed in the late 1960s and early 1970s when *Preachers Not Judges* was written.

[98] Mitchell, *The Society*, p. 85; Ahmad al-Baquri *Baqaya Dhizkrayat* (Remains of Memories), Cairo: Markaz al-Ahram, 1988, p. 92; Abdul Azim Ramadan, *Al-Ikhwan al-Muslimun wa al-Tanzim al-Sirri* (The Muslim Brothers and the Secret Organization), Cairo: al-Haya al-Amma lil Kitab, 1993, p. 94; Farid Abdul Khaliq, *Al-Ikhwan al-Muslimun Kama Yarahum Farid Abdul Khaliq* (The Muslim Brothers as perceived by Farid Abdul Khaliq). Interview by Ahmad Mansur in Shahid ala al-Asr, Al-Jazeera Satellite Channel, 7 December 2003 to 7 March 2004, episode 8; Hasan Al-Hudaybi, 'Hiwar Ma' Hasan al-Hudaybi (Interview with Hasan al-Hudaybi)', *al-Jumhur al-Masry*, 15 October 1951, p. 3.

[99] Al-Hudaybi, 'Hiwar Ma' Hasan al-Hudaybi' (Interview with Hasan al-Hudaybi), p. 3. That was however inaccurate, since the MB's leadership in al-Isma'iliyya declared *jihad* against the British in the same year (see for example Mitchell 1979, p. 191; see also the commentary of Abu Ruqayq on Mitchell 1979, p. 192). Also, the involvement of the SA/SO and its future commander Yusuf Tal'at (1953–54) in the Canal Zone has been well documented. Mitchell mentions that at least 300 MB and SA members participated in the Canal fighting in 1951: see Mitchell, *The Society*, p. 193.

lead to the departure of the British from Egypt.[100] In post-Saddam Iraq the Islamic Party, the MB's official branch in Iraq, has cooperated with the United States and participated in various governments under US military presence, rather than engaging in armed resistance. Tariq al-Hashimi, the former head of the Islamic Party, is currently the Vice-President of Iraq. This shows that it is possible for a Muslim Brotherhood autonomous branch to move to de-radicalize under foreign military presence, as well as to cooperate with the occupier.

Certain conditions still apply in the case of Hamas, however. In any successful Islamist de-radicalization process, the leadership has a crucial role. A leadership with theological credentials,[101] a history of 'struggle',[102] and a senior standing[103] in the organization is able to exert considerable influence in supporting de-radicalization processes.[104] Also, a leader who has a history of rising above organizational factionalism would be more likely to influence de-radicalization efforts.[105] In Hamas, the major 'centres of power' are the political leadership in Gaza and Damascus and the leadership of the QB. Between these factions, there are considerable differences over major issues, like the borders of the state of Palestine, Israel's existence, the legitimacy and feasibility of armed confrontation with the PA, and the role of the armed wing. For example, whereas some of the leaders on the 1967 borders and the *de facto* recognition of Israel adopted the stance previously mentioned, others like Mahmoud al-Zahar, the Foreign Minister in the Hamas government of Ismail Haniya, state that Hamas 'will not concede an inch of historical [mandated territory] Palestine.'[106] Military escalations with the PA and Fatah and the takeover of Gaza via armed confrontation also caused severe internal tensions, this

---

[100] Ibid.

[101] These could range from a degree from a prestigious university like al-Azhar of Egypt (for example, Umar abd al-Rahman and other IG leaders) or Umm al-Qura in Mecca (for example, Safar al-Hawali) to informal self-teaching and, based on that, a proven command of theological knowledge and issuing of *fatwas* (as for example al-Maqdisi of Jordan and the al-Sharif of al-Jihad Organization).

[102] Usually participating in armed action against a perceived 'secular', repressive regime or against foreign forces would count as a history of struggle in the eyes of the followers.

[103] Like being the emir, the former emir or a member in the leadership council (usually called the consultative council or the elite council in armed Islamist movements).

[104] Ashour, *The De-Radicalization of Jihadists*, p. 137.

[105] Ibid., p. 139.

[106] Mahmoud al-Zahar. 'Hiwar Ma' al-Zahar (Interview with al-Zahar).' Interview by Muhammad Mostafa, *al-Ahram*, 14 June 2004, p. 7.

time arising from criticism by the leadership in the West Bank, who perceived the actions in Gaza as unnecessary and exposing them to the risk of Fatah's reprisals in a region where the QB is not as powerful as it is in Gaza.[107]

Although there are common accusations that the Hamas politicians based in Damascus are the 'hardliners' compared to the political leaders in Gaza, the factional map of Hamas is much more complex and dynamic. In general, however, the political leadership in both Gaza and Damascus employs a more pragmatic rhetoric than the one employed by the QB and the QBIO, where the emphasis is more on '*jihad*', 'victory' and/or 'martyrdom'. At all times, Hamas strongly denies that is any internal division among its leadership, and the movement is quite successful in keeping its internal differences away from the public, the media, and even their own grassroots and junior ranks. Indeed, the movement has not witnessed any major splits.

## Conclusion: a de-radicalization of Hamas?

In light of the previous model of de-radicalization and the overview of Hamas history, structure, ideology and behaviour, and the suggested comparative de-radicalization case of the SA, it can be concluded that some of the necessary conditions for de-radicalization are present. Those are mainly repression and internal and external interaction with the 'other'.[108] However, when it comes to leadership and inducements, those variables are well below what is required for de-radicalization. A charismatic, unifying figure, above factionalism, who can give legitimacy to a de-radicalization process, seems to be non-existent within Hamas currently. Ahmad Yassin, the founder of the movement, could have played that role at the right timing. However, he was assassinated by Israel in March 2004. Eliminating spiritual leaders (as opposed to organizational commanders) of a militant movement could be perceived as a media/psychological victory for a government but would make a comprehensive or a substantive de-radicalization process less likely to succeed. Those leaders are necessary to legitimatize de-radicalization and initiate a genuine dialogue with their followers (internal interaction) to limit mutiny and splintering. As the case of Hamas and others clearly demonstrate, decapitating the spiritual head of the movement will not necessarily mean a collapse of the 'headless' movement. Decapitation of spiritual leaders, however, would make negotiations to

---

[107] Ahmad Shaki, '*Khilafat Dakhil Hamas...wa la Inshiqaq* (Divisions within Hamas...but no splits)', *Al-Akhbar*, 11 February 2008, p. 3.
[108] Including international organizations and secular movements and figures.

de-radicalize less likely to succeed because of factionalism. Therefore, in the absence of a leadership with similar credentials like that of Yassin, and in the absence of more worthwhile selective inducements, a comprehensive de-radicalization of Hamas will be less likely to occur in the near future.

# 9

# Armed Groups and Fragmentation and Globalization in Iraq

*Eric Herring*

What are the relationships between violent non-state actors (VNSAs), world politics and the state in post-invasion Iraq? That is the question addressed in this chapter. VNSAs are diverse actors which can be a resource for state building but can also threaten the state in various ways, for example by taking control of economic activity and having a vested interest in continuing armed conflict to continue controlling it, or by developing a base of popular support so that they challenge the state's claim to a monopoly of legitimate violence. World politics is usually portrayed as playing contradictory roles in the relationships between VNSAs and the state. On the one hand, economic globalization creates demands on the state with which it may be unable to cope, thus fuelling the rise of VNSAs, and external backing for VNSAs may come from other states pursuing regional rivalries or global agendas. On the other hand, the 'international community' of states and international organizations seek ways of co-opting, marginalizing or defeating to strengthen the state, using a range of economic, military and political means. On top of this, the end of the Cold War and the coming of the US 'war on terror' (and continuing policies which avoid that phrase) produced a tendency to frame many VNSAs as so threatening and illegitimate that they must be eliminated by any means available. While some states play on this to secure US backing, that backing can generate support for VNSAs.

There is an extensive literature on the existence of all of these dynamics. This chapter seeks to make a contribution to the literature at two levels. First, it proposes an ontology placing much more emphasis on the overlap between VNSAs, the state and globalising forces, and their mutual constitution, and, related to that, more consideration of contemporary trends in globalization. At the same time it suggests referring to armed groups rather than VNSAs, and conceiving the Iraqi state as fragmented and globalising rather than failed or fragile. Second, it explores how these general themes play out distinctively in the case of Iraq and argues that armed groups are both responding and contributing to the fragmentation and globalisation of the Iraqi state. This includes an assessment of whether the reduction in violence in Iraq since September 2007 indicates that Iraq's fragmentation is being overcome as its globalisation proceeds.

## The Iraqi state: failed, fragile—or fragmented and globalizing

A widely held view up to the end of 2007 was that Iraq was a failed state, that this was triggered by the invasion (because of pre-existing weakness from the Saddam Hussein era, or else because of blunders in US occupation policy) and that armed groups filled the vacuum that resulted. It was seen as, and for some still is, a failed state in terms of not meeting the basic needs of most of the population or not exercising the most elementary of functions in external relations as well as domestic order. The international policy responses then clustered around a range of options.

The containment perspective was that the failed Iraqi state was replaced by myriad armed groups of many types which blur the economic and political in their motivations and whose interests depend on preventing the re-establishment of effective state authority. The associated international policy response was to contain the threat such actors pose to the outside world in terms of population movements, the informal economy, terrorism and disruption of oil supplies. The tools of this containment were selective armed intervention, humanitarian aid, deals with local armed groups, and rubber-stamping by the vestigial powerless 'state'. Iraqi state failure was often treated as something that could not be overcome for the foreseeable future and so must be managed. The partitionist perspective also concluded that the Iraqi state was a failed state. However, the armed groups were seen as clustering into ethno-sectarian Kurdish, Sunni Arab and Shi'a ones in the north, centre and south of Iraq respectively, which could not be defeated. In this case, the task of international actors was seen as assisting in the emergence of these three new states, with partition as a necessary condition for effective state building to begin.

The state building perspective has a more positive view of the situation and has become the predominant view on account of the reduction in violence since late 2007. In this framing, the Iraqi state is fragile rather than failed, with the state meeting some basic needs and carrying out some external and internal functions. With international assistance the Iraqi state has, according to this view, a reasonable chance of overcoming the armed groups it faces by co-opting, defeating or marginalizing them, and is making progress in doing so. For some, state building is most likely to be effective and lasting if carried out by an authoritarian centralized state, at least in the centre and south. For others, Iraq's future will be more democratic and loosely federal (if not particularly liberal), either on ethno-sectarian lines (because of the incoherence and weakness of an Iraqi identity and suspicion of centralized coercive power as a legacy of Saddam Hussein's rule) or with a range of versions that cut across ethno-sectarian lines (according to governorate-level political views on the best form and degree of federalism).

All of these perspectives are represented in the literature in various ways, but they are ideal types and so I will not oversimplify by forcing the various contributions into any particular category.[1] Any particular author's view may cut across some of the categories, and their views may evolve. In particular, as of the last quarter of 2007, with a dramatic fall in the amount of violence, more may accept that Iraq is a fragile rather than a failed state.

It is more helpful to categorize Iraq as a fragmented state, that is, one in which there is some state authority but a great deal of dispute over the location of that authority and over means of resolving such disputes.[2] The concept

---

[1] Relevant studies include Frederick W. Kagan, *Iraq: The Way Ahead—Phase IV Report*, American Enterprise Institute, 24 March 2008; Liam Anderson and Gareth Stansfield, *The Future of Iraq: Dictatorship, Democracy or Division?*, London: Palgrave Macmillan, 2004; David C. Hendrickson and Robert W. Tucker, 'Revisions in Need of Revising: What Went Wrong in the Iraq War', *Survival*, 47, 2005, pp. 7–32; Ahmed S. Hashim, *Insurgency and Counter-Insurgency in Iraq*, London: Hurst and Ithaca: Cornell University Press, 2006; Daniel L. Byman and Kenneth M. Pollack, *Things Fall Apart: Containing the Spillover From an Iraqi Civil War*, Washington: Brookings Institution Press, 2007; Reidar Visser and Gareth Stansfield (eds), *An Iraq of its Regions: Cornerstones of a Federal Democracy?*, London: Hurst, 2007; Toby Dodge, 'The Causes of US Failure in Iraq', *Survival*, 49, 2007, pp. 85–106; and Ali Al Allawi, *The Occupation of Iraq: Winning the War, Losing the Peace*, London: Yale University Press, 2007.

[2] This argument builds on Eric Herring and Glen Rangwala, 'Iraq, Imperialism and Global Governance', *Third World Quarterly*, 26, 2005, pp. 667–83; Eric Herring and Glen Rang-

of state fragmentation has two advantages over notions of state failure or fragility. First, it rejects the ontology of VNSAs, the Iraqi state and the international (such as the US, regional states, international organisations and transnational corporations) as essentially separate entities which interact and sometimes overlap. Instead, it involves more focus on their mutual constitution and varying degrees of overlap. To begin with, the armed groups in Iraq are not simply non-state: the line between them and the state is blurred and fluid. The same can be said in relation to armed groups and the international, as discussed below. Furthermore, there is a lot more to them than violence and often violence is not their primary instrument.

The term 'violence' often implies illegitimacy (though not in Weberian terms) in comparison with the force or war (distinct from violence) used by the state and international coalitions and actors with UN authority, but if they are blurred and mutually constitutive, that contrast is also undermined. Second, the concept of state fragmentation can be used to historicise this mutual constitution in relation to globalization, that is, the process by which all parts of the world are deeply connected and mutually constituted in all spheres (militarily, culturally and ideationally as well as economically and politically) so that the meaning of the local—including failure or fragility—is inevitably produced to a significant degree by this worldwide process, and vice versa.[3]

At this stage of world history, overcoming the fragmentation of political authority is less likely to produce a sovereign state (coherent, legitimate and legal political authority at the national level which can assert itself effectively against internal and external actors) than a governance state (coherent, legitimate and legal political authority involving corporate and public actors at the local, national and international levels, with local-local and local-international authority not necessarily mediated via the national).[4] Underlying this shift is

---

wala, *Iraq in Fragments: The Occupation and its Legacy*, London: Hurst and Ithaca: Cornell University Press, 2006, and Eric Herring, 'Neoliberalism Versus Peacebuilding in Iraq' in Neil Cooper, Michael Pugh and Mandy Turner (eds), *Whose Peace? Critical Perspectives on the Political Economy of Peace Building*, London: Palgrave Macmillan, 2008, pp. 47–64.

[3] See Tarak Barkawi, *Globalization and War*, Oxford: Rowman & Littlefield, 2006.

[4] This does not mean that advanced industrial political economies (even within the European Union) have seamlessly coordinated governance or that there is a direct link between decreased welfare and increased economic competitiveness. See Paul Hirst and Grahame Thompson, *Globalization in Question: The International Economy and the*

the neoliberal phase of capitalism, a phase that has been in crisis since 2007 owing to the global credit crunch. Neoliberalism may be coming to an end, replaced by a massive increase in state ownership and regulation in the financial sector, or it may be entering a new phase: it is too early to tell. In the neoliberal phase of capitalism, the welfare model of political economy characterized by the national state taking the lead in ensuring full employment, consumption and welfare, regulating business and correcting for market failure in a relatively closed national economy was increasingly squeezed out. Instead, the trend has been towards a neoliberal or competition political economy in which capital is provided with incentives such as deregulation to promote competitiveness, welfare is not a right but an instrument of promoting competitiveness, and decision-making is geared towards governance rather than sovereignty.[5]

Since the invasion, Iraq's welfare political economy, already in tatters from years of war, sanctions and misrule, has been targeted for neoliberalization, although a host of problems, not least armed opposition, have forced a scaling back of short-term ambitions if not long-term goals. The outcome is that most of the Iraqi population find themselves with very limited access to either a welfare or a competition political economy: they are part of the global South—marginalized, consuming minimally, uninsured, but policed and if necessary repressed. Meanwhile, elements of the Iraqi political and business elite have been internalizing neoliberalism and taking their place as part of the global North—deeply integrated into advanced capitalism, wealthy, and benefiting from containment and securitization of the global South. In other words, the fighting in Iraq is not just another civil or insurgent war: it derives

---

*Possibilities of Governance*, Cambridge: Polity, 1999, 2nd edn. Coherence is in effect managed conflict that can evolve to overwhelm a system's ability to manage it. Graham Harrison and, following him, Mark Duffield use the term 'governance states' in a slightly different way from mine in this chapter. They have in mind states in the South in which the 'international community' is thoroughly integrated to monitor their performance and shape their decisions in a top-down manner. See Graham Harrison, *The World Bank and Africa: The Construction of Governance States*, London: Routledge, 2004; also Mark Duffield, *Development, Security and Unending War. Governing the World of Peoples*, Cambridge: Polity Press, 2007. In this chapter, I do not build top-down control into the definition of a governance state. We do need a label for such states—perhaps something old-fashioned like 'client states'.

[5] See especially Bob Jessop, *The Future of the Capitalist State*, Cambridge: Polity, 2002, and David Harvey, *A Brief History of Neoliberalism*, Oxford University Press, 2005.

a crucial part of its meaning from the dynamics of global neoliberalization, though its meaning is not reducible to it.

Within this, the US is the single most influential actor globally, seeking to balance its own immediate interests with its longer-term interests of system maintenance and keeping the other leading actors on board. Armed opposition to the US occupation of Iraq is not necessarily opposition to Iraq's neoliberal globalization; although the two have tended to be linked, it has been more of the former than the latter. Furthermore, the militia-based Kurdish and Shi'a parties at the heart of the Iraqi government have shown themselves to be willing to rely on neoliberalized security in the form of some 182,000 private security contractors (118,000 of them Iraqi, 21,000 US and 43,000 citizens of third countries) from well over 100 companies who effectively have impunity in relation to Iraqis.[6] In comparison, the US had 158,000 troops in Iraq in March 2008.[7]

Three more observations are important. First, working with the definitions offered above, globalization does not necessarily produce governance. Post-invasion Iraq has been increasingly globalized, but that effort and opposition to it have for most of that time produced fragmentation writ large rather than governance. Second, this has been fragmentation and globalization from below as well as from above, because of connections to Jihadist and Islamic imaginaries and the global informal economy (not least the trade in smuggled oil), as the global justice movement has looked on with little affection for any of the main protagonists. Third, state building (a deliberate project by political agents to create a state) should be distinguished from state formation (the emergence of a state independently of the intentions of political agents to build a state), just as globalization as a deliberate project should be distinguished from globalization as a process that occurs even when political agents are not attempting to promote it.[8] In other words, as actors engage in immediate struggles for power and security, they can create systems of coherent

---

[6] Human Rights First, *Private Security Contractors at War: Ending the Culture of Impunity*, 2008; Jennifer K. Elsea and Nina M. Serafino, *Private Security Contractors in Iraq: Background, Legal Status, and Other Issues*, CRS Report for Congress, updated 11 July 2007. However, in February 2009 the Iraqi government refused to licence the private security firm Blackwater to continue to operate in Iraq because of the killing of 17 Iraqis in Baghdad in September 2007. Associated Press (AP), 'US nixes Blackwater contract for Iraq', CBS News, 10 March 2009.

[7] AP, 'Bush resolute in face of Iraq death toll', MSNBC, 24 March 2008.

[8] Bruce Berman and John Lonsdale, *Unhappy Valley: Conflict in Kenya and Africa*, London: James Currey, 1992.

authority without having had a prior long-term vision of a state with these struggles as means to achieve it. Alternatively, there may be a particular vision of the state that is frustrated by immediate struggles, so that a different type of state emerges. In the case of Iraq, the US attempt at state building and the opposition it has generated have been counter-productive for the formation of the post-Saddam Hussein state. The fragmented, globalized state that is forming is not the neoliberal governance state the US sought to create.

With this theoretical framework in place, I can now explore the interaction of the local, national and international in Iraq since the invasion in relation to these central themes.

## The interaction of the local, national and international

The Kurdish Autonomous Region (KAR) of Iraq has had self-rule since the Gulf War of 1991, including the post-invasion period, and has mostly remained outside the area of US military occupation. Collectively, the territory of the KAR plus Ninewa and At Tamim province are what I refer to as northern Iraq. The Kurdish Regional Government (KRG) which runs the KAR is part of Iraq's formal state structure, but to a considerable degree operates unilaterally. The area is unstable, as it is the site of multiple vectors of potential and ongoing armed conflict, and the semi-detached state structures have only fragile and shallow unity. This is a hindrance to the establishment of either a sovereign or a governance state in Iraq and belies the area's image among some as an island of peace and stability. The leaders of the two dominant Kurdish parties, Massoud Barzani of the Kurdistan Democratic Party (KDP) and Jalal Talabani of the Patriotic Union of Kurdistan (PUK), the latter also being President of Iraq, are both secular Sunni Kurds. They were able to operate in the north outside Baghdad's control through the 1990s, where they built up their militias, institutions and stable bases of support. Estimates of Kurdish *peshmerga* (meaning 'those who face death') fighters' numbers vary widely but tend to be around 140,000.[9] The PUK and KDP were unable to share power and engaged in armed conflict with each other intermittently through much of the 1990s and especially in 1994. In 1996, despite the atrocities of the gassing of Kurds in Halabja in 1988 and Saddam Hussein's broader murderous Anfal campaign against the Kurds, the KDP invited his forces into the region to push the PUK out of Irbil and Sulaymani-

[9] e.g. Reuters, 'Militias and security forces in Iraq', 19 Feb. 2007.

yya. For its part, the PUK allied with Iran against the KDP and retook Sulaymaniyya. Fighting could break out again between the PUK and KDP and, even if they do not fight each other, the *peshmerga* forces are primarily Kurdish rather than Iraqi in loyalty.[10]

Since the invasion in 2003 the PUK and KDP have generally managed to put on a broadly united front in the pursuit of as much autonomy, territory and resources as they can secure for their region. During 2005 they were finally able to cooperate sufficiently well to convene the KRG National Assembly, but they continued to run separate regional governments (the PUK in Sulaymaniyya and the KDP in Irbil and Dahuk) as they were unable to agree on a joint cabinet or the duration of its period of service before the holding of parliamentary elections.[11] In January 2006 they formally announced the unification of their government, but party divides remain locally.[12] Kurdish security forces (the *Asayish*) are divided between PUK and KDP forces which have their own prisons. These forces are mainly detaining Iraqi Kurds within the KAR, but the detainees include Iraqi Arabs taken from Kirkuk, Mosul, Salah ad Din, Anbar, Diyala and Baghdad.[13] Detainees are often tortured and denied due process.[14] Although the Kurdish *peshmerga* militia is formally part of the Iraqi armed forces and legal, in reality it is split between those forces loyal to Talibani and those loyal to Barzani, despite formal agreement to merge them in the Unification Agreement of 2006. The former forces are on occasion deployed elsewhere in Iraq such as Mosul and Baghdad. The latter generally remain in the Irbil area but were deployed to the Sinjar area west of Mosul in August 2007 by Barzani: this appears to have been an effort to win friends among the Yezidis of this area after over 500 local people were killed and injured in bomb attacks in one day.[15] Violence in

---

[10] Tom Lasseter, 'In Iraq, Kurdish militia has the run of oil-rich Kirkuk', McClatchy Newspapers, 16 Feb. 2007.

[11] Inur Levik, 'Talabani: visit of Barzani to White House is recognition of identity of Iraqi Kurdistan', *New Anatolian*, 30 Oct. 2005.

[12] Kurdistan Regional Government (KRG), 'Kurdish Regional Government Unification Agreement', 21 Jan. 2006.

[13] Human Rights Watch (HRW), *Caught in the Whirlwind: Torture and Denial of Due Process by the Kurdistan Security Forces*, July 2007, p. 9.

[14] HRW, ibid., pp. 8–9; UN Assistance Mission for Iraq, *Human Rights Report*, Jun. 2007, pp. 5–6, 28–32; Kamal Said Qadir, 'Iraqi Kurdistan's Downward Spiral', *Middle East Quarterly*, Summer 2007.

[15] 'Kurdish Peshmerga force deployed to Sinjar District for protection', *Voice of Iraq*, 17 August 2007.

Mosul, which may have an Arab majority (there is no recent census), was only sporadic until the US assault on Falluja in November 2004, at which point the largely Sunni Arab police force of the city either resigned or joined the insurgents. Kurdish *peshmerga* forces were subsequently deployed to recapture the town.[16] Since then, violence has become more widespread in Mosul with insurgents and their supporters in the police on one side lined up against US forces, Iraqi army units and Kurds on the other.

The KDP and PUK are struggling to manage a series of issues related to armed groups. First, Sunni Islamic fundamentalists are a threat to Yezidis and more secular Kurds alike. There are perhaps 200,000 Yezidis in mainly Kurdish areas of Iraq (though estimates vary widely), some of whom regard themselves as ethnically Kurdish while some see themselves as ethnically Arab. Yezidis are targeted by Islamic fundamentalists as unbelievers and devil-worshippers. In August 2007, four coordinated suicide bomb attacks killed 250 to 500 Yezidis in two villages near the border with Syria in Nineveh province.[17] The Islamic fundamentalist group Jund al-Islam (later renamed Ansar al-Islam before merging into the Ansar al-Sunnah Army umbrella group) carries out suicide bomb attacks on PUK and KDP offices, most recently in May 2007.[18]

Second, the fact that there are large Kurdish minorities and Kurdish armed groups in Iran and Turkey ensures there are ongoing international tensions. The Kurdistan Free Life Party (PEJAK) launches attacks into Iran from bases in the mountains of the Iran-Iraq border: it has around 1,000 fighters and appears to have links with the Kurdish Workers Party (PKK) which operates on the Turkey-Iran border and is thought to have some 3,000 fighters.[19] There are sporadic incursions and shellings by Iranian forces into Kurdish Iraq, targeted at the PEJAK, and others by Turkey (with US political support and military intelligence), targeted at the PKK. The KRG has distanced itself publicly from the PEJAK and the PKK but their exact relationship is unclear. In February 2008, again with US support, around 10,000 Turkish troops crossed the border into Northern Iraq. Kurds suspect that Turkey may be

---

[16] Charles Glass, 'Diary', *London Review of Books*, 16 Dec. 2004, pp. 34–5; Michael Howard, 'Insurgents step up the battle for Mosul', *Guardian*, 25 Nov. 2004.

[17] AP, 'Bombings are deadliest since Iraq war began', 15 Aug. 2007, MSNBC.

[18] Daniel Kimmage and Kathleen Ridolfo, *Iraqi Insurgent Media*, RFE/RFL Report, Jun. 2007, p. 41.

[19] AP with Today's Zaman, 'PKK-PEJAK Militants Train For Battle Against Iran', *The Journal of the Turkish Weekly*, 5 Feb. 2007.

sending a signal to the KRG not to move towards independence for the KAR or try to incorporate Kirkuk into the KAR.

The biggest issue in the north connecting local armed groups and international relations is the struggle for Kirkuk. The Kurdish political leaders secured guarantees of federal government in the new constitution, and their next goal was to win the referendum mandated in the constitution on whether or not Kirkuk should become part of the KAR. They had long laid claim to the oil-rich areas of Mosul in Ninewa province and especially Kirkuk province as parts of Kurdistan, against the objections of everyone else, including the Sunni Arabs, Turkmens and Assyrians. Escalation to large-scale violence between Kurds on the one hand and Turkmens and Arabs on the other in Kirkuk has been made more likely by the lack of a coherent and authoritative national level political process to address the issues in dispute.

Around 750,000 people live in the city of Kirkuk, making it Iraq's fourth largest city, behind Baghdad, Basra and Mosul. Figures for its ethno-sectarian composition are rough estimates and vary widely, especially given the degree of internal migration and displacement. In October 2005 between a third and something over a half the city's residents were Kurdish, with the remainder equally divided between Arabs and Turkmens, plus a small number of Assyrian and other Christians. Turkey perceives itself as having a strong ethnic affinity with Turkmens and as being the guardian of Turkmen rights. Many of the city's Arabs, largely Shi'a transported from the South, moved to the northern region under the Arabization policy of the central government, especially from the early 1970s onwards, a policy that also involved the forcible removal of 250,000 Kurds from Kirkuk.[20] As Saddam Hussein's regime collapsed, many Arabs fled south as the KDP and PUK militias advanced with US special forces' support, fearing Kurdish revenge.

The Iraqi constitution requires that a referendum to settle Kirkuk's status should be held by the end of 2007. Kurds pushed for this referendum in the expectation that they would win it. However, for precisely this reason, Iraqi Arabs and Turkmens opposed it. Rather than risk confrontation, the Kurds are continuing to try to find a negotiated way forward without dropping the demand for a referendum.[21] In December 2007, the KRG National Assembly voted to approve the UN's proposal that the referendum be delayed for six

[20] International Crisis Group (ICG), *Iraq's Kurds: Towards a Historic Compromise?*, 8 April 2004.

[21] ICG, *Iraq and the Kurds: Resolving the Kirkuk Crisis*, 19 April 2007; ICG, *The Brewing Battle Over Kirkuk*, 18 July 2006.

months.[22] This did not resolve the problem, and a further delay was certain as June 2008 approached.

The fate of the KAR is intimately connected to the other areas of Iraq. The mainly Sunni Arab armed groups in central Iraq are rooted in numerous personal, family, tribal, political, geographical and sectarian ties and have drawn strength from resentment at the occupation and the way it has been conducted. By central Iraq I mean the provinces of Anbar, Salah Ad Din, Diyala and Baghdad. Occasionally claims are made that Iran is providing money and weapons to Sunni Arab insurgents even though those groups are predominantly anti-Shi'a and tend to refer to all Iraqi Shi'a pejoratively as Iranians or Persians.[23] Such support may be a product of the dictum that the enemy of my enemy is my friend, or there may be low level profiteering connected to smuggling. It does not seem to be a central plank of Iranian policy in Iraq and or a key factor in ensuring the survival of armed opposition to the US in Iraq. Although Iraq's porous borders allow the conflicts to have an international dimension, especially in terms of foreign volunteers, the militia and insurgent armed groups in central Iraq are overwhelmingly Iraqi in terms of personnel and resources. When Coalition forces capture people who are indisputably insurgent combatants, they are rarely non-Iraqi.

A substantial number of Sunni Arab armed groups in central Iraq reject negotiations with the United States or the Iraqi government, reject the whole idea of a modern Iraqi state in favour of a wider Caliphate of all Muslims focused solely on implementing Shari'a law, and hold to a version of Sunni Salafist doctrine that regards Shi'a as *kuffar* (unbelievers in or concealers of the truth). They seek to expel or kill all those who deviate from this position, and engage in *takfir* against all other Muslims (that is, declaring them to be *kuffar* and hence apostates).[24]

The most important of these groups has been the Monotheism and Jihad Group, formed in 2003 and led by the Jordanian Abu Mus'ab al-Zarqawi. It changed its name to the Al Qaeda Organisation in the Land of Two Rivers (or sometimes 'Al Qaeda in Mesopotamia' in Western commentary); this indicated its ideological outlook towards, rather than organizational integration into, Al Qaeda. In January 2006 six groups (the Al Qaeda Organization in the Land of the Two Rivers, the Jaish al-Taifa al-Mansoura, the al-Ahwal Brigades, the Islamic Jihad Brigades, the al-Ghuraba Brigades, and the Saraya Ansar

[22] KRG, 'Kurdistan's Parliament Approves Kirkuk Referendum Delay', 28 Dec. 2007.
[23] 'Kuwait militant says Iran supports Sunni fighters in Iraq', *Kuwait Times*, 8 May 2008.
[24] ICG, *Understanding Islamism*, 2 March 2005.

al-Tawhid) announced that they were forming the Mujahideen Shura Council.[25] It claimed that Zarqawi (who was killed by US forces in June 2006) had stepped down in favour of Abdullah Rashid al-Baghdadi (probably a pseudonym) as emir or leader. The creation of the Islamic State of Iraq (ISI) organization was announced in October 2006 by the Mujahideen Shura Council, the Jaish al-Fatiheen, the Jund al-Sahaba, the Kataeb Ansar al-Tawheed wal-Sunnah and some Sunni Arab tribal chiefs as the Pact of the Scented People under Baghdadi's leadership.[26]

These groups have had the largest number of non-Iraqi leaders and volunteers (mainly Saudi but also Syrian and North African) compared with other Sunni Arab armed groups, but they have still been predominantly Iraqi.[27] Despite the changes in nomenclature of what is now the ISI, the US and many Iraqis call it Al Qaeda in Iraq (AQI) or simply Al Qaeda. Furthermore, in central Iraq, the US routinely refers to insurgent attacks or targets as AQI or Al Qaeda. However, it is often unlikely that this is the case.[28] In March 2007, of attacks claimed on the Internet, the ISI only claimed 13 out of 357 on US forces, 40 out of 296 on Iraqi government forces, three out of 143 on Shi'a groups and militias and six out of 12 on Kurdish targets.[29] Indeed, while in July 2007 the US military estimated AQI to be responsible for 15 per cent of attacks in the first half of 2007, some intelligence specialists put it at 8 per cent. In 2006 the US State Department estimated the membership of AQI at 'more than 1,000', while in August 2007 the US military said that of its 24,500 detainees in Iraq, 1,800 were AQI supporters.[30]

From the time of its formation, the ISI demanded that the other insurgent groups subordinate themselves to it and began to kill some of their members, while continuing its attacks on civilians. This strategic blunder pushed the other insurgent groups and tribal leaders to fight back from around April 2007.[31] Various mainly Sunni Arab tribes, and to a lesser extent insurgents,

---

[25] Memorial Institute for the Prevention of Terrorism (MIPT) Terrorism Knowledge Base (TKB), 'Group Profile—Mujahideed Shura Council', 2007.

[26] Ibid.

[27] ICG, *In Their Own Words: Reading the Iraqi Insurgency*, 15 Feb. 2006, especially pp. 1–2, 12–13; Kimmage and Ridolfo, *Iraqi Insurgent Media*, p. 40.

[28] Andrew Tilghman, 'The Myth of AQI', *The Washington Monthly*, Oct. 2007.

[29] Kimmage and Ridolfo, *Iraqi Insurgent Media*, p. 11.

[30] Tilghman, 'The Myth of AQI'.

[31] Kathleen Ridolfo, 'Iraq: Al-Qaeda in Iraq leader struggles with native insurgents', RFE/RL News Analysis, 1 May 2007; Kathleen Ridolfo, 'Iraq: Al-Qaeda tactics lead to split among insurgents', RFE/RL News Analysis, 17 Apr. 2007.

formed the Anbar Salvation Council to cooperate with the US and the Iraqi government against what they saw as the more immediate threat from the ISI and those tribes working with it. This rapidly spread into what have become the Awakening (*Sahwa*) groups across central Iraq. In some cases the US called them Concerned Local Citizens groups (especially where these were urban neighbourhood militias rather than being primarily tribal) and then, from January 2008, the Sons of Iraq (*Abna al-Iraq*). With local knowledge and support, the Awakenings movement has had dramatic success against the ISI, especially in western Iraq, but has faced counter-attacks. Tens of thousands are being armed and paid by the United States—according to the US, 43,000 in 17 districts of Baghdad alone. However, there is a possibility, accepted by the Coalition and the Iraqi government, that should the ISI be defeated, the Awakening groups and the Reform and Jihad Front could turn their full attention to armed opposition to the Coalition and the Iraqi government. Furthermore, the dominant view among those in the Awakening groups appears to be that they can trust the United States a great deal more than they can trust the Shi'i who dominate the Iraqi government.[32]

In May 2007 the Islamic Army of Iraq, the Ansar al-Sunna Shari'a Council and the Mujahideen Army announced the formation of a new Reform and Jihad Front (RJF): rather than being a settled group, it is merely one of the most prominent of many ambiguous announcements of groupings. Its official aim is to establish an Islamic state within Iraq's current borders and is anti-Iranian, but claims not to target Shi'i. The RJF has the backing of the mainly secular Arab Ba'th Socialist Party (ABSP), the Islamic Front of Iraqi Resistance-Hamas-Iraq, and possibly also the Army of Mohammed which effectively became the military wing of the ABSP and the 1920 Revolution Brigades.[33] Officially the RJF is equally opposed to the US and the Iraqi government on the one hand and the ISI on the other. However, the Islamic Army of Iraq has turned out not to be averse to coordination with the US and the Iraqi government in its fight against the ISI. For example, in November 2007, the Islamic Army of Iraq ambushed ISI fighters near Samarra north of Baghdad, having contacted the Iraqi police in advance and requesting US forces to stay away.[34]

---

[32] Alissa J. Rubin and Damien Cave, 'In a force for Iraqi calm, seeds of conflict', *The New York Times*, 23 Dec. 2007.

[33] Evan F. Kohlmann, *State of the Sunni Insurgency in Iraq*, NEFA Foundation, Aug. 2007; Kimmage and Ridolfo, *Iraqi Insurgent Media*, pp. 40–2; and ICG, *Iraq After the Surge 1: The New Sunni Landscape*, 30 Apr. 2008.

[34] AP, 'Clash between ex-insurgents, al-Qaida in Iraq kills 18 in terror group', *International Herald Tribune*, 9 Nov. 2007.

The 1920 Revolution Brigades or at least major elements of it have gone even further, have abandoned the Reform and Jihad Front and are working directly with US forces as scouts and intelligence gatherers. For example, in Diyala in November 2007, the Brigades attacked the ISI in the vicinity of Buhriz and, according to the Iraqi Army, captured 60 suspected ISI members whom they handed over to the Iraqi Army.[35]

The ISI has been weakened in Anbar and Baghdad as most insurgents and tribal militias have stopped attacking US and Iraqi government forces and have worked with them to take on the ISI.[36] In contrast, the level of violence escalated throughout 2007 and stayed high in Salah ad Din, Ninewa and Diyala. For example, media-confirmed violent civilian deaths in Diyala were 255 per 100,000 inhabitants in 2007, compared with 120 for Salah ad Din and 100 for Ninewa (and 164 for Baghdad, 122 for Anbar).[37] These provinces are majority Sunni Arab with a large representation of Shiʻa, Kurds and Turkmens. US-led Kurdish and Shiʻa Iraqi government forces have been engaged in offensives in Sunni Arab dominated areas and so have met fierce opposition: in addition, the ISI has a substantial presence and local tribal alliances there.

Baghdad is the focal point for connecting the conflicts in the rest of central Iraq with the rivalry between Shiʻa armed groups in the capital and the south of the country. The Shiʻa Sadr movement split in July 2003 between the two figures who claimed that Ayatollah Muhammad Sadiq al-Sadr (assassinated on Saddam Hussein's orders) had left his mantle to them: his son Muqtada

---

[35] Ibid.

[36] There have been many more Sunni Arab armed groups in addition to those discussed here. See, for example, those listed by Hashim, *Insurgency and Counterinsurgency in Iraq*, pp. 170–6. Furthermore, the evolving complexities of networked, cell and hierarchical structures mean that there is considerable uncertainty about any attributions of position or policy. In addition, it is worth noting the presence of the Mujahedeen-e Khalq (MEK) in al-Khalis in Diyala province. It seeks the overthrow of the current Iranian government and has around 3,000 personnel. Placed on the US Department of State list of terrorist organizations for past acts, it was disarmed by the US in 2003 and has been confined to Camp Ashraf, a former military base, ever since. Whether to release or detain its personnel or take it off the terrorist list and use it against Iran is a matter of continuing debate in the United States. Holly Fletcher, 'Mujahadeen-e-Khalq (MEK) (aka People's Mujahedin of Iran or PMOI)', Council on Foreign Relations, updated 18 April 2008. In May 2008, the British courts ruled, against the opposition of the British government, that it should no longer be proscribed as a terrorist organization.

[37] IBC, *Civilian Deaths*. It should be emphasized that these are counts based on media reports, not overall estimates, and so the real figures could be multiples of these counts.

al-Sadr, leader of the Mahdi Army, and Shaykh Muhammad al-Ya'qubi, founder of the Fadila Party.[38] The Mahdi Army's main area of control is the Sadr City district of Baghdad, a particularly poor area with a population of some 2.5 million, and it is also a central actor in Basra. The Mahdi Army is not part of a formal political party and Sadr himself has disclaimed any intention of seeking political office. However, the two wings of the Sadr movement (Fadila and Sadrist) were integrated into the almost exclusively Shi'a United Iraqi Alliance (UIA) with the Supreme Council for the Islamic Revolution in Iraq (SCIRI) and Da'wa in 2004. The Sadrists became the largest group within the UIA in the December 2005 elections, and held office in the Iraqi government before withdrawing from it in 2007.[39]

The US alleges continuing organizational links between the Mahdi Army and the Special Groups of the Iranian Revolutionary Guards-Qods Force and in particular the Ramzan Corps, which it maintains is responsible for most Qods Force operations in Iraq.[40] There appear to be links between the Mahdi Army and Iran, but the Mahdi Army is not merely an Iranian proxy and frequent US allegations of systematic and large-scale Iranian supply of weapons have not been substantiated.[41] Indeed, the Mahdi Army is more nationalist, and more independent from Iran, than SCIRI (which renamed itself the Islamic Supreme Council of Iraq or ISCI in May 2007). Estimates of Mahdi Army numbers are now usually in the tens of thousands, based mainly in Baghdad, Basra and holy cities such as Karbala and Najaf.[42] In a major show of force in November 2007, tens of thousands of Mahdi Army militiamen were brought to Najaf for a rally commemorating the ninth anniversary of the killing of Ayatollah Sadr.[43] In addition to having its own units, it plays a major

[38] Patrick Cockburn, *Muqtada al-Sadr and the Fall of Iraq*, London: Faber & Faber, 2008.

[39] Herring, Rangwala, *Iraq in Fragments*, p. 167; 'Sadr loyalist ministers quit Iraq government', *Guardian*, 16 April 2007.

[40] Bill Roggio, 'US Kills 25 Special Groups Fighters in Diyala', *The Long War Journal*, 5 Oct. 2007.

[41] Leila Fadel, 'Chilling Stories From the Mahdi Army', McClatchy Newspapers, 22 June 2007; Tina Susman, 'Iraq: The Elusive Iranian Weapons', Babylon and Beyond Blog, *Los Angeles Times*, 8 May 2008; Kenneth Katzman, *Iran's Activities and Influence in Iraq*, CRS Reports for Congress, updated 9 April 2008.

[42] e.g. 60,000 in *Independent Commission on the Security Forces of Iraq*, Report to Congress, General James L. Jones, USMC (Ret.), Chairman, 6 Sept. 2007 [Jones Commission], p. 30.

[43] Sam Dagher, 'Iraq's Sadr uses lull to rebuild army', *Christian Science Monitor*, 11 Dec. 2007

role in the 140,000–strong Facilities Protection Force, some of its members are police by day and militiamen by night, and others operate under cover of being members of the Iraqi army.[44] While infiltration is thought to be more extensive in the police than in the army, it is substantial in both cases.

The Mahdi Army has offices and spokesmen openly in many locations across central and southern Iraq. This makes it a prime target for attacks and raids by US and Iraqi government forces and unknown assailants usually assumed to be from ISCI, Fadila, Sunni Arab insurgents or tribal enemies.[45] Its local representatives are often quite high profile and have the authority or at least the power to conduct negotiations with government officials. Its activities can be popular in terms of a range of basic services such as food, medicine and resettlement, to the point where it is a state within a state in Sadr City.[46] It is often brutally repressive also. In June 2007, a Mahdi Army anti-Sunni death squad was dominant in the Adhimiyah and Hai al Salam districts of Baghdad, terrorising, torturing and killing—withdrawing when US forces patrolled and returning when they left.[47] Some Mahdi Army members torture and kill any Sunnis and fellow Shi'a who are followers of the more moderate Grand Ayatollah Ali al-Sistani. Although some identify themselves by wearing all-black clothes, this is not standard practice and it is not obvious who is and is not an ordinary member. In July 2006, a report by the International Crisis Group argued that the Mahdi Army had a much looser structure than was often thought.[48] This looseness was confirmed by reports of fighting in Baghdad between factions within the Mahdi Army, partly over control of property from Sunnis driven out of the city which can then be rented out and used to buy weapons and pay the salaries of militiamen.[49] Indeed, both the US and the Mahdi Army leadership agree on the general trend that, as the Mahdi Army

---

[44] Jeremy M. Sharp, *The Iraqi Security Forces: The Challenge of Sectarian and Ethnic Influences*, Congressional Research Service Report for Congress, 18 Jan. 2007, p. 5; Ned Parker, 'Shiite militia infiltrates Iraqi forces', *Los Angeles Times*, 16 Aug. 2007.

[45] e.g. 'Assassinating a member from al-Sadr movement in al-Basra', PUKmedia, 14 Jan. 2008.

[46] Dagher, as note 43; Shashank Bengali, 'Charity work shows another side to Sadr's movement in Iraq', McClatchy Newspapers, 8 May 2008; Kristele Younes and Nir Rosen, *Uprooted and Unstable: Meeting Urgent Humanitarian Needs in Iraq*, Refugees International, April 2008, p. 3.

[47] Fadel, as note 41.

[48] ICG, *Iraq's Muqtada al-Sadr: Spoiler or Stabiliser?*, 11 July 2006, p. 24.

[49] Paul Wood, 'The uniformed kidnappers of Baghdad', BBC, 16 Jun. 2007.

has grown, top-down control has weakened.[50] In response, in late 2007 the Mahdi Army movement leadership began a purge to strengthen top-down control.[51] Between then and March 2008, when the US attacked Mahdi Army units, it claimed to be going after splinter groups, and there was speculation that the Sadr movement leadership was quietly providing the US with intelligence to enable it to do so.[52]

The main rival to the Mahdi Army is ISCI, led by Abd al-Aziz al-Hakim, and its (officially demilitarized) Badr Organization militia, led by Hadi al-Amiri who is a member of the Iraqi parliament.[53] Established in Iran, it fought on the Iranian side in the Iran-Iraq war of the 1980s. There is no Badr uniform, but Badr members often engage in their activities when in Iraqi police uniform and some wear a Badr T-shirt under their uniform. It has around 15,000 members with light weapons and through ISCI dominates the Ministry of the Interior.[54] In a notorious case, US forces and Iraqi police discovered in November 2005 a Ministry of the Interior dungeon thought to be under Badr control with 175 people in it, many showing evidence of torture.[55] In February 2006, the US military reported evidence of Badr-Interior Ministry death squad activity directed at Sunnis.[56] Badr members are thought to control the elite paramilitary police, which have the authority to operate anywhere in Iraq.[57] Badr and the Mahdi Army have fought each other repeatedly in Baghdad, Basra, Karbala, Najaf and elsewhere. It is ironic that ISCI is more sectarian, fundamentalist, Iranian-rooted and pro-Iranian than the more popular Mahdi Army but is much closer to the United States: this is due to an alliance of convenience, as the US has needed an armed ally and ISCI has needed a political ally to move to centre stage in Iraq.

The armed struggle for control of southern Iraq—that is, the provinces of Karbala, Babil, Wasit, Najaf, Qadisyah, Muthanna, Dhi Qar, Maysan and

[50] Patrick Jackson, 'Who are Iraq's Mehdi Army?', BBC, 30 May 2007.

[51] Ned Parker and Haidar Azzawi, 'Beatings, abductions, shootings: on patrol with the al-Mahdi Army', *The Times*, 3 Oct. 2006.

[52] AP, 'U.S. troops kill 11 members of Mahdi Army splinter group', *Baltimore Sun*, 28 Dec. 2007.

[53] AP, 'Iraq's Badr Organization denies it's a militia', *International Herald Tribune*, 21 April 2008.

[54] Jones Commission, as note 42, p. 30.

[55] Kim Sengupta, 'Raid on torture dungeon exposes Iraq's secret war', *Independent*, 16 Nov. 2005.

[56] 'Iraq death squad "Caught in Act', BBC, 16 Feb. 2006.

[57] Sharp, *The Iraqi Security Forces*, p. 5.

Basra—has overwhelmingly been among Shi'a. However, this does not mean that the struggle has been primarily about differing interpretations of Shi'ism; more prominent have been divisions over class (with the Mahdi Army supported by the poorest and ISCI supported by the religious and business establishment), federalism (with the Mahdi Army favouring a strong central government and ISCI preferring a strong federation of southern provinces), money (with both seeking control of religious, state and informal economy funds) and nationalism (with the Mahdi Army anti-occupation and ISCI willing to work with the US). During the period of formal occupation, the southernmost provinces of Basra, Dhi Qar, Maysan and Muthanna were part of a military command with overall British responsibility and a Coalition Provisional Authority civilian authority which was mainly British. Around 90 per cent of central government revenue is from oil produced in these governorates and Basra, Iraq's second largest city, is the main source of support outside Baghdad for the Shi'a political parties.

With few military resources, little political will and almost no interest from the Coalition leadership in Baghdad, efforts to confront armed groups locally were half-hearted. This has allowed Shi'a militias, especially those of the Mahdi Army, Fadila and SCIRI/ISCI, to dominate. Fadila took part in the governorate elections there in January 2005, and had the support of Mahdi Army members in its campaign. It won 21 per cent of the vote, coming second to the 'Islamic Basra' slate that included SCIRI and al-Da'wa, which won 33 per cent. However, subsequently it managed to put together a coalition with minor parties that gave it 21 out of the 41 seats on the governorate council, and thus won the governorship position for a Fadila party member, Muhammad Musabih al-Wa'ili, who has on occasion taken an independent stance.[58]

Southern Iraq has been vulnerable to the partly political, partly economic mafia armed struggle between ISCI, the Mahdi Army and Fadila; to vigilante gangs of Islamic fundamentalists from within and beyond those groups attacking those they deem to be apostates, unbelievers, immoral or immodest; and to violent criminal gangs.[59] Many of the Iraqi police actually owe their primary loyalty to these groups, and police who act against any of them have routinely faced intimidation and murder. Fadila has controlled the Oil Protection Force, the Hizbollah Party has been a major actor in the Customs Police

[58] Edmund Sanders, 'Power struggles stall Iraqi provincial councils', *Los Angeles Times*, 6 April 2005.
[59] ICG, *Where is Iraq Heading? Lessons From Basra*, 25 June 2007.

Force, and the Mahdi Army has controlled the Facilities Protection Service and much of the police force.[60] Periods of reduced violence have reflected the aftermath of the murder or driving out of perceived enemies or uneasy compromises, rather than stability and the rule of law.

What political authority there has been in the South has often been fragmented: governorate councils sometimes reject the authority of national ministries and the national government itself, and political factions run their own militias. British forces made reconstruction, anti-militia and anti-corruption efforts such as Operation Sinbad which ran from late 2006 to early 2007. However, because of a continual fear of being overrun, the priority of British forces was to avoid antagonizing excessively local armed political actors, and the US increasingly took on a combat role in the south in 2007–8. Around 4,500 British forces remained in Basra into early 2009 at the airport, having withdrawn from their bases in Muthanna, Dhi Qar and Maysan provinces and with the intention to leave around one tenth of this number in a purely training role; this has now been carried out. An Iraqi government attempt in the spring of 2008 to destroy the Mahdi Army and Fadila in Basra soon ran into trouble and around 1,000 Iraqi troops mutinied; the US and Britain provided air strikes to assist and a ceasefire was announced in early May 2008.[61]

## Explanation and significance of the reduction of violence since September 2007

According to the Iraqi government, the number of violent civilian deaths in Baghdad in December 2007 was 7 per cent lower than a year earlier.[62] While the exact figures are a matter of debate, the downward trend here and across most of Iraq is much more evident, although the level of violence in 2008 was still in the vicinity of the level in 2004, at the time seen as high. Iraq Body Count (IBC) collates media reports of violent civilian deaths;[63] it counted 10,759 such deaths in 2004 and 9,204 in 2008. However, two-thirds of those deaths were recorded in the first half of 2008. What are the reasons for this pattern?

---

[60] ICG, *Where is Iraq Heading?*, pp. 11–12.

[61] Leila Fadel, 'Sadr City residents fear a cease-fire means more violence', McClatchy Newspapers, 11 May 2008; Gulf News, 'Guns fall silent in Baghdad militia bastion of Sadr City', Iraq Updates, 12 May 2008.

[62] Ross Colvin, 'Civilian casualties drop dramatically in Iraq', Reuters, 31 Dec. 2007.

[63] IBC, *Database*, n.d. Accessed 2 March 2009.

First, sectarian separation occurred on a massive scale during 2007, especially in central Iraq.[64] According to the US National Intelligence Estimate of August 2007: '[w]here population displacements have led to significant sectarian separation, conflict levels have diminished to some extent because warning communities find it more difficult to penetrate communal enclaves.'[65] In July 2006, around one third of Baghdad was at least 7 per cent Sunni or Shi'a, but by July 2007 nearly all areas of the city were at least 75 per cent Sunni or Shi'a, with the Shi'a areas very predominant.[66] Some tens of thousands of refugees have returned to Iraq (a tiny proportion of the two million, leaving aside a further two million internally displaced), some because of increased security and some because of poverty. As of February 2009, new displacements were rare and returnee levels were increasing but were still very low.[67] The US has expressed concern that the returns, if not managed properly, could spark new violence, and considers that the necessary management is not occurring.[68] Nevertheless, any large-scale reversal of sectarian separation seems unlikely until a major shift occurs in the political and security environment

Secondly, as indicated above, a large proportion of the mainly Sunni Arab tribal militia and insurgent groups decided to work with the Coalition, either against the ISI or to take control of their own neighbourhoods to protect them from militias or government forces dominated by Shi'a. Both of these developments are independent of the small increase in US forces and are not a stable basis to prevent a return to increased violence or promote political integration. The Awakening Councils started to come under increasing attack as of January 2008, especially in Baghdad, with Awakening Council members asserting that the Iraqi government was not providing them with sufficient security and attributing this to Iranian or Mahdi Army influence, and even claiming that the Iraqi government was involved in the attacks.[69] Just as the

---

[64] Hannah Allam, 'Survey: Many Iraqis in Syria fled during U.S. troop buildup', McClatchy Newspapers, 14 Dec. 2007; IPSOS, *Second IPSOS Survey on Iraqi Refugees (November 2007) Preliminary Results*, Dec. 2007.

[65] US National Intelligence Estimate, *Prospects for Iraq's Stability: Some Security Progress but Political Reconciliation Elusive*, 23 Aug. 2007, p. 3.

[66] Jones Commission, as note 42, p. 34.

[67] International Organization for Migration, *Three Years of Post-Samarra Displacement in Iraq*, 22 February 2009.

[68] Michael R. Gordon and Stephen Farrell, 'Iraq lacks plan on the return of refugees, military says', *The New York Times*, 30 Nov. 2007.

[69] Juan Cole, '24 dead in Sunni counter-attacks', Informed Comment, 8 Jan. 2008 and 'Sunnis fear return of Baghdad violence', Informed Comment, 9 Jan. 2008.

Awakening Councils show substantial distrust towards the Iraqi government, so the Iraqi government is showing lack of trust in them in not integrating them into its security forces or public works units, despite US pressure.[70]

The view of the US military that the situation is unstable, and one in which the Awakening Councils could turn on it and the Iraqi government, seems to be accurate.[71] On the edge of Baghdad in January 2008, the US military felt it necessary to use air strikes in an area that had been thought to be secured.[72] Sunni Arab armed groups of all kinds retain their determination to end the US occupation, to promote Sunni Arab interests as they see them in the government, the security services and the constitution, and to roll back 'Iranian' (often a pejorative term for Shi'a, including Iraqi Shi'a) influence.[73] In May 2008 a new US-backed offensive began in Mosul to try to defeat Sunni Arab insurgents there.[74] Such offensives could contribute to a breakdown of Sunni Arab cooperation with the US. Furthermore, the Sunni Arab parties in parliament do not speak on behalf of the Awakening groups or the Reform and Jihad Front, and dangerous new rivalries among Sunni Arabs exist. For example, the Awakening groups in Anbar in March 2008 threatened to attack the Sunni Arab Iraqi Islamic Party led by Iraq's Vice-President Tariq al-Hashimi if it did not cease to operate in the province.[75]

Thirdly, Muqtada al-Sadr officially suspended the armed operations of the Mahdi Army and agreed a ceasefire with ISCI in October 2007: neither cessation of fighting held fully before the anti-Mahdi Army offensive in March 2008.[76] His motivation appears to have been mixed: seeking to avoid being targeted by the US military surge in Baghdad or fighting ISCI elsewhere, while purging the Mahdi army of undisciplined elements and positioning it to take advantage of the expected provincial elections.[77] In the offensive the

---

[70] Peter Spiegel, 'U.S. shifts Sunni strategy in Iraq', *Los Angeles Times*, 14 Jan. 2008.

[71] Ibid.

[72] Jamie Gumbrecht and Nancy A. Youssef, 'In Iraq, U.S. airstrikes target insurgents near supposedly safe zone', McClatchy Newspapers, 10 Jan. 2008.

[73] Hala Jaber, 'American backed killer militias strut across Iraq', *Sunday Times*, 25 Nov. 2007.

[74] Alexandra Zavis, 'Long-promised offensive catches Mosul off guard', *Los Angeles Times*, 12 May 2008.

[75] Fadhil Ali, 'Sunni Rivalries in al-Anbar Province Threaten Iraq's Security', *Terrorism Focus*, Vol. 5, No. 10 (11 March 2008).

[76] Ross Colvin, 'Civilian casualties drop dramatically in Iraq', Reuters, 31 Dec. 2007; ICG, *Shiite Politics in Iraq: The Role of the Supreme Council*, 15 Nov. 2007, p. 20.

[77] ICG, *Iraq's Civil War, the Sadrists and the Surge*, 7 Feb. 2008.

Mahdi Army suffered reverses but not a strategic defeat. The Sadrists are increasingly, and increasingly effectively, taking part in the political process, but their positions are usually not ones favoured by the United States.

Fourthly, the US has actively sought to work with the new political trends of sectarian separation, Sunni Arab armed opposition to the ISI and, less consistently, the Mahdi Army ceasefire. In January 2007 the Bush administration announced its Iraq strategy review, with its 'The New Way Forward' plan which became known as the 'surge'.[78] Its primary focus was to be on providing security for the population (especially in Baghdad), using Iraqi security forces with a temporary, modest increase of some 30,000 in US troops to 160,000, and reaching out to tribal and insurgent groups willing to work with it. There has been extensive use of measures to restrict freedom of movement, such as building barriers or temporary bans on the use of motor vehicles.

The main aim of the surge was to create the space for political reconciliation. The Iraqi government became increasingly narrow in its base owing to the withdrawal in 2007 of its Sadrist members. The mainly Sunni Arab Iraq Accordance Front (also known as the Tawafuq Party and composed of the General Council for the People of Iraq, the Iraqi Islamic Party and the Iraqi National Dialogue Council) also withdrew in 2007 but rejoined the government in April 2008.[79] Fundamental issues such as finalization of the constitution, the future of Kirkuk, sharing oil revenues and agreeing the balance of federal and national powers remain unresolved and not obviously closer to resolution as of early 2009.[80]

There have been efforts to develop an Iraqi nationalist political coalition emphasizing strong central government, national level control of Iraqi oil revenues, opposition to ethno-sectarian quotas in government and a timetable for withdrawal of US and other Coalition troops. The discussions have included the supporters of Muqtada al-Sadr, Fadila, the National Dialogue Front of Sunni Arabs (led by Saleh al-Mutlaq and composed of the Iraqi National Front, the National Front for a Free Iraq, the Iraqi Christian Democratic Party, the Democratic Arab Front and the Sons of Iraq Movement) and the secular Iraqi National List of Iyad 'Allawi. An important point is that this

---

[78] US National Security Council, *Highlights of the Iraq Strategy Review*, Jan. 2007.

[79] Eli Lake, 'Iraqi political crisis near end as Tawafuq chief quits', *New York Sun*, 6 July 2007; 'Obstacles diminish for the Sunnis' return to Iraqi gov't', Xinhuanet, 27 Dec. 2007; James Glanz, 'Top Sunni bloc is set to rejoin cabinet in Iraq', *The New York Times*, 25 April 2008.

[80] ICG, *Iraq After the Surge II: The Need for a New Political Strategy*, 30 April 2008.

loose and fluid grouping increasingly includes the Prime Minister Nour al-Maliki and elements of the Da'wa party. As this nationalist coalition is opposed to the US military presence and many of the fundamental assumptions of US policy (for example, that state building in Iraq requires a loose federation and ethno-sectarian quotas), the US has not welcomed these developments, but it has been unable to stop them.[81] Instead, it continues to back the ISCI-PUK-KDP grouping, but with declining effect.

The 31 January 2009 provincial elections (held owing to pressure from the nationalist coalition) produced a major strengthening of the various Da'wa factions and less sectarian, more secular Sunni Arab parties, and dramatic losses for ISCI, Fadila and the Iraqi Islamic Party compared with the January 2005 elections, with the Sadrists almost catching up with ISCI overall.[82] This is a clear shift away from the advocates of ethno-sectarian decentralized federalism, with secular parties making gains also, though to a lesser degree.

From this it can be seen that there has been a sustained reduction in the overall level of violence, but much more limited progress in eliminating or marginalizing Iraq's armed groups or co-opting them into state building (especially of the sort favoured by the United States). The US Department of Defence assessment that the gains are significant but fragile and reversible is an accurate one.[83] However, the view of most Iraqis across Iraq and without fundamental variation related to ethno-sectarian background, according to focus groups held on behalf of the US military in December 2007, is that the main reason for the violence in Iraq is the US military presence, and that the prospects for national reconciliation would improve if US forces left.[84] These results are in line with many previous polls and are the opposite of the official US view and until recently the Iraqi government view, which is that the US military presence is necessary to help create the conditions for national reconciliation.

No united anti-occupation front has emerged with a shared vision of the state and Iraqi identity to force the end of the occupation so as to implement

---

[81] Reidar Visser, 'The 22 July opposition alliance is still alive and well—and gets some support from Maliki', 8 February 2009, http://gulfanalysis.wordpress.com/2009/02/08.

[82] Reidar Visser, 'No longer supreme: after local elections, ISCI becomes a 10 per cent party south of Baghdad', 5 February 2009, http://www.historiae.org/ISCI.asp, and 'The provincial elections: the seat allocation is ffficial and the coalition-forming process begins', 19 February 2009, http://www.historiae.org/allocation.asp.

[83] US Department of Defence, *Measuring Security and Stability in Iraq*, Report to Congress, December 2008, p. iv.

[84] Karen De Young, 'All Iraqi groups blame U.S. for discord, study shows', *Washington Post*, 19 Dec. 2007.

its own project for a sovereign or governance state. Nevertheless, Maliki and the Da'wa party are increasingly following the centralist nationalist trend which may hold out more promise for coherent state authority than the model that has been favoured by the United States. In a deal signed in November 2008 and ratified by the Iraqi Presidency Council the following month, the outgoing Bush administration agreed with the Iraqi government that that all US forces would withdraw from Iraqi cities, villages and localities no later than 30 June 2009 and would withdraw from Iraq completely no later than 31 December 2011.[85] In February 2009, President Obama announced that the US combat mission in Iraq would end on 31 August 2010, with 35–50,000 support troops staying on until 31 December 2011 to train, equip and advise Iraqi security forces deemed to be non-sectarian; engage in counter-terrorism operations; and provide protection for those engaged in the first two missions.[86] The Iraqi military continues to be reliant on the US for logistics, surveillance, air power and other support, and the timeline for US withdrawal is not as rapid as the more nationalist grouping wanted, but the underlying direction is towards decreasing freedom of manoeuvre for the United States.

## Conclusion

In many cases the line between the state, parties, militias, insurgents and the international is blurred in Iraq. This creates a fundamental problem in that efforts supposed to strengthen the state (by means of weapons, training, intelligence and other support) are often exploited by militias and insurgents within the state apparatus for their own ends. Even where there is cooperation with the US and the Iraqi government, there can be no confidence that this cooperation can be relied upon to continue. The independent and semi-independent organized armed groups have often shown their resilience against armed attack and their unwillingness to integrate fully into the state. There are still numerous ongoing armed conflicts in Iraq and the main focus of conflict has moved through a number of phases—multiple local mobilizations, then insurgency and counter-insurgency, then sectarianism and now power

[85] US-Iraq, *Agreement Between the United States of America and the Republic of Iraq On the Withdrawal of United States Forces from Iraq and the Organization of Their Activities during Their Temporary Presence in Iraq*, December 2008. See also US-Iraq, *Strategic Framework Agreement for a Relationship of Friendship and Cooperation between the United States of America and the Republic of Iraq*, December 2008.

[86] Barack Obama, 'Text: speech at Camp Lejeune, N.C.', *The New York Times*, 27 February 2009.

struggles that are not primarily about sectarian doctrine even though they are between groups of the same sect—while secondary strands of armed conflict have flared up or died down mainly according to their own logics. Up to the end of 2007 these phases represented the opposite of an evolution towards the creation of a coherent sovereign or governance state in Iraq: since then there have been at least some limited signs of increased coherence.

In the meantime Iraq is a fragmented state in the sense that there is some state authority but a great deal of dispute over the location of legitimate authority and over the means of resolving such disputes. This contrasts with the categorization of Iraq as a failed or fragile state, which implies the absence of state authority or else implies that it is weak but centralized. The Iraqi state is failing some of the people all of the time, all of the people some of the time, but it is not failing all of the people all of the time. It provides some services and the existence of a variety of state functions is partly what ensures continuing competition over control of them. The Iraqi state is indeed fragile in that it is frequently and easily challenged when it attempts to assert itself, but state authority is not merely weak, it is fragmented. Furthermore, both the failed state and fragile state categories are strongly associated with rationales for international armed intervention to create or strengthen state authority, when international armed intervention has actually been central to fragmenting Iraq.

Iraq is not, as is often claimed, fragmenting into three ethno-sectarian entities based on a Kurdish north, Sunni Arab centre and Shi'a south, whether as states or federal regions. The fragmentation manifests itself across many axes—between and within regions, urban-rural, class, tribe, party, political ideology etc., as well as ethnicity and sect—and these can be cross-cutting rather than mutually reinforcing. Diversity is compatible with a coherent state, but in Iraq that diversity is channelled into, and magnified by, political paralysis, mistrust, short-termism and violence. Disputes over formulating, passing, implementing and interpretation legislation regarding oil, federal powers, local elections, de-Ba'thification and the constitution are over specific substantive issues and over differences in identity, values, interests, strategies and goals. However, political fragmentation is not just a reflection of political incompatibility on specific issues or differences between actors: it encourages those involved, including armed groups, to see what divides them as insurmountable. In this melee, the US has sought and failed to find a way to retain a privileged position in Iraqi politics without backing political parties and armed groups inside and outside the government that have shown little interest in a shared vision for a coherent Iraqi state.

# 10

# Al Qaeda

## From the Near to the Far Enemy and Back
## (1988–2008)

### Mohammad-Mahmoud Ould Mohamedou

*All hopes to the contrary notwithstanding, it seems as though the one argument that the Arabs are incapable of understanding is force.*

– Hannah Arendt\*

By the mid-to-late 2000s, Al Qaeda had essentially completed the mission it set out to achieve twenty years earlier. For all practical purposes and against all odds, the subsequent phases that have been discerned in the conflict with its foes were in effect just additional opportunities for the group's existing global gains; it has outlived the George W. Bush administration, has engineered further political decrepitude in Iraq, Afghanistan, and Pakistan, and threatens to conduct potential new attacks on Western targets. The conventional wisdom, rehearsed from 2004 on, held that it was the transformation of Al Qaeda that had been the key reason for its survival and resurgence. Close examination of the group's history reveals that the strength of Al Qaeda lies, in point of fact, not so much in its post-September 11 mutation—a logical evasive step which many other terrorist or insurgent groups had enacted

---

\* 'Peace or Armistice in the Near East', *Review of Politics*, January 1950, p. 56.

previously—but more in its inherent adaptability and its faculty to innovate constantly. In contrast to its state adversaries who profess to be on the offensive in the 'war on terror' but are more often than not confined to a structurally defensive position, not knowing how, where, when, and under what guise to expect an assault, this transnational non-state armed group has been writing its own story.

The staying power and uniqueness of the group cannot be overstated. But almost two decades since its creation and several years into its stalemated conflict with the world's most powerful nation. Al Qaeda reached a paradoxical milestone in that narrative. By virtue of its very ability to escape defeat at the hands of the United States, and in spite of the constant increase in its global impact, the organization has found itself immersed increasingly in the local management of conflicts with states. Since the September 11 attacks it conducted on the United States, this strategic about-face and proactive design have played out on evolving parallel tracks with a common and urgent concern, namely the avoidance of predictability. Whereas the fourfold *ghazzou* (raid) on New York and Washington endowed Al Qaeda overnight with global notoriety status, the group's leaders, Osama Bin Laden and Ayman al Dhawahiri (Zawahiri),[1] did not seek reflexively to replicate those strikes by immediately engineering further attacks on the United States. Expectations of a second wave were high in the United States during the autumn of 2001 and throughout 2002, and the country braced itself for such a follow-up assault. Instead, blurring the picture, the group opted to shift its attention to Europe where it targeted those states—Spain on 11 March 2004 and the United Kingdom on 7 July 2005—which had actively assisted the United States in its war in Iraq.

When that pattern proved successful, putting on high alert other European states (Italy, Norway, and France notably) that had been warned by the group about their military activity in Iraq and Afghanistan or their perceived hostility to Muslim populations,[2] Al Qaeda did not expand it. Ushering in a third phase in its post-September 11 strategy, it proceeded, instead, to concentrate on the conflict in Iraq, where it had been dealing blows to the US and coalition forces since mid-2003. After spearheading the insurgency in that country

---

[1] The common 'Zawahiri' spelling in English is due to the use of an Egyptian colloquial mispronunciation of the Arabic letter 'dha' as 'za'. Al Dhawahiri is an Egyptian national.

[2] France did not join the United States in Iraq, but, in a taped message aired on 24 February 2004 it was threatened by Ayman al Dhawahiri following its adoption of legislation banning Islamic headscarves in public schools.

and setting it in motion dramatically under the local leadership of Abu Musab Al Zarqawi—notably with an *uptempo* series of attacks in 2004–the organization in essence took a back seat in relation to that battlefront and moved on, in 2006, to support the resurgence of the Taliban in Afghanistan. By 2008, reports of Al Qaeda-supported Taliban units in near-total control of parts of Afghanistan as well as the Tribal Areas in Pakistan (known officially as the Federally Administered Tribal Areas) and the upheaval in that country following the 27 December 2007 killing of the former Prime Minister Benazir Bhutto indicated the organization's revitalization in that region.

However, there has been an unexpected twist, illustrated by the return of Al Qaeda to its initial ground and to the very aim it had originally sought to steer away from: engaging local rulers. The historical implications of this development for the countries of the Middle East and North Africa and that region's interaction with its neighbours are profound.

## Rebellion as export: the emergence of Al Qaeda

If, by the late 2000s, the group led by Osama Bin Laden and Ayman al Dhawahiri had mutated into a *sui generis* powerful global private entity, the transnational war inaugurated by Al Qaeda in the late 1980s represented initially merely a change of scale in the post-colonial struggle in the Arab and Muslim region. This ethnogenesis owed much to an original displacement of the focus of opposition of several Islamist groups from battling local regimes, denounced as authoritarian, corrupt, and repressive, to fighting the United States directly for its support of those regimes. Such a change—described as a move from *al adou al qareeb* (the near enemy) to *al adou al ba'eed* (the far enemy), in the literature of the Islamist groups—represented a conscious choice on the part of a number of Islamist leaders who had gathered in Afghanistan during the period of the Soviet invasion of that country. The strategic shift was also the objective result of the stalemated and at times counterproductive results of the campaigns which many of these Islamist groups had led in their respective countries, notably in Egypt, Saudi Arabia, Jordan, Syria, Yemen, and Algeria.

Historically, from the early 1950s to the mid-1990s, the majority of Arab and Muslim states had been faced, to varying degrees, with steadily mounting Islamist opposition. The context of these conflicts was fourfold. First, in many of these places, the post-colonial governments that had inherited power following the countries' respective independence had often simply imposed their policies over existing religious options put forth by alternative (Islamist) groups. Consequently, the initial contest fought around the founding of the state persisted beyond the time of the induction of the nationalistic regimes: an often violent engagement playing out at times underground, at other times on the front pages of newspapers.

Second, the new regimes rapidly, if not immediately, displayed authoritarian tendencies of which the Islamist groups, by virtue of their oppositional nature and their threatening potential, bore, first and foremost, the full brunt. Egypt, in particular, was the theatre of a violent struggle between the regime of Gamal Abdel Nasser and the Muslim Brotherhood. The writings of one of the figures of that movement, Sayyid Qutb, executed in August 1966, would in time become a leading ideological reference for Al Qaeda and an influence on many of its actors, Ayman al Dhawahiri in particular.

Third, those regimes' failed political performance and poor socioeconomic record pushed many segments within these societies into the open arms of the Islamists. From being a peripheral option, the alternative choice (and social services) offered by the groups therefore gained ground, ultimately reaching mainstream appeal in many Muslim theatres. In Algeria, for instance, the Islamic Salvation Front (FIS), better organized and more committed than the ruling National Liberation Front (FLN), earned the support of many Algerians in the period 1988–91, leading to a thwarted electoral victory in December 1991. Finally, the multifaceted links—political, economic, military, and of a security type—that most of these governments came to enjoy with the United States allowed the Islamist groups, insofar as that country provided support to the Israeli occupation of Palestine, to denounce the 'corruption' and 'crimes' both against their specific countries and against the *umma* (Islamic community) at large.

Underlying this tapestry were accusations levelled by the Islamist groups against unmet expectations and ineffective state-building by the post-colonial regimes. Religious considerations aside, the arguments centred on the fact that in failing to resist the influence of the United States (and the West generally), the various successive governments in the region had defrauded their people. Consequently, it was argued, these states were illegitimate and had to be removed, by means including force. It is important to recognize this often overlooked motivation of most Islamist groups, including Al Qaeda, which, as it were, claim much legitimacy from the very illegitimacy that resulted from the post-colonial state's performance and behaviour. This state-building dimension should not—particularly in the aftermath of the 2003 United States war on Iraq—be confused with the state fragmentation scenario. In practice, the latter occurs when claims of particular actors to exercise legitimate governmental authority remain fundamentally disputed, both in principle and in practice, and there are no clearly agreed procedures for resolving such disputes.[3] When the contemporary Islamist movements were set in motion, such procedures did exist and the differences concerned merely the identity of those who would be allowed to capture the state to conduct the 'building' work. In a situation like that in Iraq after the American and British invasion, or indeed in Afghanistan for most of the second half of the 20th century and into the 21st, the contest was far more primal and encompassed wider ethnic, tribal, and sectarian dimensions.

In contrast, state-building is an exercise that cannot be posited in a vacuum.[4] It is also neither finite state-formation (concretization of statehood) nor the looser nation-building (the process by which the national consciousness appears and becomes institutionalized in the structures of society). State-building is an open-ended set of tasks. To the extent that the state itself is an abstract, continuous, survival-seeking, resource-gathering entity, and policy is the process that flows from its very existence, state-building has to be a political activity. There is, too, a radical difference between state-building as an internal mission (even when assisted from abroad) and external state-building resulting from intervention (even when triggered by a mechanism like the 'responsibility to protect'). The difference lies in the nature of the order built and the ability of that construct to stay the course.

Classically, the Weberian state (sovereignty, territory, population, monopoly on the legitimate exercise of violence) comes into existence after it brings preexisting modes of domination (patriarchy, feudalism, tribalism) to an end. Its birth marks the end of patrimonialism as the state becomes a distinct, *primus inter pares*, institution within society. Yet there is a vision different from the Weberian one, namely one that places emphasis on the historical changing dynamics and societal actors that affect the state. Indeed, there are places where such independent forces did not disappear, (re)gained strength and sometimes sought forceful ways to accommodate their alternative vision in the state polity. In many parts of the non-Western world, what still provides direction and impetus to the political process is not what merely represents it formally but what shapes the building of that state. An example, among

---

[3] Eric Herring and Glen Rangwala, *Iraq in Fragments: The Occupation and its Legacy*, London: Hurst & Company, 2006, p. 50. See also Herring's Chapter 9 in this volume.
[4] See Mohammad-Mahmoud Ould Mohamedou, *Iraq and the Second Gulf War: State-Building and Regime Security*, San Francisco: Austin and Winfield, 2001.

others, of this is the evolution that the Lebanese state has followed of late. Following years of war, it seemed the country was back on its feet in the mid-1990s only, in the mid-2000s, to again become the terrain of both domestic and international struggles, involving a powerful Islamist group, and lapsing anew into strife. Hence, it is often the sedimentation of cumulative historical pathologies and the instrumentalization of these states' building processes that account primarily—maybe more than the familiar theories of ethnic and sectarian conflict—for their weakness and vulnerability.

In such a general context of Arab and Islamic world state-building or lack thereof, Al Qaeda sprang forth as a politico-religious project built on (i) the relocation of authority, (ii) the circumventing of the state, and (iii) the militaristic empowerment of a non-state actor. Capitalizing on waves of riots and uprisings (notably in Cairo, Casablanca and Algiers in the 1980s), which had sealed the historical failure of the post-colonial Arab state—painting a compelling picture of resentment, alienation, and anomie—a modern-day Islamist movement came to be born from the very factor alternatively enabling state-building, namely the reinvention of the political sphere. In that sense, Al Qaeda's action was something akin to a statement that there is nothing inevitable about the vulnerabilities of states; that their conditions are but products of a history and as such can be remedied similarly; and, a more revolutionary notion, that violence—including offensive international force—is not solely a state prerogative. Thus, usurping authority that traditionally accrued to the state and offering a prescriptive agenda unacceptable internationally, Al Qaeda was from the very beginning immune to statist deterrence.

The movement's assertiveness sprang as well from its battle-hardened status. Starting in the early 1980s, a number of Islamist militants began migrating to Afghanistan to take part in the resistance against the Soviet occupation of that country. Later known as the 'Arab Afghans', these operators rapidly formed a relatively contiguous group which achieved both regional notoriety and substantial success in its *jihad* against the Soviets. In particular, while liaising with the local Afghan Islamist factions—in time building an alliance with the Taliban (who would take over the country in 1996) and leaders such as Gulbuddin Hekmatayar and Abdul Rasul Sayyaf—these Arab fighters came to be organized under the umbrella of a coordinating office known as the *Maktab al Khadamat lil Mujahideen* (office of work for the combatants). The office was led initially by Abdallah Youssef 'Azzam, who was replaced in mid-1988 by Osama Bin Laden in association with Ayman al Dhawahiri. Azzam and his two sons were assassinated on 24 November 1989 in Peshawar in Afghanistan.

Started in May 1988 and completed in February 1989, the Soviet withdrawal from Afghanistan was a watershed moment—more so, in a sense, for the nascent international Islamist movement than for the country itself. If the full nature of their military contribution to the Soviet defeat[5] remains imperfectly known—a realistic assessment is that it was substantial but not decisive—the 'Afghan Arabs' (many of whom were not, in fact, ethnic Arabs) nonetheless yielded maximum dividends from their involvement in this conflict. Yet for all the mythology that developed around them, attracting in turn additional recruits and worldwide funding, like any victorious army with time and energy on its hands this newly-gathered population was in need of a mission—and a mission that would up its own ante. Hence, in a further flight from their respective domestic terrains, the leadership of these men decided on the creation of an international army of Islamist fighters that would concentrate its forces on targeting the one party that, they argued, had long been weakening the Arab and Islamic world, notably through its support of Israel: the United States. Thus was Al Qaeda born.

How the group went on subsequently to assemble a force of several thousand foot soldiers, trained in a dozen or so camps throughout Afghanistan, supported by a guild of senior operators (Abu Ubaida al Banshiri, Abu Hafs al Masri, Abu Zubaydah), headed by a charismatic leader (Osama Bin Laden) and his authoritative deputy (Ayman al Dhawahiri), and paralleled by several secret transnational cells implanted in Europe and the United States, is what came to constitute the *differentia specifica* of Al Qaeda, and the culmination of that design in the September 2001 attacks on the United States.[6]

To the extent that the 'Arab Afghans' were indeed the core membership of Al Qaeda and that their role was instrumental in subsequently establishing Al Qaeda as a successful venture throughout the 1990s and more so in the 2000s, it is important to note that we can, in retrospect, identify three such successive

---

[5] The Soviet Union lost the war in Afghanistan because of a classical pattern that has long plagued conventional armies battling insurgencies. Unable to significantly break a stalemate that settled rapidly after the 1979 invasion, the Soviets were faced with lack of control of territories beyond Kabul, difficult mountainous terrain, an agile resistance movement supported by the population and by international fighters, large-scale sabotage operations, and, ultimately, mounting casualties and the heavy domestic political and financial toll of an unpopular war.

[6] For a history of Al Qaeda see, notably, Abdel Bari Atwan, *The Secret History of Al Qaeda*, London: Saqi Books, 2006; and François Burgat, *L'Islamisme à l'heure d'Al Qaida*, Paris: La Découverte, 2005.

waves of 'Arab Afghans'. A first group establishing itself as early as 1980, following Abdullah Azzam's *fatwa* declaring it was a '*fard ayn*' (personal) obligation on all Muslims to fight the Soviets in Afghanistan,[7] comprised ready-made Islamists, in their majority from the Gulf states, who had already gone through significant struggles with the local governments during the 1970s. While these individuals brought in a seasoned dimension to their militancy, they also looked upon the migration to Afghanistan as relief from the stalemated fight against their 'near enemy'. The coming of a second contingent, largely North African, was clustered in mid-1986 in the aftermath of the successes of the original group in the insurgency against the Soviets, and ahead of the increasing prospect of the latter's withdrawal. Following the formal establishment of Al Qaeda in 1988–89, a third layer, including arrivals from Europe and the United States, added strength to the organization and was instrumental, in particular, as preparations proceeded for a series of assaults on US targets round the world. Moreover, with the departure of a number of first and second wave fighters (either to their home countries, notably Algeria where the Islamic Salvation Front was becoming engaged in a violent conflict with the government, or to take part in the conflict in Bosnia), there was a measure of natural filtering among the fighters of the new generation. Whereas the first group brought in commitment and energy, and the second added numbers and dedication, the third group injected renewal and focus at a crucial phase.

Arising from these specific antecedents, by the mid-1990s, without the knowledge of most observers including intelligence services, Al Qaeda was well on its way to becoming a transnational non-state armed group of a new calibre. As such, the organization had become an entity that could attack within and across state boundaries, based on sophisticated networks of communication and information, and empowered by globalization and information-age technologies. Asymmetrically, such clandestine and information technology-based operations can bypass superior military power of nation-states to attack political, economic, and other high-value targets.[8] In fact the

---

[7] Azzam had declared that: 'Whoever can, from among the Arabs, fight jihad in Palestine, then he must start there. And, if he is not capable, then he must set out for Afghanistan.' See Sheikh Abdullah Azzam, *Defense of the Muslim Lands: The First Obligation after Iman* [belief], 1984. Audio footage of Azzam making the same point was integrated in a 4 July 2007 message by Ayman al Dhawahiri.

[8] See Andrea J. Dew and Mohammad-Mahmoud Ould Mohamedou, *Empowered Groups, Tested Laws, and Policy Options: The Challenges of Transnational and Non-State Actors,*

novelty goes beyond the transnationality element; it triggered, arguably, new types of terrorism as well as novel forms of insurgency.[9]

This protean sophistication was husbanded with one main objective in mind, to attack the United States in an unprecedented and unexpected way: first through the targeting of US assets in different parts of the world (particularly those regions, like East Africa, where Al Qaeda was in the process of establishing solid operational networks) and, subsequently, through attacks on US soil itself. As it was setting this plan in motion, Al Qaeda paid close attention to the public perception of its activities and its martial logic. Accordingly, on 23 August 1996, Al Qaeda issued a declaration of war on the United States entitled 'Declaration of War against the Americans Occupying the Land of the Two Holy Places' (meaning Saudi Arabia. Mecca and Medina being the two main holy cities of Islam). Subsequently, on 23 February 1998, a second declaration of hostilities was released similarly by the group, 'Jihad against Jews and Crusaders'. The original declaration (reproduced in the London-based Arabic language newspaper *Al Qods al Arabi*) was issued by Osama Bin Laden himself. The second was released on the occasion of a meeting of Al Jabha al Islamiya al Alamiya li Qital al Yahud wa al Salibiyin (the World Islamic Front for Jihad against the Jews and the Crusaders), at a joint conference in Afghanistan with Bin Laden, Ayman al Dhawahiri, and three other Islamist leaders—Abu Yasir al Rifai Ahmad Taha (Egypt), Sheikh Mir Hamza (Pakistan), and Fazlul Rahman (Bangladesh)—in attendance.

Although these statements have not been taken seriously by the United States, and are often derided by commentators who insist on their illegitimacy and insincerity, the singular *casus belli* articulated by Al Qaeda in those two founding texts has remained cogent and consistent, unacceptable as that may be to the US. An expert—Thomas Joscelyn of the Claremont Institute—remarks that Bin Laden's 'explanations make no rational sense'.[10] More observant analysis is provided by another who remarks that: 'To this day, we do not know quite how much relative weight Osama Bin Laden attributes to his religious and his political goals. The manner in which he has altered the listing

---

Cambridge, MA: Harvard University, 2007, available at www.tagsproject.org/_data/global/images/Report_Empowered_Groups_Nov2007.pdf.

[9] See David Tucker, 'What is New about the New Terrorism and How Dangerous Is it?', *Terrorism and Political Violence*, Vol. 13, Autumn 2001, pp. 1–14; and David Kilcullen, 'Countering Global Insurgency', *The Journal of Strategic Studies*, Vol. 28, No. 4, August 2005, pp. 597–617.

[10] 'Symposium: Al Qaeda: What Next?', frontpagemagazine.com, 15 June 2007.

of his various aspirations in his various statements suggests that the political is primary and religion a tool.'[11] Indeed, the three reasons named by Al Qaeda as its justification for going to war against the United States—the presence of US troops in the Middle East, the country's support for Israeli occupation of Palestinian territories, and its support for repressive Arab and Muslim regimes—have remained the group's focal political reference. In their respective messages (some sixty altogether) sent since the September 2001 attacks, Bin Laden and al Dhawahiri have systematically made references to parts or the whole of this oppositional narrative.

Ten years after the first declaration, Al Qaeda released on 29 May 2007 a videotaped message, delivered by one of its senior officers, the American-born Adam Gadahn, in which these three main components of the *casus belli* were restated almost verbatim. Entitled 'Legitimate Demands', the message rehearsed the familiar three elements and added another three demands: ceasing 'interference in the religion, society, politics, and governance of the Muslims world'; putting 'an end to all forms of interference in the educational curricula and information media of the Islamic world'; and freeing 'all Muslim captives from your prisons, detention facilities, and concentration camps, regardless of whether they have been recipients of what you call a fair trial or not'. The new demands emerged as a reaction to developments since the September 11, 2001 attacks, in particular the invasions of Afghanistan and Iraq, the launching of a number of media outlets aimed at the region (such as the news channel *Al Hurra*), and the incarceration of Islamist militants in a number of places round the world, notably the prisons in Bagram, Abu Ghraib and Guantánamo Bay and secret locations in Europe.[12]

## Retreat and advance: managing the post-9/11 period

The September 2001 attacks on the United States marked the culmination of a tactical battleplan set in motion since 1996. That plan was part of a strategy of '*jihad* displacement' in which Al Qaeda's very creation was anchored. Al Qaeda advanced, then, throughout the 1990s with an eye cast mostly on its

---

[11] Louise Richardson, *What Terrorists Want: Understanding the Enemy, Containing the Threat*, New York: Random House, 2006, p. 63.

[12] On the secret prisons in Europe (notably in Poland and Romania), see Council of Europe, Parliamentary Assembly, *Secret Detentions and Illegal Transfers of Detainees Involving Council of Europe Member States: Second Report*, available at http://assembly.coe.int/Documents/WorkingDocs/Doc07/edoc11302.pdf., 11 June 2007.

operational and logistical preparations. Acquiring capacity—following the gathering of experience through the Afghanistan conflict—was the order of the day. As a series of spectacular operations in the period 1995–2000 demonstrated, the group was proving adept at this new form of war. These were the 13 November 1995 bombing of a Saudi-American base in Riyadh, Saudi Arabia; the 25 June 1996 attack on the Al Khobar towers near Dhahran in Saudi Arabia (the living quarters of the crews enforcing the no-fly zones over Iraq); the simultaneous bombings of the US embassies in Nairobi in Kenya and Dar es-Salaam in Tanzania on 7 August 1998; and the speedboat attack against the USS Cole off the coast of Aden in Yemen on 12 October 2000.

Ostensibly, the 2001 attacks marked a clear phase of geographical expansion of the group's mission. From a military ambition—Al Qaeda al 'Askaria (the Military Base) and al Jaysh al Islami (the Islamic Army) were early appellations of Al Qaeda, which was also created in the immediate aftermath of a war—it was moving to a strategic design meant to channel and cross-pollinate the experience, capacity, and energy henceforth gathered into a direct push on the United States. That progression persisted in the post-September 11 phase, and with the dramatic acceleration due to the lethal character of the attacks, as well as the United States' reaction in Afghanistan and Iraq, took on a political ambition on a far larger scale. Yet that evolution did not take Al Qaeda by surprise. The group was by design transnational and its aim all along had been precisely to lure the United States into battling it on its deterritorialized terms—a result which, strategically, would endow Al Qaeda with preeminent status among Islamist groups and, tactically, more engagement options to choose from. In that sense, Al Qaeda's advantage over the correlation of forces arraigned against it is that it has remained always proactive—seldom, if ever, reactive.

Specifically, such evasive and forward-looking planning played out on three fronts in the 2002–5 period. First, with the US invasion of Afghanistan in October 2001, even though the group had forecast some major reaction by the United States and had prepared for it (as attested to by the rapid disbandment of units previously housed in the training camps in Afghanistan), Al Qaeda nonetheless found itself on the defensive. Indeed, it was forced to abandon important terrain it controlled and retreat into the areas on the border between Pakistan and Afghanistan. Yet for all the talk of Al Qaeda being defeated by the US military in Afghanistan in 2002, no such picture emerged unambiguously. Indeed, arguably most of those detained by the United States during those engagements were either Taliban militants or non-Al Qaeda Islamists to whom Afghanistan had become home over the past years.

Certainly a number of Al Qaeda operatives were either killed, notably the military chief Mohammed Atef (Abu Hafs al Masri), hit during a US airstrike near Kabul on 16 November 2001, or arrested—in particular Ramzi Bin al Shaiba and Khaled Sheikh Mohammed, respectively coordinator and organizer of the September 2001 attacks on New York and Washington, who were detained on 11 September 2002 in Karachi and on 1 March 2003 in Rawalpindi in Pakistan, and Zein al Abidin Mohammad Hussein (Abu Zubaydah), senior chief of operations, captured in Faisalabad in Pakistan on 28 March 2002. However, none of these setbacks contributed significantly, much less lastingly, to the weakening of an Al Qaeda leadership which had mostly moved away already and by the time of the December 2001 Tora Bora battle was essentially unreachable. In dissolving its physical, pinpointable presence, Al Qaeda rendered its centre of gravity fluid and itself evanescent. In so doing, it also frustrated the advancing US Special Forces bracing for a fight, luring them into a cat-and-mouse game which remained undecided several years later.

Second, rather than attempting a repeat of the attacks on the United States (not necessarily in the form of another aircraft hijacking operation), Al Qaeda opted to forestall and relocate its attacks on that country's allies round the world. Accordingly, the group conducted eight medium-scale operations in Karachi in May and June 2002; in Sana'a in October 2002; in Riyadh in May and November 2003; in Casablanca in May 2003; in Istanbul in November 2003; and in Amman in November 2005. In parallel there were two major operations in Madrid on 11 March 2004 and in London on 7 July 2005.

Finally, following the American and British invasion of Iraq in March 2003, and the rise of a multifaceted insurgency dominated by the Jordanian Islamist Ahmad al Nazal al Khalaylah (Abu Musab al Zarqawi), Al Qaeda actively supported the fight against US and coalition troops in that country and agreed subsequently to the opening of a local branch, Al Qaeda fi Bilad al Rafidayn (Al Qaeda in the Land of Mesopotamia).

These three synchronized steps, in particular the latter, went along with an accelerated decentralization strategy which eventually saw the organization embrace rapidly the international appeal and influence it had come to exert over other Islamist groups. Accordingly, in a span of two years (2004–6), it established six official branches: Al Qaeda in the Gulf, Al Qaeda in Europe, Al Qaeda in Iraq, Al Qaeda in Egypt, Al Qaeda in the Islamic Maghreb, and Al Qaeda in Afghanistan (led by Mustapha Abu Al Yazid who pledged allegiance to Bin laden and al Dhawahiri in a 23 May 2007 videotape).

Akin to franchises and with some differences, these operationally-independent regional organizations followed the methods and signature of the central organization, a 'mother' Al Qaeda or Al Qaeda al Oum. Announced formally in audio- or videotaped messages by Ayman al Dhawahiri, the creation of these units was in itself a telling sign of the group's global reach and the coalescence of its design. In Europe, the Jamaat al Tandhim al Sirri li Munadhamat Qaedat al Jihad fi Europa (Group of the Secret Organization of Al Qaeda in Europe) claimed within hours the 7 July 2005 multiple bombings in London. Posted on a site (www.qal3ati.com) now closed down, its online release declared: "As retaliation for the massacres which the British commit in Iraq and Afghanistan, the mujahideen have successfully done it this time in London. And this is Britain now burning from fear and panic from the north to the south, from the east to the west. We have warned the British government and British nation several times. And, here we are. We have done what we have promised. We have done a military operation after heavy work and planning, which the mujahideen have carried out, and it has taken a long time to ensure the success of this operation." The language used was strongly reminiscent of that of Bin Laden in the aftermath of the September 11 attack ("There is America, full of fear from its north to its south, from its west to its east", 7 October 2001 message). A year later, on 7 July 2006, Al Dhawahiri confirmed that the attacks were the work of Al Qaeda and that two of its perpetrators (Shehzad Tanweer and Mohammad Sidique Khan) had met the organization's leadership in Pakistan.

In Saudi Arabia, the group went on to actively challenge the local House of Saud rulers with a series of high-profile and unprecedented attacks in the country, including attacks on oil facilities (May 2004), the Ministry of the Interior (December 2004), and the US Consulate in Jeddah (December 2004). Following the killing of the branch's original leaders (Abdelaziz al Moqrin and Salah al Oofi), the group adopted a lower profile, indicating both operational challenges and semi-successful police work in the country, but also the migration of many operators to Iraq, where, according to one estimate, Saudi nationals came to represent close to 45 per cent of the foreign insurgents.[13]

[13] Ned Parker, 'Saudis' role in Iraq insurgency outlined', *Los Angeles Times*, 15 July 2007. Also see Dan Murphy, 'All-out war between Al Qaeda and the House of Saud under way', *The Christian Science Monitor*, 3 June 2004; and Jefferson Morley, 'Is Al Qaeda winning in Saudi Arabia?', *Washington Post*, 18 June 2004. In Iraq, the local antipathy towards Al Qaeda-related Saudis was expressed by a number of Shiite factions, which often decried in their statements the 'Wahhabi invasion'.

The case of the Iraqi branch illustrates Al Qaeda's deployment strategy particularly well. Although, as noted, Al Qaeda al Oum had supported the Iraqi insurgency (in its statements) from the very beginning, and was seen as a rising menace in that theatre,[14] it was not formally present in the country until, on 28 October 2004, Abu Musab al Zarqawi—who had rapidly emerged as the most lethal threat to US and coalition forces in Iraq, notably following his 2003 back-to-back attacks on the Jordanian embassy on 7 August, the United Nations offices in Iraq on 19 August, and the International Committee of the Red Cross (ICRC) on 27 October—sent a public letter to Osama Bin Laden praising his leadership and requesting that his own organization (Al Tawhid wa al Jihad) should receive Al Qaeda's imprimatur. A sign of the times, such a modern-day merger of a successful local start-up with an established and recognizable global brand was also equally in line with age-old *bay'a* ceremonials among Arab tribes whereby one swears an oath of allegiance to a leader and receives the latter's blessing. In an equally public message, Bin Laden responded the following 27 December welcoming this initiative as 'an important step in unifying the fighters in establishing the state of righteousness and ending the state of injustice.' Two days after the killing of al Zarqawi in June 2006, his replacement, Abu Hamza al Muhajir, confirmed the *bay'a* addressing Bin Laden thus: 'We are at your disposal, ready for your command.'

This jigsaw matrix was replayed on 5 August 2006 with an announcement by Ayman al Dhawahiri that the Egyptian Islamic Group (Al Jama'a al Islami-yya) had joined Al Qaeda to form a branch in Egypt under the leadership of Mohammad Khalil al Hukayma. Appearing in the video to support the claim, the latter was indeed a member of the Jama'a but of junior rank. The Group subsequently denied al Dhawahiri's allegation[15] but the purpose was already achieved, namely the external empowerment of an internal officer with a view to bringing into Al Qaeda's fold one of the most important and (considering the Jama'a as an offshoot of the older Muslim Brotherhood) longest-established Islamist organizations. The move in Egypt was particularly adroit, representing a sort of long-distance coup d'état conducted by Al Qaeda against the prominent, decades-old Islamist organization which had renounced violence in the 1970s. Al Qaeda accomplished this by drafting a lesser member of the Muslim Brotherhood and, in effect, painting its older

---

[14] Richard C. Paddock, Alissa J. Rubin, and Greg Miller, 'Iraq seen as Al Qaeda's top battle-field', *Los Angeles Times*, 9 November 2003, p. 1.

[15] Interview of Najih Ibrahim with *Al Sharq Al Awsat* (London), 13 August 2006, p. 1.

figures either as obsolete or incapable of leadership (partly as their own followers were apparently joining Al Qaeda).[16]

Such tactical manoeuvring was not needed in the case of another leading North African Islamist group. The following month, al Dhawahiri announced, on 11 September, that the Algerian Salafist Group for Preaching and Combat (GSPC, from its commonly-used French appellation, Groupe Salafiste pour la Prédication et le Combat) was also joining Al Qaeda to lead the fight in the wider Maghreb. Accordingly, the GSPC altered its name and, on 11 January 2007, became Al Qaeda in the Islamic Maghreb (Al Qaeda fi Bilad al Maghrib Al Islami). Subsequently, in a videotaped message aired on 3 November 2007, al Dhawahiri announced that a Libyan group, the Libyan Islamic Fighting Group,[17] had joined Al Qaeda in the Islamic Maghreb and urged the *mujahideen* in North Africa to topple the leaders of Libya, Tunisia, Algeria, and Morocco. The fifth Maghrebi country, Mauritania, was conspicuously absent though, paradoxically, it had been the target of a GSPC attack on a Mauritanian military base (in the northeastern area of Lemgheity) in June 2005. In the aftermath of al Dhawahiri's call, four French tourists were murdered in southern Mauritania and, two days later, three Mauritanian soldiers were killed in an ambush in the northern area bordering Algeria. The attacks were claimed by Al Qaeda in the Islamic Maghreb.

The November 2007 announcement might also have been prompted by the increasing perception that, for all its regional mission, Al Qaeda in the Islamic Maghreb had remained up to that point mostly an Algerian affair. In Morocco, besides the 16 May 2003 operation in Casablanca against several Western-related buildings (before creation of the new entity),[18] there had indeed been recent Al Qaeda activity as illustrated by the death of suspected kamikazes

---

[16] Mohammad-Mahmoud Ould Mohamedou, 'The Dividends of Asymmetry: Al Qaeda's Evolving Strategy', opendemocracy.net, 18 December 2006, www.opendemocracy.net/conflict-terrorism/asymmetry_4195.jsp.

[17] The Libyan Islamic Fighting Group is a little-known Libyan organization which first appeared in 1995, vowing to overthrow the Libyan leader Muammar Gaddafi.

[18] The Moroccan Islamist Combatant Group, whose leader (Abdelaziz Benyaich) was arrested after the 2003 Casablanca attacks, as well as the Salafiya Jihadia in Morocco, had not been so active. Similarly in Tunisia, the Tunisian Combatant Group has kept a low profile. In late December 2006–early January 2007, a group of 23 Tunisian Islamists, mostly Tunisians coming from Algeria where they had been crossing since 2005 and led by a former Tunisian security forces officer, Lassaad Sassi Al Muritani, was apprehended by the Tunisian authorities. Al Muritani was killed on 3 January 2007 by Tunisian police.

(Mohammed Mentalla and Mohammed Rachidi) about to be arrested by the Moroccan police on 10 April 2007. A month later, another kamikaze (Abdelfateh Raydi) was killed in a Casablanca cybercafé, and an alleged accomplice (Youssef Khoudri) was injured. Yet besides these developments and *ad hoc* statements by individual Islamists in Mauritania,[19] the North African Al Qaeda scene remained dominated by the former, now reformed GSPC. In a sense the GSPC had unilaterally pledged allegiance to Al Qaeda in September 2003, and had also shared a long-distance anti-French strategy with al Zarqawi after the latter threatened France on 18 May 2005 for its treatment of Muslims. In a confidential memorandum dated 16 December 2005, the French Anti-Terrorist Struggle Coordination Unit (Unité de Coordination de la Lutte Antiterroriste, UCLAT)—which oversees liaison between French intelligence, the police force, and the Homeland Security-like Direction de la Surveillance du Territoire (DST)—estimated subsequently that the Al Qaeda threat against France was 'particularly elevated' as a result of these pronouncements.

In many ways the regionalization of the GCSP was but a replay of Al Qaeda Al Oum's own expansion strategy. The GSPC had been set up in 1998 by Hassan Hattab, who led the group until he was replaced by Nabil al Sahraoui in August 2003; al Sahraoui, in turn, was killed by the Algerian army in June 2004 and replaced by Abdelmalek Droukdel (also known as Abou Moussab Abdelweddoud) as 'national emir'. The resurgence of the GSPC then began in earnest in 2003 when its southern region leader, Amari Saidi (subsequently arrested by the Algerian authorities), kidnapped 32 European tourists and released them after the German government agreed to pay a ransom of five million euros. The group was then divided into six sectors, the most active being the ones headed respectively by Abderrezaq 'El Para' and Mokhtar Ben Mokhtar. The attraction that Al Qaeda had for the North African group was first expressed through public correspondence that Droukdel maintained with al Zarqawi, each congratulating the other on respective actions. Bin Laden and al Dhawahiri, however, had long been in close ties with the area's militant Islamists. A first contact was established through the Algerian Armed Islamic Group (Groupe Islamique Armé, GIA) and its regional head in Europe, Abu Qotada al Filistini. A Yemeni Islamist (Abdelwahab al Wani) visited Algeria in 2000 on behalf of Bin Laden, and was killed there in September near the

---

[19] Five individuals had been arrested in Nouakchott, capital of Mauritania, on 19 October 2007 and accused of links with Al Qaeda in the Islamic Maghreb.

city of Batna. It was reported that al Wani had discussions with his local contacts—in particular 'El Para', who moved further south in Algeria[20]—about the establishment of an Al Qaeda fi Bilad al Berbar (Al Qaeda in the land of the Berbers).

The constant radicalization of Al Qaeda's branch in the Maghreb is certainly cause for concern among the states of the region as it aims to target the wider region.[21] From islands of connection but no full picture of regional and intercontinental cooperation, the move has increasingly been towards more formal expansion underscored by the renewed local preoccupations of the 'mother Al Qaeda'. In June 2007, there was even a spin-off from the new (Al Qaeda in the Islamic Maghreb) spin-off: Ansar al Islam fil Sahra (the Partisans of Islam in the Sahara). In a video message aired online that month, the previously-unknown group threatened to attack North African and Western European countries as well as the United States.

Control over the offshoots—whether spun (Iraq), attracted (Algeria), or inspired (Somalia)—was also evidenced by the fact that these new branches rapidly displayed Al Qaeda's *modus operandi*, in particular (i) high-profile and coordinated attacks against symbolic targets, (ii) active use of the media and the Internet, and (iii) investment in lengthy preparations and timing. Thus the Al Qaeda in the Maghreb-led twin bombings in Algiers on 11 April 2007 targeted a government building (an explosive-packed vehicle ran through the gate of the six-storey prime minister's office) and the Bab Ezzouar police station housing special police forces. Much like the operations conducted by the Hamburg or Madrid cells, the attacks were the work of a small commando, in this case three individuals—known by their *noms de guerre* Al Zubair Abu Sajeda, Mu'az Ben Jabal, and Abou Dejna—whose videotaped wills were circulated immediately by the group. (An earlier attack by the group had resulted in six deaths in Algiers on 13 February 2007.) Furthering that pattern and echoing Al Qaeda in Iraq's own 2003 attacks on the UN and the ICRC, Al Qaeda in the Islamic Maghreb struck anew on 11 December 2007 with near-simultaneous twin bombings in Algiers targeting buildings housing the United Nations representation and the Algerian Constitutional Council. The same day, the group announced that the attacks

---

[20] See Salima Mellah and Jean-Baptiste Rivoire, 'El Para, the Maghreb's Bin Laden', *Le Monde Diplomatique* (English edition), February 2005, p. 1, http://mondediplo.com/2005/02/04algeria.

[21] Craig S. Smith, 'North Africa feared as staging ground for terror', *The New York Times*, 20 February 2007, p. A1 and A6.

had been conducted by two of its members, Ibrahim Abu Othman and Abdulrahman al Asimi.

Even in the context of a violence-beset country such as Algeria, the difference in scale and method used by the new entity was noticeable. No such spectacular bombings had been resorted to by the various factions at war during the 1990s civil war in the country. With the exception of the 26 August 1992 bombing at the Algiers airport, the violence had taken the form of targeted assassinations and large-scale reprisal massacres (notably in the villages of Rais and Bentalha in August and September 1997),[22] not regular bombings, nor indeed anything to confirm worrying reports that the GSPC had, possibly, access to chemical weapons.[23]

At the end of this phase, Al Qaeda had been able to advance globally, cumulatively, and against important odds. During this period, for each tactical loss, Al Qaeda won a strategic gain: retreat in Afghanistan but advance in Iraq; confined leadership but proliferating cells; curtailed physical movement but global, transnational impact; additional enemies but expanding recruitment.[24] Similarly, its leadership embraced a loose approach to influence with the bicephalous Bin Laden-al Dhawahiri leadership morphing into a meta-command now issuing directives, now welcoming initiatives, and regularly offering politico-religious and militaro-strategic commentary.

In parallel, Al Qaeda's official media branch, Moussassat al Sihab (the clouds' organization) increased both the quantity and quality of its output. No longer merely releasing semi-annual static videos of Bin Laden or al Dhawahiri delivering lengthy statements in the form of tapes sent to the Doha-based Arabic all news channel Al Jazeera, it added a variety of formats (including hour-long online documentaries with graphs and computer simulation) and articulate speakers (such as Adam Gadahn[25]) to its releases (up to 58

---

[22] Although attributed to Islamist factions, the two massacres may in fact have been conducted by other actors, and accusations have been pointed towards governmental circles. See Nesroulah Yous, *Qui a tué a Bentalha: chronique d'un massacre annoncé*, Paris: La Découverte, 2000.

[23] Faycal Oukaci, 'Mutations logistiques du terrorisme au Maghreb: des produits tetatogènes dans l'arsenal du GSPC Al Qaida', *L'Expression* (Algiers), 26 March 2007, p. 6.

[24] Mohammad-Mahmoud Ould Mohamedou, 'Towards the Real Al Qaeda', *opendemocracy. net*, 10 September 2007, available at www.opendemocracy.net/article/democracy_terror/real_al_qaida.

[25] Among those that have had particular prominence in the upper echelons of the post-September 11 Al Qaeda is Adam Yahiye Gadahn, known as Azzam al Amriki or Azzam

in 2006 and 67 in 2007). In late 2007, the group innovated further through an open interview with al Dhawahiri. In a 16 December release by Moussassat al Sihab, private individuals, journalists, and organizations were invited to submit, within a month-long frame, questions sent to specific Islamist websites to which al Dhawahiri would subsequently respond.

While al Dhawahiri increased his output, Bin Laden, in contrast, released fewer messages after 2004. None in 2005, four in 2006–a truce offer to the United States (19 January), a message to Americans about their 'complicity' in their government's actions (23 April), a clarification about non-involvement of Zacarias Moussaoui in the September 2001 plot (24 May), and a eulogy of al Zarqawi (1 July)—and five in 2007. The 2007 messages were a homage to the members of the September 11, 2001 commando (11 September), messages to the Pakistanis (20 September), to the Iraqis (23 October) and to the Europeans (29 November), and a commentary on the US presence in Iraq (29 December).[26] The absence of video footage was particularly important. On 16 July 2007, however, Mouassassat al Sihab released a video on the group's fighters which included previously unseen and undated footage of Bin Laden, discussing the value of martyrdom; although that did not constitute a new appearance as such, the short footage in the forty-minute video created media stir and political rumblings.

---

the American ('*azzam* means courageous in Arabic). Oregon-born, California-raised, Gadahn is a thirty-year-old American sought by the FBI since May 2004 and indicted since October 2005 (following the airing of a videotaped message in which he threatened attacks against the United States) for material support to Al Qaeda, and, in October 2006, for treason. He is currently on the US government's most-wanted terrorist list with a million dollar bounty for his capture. Of a Jewish-Protestant father and a Pennsylvanian mother, Gadahn converted to Islam in November 1995 and travelled in late 1997 to Pakistan, where he allegedly linked up with Abu Zubaydah. See Raffi Khatchadourian, 'Azzam the American: The Making of an Al Qaeda Homegrown', *The New Yorker*, 22 January 2007, pp. 50–63.

[26] This author has reservations as to the authenticity of the tape released on 7 September 2007 allegedly featuring Bin Laden. In important ways, it does not conform to Al Qaeda's previous releases. The form of this release (a pre-announced posting, copy obtained by US authorities though an advocacy anti-terrorism research site and subsequently leaked to Reuters) and the video's poor quality (showing the leader in an almost identical outfit as in the October 2004 tape, with an inexplicably darker beard) cast doubts on it. More importantly, the film features minimal motion, and is a still image from minute 2 to minute 12:30 and from minute 14 to the final minute 26. It is hardly conceivable that Al Qaeda would spend the previous years dramatically improving its visuals only to mark the (video) comeback of its leader with the most amateurish tape it had yet produced.

An important anomaly and an indication that Al Qaeda's network—or at least its distribution circuit—could be penetrated took place in September 2006 when the unedited outtakes of the filmed wills (*wasiyyat*) of Mohammad Atta and Ziad Jarrah were leaked to the London-based British newspaper *The Sunday Times*.[27] The hour-long raw footage dated 18 January 2000 depicting the two men, together and in separate filming sessions, bearded and sitting next to an AK-47, was allegedly made available to the newspaper 'through a previously tested channel'. The recording features no sound track and footage from the same tape, dated 8 January 2000, depicts a meeting with Bin Laden and about a hundred men in the open air, presumably at one of the camps in Afghanistan, possibly the Tarnak Farm on the outskirts of Kandahar.

All in all, the routinization of messages, their customization, integration of external footage about Al Qaeda, and addressing of different audiences spoke, first and foremost, to a strategy of diversification and decoupling. In that sense, Al Qaeda's ability to persuade local groups to link their struggles with a broader, pan-Islamist campaign is arguably the organization's signal achievement.[28] It also unveiled a desire on the part of Al Qaeda to establish the 'normality' of such long-term process whereby these activities on the part of the organization are to be expected regularly ('this year, next year, the year after that, and so on' as Gadahn stated in May 2007). To the extent that the release of a message was no longer an event in and of itself (as was the case in 2001–2), it became important to distinguish the specific purpose of each release; hence the use of titling (e.g. 'Message of One Concerned', 'The Power of Truth', 'The Wills of the Heroes of the Raids on New York and Washington', 'One Row', 'Legitimate Demands'—the latter, noted one analyst, being a 'supremely confident presentation... studded with contemporary [English-language] slang and catch-phrases' characterized by an 'almost complete lack of Islamic terminology and allusions'[29]). Paradoxically, this controlled proliferation effort also rendered obsolete the United States' attempt to play down the impact of each new message coming from Al Qaeda.

[27] Yosri Fouda, 'The Laughing 9/11 Bombers: Exclusive Film of Suicide Pilots at Bin Laden's HQ', *The Sunday Times*, 1 October 2006, p. 1.

[28] Angel Rabasa *et al.*, *Beyond Al Qaeda: Part One: The Global Jihadist Movement*, Santa Monica, CA: Rand Project Air Force, 2006, p. xxv.

[29] Michael Scheuer, 'Al Qaeda's American Recruit Releases Something Entirely New', *Terrorism Focus*, IV, 17, 5 June 2007, p. 6.

## Discontinuity and continuity: back to the future

For all practical purposes, Al Qaeda had handed the United States a defeat in Iraq within three years of the parties' encounter in that country. Certainly the fiasco there was hardly the result of actions engineered solely by Al Qaeda; most of it had to do with the United States' self-undermining choices. The Islamist group was, however, instrumental in manifold ways in the US rout and capitalized on that situation. With all the envisioned strategic mishaps forewarned from September 11, 2001 to March 19, 2003 about an invasion of Iraq having come to pass—civil war, factionalism, ethnic cleansing, empowerment of armed groups, regional instability, authoritarianism, militarization[30]—Al Qaeda did not need further arguments to make the point about the United States' miscalculation. Yet adding insult to injury, the organization recognized that it was ahead of its foe, stated it resoundingly, and moved on: both physically (on to Afghanistan and North Africa) and conceptually (regrouping and organizing). On 10 November 2006, two days after the Republican Party had lost control of both houses of the US Congress to the Democrats, Abu Hamza al Muhajir (also known as Abu Ayub al Masri)—al Zarqawi's replacement as head of Al Qaeda in Iraq—announced 'victory' over the United States, claimed to be at the helm of a 12,000–strong force, and invited the United States to remain in the country so that his organization would enjoy more opportunities to kill American soldiers.

Al Muhajir's taunting assessment was only partly sarcastic. Indeed, Al Qaeda had done much to secure this 'victory' after taking charge of the embryonic insurgency in Iraq with contacts as early as May-June 2003. By December 2006, Al Qaeda had managed to offset the United States' plans, outpace the other insurgent groups (in effect setting standards of both type and ferocity of attacks against the foreign troops and other local actors), and throw off any plans of establishing normalcy in that country (declaring that his fighters in Iraq had 'broken the back of America', al Dhawahiri made mention, in May 2006, of eight hundred attacks led by Al Qaeda in the country.) When al Zarqawi made the tactical mistake of declaring war on the Shia, the 'headquarters' in Afghanistan was able to pull him back from that strategy and, following his death, gradually retreated from it through an agreement to operate under the banner of a multi-party Islamist entity known as Al Dawla al Islamiya fil Iraq (the Islamic State in Iraq). Possibly as preparation for such a

---

[30] On the barbarization of Iraq, see Nir Rosen's vivid account, 'Anatomy of a Civil War: Iraq's Descent Into Chaos', *Boston Review*, 31, 6, November/December 2006, pp. 7–21.

change, Al Zarqawi had been, in effect, noticeably absent from the Iraqi operation scene from the late autumn of 2005 to the early spring of 2006, only reemerging in late April, six weeks before his death on 7 June, with a discourse and behaviour closer to Bin Laden's and al Dhawahiri's demeanour than at any time before.

Attacks in Iraq and Afghanistan aside, Al Qaeda did not conduct any major international operation between mid-2005 and early 2008. The absence of such assaults was hardly fortuitous. Neither was it due to the impossibility of conducting such attacks, or to the—limited—success of counter-terrorism policies. Given the group's assertive approach to strategy making, if Al Qaeda had broken a well-established pattern, surely it was deliberately. A July 2007 estimate by the United States National Intelligence Council (summarizing the conclusions of sixteen US intelligence agencies) concluded: 'Al Qaeda is and will remain the most serious terrorist threat to the Homeland, as its central leadership continues to plan high-impact plots... Al Qaeda will continue to enhance its capabilities to attack [the United States] through greater cooperation with regional terrorist groups... [P]lotting is likely to continue to focus on prominent political, economic, and infrastructure targets with the goal of producing mass casualties, visually dramatic destruction, significant economic aftershocks, and/or fear among the US population.'[31] The lack of operations was also a conscious choice meant to keep its enemy in a constantly defensive position by, in effect, rebooting international terrorism. Honed in Iraq, the terror tactics were being exported to the Levant, the Gulf, North Africa, and Europe, and the strategy was moving from 'wait-and-wait-and-attack' to 'wait-and-wait-and-deceive-and-attack'.

The two years during which Al Qaeda had been relatively silent internationally were those when its leadership (i) asserted greater control of its activities and (ii) developed greater speed in responding to key international developments.[32] On a more secure footing about its own safety, Al Qaeda's central leadership reestablished core functions in Pakistan's tribal areas. A

---

[31] National Intelligence Council, 'The Terrorist Threat to the US Homeland', National Intelligence Estimate, July 2007. Also see Peter Grier, 'Why US sees Al Qaeda as a growing threat', *The Christian Science Monitor*, 17 July 2007; Mark Mazzetti and David E. Sanger, 'Al Qaeda threatens, US frets', *The New York Times*, 22 July 2007; and Michael Moss and Souad Mekhennet, 'Militants widen reach as terror seeps out of Iraq: start of trend is seen', *The New York Times*, 28 May 2007, pp. A1 and A8.

[32] See Paul Haven, 'Al Qaeda ops show leadership in control', Associated Press, 13 July 2007.

reaction period of about five weeks was reduced to an average ten days needed to release fully-produced videotaped messages—eleven after Hamas' takeover of Gaza in May 2007 or eight after the Red Mosque siege in Pakistan, a few weeks later. Similarly, the leadership (iii) oversaw the emergence of a new generation of leaders (such as Abdelhadi al Iraqi), under the direct control of the 'mother Al Qaeda'. This consolidation of power was also recognized by US authorities.[33] Al Qaeda's self-control and choice to regroup deeper are important in light of the fact that, as a former inspector general of the US Department of Homeland Security noted in 2007, 'it is only marginally harder for terrorists to enter the United States now than it was before September 11, and once they're inside our borders the potential targets are infinite.'[34] In many ways, one of Al Qaeda's greatest strength is indeed its human resource management. It scores high on programme management as relating specifically to the uniqueness, temporariness, and predefined goals of its projects.[35]

Yet in this context, another dimension was emerging slowly: Al Qaeda had in effect, through premature and amplified success, reached the limit of what a transnational non-state armed group could realistically achieve in opposing (powerful) states. Only naturally, it then turned its attention to its old nemeses, the weak and weakened regimes of the Arab and Islamic world. In a 20 September 2007 audiotaped message, Osama Bin Laden called on the Pakistanis to overthrow President Pervez Musharraf. A month later, on 22 October Bin Laden spoke to the Iraqis urging them to unite and avoid factional infighting. Ten days later, on 2 November, Ayman al Dhawahiri called for the removal of the leaders of Libya, Morocco, Algeria, and Tunisia.

## Conclusions

The impact of Al Qaeda on global politics is an affair of long standing. Its inception goes back two decades to the contemporary emergence and transformation of a non-state armed group which has sought to create original

---

[33] Mark Mazzetti, 'New leadership is seen on rise within Al Qaeda', *The New York Times*, 2 April 2007, pp. A1 and A11.

[34] Clark Kent Ervin, 'Answering Al Qaeda', *The New York Times*, 8 May 2007, p. A23.

[35] See Ofer Zwikael, 'Al Qaeda's Operations: Project Management Analysis', *Studies in Conflict and Terrorism*, Vol. 30, 2007, pp. 267–80. Zwikael concludes that 'unlike Western organizations, Al Qaeda's project management strengths in human resources and communications management are aligned with the areas that are most valuable to project success' (p. 280).

regional and international dynamics anchored in a privatized use of force for a political purpose. Beyond solely triggering domestic or foreign crises, this organization has aimed, in particular, to adapt, achieve, and prosper open-endedly as it pursued such a novel strategy. It is in that sense that the meta-morphosis of Al Qaeda was planned in advance. From the very beginning, this was an inevitable way to ensure its continuation and set it apart from previous and subsequent Islamist groups.

This central characteristic of Al Qaeda, its transformation and continued mutation, is what makes counter-terrorism measures against it so difficult, almost doomed to failure in the face of an evanescent organization.[36] The strength of Al Qaeda has lain, too, in its proactive, secure, and dedicated approach. Whereas the most established analysts, too often indulging an emo-tional reading, misread the complex nature of the movement, Al Qaeda has invariably been ahead maintaining ideological consistency and displaying constant operational novelty. By 2007, and mostly because of the failure in Iraq, policy thinking in the United States started recognizing in retrospect that 'just a year after the start of the war on terror, the terrorist threat started to evolve'.[37] Even such a late assessment is, however, faulty. This 'threat' never ceased to evolve and was largely resilient in facing what came to be known as the 'war on terror', namely the US' own tardy response to Al Qaeda.

Paradoxically, twenty years into this design, the dominant narrative about Al Qaeda almost systematically tends towards awkward scientific resistance to registering the success and innovation, indeed the visionary quality of Al Qaeda's project. From hatred, barbarity, and irrationality, we are merely being presented with a brew of elements rooted in denial, reductionism, and personalization of martial revolution. Martin Van Creveld, for instance, tells us that: 'All [the men of the 9/11 commando]... had been driven to that position by their experience of living in the West and trying, vainly, to assimilate'.[38] (In point of fact, fifteen of the nineteen men arrived in the

---

[36] For a discussion of these type of challenges, particularly as regards Al Qaeda's activities in the Gulf and in Iraq, see Bruce Hoffman, 'The Changing Face of Al Qaeda and the Global War on Terrorism', *Studies in Conflict and Terrorism*, Vol. 27, No. 6, December 2004, pp. 549–60.

[37] Peter Brookes and Julianne Smith, 'Course Correction in America's War on Terror', Bridging the Foreign Policy Divide Project, Muscatine, Iowa: The Stanley Foundation, May 2007, p. 2.

[38] Martin Van Creveld, *The Changing Face of War: Lessons of Combat from the Marne to Iraq*, New York: Ballantine Books, 2007. Van Creveld presents the case of the British army against the Irish Republican Army and the Syrian army against the Islamist rebel-

United States between May and July 2001. The other four, who included a *summa cum laude* PhD graduate and a polyglot playboy, had led successful lives in Europe before going to the United States.[39]) Some attempt to discern the mechanics of what would make Al Qaeda disappear, thus bypassing the lasting impact of a group which has already reached the status of being emulated (in Lebanon, Algeria, Iraq, etc.).[40] Others acknowledge the potential value of non-military engagement with armed Islamist groups, but de-emphasize the importance of Al Qaeda as a consequential actor, arguing instead, in pursuit of the safety of the familiar, that peripheral engagement with secondary groups might prove more fertile.[41]

All along, the dominant framework of thinking is that 'terrorist groups move along the same path—sustaining their ideology, objectives, and tactics—until some outside force causes them to shift'[42] and that 'terrorist organiza-

---

lion in Hama in 1982 as successful approaches to tackling such asymmetrical threats. The analogies are misleading militarily—the British exercised some restraint in Ireland and little is known about what really transpired in Hamas—but it is his conclusions that are astonishing: 'There are situations in which it is necessary to resort to cruelty' and 'once you have made up your mind to strike, you cannot strike hard enough' (p. 241). The distinguished scholar writes: 'Let there be no apologies, no kvetching [sic] about collateral damage caused by mistake, innocent lives regrettably lost, 'excesses' that will be investigated and brought to trial, and similar signs of weakness. Instead, make sure that as many people as possible can hear, smell, and touch the results; if they can also taste them, such as by inhaling the smoke from a burning city, then so much the better. Invite journalists to admire the headless corpses rolling in the streets, film them, and write about them to their hearts' content. Do, however, make sure they do not talk to any of the survivors so as not to arouse sympathy.' (p. 245) Referring to the 'developed world', Van Creveld concludes his book by remarking that 'the choice, as always, is ours'. In fact, that may not be the case here. In bringing down the pillars of such blinding certainty, Al Qaeda has done nothing less than displace the strategic locus of offence. A constantly mutating group of a few thousand men has been keeping the 'developed world' on its toes for the past decade facing an enemy which no one knows how to defeat. For once, the choice, it seems, is theirs.

[39] For a detailed account of the men's lives, see Mohammad-Mahmoud Ould Mohamedou, *Contre-croisade: Origines et conséquences du 11 septembre*, Paris: L'Harmattan, 2004.

[40] See, in particular, Audrey Kurth Cronin, 'How Al Qaeda Ends—The Decline and Demise of Terrorist Groups', *International Security*, 31, 1, Summer 2006, pp. 7–48.

[41] Ram Manikkalingam and Pablo Policzer, 'Al Qaeda, Armed Groups, and the Paradox of Engagement', March 2007, available at www.tagsproject.org/_data/global/images/Policzer%20and%20Manikkalingam.pdf.

[42] Angel Rabasa, Cheryl Benard, Peter Chalk, R. Kim Cragin, Sara A. Daly, Heather S. Gregg, Theodore W. Karasik, Kevin a. O'Brien and William Rosenau, *Beyond Al*

tions such as Al Qaeda face difficulties in almost any operational environment, particularly in terms of maintaining situational awareness'.[43] Hence 'attacking the ideology', 'breaking links', 'denying sanctuary', or indeed 'engaging peripherally' remained analytical lines that held sway among many. These analyses share a common emphasis on locating the initiative on the states' side, painting the misleading portrait of a reactive Al Qaeda only moving about along gaps created by these states' actions and inactions, when it is precisely the opposite that has often proved true.

Although there has been an increasing recognition of 'structural' reasons that allowed for Al Qaeda to blossom—'thanks to a series of organizational technological innovations, guerrilla insurgencies are increasingly able to take on and defeat nation-states' writes one analyst in a mainstream forum[44]—the overall perception persists that this 'superempowered competition'[45] is a reality guided by the centre. Whereas it can be argued that by forcing its enemy to allocate attention and resources (including political capital and military matériel) in areas unforeseen originally in this conflict,[46] Al Qaeda is impacting events more from the periphery inward.

In the post-September 11, 2001 period, Al Qaeda has remained a security threat of the first order to many Muslim and Western states for at least seven reasons. First, the group designed and implemented a successful battle plan. It forecast most of the reactions of its enemy and dealt adroitly with a large-scale global counterattack by the world's superpower and its strong allies. Most important, it set its struggle on a long-term track from the beginning. A philosophy borrowed, to be sure, from earlier movements, as summarized thus:

The guiding principle of the strategy of our whole resistance must be to prolong the war. To protract the war is the key to victory. Why must the war be protracted? ... If we throw the whole of our forces into a few battles to try to decide the outcome, we shall certainly be defeated and the enemy will win. On the other hand, if while fighting we maintain our forces, expand them, train our army and people, learn military

*Qaeda: Part Two: The Outer Rings of the Terrorist Universe*, Santa Monica, CA: Rand Project Air Force, 2006, p. 2.

[43] Combating Terrorism Center, *Harmony and Disharmony: Exploiting Al Qaeda's Organizational Vulnerabilities*, United States Military Academy, Department of Social Sciences, 14 February 2006, p. 2.

[44] David Brooks, 'The insurgent advantage', *The New York Times*, 18 May 2007, p. A25.

[45] As John Robb calls it. See his *Brave New War: The Next Stage of Terrorism and the End of Globalization*, Hoboken, NJ: John Wiley and Sons, 2007.

[46] That is the case for instance with the Sahel. See Lawrence Cline, 'Counterterrorism Strategy in the Sahel', *Studies in Conflict and Terrorism*, Vol. 30, 2007, pp. 889–99.

tactics… and at the same time wear down the enemy forces, we shall weary and discourage them in such a way that, strong as they are, they will become weak and will meet defeat instead of victory.[47]

Second, in the face of a massive invasion of the country that had sheltered it for several years (an attack supported by a key force in that country, namely the Northern Alliance), Al Qaeda implemented successfully a layered tactical retreat instead of succumbing to the cut-and-run syndrome that has often marked the end of less organized terrorist groups. Focusing on evading, regrouping and downsizing, the changing organization multiplied attacks across the globe in places where the United States did not expect it to strike, and refrained from attacking America anew. Al Qaeda's inaction during that period confused its enemies who oscillated between expectations of imminent attacks and totemic conclusions that there were no longer any terrorists: 'Why have they not been sniping at people in shopping centers, collapsing tunnels, poisoning the food supply, cutting electrical lines, derailing trains, blowing up pipelines, causing massive traffic jams, or exploiting the countless other vulnerabilities.'[48]

Third, its losses during this phase were minimal and, for a group of this sort, strategically acceptable. Some setbacks took place but few significant leaders were killed or arrested. A new generation of leaders was brought forth and the ultimate disappearance of the bicephalous Bin Laden-al Dhawahiri leadership prepared for. By early 2007, that new generation was apparently in control of operational levels (about which little is known), including those in the tribal regions near the Afghan border.[49] (Only one known leader from among the new Al Qaeda generation—Abdelhadi al Iraqi, detained in Turkey—has been captured.)

Fourth, Al Qaeda's main leadership remained intact (and 'if you can't find, you can't fight'[50]), acquiring instant global visibility for its cause after the

---

[47] Dang Xuan Khu, *Primer for Revolt*, New York: Praeger, 1963, pp. 11–12. Khu was a leading Vietnamese Communist leader and theoretician.

[48] John Mueller, 'Is there Still a Terrorist Threat?', *Foreign Affairs*, September/October 2006.

[49] Mark Mazzetti and David Rohde, 'Terror officials see Qaeda chiefs regaining power', *The New York Times*, 19 February 2007, pp. A1 and A7. Cited in the assessment, former Director of National Intelligence John D. Negroponte declared that 'Al Qaeda's core elements are resilient. [The organization] is cultivating stronger operational connections and relationships that radiate outward from their leaders' secure hideout in Pakistan to affiliates throughout the Middle East, North Africa, and Europe.'

[50] John Arquilla, 'The War on Terror: How to Win', *Foreign Policy* 160, May-June 2007,

attacks on New York and Washington. That elevation was capitalized on for several years and, through the nurturing of a certain 'nobility' associated with battle going back centuries in Arab mythology,[51] a prototype of the young Muslim fighting for his ancestral religion and identity in the modern world was reinvigorated in both the centre of the Western metropoles and the outer rings of the Islamic lands—not least, paradoxically, by way of ultra-modern technological tactics bridging these two worlds. Such new mythology was framed around the contemporary actions of the '*murabitoun ulama* warriors' as Ayman al Dhawahiri refers to them (such as Abd al Rashid al Ghazi, Abdullah 'Azzam, Mullah Daddulah, Abu Omar al Sayf, Abdallahi al Rashood, Hamoud Al 'Uqla, himself implicitly and, of course, Bin Laden). In addition, with its truce offers to Europe (April 2004) and the United States (January 2006), Bin Laden positioned himself as having 'given peace a chance', an argument he could come back to in the rationalization of potential further violence. Hence, to the 'bureaucratized and professionalized warfare'[52] of the West, Al Qaeda responded with a throwback to ancestral Islamic martial values coupled with modern-day technology. As Richard Shultz and Andrea Dew remark: 'When policymakers send soldiers to fight warriors, they must be aware that, for warriors, traditional concepts of war remain highly relevant. What is more, these traditional concepts will invariably take protracted, irregular, and unconventional forms of combat 'on the ground'.'[53]

Fifth, Al Qaeda turned its enemies' strategic miscalculations against them. The war in Iraq, in particular, was used opportunistically as a battleground to defeat the United States through a spearheading of the local resistance movement. Yet Al Qaeda, here, sought ultimately not to enjoy local decision-making but to provide decisive support and oversight.[54] The dialectic between

---

p. 45. Arquilla notes that 'there has been hardly a hint that the pursuit of Al Qaeda and its allies is guided by any serious thinking about the new types of problems posed by adversaries who operate in small, interconnected bands with minimal central control.'

[51] See Michael Bonner, *Aristocratic Violence and Holy War: Studies in the Jihad and the Arab-Byzantine Frontier*, New Haven: Yale University Press, 1997; and, for the larger narrative, John Wansbrough, *The Sectarian Milieu: Content and Composition of Islamic Salvation History*, Oxford University Press, 1978.

[52] David Kennedy, *Of War and Law*, Princeton University Press, 2006, p. 165.

[53] Richard H. Shultz Jr. and Andrea J. Dew, *Insurgents, Terrorists, and Militias: The Warriors of Contemporary Combat*, New York: Columbia University Press, 2006, pp. 269–71.

[54] In that sense, at the height of a mid-2007 US-supported Sunni push on Al Qaeda, Harith

*jihad* export as necessity and as improvised design was, here, quite fertile. As one analyst remarks:

Wilderness Ghazi groups like Al Qaeda have only one path open to them: to aspire to eventual political leadership. They must use their symbolic authority to assert a supra-national political authority. As a result all fighter groups begin locally but then shake off their small town roots. Only by leaving Arabia could Al Qaeda announce a bigger vision. So the wilderness framework not only plays to piety by tracing the steps of Muhammad. It also plays to deep chords of Muslim universalism. Nevertheless, Al Qaeda shows that playing to the world, or even creating a physically international network does not necessarily lead to Pan-Muslim political authority, and so their franchises tend to express the local identity of the places where they do business.[55]

Sixth, an international strategy of decentralization was pursued successfully. Assembling, as it were, 'near' and 'far' all-volunteer allies in Pakistan, Afghanistan, Iraq, the Gulf, the Levant, East Africa, North Africa, Europe, and possibly the United States, the leaders of Al Qaeda have extended the reach of their virtual dominion.[56] An impact captured by Shakir Al Abssi, leader of the Lebanese Fatah al Islam (a group which, emulating Al Qaeda's asymmetrical tactics, had in May-June 2007 dealt serious blows to the Lebanese army[57]):

---

al Dari, Secretary-General of the Union of Islamic Ulama in Iraq, stated revealingly: 'We do not accept Al Qaeda's activities, and we have rejected Al Qaeda's actions. However, Al Qaeda remains part of us and we are part of it. The majority of Al Qaeda are Iraqis and are not foreigners coming from abroad. Ninety per cent of Al Qaeda today are Iraqis. We can enter in discussions with them... That we would fight them, however, next to the occupation forces is unthinkable.' Interview with Al Jazeera, 5 October 2007.

[55] Michael Vlahos, 'Two Enemies: Non-State Actors and Change in the Muslim World', Strategic Assessments Office, National Security Analysis Department, Johns Hopkins University Applied Physics Laboratory, January 2005, p. 13. Also see by the same author, 'Fighting Identity: Why We Are Losing Our Wars', *The Military Review*, November/December 2007, pp. 2–12

[56] We should also note the accusations of collaboration with Hezbollah (see Bilal Y. Saab and Bruce O. Riedel, 'Hezbollah and Al Qaeda', *International Herald Tribune*, 9 April 2007, who note several strategic and behavioural differences between the two groups and call for more discernment) and the alleged links with the Palestinian Jaysh al Islam, which kidnapped the BBC journalist Alan Johnston in May 2004 (the announcement of the kidnapping was posted on www.alhesbah.org, a site often associated with Al Qaeda).

[57] Hassan M. Fatah and Nada Bakri, 'Lebanese troops fight Islamists; dozens are slain—sympathizers of Al Qaeda', *The New York Times*, 21 May 2007, pp. A1 and A10. The Fatah al Islam fighters in Nahr al Bared were led by operators originating from the Iraq battle zone. See Bernard Rougier, *Everyday Jihad: The Rise of Militant Islam among Palestinians in Lebanon*, Cambridge, MA: Harvard University Press, 2007.

'Osama Bin Laden does make the fatwas. Should his fatwas follow the Sunnah, we will carry them out.'[58] Such exaltation led US intelligence to conclude that the challenge of defeating Al Qaeda has become more complex than it was in 2001, and that the organization is a more dangerous enemy today than it has ever been before.[59] Consequently, the focus is not on the end of the conflict but on the end of the organization itself—an exercise at times centred merely on the quantitative disruption of cells.[60]

Seventh, in all these steps and in its conscious engineering of its own self-sustaining *Al Qaedaism* mythology, Al Qaeda remained consistently ahead of its enemies and made innovative use of time and space as regards its martial strategies. While maintaining cogency and consistency in its political message, it introduced improvisations (such as geographical indeterminacy of theatre of operations, concurrent acceleration and deceleration of engagement, weaponization of civilian assets) which were novel by fourth generation warfare standards.

In the final analysis, Al Qaeda's war of detachment vis-à-vis its 'near' Muslim enemies, which had prompted it at birth to orient its energy abroad, might have entered a new phase as a result of these manifold developments. The group is today an intensely complex global network, with a decentralized, flexible structure that enables it to spread in all directions across the Arab world, Africa, Asia, and Europe.[61] Yet by repatriating its energy 'prematurely', Al Qaeda may in fact have given in to reaction for the first time in its history. For once, it seemed to be following developments independent of its design, which give at least three reasons for its return to the region: (i) a desire to fight on a territory where it can move about and inflict direct losses on the United States; (ii) the renewed activism of the authoritarian regimes, which, if structurally weak, used the opportunity of the 'war on terror' to extend their

---

[58] Michael Moss and Souad Mekhennet, 'Jihad leader in Lebanon may be alive', *The New York Times*, 11 September 2007, p. A14.

[59] Bruce Riedel, 'Al Qaeda Strikes Back', *Foreign Affairs*, Vol. 86, No. 3 May/June 2007, pp. 24–40.

[60] See Jonathan David Farley, 'Breaking Al Qaeda Cells: A Mathematical Analysis of Counterterrorism Operations (A Guide for Risk Assessment and Decision Making)', *Studies in Conflict and Terrorism*, Vol. 26, No. 6, November/December 2003, pp. 399–411.

[61] Soumaya Ghannoushi, 'The West has created fertile ground for Al Qaeda's growth', *The Guardian*, 21 June 2007. Also see by the same author, 'The Erosion of the Arab State', 24 September 2006, aljazeera.net. Ghannoushi notes: '[S]ome Arab states are unable to respond to ever-mounting external threats, and…the burden of homeland protection is increasingly shifting from the standard political order to non-state actors.'

leases on their countries; and (iii) the difficult conditions in penetrating Western metropoles to conduct complex operations. In 'The Evolution of a Revolt', a 1920 essay he published in the British *Army Quarterly and Defence Journal* after his return from his campaigns in Arabia, T.E. Lawrence remarked that the virtue of irregulars lay in depth, not in face, and that it was the threat of attack by them that in effect paralyzed their enemies. Such depth of engagement is precisely what Al Qaeda achieved ultimately in the course of its meta-strategy towards both its 'near' and 'far' enemies.

# 11

# The Role of Sub-National Actors in Afghanistan

*Amin Saikal*

Afghanistan has historically been made up of numerous micro-societies, with the powers of the central authority often determined by the nature of its relationship with various local centres of power and their cross-border ethnic ties with Afghanistan's neighbours. Hence it has been a prime example of a country where sub-national actors have frequently played a debilitating role in preventing it from consolidating its position as a viable unit. The country has traditionally been marked by a weak state and strong society ever since its establishment as an identifiable political and territorial unit from the middle of the 18th century. It has been unable to develop solid domestic structures of stability, security and viability, and so has remained vulnerable to frequent outside interventions and invasions, which in turn have exacerbated its weak domestic conditions. This situation has largely contributed to the latest phase of bloodshed and conflict that has gripped the country from the late 1970s. Unless Afghanistan is put on a path of political, economic and security building that will enable it to develop an effective system of governance to reassure its micro-societies in relation to one another and the central authority, as well as to deter Afghanistan's predatory neighbours, the future of the country looks likely to be as bleak as its past. This is not to suggest that Afghanistan will disintegrate. It is primarily to claim that the country is likely to remain in the throes of instability and insecurity for a long time to come.

This chapter has three main objectives. The first is to look at the mosaic nature of the Afghan society and the difficulties that this has historically created for the country to become a strong state. The second is to identify the main sub-national actors—more saliently the Taliban—and examine their contributions to Afghanistan's instability in recent times. The third is to assess some of the vulnerabilities that have prevented the central government of President Hamid Karzai and its international supporters, especially the US and its NATO allies, from putting Afghanistan on a culturally relevant, stable path of change and development.

## Mosaic make-up of society

The evolution of Afghan politics and society has traditionally been affected by a number of critical variables. The first is that, although a Muslim country, Afghanistan is made up of numerous ethnic, tribal, linguistic, cultural and sectarian clusters. The ethnic Pashtuns have traditionally formed the largest cluster, constituting about 43 per cent of the total population,[1] and dominated the political leadership and the armed forces. However, they have not been homogeneous, given their division along various tribal, clan and family lines. The next group after the Pashtuns is a cluster of ethnic Tajiks, who have formed about 25–30 per cent of the population but, somewhat similarly to the Pashtuns, have been divided along various sub-ethnic and family lines. The rest of the population has come from various other ethnic origins, such as Turkmen, Uzbek, Nooristani and Hazara. The two main official languages spoken in the country are Pashtu and Dari (both Indo-European languages, the latter being a dialect of Persian), but there are also many localized languages, and varying dialects that are spoken within each of the two main ones. While some 80 per cent of the Afghan population are followers of the Sunni branch of Islam, the remainder belong to the Shi'ite branch of the religion, with different schools and orders causing widespread variations in the practice of both sections.[2]

[1] For a figure of about 40 per cent in the 1990s, see Ralph H. Magnus and Eden Naby, *Afghanistan: Mullah, Marx and Mujahid*, Boulder: Westview Press, 1998, p. 93; Alfred Janata, 'Afghanistan: the Ethnic Dimension', in Ewan Anderson and Nancy Hatch Dupree, *The Cultural Basis of Afghan Nationalism*, London: Pinter Publishers, 1990, p. 64.

[2] For a detailed discussion see Amin Saikal, *Modern Afghanistan: A History of Struggle and Survival*, London: I.B. Tauris, 2006, Ch. 1; Magnus and Naby, *Afghanistan: Mullah,*

The second variable relates to the Islamic-based practice of polygamy. From shortly after the foundation of modern Afghanistan until the pro-Soviet communist coup of April 1978, Afghanistan suffered terribly from this practice. It divided successive royal families into rival branches, competing for power at the cost of the unity of the ruling elite, effective governance and national cohesion.[3]

The third variable is the geostrategic location of Afghanistan, at first between the rival Russian and British powers and then, following World War II, between the US and its global Soviet competitor until the disintegration of the USSR and end of the Cold War in 1991. The fourth is the status of Afghanistan as a landlocked country, with extensive cross-border ties with its neighbours. This has meant that, on the one hand, Afghanistan has been very dependent on its neighbours for its existence and, on the other, it has remained vulnerable to its neighbours' pressures and manipulation of Afghan micro-societies against one another and the central government whenever these neighbours have deemed it desirable.

All these factors have interactively set the parameters within which Afghanistan could coalesce, function and develop as a state. They have played a profound role in preventing Afghanistan from nurturing firm domestic structures and a capacity to fend off the predatory actions of its neighbours and the competitive behaviour of big powers. The overall result has been that Afghanistan has evolved as a weak state in dynamic relationship with a strong society.[4] Two important characteristics of such a state are worth emphasizing. The first is that while a state may have a central authority, that authority and the functioning of the state can be very much at the mercy of numerous internal sub-actors and external actors who can manipulate various sub-actors for their purposes. The second is that the political stability and security of such a state can be ensured not so much through the adoption of rational-legal frameworks and the enforcement of central authority, but rather through relationships and alliances that the central authority can forge with sub-national

---

Marx, and Mujahid, Ch. 1; Louis Dupree, *Afghanistan*, Princeton University Press, 1980, Part II; William Maley, *The Afghanistan Wars*, London: Palgrave/Macmillan, 2002, Ch.1; Barnett R. Rubin, *Fragmentation of Afghanistan*, 2nd edn, New Haven: Yale University Press, 2002, Chs. 2–3.

[3] Saikal, *Modern Afghanistan*, Chs. 2–4, 6–7.

[4] For a theoretical discussion of such a state, see Joel S. Migdal, *Strong Societies and Weak States: State-Society Relation and State Capabilities in the Third World*, Princeton University Press, 1988.

actors, especially the most powerful and influential among them, and through the balance that it can achieve between external actors.

Against this backdrop, Afghanistan has always been a land of 'strong men', local power holders and regional figures—some with more distributive and dispensary powers than others. Prior to the rise of the communist rule and the Soviet invasion of Afghanistan in late December 1979, the people who filled these positions were called Khans, Sardars, Maleks, Mullahs and Pirs. The best way that the Afghan monarchy could rule and expand its writ from 1929 to 1973 was to establish a pattern of rule based on a triangular relationship between the monarchy, the local power holders and the religious establishment. This proved quite effective in helping Afghanistan to be one of the most stable and secure countries in the region during this period. However, this situation was disturbed from July 1973, when Mohammad Daoud overthrew his cousin and rival King Zahir in a bloodless coup and declared the country a republic, resorting to a greater degree of power centralization based not so much on the politics of a triangular relationship but rather on imposition from the centre.[5]

A greater accretion to the sub-national layers of power and authority occurred following the pro-Soviet communist coup of 28 April 1978 by the People's Democratic Party of Afghanistan (PDPA), which declared Afghanistan a Democratic Republic, with 'fraternal ties' with the Soviet Union. Since the PDPA was highly factionalized and at the same time lacked popularity, historical legitimacy and administrative competence, its Stalinist behaviour rapidly alienated a majority of the Afghan people, prompting many of them to engage in an Islamic resistance. When the PDPA's rule faced collapse, the USSR invaded Afghanistan in late December 1979 to save not only PDPA rule but also the long-standing Soviet political, economic and military investment in Afghanistan since the mid-1950s. The invasion only worsened the situation for the Soviets and their surrogates. The Afghan people now had greater cause to join the opposition that rapidly coalesced around Islam as an ideology of resistance and salvation. They supported various armed Islamic resistance groups—the Mujahideen—to fight the invaders and their supporters. Most in the Muslim world and the US and its allies immediately backed them in what became known as the Afghan *jihad* or holy combat.[6]

---

[5] Saikal, *Modern Afghanistan*, Ch. 7.
[6] For details, see Maley, *The Afghanistan Wars*, Chs. 3–6; Saikal, *Modern Afghanistan*, Ch. 8.

In this context, a new breed of armed local power holders and strong men emerged to dominate the scene. They were either commanders belonging to different Mujahideen groups, or those individuals who managed to gather sufficient arms and money to head localized militias in opposition to or in support of Soviet occupation. Backed by various regional and international actors, notably the United States, these figures rapidly emerged to eclipse and in many cases replace the traditional sub-national actors in the country. They became popularly known as 'warlords'. Some of the figures boasted highly personalized and localized power bases and agendas, and others claimed wider popularity and programmes of action, with some also projecting a national vision and consciousness.[7] These actors progressively carved up the areas outside the control of the Soviets into distinct units over which they sought to impose their varying jurisdictions and to defend them in the manner that they saw fit.

The power of the gun and support from local and foreign aid sources that empowered them to provide people with security and livelihoods, and to build patronage, rapidly enabled them—as individuals and in alliances with one another—to gain greater prominence than many of their traditional counterparts. They exerted control over the areas under their control in proportion to their influencing capacity. For example, while the resistance commander Ahmed Shah Massoud consolidated a hold on his native Panjshir Valley and several northern and north-eastern provinces, other prominent Mjuahideen leaders, such as Ismail Khan, Yunous Khalis and Abdul Rasul Sayyaf, established themselves in areas to the west and east of Afghanistan respectively, and Gulbuddin Hekmatyar carved a territorial niche to the southeast of the country.[8] They thus emerged as critical players not only in the resistance, but also in the shaping of Afghan politics and society.[9]

This remained the case following the Soviet troop withdrawal in May 1989, the collapse of the Soviet-backed regime of Najibullah three years later and its replacement by the Mujahideen Islamic government. A majority of the Afghan people, in rural areas in particular, seemed to view this development as something to which they had grown accustomed. This exacerbated and reinforced the patterns that had historically impeded the processes of building a strong state, capable of defending Afghanistan against its neighbours' preda-

---

[7] Magnus and Naby, *Afghanistan: Mullah, Marx and Mujahid*, Ch. 6.

[8] Amin Saikal and William Maley, *Regime Change in Afghanistan: Foreign Intervention and the Politics of Legitimacy*, Boulder: Westview Press, 1991, Ch. 4.

[9] Amin Saikal, 'Afghanistan's Ethnic Conflict', *Survival*, 40 (2), Summer 1998, pp. 115–26.

tory behaviour. The neighbour that now found it opportune and desirable that Afghanistan should serve its regional interests was Pakistan, with which Afghanistan shares a treacherous 2,400–km border and extensive cross-border ethnic ties.

## The Taliban

It was in this setting that two more sub-national militia-actors emerged and rapidly dominated the Afghan political landscape. They were the Taliban and Al Qaeda, the former being composed largely of ethnic Pashtuns, mostly from Afghanistan but some also from Pakistan, and the latter of Arabs, some of whom had participated as volunteers in the Afghan *jihad*, with logistic support from Pakistan's powerful military intelligence (ISI) and the CIA—the two organizations that had coordinated and distributed international, especially American, assistance to the Mujahideen during the Soviet occupation.[10] It is now established that the Taliban were essentially a creation of the ISI, which had been entrusted with the conduct of Pakistan's Afghanistan and Kashmir policies since the early 1980s and had grown to function in Pakistan as a government within the government—which still remains the case. Pakistan raised, armed, trained and logistically supported the Taliban from mid-1994, when the militia carried out its first operation to protect a Pakistani convoy of goods destined for the newly independent Muslim states of the former Soviet Union in Central Asia.[11]

Islamabad wanted influence in these states not only to access their natural resources and markets, but also to prevent advances by Iran and India. In this respect (although not so much in relation to India), Pakistan's policy actions suited Washington's objectives and those of its three other regional allies, Saudi Arabia, the United Arab Emirates (UAE) and Turkey, which were also keen to see Iran's regional activities and influence contained. Thus, the US and its regional allies had a vested interest originally in seeing Islamabad do whatever was necessary to stabilize Afghanistan as a direct corridor to Central Asia. The US had achieved its overriding goal of inflicting a mortal blow to

[10] For details see Chapter 10 in this volume. See also John K. Cooley, *Unholy Wars: Afghanistan, America and International Terrorism*, London: Pluto Press, 1999; George Frile, *Charlie Wilson's War: The Extraordinary Story of the Largest Cover Operation in History*, New York: Atlantic Monthly Press, 2003.

[11] For a detailed discussion, see Ahmed Rashid, *Taliban: Militant Islam, Oil and Fundamentalism in Central Asia*, New Haven: Yale University Press, 2002.

the Soviet Union as part of its long-term policy of containing the USSR by forcing the latter to retreat in defeat from Afghanistan. It was now quite content to let its regional allies, principally Pakistan, take care of the post-communist management of Afghanistan. Islamabad therefore made the Taliban operational with, if not the direct, at least the indirect support of Washington, and the direct political and financial backing of Saudi Arabia and the UAE.

Meanwhile, the Taliban proved to be very radical in their ideological disposition, military operations and methods of governance. They set out to upstage the moderate Islamic government of Burhanuddin Rabbani and Ahmed Shah Massoud, which had assumed power following the collapse of the communist government in Kabul, and to overcome many local power-holders in different parts of the country. In ideological terms, the militia espoused an extreme form of Wahhabi-Deobandi Sunni Islam, which sought a transformation of Afghanistan into a puritanical Islamic state, based on what it propagated as the Islam of the time of the Prophet Mohammad and his Companions. Led by a one-eyed former Mujahideen commander, Mullah Mohammad Omar, whose followers subsequently declared him Amir al-Mo'mineen (the Commander of the Faithful), the militia soon proved to be opposed to whatever aspect of modernity and cultural and social activities did not conform to its version of pristine Islam.

The Taliban adopted a patrimonial, medievalist approach to the application of Islam, highly discriminatory against not only the Shi'ites and women, but also any Sunni group that did not subscribe to its brand of Islam.[12] They combined military operations with buying off various local power-holders whenever feasible and required. They did so with the help of a large amount of cash channelled through the ISI from Saudi Arabia and the UAE. Whenever they took over a piece of territory, they immediately imposed a theocratic order based on their leadership's rigid version of Islamic law and justice, and a closed system of governance, in order to subordinate the population and to bring 'peace' and 'security' to that area.[13] They adopted a faceless approach to governance, whereby none of its leaders could be photographed.

Although their extremist Islam was alien to the Afghan people, who had historically practised a moderate Islam, largely at the village level, the Taliban

---

[12] For an evaluation of Taliban and Talibanism in a historical setting, see Nazif Shahrani, 'Taliban and Talibanism in Historical Perspective', in Robert D. Crews and Amin Tarzi (eds), *The Taliban and the Crisis of Afghanistan*, Cambridge, MA: Harvard University Press, 2008, Ch. 4.

[13] Ibid., Parts I–II; Neamatollah Nojumi, 'The Rise and Fall of the Taliban', in Crews and Tarzi (eds), *The Taliban and the Crisis of Afghanistan*, Ch. 3.

approach initially worked among a people who were exhausted by fighting, bloodshed, insecurity and divisions under the rule first of the communists and then of the rival Mujahideen groups. Many people were willing to tolerate the Taliban's theocratic imposition if it could bring them peace, security and an improvement in their impoverished living conditions. This, together with massive Pakistani logistic support, enabled the Taliban to succeed rapidly in first establishing themselves in the southern Afghan city of Kandahar (quite close to the Pakistani border city of Quetta, the capital of Pakistan's Baluchistan province) as their heartland, and then expanding their territorial control towards Kabul. By September 1996, they took over Kabul, forcing the Rabbani-Massoud government to retreat to the north, with Massoud repositioning his forces in his native Panjshir Valley to resist what was now widely viewed as 'Pakistan's creeping invasion' of Afghanistan. By late 1988 the Taliban took over most of Afghanistan, confining the Rabbani-Massoud government and its forces to north-eastern areas.

Meanwhile, soon after the Taliban's capture of Kabul, another sub-national actor—Osama Bin Laden and his Al Qaeda network, with an international agenda—came to join forces with the Taliban under the watchful eyes of the ISI. Bin Laden had been expelled from his native Saudi Arabia for opposition to the Saudi regime and its close alliance with the US, as well as to American troops deployed in Saudi Arabia for the efforts to reverse the August 1990 Iraqi invasion of Kuwait.[14] Afghanistan was not a strange land for either Bin Laden or some of his accompanying operatives. He had participated in the Afghan *jihad* against the Soviets and taken much pride in the success of that *jihad*. As before, this time too the ISI facilitated his return through Pakistan, for Afghanistan's other neighbours had closed their borders with the country out of opposition to the Taliban. Bin Laden immediately forged an alliance with Mullah Mohammad Omar and brought Arab money and fighters to the Taliban in return for a safe haven and freedom to use Afghan territory for whatever purposes he desired. Al Qaeda's position was further boosted when the leader of the Egyptian Islamic Jihad, Ayman al-Zawahiri, came to Afghanistan and merged his organization with Al Qaeda in 1997, and formed the World Islamic Front for Jihad the following year.[15]

It was not until the end of 1997 that the US Secretary of State, Madeleine Albright, and the First Lady, Hillary Clinton, criticized the Taliban for their

---

[14] For background discussion, see Jason Burke, *Al Qaeda: The True Story of Radical Islam*, London: Penguin Books, 2004.

[15] Abdel Bari Atwan, *The Secret History of Al-Qae'ida*, London: Abacas, 2006, p. 47.

brutal theocratic and discriminatory rule, with Albright also claiming that the Taliban should not be the only force to govern Afghanistan.[16] However, a concerted US effort to counter Al Qaeda did not begin until the network's attacks against US embassies in Kenya and Tanzania in August 1998, in which many Americans and hundreds of locals were killed. Those attacks galvanized the Clinton Administration to focus on three things. The first was to coordinate a counter-terrorism strategy with India, which had been complaining about Pakistan's support of cross-border terrorism for years, and Russia, which had become increasingly concerned about the Taliban's and Al Qaeda's support for Chechen separatists. The second was to authorise the CIA to see if it could snatch Bin Laden out of Afghanistan. The third was to limit unofficial American dealings with the Taliban and to seek stronger diplomatic pressure on the militia through a series of UN sanctions.[17]

Yet none of these measures, nor the American cruise missile attack on Al Qaeda's training camps in Afghanistan following the bombing of the US embassies in Africa, diminished Al Qaeda's capacity to press on with its apocalyptic agenda or the Taliban's resolve to continue to harbour the network's leadership. As long as the Afghan-Pakistan border remained wide open and Islamabad did not find it imperative to back away from the Taliban and the Taliban-Al Qaeda alliance, no American pressure short of taking on Islamabad could work. As for how to counter the role of nuclear armed Pakistan in all this, Washington found itself impaired by the fear that if it pressured the country too much it could possibly implode and this would land the US with more problems than it was worth.[18]

Although Pakistan was 'Terrorism Central', it was from Afghanistan that Al Qaeda masterminded a number of operations against the US and its allies, the largest being the attacks of 11 September 2001 on the US. The last event changed the picture for all sides involved. It finally propelled the US to launch Operation 'Enduring Freedom' as part of a wider enterprise, which shortly thereafter President George Bush called the 'war on terror'. The purpose was

---

[16] *Reuters*, 18 November 1997.

[17] Richard Clark, *Against All Enemies: Inside America's War on Terror*, New York: Free Press, 2004, Ch. 6.

[18] For a detailed discussion of US-Pakistan relations, see Ahmed Rashid, *Descent into Chaos: The United States and the Failure of Nation Building in Pakistan, Afghanistan, and Central Asia*, New York: Viking, 2008, Ch. 3; Steve Coll, *Ghost Wars: The Secret History of the CIA, Afghanistan, and Bin Laden, From the Soviet Invasion to September 10, 2001*, New York: Penguin Press, 2004.

to eliminate Al Qaeda and topple the Taliban's regime in favour of an internationally backed government in Afghanistan. A majority of the Afghans welcomed this development with a sigh of relief at the prospect of liberating themselves from the politically and culturally suffocating rule of the Taliban and their Al Qaeda allies, whom they viewed as outsiders using their territory for their messianic purposes. By late November 2001 the US, assisted by the anti-Taliban forces of the United Front for Islamic Salvation of Afghanistan or what was popularly referred to as the Northern Alliance—whose leader, Massoud, had been assassinated by Al Qaeda agents on 9 September—had brought about the overthrow of the Taliban regime and the disintegration of Al Qaeda's leadership and structures in Afghanistan. This was followed by the signing of the Bonn Agreement on 5 December 2001, according to which the administration of Hamid Karzai came into existence, and the role of the UN and outside military forces in the processes of Afghanistan's reconstruction and security building were legitimized.[19]

However, the Taliban were toppled but not defeated, and Al Qaeda was dispersed but not eliminated. Their leaders and top operatives remained at large, with the potential to regroup and rebuild their capacity to fight the Karzai government and its international backers another day. Most of the Taliban leaders, commanders and foot soldiers simply melted away among the Pashtun population on both sides of the Afghan-Pakistan border. They managed to keep their power structure at the leadership level quite intact and to store away many of their financial and military assets. Although the Pakistani military regime of Pervez Musharraf formally turned its back on the Taliban under a US ultimatum to side with either the US or terrorism, the Taliban continued to enjoy support from elements within the Pakistani military—the ISI in particular—and radical Islamic circles, especially along the border with Afghanistan. What motivated these elements was both strategic considerations and ethnic and Islamic solidarity. This meant that Pakistan remained a ready sanctuary with critical sources of human and material support for the Taliban—a fact that President Musharraf partially acknowledged at a joint Afghan-Pakistan tribal peace assembly in Kabul in August 2007.[20]

---

[19] For a discussion of the Bonn Agreement and its implementation, see Amin Saikal, 'The Changing Geopolitics of Central, West and South Asia after 11 September', in Ramesh Thakur and Oddny Wiggen (eds), *South Asia in the World: Problem Solving Perspectives on Security, Sustainable Development, and Good Governance*, New York: United Nations University Press, 2004, Ch. 24.

[20] *Reuters*, 12 August 2007. The continued ISI support for the Taliban has lately become a

## Vulnerabilities

Meanwhile, the policy approach pursued by the US and its Afghan and non-Afghan allies in dealing with the post-Taliban management and rebuilding of Afghanistan provided the Taliban and their supporters with unique opportunities to reorganize and reinvent themselves rapidly. Less than eighteen months after losing power, they re-emerged as a critical sub-national actor, mounting a serious political and security challenge to the Karzai government and its foreign supporters. Several factors proved critical in this respect.

First, the US and its allies failed to deploy enough forces to capitalize on their initial successes to ensure the transformation of Afghanistan from a war-torn and debilitated state to a stable and secure state. The US originally deployed about 10,000 troops and supported the deployment of another 5,000–strong force, made up of troops from its NATO allies, as the International Security Assistance Force (ISAF). This was against the better judgement of a number of seasoned scholars and observers of the Afghan situation, who recommended a force of at least 50,000 troops as necessary to secure not just Kabul but also other major cities as well as the main strategic means of communication and border points of entry. The primary focus of the US forces, which together with some contribution from US allies formed what become known as the 'Coalition Forces', was to hunt down the Al Qaeda and Taliban leaders. For this purpose, Washington also armed and financed, as a necessity under the circumstances,[21] a number of existing local power holders and their militias which operated independently of the Afghan central government, and over which the US could not ensure control in the medium-to-long run. In the meantime, ISAF was mandated only to provide security for Kabul and the Karzai government.

These forces soon proved to be inadequate. The field was left wide open for many sub-national actors, including local chieftains, drug traffickers and powerful poppy growers, to re-emerge on the Afghan scene. Most important, it provided a valuable opportunity for the Taliban and their Pakistani backers to re-establish themselves in the provinces along the border with Pakistan. With the US-led Coalition forces spread very thinly in the southern and eastern

---

major issue of concern for the US government. See Mark Mazzetti and Eric Schmitt, 'Afghan strikes by Taliban get Pakistan help, U.S. aides say', *The New York Times*, 26 March 2009.

[21] See the comments at the time by US envoy, Zalmy Khalilzad, *Afghanistan Online Press*, 15 June 2002, www.afghan-web.com/aop

Afghan provinces, by the turn of 2004 the Taliban were in a position to augment their military operations, preventing the Coalition forces from consolidating a hold especially in the Taliban's heartland in the provinces of Kandahar, Helmand and Uruzgan. Although from 2006 the US and its allies boosted their troop deployment to a level of 57,000 by 2008, this did little to compensate for earlier mistakes or to make a great difference in overcoming security challenges.

Further, the Karzai leadership and its international backers, especially the US as the dominant actor, incrementally failed to develop an effective system of governance. From the start they were seductively lured by the idea of centralized power and authority within a strong presidential framework—something akin to the American system. Despite warnings by informed scholars against adopting a strong presidential system of governance as totally inappropriate for a war-torn state with a myriad social divisions, they failed to appreciate that such a system typically produces only one winner, and many disgruntled losers intent upon challenging or undermining the victor's position. In addition, it can result in concentration of too much formal power in the winner's hands, leading to personalized politics in which access to the president becomes a prized opportunity over which lesser politicians fight viciously. Yet paradoxically, the effective powers of the president may be less than they appear on paper, while the responsibilities of the office, and the expectations which citizens hold of the president, may be unrealistically heavy, making the job extremely difficult for one person to perform satisfactorily.[22]

The result has been the growing isolation of President Karzai from the public, and the construction of a dysfunctional and corrupt government, where senior governmental positions have been filled on the basis not of merit, but of family, tribal, ethnic and factional connections. Afghanistan does have a parliament, which although far from perfect has nonetheless provided a venue for a range of voices to be heard. However, the executive branch of the government has seen no compelling reason to coordinate its functions with the legislative branch.

Given Afghanistan's historical experience as a weak state with a strong society, what the country required was a more inclusive, parliamentary system of government, with the government made and unmade in the Wolesi Jirga (Lower House), and strong emphasis on legitimate local government structures to give ordinary Afghans a sense of connectedness to the political sys-

---

[22] Amin Saikal and William Maley, 'The president who would be king', *The New York Times*, 6 February 2008.

tem. The current political system has increasingly cracked under the weight of the burdens it is expected to carry.[23] This has generated a massive political and administrative vacuum, which the Taliban and their supporters have skilfully exploited against the Karzai government and its supporting foreign forces.

Meanwhile, the US and its allies failed initially to make sufficient investment in Afghanistan's reconstruction.[24] President Bush originally endorsed the idea of something along the lines of the Marshall Plan for Afghanistan, but he never put it into practice, presumably on the assumption that a small amount of money could go a long way in a country like Afghanistan.[25] According to a major report by the Agency Coordinating Body for Afghan Relief (ACBAR), of the more than $20 billion promised by the international donors between January 2002 and January 2008, some $9 billion still needed to be delivered. Of the amount distributed, 40 per cent went back to the donor countries in consultancy fees and expatriates' pay, with most of the remaining funds being spent on UN and non-governmental organizations' operations and foreign contractors and sub-contractors. USAID dispensed two-thirds of the aid it had pledged, but only 6 per cent of it was spent through the Afghan government, which indicated a clear lack of trust in the government and concern about growing insecurity in the country. The same report makes it clear that 'while the US military spends $100 million a day, the average amount of aid spent by all donors combined has been just $7 (million) a day since 2001'.[26]

The result has been far less investment in the reconstruction of Afghanistan per head of the population than has been made in three concurrently disrupted states: Bosnia, Kosovo and East Timor. This has meant that a majority of the Afghans have not benefited from the post-Taliban reconstruction and have not experienced a positive change in their living conditions.[27] By the same token, they have not developed confidence in the government and its

---

[23] For an analysis of the problems of the political system, see William Maley, *Rescuing Afghanistan*, Sydney: University of New South Wales Press, 2006, Ch. 2.

[24] See Wolfgang Danspeckgruber and Robert P. Finn, 'The Afghan Economy', in Wolfgang Danspeckgruber with Robert P. Finn (ed.), *Building State and Security in Afghanistan*, Princeton: Woodrow Wilson School of Public and International Affairs, Princeton University, 2007, Ch. 8.

[25] James Dao, 'A nation challenged: the President; Bush sets role for U.S. in Afghan rebuilding', *The New York Times*, 18 April 2002.

[26] *BBC News*, 25 March 2008.

[27] For a detailed discussion, see Maley, *Rescuing Afghanistan*, Ch. 4.

foreign backers, and as a consequence have remained vulnerable to the Taliban's offer of security and better living.

In addition, the US tied its intervention in Afghanistan to the wider 'war on terror' and the critical role that Pakistan could play on both of these fronts. This had two important consequences. The first was that US efforts were focused on Afghanistan with the overriding goal of winning the war on terrorism, which in itself has grown as elusive as its targets. The second was that nuclear armed Pakistan—the original source and sponsor of Muslim extremism—was allowed to get away with making as little structural adjustment in its approach to Afghanistan as possible. The Musharraf regime (1999–2008) dwelt heavily on its status as the US's closest partner in the war on terror and its elevation, from 2005, as one of America's major non-NATO allies to press for what it deemed desirable in support of its interests, rather than what the US wanted in terms of its goals in the region. While being showered with massive US economic and military assistance, amounting to more than $10 billion by 2007,[28] it did not find it imperative to do whatever it took to deny the Taliban sanctuary in and logistic support from Pakistan. If anything, its policies contributed substantially to the Talibanization of Pakistan's border areas with Afghanistan, undermining any efforts on the part of the US and its NATO allies to enhance Pakistan-Afghanistan border security, but placing the Taliban in an increasingly large comfort zone. This has been instrumental in widening the Taliban's networks of support in Pakistan and strengthening their capacity to augment their cross-border operations in Afghanistan. Whenever Washington sought to exert some pressure on Islamabad to do more against the Taliban, the Musharraf regime was able to warn it that pressure could only result in a popular backlash, causing Pakistan to implode and the war on terror to fail.[29]

In addition, the Karzai government and its international backers failed from the outset to develop a national ideology of state building that would be culturally relevant and capable of countering the effect of the Taliban's reliance on Islam as an ideology of resistance and human dignity. While Islam is enshrined as state religion in the new Afghan Constitution of 2004, the Karzai government has largely pursued a strategy of promoting secular politics, and has tolerated the kind of social and cultural practices by the ruling elite

[28] Nathaniel Heller, Sarah Fort and Marina Walker Guevara, 'Pakistan's $4.2 Billion 'Blank Check' for U.S. Military Aid', The Center for Public Integrity, 27 March 2007.

[29] For a detailed discussion of Musharraf's policy responses, see Rashid, *Descent Into Chaos*, Ch. 8.

and expatriates that have left it vulnerable to the accusation of acting contrary to the spirit of Islam and behaving at the behest of 'occupying powers'.

This has substantially aided the Taliban to lure many Afghans away from the government and its international supporters. The movement's deployment of Islam as an ideology of action has proved effective particularly in view of other factors such as poor governance, the slow pace of reconstruction, and ill-conceived US and NATO actions, which have resulted in numerous civilian deaths, human rights violations and religious-cultural humiliation. This, together with the Taliban's offer of religious rewards in the hereafter and higher pay than the average government salary of $50–70 per month, have led many disgruntled Afghans to become, if not active supporters, at least sympathetic and tolerant towards the Taliban. Beyond this, the fact that the Taliban have fielded more honest representatives in the areas under their control, to help people resolve their daily problems and so remove the need for them to refer to corrupt government officials for assistance, has given the militia more popular standing than they could have dared hope to attain.

The shortcomings in all these areas have been matched by a lack of well-crafted, coherent international civilian and military strategy. This has been reflected in the lack of effective coordination between the government and the international actors in Afghanistan on the one hand, and among the international actors themselves on the other. As the Karzai government has failed to consolidate itself as a reliable or trustworthy partner, the US and its allies have also remained very divided in their approach and commitment, and thus have not been able to forge the needed common strategy. Whereas Washington has continued to pledge an open-ended commitment to Afghanistan as part of its wider war on terrorism strategy, most of its allies have treated their involvement in Afghanistan as a short-term measure and also as a way of avoiding participation in the Iraq fiasco, which has drained US resources away from Afghanistan. While the US stood fast until recently in its determination to eliminate the Taliban and Al Qaeda leaderships, many of its European allies and indeed the UN have increasingly wanted to focus on an approach that could enable them to disentangle themselves from Afghanistan sooner rather than later. It is against this backdrop that the Karzai government has increasingly become receptive to dialogue and some kind of power-sharing arrangement with the Taliban, as a way of taking the sting out of the militia's growing insurgency. However, the Taliban have made any negotiation with the government conditional on the departure of foreign forces.

NATO members continue to have serious disagreements over their approach, the depth and length of their involvement, and the degree to which they could coordinate with the Afghan government and among themselves. They have remained baffled not only about how to differentiate between 'core Taliban' and 'non-core Taliban' as well as between the 'old Taliban' and the 'new Taliban',[30] but also about how to stem the tide of opium production in Afghanistan, which made the country the largest producer in 2007.

For all practical purposes, Afghanistan has already become a narco-state, which means that even if the Taliban are eliminated and peace and security are returned, Afghanistan will still be in the grip of a narco-economy on a long-term basis. Today, the Afghan economy is based on a 40 per cent contribution from opium, 50 per cent from foreign aid and 10 per cent from internal sources. Proceeds from opium, heroin production and drug trafficking have not only substantially funded the Taliban's operations and helped the growth of many other private militias, but have also become a lucrative source of income for many government officials, who have been heavily involved in the industry.[31] The government and its NATO backers have not been able to come up with a common approach to tackle the problem. Whereas the US has favoured aerial spraying as the best solution, the Afghan government and many European actors have opposed the US prescription on the grounds that it will deprive many poor Afghan farmers of a critical means of livelihood and result in alienation of more Afghans from the government and foreign forces. Meanwhile, they have not formulated viable alternative strategies such as crop substitution or monetary compensation to address the problem.[32]

During their rule, the Taliban had issued an Islamic *fatwa* (ruling) against poppy growing and drug trafficking. But this is not an option available to the Karzai government, because of its lack of credentials as an Islamic authority.

---

[30] For a discussion of various categories of the Taliban, see Robert D. Crews, 'Moderate Taliban?', and Amin Tarzai, 'The Neo-Taliban', in Crews and Tarzi (eds), *The Taliban and the Crisis of Afghanistan*, Chs. 7 and 8.

[31] This has led the new US Secretary of State, Hillary Clinton, to describe Afghanistan during her confirmation hearing as a 'narco-state', 'with the Afghan government plagued by limited capacity and widespread corruption'. Helen Cooper, 'Obama's war: fearing another quagmire in Afghanistan', *The New York Times*, 24 January 2009.

[32] See Barnett R. Rubin and Jake Sherman, *Counter-Narcotics to Stabilise Afghanistan: The False Promise of Crop Eradication*, New York University, February 2008. For an optimistic view of the situation, see Joanna Wright's interview with General Khodaidad, Afghanistan's Acting Minister for Counter-narcotics, entitled 'Poppy Purge', *Jane's Intelligence Review*, 20 (2), February 2008, p. 58.

Even at the Bucharest summit on Afghanistan in April 2008, the NATO and non-NATO participants remained divided on the additional number of troops they could send and how to deal with the drug problem. France pledged to dispatch another 1,000 troops but this was well short of the 5,000 needed. The call by the Australian Prime Minister Kevin Rudd for a decisive approach to the drug issue produced little result.[33] As a consequence, while Afghanistan remained the leading source of opium and heroin in the world, the Taliban could count on the continuation of their major source of income for the foreseeable future.

All this has been extremely helpful to the Taliban leadership and its supporters, enabling them to highlight the disunity among NATO members and the temporary nature of the alliance's involvement against the permanency and saliency of their cause. They have become convinced that despite its public rhetoric, NATO will not and cannot afford to endure the burdens of Afghanistan indefinitely.

The fact is that the Taliban are not the best trained, equipped and led force. The movement is largely made up of self-styled but poorly trained, fed and clothed Jihadis, with no major power behind them. They have largely relied on such means as light arms, roadside bombs, suicide attacks, ideological purity and a sense of nationalism to tie down the resources of the Karzai government and NATO. The insurgency has so far prevented the government and NATO from rebuilding and securing Afghanistan to the extent that is needed to de-legitimize the Taliban's position. The Taliban, for their part, have made a comeback to fill the very vacuum which has been created by the political and strategic failures of the Karzai government and its foreign allies. Whatever the rights and wrongs of the Taliban's approach and goals, they have now re-emerged as a critical sub-national actor that can influence and shape the politics, society and foreign relations of Afghanistan. In the process, they have succeeded in widening the space for many other smaller sub-actors to operate independently of the Kabul government, which, according to the US Director of National Intelligence, Michael McConnell, by early 2008 controlled no more than 30 per cent of Afghanistan.[34]

The new US President Barack Obama, who took office on 20 January 2009, has now revised his predecessor's policy approach to Afghanistan. The revised policy not only places greater emphasis on an integrated approach to rebuild-

---

[33] Steve Lee Myers and Thom Shanker, 'NATO expansion, and a Bush legacy, are in doubt', *The New York Times*, 15 March 2008.

[34] *Voice of America*, 27 February 2008.

ing and securing Afghanistan, with deployment of 17,000 additional troops and 4,000 military personnel to accelerate the building of the Afghan National Army, Police and Border Guard, and larger reconstruction investment. It also recognizes strongly that Afghanistan's problems are intertwined with those of Pakistan as a critical source of support for the Taliban and their Al Qaeda allies. The policy underlines the importance of seeking to stabilize Afghanistan and Pakistan concurrently by also injecting more aid into Pakistan to support its economic-social development and democratic transformation. Beyond this, it postulates wider cross-border operations from Afghanistan to target Taliban and Al Qaeda sanctuaries in Pakistan. The Obama Administration has accompanied this with intensified efforts to stimulate NATO allies to do more in the area of state and security building in Afghanistan and to build up a regional consensus in pursuit of stability there.[35]

Obama's approach has generated optimism among some policy makers and military analysts in the US and its allies. However, the test of it will be very much in its implementation and outcome. The heart of the Afghanistan crisis is how to generate the necessary conditions for the creation of an appropriate and effective system of governance, provision of human security, an accelerated process of economic rebuilding from which most Afghans (not just a tiny minority) could benefit, the development of a culturally relevant national ideology of state building, eradication of the drug problem on a systematic but humane basis, enhancement of border security between Afghanistan and Pakistan, and transformation of Pakistan into a stable pluralist state free of extremism.

These issues require costly and, in some cases, painful policy actions over at least the next ten years. Should the Afghan government and its NATO and non-NATO allies fail to move in this direction, the national and regional conditions as well as time can only favour the continuation of the Taliban's insurgency at the cost of more violence and hardship for the Afghan people and humiliation for the international community. This would be particularly true for the US, which may find itself inextricably involved in what increasingly looks like a quagmire.

[35] *BBC News*, 27 March 2009.

# 12

# Militia Formation and the 'Nationalization' of Local Conflict in Liberia*

*Morten Bøås*

## Introduction

During the period from 1980 to 2003 Liberia become synonymous with war, chaos and destruction. Fragmented by different militias that seemingly fought each other for no better reason than plunder and theft, the country was presented as a primary example of a 'new war'.[1] There is little doubt that economic motives were important for the war and the establishment of many of the militias involved. However, the reasons behind the formation of militias during the Liberian war are also deeply entrenched in history. The only way to understand this dimension of the war is therefore to come to terms with this history and its ramifications. The Liberian war was not a 'new' war, but a 21st century manifestation of conflicts that had started much earlier, some of them even preceding the first settlers that arrived in the early

* The research on which this chapter is based was funded by the Norwegian Research Council (grant 174582/S30) and the Norwegian Ministry of Foreign Affairs (grant QM14072075). Both grants are gratefully acknowledged.
[1] Mary Kaldor, *New and Old Wars: Organized Violence in a Global Era*, Cambridge: Polity Press, 2001.

19th century.[2] The 'ghost' of war was not new to Liberia. Indeed, the argument could be made that Liberia has been at 'war' with itself from the very beginning of its existence as an independent state:[3] a 'war' concerning the questions of what it meant to be a Liberian, and how the polity of the country should be constituted and resources distributed.

The Liberian civil war is hardly ever mentioned without reference to ex-President Charles Taylor. Both the media and international organizations (governmental and non-governmental) have contributed to a personalization of the Liberian war through the emphasis placed on Taylor, both in fuelling the Liberian war and in the making of a larger war zone in the Mano River area. There is no doubt that Taylor murdered, plundered, and treated the presidency as his personal bank account. However, this does not mean that we can assume that the Liberian conflict was the consequence of one man's criminal behaviour. Such an approach is at best misleading, and in this case clearly wrong. This chapter therefore also seeks to issue a rejoinder to the many simplistic analyses of the Liberian conflict presented not only in international media, but also in work of a supposedly more scholarly character.[4]

## Liberia—the 'nationalization' of local conflict

The Liberian conflict was not just one war. As the case of Lofa County will illustrate, it was a series of local conflicts tangled up in each other, as Taylor's rebellion against Samuel Doe's dictatorship pushed the Liberian state over the edge and into the abyss. This 'nationalization' of local conflicts created a 'logic of the war' that dramatically affected the course of the conflict, the decision making of the individuals involved, and the subsequent militia formation.[5]

Even prior to the war, Liberia was characterized by corruption, political and economic violence, identity crises, generational and other group clashes, and

---

[2] See also Morten Bøås, 'The Liberian Civil War: New War/Old War?', *Global Society*, Vol. 19, No. 1, 2005, pp. 73–88.

[3] Morten Bøås, 'Liberia: the Hellbound Heart? Regime Breakdown and the Deconstruction of society', *Alternatives*, Vol. 22, 1997, pp. 350–80; Mary H. Moran, *Liberia: the Violence of Democracy*, Philadelphia: University of Pennsylvania Press, 2006.

[4] One illuminating example is the book written for the International Peace Academy by a former US ambassador to Sierra Leone. See John L. Hirsch, *Sierra Leone: Diamonds and the Struggle for Democracy*, Boulder: Lynne Rienner, 2001.

[5] Morten Bøås and Anne Hatløy, 'Getting in, Getting out: Militia Membership and Prospects for Re-integration in Post-war Liberia', *Journal of Modern African Studies*, Vol. 46, No. 1, 2008, pp. 33–55.

widespread poverty.[6] Local chiefs were incorporated into the structure of the True Whig Party (TWP) through a combination of brute force and neopatrimonial indirect rule through district commissioners. This created a rural elite which cemented ethnic differences that, through fosterage and intermarriage, used to have a relatively flexible nature.[7] The result was a highly competitive patrimonial environment where various local elites were locked into struggles over state resources, often but not exclusively built on ethnic affiliation, and exclusionary practices that shaped politics and the control of state institutions as a zero-sum game.

Liberia consists of 16 major indigenous groups of people, each possessing its own traditions, customs, religious philosophy, and languages and dialects.[8] However, in order to understand the background for militia formation, we must also take into consideration the group of freed slaves repatriated from the United States between 1822 and 1861 to this part of the West African coastline.[9] These freed slaves established the Republic of Liberia and became known as the Americo-Liberians.

The intention was to create a safe haven for freed slaves; the problem, however, was that they were just as much strangers in Liberia as they had been in the United States. Given a land to govern, they built their system of rule on the only political and administrative system with which they were familiar: the system of the plantations in the Deep South of the United States. The

---

[6] Morten Bøås and Kevin C. Dunn, 'African Guerrilla Politics: Raging against the Machine?', in Morten Bøås and Kevin C. Dunn (eds), *African Guerrillas: Raging Against the Machine*, Boulder: Lynne Rienner, 2007, pp. 9–37; Stephen Ellis, *The Mask of Anarchy: the Destruction of Liberia and the Religious Dimension of an African Civil War*, London: Hurst & Co., 1999; William Reno, *Warlord Politics and African States*, Boulder: Lynne Rienner, 1998; William Reno, 'Liberia: the LURDs of the New Church', in Morten Bøås and Kevin C. Dunn (eds), *African Guerrillas*, pp. 69–80; Amos Sawyer, *Beyond Plunder: Toward Democratic Governance in Liberia*, Boulder: Lynne Rienner, 2005; Mats Utas, *Sweet Battlefields: Youth and the Liberian Civil War*, Uppsala: University of Uppsala Press (Dissertation in Cultural Anthropology), 2003.

[7] Warren d'Azevedo, 'Tribe and Chiefdom on the Windward Coast', *Liberian Studies Journal*, Vol. 14, No. 2, 1989, pp. 90–116.

[8] These are the Bassa, Belle, Dey, Gbandi, Gio, Gola, Grebo, Kissi, Kpelle, Krahn, Kru, Loma, Mandingo, Mano, Mende and Vai.

[9] The number of repatriates was relatively small, between 1822 and 1861 about 12,000 colonists landed in Liberia. Of these, 4,500 were freeborn (all the first five presidents had been born in freedom) and about 7,000 were born in slavery. In addition, about 6,000 Africans were freed from slave ships and resettled in Liberia; in one 18–month period in 1860 more than 4,000 were settled along the coast. See Paul Gifford, *Christianity and Politics in Doe's Liberia*, Cambridge University Press, 1993.

main difference of course was that this time they were the 'masters' and the indigenous people the 'servants'.[10] Trapped within this model, they embarked on a political strategy of division between the self (perceived as the civilized, educated class) and the other (perceived as the savage, a native underclass to be kept in place by hard work and discipline). The indigenous population revolted on several occasion, but these rebellions were crushed with military help from the United States.[11]

When the Republic of Liberia was established in 1847, a constitution based on the American model was adopted. According to the Liberian constitution, all men are born equally free and independent and have certain natural, inherent and inalienable rights. However, 'all men' did not mean all men who inhabited the area to which the constitution laid claim; on the contrary, the constitution strongly delineated between the repatriates and the indigenous population. The members of the so-called 'native tribes' were not eligible for election or voting. A firm division between these two groups were therefore institutionalized, laying the foundation for entrenched alienation between the different ethnic groups in Liberia, and between these groups and the new upper class constituted by the Americo-Liberians.

In 1870 the TWP was established, and for the next 110 years Liberia was *de facto* a one-party state. However, it can be questioned whether Liberia would have survived as an independent state if had not been for the diplomatic and military support of the United States, which prevented France and the United Kingdom from carving up the territory of Liberia and sharing it between them.[12] The military support from the US also made it possible for Americo-Liberian rule to survive the various rebellions from indigenous groups. The Liberian army, then known as the Liberian Frontier Force (LFF), was led by an Americo-Liberian corps of officers supported by black soldiers and NCOs from the US army.[13] Despite the overwhelming military superior-

---

[10] Bøås, 'Liberia: the Hellbound Heart?'

[11] Levitt describes 15 major wars between the Liberian state and indigenous groups in the period between 1822 and 1915. Jeremy I. Levitt, *The Evolution of Deadly Conflict in Liberia: from Paternaltarianism to State Collapse*, Durham: Carolina Academic Press, 2005.

[12] Considering recent events in Liberia it is therefore of more than historical interest to note that in the tales the Mandingo people tell about their origin in Liberia, they claim that Lofa became a part of Liberia because the powerful Mandingo chief, Chief Bongo, preferred to join Liberia rather than French Guinea.

[13] Harison O. Akingbade, 'The Role of the Military in the History of Liberia, 1822–1947', PhD Thesis, Howard University, Washington, 1977.

ity of the Liberian army, the Liberian hinterlands were not completely pacified until the 1930s.[14]

Military force was one important element in the constitution of Americo-Liberian hegemony; another was the administrative boundaries and the practice of indirect rule.[15] This system was quite similar to the practice of indirect rule established in British colonies. The TWP regime ruled the Liberian hinterlands through district commissioners, who in turn ruled through local chiefs. This type of rule cemented differences between the many ethnic groups of Liberia. Before the establishment of the administrative boundaries of the TWP state, the ethnic structure of Liberia had a relatively flexible character. One example is the Krahn, an ethnic group which has been at the centre of the Liberian civil war. Initially, the Krahn were not so much a clearly defined ethnic group as several smaller groups of people (that is, clans) whose dialects belonged to the same type of language (Krahn) and who happened to live within the same administrative boundary. Even today, one usually refers to an eastern and a western dialect of Krahn. These two dialects are so different that an eastern speaker has problems understanding a western speaker and *vice versa*; the French language came to influence the western variant, whereas the eastern type borrowed extensively from English.[16] The Krahn as a distinct ethnic category are therefore a relatively recent creation.

In fact not only the Krahn, but also many of the other ethnic divisions that currently exist and informed the formation of militias during the civil war were sharpened by the administrative boundaries imposed by Americo-Liberian rule. This also suggests that ethnicity should not necessarily be viewed as a monolithic factor in the civil war, but as a social construction. The different armed factions were mostly built around ethnic groups, but these should not be seen as objective entities, but as social formations created by first the administrative practice of the state and then later by the dynamics of a war fought on the ruins of a dysfunctional neopatrimonial state.

---

[14] Robert Kappel, 'Resistance of the Liberian People: Problems of the Ignored Facts', in Eckhard Hinzen and Robert Kappel (eds), *Dependence, Underdevelopment and Persistent Conflict: on the Political Economy of Liberia*, Bremen: Übersee-Museum, 1980, pp. 169–96.

[15] Levitt, *The Evolution of Deadly Conflict in Liberia*.

[16] Günter Schröder and Dieter Seibel, *Ethnographic Survey of Southeastern Liberia: the Krahn and the Sapo*, Newark: Liberian Studies Association in America Monograph Series No. 3, 1974.

## The Americo-Liberian state

By the early 1920s, the Americo-Liberian elite had secured its rule through this combination of force and clientelistic arrangements. A complex system of pyramidal patron-client relationships throughout Liberian society, with the Americo-Liberians at the top, maintained settler rule.[17]

With the accession of President William Tubman in 1944, some cosmetic changes in the system were implemented. Officially, Tubman advocated a policy of unification, designed to incorporate the indigenous people of the Liberian hinterland into the political and economic system of the state. However, it was also under Tubman that the cult of the presidency reached its peak as he subverted every institution of society into an image of Tubman as the national symbol of sovereignty. When Tubman died in office in 1971, he left behind a state dominated by a circle of relatives running an aggressive business establishment, other Americo-Liberian families of importance, and some tribal entrants more recently assimilated into his 'honourable' class.[18]

Such a neopatrimonial system can be remarkably stable as long as the resources necessary to maintain it are available. Until the 1970s, this was the case in Liberia. The neopatrimonial state provided social order and stability through the maintenance of a social structure ensuring that the Americo-Liberians remained in power.

When Tubman died, his Vice-President William Tolbert succeeded him. At the start of his presidency, Tolbert tried to introduce some degree of reform; among other things he established an anti-corruption commission. However, since he, his family and government ministers were among the main offenders, it was clear that this move was nothing but a mere facade. As the Tolbert regime's corruption and misuse of public funds increased over time—while at the same time it did not show the same ability and willingness to use coercion and patronage as the Tubman regime—it became clear that Tolbert's position was insecure.[19] In April 1979, riots broke out. Trying to secure his position, Tolbert declared a state of emergency and put down the riots with full force. Most leaders of the small and fragmented opposition that had emerged under his rule were arrested. However, only two days before their

---

[17] Paul Gifford, *Christianity and Politics in Doe's Liberia*, Cambridge University Press, 1993.

[18] Reno, *Warlord Politics and African States*.

[19] See S. Byron Tarr, 'Founding the Liberian Action Party', *Liberian Studies Journal*, Vol. XV, No. 1, 1990, pp. 13–47.

cases were due to appear in court, a group of 17 enlisted men killed Tolbert, overthrew the government and executed several of the ministers at the beach in Monrovia.[20]

Before we continue our review of the background for militia formation in Liberia, it is important to underscore that the heritage from Tubman's rule has been extremely enduring in Liberia. In fact, it can be argued that the rulers and would-be rulers (such as warlords) who appeared after Tubman all tried to recreate the glamour of his era. These attempts have not been successful. Rather they have ended up as an inverse, perverted mirror-image of the well-structured neopatrimonialism of the Tubman era.[21]

## The warlords: Samuel Doe, Charles Taylor and their lot

Samuel Doe, a young man of Krahn origin, led the group of young officers that killed Tolbert and assumed state power.[22] Initially, the coup was well received among ordinary Liberians. For the majority of the population the removal from power of the TWP regime was seen as a blessing, and many envisioned a new era for Liberia in which finally 'all men would be equal'.

However, it soon became obvious that the soldiers who had assumed control of the state were not able or willing to even attempt to dismantle the neopatrimonial state. On the contrary, they themselves became captives of the logic of such a state. As the people in the interior assumed that the new leaders would provide them with employment, education and other resources, the ruling junta—the People's Redemption Council (PRC)—became a vehicle for enrichment of its members and the elite of the group to which they belonged. The result was a competitive relationship within the PRC, cementing the ethnicization of Liberian politics that had begun with the administrative boundaries established by the TWP. Ethnicity, therefore, became even more politicized and polarized as the social construction of difference between

---

[20] The current president, Ellen Johnson-Sirleaf, was Minister of Finance in Tolbert's last government. She was one of only four ministers not to be executed on the beach in Monrovia after Samuel Doe's coup.

[21] See Morten Bøås, 'Liberia and Sierra Leone: Dead Ringers? The Logic of Neopatrimonial Rule', *Third World Quarterly*, Vol. 22, No. 5, 2001, pp. 697–723.

[22] What exactly happened the night of 12 April 1980 when Tolbert was killed is still unclear. Some claim that Samuel Doe himself hid in the garden outside the Executive Mansion while his men killed Tolbert, whereas other sources claim that it was Doe who killed Tolbert. No matter who actually pulled the trigger, this meant that the decades of TWP rule had finally come to an end.

various groups increased. It soon became apparent that the only thing separating Doe's regime from his predecessors' was that the new regime lacked the facade of glamour and elegance with which the previous regime had surrounded itself.[23] However, despite the brutal and despotic nature of Doe's rule, Cold War geopolitical considerations meant that he could count on support from the United States. Indeed, the extremely bent election that Doe organized in 1985 was lauded by the US government as a major step towards the consolidation of democracy in Africa, and Doe himself was received in the White House as one of America's main African allies.[24]

Shortly after the shamelessly flawed 1985 election, an attempted coup by a popular Gio soldier, Thomas Quiwonkpa, was brutally suppressed by Doe's troops. After the coup had been prevented and Quiwonkpa killed, those troops, the by now thoroughly Krahn-dominated Armed Forces of Liberia (AFL) engaged in reprisals against real and suspected opponents and their home communities, targeting mostly Gio and Manos in Nimba County. This violence prepared the stage for the civil war that was to follow.

The last five years of Doe's reign are a story of petty corruption, grand theft of state resources, murder, rape, torture and other human rights abuses. The traditional structure of society fragmented, and people sought refuge in magic and in the many secret societies of Liberia. In previous decades these secret societies had played an integrative, albeit hierarchical effect, but as the conflict increasingly revolved around ethnicity they contributed to the eventual fragmentation and breakdown of Liberian society. As the civil war started, the kind of social practice represented by the secret societies ceased to be embedded in their respective local communities and traditional structures. Part of the violent practices that emerged during the civil war can be seen as a perversion of socio-economic practice in a period of extreme social stress.[25]

On Christmas Eve 1989, the National Patriotic Front of Liberia (NPFL), a small rebel army led by Charles Taylor, crossed the border into Liberia from

---

[23] Morten Bøås, 'The Liberian Civil War: New War/Old War?' *Global Society*, Vol. 19, No. 1, 2005, pp. 73–88.

[24] See Mark Huband, *The Liberian Civil War*, London: Frank Cass, 1998. During the 1980s the Doe regime received more financial support from the United States than any other government in Sub-Saharan Africa. Despite the brutality and extreme levels of corruption of Doe and his associates, the United States continued to support him, nearly to the very end. See also George K. Kieh, 'Merchants of Repression: an Assessment of United States Military Assistance to Liberia', *Liberia Forum*, Vol. V, No. 9, 1989, pp. 50–61.

[25] See Bøås, 'Liberia: the Hellbound Heart?'

Côte d'Ivoire.[26] Although their forces only numbered about 100 lightly armed men when they crossed the border, they expanded rapidly. By June 1990, Taylor's army had grown to almost 5,000 men, women and children; in the next three months, it doubled again. Doe fought back with all the force he could muster. He knew that the manpower and support for Taylor's forces mainly came from Gio and Mano communities, particularly in Nimba County, and so Doe ordered his army to attack such villages where Taylor's troops could be hiding. Taylor, on the other hand, unleashed his rebels on Krahn and Mandingo communities which were known to support Doe.[27] This created a lasting pattern, in which Gio and Mano communities—particularly in Nimba County—were Taylor's most faithful allies, while the Krahn and the Mandingo formed their own militias after Doe's murder in September 1990. Indeed, the same pattern was evident during the summer of 2003: Taylor's last bastion of support was in the Gio and Mano communities in Nimba County. The Liberians United for Reconciliation and Democracy (LURD) militia was a Mandingo project and the other main rebel group in the latter part of the Liberian civil war (1998/99–2003) was the Krahn-based Movement for Democracy in Liberia (MODEL). The killings of civilian Gios and Manos in Nimba County by these two rebel forces in the wake of Taylor's departure on 11 August 2003 was therefore part of a larger web of ethnic polarization and revenge.[28]

In the summer of 1990 the other West African states also became involved in the war through the Economic Community of West African States (ECOWAS) and its ECOWAS Ceasefire Monitoring Group (ECOMOG). Formally, the objective was to impose a ceasefire and help to form an interim government that could hold elections within 12 months. Unofficially, the mandate was much simpler: to keep Taylor away from the presidency. In order to achieve the latter goal, ECOMOG accepted the assistance of other, newly

---

[26] Taylor, the son of a Liberian mother and a father believed to have been Americo-Liberian, was raised in Liberia, but educated in the United States, and worked there as well. He returned to Liberia just after Doe's coup in 1980 and was given a post in Doe's cabinet. Quite soon, Taylor ran into trouble with Doe and in 1983 he was accused of stealing nearly US$1 million from the national treasury. He fled from Liberia and went first to the United States were he was arrested, broke out of jail and returned to Africa, where he gradually acquired support for his anti-Doe rebellion. This included a stay in Libya where he received some military training.

[27] Many people of Krahn origin supported Doe because he was one of their kin, whereas the Mandingo people, as a minority group everywhere in Liberia, has traditionally allied itself with whoever sits in the Executive Mansion.

[28] Mark Doyle, 'Call for huge UN force in Liberia', Monrovia: BBC, 5 September, 2003.

emerging militias in fighting Taylor's rebels.[29] In doing so, ECOMOG dropped what little impartiality it may have had. The main reason behind ECOMOG's decision was that the new militias were not only an effective proxy force that ECOMOG could use to fulfil its objective of defeating Taylor, but also that by assisting these insurgency groups ECOMOG soldiers and generals could gain an advantageous position in the emerging underground economy of the civil war.[30]

These new militias were mainly established according to the politics of place and identity of Liberia, and included the forerunner of both LURD and MODEL. This faction was called the United Liberian Movement for Democracy (ULIMO), and it was initially started as a co-operative arrangement between Krahn and Mandingo leaders with the shared goal of keeping Taylor as far away from power as possible. This was a weak basis for a sustainable political alliance, and open conflict in the movement followed. In 1995, ULIMO split into two groups: ULIMO-K, the Mandingo faction, and ULIMO-J, the Krahn faction. LURD was based on the old ULIMO-K, whereas MODEL was a new version of the defunct ULIMO-J. Another militia that emerged through ECOMOG support was the Liberian Peace Council (LPC) led by George Boley, and in addition several smaller community-based insurgencies were also established; one of these was the Loma militia, the Lofa Defence Force (LDF), that fought in Lofa County together with Taylor's NPFL against ULIMO.

No one knows how many people died in the first part of the Liberian civil war (1990–97); some say 60,000, while others claim casualties as many as 250,000. The first estimate is probably more realistic than the latter. What is obvious, however, is that the level of human suffering created by the war was enormous, and the war also spilled over to other West African countries. Consequences of the Liberian civil war—including refugee flows, political and economic destabilization, the creation of new military alliances, and incorporation into the underground economy of the Liberian civil war—could be identified in Burkina Faso, Côte d'Ivoire, Guinea-Bissau, Guinea, Nigeria, and of course Sierra Leone.

---

[29] Morten Bøås, 'Nigeria and West Africa: from a Regional Security Complex to a Regional Security Community', in Einar Braathen, Morten Bøås and Gjermund Sæther (eds), *Ethnicity Kills? The Politics of War, Peace and Ethnicity in Sub-Saharan Africa*, London: Macmillan and New York: St Martin's Press, 2000, pp. 141–62.

[30] See Herbert M. Howe, *Ambiguous Order: Military Forces in African States*, Boulder: Lynne Rienner, 2001.

Factions' leaders and the Nigerian generals in ECOMOG became important actors in the regional underground economy that was created around the Liberian civil war.[31] Although many ordinary Liberians lost all their personal belongings several times during the war, faction leaders and several Nigerian generals amassed huge riches for themselves. As the war went on, economic incentives came to play an increasingly important role.[32] That said, underlying and, to a certain extent, delineating the Liberian war economy was the historical dimension to the conflict. Although the political economy of conflict that the war established created its own logic—in which war was both a way of life and a mode of production—the conflict lines around which the war initially started remained present. Specifically, the questions concerning what set of rights and obligations should underwrite a common Liberian identity remained a focal point for militia formation, and this issue is still not properly addressed.

*Lofa County: a microcosm of the Liberian war.* Lofa is the northernmost Liberian county, and Voinjama is the largest city and county capital. Although Kissi, Kpelle and Mano communities also exist in Lofa County, the two main groups are the Loma and the Mandingo. Lofa has always been a world apart from Monrovia and central Liberia, but nonetheless the county was quickly integrated into the Liberian civil war. This was partly due to the dynamic of the war itself, but the pattern of militia formation in Lofa also followed pre-existing patterns of tension between the Loma—who consider themselves autochthonous to the area—and the Mandingo, who are generally seen as latecomers and immigrants.[33]

Different stories are told about the settlement of Lofa, but most scholars believe that the Loma arrived prior to the Mandingo (perhaps as early as the late 16th century), whereas the first people of Mandingo origin arrived in the latter part of the 17th century, and it was only as late as the second half of the 19th century that more substantial groups of Mandingo people immigrated into Lofa from southwestern Guinea.[34] This migration changed the social and

---

[31] See Ellis, *The Mask of Anarchy.*

[32] Reno, *Warlord Politics and African States.*

[33] In 1909, when most other indigenous groups were granted full citizenship, the Mandingo continued to be classified as an 'ethnic minority'. See Augustine Konneh, *Religion, Commerce, and the Integration of the Mandingo in Liberia,* Lanham: University Press of America, 1996.

[34] See ibid., as well as Christian Kordt Højbjerg, *Resisting State Iconoclasm Among the Loma of Guinea,* Durham, NC: Carolina Academic Press, 2007

political life of Lofa, as it brought both Islam and the Mandingo trade networks to this area. For many people of Loma origin, a narrative of Mandingo expansion and imperialism is an integral part of their cosmology. However, the basic problem is that, in Lofa as in other parts of Liberia (Nimba in particular), people of Mandingo origin are not considered proper Liberians, but seen as strangers and foreigners.[35]

Consequently, the relationship between the two main ethnic groups of Lofa has been tense and hostile, particularly since the beginning of the civil war in 1989–90. The Mandingo accuse the Loma of supporting Taylor's forces when they reached this part of Liberia in the autumn of 1990, whereas the Loma believe that the attacks by ULIMO on Loma towns in 1992 were unjustified and mainly carried out in order to take their land and steal their belongings. A similar pattern is evident after LURD crossed over the border from Guinea in 1998–99; the Loma claim that the Mandingo-dominated LURD forces attacked their villages indiscriminately. Because of the nature of the war in Lofa, the Loma also established their own militia, the LDF. It was established in 1993–94 with the support of the Poro society. Its political leader was Francois Massaquoi.[36]

The same pattern also came to the forefront during the elections in October and November 2005. In the first round of the presidential elections the Mandingo voted for their candidate, the former warlord Alhaji Kromah, and his All Liberian Coalition (ALCOP). In the Mandingo towns along the border with Guinea, Kromah received over 95 per cent of the votes. However, as the Mandingo only constitute a majority in a few places in Lofa, mainly along the border, Kromah only received 18 per cent of the total votes in the county, taking him to second place in the first round of presidential elections in Lofa. The main reason for the Mandingo's support for Kromah is that they view the former warlord and militia leader as a hero, the one that defended them not only against Taylor's forces, but also against Taylor's allies among the Loma.[37] In this regard, the establishment of a militia fiefdom during the war is understood not as an act of personal enrichment, but as an attempt to protect their people under the extreme circumstance of civil war.[38]

In the collective memory of the Mandingo, the massacres in Bakiedou in 1990 and in other Mandingo towns, and the wartime burning of their

---

[35] See Bøås, 'The Liberian Civil War: New War/Old War?'
[36] Ellis, *The Mask of Anarchy.*
[37] Bøås and Hatløy, 'Getting in, Getting out'.
[38] See Bøås and Dunn, 'African Guerrilla Politics'.

mosques, are very much alive.[39] Their dual sense of ethnic solidarity and uncertainty—given the fact that their overall position in the Liberian polity is contested—is an integral part of daily life for the Mandingo, and contributed to their participation in militia formation during the war. Thus the war, both in its physical destruction and in terms of memory and identity, is still present in Lofa. The Mandingo are not completely alone in this 'battle', either. Their ethnic relatives, the Konianké, live right across the border in Guinea's Forest Region, and they face similar problems there. Renewed tension in Lofa or Nimba, or a complete breakdown in Guinea, could easily unite these conflicts and reignite this part of the Mano River area, and the consequence would be devastating.

## Taylor, LURD and the second part of the civil war

Between 1994 and 1996 several attempts to implement a peace agreement in Liberia failed, mostly because of the unwillingness of Nigeria to accept a deal that included Charles Taylor. However, in 1996, Taylor and the then Nigerian ruler Sani Abacha reached an agreement, and elections were carried out in July 1997. In relatively free and fair elections supervised by international election observers, Taylor won about 75 per cent of the votes, whereas Ellen Johnson-Sirleaf received nine per cent and Alhaji Kromah, the leader of ULIMO-K (the predecessor to LURD) only about four per cent.

Taylor's election victory cannot simply be attributed to the fact that he had enough weapons and soldiers to continue the war if he lost, as this was also the case for most of the other factions and leaders; the emergence of LURD and MODEL clearly proves this point. More important at that particular stage in Liberian history was that Taylor's movement was the most ethnically diverse of all Liberian factions, whereas each of the other armed insurgency groups was the project of one particular ethnic group, as for example the Mandingo and ULIMO-K, the Krahn and ULIMO-J and the Loma and LDF. The civilian opposition, on the other hand, was too fragmented and disorganized to be able to put up a real challenge to Taylor and his NPFL.

From 1997 to 2000, the situation in most parts of Liberia was relatively peaceful. However, in the northern territory of Lofa County, instability and low-level conflict continued as the Mandingo felt that their Loma neighbours

---

[39] Morten Bøås and Anne Hatløy *After the Storm: Economic Activities Among Returning Youths: the case of Voinjama*, Oslo: Fafo (Fafo-report 523), 2006.

had gained the upper hand in local affairs after Taylor's victory in the 1997 elections. Increased discrimination and harassment of young Mandingo men led many of them to seek refugee across the border in Guinea, from where they organized the first cross-border raids as early as 1998. However, LURD as a formal organization was not formed until February 2000 when its establishment was announced in Freetown, capital of Sierra Leone.[40] The place of announcement apart, LURD's centre of gravity was Guinea and President Lansana Conte played an important role in the process. Conte had supported the struggle against the Revolutionary United Front (RUF) in Sierra Leone, and by doing so he had also established himself as one of the most useful allies of the United Kingdom and the United States in the region. It is hard to imagine that the war against Taylor would have been so successful had it not been for Conte's support for LURD.

Ethnicity is one factor in this relationship as the Mandingos are also an important group in Guinea and Conte belongs to an ethnic group that historically has used the Guinean Mandingo as an ally in domestic power struggles. This is one reason why the LURD leadership was able to harvest support for its desire to continue the war against Taylor. Personal relations also played an important role; Sekou Conneh, a used-car dealer from Bong County, was chosen as the LURD leader not because of his political or military capabilities, but because his wife, Ayesha, had become Conte's spiritual adviser on the basis of her premonitions of the 1996 coup attempt and a warning that allowed him to prepare for the event.[41] This gave LURD direct access to the President of Guinea.

By 1999 the second phase of the Liberian civil war was well on its way. The battles were initially concentrated in Lofa County along the border between Guinea and Liberia, without much progress being made by either side. Taylor was not able to eliminate LURD, whereas the rebels were not a major threat to Taylor. The real losers were the civilians who lived in these areas. First LURD would occupy a village and goods would be taken away. Then Taylor's forces would come and chase LURD away, and in turn plunder what was left. This was a common pattern in the Liberian civil war, and helps explain why so many children and youths joined the various factions: they joined for the enhancement of their own as well as their family's security.[42]

---

[40] William Reno, 'Liberia: the LURDs of the New Church', in Morten Bøås and Kevin C. Dunn (eds), *African Guerrillas: Raging Against the Machine*, Boulder: Lynne Rienner, 2007, pp. 69–80.

[41] See also ibid.

[42] See Bøås and Hatløy, 'Getting in, Getting out.'

As the war continued, Taylor was weakened by the United Nations sanctions imposed on his regime for its support of the RUF. The UN placed Taylor under strict surveillance, and it became increasingly more expensive for him to arm and pay his soldiers. LURD and MODEL, however, were not targeted by similar sanctions, and could therefore restock their military capacity without much hindrance or interference. During the summer of 2003, this advantage became obvious. In June 2003 LURD's offensive was about to stop; the movement seemed to lack both the weapons and ammunitions needed to break down Taylor's defences around Monrovia. Three weeks later, however, LURD's forces were pushing Taylor's aside as they shelled Monrovia with mortars and other artillery. Lansana Conte and the government of Guinea were responsible for enabling LURD to restock its military capability so quickly. It is an open secret that LURD would never have been able to take on Taylor the way it did without the military support from Guinea; in this regard, it is of considerable interest that Guinea is a major recipient of military aid from the United States, some of which was transferred from the Guinean army to LURD. The US government must have been aware of this.[43]

## The 'nationalization' of conflict: the Ivorian connection

When Taylor started the war in 1989 he received covert support from Côte d'Ivoire, as the then President, Houphouët-Boigny, was concerned that the close relationship between Samuel Doe and the Nigerian military leadership would negatively influence his own regional system of personal relations. As Stephen Ellis also emphasises,[44] the Doe-Babangida axis during the late 1980s was seen by Houphouët-Boigny not only as the perpetuation of the personal humiliation he had suffered when the upstart Doe had been responsible for the murder of his son-in-law, but also as the reversal of a previous diplomatic alliance between Abidjan and Monrovia.[45]

At the heart of these relationships of personal politics were networks of trade and commerce and the question of access to and control of Liberia's natural resources. Of particular importance were the iron ore deposits in

---

[43] Peter Takirambudde, 'Liberia: where the arms come from', *International Herald Tribune*, 17 September 2003, www.iht.com/articles/110148.html.

[44] Ellis, *The Mask of Anarchy*.

[45] Houphouët-Boigny's goddaughter had been married to a son of William Tolbert. Doe and his men killed both William Tolbert and his son. Houphouët-Boigny's goddaughter, however, survived and moved to Burkina Faso.

Nimba County, one of the most valuable in the world, much sought after by French as well as American and other European firms. Côte d'Ivoire's support for Taylor's NPFL was therefore at least partly related to access to the iron ore deposits, and in this the government of Côte d'Ivoire had the support of French business interests. These made it possible for Taylor to tap into the concerns of French government officials that the Nigerian-led ECOMOG intervention in Liberia signalled an Anglophone intrusion into a part of Africa historically within the French sphere of interest.[46] Thus, at the very top, the politics of personal relationships constituted a sinister cobweb of neatly interwoven regional alliances that could be exploited by insurgency groups in the making. Somewhat similar to the feudal system of alliance-building through marriages and other means of forging personal relations, these alliances represented both personal and national aspirations and ambitions, and in the first part of the Liberian civil war they drew Côte d'Ivoire into the quagmire of informal politics that the Liberian war was becoming.[47]

At the end of Taylor's reign in Liberia the picture presented above had been turned completely upside down, and relations between his regime and the government of Laurent Gbagbo were bordering on open war. What had caused this change was the attempted coup in Côte d'Ivoire on 19 September 2002 when a group of about 700 soldiers simultaneously attacked the cities of Abidjan, Bouaké and Korhogo. When they failed to take Abidjan, the soldiers retreated to Bouaké and re-emerged as the Mouvement Patriotique de la Côte d'Ivoire (MPCI). One month later two other insurgency groups also appeared, this time in the Western regions bordering Liberia. The Mouvement Populaire du Grand Ouest (MPIGO) and the Mouvement Pour la Justice et la Paix (MPJ) demanded revenge for the killing by government forces on 19 September 2002 of Robert Gueï, the leader of the military junta that had ruled Côte d'Ivoire from 1999 to 2000, and expressed their determination to remove President Gbagbo from power.

The reasons behind the civil war in Côte d'Ivoire are not connected to the Liberian conflict. The Ivorian war is in essence a national conflict concerned with the rights (or lack of such) of immigrants from northern neighbouring countries as well as those of northern Ivorian origin, who together had been relegated to the status of second-class citizens by the discourse of *ivoirité*, a discourse manipulated both by Henri Konan Bédié and current president

---

[46] Reno, *Warlord Politics and African States*.
[47] Bøås, 'Nigeria and West Africa'.

Laurent Gbagbo and his supporters.[48] However, the rebellion also had a regional component.

The original coup attempt and the MPCI were planned and implemented by former Ivorian soldiers living in exile in Burkina Faso, and a former Sierra Leone warlord, Sam 'Maskita' Bockarie, who at this time was supposed to be in Taylor's service, was involved in the Western regions with both MPIGO and MPJ. Other Taylor cronies involved included several who were well known for having collaborated with MPIGO's official leader Felix Doh, who had been living in exile in Liberia since Guei was removed from office in 2000.[49]

Many of those who ended up fighting with MPIGO and MPJ had a background as Gueï supporters, and Taylor himself had known Gueï ever since the Liberian war started, as Gueï had been the senior Ivorian officer in charge of supporting Taylor's rebels. It was probably on this basis that Taylor continued to support Gueï when the latter, after losing power in 2000, retreated to his fiefdom close to the western border with Liberia. Here Gueï, himself a Yacouba, recruited fighters from that group's ethnic cousins over the border, the Gio, who also constituted an important component in Taylor's army. The border between Liberia and Côte d'Ivoire, always porous, became effectively nonexistent when Liberia's war propelled into Côte d'Ivoire's territory and *vice versa*, creating a spiral of inter-ethnic violence.

Gbagbo's response was to activate his longstanding anti-Taylor connections among Liberians living in exile in Côte d'Ivoire, mainly of Krahn decent. Thus, in order to retaliate, he allowed the anti-Taylor MODEL group to establish bases along the border with Liberia. Weapons and ammunition were delivered to these bases by the Ivorian army. Their incursions into Liberia were supported by the Ivorian army as well as the local pro-Gbagbo militia, the Forces de Libération du Grand Ouest (FLGO), recruited from the Ivorian

---

[48] Richard Banegas and Ruth Marshall-Fratani, 'Côte d'Ivoire: Negotiating Identity and Citizenship', in Bøås and Dunn (eds), *African Guerrillas*, pp. 81–111.

[49] We still do not know whether this was on Taylor's direct order or if they acted independently as they had began to realize that Taylor's ability to pay for their services was becoming more limited. It is somewhat strange that a cunning strategist like Taylor would chose to open a second front as LURD rebels crossing the border from Guinée Forestière simultaneously pressured him from the north. Taylor may, however, have seen the war in Côte d'Ivoire as a way of providing him both with the opportunity to arrange an 'Operation Pay Yourself', for his mercenaries as well as laying his hands on huge quantities of Ivorian cocoa.

Guéré,[50] who are ethnic relatives to the Liberian Krahn. This alliance was therefore situational, but also built on ethnic affiliation, support and solidarity. Many Ivorian Guéré claim that Samuel Doe was originally an Ivorian, and the connections between the two groups have been cemented by the Liberian civil war that sent thousands of Liberians to seek refugee in western Côte d'Ivoire. Most of these refugees were of Krahn origin and many lived among their ethnic 'cousins' the Guéré. The latter group has traditionally supported Gbagbo and his Front Populaire Ivorien (FPI).

The outcome was a significant number of Ivorian Guéré in MODEL, leading some observers to claim that Gbagbo at a time had more control over MODEL than the political leadership of the movement.[51] Either way, the result was another cross-border ethnic alliance that embedded the southern part of Liberia firmly into the conflict in Côte d'Ivoire.

## Conclusion: endgame Taylor

The consequence of the Guinean and Ivorian involvement, through LURD and MODEL respectively, was that Taylor was forced to fight a two-front war that was far beyond his military capacity. The battles intensified, and the conditions for the civilian population got increasingly worse. This was the background to the peace negotiations that started in Ghana in the first half of June 2003, which themselves were the result of over a year of effort by West African diplomats. In June 2003 ECOWAS finally managed to bring all parties to the negotiating table.

ECOWAS conducted quite a remarkable piece of regional diplomacy when it managed to bring all major parties to the negotiating table in Ghana. However, there were other actors involved, with their own agendas. One was David Crane, the prosecutor at the Special Court for Sierra Leone. The same day that the negotiations started in Ghana, he published his indictment against Taylor and asked the Ghanaian government to hand him over to the Special Court. The Ghanaian government ignored this request, but Taylor and LURD acted immediately: Taylor left the negotiations and flew back to Monrovia, while the LURD leadership ordered its field commanders to attack Monrovia. Subsequently, the negotiations broke down, and the summer of 2003 turned into a disaster for the inhabitants and the internally displaced in

---

[50] The Guéré are sometimes also referred to as the We.
[51] International Crisis Group (ICG), 'Côte d'Ivoire: The War is not yet over', Brussels, 2003.

Monrovia.[52] The fighting therefore continued until Taylor rather surprisingly gave up and accepted a Nigerian offer of exile on 11 August 2003. Contrary to common wisdom, Taylor was not completely defeated. LURD had still not been able to cross the main bridges at Providence Island leading into the centre of Monrovia, and even if Taylor did not want to continue the battle in Monrovia he could easily have escaped up north to Nimba County and continued the war from there, as he still had soldiers and militia men there as well as genuine support from Gio and Mano communities.[53]

In August 2003 Liberia thus finally emerged from a devastating 14 years of civil war (with just a three-year break) with almost every single piece of institution and infrastructure broken and bent. When Taylor went into exile power was first transferred to his Vice-President Moses Blah, before the National Transitional Government of Liberia (NTGL) was established under the leadership of Gyude Bryant to steer Liberia through the two-year transition phase agreed upon in the Comprehensive Peace Agreement (CPA). Together with the United Nations Mission in Liberia (UNMIL), the NTGL managed to conduct the relatively free and fair elections that brought Ellen Johnson-Sirleaf to power, but a lot of problems were also encountered on the way that will have long-term implications for peace and security in Liberia.

The main challenge is that the composition of the NTGL was not much different from previous power-sharing arrangements, including the PRC. Like previous Liberian governments, the NTGL was basically a highly competitive patrimonial environment where various elites were locked into struggles over state resources—often but not always built on ethnic affiliation and exclusionary practices that shaped politics and the control of state institutions as a zero-sum game.[54]

A few representatives from the private sector and civil society were included in the NTGL, but by and large the transitional government reflected the prevailing military power balance between the three main factions—Taylor's forces, known in the NTGL as the Government of Liberia (GoL), and the Mandingo-controlled LURD and the Krahn-dominated MODEL. The two most prominent civilian leaders were the Chairman, Gyude Bryant, and the

---

[52] The indictment of Taylor is correct, in terms of the abuses of power and criminal acts committed while he was president. Its timing, however, was a disaster in humanitarian terms. See Bøås, 'The Liberian Civil War'.

[53] One obvious place would have been Ganta who had been retaken by Gio and Mano groups after the town had been taken by LURD earlier in 2003.

[54] Bøås and Anne Hatløy, 'Getting in, Getting out'.

Vice-Chairman, Wesley Johnson.[55] Other important members included Thomas Nimley, a MODEL leader who was the foreign minister, and Lusinee Kamara, the Finance minister, who was appointed to this position by Sekou Conneh, the LURD leader. Thus, even if the NTGL included some important business and civil society representatives, it was nonetheless a government based on a compromise between the three main factions in the second phase of the Liberian civil war—the GoL, LURD and MODEL—and the international community, meaning that the real powers in the NTGL were the members of the former warring factions. Part of the current security predicament in Liberia is that the ramifications of this compromise are not fully acknowledged.

LURD and MODEL had won the war, but there was no way that these groups could win the peace. LURD was a Mandingo-dominated group, which would never ever be able to win a national election. The Krahn on the other hand are also a relatively small group, and they are also still marked by the fact that many other Liberians believe that they were the favoured group during Samuel Doe's dictatorship.[56] Their interest in the NTGL was therefore not the transition as such; rather, it represented a last chance of enrichment before multi-party election would blow them into oblivion. Acutely aware of this, faction leaders even openly traded in NTGL positions selling them to the highest bidder. Part of the legacy that Ellen Johnson-Sirleaf's government now has to struggle with is related to the fact that those that won the war could not win the peace. This gave their leaders the incentive to treat the NTGL as a means to milk the traditional cash cows of the Liberian state such as the ports, the airports and the customs, but it also entailed that certain tensions between some peripheral groups and the state were embedded without any solution into the new democratic Liberian polity. Elections in conflict-ridden and sharply divided countries such as Liberia will not on their own bring society together, but may just as well cement these differences and thereby also constitute a new platform for militia formation if the current process of state building breaks down.

---

[55] Gyude Bryant, of Grebo origin, was chosen as NTGL chairman as he was perceived as relatively unattached either to the rebel movements or to Taylor's forces, whereas Wesley Johnson got his position from having been one of the leading members of the civilian opposition to Taylor.

[56] See also Huband, *The Liberian Civil War*; Ellis, *The Mask of Anarchy*.

# 13

# Understanding the Character and Politics of the Revolutionary United Front in Sierra Leone

*Kwesi Aning*

## Introduction

The spill-over of the Liberian civil war into Sierra Leone and the outbreak of war in that country represent one of the most phenomenally devastating dynamics of warfare in post-Cold War sub-Saharan Africa. The popularity of the war in intellectual discourse and literature is partly due to its peculiar nature and impact on Sierra Leone and the entire West African sub-region.

As in some other wars in Africa, belligerents in the Sierra Leonean war employed particularly vicious violence against non-combatants as an insurgency strategy when the war commenced in March 1991. Studying and attempting to appreciate the dynamics of the processes leading to the destruction unleashed by the Sierra Leone fighting groups remain popular among scholars of violent non-state actors (VNSAs), owing to the high intensity of the violence employed, most especially the graphic mutilations of victims. The Revolutionary United Front (RUF) insurgents, the West Side Boys (WSB) and the Armed Forces Revolutionary Council (AFRC) junta, for example, all employed the gruesome tactic of severing the limbs of non-combatant civilians either at the elbow or at the wrist as a particular strategy to sow fear. These graphic mutilations, named Operations *'No hands'* and

*'Pay-for-Yourself'*,[1] served as exemplary but gruesome ways in which these groups displayed particularly horrific forms of violence with the ultimate aim of undermining the sense of security of the populace by sowing fear and hatred, as a way to destabilize the country. By the end of the war in 2002, an estimated 50,000 Sierra Leoneans had been killed, over one million displaced from their homes, and thousands had become victims of brutal amputations, rapes, and other violent assaults.[2]

The violent nature and unpredictable dynamics of the war arose largely from the character and politics of those actors involved, particularly, the RUF as the major insurgent group, and later the West Side Boys.[3] The character and politics of the RUF, in particular, greatly dictated the direction, duration and intensity of the war. Among violent non-state actors in West Africa, the RUF has been variously described in the literature as irrational, mad, uncontrollably violent, lacking in political ideology and basically representative of the raga-muffins in society.[4] In attempts to understand the roots and causes for the nature and character of VNSAs, many thoughts and arguments have been advanced that touch on the 'greed and grievance' factor among the factors in the war.[5] However, in an earlier study, McIntyre, Aning and Addo argued that a useful way of understanding the violence of such groups is to situate them within the context of 'constructive social incentives'. They argue that:

Those elements within a society that contribute to stability, and order, as opposed to violent, social change ... constitute the broad range of elements that shape people's choices, including those of youth. The erosion of incentives can be brought about by warfare, taking the form of disintegration of family and community cohesion, educational and economic opportunities; narrowing the available choices and survival strategies and ultimately, the protracted social spaces afforded to young people for growth and achievement.[6]

---

[1] Both 'operations' resulted in wanton and barbaric destruction of human lives. In *'Operation No Hands'*, for instance, victims were asked whether they wanted a *'short-sleeve'* with limbs cut at the elbow and *'long sleeve'* with hands severed at wrist.

[2] Human Rights Watch. 'Sierra Leone: Getting Away with Murder, Mutilation, and Rape.' New York: Human Rights Watch, 1999.

[3] Mats Utas & Magnus Jorget. 'The West Side Boys: military navigation in the Sierra Leone War', mimeo, 2008.

[4] See A. McIntyre, E.K. Aning and P. Addo. 'Politics, War and Youth Culture in Sierra Leone: an Alternative Interpretation', *African Security Review*, Vol. 11, No. 3, 2002. pp. 7ff.

[5] This argument became particularly popularized by Paul Collier, but see also M. Berdal and D. Malone, *Greed and Grievance: Economic Agendas in Civil Wars*, Boulder: Lynne Reinner, 2000.

[6] Ibid., p. 8.

This chapter attempts to understand the character of non-state actors by using the RUF of Sierra Leone as a case study. It argues that the distinctive nature of political and economic governance processes in Africa contributes largely to the way in which people decide to employ violence as a characteristic aspect of their response to governance deficiencies and weaknesses. Such distinctive types of both elite and mass politics, which usually lack deeply engrained bureaucratic processes and mechanisms, contribute to a particular type of governance process usually characterized by violence.

The nature of post-independence politics in Sierra Leone reflected the type of political and economic governance processes which lacked structured and organized forms of bureaucratic control and oversight. Because of these inherent weaknesses in the state structure, Sierra Leone was to spawn several violent groups which in the literature are basically treated as bandits and vermin.

This chapter seeks to present the results of an empirically based study from fieldwork carried out in 2002–3 with different groups of youths who participated in Sierra Leone's war from 1991 to 2001. While the focus of the study will be on the best known of these groups in terms of the political dynamics within the state that led to their establishment, it will also argue that a nuanced and differentiated approach is needed to understand the complexity of violent non-state armed groups in Sierra Leone. It will argue that, while the most internationally known among such groups, the RUF/SL, is usually perceived as an independent, stand-alone group, this notion is not borne out by empirical research. Rather, it demonstrates that the RUF also formed a political and economic alliance with the official Armed Forces of Sierra Leone, enabling it to gain and hold power albeit for a brief period.

It is this capacity of a violent non-state actor to form alliances with state institutions and other violent non-state actors, and manipulate both political and economic processes with the active connivance of individuals and groups representing the state, that makes the RUF/SL's role and prominence in the Sierra Leone civil war worthy of study.

## Post-independence political and economic governance in Sierra Leone

Sierra Leone became independent in 1961. Its politics was dominated by two parties, the Sierra Leone People's Party (SLPP) and the All Peoples Congress (APC). The nature of post-independence political and economic governance in Sierra Leone under the various regimes, and particularly under Siaka

Stevens—the country's first President after the introduction of a presidential Republican constitution—indicates how the country later spawned violent non-state actors that made violence an inevitable part of their response to governance and economic deficiencies.

After the APC had won elections in 1967 and its leader Stevens was about to become Prime Minister, he was put under house arrest by Brigadier David Lansana, a prejudiced and ethnocentric client of the defeated Prime Minister, Sir Albert Margai. Stevens sought exile in Guinea and whilst there is alleged to have started training a group of guerrillas to overthrow the National Reformation Council (NRC) under Major Juxon-Smith, a group of middle ranking officers who usurped David Lansana a day after his intervention.[7] When a group of junior officers took power and formed the Anti-Corruption Revolutionary Movement (ACRM) in April 1968 and quickly called on Stevens to return, he is alleged to have integrated his former guerrilla group into the national army.[8]

Under Stevens the political attitude of the APC became markedly different from what it used to be in opposition or when the APC controlled the Freetown City Council.[9] His first decade in power became characterized by growing alienation from his political roots and the abandonment of virtually all objectives that were prominent within his party when it was in opposition, except probably for the objective of national unity.

By conscious efforts the APC succeeded in reducing the number of opposition SLPP members in the House of Representatives through questionable election petitions which the judiciary accepted, and successfully dismantled the national coalition cabinet that had been instituted in 1968. The government became totally opposed to politically dissenting opinions and groups, to the extent that all attempts were made to stifle the opposition, particularly the SLPP, and any other form of organized opposition. This was characterized by an atmosphere of violence in which many influential members of the SLPP were arrested and detained.

---

[7] A.M. Lavalie, 'Government and Opposition in Sierra Leone, 1968–78', in A. Jones and P.K. Mitchell (eds), *Sierra Leone Studies at Birmingham*, Birmingham: University of Birmingham's Centre for West African Studies, 1985, pp. 77ff.

[8] A.B. Zack-Williams, 1999. 'Child Soldiers in the Civil War in Sierra Leone' Paper Presented at the Development Studies Association Conference, 12–14 September, University of Bath.

[9] I. Abdullah, 'The Path to Destruction: The Origin and Character of the Revolutionary United Front of Sierra Leone' *Journal of Modern African Studies*, Vol. 36, No. 2 (June 1998), p. 206.

The police and army were employed in brutalizing political opponents and groups with dissident views. During this period, the rule of the APC witnessed many States of Emergency during which the ex-guerrilla sections of the army were used prominently to intimidate opponents and those with dissenting views in Sierra Leone.[10] During one such State of Emergency the police and army executed a joint operation in the Southern and Eastern Provinces which resulted in the mass arrest and brutalization of not only SLPP members, but also their supporters, including chiefs. Besides intimidating and brutalizing the people involved, the operation resulted in looting and damaging of property as well as fatal shootings.[11] In what became known as the 'Taninahun Massacre', a joint army-police operation led to the death of a large number of innocent people in the Kenema district town of Taninahun.

By the time a one-party dictatorship was instituted, the SLPP had been practically weakened and disabled by Stevens' extensive use of cooptation and oppression of the opposition. This gave way to the centralization of power in President Stevens and the APC. That is visibly the most notable point when the culture of political violence among the youth, which was later to become problematic, surfaced in the politics of the country. At this time the character and name of the youth of the APC, for instance, became generally associated with political violence and vandalism.[12]

Membership of the APC then became a deciding factor in political survival and progress as well as individual and group access to resources. Non-members were sidelined as membership of the APC became 'a *sine qua non* to get by; exclusion literally meant death by attrition.'[13] The public and civil service and the judiciary persistently suffered interference from the APC politicians. SLPP politicians in parliament were allowed to remain as APC supporters and some were given cabinet positions.

Through his control of the diamond sector, Stevens succeeded in extending clientelist, neo-patrimonial and exclusionary politics to the industry. Thus networks of informal markets evolved with which he rewarded his cronies and supporters and also chastized his opponents. Chiefs and individuals supporting the APC were rewarded while opponents of his political posture were removed and/or punished.

In his attempt to strengthen his hold on power, Stevens inadvertently attracted many more opponents across the country. However, rather than

[10] Lavalie, 'Government and Opposition in Sierra Leone', pp. 85–7.
[11] Ibid.
[12] Zack-Williams, 'Child Solidiers', p. 4.
[13] Abdullah, 'The Path to Destruction', p. 206.

leading to a reduction in the regime's use of repression and cooptation of opponents, this gave the regime a further incentive to extend its power through the use of suppression and cooption. For instance, owing to resistance to the government's use of violence in the Southern and Eastern Provinces, the Public Order Act of 1965 was invoked by the government and was used by its forces to strike at the very heart of opposition strongholds. However, rather than stem the tide of opposition, the SLPP rather organized an anti-APC campaign strategy based on the use of the male secret society, the Poro, which is popular among the Mende and Temne ethnic groups of south-eastern Sierra Leone and south-western Liberia.[14]

In this context of a weakened opposition, centralized power and violent political culture during Stevens' rule, structured political and bureaucratic processes for addressing public grievances became stifled.[15] This was the background for the many attempts to overthrow Siaka Stevens through a coup d'état, one of which was led by Muhammed Sorie Forna and fourteen others including Foday Sankoh, and the student-led demonstrations in 1977. Whilst not attempting to advance a justification for any of them, one may argue that the lack of a vibrant opposition provided the leeway for students and the youth to emerge as a daring alternative opposition to the APC regime and eventually led to the use of Sierra Leonean youth as a political group with a distinct identity. Also that the culture of violence and the lack of workable political and bureaucratic processes for addressing political and social grievances encouraged students and youths to employ demonstrations and sometimes violence as a medium of communicating their grievances and opposition to government.

Prior to the 1977 general elections, widespread popular student-led demonstrations registered the extent of opposition to Stevens' government amid the mounting economic disarray that Sierra Leoneans grappled with. Consequently, despite the violence and rigging that characterized the elections, the SLPP still managed to garner enough support to gain 15 seats. The demonstrations, which registered the existence of popular opposition among the country's students, then bolstered the confidence of the opposition which had by then been crushed by the APC to its lowest ebb of performance.

[14] Lavalie, 'Government and Opposition in Sierra Leone', pp. 78–81; See also S. Ellis, 'Liberia 1989–1994: A Study of Ethnic and Spiritual Violence', *African Affairs*, Vol. 94, No. 375, April 1995.

[15] L.D. Fashole, and S.P. Riley, 1989. 'The Politics of Economic Decline in Sierra Leone', *Journal of Modern African Studies*, Vol. 27, No. 1., p. 135.

Under Stevens, initially the economy of Sierra Leone improved through better efforts to rationalize the extraction of minerals. However, by the 1980s the economy had gone so far downhill that there were food shortages, price rises and non-payment of salaries that led to discontent across the country. The trend of economic non-performance or retrogression was basically due to over-spending, clientelism, neo-patrimonialism and the privatisation of state structures that became characteristic of the Stevens regime. An estimated US$10 million is said to have been spent on the 1980 Organisation of African Unity (OAU) summit conference in Freetown, for instance,

As noted above, the diamond sector, a major mainstay of the Sierra Leone economy, suffered political interference. Similarly, the Kailahun district, renowned for agricultural exports, was interfered with. During this period, one group that markedly benefited from the clientelist and neo-patrimonial economic and political direction of Stevens was the Lebanese and Afro-Lebanese component of Sierra Leone's business population. These people allied themselves with Stevens' leadership and so, though excluded from any formal political roles, many of them wielded considerable influence in the country derived from their connection with and support for the ruling APC. Consequently such people also held considerable economic power and dominated the gold, diamond production and marketing, fisheries, transport, tourism, trading, banking and financing, construction, engineering, and other sectors of the country's economy.[16]

So Sierra Leone's political and economic governance under President Stevens can be said to be characterized by a culture of violence, repression and cooptation of the opposition, the lack of appropriate bureaucratic processes for addressing grievances, the centralization of power and a lack of appropriate institutions for managing the economic sector of the country. I argue that these characteristics produced an inherent economic and political weakness which created the enabling environment for several violent non-state actors, particularly the Revolutionary United Front (RUF).

Major-General Joseph Momoh, who succeeded Stevens as President in 1985, inherited these weaknesses and rather than stemming them, perpetuated them considerably. He declared a State of Emergency under which sweeping powers were bestowed on the government to clamp down on the activities of corrupt government officials, gold and diamond smugglers, and

---

[16] A. Hoogvelt. 'IMF Crime of Conditionality', *Review of African Political Economy* (Sheffield), Vol. 38, 1987, pp. 80ff.; See also 'Business Profile: Jamil Said Mohammed', in *South: the Third World Magazine* (London), December 1982, p. 64.

hoarders of essential commodities and local currency. In addition he implemented a wide range of structural adjustment policies, under Sierra Leone's Economic Recovery Programme. Even though Momoh vigorously implemented economic recovery recommendations, no effort was made to rationalize the economic governance processes in the country. Corruption was still rife in all parts of society. By 1987, the country's treasury was unable to pay the salaries of government employees; there was also a severe shortage of currency in the banks due to the hoarding of money. The economic decline that had started during Stevens' regime, therefore, worsened to the extent that at the time of the outbreak of the war, the country had the lowest living standards of any country in the world whilst the political leadership wielded political violence against opponents and yet did little about social services such as health and education.[17]

Politically, Momoh attempted to sustain the culture of violence, intimidation and repression against the opposition. But during his time in office, the wave of multi-party politics was advancing across the African continent, and it now became a popular requirement for political reforms. In the face of popular demand for multi-party politics in Sierra Leone by the Sierra Leone Bar Association (SLBA), the university community, students and the general populace, Momoh's government at first responded only by warning that any talk of multi-party democracy in the country would be punished with the full rigour of the law since such discussions, agitations and demands were illegal under the one-party system.[18]Momoh attempted to preserve the existing order and thus predisposed the country to an implosion which would open the way for violent non-state actors.

## The emergence of youth as alternative opposition

As discussed earlier, Stevens's use of repression and cooptation against political opposition further weakened the activities of the SLPP and other opposition groups in the country. The persistent use of political violence by the government and the exploitation of youths and youth groups by the APC, in the midst of increasing economic decline and unemployment among young people, almost naturally led to resistance from students and other daring

---

[17] United Nations, *Human Development Report 1993*, New York: United Nations Development Programme, Oxford University Press; see also W. Reno. *Corruption and State Politics in Sierra Leone*, Cambridge and New York: Cambridge University Press, 1995.
[18] Zack-Williams, 'Child Soldiers', p. 9.

youth components of the country. Student-led demonstrations thus became prominent aspects of political opposition. The general elections of 1977, for instance, came in the wake of student-led demonstrations across the country. Radical youths and students coalesced around radical political colleagues, particularly those who had been expelled from Fourah Bay College (FBC). Ibrahim Abdullah and Ismail Rashid argue that to appreciate the role of youth in galvanizing opposition to government, this should be situated during the period when the expelled FBC students became principal architects of radicalizing their colleagues and particularly the young urban unemployed.[19]

The Sierra Leone intellectual community, by using pan-Africanism and an anti-apartheid stance, started an informal youth-led opposition against the APC's repressive governance. By 1982, this idea had culminated in the establishment of the Pan-African Union (PANAFU) which was dedicated to the anti-apartheid struggle in South Africa. Other groups such as the Mass Awareness and Participation (MAP), the Green Book Study Group, the Juche Idea Study Group and the Socialist Cub had also emerged on university campuses in Sierra Leone, particularly the FBC campus. Within these groups members shared and discussed radical political ideologies and the examples of other countries in the sub-region as a basis for motivating themselves to resist the APC's repressive regime.

Whilst this was taking place among students, the majority of the unemployed urban youth were already coalescing around interests such as smoking, music, drugs, and the establishment of independent neighbourhoods. Even though in the past the students and the urban unemployed youth had very little in common and were separated by their class positions in society, they began coalescing around common interests and experiences, especially culture and the worsening economic conditions in the country that affected all citizens. This provided a convergence point which offered the radical students the opportunity to share their radical political ideas with the unlettered but disaffected youth. What is notable is that this convergence, apart from widening the existing base of opposition among young people in the country, also led to acquaintances among young people some of whom were later to become important actors in the country's political history.

In the wake of the APC's treatment of the opposition, the expanded base of opposition among the young elites and urban unemployed increasingly

---

[19] I. Abdullah and Rashid Ismail, 'Rebel Movements' in Adekeye Adebajo and Ismail Rashid (eds), *West Africa's Security Challenges: Building Peace in a Troubled Region*, Boulder: Lynne Rienner Publishers, Inc., 2004, p. 178.

grew to believe that because of the lack of political processes for change, violence was their only bargaining chip to change the existing regime or was the only language the regime would understand. This idea gained popularity especially after the election violence. On the basis of this idea, the bulk of unemployed urban youth who, hitherto, had been considered a violent and grossly undisciplined mass became relevant training ground for would-be revolutionaries for Sierra Leone.[20] The 1985 rustication of 41 students of Fourah Bay College and the subsequent disbanding of MAP gave such victims the motivation and also room to garner support for a vibrant youth opposition as an alternative to the weakened SLPP.

But to understand the urban and 'youth' background of these non-state violent groups in Sierra Leone, one needs to appreciate the central element of the role of youth in Sierra Leonean politics, and possibly in the wider politics of West Africa: what can basically be described as the 'crisis of youth'. It has been argued that,

The phenomenon of youth participation in African conflicts is deeply rooted in the crisis of governance that characterizes most post-colonial African states. This crisis has over the years been manifested in various forms, including conflicts over power sharing; incapacity of the state to provide for and protect its citizens; the solitary exercise of political power; mismanagement of state resources, abuse of power and in the collapse of economic and social structures and institutions.[21]

Thus the 'youth' background of the RUF and the West Side Boys was rooted in the corruption and maladministration that characterized the Sierra Leonean state. In the end, what motivated young people's decision to join the armed groups, especially the RUF and the West Side Boys, was as varied as the extensive variety of economic, familial, personal, and political influences in their lives. Thus recruitment potential was seen as arising from their vulnerability, as opposed to resilience.[22]

---

[20] Ibid., 179.

[21] Cited in McIntyre, Aning, and Addo, 'Politics, War and Youth Culture in Sierra Leone'.

[22] The point about resilience is important and needs to be understood. Resilience is best developed when there is a core of values that provides a certain minimum of survival. These can be related to the home and community. In cases where these are undermined, it is highly probable that people may turn to other forms of participation, recognition and empowerment, characterized by an aggressive stance towards established institutions and practices.

## Spawning the RUF

The rustication of the 41 students from FBC in the midst of a troubled economic and political situation opened a Pandora's Box in three important ways:

(a) It provided the rusticated students with the opportunity to exploit the hardships in the country and the repressive policies of the APC to sell their radical political ideas among all sections of the country's youth, particularly the poor and unemployed urban groups who hitherto were not privileged enough to access such radical political ideology. It can be argued that the obvious motivation for such a project, on the part of the rusticated students and other radical political ideologues, was the state of affairs in the country. This broadened the opposition base among the young people in the country and against the APC.

(b) Members of such youth and radicalized political groups became available for training outside the territory of Sierra Leone, and many of them further entrenched their radical stance by learning from the experiences and motivation of similar groups in other countries, particularly Liberia, Ghana and Libya. For instance a section of these groups travelled to Ghana where they were supported by Ghanaian student radicals who shared their experiences and vision of an egalitarian society,[23] and

(c) They were able to exploit training opportunities. This led to the recruitment of individuals for training in Libya, some of whom were later to be deciders of the country's fate through their activities in the RUF.

## Character and politics of the RUF

The nature of the politics and the political character of the state instituted by Siaka Stevens and sustained by Joseph Momoh had important implications on the formation and character of the RUF. First, the inherent political and economic weaknesses created the conditions favourable for the emergence of radical elements whose brainchild became the RUF. Secondly, the nature of violence perpetuated by the radical youth of the ruling APC, particularly under Stevens, in settling political scores introduced individuals who later led the RUF to a culture of violence and an idea that the violent nature of the political system could only be confronted and changed by an equally violence-

[23] See *Africa Development*, XXII (3/4), 1997, pp. 172ff.

based strategy. According to one FBC student who claimed to belong to a movement known as the Sierra Leone Democratic Movement/Front (SLDFM), they aimed at 'democracy and destroying the APC, maybe by military means' and preferred a coup to a protracted military struggle.[24]

Thirdly, as a fallout from the violent culture and from the example of use of young people (youth wings) of the APC to execute political vandalism against opponents, the RUF when it needed combatants at the onset of the war employed child soldiers extensively. Fourthly, the RUF attempted to seize control of the economic hub of the country by controlling the districts of diamond production. Another political feature of the RUF was the apparent lack of a focused political ideology with which it could realise its goal of revolutionalizing the country. In the ensuing sub-sections, I will attempt to draw empirical linkages between these features of the RUF and the political and economic events that preceded its emergence.

*Violence against non-combatants.* Young people became involved in the politics of the country in the immediate post-independence era mainly as foot soldiers of the various political parties, especially the APC and the SLPP. Within the various political parties their critical role usually came into play during crisis moments when they were called upon to execute the 'dirty jobs' which sometimes included violent activities such as the 1970 arson at the Ginger Hall in Freetown and also the 1977 assault on FBC students.[25]

Most of the young people who did the dirty jobs of violence were urban-based unlettered and unemployed youth who were active in the various underground economies of the country and were noted for crime, violence and indiscipline. By doing the dirty jobs, they acted as thugs for politicians.[26] This implies that they became exploitable agents for any repressive tendency of politicians who favoured violence.

The dwindling of the gap between radical students and the unlettered urban unemployed who were usually the 'dirty job' doers led to the emergence of a cocktail of radicalism involving the indiscipline of the latter and the political ideas of the former. As part of this radicalism, an idea evolved that

[24] D. Keen, *Conflict and Collusion in Sierra Leone*, New York, International Peace Academy, 2005, pp. 46ff.

[25] I. Abdullah, 'The Path to Destruction', p. 207; See also G.O. Roberts, *The Anguish of Third World Independence: The Sierra Leone Experience*, Lanham, MD: University Press of America, 1982,

[26] I. Abdullah, 'The Path to Destruction', p. 208.

violence was necessary in changing the political system or registering grievances with the political system of Sierra Leone. I argue that this complex trajectory is an important factor in understanding the violent character of the RUF, since some members of this group of people who witnessed political violence under the various regimes and were also introduced, through participation, to political violence against the opposition ended up in the ranks of the RUF.

First of all, it can be argued that the emergence of the idea that violence was necessary in transforming the prevailing political and economic system informed the attack on 23 March 1991 in the Kailahun district which marked the beginning of the war. After the attack, the extent of the violence and the tactics employed then gave ample evidence of the extent to which violence was inherent in the rank and file of the RUF. It is ironic, however, that the leadership of the RUF thought it could garner the support and allegiance of the population by terrorising people.

*Recruitment of child soldiers.* The RUF is known to have used no fewer than 3,000 child soldiers in the war, and it is estimated that about half of the RUF fighters were between eight and 14 years old.[27] This strategy of recruiting children as combatants offered the RUF certain advantages such as ease of recruitment, ease of conditioning for battle, reduced likelihood of boredom and desertion of the movement, and unreasonable destructiveness. I argue, however, that apart from these factors, the fact that both government and rebel groups relied heavily on the youth components of the population, people who could be trusted to mete out considerable violence to opponents, may have increased the RUF's difficulty in recruiting young adults, and hence the group's resort to children. Whilst this point is contestable, the extent to which the RUF evolved from an environment of violence dominated by radical youth, many of whom were unlettered and grossly undisciplined, could have a link with the group's use of young people including children. At the onset of the war, the RUF had few fighters and so was desperately in need of combatants. Given the difficulty in recruiting adult combatants, it made sense for them to resort to children who could be forcibly recruited and conditioned for war and asked few questions about the consequences of their actions.

---

[27] R. Brett and M. McCallan, *Children: The Invisible Soldiers*, Radda Barnen, Save the Children, 1998. See also K. Peters, and P. Richards, 'Why We Fight: Voices of Youth Combatants in Sierra Leone', *Africa*, 68 (2), 1998, pp. 185ff.

*Attempts to control diamond fields.* Many arguments have been advanced for the RUF's interest in seizing diamond fields in the war. One popular argument is that rebels could depend upon it as a fungible good to fund the war. Indeed some rebels were reported to have sold diamonds in Koindu and with the proceeds bought weapons from Guinean soldiers.[28] In the case of the RUF, given the unreliability of the funding Charles Taylor initially gave them, this point is valid in explaining their quest to seize control of diamond fields in some parts of the country. However, it is also important that given the general lack of transparent economic processes in the country and the country's inability to impose control on its economy, leading to inequitable distribution of national resources, the RUF leadership thought that in meeting its targets under the revolution (and the 'paradise' they promised their followers, supporters and sympathisers in Sierra Leone), the quickest way would be to take control of the diamond fields and also trade routes.[29] To get direct access to resources, therefore, the movement then decided to seize districts and towns that were prominent in such important economic activities.

Notwithstanding the objective, the tactic employed by the RUF in achieving the desired control of the targeted regions can be said to be similar to the tactic the Siaka Stevens regime employed in some of the districts that housed major economic activities in the country, particularly agriculture and mining. Under Stevens, for instance, the APC's tactic was to recruit vandals from the Kono District and the Northern Province into the Kailahun district under the supervision of APC stalwarts and MPs to brutalize people, burn houses and on polling days turn people away from voting so as to assist APC candidates to gain advantage over their opponents.[30] Whereas this tactic was used by the APC, the RUF was later to adopt similar tactics against civilians in their battle to control the diamond fields. Whilst the RUF's employment of the same tactic could be said to be merely coincidental, it does not rule out idea that the RUF could have borrowed the tactic from the APC's earlier usage.

*The political character of the RUF.* Even though the RUF theoretically proclaimed political motives in terms of calling for political change and sharing a

---

[28] See *West Africa*, 23–29 October 1995; *Concord Times*, 21 June 1995.

[29] David Keen shares a similar argument. For his view on this point see D. Keen, *Conflict and Collusion*, pp. 50ff.

[30] Lavalie, 'Child Soldiers', p. 81. See also Zack-Williams, 'Child Soldiers', pp. 6ff.

somewhat fluid and abstract cocktail of socialist ideals, its activities at the onset of the rebellion make it difficult to fully interpret their political character. According to some escapees from rebel camps, the rebels shared their ideal of how Sierra Leone should be run and condemned prevailing forms of corruption, inequitable distribution of state resources, clientelism and neo-patrimonialism. In addition, the rank and file of the movement, and particularly the leader Foday Sankoh, seem to have held on to the goal of taking over the leadership of the country. But any shade of ideology with which the RUF can be said to have identified fades into irrelevance beside the wanton use of brutalities that the group meted out to civilians.

Whilst the RUF has been viewed and analyzed extensively as a stand-alone entity distinct from the national army, I argue that the May 1997 coup d'état led by Johnny Paul Koroma is a significant event in understanding the complex political character of the RUF and its ability to negotiate both political and economic alliances with other groups within and/or outside Sierra Leone. The military regime of the Armed Forces Revolutionary Council (AFRC) under Koroma was allied to the RUF, which moved into Freetown to help it rule. Thus the RUF was able to gain the support of the official army, with which it took power in 1997, albeit for a brief period.

In considering the RUF's association with the army, even though much detail has remained unclear, one may consider that some of the youth who interacted with the urban unemployed in the earlier year may have ended up in the army, and therefore on the basis of familiarity shared informal acquaintance with some combatants of the RUF or become sympathetic to their goal. Another explanatory argument can be posited within the wider debate on 'greed' or the economic underpinnings of the war. The RUF rebellion provided a way for certain elements in the country's army and also civilians to enrich themselves through the underground economy that emerged around the war. Against this background, the point of convergence then became the economic incentives motivating the rank and file of both the RUF and the official army, or a common dissatisfaction with the political attitude of various leaders of the country.[31] Whilst these suggestions remain speculative, the RUF was certainly able to join with the army to gain and hold power for a brief period in 1997–98.

[31] Both the RUF and the SLA were widely implicated in the abuse of civilians, through looting, forced labour and recruitment (of children among others), sexual violence, and indiscriminate killing. See Dan Smith, 'Trends and Causes of Armed Conflict', Berghof Research Centre for Constructive Conflict Management, 2004.

## Conclusion

The lack of a coherent economic and political governance process in Sierra Leone was critical in the emergence of a culture of violence which ultimately contributed to the creation of violent non-state actors such as the RUF in Sierra Leone. That group, upon its emergence onto Sierra Leone's political space, borrowed extensively from experiences of suppression of the opposition, violence, and cooptation. Consequently the inherent weaknesses within Sierra Leone's economic and political governance processes can be said to have had an important impact on the character and politics of the group.

The RUF's dynamic politics gave it the opportunity to form alliances both within and outside the country, including an alliance with the formal army of Sierra Leone. Whilst the group is usually considered a stand-alone entity, this political character enabled it to navigate its way around the many hurdles that the murky situation of war and rebellion created, to the extent that it was able, together with the formal army, to take over power for a brief period of time.

Thus, from the example of the RUF in Sierra Leone, it can be established that the nature of post-independence politics in Africa, reflecting inherent weaknesses in the political and economic governance processes of states, has grave implications for the security of states; in particular, it can lead to the emergence of groups generally describable as irrational, mad, uncontrollably violent, lacking in political ideology and basically representative of those often seen as ragamuffins in society, even as bandits and vermin.

# 14

# UNITA's Insurgency Lifecycle in Angola

*Assis Malaquias*

In the 1980s, Angola was one of the main battlegrounds of the Cold War and a key front in the Reagan Doctrine's strategy to 'roll back' communism. Given the critical importance of local insurgencies in this global strategy, UNITA[1] became a major recipient of both covert and overt American assistance. Added to the support from the apartheid regime in South Africa, American assistance enabled UNITA to develop into one of the most formidable violent non-state actors (VNSAs) in Africa. By the mid-1980s, UNITA controlled and administered significant portions of rural Angola and posed a serious military threat to the MPLA[2] government which, at the time, was a major recipient of Soviet and Cuban support. At the end of the decade, with the MPLA government on the defensive owing to the momentous global geopolitical changes precipitated by the collapse of the Soviet bloc, UNITA seemed poised to finally gain the upper hand on the battlefield as a prelude to gaining political power. But this optimism was misplaced; UNITA failed to seize political power and, within a decade, this once powerful political and military machine was in a shambles—its long-time leader Jonas Savimbi was killed in combat and his defeated army surrendered within weeks of his death. What

---

[1] União Nacional para a Independência Total de Angola (National Union for Total Independence of Angola).

[2] Movimento Popular de Libertação de Angola (Popular Movement for the Liberation of Angola).

accounts for the political and military failures that led to UNITA's collapse and its decreasing relevance in Angolan politics?

This chapter reviews the key factors leading to the emergence and development of UNITA's insurgency in Angola and focuses on the dynamics—both internal and external—that combined to precipitate its downfall. At the internal level, UNITA was unable to overcome peacefully the multiple crises it confronted throughout the various phases of the conflict. As a result, it resorted to internal purges that, while 'cleansing' the group of perceived obstacles, left it profoundly debilitated politically and militarily, constantly undergoing forced metamorphoses to survive. At the external level, these metamorphoses led to frequently changing alliances. Ultimately, UNITA's ability to win influential external allies—however odd they might have been—could not compensate for its internal weaknesses nor, even more important, avert its eventual downfall. When, at the end of the Cold War, UNITA faced the prospect of survival without major external backers, it resorted to criminal violence: its strategy for seizing power now necessitated control of important natural resources, especially diamonds, to sustain the insurgency. The administration of 'liberated areas'—once a source of internal legitimacy and external prestige—was no longer a centrepiece of UNITA's strategy to deny the government control of the countryside as a part of the campaign to overthrow it. This change—from liberation movement to criminal insurgency—sealed UNITA's fate.

## Nationalist responses to colonialism in Angola

Portuguese explorers first arrived in Angola in 1483 and found the Kongo kingdom at the height of its power, dominating the west coast of central Africa. The Portuguese were treated not so much as explorers or conquerors but as citizens of a distant but equal power with whom Kongo initially sought to establish a mutually beneficial relationship. This relationship rapidly deteriorated, however, as the explorers redirected their attention towards exploiting Kongo's vast human and natural resources. The ensuing slave trade that soon came to dominate Portuguese-Kongo relations was a direct result of this fundamental shift which, in turn, seriously weakened Kongo and opened the door for Portuguese conquest. From Kongo, the Portuguese proceeded to conquer the entire territory of present-day Angola. By the late 17th century, the Portuguese had a significant presence along the coast and were penetrating toward the central highland kingdoms. At the Berlin conference of 1884–85 Portugal could claim Angola as its territory.

Portugal's attempts to consolidate its presence in Angola after the Berlin conference yielded mixed results. The process of colonial domination accelerated in the 1920s. The colonial regime was reinvented after the May 1926 military coup that led to the establishment of a one-party regime, known as the *Estado Novo* (New State). The *Estado Novo*, especially through its Colonial Act of 1930, changed the relationship between Portugal and its 'overseas possessions'. Those territories became 'provinces' and were regarded as integral units of both the Portuguese nation and the colonial state. For colonial Portugal—a decaying, resource-poor empire—this constituted a convenient way to continue exploiting conquered territories. It also provided a legal framework for decades of colonial violence.

During almost five centuries, Portugal used a variety of violent means—physical, psychological, and structural—to exercise and retain control over the colony. This included slavery until the late 17th Century and forced labour well into the 20th. Under the 1878 *Regulamento para os contratos de servicais e colonos nas provincias de Africa* (Regulation for contracts of servants and colonists in the African provinces) Portugal substituted slavery with forced labour by renaming slaves 'contract labourers'. The *Regulamento* included a 'vagrancy clause' which stipulated that all those Angolans not fully employed were considered vagrants and could therefore be forced into contracts for up to five years.

In addition to slavery and forced labour, colonialism subjected Angolan society to racial stratification. The political economy of colonialism placed the minority white settler community at the top of the social structure while *indigenas* (indigenous) peoples were relegated to the bottom, with mulattos and *assimilados* (assimilated) Africans occupying the middle rungs. Assimilation was a form of psychological violence against Angolans in the sense that it involved an experience akin to 'a process of cultural decomposition that aimed at producing a *colonial subject*.'[3] It separated Angolans from their pre-colonial identities, values and languages while teasing them with socio-economic and cultural conditions they could never fully reach. Within a fundamentally oppressive colonial society, Angolans could only achieve the purported goals of assimilation—to be certified as 'civilized' and thus become a Portuguese citizen—by rejecting their past and embracing alien identities, values, and languages in what MPLA referred to as 'cultural genocide.'[4]

[3] Tarsis Kabwegyere, 'The Dynamics of Colonial Violence: The Inductive System in Uganda', *Journal of Peace Research*, Vol. 9, No. 4, 1972, pp. 303–14.
[4] MPLA, 'Cultural Racism', in Aquino de Bragança and Immanuel Wallerstein (eds), *The*

As would be expected, Angolans resisted this kind of domination, humiliation, and exploitation. During the 1930s and 1940s several social, cultural, and sports groups emerged in colonial Angola, particularly in urban areas, to coordinate various emerging forms of anti-colonial resistance. These associations, including LNA[5] and ANANGOLA[6], became important sites for aggregating and articulating revolutionary ideas arising from continuing and intensifying colonial exploitation, violence and humiliation, especially the tensions arising from the large influx of settlers after the end of World War II. In the 1950s these associations became increasingly politicized. In many important respects, such associations constituted the embryos of the independence movements that led the armed anti-colonial struggle starting in 1961. UNITA was one of these nationalist movements.

## UNITA's character

UNITA emerged in 1966 to give a revolutionary political voice to the Ovimbundu, Angola's largest ethno-linguistic group. The Ovimbundu represent 35–40 per cent of Angola's population and dominate the areas with the highest population density in the country—the central plateau provinces of Huambo, Bié, and Benguela. Many Ovimbundu believed that, as the largest community in Angola, it was critical to have their own liberation movement to counterbalance the role and power of the movements representing the other two major ethnic communities. Thus, there was a strong ethnic rationale behind the creation of UNITA.

This ethnic rationale notwithstanding, the birth and development of UNITA are inextricably associated with the determination and vision of one man: Jonas Savimbi. Early in his political career, he had been inclined to join Agostinho Neto's communist-influenced MPLA because it had a progressive programme and Savimbi 'did not want to be on the right wing.'[7] However, the dominance of mulattos in MPLA's leadership positions dissuaded the young nationalist leader from joining this already established political organization. Savimbi was also deeply suspicious of the *assimilados*.

---

*African Liberation Reader*, Volume 1, *The Anatomy of Colonialism*, London: Zed Press, 1982, p. 139.

[5] Liga Nacional Africana (African National League).

[6] Associação dos Naturais de Angola (Association of Natives of Angola).

[7] Fred Bridgland and Jonas Savimbi, *A Key to Africa*, New York: Paragon, 1987, p. 45.

After rejecting MPLA because it was dominated by mulattos and *assimilados*, Savimbi joined UPA[8] on 1 February 1961 even though he had found its leader Holden Roberto to be uninspiring.[9] By the time UPA initiated its military campaign against Portuguese colonialism on 15 March 1961, Savimbi had risen to the rank of secretary-general. In that capacity, he played an important role in the merger between UPA and the smaller PDA[10] to create FNLA[11] in 1962. A week later, after FNLA formed the GRAE,[12] Savimbi was given the foreign secretary position. But Savimbi eventually became disappointed with Roberto's autocratic leadership style and his keenness to fill the organization's executive posts with relatives and members of his community. He resigned from FNLA/GRAE in July 1964, travelled to China in 1965 with several followers to receive training in Maoist guerrilla warfare at Nanking Military Academy, and returned to Angola to create UNITA on 15 March 1966.

Initially, UNITA opted for spectacular military actions for maximum publicity. Thus, in December 1966, after its first commanders returned from military training in China, UNITA mounted its first two military attacks against Portuguese targets. The first attack, personally planned and led by Savimbi, was against the small town on Cassamba in Mexico province. Cassamba was a soft target, 'a small timber outpost' where Portuguese lumberjacks lived with their families and several hundred Angolans under the protection of 'a couple of hundred Portuguese soldiers'.[13] According to Savimbi's own account of the attack, 'it was a disaster.'[14] Against the advice of David 'Samwimbila' Chingunji—a top military commander who had also received training in China—Savimbi led 60 poorly trained villagers on the Cassamba attack. The attackers were easily beaten back, suffering many casualties; not a single Portuguese was killed.

UNITA's wish to grab international attention would have to wait until Christmas day 1966 when troops led by Samuel Chiwale, also trained in China, attacked Teixeira de Sousa (Luau), an important town at the end of the Benguela Railway. This was an important propaganda coup because it

[8] União dos Populações de Angola (Union of the Peoples of Angola).
[9] Bridgland and Savimbi, *A Key to Africa*.
[10] Partido Democrático de Angola (Democratic Party of Angola).
[11] Frente Nacional de Libertação de Angola (National Front for the Liberation of Angola).
[12] Governo Revolucionário de Angola no Exilio (Angola's Revolutionary Government in Exile).
[13] Bridgland and Savimbi, *A Key to Africa*, p. 71.
[14] Ibid.

disrupted for a week the shipment of Zambian and Congolese copper to the Lobito port via the Benguela Railway. However, from a military perspective, the attack could not be considered a success inasmuch as UNITA—again using poorly armed recruits with little guerrilla training—lost half of its 600 fighters against six Portuguese killed, including the town's chief of the secret police.[15] But, strategically, the negative consequences of this attack extended much beyond the casualty count. It led to UNITA being 'outlawed in Zambia'[16] in early 1967. Given its dependence on copper exports through the Benguela Railway as a source of foreign exchange, Zambia could not tolerate UNITA's disruption of this critical commercial link. Zambia's actions against UNITA—perhaps as much as the organization's leadership training in Mao's China—forced UNITA to operate completely inside Angola. Initially, UNITA made a virtue out of this necessity by claiming that, unlike MPLA and FNLA who operated from bases outside the country, it was the only genuine liberation movement. But this bravado hid an untenable situation for UNITA. For the next two years, UNITA's main struggle was not against the Portuguese army—it was for its own survival.

By 1971, the Portuguese colonial army was in a position to eliminate the several hundred UNITA guerrillas that remained active in isolated pockets around Moxico region. However, the Portuguese army spared UNITA because 'from a military point of view it was better to use them against the MPLA.'[17] Minter quotes General Costa Gomes—commander-in-chief of the Portuguese forces in Angola from April 1970 to August 1972 and who later became President of Portugal some months after the 25 April 1974 coup—as saying that 'it was understood that Portuguese and UNITA forces would not fight against each other. UNITA captured food and armaments from the MPLA, while the Portuguese gave them ammunition (not guns), as well as medical and school equipment. The area reserved for UNITA was the Lungue-Bungo river area, between Luso and Bie.'[18] Minter also reproduces documents indicating that Savimbi sought, and the Portuguese authorities seriously considered, his and his group's 'reintegration' into 'the national community.'[19]

---

[15] John Marcum, *The Angolan Revolution*, Vol. II, *Exile Politics and Guerrilla Warfare 1962–1976*, Cambridge: MIT Press, 1987, pp. 191–2.

[16] Bridgland and Savimbi, *A Key to Africa*, p. 75.

[17] William Minter, *Operation Timber: Pages from the Savimbi Dossier*, Trenton: Africa World Press, 1988, p. 18.

[18] Ibid.

[19] Ibid., pp. 83–5.

In other words, Savimbi was ready to cut a political deal with the Portuguese authorities that would result in his return to the colonial society he had sought to liberate the Ovimbundu people from. The 'gentlemen's agreement' between UNITA and the Portuguese colonial army lasted from 1971 until early 1974,[20] just before the military coup in Portugal.

The coup in Portugal marked the beginning of the end of the colonial presence in Angola. But it also marked the beginning of Angola's civil war. This conflict was caused mainly by the liberation movements' inability to agree on a blueprint for post-colonial political power-sharing and economic development. Attempts to reach such an agreement, like the power-sharing formula that constituted the Alvor Accord, failed because they were founded on the premise that the nationalist movements would be willing to work cooperatively. Instead, shortly after it was signed, the Alvor Accord and the transition government it brought into being were rendered irrelevant as MPLA expelled FNLA and UNITA from Luanda and the country descended into civil war. The nationalist leaders had placed personal and group interests—not national aspirations—at the top of their political calculations as MPLA, FNLA, and UNITA engaged in a zero-sum fratricidal struggle for supremacy.

Since neither was sufficiently strong to overcome the other, they all sought external assistance. In the early stages of this internationalized civil war Cuban troops helped MPLA prevail over both UNITA, which was backed by a South African army lacking the political will to fight, and FNLA which was supported by a Zairian army lacking professionalism. Demoralized and humiliated for failing to install their respective allies in power, both the South African and the Zairean armies retreated within months of independence. However, independence and the defeat of the UNITA/SADF[21] and FNLA/Zairian forces in 1976 constituted a short pause in the civil war. The conflict continued with greater intensity, having mutated into a protracted guerrilla war, proving that it was fundamentally a continuation of the unresolved struggles and contradictions within the anti-colonial movement predating independence.

## Adapt or perish

The withdrawal of the invading South African troops from Angola in February 1976 after failing to prevent the post-colonial MPLA takeover left

[20] Ibid., p. 18.
[21] South African Defence Force

UNITA virtually destroyed. But although MPLA had prevailed over invading armies and internal enemies like UNITA, it had been traumatized by the complex and violent birth of the new state. It also recognized that, surrounded by enemies like South Africa and Zaire, it would indefinitely remain on life-support. Thus, from independence, the MPLA regime viewed its long-term security as being intrinsically tied to its ability to foster a friendlier regional environment. This led it to actively support domestic opponents of the regimes in South Africa and Zaire. The new Angolan government provided open and unconditional military and diplomatic support for South Africa's ANC, Namibia's SWAPO and Zaire's FNLC.[22] The South Africa and Zairean regimes responded by supporting their own proxies in Angola. With FNLA out of commission as a military force, UNITA became the proxy of choice.

South Africa's response to the perceived threats emanating from the new Angolan state came in the form of the so-called 'total strategy'. This involved a set of policies aimed at ensuring the survival of the apartheid system through a combination of reform and repression at home and coercive regional intervention aimed at preventing neighbouring states from actively supporting the armed liberation struggle in South Africa and Namibia. Therefore, Angola became one of South Africa's principal targets in the region because of its position as the main SWAPO[23] sanctuary and an important ANC[24] base. Consequently, from the late 1970s through the 1980s, Angola suffered the brunt of the apartheid regime's total strategy. South Africa used two main instruments to threaten Angola's territorial integrity: first, frequent and well-planned military invasions deep into Angolan territory; second, the instrumentalization of UNITA as a proxy in its regional destabilization policies. UNITA in the mid-1970s, faced with a situation peculiarly similar to its predicament a decade earlier, willingly accepted a new proxy role as a means of ensuring its own survival.

Between its withdrawal in 1976 and its final disengagement in 1988, the SADF carried out twelve major military operations in Angola. These actions, carried out under the pretext of responding to increased SWAPO attacks in northern Namibia from bases in southern Angola were also crucial for UNITA's development as a major military force. Although virtually destroyed by MPLA and Cuban troops in 1975–76, UNITA was reorganized into a sig-

---

[22] Front National pour la Libération du Congo (National Front for the Liberation of Congo).

[23] South West Africa People's Organization.

[24] African National Congress.

nificant military force by 1979. UNITA entered the 1980s fully restructured by the South Africans along the lines of a conventional army, with brigades, regular battalions, semi-regular battalions, and 'special forces' or small groups of a few dozen men normally used for sabotage operations. Thus reorganized and revitalized, UNITA took advantage of South Africa's regular incursions to advance behind SADF, occupy 'liberated' territory, and defend it with weapons captured by the South African army. Thus, while SADF threats kept the government occupied, UNITA was able to expand its guerrilla activity throughout most of the country. The regional environment, then, had a major influence on UNITA's development as a post-colonial insurgency. Specifically, South African support enabled UNITA to seriously disrupt food production in rural areas, bring the vital Benguela Railway to a standstill, and to threaten onshore oil production and disrupt diamond exploration.

## Cold War connections

Since the outcome of the Angolan conflict was expected to have significant geostrategic implications for southern Africa, Angola quickly became an important Cold War battleground with the United States and the former Soviet Union attempting to place their respective clients—FNLA and MPLA—in power. But in the mid-1970s the two superpowers had different approaches to intervention around the world. In the aftermath of Vietnam, the United States was averse to engage in major foreign military interventions. Thus, it did not provide effective support to enable FNLA to seize power after the collapse of the colonial regime. The former Soviet Union acted differently. Emboldened by American failure in Vietnam, the Soviet Union's more forceful behaviour on the world stage included an effective intervention in Angola which enabled its client, MPLA, to achieve power by overcoming its domestic rivals, militarily defeating FNLA and seriously weakening UNITA.

The US did not welcome MPLA's victory. Henry Kissinger, US Secretary of State at the time, said that the US would not recognize the MPLA because it had seized power 'through a very substantial inflow of communist arms.'[25] Additional impediments to diplomatic recognition of the new Angolan state included the fact that MPLA maintained itself in power with Soviet and Cuban assistance and had not resolved 'the problem of internal reconciliation

[25] Nina Howland, 'The United States and Angola, 1974–88: A Chronology', *Department of State Bulletin*, February 1989.

among the various factions in Angola.'[26] It took two decades before the US recognized the Angolan government, and this occurred only after American demands—withdrawal of Cuban troops and national reconciliation—were met. To achieve these objectives, the US used UNITA as an important tool to pressure the MPLA government.

Beginning in the early 1980s, through the implementation of the Reagan Doctrine, the US pursued a clear and unambiguous policy to induce changes in the MPLA regime. The Reagan Doctrine was conceived as a robust global strategy to 'roll back' communism in the 'Third World' to complement the policies to 'contain' the former Soviet Union. One of the main components of this doctrine was a US commitment to support anti-communist guerrilla movements around the world, including UNITA in Angola. In 1981, the Reagan Administration formally asked Congress to repeal the 1976 Clark Amendment prohibiting US assistance to the Angolan rebels. The repeal of this amendment in 1984 had an almost immediate impact on the Angolan civil war as UNITA became a major recipient of sophisticated American weaponry, including 'Stinger' anti-aircraft missiles that upset the air supremacy once enjoyed by the MPLA government. Consequently, all major military offensives mounted by the MPLA/Cuban/Soviet forces to dislodge UNITA rebels from their bases in southern Angola ended in failure.

US support for UNITA in the 1980s had more than military significance. At the political level, UNITA shed the international pariah status it had acquired on account of its role as a proxy of South Africa's apartheid regime. No longer isolated diplomatically, UNITA spent the 1980s renewing its relationships throughout the world. By the end of the decade, this rebel organization had a significant diplomatic and/or public relations presence in most West European and African capitals. The global environment, then, also played a significant role in UNITA's development as an insurgency, especially during the 1980s.

Significantly, increased American help to UNITA through the 1980s coincided with the decline of the Soviet Union's support for MPLA. By the end of the decade, the USSR was seeking ways to disengage from its commitments around the world, including Angola, because of mounting domestic problems. Without Soviet assistance, and with the US continuing to support UNITA, the MPLA regime was forced to accept an American framework to end the

---

[26] Facts on File, 'Angola Requests U.S. Relations', Facts on File, *World News Digest*, 28 July 1978, p. 562 F1.

civil war and accommodate UNITA. Thus, on 1 February 1988, Angola 'for the first time affirmed its acceptance of the necessity of the withdrawal of all Cuban troops.'[27] This led to the signing of the New York Accord of 22 December 1988 between Angola, Cuba, and South Africa. The Accord included provisions for implementation of United Nations Security Council Resolution 435 on Namibian independence and for the withdrawal of all Cuban troops from Angola. The New York Accord opened the way for a negotiated settlement of the civil war via the 1991 Bicesse Peace Accords between MPLA and UNITA.

The Bicesse Accords aimed to end the civil war by creating a framework for Angola's transition to elected government. However, they ended only the proxy war stage of the conflict. In November 1992, in the aftermath of a failed electoral process, MPLA and UNITA initiated another round of fighting, this time using mostly domestic resources—oil and diamonds—that they controlled. Ironically, UNITA refused to accept one of the main goals of American policy toward Angola—national reconciliation through elections and power sharing. However, the United States under President Bill Clinton fulfilled its promise by extending diplomatic recognition to Angola's government after the electoral exercise.[28] This effectively ended US backing for UNITA. Without American assistance, UNITA found it difficult to obtain the necessary external support needed to carry out the insurgency. Its diamond resources could only go so far in removing the obstacles arising from external isolation. Consequently, within a decade of its return to war, UNITA had been destroyed as a military force.

## UNITA's strategic miscalculations

UNITA's development as a powerful military force created the conditions for a negotiated settlement of the civil war in 1991 through the Bicesse Peace Accords which, in turn, led to the 1992 elections. But UNITA failed to duplicate its battlefield performances in the political arena and, consequently, lost the elections. Electoral defeat can be attributed primarily to the group's idiosyncrasies. Specifically, Savimbi's paranoid and authoritarian leadership led to UNITA's propensity for self-mutilation. Permanently bleeding at the leader-

[27] Samantha Sparks, 'Angola: U.S. Sees Progress in Talks', *Inter Press Service*, 1 February 1988.

[28] Steven Holmes, 'Washington Recognizes Angola Government', *The New York Times*, 20 May 1993, p. A9.

ship level, the party lacked sufficient flexibility to make fundamental corrections in the conduct of the insurgency. Ultimately, by emphasizing military over political means, UNITA alienated a significant segment of its traditional support base, with negative electoral consequences.

But the internal factors that eventually led to UNITA's decline and Savimbi's death were apparent since the initial stages of the anti-colonial struggle. Savimbi never succeeded in developing his organization into a liberation army. Hence its survival depended mainly on the degree to which it was useful as a tool in the hands of external forces. This inability to transform itself into a liberation army had negative impacts on the internal dynamics of the organization and, more generally, on the way the civil war was fought. UNITA, unlike classical guerrilla insurgents, did not adequately resolve the strategic relationship between political ends and military means. This partly explains why Savimbi apparently did not perceive the fundamental contradictions inherent in his organization's problematic relationships with the Portuguese army and secret police during the liberation struggle and, later, with the South African apartheid regime.

Above all, however, the character of Savimbi's leadership robbed UNITA of the flexibility it needed to face changing political circumstances at both domestic and international levels. By the time of its mauling at the hands of MPLA in 1975–76, UNITA was already in advanced stages of its transformation from a rag-tag rebel group that barely survived the anti-colonial armed struggle into a fanaticized, even if not yet powerful, military organization occasionally masquerading as a political party. Its main functions included enforcing an internal personality cult of the leader while wreaking havoc throughout the country. The first function led to the politics of fear as UNITA robbed most of its members of their basic sense of individual identity. Although initially many people filled UNITA's ranks voluntarily, exit was rarely an option. Given UNITA's military character, deviance was dealt with through severe punishment. Such punishment was particularly severe against those members who were perceived by Savimbi as a potential threat to his leadership. Thus, Savimbi eliminated most of his party's most promising political and military cadres including Jorge Sangumba (foreign secretary), Pedro 'Tito' Chingunji (foreign secretary and deputy secretary general), Wilson dos Santos (international cooperation), Eunice Sapassa (president of UNITA's women's organization), António Vakulukuta (UNITA's top Ovambu leader), Valdemar Chindondo (chief of staff), José António Chendovava (chief of staff), and Mateus Katalaio ('interior minister'), among others.

Bizarrely, Savimbi did not just kill his close assistants; he also had all their families killed, including small children. To instil fear among his followers, Savimbi often meted out punishment in public. These public punishment events ranged from beatings to a variety of the most horrific killing methods: burning at the stake, use of heavy vehicles to crush victims, smashing of the victims' children's skulls against trees, and death by firing squad. An infamous episode of this sort took place at UNITA's former headquarters in Jamba on 7 September 1983. After a group of women and children were accused of witchcraft, they were burnt to death on a giant bonfire under Savimbi's personal supervision. This level of intra-party violence was symptomatic of a seriously dysfunctional organization. But it only represented the tip of a much larger structural problem that contributed to UNITA's electoral defeat and eventual demise as an insurgency.

Beyond the leadership problems and concomitant intra-party violence, in the early 1990s UNITA faced serious structural challenges as it approached a new era of multi-party politics. For much of its post-colonial insurgency, UNITA attempted to cultivate the image of a champion of peace, freedom and multi-party democracy. Thus, it attempted to present itself as the main catalyst for all the political and social transformations that took place in Angola. Ironically, UNITA itself was unprepared for the new realities of multi-party politics. It was very slow in adjusting from war to peace, from a guerrilla group to a political party.

The complexities involved in UNITA's transformation were colossal. As Savimbi made clear in a speech to the Seventh UNITA Congress, on 12 March 1991, 'UNITA was not born as a political party, but as a military force with a political outlook.'[29] Thus, the end of the civil war posed stark choices for UNITA: either find additional justifications and/or rationales for continued fighting or reinvent itself to face a new political reality for which it was unprepared. Specifically, this involved organizing an inclusive political party, developing a coherent electoral strategy, and carrying out an election campaign with a viable alternative programme of government. In other words, UNITA cadres would have to do precisely the opposite of what their leader ordered them to do at the March 1991 Congress—'think politically in order to find the best way of fighting.' The new era of multi-partyism required UNITA to develop winning strategies to fight politically.

[29] Voice of the Resistance of the Black Cockerel (UNITA clandestine radio station), 14 March 1991.

The political fight against the MPLA posed serious problems for UNITA inasmuch as the former clearly had some clear advantages. Savimbi publicly recognized this also at the Seventh Congress when he pointed out that 'MPLA will benefit from certain advantages because it has been a politically inspired and motivated organization, whereas we have always been guided by our political thought but with emphasis on the armed struggle.' Thus UNITA made an attempt to acquire a political outlook by seeking to adapt its structures to the new political conditions.

Some changes were announced at the Seventh Congress held just before the signing of the Bicesse Accords. Thus UNITA kept the Party Congress, which convened every four years, as its supreme organ. It also kept the Central Committee to represent various political, economic, and religious interests. But the Central Committee was relieved of all decision-making powers and assumed a merely consultative role. UNITA's decision-making powers were transferred to the new Political Commission. In effect, the Political Commission thus gained all the powers that were once in the hands of both the Central Committee and Political Bureau. The latter was kept with the sole function of advising the party's president. UNITA's Executive Committee, or 'government-in-waiting', was charged with the responsibility of executing the decisions of the Political Commission.

These political transformations in UNITA's structures, however, did not change its public perception as an extremist military organization. The serious divisions that occurred within the organization soon after the signing of the Bicesse Accords further reinforced this view. Two prominent UNITA figures—Tony da Costa Fernandes, one of UNITA's co-founders, and Miguel N'Zau Puna, UNITA's deputy leader for nearly 24 years—defected on 29 February 1992. Both accused Jonas Savimbi of serious human rights abuses, including the execution of prominent UNITA figures. The defection of Puna and Fernandes represented the first serious crack in UNITA's outward façade of unity. No longer captive, many close associates of Savimbi could now break away from UNITA's rigid society and integrate into the wider Angolan society, even though the latter also showed signs of rot.

In addition to corroborating information about the nature of Savimbi's leadership, Fernandes and Puna ominously publicized UNITA's lack of commitment to the peace process. The defections exposed for the first time the rebel group's intention to block moves toward a genuine democracy in Angola. Fernandes and Puna claimed that UNITA was preparing to use military force to usurp power if it failed to win the elections. Tony Fernandes declared, for example, that Savimbi maintained a secret army in UNITA-controlled areas on the border with Namibia.

Why would UNITA insist on pursuing a military path to power? Throughout the years of insurgency, UNITA did not demonstrate that it was any better equipped to establish a new form of governance than MPLA. As mentioned before, after losing a pre-independence power struggle with MPLA, UNITA returned to the countryside and waged a devastating guerrilla war. By the time the Bicesse agreements were signed, the rebels controlled most of the southeastern portion of Angola. However, for several reasons, political participation in those areas was even more problematic than in government-held zones. Although UNITA portrayed itself as a democratic organization, it developed highly centralized structures at both the political and military levels. Peculiarly, its military structures dominated the organization in the sense that few civilians held leadership positions. For example, all members of UNITA's Politburo and Political Commission had a military rank. The primacy of the military over politics gave UNITA a particularly rigid and non-revolutionary character.

Second, open political competition with MPLA within a multiparty system was not UNITA's preferred option. It was a direct result of the major global and regional changes that took place in the late 1980s and early 1990s. The end of the Cold War and the collapse of the minority regime in South Africa threatened UNITA with irrelevance at the international and regional levels. This would inevitably have negative effects at the domestic level as well. These momentous changes presented UNITA with important challenges. The rebels could no longer count on the generosity of external benefactors to ensure survival, let alone victory. Thus UNITA reluctantly joined an externally driven peace process aimed at ending the civil war. However, it did not completely abandon its long-term goal of capturing state power by force. Instead, the rebels used the peace process as an opportunity to reorganize for a planned new phase of the war. Savimbi believed that the MPLA regime was irremediably debilitated by long years of economic mismanagement, internal squabbles, and civil war. More important, the regime could no longer count on 50,000 Cuban troops that had kept it in power since independence. Moreover, the peace process would enable Savimbi to move his best troops from southeastern and central Angola into the diamond producing regions of Lunda Norte, Lunda Sul, and Malange; thus the loss of American and South African support would be more than offset by the newfound diamond wealth.

UNITA guerrillas initiated their northward movement immediately after the signing of the Bicesse Peace Accords. The process of demobilizing excess government and UNITA soldiers as part of the peace process provided the ideal pretext inasmuch as both government and rebel troops were expected to assemble with their weapons in various predetermined sites around the country. But UNITA did not send its best soldiers to the demobilization centres; these were hidden to fight another day. But, in the end, UNITA's post-electoral gambit failed because it had little popular support, even from the Ovimbundu who had also been alienated by UNITA's indiscriminate violence.

## Aftermath of defeat: criminal insurgency

Angola after the Cold War no longer offered conditions for a successful insurgency. And UNITA could no longer place its insurgency within a larger international ideological context—a critical element for sustaining external backing. At the domestic level, the insurgency had lost much of its support because the rebels abruptly reneged on the very key issues they were purportedly fighting for—democratic elections—to put an end to MPLA's political monopoly. To survive, let alone succeed under such conditions, UNITA's insurgency would have required an even greater Clausewitzian content—the population had to be convinced that a higher political goal existed to justify the suffering involved in the conflict. But UNITA had long abandoned the strategy of creating an intimate and reciprocal relationship between the political and military aspects of insurgency. It did not use its insurgency as a means to achieve clearly discernible political objectives. In other words, war was not regarded as part of a broader contest for political loyalty and legitimacy involving, first and foremost, winning 'the hearts and minds' of the people. In fact, for UNITA, the people came to be regarded as a burden whose displacement by military means was often justified. For example, by removing people from diamond producing areas, rebels could enrich themselves without the political and administrative costs of governance.

After resuming the war, UNITA demonstrated neither the ability nor the inclination to bring new, more effective and inclusive forms of governance to the portions of Angola it controlled. More significantly, it was unable to articulate a coherent set of political objectives for the new phase of the civil war. In fact, the insurgency acquired a more pronounced criminal character. After returning to war, UNITA held fast to its strategy of rendering the country ungovernable to induce an implosion that would finally enable it to achieve power amidst the expected chaos. Thus the rebels increased pressure on infrastructure targets such as water and electricity while continuing to attack small towns and villages throughout the country, resulting in countless civilian casualties and the displacement of 1.3 million people, about ten per cent of the population. UNITA also stepped up terror actions against the population including the use of torture, summary executions, indiscriminate killing of civilians in operational areas, forced displacement, and continuous mine-laying.

Peculiarly, for the first time since the civil war began in 1975, UNITA reversed its longstanding practice of forcing people into its controlled areas. Instead, it pursued a policy of forcibly pushing civilian populations into government-held cities and towns to overwhelm already strained state structures and thus demonstrate governmental incapacity to provide internally displaced persons (IDPs) with the basic means to survive—food, shelter, clothing, drinking water, and medical assistance—besides emphasizing the state's inability to provide basic security to its citizens, because UNITA was able to bombard many areas under government control. UNITA, it appeared, could use military means to bring the government to its knees. However, as discussed below, the combination of popular alienation and the choice to pursue a more conventional military strategy ultimately led to UNITA's demise.

After losing and rejecting the results of the first multi-party national elections of September 1992, UNITA used conventional military tactics to overrun most government positions around the country and seriously threatened the capital, Luanda. It took two years for the Angolan government to beat back UNITA's pressure. In November 1994 Angolan government forces captured Huambo, UNITA's main stronghold, only days before the two sides were due to sign the Lusaka Peace Protocol to end the post-election violence. Ominously, Jonas Savimbi did not personally endorse this agreement. Instead, he retreated to Bailundo and Andulo to set up his group's new headquarters.

Gaining control of these two strongholds then became a top political and military priority for the government. First, its post-electoral programme rested heavily on the ability to fully implement the Lusaka Protocol which provided the government with both a mandate and a timetable to reestablish state authority in all areas still under rebel control. Secondly, UNITA's headquarters were highly symbolic: Bailundo was regarded as the cradle of Ovimbundu nationalism while Andulo was Savimbi's hometown. But these towns were also significant from a military standpoint: they were the main nerve centres for UNITA's then impressive military machine. Andulo, for example, was the main operational centre for supporting UNITA forces fighting on the various fronts. Equally important, those towns' geographic position in the centre of the country was of particular concern for the government inasmuch as, from there, UNITA could continue to spread its political and military activities throughout the country. By retaking Bailundo and Andulo, the government could force UNITA forces to disperse into various unconnected regions, thus making communication, coordination, and control as well as logistical support more difficult for the rebels. In other words, without its central headquarters, UNITA could not retain a conventional military posture which was so threatening to the government. Conversely, from the rebels' point of view, this meant that Bailundo and Andulo had to be defended at all costs.

Initially, guided by the provisions of the Lusaka Protocol, the government embarked on an attempt to regain control over these two areas through negotiations. However, after four years of failed efforts, the government changed course. On the eve of its fourth Congress, the governing MPLA blamed UNITA's 'warmongering wing' for obstructing implementation of the Lusaka Protocol by refusing to demilitarize and thus preventing the government from restoring administration in all areas of Angola. Therefore, it decided to discontinue talks with the rebels while condemning their leader as a 'war criminal'. The government promptly directed the armed forces to retake the two UNITA strongholds. At the time, however, UNITA was strong enough to withstand this offensive. In fact, buoyed by newly acquired war material, the rebels responded by mounting military offensives of their own.

After successfully stopping the March 1999 offensive by the FAA,[30] UNITA escalated its military operations and brought them, as in 1992, closer to the capital city. Thus, on 20 July 1999, UNITA rebels mounted a daring and surprise attack on the town of Catete, just 60 km from Luanda. Catete represented a clear warning to the government that Luanda itself could be the next target.

UNITA's military and political calculations, however, reflected its continuing inability to carefully assess the realities on the ground. This would, again, lead to major operational errors for the rebels. For example, UNITA's pressure on Luanda could not be sustained for any prolonged period. First, the FAA had significant concentrations of military power in the capital. Second, the

---

[30] Forças Armadas de Angola.

civilian population in Luanda was heavily armed as a result of the government's distribution of surplus army rifles to its sympathizers in the aftermath of the electoral fiasco of 1992. More important, while UNITA was putting pressure on Luanda, the FAA were fortifying their positions in the central highlands, in preparation for their long-delayed *cacimbo* (cold season) offensive against Savimbi's headquarters in Andulo and Bailundo.

Operationally, instead of preparing to attack Luanda, UNITA was in a better position to deny government troops the ability to mount the much-anticipated *cacimbo* offensive. This would have necessitated continuing the sieges of Huambo, Kuito, Malanje and Menongue, all government-controlled cities where the FAA would have to build up their forces before attacking UNITA bases in Andulo and Bailundo and rebel positions around the Nharea diamond mines. What led UNITA into such operational blunders?

First, UNITA had lost most of its top military leaders to the government in the context of the demobilization and reintegration processes stipulated by the Bicesse Peace Accords and the Lusaka Protocol. In 1990, on the eve of the failed peace process, UNITA had a sixteen-member top military command.[31] Of these, only generals Sapalalo (Bock), Dembo, and Kamalata (Numa) remained with Savimbi as UNITA entered the critical last phase of the conflict. In other words, after the resumption of the war in the aftermath of the 1992 elections, UNITA forces were led by mostly inexperienced second-tier military officers. Many of those who had commanded the bulk of UNITA troops were, ironically, now commanding the very government troops that would pursue Savimbi to his death.

Second, and not unrelated, UNITA lacked the ability to properly interpret what appeared to be conflicting messages from senior FAA officers and members of the Angolan government regarding their perceptions and interpretations of the rebel military threat. Some FAA officers expressed overt pessimism about the government's ability to defeat UNITA militarily. For example, in June 1999, in a report to the Angolan parliament, the army chief of staff, Lieutenant-General José Ribeiro Neco, admitted that 'UNITA has the upper

---

[31] Jonas Savimbi, Arlindo Chenda Isaac Pena (Ben Ben), Andrade Chassungo Santos, Altino Bango Sapalalo (Bock), Renato Sianguenhe Sakato Campos Mateus, Augusto Domingos Lutoki Liahuka (Wiyo), Peregrino Isidro Wambu Chindondo, Jeronimo George Ngonga Ukuma, Demostenes Amos Chilingutila, Geraldo Sachipengo Nunda, Antonio Sebastiao Dembo, Abilio Jose Augusto Kamalata (Numa), Carlos Tiago Kandanda, Jeremias Kussia Chihundu, Carlos Veiga Morgado, and Daniel Zola Luzolo (Mbongo-Mpassi).

hand and the Angolan army is largely on the defensive.'[32] Even the Angolan president was publicly seeking support from regional allies to deal with UNITA. Regardless of whether or not such signals where intended to confuse the rebels, they all reinforced UNITA's misperceptions of its own military capacity.

UNITA exhibited this exaggerated sense of confidence when it claimed to control 70 per cent of the country in the semi-circular zone adjoining the Democratic Republic of Congo, Zambia and Namibia while 'the regime control[led] only 30 per cent of the territory, mainly the coastal band about 100–175 km wide.'[33] From this delusional position of strength, Savimbi would threaten to enter Luanda. In a letter to the ruling MPLA, he stated that 'this time, UNITA may reach Futungo (the presidential palace) before the Angolan armed forces reach Andulo.'[34] But government forces were not as unprepared as Savimbi expected. In fact, they were openly preparing for a decisive offensive against UNITA. For example, the Deputy Minister of Defense Armado Cruz Neto confirmed that the FAA were 'preparing for a decisive offensive against UNITA' and repeated his government's intention 'to wipe out' the rebels.[35] Other senior FAA officers maintained that the government was 'very close to cancelling UNITA's military advantage, especially in the area of long-range artillery'[36] which had been primarily responsible for UNITA's ability to block previous FAA military offensives aimed at reoccupying Andulo and Bailundo in March 1999.

Self-deceivingly, until the eve of their defeat in Bailundo and Andulo, UNITA demonstrated a total disregard for the conditions on the ground and chose to believe only those reports that presented the insurgents as the stronger force. Thus, the rebels did not appear to fully appreciate the previously mentioned political and military factors driving MPLA's strategy. Consequently, they seemed both surprised by and unprepared for the scale of the FAA's much anticipated offensive that began on 14 September 1999. The government formally announced the capture of Bailundo and Andulo on 20 October.[37] The following day, Angolan television showed pictures of then

---

[32] Suzanne Daley, 'Hunger ravages Angolans in renewed civil war', *The New York Times*, 26 July 1999, p. A1; Chris McGreal, 'Profits fuel Angola's war', *Manchester Guardian Weekly*, 14 July 1999, p. 3.

[33] BBC, 31 August 1999.

[34] Ibid.

[35] Xinhua News Agency, 13 July 1999.

[36] BBC, 21 July 1999.

[37] BBC, 25 October 1999.

FAA chief of staff, General João de Matos, in Andulo. Despite UNITA's deployment of some of its most experienced troops back to Andulo from the siege of Malange for a final stand on the outskirts of the town, the government advance was so powerful that Andulo was evacuated without heavy fighting. In the disorderly evacuation, the rebels abandoned large quantities of war matériel including heavy guns and vehicles. They also abandoned other valuable possessions including their leader's Mercedes limousine. As he moved east into Moxico province toward his last dead-end, Savimbi would not need such luxurious means of transport. He was now moving on foot, heading back into where his journey as UNITA leader had began in 1966, taking his rebel group into one last grand act of self-destruction. The insurgency was crushed within two years of the taking of Bailundo and Andulo.

The loss of Bailundo and Andulo affected the insurgency in several important ways. It was a major political and psychological setback for UNITA. It proved its inability to hold on to two key symbolic bastions. From a military perspective, the loss of the two towns threw the insurgency into disarray because it robbed the rebels of important command, control, and communication systems. Beyond these two factors, however, the demise of UNITA's insurgency can be attributed to Savimbi's fateful strategic decision to de-emphasize guerrilla warfare in favour of more conventional military operations to engage government forces. This decision was inspired by the rebels' control of important diamond revenues that could be used to purchase vast quantities of war materiel. But the rebels seriously misjudged the degree to which control of significant diamond revenues could be translated into military power.

*The role of diamonds.* By the early 1990s, UNITA's resources were mainly drawn from diamonds. From 1992 until 1999, the rebels obtained US$ 400 million to US$ 600 million per year in income from key diamond producing regions they controlled.[38] UNITA's wealth came at a time when the acquisition of weapons to support insurgencies had become considerably less complicated. In the post-Cold War era, diamond smuggling from rebel controlled areas took place within a context of unprecedented worldwide proliferation of light weapons. While during the Cold War the United States and the former Soviet Union often supported their respective clients with weapons, such support—whether to governments or liberation movements—took place

---

[38] Christian Dietrich, 'UNITA's Diamond Mining and Exporting Capacity', in Jakkie Cilliers and Christian Dietrich (eds), *Angola's War Economy: The Role of Oil and Diamonds*, Pretoria: Institute for Security Studies, 2000, p. 275.

mostly through 'official' channels. In the post-Cold War era, however, many states and manufacturers were eager to empty their arsenals and warehouses of weapons that were no longer needed either because of the momentous global political changes of the previous decade or simply because they had been made obsolete by technological innovation. Places like Angola became some of the few areas in the world where civil wars created irresistible markets for arms traders.

The relatively easy availability of both diamonds and weapons created a particularly nightmarish situation in Angola. There, UNITA used its considerable diamond revenues to evolve from a guerrilla group into a quasi-conventional army, with near catastrophic consequences for the government. But the availability of such enormous amounts of money created premature overconfidence within UNITA, leading the rebels into committing major military and political errors. Specifically, control of diamond revenues led to an illusion of military capacity. This illusion, in turn, caused serious strategic and operational miscalculations: UNITA used its newly acquired wealth to transform itself too rapidly from a guerrilla group into a quasi-conventional army. In the end, UNITA's option to use conventional warfare operations—complete with deployment of large infantry units, mechanized units, and heavy artillery—to face government forces proved fatal for the rebels. They were simply not ready to confront Angolan government forces in successive conventional battles. After all, since coming to power in 1975, the government had moulded its own former guerrilla army into a powerful fighting force with the help of Cuba and the Soviet Union. Although UNITA had important advantages—a plentiful supply of seasoned troops and, since the early 1990s, access to important sources of revenue to purchase enough supplies to equip a sizeable conventional army—the rebels grossly underestimated the government's military advantages, particularly in the air but also in artillery and logistics.

At the political level, UNITA's control of important diamond mines also induced the rebels into committing significant blunders, especially after the Bicesse Peace Accords. For example, as argued above, UNITA failed to position itself as the natural political alternative to the governing MPLA. Specifically, UNITA did not offer a clear programme to satisfy national aspirations for change, particularly in terms of good governance and respect for the fundamental rights of the citizen. Instead, its misplaced overconfidence led UNITA to underestimate MPLA's determination to stay in power and the regime's willingness to employ all available means to achieve this objective.

Conversely, UNITA's relations with the population grew increasingly hostile and violent. For the rebels—no longer dependent on the population for food and other necessities because those goods could now be purchased abroad with diamonds and flown into rebel controlled areas—people became both dispensable and disposable. Consequently, from a strategic point of view, control of resources, not people, became the rebels' primary concern. Operationally, this was consistent with a movement away from guerrilla warfare towards more conventional forms of combat to secure control of diamond-rich territory.

UNITA used its substantial diamond revenues to undertake a fundamental military reorganization away from its traditional posture as a guerrilla army into a more conventional disposition, in preparation for delivering a final victorious blow against government forces and finally seizing state power. To this end, the rebels engaged in a major military procurement programme. The Fowler Report[39] prepared in compliance with UNSC Resolution 1237 (1999) presented a detailed account of UNITA's activities in acquiring arms and military equipment. It established, for example, that UNITA used several international arms brokers as well as connections in several African states—especially Burkina Faso and Togo—to facilitate delivery of large quantities of weapons imported from Eastern Europe, including 'mechanized vehicles such as tanks and armored personnel carriers, mines and explosives, a variety of small arms and light weapons, and anti-aircraft weapons, and a variety of artillery pieces.'[40] This evidence corroborated previous reports that, between 1994 and 1998, UNITA had purchased military hardware from Eastern Europe, particularly Ukraine and Bulgaria, including about 50 T-55 and T-62 tanks; a significant number of 155–mm G-5, B-2, D-2 and D-30 guns; medium-and long-range D-130 guns; BMP-1 and BMP-2 combat vehicles; ZU-23s anti-aircraft weapons; and BM-21 Multiple Rocket Launchers.[41] In the end, however, as discussed above, UNITA's attempts to topple the government through conventional means backfired.

In sum, UNITA's own errors ultimately contributed to the Angolan government's victories both in the political arena and on the battlefield. In the end, these errors left the rebels with only one viable option—another return to guerrilla warfare. However, given the rebels' violent track record, the rural populations were particularly loath to aid them, making it impossible the

---

[39] Available at: http://www.un.org/News/dh/latest/angolareport_eng.htm
[40] Ibid., paragraph 48.
[41] BBC, 17 August 1999.

return to the classical Maoist framework. Defeat, in such circumstances, was just a matter of time.

## Conclusion

UNITA, created in the mid-1960s as a liberation movement, achieved great prominence from the 1970s through to the 1990s both within the national politics of Angola and in the international politics of the Cold War. Its protracted political and military struggle to overthrow the newly established Marxist regime in Angola lasted from independence in 1975 until its implosion in 2002 after the killing in combat of its leader.

The fact that this political and military organization—once powerful enough to bring a state to the verge of collapse—imploded within days of the killing of its leader points to the individual and organizational dimensions as the key categories to understand UNITA as a failed insurgency. Although the colonial environment that created the conditions for UNITA's emergence had disappeared, the post-colonial environment was still conducive for an insurgency because it excluded significant numbers of the citizens from participation in politics. In fact, politics became the exclusive arena for those who sympathized with one of the three main political forces in the country: the governing MPLA. UNITA and FNLA members and sympathizers were excluded. This political exclusion had important implications in other key social and economic domains as well, as avenues for achieving status and wealth necessarily passed through MPLA membership. This disenfranchised most citizens. Predictably, many deposited their hopes for changing the situation on a successful insurgency. But peculiar internal dynamics—organizational and individual—prevented UNITA from fulfilling the aspiration of those who had been disenfranchised by the post-colonial system imposed by MPLA.

At the organizational level, UNITA's penchant for self-mutilation in the form of regular purges slowly destroyed its core. The superficial appearance of cohesiveness—derived partly because of the ethno-linguistic homogeneity of the organization—hid incredibly destructive forces: fear, deceit, lies and, perhaps most destructive of all, an oppressive cult of personality. Ultimately, it became apparent that the insurgency was driven more by its leader's megalomaniac designs than by a coherent ideology or vision for the country. Savimbi's authoritarian control over the organization made it highly inflexible and the propensity to kill his brightest lieutenants depleted UNITA of its most capable political and military leaders. In many respects, Savimbi did not make a distinction between himself and the organization; he created the organization, he was the organization.

Although UNITA did not completely disappear after Savimbi's death, today it is a spent force. Politically, it is undergoing a difficult process of transition as it seeks to adapt yet again to a set of conditions it is powerless to influence. Still, many of the internal conditions that sustained its insurgency for almost three decades remain: Angola is still a deeply divided society. Specifically, there is increasing concern about the concentration of power and wealth in the hands of the few—not completely unlike the conditions under settler colonial rule and, afterwards, during MPLA's one-party system. But although the conditions for resurrecting insurgency remain favourable, UNITA is no longer in a position to lead it because it has lost all legitimacy as a violent non-state actor.

# 15

# Violent Non-State Actors in Sudan

## William Reno

Anti-government insurgents provide the classic picture of violent non-state actors in Africa. Anti-colonial and anti-apartheid insurgencies up through the 1980s and insurgencies in Uganda, Ethiopia and Rwanda in the 1980s and 1990s fought to replace existing regimes with better organized and more efficient alternatives. Their struggles to control the state envisioned installing stronger and more effective administrations and promised political programmes to mobilize people against a central government that was too distant, too corrupt or too illegitimate to command popular support. Most of these insurgents went to considerable effort to implement their visions of the societies of the future and shield their supporters in their liberated zones from the wrath of incumbent regimes.

Sudan's violent non-state actors present a different picture, representing an extreme version of what has become an increasingly common pattern of conflict in Africa. In contrast to other insurgencies of the past and present, violent non-state actors in contemporary Sudan include more than fifty small, diverse and autonomous groups of local community activists, ambitious national politicians, tribal and clan leaders, and criminal gangs. These groups are atomized into loose, decentralized networks and resist attempts in their own ranks and among outsiders to consolidate them into a smaller number of organizations. They share information and resources and coordinate their actions to varying degrees. In spite of these connections, these groups generally fail to synchronize their actions for long. Within their own organizations, some

319

encounter great difficulties in sustaining a core ideology or a comprehensive political programme. Others put little effort into this task. In the areas where they operate they are not very effective at protecting local people, even when they declare that they are defenders of an ethnic or clan group. Their main goal often is simply to secure their continued existence and the changing personal, clan or tribal interests and ambitions of their leaders.

This chapter explains why such an intense fragmentation of violent non-state actors occurs in Sudan's contemporary conflict. The next section explains why Sudan hosts so many violent non-state actors. The political strategies of state officials are identified as the primary cause of this development. The analysis of the current situation in Darfur that follows illustrates how fragmentation occurs. The consideration of earlier conflict in Southern Sudan that follows provides a contrasting experience of insurgent organization and behaviour in similar broad circumstances to shed further light on the process of fragmentation. The conclusions drawn in this analysis emphasize the consequences for state politics of this fragmentation of violent non-state actors for states and the impact of changes in international responses to the violence and political instability that these strategies create.

## The context of fragmentation

It is easy to say that the fragmentation and disorganization of Sudan's violent non-state actors reflect local social structures. Clans and tribes, sectarian differences, occupational patterns, and local struggles over resources do shape the organization and behaviour of these groups. For example, one might observe that factional splits and struggles parallel divisions among clans and tribes of Darfur and in Southern Sudan, and that these are hostage to local struggles for resources, and are prone to spark the ambitions of local strongmen. But even though examples of fragmentation on personal and social grounds were hardly absent from classic insurgencies, Sudan's situation presents a stark contrast to the Eritrean People's Liberation Front's integration of women into the front ranks of fighters, or the capacity of Uganda's National Resistance Army to bring together southern Uganda's ethnic groups to overthrow a dictatorial regime.

The fragmentation of violent non-state actors is not inevitable, however, even in societies that are more intensely segmented and—unlike Eritrea or southern Uganda—have more limited historical experiences with forming centralized states. After all, Somali factional leaders were able to motivate fighters and others in Mogadishu to join forces to battle and drive off American soldiers in 1993. Something close to a broad-based coalition in Sudan appeared in the 1980s in Southern Sudan under the banner of the Sudan People's Liberation Army (SPLA). Even when the SPLA's organization fragmented in the 1990s, many who had become rivals later rejoined the group as it succeeded in becoming a broader-based political coalition.

A critical factor explaining the divergence of Sudan's violent non-state actors from classic experience lies in these groups' relations with state power. The old pattern was that insurgents organized in social and political spaces separate from and in opposition to the state. Sudan's contemporary violent non-state actors, however, are integral to the exercise of state power. Politicians in the capital use violent non-state actors as proxies in struggles among the factions at the centre of power. These politicians also use violent non-state actors to exercise control over people and territory in distant parts of the country. In the late 1980s, an observer noted that in Sudan 'tribal militias, non-existent in the Madhist state of the 1880s, now thrive with support (direct and indirect) from the government'.[1]

This strategy reflects the administrative weakness of successive governments in Sudan. These areas cannot be controlled directly through strong security services or extensive local administrative apparatuses. The latter are beyond the financial means of the government and are controversial among local people who resent the heavy hand of capital-based politicians imposing a vision of national identity on local communities. The former—control through security services—presents dangers to incumbent politicians. Since independence in 1956, Sudan's rulers have faced numerous serious threats to their hold on power. A coup in 1969, coup attempts in 1970 and 1971, a coup in 1985, another in 1989, a state of emergency in 1999 and a coup attempt in 2003 demonstrate the need for strong security forces to protect regimes, but also the danger that these same forces will be used against those who they are supposed to protect.

The alternative is to use violent non-state actors as proxies to assert domestic political control. This strategy takes account of the administrative weakness of the state and projects power through flexible and politically contingent alliances with violent non-state actors. These shifting alliances exploit the segmentation of local societies that ideologically minded insurgents try to

---

[1] M.A. Mohamed Salih, "'New Wine in Old Bottles': Tribal Militias and the Sudanese State', *Review of African Political Economy*, Vol. 45/46, 1989, p. 169

overcome. They bring localized lineage disputes directly into wider politics. Individuals or groups that are marginalized in local politics or who share some other grievance can look to the capital for resources and political support, at least until they become too effective or popular in the eyes of their backers.

This shifting support and the rotation of appointments of co-opted local leaders prevent the rise of strong local elite groups that might have the resources or authority to lead a broad-based rebellion. To the extent that control over land and other resources become entangled in these externally manipulated local struggles, neither local custom nor state regulation offers reliable protection of property rights. The uncertainty that this local turmoil creates inhibits the emergence of a strong local commercial class that would command the resources to build its own political base beyond lineage and tribe. Thus most conflicts involving violent non-state actors having this sort of relationship with state elites can be said to involve struggles over land and other assets. Control over land, local office and commercial opportunities are potential points of contention in most societies, and are pivots on which state officials can use their positions to exploit divisions among opponents. Classic insurgents take great care to settle these issues and harness them to organize and unify communities to create a sort of state in waiting in liberated zones and eventually to overthrow an incumbent regime.

This close connection between state power and violent non-state actors beyond the weak administrative realm appears in regional politics. Governments in many of Sudan's neighbours—Libya, Chad, Uganda, Ethiopia and Eritrea—have cultivated alliances with violent non-state actors in Sudan. Sometimes they do this to destabilize Sudan's government and assert their own interests. At other times, they are anxious to prevent the organization of insurgents against their own power using Sudan as a refuge. Like Sudan's rulers, they are keen to avoid any signs that these groups are developing support among local people to the extent that they can consolidate control to pursue their own more autonomous political agendas without regard for the interests of their patrons.

Even governments and international organizations that do not intend to influence groups as proxies can unintentionally contribute to the incentives for violent non-state actors to split into more factions. The prospect of joining a coalition government, or just simply of having one's community's demands inserted into high level talks, may entice subordinate commanders to break with their superiors and claim to be leaders of a new faction. Such incentives can contribute to a state policy to divide rebel factions. Negotiations that welcome all armed factions can thus serve state interests and advance state agendas in wartime. These venues foster the ambitions of commanders in negotiation delegations and show those left behind on the ground in the conflict zone that creating one's own faction earns one a place at the bargaining table.

The irony of contemporary state power in Sudan is that it is both quite weak and quite strong. It is weak in the administrative sense that measures the provision of services to citizens, or even basic public goods such as security beyond a core area around the capital and major cities. At the same time it is strong in terms of exercising influence over the course of multiple rebellions. None among the many violent non-state actors in Sudan is likely to march to the capital and install itself or some alliance of groups as the new government of Sudan (unless it has help from a faction of insiders within the government). To the extent that they represent a threat to state power, danger lies in the possibility that some faction in the capital will ally itself with a coalition of violent non-state actors as part of its political strategy. But Sudan's government, or at least those who hold the bulk of power in it, have proved adept at preventing this. Thus the intense fragmentation of violent non-state actors has been an integral element of a durable system of authority in Sudan's contentious political environment. The irony is that efforts to build a stronger state in Sudan (as conventionally understood in the bureaucratic sense) might risk undermining this strategy and leave opposition groups in better positions to form stronger and more unified armed challenges to the state.

The development of this politics of violent non-state actors points to similar strategies in other countries. Nigeria's government has selectively patronized local armed groups to prevent the emergence of a broad-based alternative. Lineage and local factional politics also plays a large role in the shifting alliances and fragmentation of these groups. Chad's government attempts to use similar techniques, though with varied results. Some violent non-state actors there have managed to fight their way to the capital and seize state power. Chad's current president, Idriss Déby, seized power in 1990 at the head of the Mouvement Patriotique du Salut, a success that reflects more the intense factional nature of Chad's state politics than the popular appeal or organizational acumen of Déby's group. In any event, this state/violent non-state actor relationship shows the formation of a distinct kind of political authority in Africa. This authority rules more through formal administration in the capital and in areas that are closely integrated into the capital's economic and social networks, while areas on the political or geographic margins of capital-based power are ruled through proxies, more for the purpose of manipulating the formation of local political organizations than for the purpose of bringing state services or protection to local people.

This evolution of state relations with violent non-state actors in Sudan has significant implications for the study of insurgencies. The proposition that when the strong fight the weak they become weak finds wide acceptance.[2] The Americans' difficulties in Iraq and the general dearth of cases in which strong states have succeeded in suppressing insurgencies would suggest that efforts to build formal state capacity in Sudan to counter the threats of violent non-state actors would be futile, at least for a government that is resolute about resisting the demands of opposition groups. Sudan's rulers probably know this. Their alternative strategy shapes and makes use of the social contexts in which these groups emerge, to accomplish political and military goals at a remarkably low cost to the government. This success is not compatible with most understandings of development; nor does it bring basic security to local people. But it does sustain a state and its regime.

Darfur's current conflict provides a good illustration of how this political strategy shapes the organization and behaviour of violent non-state actors there. The next section examines this situation, and the section that follows shows how the same strategy shapes conflict in other parts of Sudan as well.

## Darfur's multiple insurgencies

Early international responses to the conflict in Darfur incorporated assumptions that this was a civil war that pitted insurgents against the Government of Sudan. It was as if there were two sides, with relatively few violent non-state actors who were not affiliated with one side or another: an assumption that became less tenable as the conflict unfolded. An international commission of inquiry in 2004 identified *janjaweed*, or local militias affiliated with Sudan's government to varying degrees, as responsible for considerable violence. The report identified two major rebel groups, the Sudan Liberation Army (SLA) and its political wing, the Sudan Liberation Movement (SLM), and the Justice and Equality Movement (JEM). There was only brief mention that some factions were emerging out of the much smaller JEM.[3] Caught between these

---

[2] Martin van Creveld, *Changing Face of War: Lessons of Combat, from the Marne to Iraq*, Novato, CA: Presidio Press, 2007.

[3] International Commission of Inquiry on Darfur, Report of the International Commis-

two sides were the Darfur civilians. Estimates of casualties during the period of most intense fighting in 2003 and 2004 varied. One estimate claimed that this violence caused 134,000 deaths, of which 35,000 were directly related to violent conflict, while others claimed that nearly 400,000 had died, 140,000 of those through direct violence.[4] In 2007, there were 2.2 million displaced people in Darfur, 242,000 refugees in neighbouring Chad and the Central African Republic, with another 420,000 displaced in those two countries as a consequence of related conflicts.[5]

By the time that the African Union (AU)-sponsored negotiations for the Darfur Peace Agreement ended in Abuja, capital of Nigeria in May 2006, the SLA had split into two main factions. The faction led by Minni Arkou Minawi (SLA/MM) signed, while the SLA faction of the SLA's original chairman, Abdel Wahid Mohamed Nur (SLA/AW), and the JEM refused to sign. By now, the JEM under the leadership of Khalil Ibrahim had suffered its own split in its military arm which left in 2004 to form the National Movement for Reform and Development (NMRD). This faction and another breakaway from JEM in April 2005, under the leadership of Mohamed Saleh Harba, did not attend the Abuja meeting.[6]

The allure of internationally mediated negotiations, offering the prize of a position in a power sharing arrangement for those who can claim leadership in a rebel faction, has long provided incentives for enterprising commanders to form new factions.[7] Moreover, these incentives can accentuate more mundane motivations such as personal grievances and personal conflicts. Several rounds of Abuja negotiations, stretching over at least two years, saw such tensions within the SLA. Moreover, the necessity for leaders to be away from the field to negotiate and to seek assistance from foreign backers—in the SLA's

---

sion of Inquiry on Darfur to the United Nations Secretary-General, Geneva, 25 Jan. 2005, on *janjaweed*, pp. 33–5; on rebel groups, pp. 39–40.

[4] The lower estimate is Debarati Guha-Sapir, Olivier Degomme and Mark Phelan, 'Mortality Estimates from Multiple Survey Data', Brussels: University of Louvain School of Public Health, 26 May 2005, p. 6; higher estimates from Coalition for International Justice, 'New Analysis Claims Darfur Deaths Near 400,000', cited at http://www.reliefweb.int/rw/rwb.nsf/db900sid/VBOL-6CRJK3? OpenDocument, accessed 9 Dec. 2007.

[5] United Nations Security Council, *Report of the Secretary-General on the Protection of Civilians in Armed Conflict*, New York, 28 Oct. 2007, p. 2.

[6] International Crisis Group Africa Briefing No. 39, *Darfur's Fragile Peace Agreement*, Brussels, 20 June 2006, p. 2.

[7] Andreas Mehler and Denis Tull, "The Hidden Costs of Power-sharing: Reproducing Insurgent Violence in Africa", *African Affairs*, 104: 416, 2005, pp. 375–98.

case, from the Sudan People's Liberation Movement (SPLM) and the government of Eritrea—fosters contention with battlefield commanders.[8] Ambitious subordinates who face day-to-day tasks of disciplining fighters and battling the enemy often build their own bases of support. They may conclude that this gives them the right to claim their own seats at the negotiating table. Ceasefire negotiations in Chad's capital N'djamena in March and April 2004 provided an additional venue for these ambitions, as did earlier talks in Abuja and Addis Ababa. It seemed, from the point of view of one commander from Southern Sudan, as though foreign negotiators intended to divide insurgent groups. Speaking of the haste of negotiations, the rebel commander wondered 'why the UN staff tries to prevent our unity and appears very keen to bring us divided to the table of talks'.[9]

Factional splits had worsened by October 2007 when Libya's government opened another round of negotiations in the coastal town of Sirte. Those who expected to appear included JEM-Collective Leadership under the direction of Bahar Idriss Abu Garda, former Vice Chairman of Khalil Ibrahim's JEM. The Revolutionary Democratic Forces Front (RDFF), an Arab-based anti-government group based in Darfur that was organized in early 2006, and the United Revolutionary Force Front (URFF), another 'Arab' anti-government group, accepted the invitation. Acceptances also came from JEM-Azraq, led by Idriss Ibrahim Azraq after breaking away from Khalil Ibrahim's JEM in 2007, the NMRD (noted above), and the Sudan Liberation Movement-G19 and the Sudan Federal Democratic Alliance (SFDA). Those not attending included Khalil Ibrahim's original JEM, the SLA/AW, the SLA/M, which was now the SLA-M/Unity in a loose alliance with fighters on the ground, and the faction of Ahmed Abdel Shafi.[10]

This situation of multiple sponsors conducting negotiations aimed at including as many of the violent non-state actors as possible contrasts with earlier practice in Africa. During the 1960s and 1970s, for example, the main anti-colonial insurgencies in the Portuguese colonies of Mozambique and Guinea-Bissau benefited from exclusive support from a neighbouring coun-

---

[8] International Crisis Group Africa Briefing No. 32, *Unifying Darfur's Rebels: A Prerequisite for Peace*, Brussels, 6 Oct. 2005, pp. 3–4.

[9] 'Darfur rebels slam UN refusal to fly them from Juba to Darfur', *Sudan Tribune*, 23 Oct. 2007, accessed at http://www.sudantribune.com/spip.php?page=imprimable&id_article=24379, 9 Dec. 2007.

[10] 'Who is attending Darfur talks, who is not', Sudan Tribune, 27 Oct. 2007, http://www.sudantribune.com/spip.php?article24453, accessed 12 Dec. 2007.

try's government which channelled international resources to those 'official' insurgencies that enjoyed considerable international legitimacy. In the case of the Southwest People's Liberation Organization (SWAPO) in Namibia, the insurgency even obtained observer status at the UN. As part of the price for this recognition, those movements had to prove that they were seriously interested in and prepared to administer territory and had to suppress factional tendencies within their own ranks. In most cases, the government in the 'home' country would also use their security services to drive out an insurgent movement's rivals and to alert its leadership to internal splits.

While this change in the international response to insurgencies may play a role in factional splits, the Government of Sudan emerges as a more important contributor to this behaviour. The ruling National Congress Party (NCP) encourages splits in violent non-state actor groups to prevent the formation of a broad-based political opposition. This is a priority in response to the Comprehensive Peace Agreement (CPA) provisions for national elections following a settlement with the SPLA insurgents in Sudan's South.[11]

One threat to the NCP government has lain in the possibility that Darfur rebels, some of whom were in contact with the SPLA and civilian opposition parties, would join in an opposition coalition to contest elections for which the CPA provided. Another has lain in the UN Security Council's decision in August 2006 to expand the mandate of the United Nations Mission in Sudan (UNMIS), which was overseeing the CPA's implementation, to include Darfur.[12] Authorized by Security Council Resolution 1769 of 31 July 2007, this force, called the Joint African Union/United Nations Hybrid Operation in Darfur (UMAMID), was authorized to include up to 19,500 soldiers and 11,500 other personnel.[13]

Another threat to the NCP government now lies in the prospect of prosecution of Sudan government officials for human rights violations. The UN's commission of inquiry (footnote 2) identified NCP officials for possible

---

[11] Protocol between the Government of Sudan (GoS) and the Sudan People's Liberation Movement (SPLM) on Power Sharing, Naivasha, Kenya, 26 May 2004, accessed at http://splmtoday.com/index.php?option=com_docman&task=cat_view&gid=15&Itemid=29, 9 Dec. 2007.

[12] United Nations Security Council, 'Security Council Expands Mandate of UN Mission in Sudan to include Darfur', 31 August 2006, http://www.un.org/News/Press/docs/2006/sc8821.doc.htm, accessed 9 Dec. 2007.

[13] United Nations Department of Peacekeeping Operations, UNAMID Deployment, Background Fact Sheet, http://www.un.org/Depts/dpko/missions/unamid/UNAMID_Deployment.pdf, accessed 9 Dec. 2009.

prosecution. In March 2005, Security Council Resolution 1593 referred the Darfur situation to the International Criminal Court (ICC).[14] On 2 May 2007, the ICC issued arrest warrants against Sudan's Minister of State for Humanitarian Affairs and against a *janjaweed* commander charged with committing crimes against humanity and war crimes, the charges being focused on the period of intense fighting in 2003–4.[15] ICC officials even went so far as to issue a warrant for the arrest of President Bashir in March 2009, to face charges of crimes against humanity and war crimes.

Thus Sudan's NCP government faced challenges to its continued hold on power and threats against specific officials both from violent non-state actors inside Sudan and from the international response to violence in Darfur. These challenges pose a dilemma for the NCP government, given its inability to directly control all of the country's territory and its lack of reliable international patrons. In this context, instigating as many splits as possible among violent non-state actor groups is a rational response, even though it promotes violence. This strategy prevents the formation of a strong domestic political opposition and complicates efforts of foreigners to intervene in Darfur's conflict. It also exploits the intended and unintended propensity of some types of international mediation to unintentionally promote the further fragmentation of violent non-state actors.

## Dividing and disorganizing

This strategy to fend off internal and international challenges exploits the fact that most insurgencies include commanders who join the fight to address community grievances or claims over land, or to pursue personal ambitions. Struggles between pastoralists and farmers over the use of land in Darfur predate the current conflict and contribute to divisions between communities. The lack of effective state provision of security in the region before and during the conflict reinforces communal divides among the population, and enhances the chance that local commanders will come from a context of grievances and claims that are very specific to a particular community.

[14] United Nations Security Council, Resolution 1593 (2005), http://daccessdds.un.org/doc/UNDOC/GEN/N05/292/73/PDF/N0529273.pdf?OpenElement, accessed 9 Dec. 2007.

[15] International Criminal Court, 'Warrants of Arrest for the Minister of State for Humanitarian Affairs of Sudan, and a Leader of the Militia/Janjaweed', 2 May 2007, http://www.icc-cpi.int/press/pressreleases/241.html, accessed 9 Dec. 2007.

The Sudan government's decision in 1994 to restore a system of local administration that relied upon customary authorities, the old model inherited from British colonial rule, gave further impetus to the segmentation of local pastoral and farming communities.[16] Officials in Khartoum used this administrative change to award chieftaincies on the basis of political support for the regime. Once installed in office, state-recognized chiefs could use their power both as leaders of local ethnic and clan communities and as heads of local administration, to allocate land and distribute guns, and to organize local PDF (Popular Defence Forces) militias. Often this distribution favoured the chief's own tribe or clan. This change gave state officials a powerful tool to shape local conflicts, since key community members had strong incentives to side with the state in order to protect or bolster their own positions.[17]

Thus local commanders and fighters in any of the main insurgent groups had to contend with local notables who might conclude that their ambitions and their community needs would be better served through an alliance with the government, which had the effect of sweeping up multitudes of divisive local issues into the wider conflict. This was true even where local authorities feared that they were marginal to the concerns of the government and had not received their fair share of government resources. At the very least, they had reason to be concerned that state officials might favour their immediate rivals in struggles over access to land or control over local militias.

This zero sum context of tribe and clan rivalry creates a situation that is fairly easily exploited from Khartoum. When, for example, the political struggles for resources and security within the region are pursued within the framework of clan and tribal structures, it is not too difficult to identify conflicts at different levels of a political and social hierarchy (see figure overleaf). This is a flexible system of control, as it allows the government to seek out alliances with sub-groups within rebel coalitions so as to undermine the cohesion of the remaining groups. Thus groups that were allies and had set aside differences on a contentious local issue would have that agreement upset by the other group's shift to the government side. This also illustrates the extent to which the Darfur conflict does not necessarily pit one ethnic group against another—'Arab' versus 'African', for example—as tensions between subgroups

[16] Christian Delmet, 'The Native Administration System in Eastern Sudan: From its Liquidation to its Revival', in Catherine Miller, François Ireton and Isabelle Dalmau (eds), *Land, Ethnicity and Political Legitimacy in Eastern Sudan*, Cairo, 2005, pp. 145–71.

[17] Alex de Waal, 'Who Are the Darfurians? Arab and African Identities, Violence and External Engagement', *African Affairs*, 104:415, 2005, p. 195.

within the larger collective become subsumed to this government strategy.[18] As international investigators found in 2004: 'The various tribes that have been the object of attacks and killings... do not appear to make up ethnic groups distinct from the ethnic group to which persons or militias that attack them belong.'[19]

Moreover, the incorporation of local customary authorities into government administration injects a multitude of controversies over lineage into the wider political arena. Especially where positions are hereditary, there is usually a family that failed to get its member appointed in the last succession. Customary authorities who are responsible for allocating land use rights also can be dragged into this wider political arena if the Khartoum government periodically shifts local administrative boundaries and switches its support for different groups' claims. Matters that previously would have been local community affairs or part of a region's affairs become much more contentious.

Figure 15.1

A

B  C

D  E  F  G

H  I  J  K  L  M  N  O

Drawing from this figure above, if the government wants to prevent the consolidation of local insurgencies, it first recognizes that H and I will join forces and act as part of D if confronted by E. B and E will act as a group if B was confronted by C. This dynamic shows how a frontal assault against Darfur by Sudan's fairly weak and politically unreliable military would produce a much stronger, more widely based and more effective insurgent response. Instead, calculating how H and I might come into conflict with each other so that they do not act as D, and so forth, would provide a sound basis for the government's counterinsurgency strategy—if one discounts concerns about human rights violations that accompany policies geared toward instigating local conflicts. This is also effective in a context where the government of Sudan abjures efforts to create an effective administration to rule these communities directly or to integrate them into the political life of the country, except on its own terms.

[18] For example, Jeffrey Gettleman, 'Chaos in Darfur on rise as Arabs fight with Arabs', New York Times, 3 Sept. 2007, A1 + A7.
[19] International Commission of Inquiry on Darfur, Report, p. 129.

The government's association with *janjaweed* militias fits within this logic. As part of a 'counterinsurgency on the cheap', those militias 'gave the government the cover of 'age-old tribal conflict'" wrote two noted scholars of Darfur.[20] A UN Panel of Experts charged with investigating the conduct of government and violent non-state actors in the conflict in Darfur concluded that it had 'found evidence of continued support by the Government of the Sudan for armed militia groups operating in Darfur'.[21] Sudan's government already had an organizational structure in its PDFs to recruit fighters from local communities for integration into government-organized campaigns.

One example of how this mobilization of local conflicts to forestall regional cooperation among VNSAs appeared among Abbala camel herders who were anxious about their tenuous land use rights to graze their herds in competition with cattle herders. This made them susceptible to the NCP's call to arms. *Abbala* Rizeigat, already more heavily armed by the NCP, were able to inflict serious damage on the Targam, even though the Targam in 2003 had participated in an NCP counterinsurgency strategy to force Fur people out and make their own claim to territory.[22] Community leaders who become allies of the government not only benefit from limits to the harm done to them by local militias; they also have support from PDFs and other official armed agencies such as the Nomadic Transhumance Route Police, Border Guards, and Central Contingency Forces.

Localized conflicts and commanders' ambitions drew some of the insurgent forces to the NCP government's side. Idriss Ibrahim Azraq's JEM faction, for example, became the Darfur Independence Front (DIF). The DIF declared that it fought for self-determination for Darfur and to dismantle Sudan 'for the benefit of all its peoples' in alliance with yet more groups, including the Revolutionary Movements and the Revolutionary Organization of the People of Darfur in the Sudan Armed Forces.[23] This simultaneous split and consolidation with its proclamations of hostility towards Sudan's government

[20] Julie Flint and Alex de Waal, *Darfur: A Short History of a Long War*, London: Zed Books, 2005, p. 57.
[21] United Nations Security Council, *Report of the Panel of Experts Established Pursuant to Resolution 1591 (2005) Concerning the Sudan Prepared in Accordance with Paragraph 2 of Resolution 1713 (2006)*, New York, 3 Oct. 2007, p. 56.
[22] International Crisis Group, *Darfur's New Security Reality*, Brussels, 26 Nov. 2007, p. 3.
[23] 'New rebel group says struggling for Darfur independence', *Sudan Tribune*, 22 Sept. 2007, accessed at http://www.sudantribune.com/spip.php?page=imprimable&id_article=23877, 9 Dec. 2007.

occurred 'amid suspicion that the NCP had bought him'.[24] Splits and repositioning of this nature occurred in the SLA factions as well. The SLA-Front for Liberation and Rebirth became SLA-Free Will, although 'aid agency sources say that SLA-Free Will is the creation of the Government of Sudan delegation in Abuja, whose goal is to split rebels along tribal lines'.[25] Higher profile shifts to the government side further exacerbated local tensions in Darfur. Minni Arcua Minnawi, the only SLA faction signer of the DPA (Darfur Peace Agreement), won an appointment as Senior Assistant to Sudan's President Omar al-Bashir. This association helped to improve the NCP government's international image, at least to the extent that it could say it was cooperating with a major signatory of the DPA. The government could at least appear to uphold the DPA and portray those holding out as enemies of peace, while heightening tensions within rival factions that complained of further marginalization to produce even more splits among those who wanted to oppose the agreement.

Such divides aggravate communal splits within these violent non-state actors. Conflicts lower down the hierarchy of leadership helped to split the SLA into what appeared to be a Zaghawa versus Fur divide, with Zaghawa clans that were divided amongst themselves. All of this contributed to more fighting on the ground between rebel factions in place of a rebel coalition poised against the NCP government.

## Cross-border politics of fragmentation in Darfur

The NCP government in Khartoum is hardly the only state actor interested in preventing the formation of violent non-state actor coalitions. The government of Chad recognizes the danger that cohesive rebel organizations can pose. Chad's President Idriss Déby himself came to power in 1990 with help from fellow Zaghawas in Darfur as the head of the Mouvement Patriotique du Salut, after taking refuge in Sudan. Déby then favoured Zaghawa recruits in his security services, which in turn earned the antagonism of other ethnic groups and even disfavoured clans within the Zaghawa. It also meant that when the Zaghawa kinsmen of the Chadian Zaghawa soldiers faced attack inside Darfur from government backed militias, Zaghawas from the Chad army started passing weapons across the border—not necessarily as official

[24] International Crisis Group, *Darfur's New Security Reality*, p. 14.
[25] Victor Tanner and Jérôme Tubiana, *Divided They Fall: The Fragmentation of Darfur's Rebel Groups*, Geneva: Small Arms Survey, 2005, p. 46.

policy—and some even fought alongside their Darfur kinsmen against Khartoum's forces.[26]

The NCP government in turn protected anti-Déby rebels in Darfur. These included the Rassemblement des Forces Démocratiques (RAFD), under the leadership of Déby's former associates among Zaghawa kinsmen, and the Rassemblement pour la Démocratie et les Libertés (RDL), led by Mahamet Nour Abdelkerim, Déby's former comrade-in-arms from the 1990 coup. Nour switched to Déby's side briefly in 2003, but then switched back to Khartoum's side. In return for his pro-Khartoum stance, Nour, son of the Tama Sultan, got assistance from *janjaweed* forces to help his small Tama ethnic group assert its claims against the Zaghawa. This also led to the recruitment of Tama fighters into the Sudanese pro-government militias.[27] Added to this crowd were members of Déby's security forces who crossed the border into Darfur to form the Socle pour le Changement, l'Unité et la Démocratie (SCUD) headed by another opponent from among the Zaghawa. Joining them was the Groupe du 8 Décembre, organized among a clan close to the former Chad president who had been overthrown by Déby.[28]

These groups tried to unite in a Front Uni pour le Changement et la Démocratie (FUCD) under Nour's leadership but failed owing to tensions between different clans. A successful alliance would not be beneficial to its Khartoum hosts, since a successful Zaghawa-based insurgency against the Chad president would present the possibility of later support for ethnic kinsmen among the anti-government VNSAs in Darfur. In any event, FUCD fighters seriously threatened Déby in April 2006 when they battled their way into N'djamena and were only repulsed with French help that included an airlift of 'supposedly Chadian troops who really belonged to JEM'.[29] In any event, the attack and continued rebel activities destabilize Déby's regime, which is a desirable situation from the point of view of the NCP government's interest in denying a rear base to rebels while preventing the formation of a consolidated political group that later might favour Darfur kinsmen over their patrons in Khartoum.

As in Sudan, negotiations led to even more fragmentation of the violent non-state armed groups on Chad's Darfur border, with the October 2007 meeting in Sirte in Libya bringing together what had now become the Union

---

[26] Victor Tanner and Jérôme Tubiana, *Divided They Fall*, p. 19.

[27] Simon Massey and Roy May, 'Commentary: The Crisis in Chad', *African Affairs*, 105:420, 2006, pp. 443–4.

[28] 'On the Frontline', *Africa Confidential*, Vol. 47, No. 7, 31 March 2006, p. 2.

[29] 'Déby Hangs On', *Africa Confidential*, Vol. 47, No. 9, 28 April 2006, p. 5.

des Forces pour le Développement et la Démocratie (UFDD), the Rassemble-ment des Forces pour le Changement (RFC), the Concorde Nationale Tcha-dienne (CNT) and the Union des Forces pour le Développement et la Démocratie Fondamentale (UFDD-F).[30] This fracturing of the Chadian VNSAs paralleled the fragmentation of groups focused on Darfur itself. For example, as the anti-Déby groups were splitting, the SLA-Minni faction spawned the Group for Development and Grievances and the Mother of All SLAs and many other groups, mostly organized around the ambitions of a prominent personality and focused on a specific community grievance.[31]

The intense division among the Darfur VNSAs had a precedent in the his-tory of insurgency in Southern Sudan. There more variation was seen in the degrees of fragmentation, in comparison to the short trajectory towards frag-mentation in the context of conflict in Darfur. Closer attention to Southern Sudan's VNSAs, the subject of the next section, highlights the elements of state strategies and the influences of regional politics on the cohesion of vio-lent non-state actors.

## The Southern Sudanese precedent

The organization of VNSAs in Darfur occurs in a broader national context. Scholars of the conflict in Southern Sudan observe that 'the use of armed militias, or 'friendlies', to harass the civilian population during pacification patrols or raids had its precedents not only in the first civil war [1955–1972], but in the Condominium period and even in the nineteenth century.'[32] This policy included instigating factional splits through enticing commanders to switch sides. Paulino Matiep's faction of Anyanya II, for example, fought against the Khartoum forces in the 1980s, then changed sides and protected oil production facilities. Moreover, government forces helped to organize local militias that resembled the *janjaweed* from among semi-pastoralist tribes embroiled in disputes over access to land and other resources in their local areas. Rolandsen adds generally that in 'those areas in the south where Khar-toum has managed to co-opt local militias, the exploitation of local disputes seems to be central, at least in the beginning.'[33]

---

[30] Jean-Philippe Rémy, 'Divisés, les rebelles tchadiens signent une trêve avec N'djamena', *Le Monde*, 7 Oct 2007.

[31] International Crisis Group, *Darfur's New Security Reality*, p. 14.

[32] Douglas Johnson, *The Root Causes of Sudan's Civil Wars*, Oxford: James Currey, 2003, p. 83.

[33] Øystein Rolandsen, 'Sudan: The Janjawiid and Government Militias', in Morten Bøas

The most dramatic break within the SPLA came in 1991 with the decision of the senior SPLA commanders Riek Machar and Lam Akol to split away from the SPLA and create SPLA-Nasir, which in March 1993 took the name SPLA-United. Just as internal negotiations to develop political strategies produced splinters in the SLA, negotiations among these dissidents produced further splits. In September 1994, SPLA-United was renamed the Southern Sudan Independence Movement (SSIM) as Machar tried to galvanize support amidst further defections. Most notably, Lam Akol maintained that he was continuing as head of SPLA-United. Other militias appeared after 1991 too. Commanders in Equatoria in 1993 set up the Patriotic Resistance Movement of South Sudan (PRMSS) and the Equatoria Defence Forces (EDF). In 1994, the South Sudan Freedom Front (SSFF) appeared, and defectors in Bahr el-Ghazal province formed the Independent Group.[34]

In April 1996, Machar and others agreed to negotiate with Sudan's government. A self-styled 'insider' who later returned to the fold of Garang's SPLA has recounted the turmoil that this decision created, and lamented Khartoum's subsequent capacity to exploit the ambitions of individual commanders. He explained the choice of the SSIM and others to negotiate as a tactical decision to get outside support in their feud with the SPLA leadership, a move that then turned into a longer-term dependence upon the government that they were supposedly fighting.[35] Johnson notes that 'the group operated within an active military alliance with Khartoum at the same time as it ostensibly fought for complete independence for the Southern Sudan'.[36]

Other groups developed contacts with Sudan's government. The EDF moved its headquarters to Khartoum in 1996 and joined rivals there. Tensions between these violent non-state actors even led to a gun battle in Khartoum in June 1998. Several factions signed the 1997 Khartoum Agreement (which made Machar an assistant to the president of Sudan) 'but operated independently and had separate lines of logistical support with the government'.[37] This

---

and Kevin Dunn (eds), *African Guerrillas: Raging Against the Machine*, Boulder, 2007, pp. 162–3, 165.

[34] Johnson, *Root Causes*, pp. 125–6.

[35] Peter Adwok Nyaba, *Politics of Liberation in South Sudan*, Kampala: Fountain Publishers, 1997, pp. 99–104.

[36] Douglas Johnson, 'The Sudan People's Liberation Army and the Problem of Factionalism', in Christopher Clapham (ed.), *African Guerrillas*, Oxford: James Currey, 1998, p. 61.

[37] John Young, 'Sudan: Liberation Movements, Regional Armies, Ethnic Militias and Peace', *Review of African Political Economy*, Vol. 30, No. 97, 2003, p. 431.

enabled them to pursue their grievances against Machar's group. During 1997–98, for example, fighters under the command of Paulino Matip Nhial split from and then attacked Machar's forces, enabling Sudan's government to occupy oil fields in the region. Matip's top commander, however, was upset over the destruction that fighting was causing in his ethnic homeland, so he defected back to Garang's SPLA.[38]

Many of these violent non-state actors in the South shifted to the side of the SPLA and its political wing, the Sudan People's Liberation Movement (SPLM), in the course of negotiations leading to the 9 January 2005 Comprehensive Peace Agreement between Sudan's government and insurgent groups in the south. This agreement provides for regional autonomy for the South, establishment of the principle of shared income from oil resources, and the integration of the SPLM and other opposition groups into politics in the capital. The behaviour of VNSAs during the CPA negotiations highlights the differences in the context of this negotiation process and the negotiations concerning the conflict in Darfur.

Sudan's government and Southern insurgents had engaged in negotiations for several years before signing the CPA. The Intergovernmental Authority on Development (IGAD) mediated a series of agreements between insurgents in various provinces and Sudan's government. These agreements under IGAD auspices offered temporary respite, an important accomplishment, but they did not challenge the underlying government strategy of dividing violent non-state actors. They still left room for incentives for ambitious commanders to form their own groups that would give them separate seats at the negotiating table.

As the IGAD process stalled, the UN Security Council and the 'Troika' consisting of the US, Britain and Norway began to pressure Sudan's government and the SPLM to conclude a comprehensive agreement. Foreign diplomats tried to get the other VNSAs to come to their own agreements with the SPLM as part of the price of having their concerns represented at the peace negotiations. This pressure introduced strong incentives for these groups to reconsider their separation from what was now the main representative of the South in the eyes of the foreign sponsors of the talks. Unlike Chad's government in its approach to Darfur's insurgents, these foreign officials saw fragmentation of these groups as an obstacle to achieving their goals. Thus,

---

[38] Jok Madut Jok and Sharon Elaine Hutchinson, 'Sudan's Prolonged Second Civil War and the Militarization of Nuer and Dinka Ethnic Identities', *African Studies Review*, Vol. 42, No. 2, Sept. 1999, p. 130.

through the two years of negotiations in Kenya, violent non-state armed groups in the South engaged in parallel negotiations with the SPLM.

Southern insurgents also maintained relative unity in the mid-1980s when the SPLA was heavily dependent upon the protection of Ethiopia's President Mengistu Haile Mariam. He provided the SPLA with access to military training, weapons, a radio station, and a rear base out of reach of Sudan's army and the pro-government militias.[39] Mengistu also used his security forces to spy on the SPLA's commanders to identify and remove dissent against Garang's leadership. Compared with Chad's President Déby, the Ethiopian president was less threatened by the presence of a strong Sudanese anti-government insurgency. Since his own rise to power had not directly involved the conflict between Southern insurgents and the government in Khartoum, Mengistu could intervene in their affairs with fewer worries about provoking opposition or opportunism from among members of his own political network.

Mengistu was more effective than Déby in using a Sudanese armed group as a proxy against his domestic security threats. His targets included the Gambella People's Liberation Front (GPLF) and the Oromo Liberation Front (OLF), both of which received help from Sudan's government. In contrast to Déby, Mengistu had no family or other deep personal connections to the communities in which these groups were based, so he could afford to intensify his own army's and the SPLA's attacks on these proxy violent non-state actors.[40]

The impact of Mengistu's patronage on SPLA unity became apparent after Mengistu's overthrow in May 1991. The evacuation of the SPLA's camps in Ethiopia forced the Southern Sudanese resistance group back into Sudan and demonstrated to the fleeing refugees that it could no longer protect its followers. Moreover, Garang's loss of exclusive political support and weapons supplies from his powerful patron left him exposed to challenges from rivals. It was only months after Mengistu's fall that Machar led his SPLA-Nasir into opposition to the SPLA and into an eventual association with Sudan's government.

Like the Troika after 2002, the Ethiopian backer's preference for unity among southern Sudan's insurgents shaped the SPLA's political goals. None of these patrons wanted the SPLA or SPLM to promote secession. This carried weight in Garang's articulation of a plan for a 'New Sudan' that was democratic in which Southern politicians could participate, rather than the

[39] John Young, *Armed Groups along Sudan's Eastern Frontiers: An Overview and Analysis*, Geneva: Small Arms Survey, 2007, pp. 21–2.

[40] Douglas Johnson, *Root Causes*, pp. 85–6.

complete separation that many intellectuals and fighters preferred. This stance also gave it a political platform upon which to make common cause with opposition political groups from other parts of Sudan. In contrast to the SSIM or some of the VNSAs in Darfur, ideology now became a better guide for the actual behaviour of the group. But when an armed group becomes the target of a government's efforts to fragment it, it does not matter so much what the group stands for; its main role becomes the disruption of similar groups around it.

## Is a strategy of fragmentation sustainable?

The CPA lessened the Sudanese government's influence over events and gave its foes and proxies a new framework of internationally monitored agreement around which to pursue their goals of regional self-determination and greater access to the levers of state power. There is some evidence that armed and unarmed opposition political groups found a new capacity to join for common causes. In eastern Sudan for example, the Beja Congress joined the National Democratic Alliance (NDA) with the SPLM. Officials in Khartoum tried to split the group through the creation of a rival Beja Congress for Reform and Development to buy off local leaders.[41] Groups like the Kordofan Association for Development (KAD) near the Abeyi oil fields take up the complaints of CPA signatories and accuse the NCP government of denying them access to resources and positions of authority in government.[42] Moreover, the SLA's declaration of political goals in 2003 echoes many of the SPLM's 'New Sudan' proposals for regional self-determination, equitable development and acceptance of cultural pluralism.[43]

Were it not for the increase in international scrutiny of Sudan's internal affairs and its involvement in regional politics, the NCP government in Khartoum would have been less constrained in continuing its strategies to divide VNSAs and the unarmed opposition. But since the end of the 1990s, Sudan's rulers have had to contend with UN and African Union peacekeeping operations in five of the nine countries that it borders. Since 2004, Sudan itself has

---

[41] International Crisis Group, *Sudan: Saving Peace in the East*, Brussels, 5 Jan. 2006, pp. 6–7.

[42] International Crisis Group, *Darfur's new Security Reality*, pp. 16–7.

[43] Sudan Liberation Movement and Sudan Liberation Army, 'Political Declaration', 14 March 2003, http://www.sudan.net/news/press/postedr/214.shtml, accessed 12 Dec. 2007.

become the host of two international peacekeeping missions, despite deep reservations about these deployments among officials in Khartoum. Multilateral international intervention has influenced the dynamics of VNSA fragmentation. These missions are charged with restoring order and overseeing the implementation of agreements. Mission leaders and foreign governments that back them—but are free from concerns that these groups will interfere in the internal political struggles of their own countries—have a strong incentive to encourage more organizational unity among violent non-state actors, so as to better monitor them and to encourage leaders to exercise more discipline over fighters. Accomplishing these tasks would turn these violent non-state actors into more reliable negotiating partners and guarantors of their parts of subsequent agreements.

This international intervention is significant in terms of numbers of soldiers committed and the diplomatic focus on Sudan's domestic affairs.[44] The UNAMID mission in Darfur received Security Council authorization in 2007 to absorb the African Union's African Mission in Sudan (AMIS) that had arrived in 2004. UNAMID was authorized to include up to 19,500 military personnel and 6,400 police to enforce an arms embargo. To the extent that it is able to enforce travel bans and asset freezes on individuals named in UN documents, it aids the ICC's pursuit of Sudanese officials and insurgents. Sudan's officials, including the president, have good reason to fear that the UN operation could facilitate the collection of further evidence for ICC indictments for war crimes. The United Nations Mission in Sudan (UNMIS) in Southern Sudan is authorized to deploy up to 10,000 military personnel and 715 police to monitor compliance with the CPA and to oversee the restructuring of the South's administration. This is especially ominous to officials in Khartoum, as external aid in setting up an effective Southern administration enhances prospects for Southerners to decide to separate from the rest of Sudan in a referendum scheduled for 2011 under the CPA.

The UN claims the right to send more than 30,000 foreign military personnel to Sudan, although an expanded deployment of this magnitude is unlikely. The threat of ICC prosecutions, however, has to be taken seriously, even if no Sudanese officials actually appear before the Court. One can argue over the effectiveness or fairness of the Court. Other tribunals prosecuted Serbia's former President Slobodan Milošević and Liberia's former President Charles

[44] UN peacekeeping figures are from the UN Department of Peacekeeping Operations web site, http://www.un.org/Depts/dpko/dpko/, accessed 13 Dec. 2007.

Taylor, the latter charged while still in office. It is reasonable to conclude that there is a non-trivial chance that major Sudanese officials will end up in jail. At the very least, this issue will continue to constrain Sudan's diplomats and policy makers as they try to manage with less room to manoeuvre in international affairs.

UN peacekeeping operations have recently appeared in Sudan's neighbours. The United Nations Mission in the Central African Republic and Chad is authorized to deploy only about 300 police and 50 military liaison officers. It works in tandem with the European Union's EUFOR TCHAD/RCA (European Force Chad/Central African Republic) operation, authorized to deploy 4,300 European Union soldiers.[45] The Mission de l'Organisation des Nations Unies en République Démocratique du Congo (MONUC) deploys over 18,300 military personnel and almost a thousand police. It also has been associated with a European force; in 2003, a French-backed force of about 1,800 to stabilize and pacify areas in eastern Congo where violence had kept MONUC out,[46] and a EUFOR force arrived in Congo in 2006 to help carry out a national election. The United Nations Mission in Ethiopia and Eritrea deploys about 1,600 military personnel on the border between the two countries alongside the African Union's small observer mission established there in 2000. In sum, Sudan's neighbours expect to host over 20,000 foreign military personnel.

The intensification of peacekeeping operations interferes with cross-border strategies of state officials to fragment VNSAs. Their enforcement of internationally mediated agreements, along with the shadow of the ICC, impinges on the autonomy of Sudan's government in pursuing its domestic strategies against armed opponents. The hybridization of peacekeeping, especially in UNAMID and across the border in the CAR-Chad MINURCAT (Mission des Nations Unies en République Centrafricaine et au Tchad) may enable some peacekeepers to exceed the UN missions' rules of engagement. As European forces have done in Congo (and the French in Côte d'Ivoire and the British in Sierra Leone), overlapping contingents may mean that higher levels of force will be used in crisis situations than is authorized in the Security Council resolutions that provide mandates for the UN peacekeepers.

[45] Humanitarian and Development Partnership Team, Central African Republic, http://hdptcar.net/blog/2007/11/14/detailed-update-on-uneu-peacekeeping-mission-to-prevent-darfur-violence-spill/, accessed 13 Dec. 2007.

[46] Kees Homon, 'Operation Artemis in the Democratic Republic of Congo', in European Commission, *Faster and More United? The Debate about Europe's Crisis Response Capacity*, 2007, pp. 151–5.

Sudan's NCP government is hardly helpless amidst these changes. It can use its existing strategy of promoting fragmentation among VNSAs to keep peacekeepers occupied with local problems of political instability. Hybrid operations are likely to suffer from disagreements among contributing governments when faced with these problems. For example, the tendency of Washington officials under President George W. Bush to make threatening statements about Sudan's government rankled more than Sudanese sensibilities. Politicians in contributing countries have to juggle competing political agendas, ranging from US concerns about the protracted conflicts in Iraq and Afghanistan to the unpopularity of overseas deployments in many European and African countries and reluctance to bear the expense and political commitment that deployment requires amidst a bewildering array of armed groups. Moreover, international intervention is bound to benefit some armed groups while disadvantaging others. This could upset the strategies that officials in Chad, for example, have relied upon to protect their vulnerable regime from violent challenge. Not taking account of that government's security concerns could lead to the possibility of international forces being stuck amidst factional fighting if the central government dissolves into competing camps as Somalia's did in 1991 or Congo's in 1996–97.

In any event, this shift in Sudan's international environment may change the organization and behaviour of Sudan's VNSAs as it shapes the range of options available to Sudanese government officials. Time will tell whether Sudan's VNSAs reverse their trend of fragmentation, although the experience of the SPLA/SPLM in the South shows that this can happen. International efforts to limit fragmentation will likely intensify as the fragmentation of VNSAs seems to raise the prospect of 'Somalization' of regional politics as large areas become insecure and, as in Chad, factional politics threatens to overwhelm these regimes.

# 16

# Non-State Actors and the Role of Violence in Stateless Somalia

*Ken Menkhaus*

Throughout the war-torn Horn of Africa, violent non-state actors (VNSAs) play a central role in their countries' politics and economies. Accurate political analysis of these pivotal actors is constrained by their relative inaccessibility—making it hard to secure interviews and reliable information about them—as well as by the very fluid nature of their membership and the loose nature of their command and control over militia. In short, VNSAs in the Horn of Africa are critically important and yet extremely difficult to assess with any degree of confidence.

Nowhere is the relocation of authority from state to non-state actors as acute as in Somalia, where the prolonged and complete collapse of the central government for 19 years has produced a context in which non-state actors have generally been the only form of political organization. Violence, or the threat of violence, is a principal (though by no means the only) unit of currency of power and the main source of individual and group security in a dangerous and often lawless environment. This has remained true despite the creation of two consecutive transitional governments since 2000. Political violence in south-central Somalia has arguably been more severe and uncontrolled in the period since 2006 than at any time in the country's two-decade-long civil war.

This chapter explores the changing use of violence by Somalia's complex galaxy of non-state actors. It records the rise of new non-state actors (NSAs) over the past 19 years—including business groups, *sharia* courts, warlord and clan militias, criminal gangs, pirates, regional and municipal polities, autonomous paramilitaries within the Transitional Federal Government (TFG), and Islamist groups—and the way each employs violence and the threat of violence in different ways. Special attention is given to the new forms of armed violence employed by the numerous Jihadists and insurgents in Somalia since 2004, including use of political assassination, remote controlled explosives, and suicide bombing. The study also examines how easy recourse to armed violence, facilitated by the availability of cheap small arms and the partial breakdown of the rule of law, has multiplied the number of potential spoilers who can block state-building and peace-building initiatives not to their liking. It argues that the composition, interests, and tactics of VNSAs in Somalia have evolved over time, and chronicles the shift from indiscriminate use of violence in the early period of the Somali crisis to a more controlled, risk-averse use of violence (up until 2007) as NSAs sought more predictable and safe environments for themselves.

It also notes that in some cases, localized forms of NSA violence are not predatory and are not bids for political power, but are rather a manifestation of defensive strategies by households and communities seeking to provide some level of physical security for themselves in a context of state collapse. This is especially important in order to understand reliance on clan and sub-clan militias as a source of deterrence against violent crime and attack, as well as the predictable problems of spiralling revenge killings that such a lineage-based system of deterrence tends to produce. It is also essential as an explanation for why Somali civic actors with an interest in peace-building have been extremely reluctant to censure or marginalize violent militia leaders from their own clan. While communities may detest these 'warlords' and Jihadists they are also dependent on them as a source of protection in the event of attack by an outside clan.

The analysis concludes by considering the implications of a Somali context in which no emerging state can reasonably expect to secure a monopoly on the legitimate use of violence for years to come, and how this context might produce conditions in which a 'mediated state'—meaning a weak central government must broker arrangements with existing NSAs to extend indirect control over parts of the country—constitutes the only viable option for state-building. For agencies tasked with promoting US national security in the Horn of Africa, this 'messy' mediated state scenario poses genuine challenges to standard operating procedures; it may require new and creative thinking about local partnerships and the management of security risks which can emerge when terrorists exploit the long transition period between state collapse and the revival of a robust state in Somalia.

## The changing Somali context

Somalia's condition of total and protracted state collapse since 1991 is an extreme manifestation of a more general phenomenon of state failure which has produced large tracts of what has been called 'ungoverned space' across much of Africa, especially in the troubled Horn of Africa region. As dramatic as Somalia's state collapse is, it is important not to overstate its importance as an explanation of the rise of NSAs in the country. Although Somalia was under the grip of the authoritarian government of Siyad Barre throughout the 1970s and 1980s, much of the remote pastoral countryside remained marginal to the state's exercising of authority, and hence a political arena of non-state actors. Most day-to-day issues of governance—settlement of disputes and crimes, and management of access to resources—were handled by traditional authorities, including clan elders and sheikhs whose reputations as peacemakers and mediators made them a preferred alternative to the corrupt and weak district court system. A central pillar of customary law—the practice of blood payments (*diya*) by kinsmen as a form of collective, compensational justice— grew less important in major urban areas but remained central in rural settings, and served to reinforce the importance of clans and clan elders as non-state actors.[1] This outsourcing of day-to-day governance to customary authorities in the countryside is by no means unique to Somalia—contemporary Yemen displays many of these political features as well. The Siyad Barre regime formally outlawed clanism, but in practice sought to manipulate it, in part by naming 'government' lineage leaders through whom it hoped to exercise control over clans and to weaken traditional authorities who commanded dangerous levels of support from their clansmen. The state did, however, seek to monopolize the legitimate use of violence, in part by interjecting its own security forces to apprehend killers when clans threatened to mobilize armed men to conduct revenge killings, and by imposing the death penalty for murder. This practice helped to reduce, though not eliminate entirely, clan clashes over resources and wrongdoings.

[1] I.M. Lewis, *A Modern History of Somalia*, 4th edition, Oxford: James Currey, 2002, p. 11; and Said Samatar and David Laitin, *Somalia: Nation in Search of a State*, Boulder: Dartmouth, 1986, pp. 29–30.

Towards the end of the Siyad Barre regime, ominous signs of the ascent of violent non-state actors began to emerge, not only in direct opposition to the state—multiple clan-based armed insurgencies eventually overthrew the government in early 1991–but also within the government itself. In the final years of the regime's existence, the armed forces broke down into clan-based units answering only to their own leaders.[2] Those leaders held the formal title of colonel or general in the army but were in fact already displaying some of the characteristics that were later labelled as warlordism. That metastasizing of army units into autonomous clan paramilitaries which later laid waste to much of the country was, in retrospect, an early warning of the breakdown of the Somali state. It is a reminder that the distinction between state and non-state actors, especially in the security sector, is not always so clear-cut when units are more likely to answer to clan patrons than to the command structure of the police and military.[3] As elsewhere, the Somali state can play host to violent non-state 'hidden powers' operating within the body politic but in pursuit of more parochial interests.[4]

Somalia's state of statelessness has changed considerably in nature since 1991, creating a new context within which non-state actors operate. First, war dynamics are quite different today by comparison with the early years of the crisis. In 1991–92 a full-fledged civil war raged between clan-based factional militias, which were unquestionably the most powerful VNSAs in Somalia. That civil war, which produced a war economy in which militias primarily engaged in looting civilians, triggered a major famine and led to the deaths of 250,000 Somalis. The 1993–95 UN Operation in Somalia (UNOSOM) halted the fighting, and although the UN mission failed to revive a central government before it departed in March 1995, it triggered changes in the subsequent scope of warfare in Somalia. From 1994 to 2005, armed conflict in Somalia became much more localized and shorter in duration. Most clashes occurred within sub-clans, rather than pitting large clan-families against one another. This pattern of highly localized armed conflict mirrored the political fragmentation which occurred in Somalia after 1994. The fighting constituted

---

[2] Africa Watch, *Somalia: A Government at War with its Own People*, New York, 1990.

[3] Bruce Baker, 'Non-State Providers of Everyday Security in Fragile African States', in Louise Andersen, Bjorn Moller and Finn Stepputat (eds), *Fragile States and Insecure People? Violence, Security, and Statehood in the Twenty-first Century*, New York: Palgrave, 2007, pp. 123–50.

[4] Finn Stepputat, 'Insecurity, State, and Impunity in Latin America', in Andersen, Moller, and Stepputat, eds, *Fragile States and Insecure People?* pp. 201–23.

a form of low-intensity war featuring periodic flare-ups of violence, usually triggered by a crime or a dispute over resources. Clashes were shorter and less lethal because clan elders were better able to intervene to stop clashes within their own lineages, because the rise of private security forces made looting less feasible, and because Somali communities and diaspora members were increasingly unwilling to contribute financially to the war coffers of militia leaders. It was at this time that the large factions which had dominated the Somali political landscape in 1991–94 gradually splintered and then dissolved into irrelevance.[5]

Until recently, this positive trajectory in armed conflict in Somalia appeared to constitute an enduring trend. In 2006, however, that trend was at least temporarily interrupted and reversed with the onset of some of the worst violence the country has seen since 1992. The new wars came in two waves. First, serious clashes erupted in Mogadishu between an alliance of militia leaders backed by the US and an ascendant Islamist movement which came to be known as the Islamic Courts Union (ICU). After several months of increasingly heavy rounds of clashes, the Courts prevailed in June 2006 and routed the militia coalition, known as the Alliance for the Restoration of Peace and Counter-Terrorism (ARPCT). After a six-month lull in which the ICU imposed the best public security Mogadishu and southern Somalia had enjoyed in two decades, rising tensions between the ICU and neighbouring Ethiopia culminated in a war between the two in late December 2006. The Ethiopian National Defence Forces (ENDF) routed the Islamists, occupied the capital city, and supported the weak Transitional Federal Government (TFG) as it sought to govern the capital for the first time since its creation in 2004. Predictably, an armed insurgency in Mogadishu arose to attack both the TFG and Ethiopian forces. The ensuing insurgency and counter-insurgency produced devastating levels of armed clashes, in which a third of the city's 1.3 million people were displaced and thousands killed.[6] The humanitarian crisis precipitated by the fighting placed 2.5 million people at risk across central and southern Somalia, and by 2007 constituted what aid officials termed the world's worst humanitarian emergency.[7] With the capital city gripped by daily

[5] Ken Menkhaus, 'Governance without Government in Somalia: Spoilers, State Building, and the Politics of Coping', *International Security* Vol. 31, No. 3, 2006/07, pp. 74–106.

[6] Ken Menkhaus, 'The Crisis in Somalia: Tragedy in Five Acts', *African Affairs* Vol. 106 no. 424, July 2007, pp. 357–90.

[7] Jeffrey Gettlemen, 'Humanitarian crisis in Somalis is worse than Darfur', *International Herald Tribune* (20 November 2007) http://www.iht.com/articles/2007/11/20/africa/somalia.php [accessed 25 May 2008].

mortar attacks, roadside bombs, gun battles, and targeted assassination, conditions of insecurity, radicalization, and militarization have produced an entirely new environment in which violent NSAs thrive. By 2008 that insecurity had spread throughout much of the countryside as well. The number of documented armed roadblocks across southern Somalia increased to 396 by April 2008, a clear indication of the proliferation of armed groups.[8]

Conditions of lawlessness have also shifted over time, following much the same path—an inverted bell curve—as have trends in armed conflict. Violent criminality bordering on outright anarchy dominated southern Somalia in 1991–92, providing an ideal environment for the rise of criminal gangs and in some instances unscrupulous business rings engaging in widespread property theft, diversion of food aid, drug-running, illegal charcoal harvesting, and dismantling of state-owned industries for export as scrap metal. During the 1990s, however, a growing number of businesspeople shifted from involvement in an economy of plunder to legitimate or quasi-legitimate businesses, including some—like telecommunications, remittance companies, import-export commerce, hotels, and light industry—that involved expensive fixed assets in buildings, equipment, and warehouses.[9]

This new commercial class was not always enthusiastic about the revival of the state—its members were, after all, profiting in a context of state collapse and feared that a revived state would tax them or nationalize their businesses. But they were increasingly strong advocates of improved street security, and by the first years of the new millennium the private security forces they hired constituted the largest militias in the capital. Local communities also formed neighbourhood watch groups and supported local *sharia* courts. All of this contributed to a decline in the type of lawlessness and criminality which had gripped the country in the early 1990s. To be sure, Somalia still had serious problems with certain types of criminality, including kidnapping for ransom, piracy, targeted assassination, and certain illegal 'white collar' crime like the environmentally-devastating export of charcoal, but the country was in a state of controlled violence, particularly on the street.[10] Violent crime dropped still further with the advent of the short but impressive administration of the CIC

[8] USAID, 'Somalia: Complex Emergency Situation Report #4 (FY2008)' (21 April 2008), posted on Relief Web http://www.reliefweb.int/rw/RWB.NSF/db900SID/EGUA-7-DWSUU?OpenDocument [accessed 25 May 2008].

[9] UNDP, *Somalia Human Development Report 2001*, Nairobi, December 2001; Peter Little, *Somalia: Economy Without State*, Bloomington: Indiana University Press, 2003.

[10] Menkhaus, 'Governance without Government'.

over most of southern Somalia in the latter half of 2006. Since 2007, however, the gradual reduction in violent crime has been reversed, as armed groups—including criminal gangs but also elements in the security forces of the Transitional Federal Government—exploit the chaos of the insurgency and counter-insurgency violence to extort, loot, rape, and assault with little fear of justice.

Finally, systems of local governance have evolved in complex ways since the early 1990s, when the massive dislocations caused by the war and the enormous scale of the violence overwhelmed customary sources of law and shattered civic organization; T-shirts worn by young gunmen emblazoned with the stark line 'I Am the Boss' captured perfectly the breakdown of authority. Over time, a variety of local sources of informal authority—clan elders, sheikhs, business leaders, women's groups, professional associations, and others—began to re-emerge and gradually rebuilt a patch-quilt of local systems of governance which, while not adding up to anything resembling a modern state, was able to provide a modicum of public security, rule of law, and modest services to the community. This phenomenon of 'governance without government' has included formal municipalities and regional administrations in some places, local *sharia* courts in others, and hybrid informal systems of governance in others again, and has constituted one of the most important political developments in the country since 1995. In some cases, informal governing arrangements have involved non-state actors seeking to use controlled violence to enforce rule of law and provide protection for the local community.[11]

## Inventory of Somali violent non-state actors

Given Somalia's protracted crisis of state collapse and the important changes in political and security conditions in Somalia since 1991, it should come as no surprise that violent non-state actors in Somalia have been both numerous and very fluid. What follows is an inventory of some of the most significant VNSAs that have emerged in Somalia from 1990 to 2009. Most of these categories are overlapping and not mutually exclusive.

It is important to note that all of these VNSAs are in violation of a UN arms embargo first established in 1992, because almost all serviceable weapons

---

[11] Ken Menkhaus, 'Local Security Systems in Somali East Africa', in Andersen, Møller, and Stepputat (eds), *Fragile States and Insecure People?* pp. 67–98.

and ammunition now in use in Somalia have arrived in the country since then. For years, blatant violations of the UN arms embargo were ignored, and the embargo was of little consequence. Somalia's Bakara market became one of the most important weapons markets in East Africa. In recent years, however, international efforts have been stepped up to document violations of the arms embargo via a UN Monitoring Group on Somalia, and discussions of targeted sanctions against individuals and groups in violation of the embargo have increased. The most recent Report of the UN Monitoring Group on Somalia is quite clear about the scope of culpability:

Although provision exists for exemptions to the embargo..., no exemption for delivery of arms and ammunition or other lethal support to any Somali armed force or group has ever been granted. Consequently, the Monitoring Group believes that every armed force, group, or militia in Somalia, their financiers, active supporters, and, in some cases, foreign donors are currently in violation of the arms embargo.[12]

The combination of the wide-reaching findings of the Monitoring Group and the growing desire in some quarters of the international community to impose targeted sanctions has major implications for Somali VNSAs and their sponsors. All the actors under review in this study are criminal as a result, and susceptible to future legal action by individual UN member states, a revived Somali state, or possibly the International Criminal Court.

## General armed groups

*Armed factions.* In the 1980s, Somali armed opposition to the Siyad Barre regime was organized around factions, nearly all of which were clan-based in composition. By early 1991, when the regime was overthrown, four large armed factions existed—the Somali Salvation Democratic Front (SSDF) (associated with the Mijerteen clan), the Somali National Movement (SNM) (associated with the Isaaq clan-family), the United Somali Congress (USC) (associated with the Hawiye clan-family), and the Somali Patriotic Movement (SPM) (associated with the Darood clan-family). Each of these factions usually featured both a political and militia wing, often with rival leaders for each wing. During the armed insurgency against the Siyad Barre government, these factions commanded thousands of armed men, drawn from whole units deserting from the army as well as untrained young men recruited mainly from pastoral areas by clan elders. With the fall of the Siyad Barre regime, the

---

[12] UN Security Council, *Report of the Monitoring Group on Somalia Pursuant to Security Council Resolution 1811 (2008)*, S/2008/769 (10 December 2008), p. 6.

southern Somali factions began fighting one another, in a conflict leading to a massive crisis of displacement and famine in 1991–92.

Command and control in these factions varied greatly. Some movements, most notably the SNM, had relatively well-developed command structures, good control over militiamen, and an organized political wing.[13] Other factions were very loosely organized, with contested authority at the top level and virtually no control exercised over armed gunmen affiliated with the militia. Indeed, because the militiamen in these factions were unpaid, their willingness to take orders was uneven; most fought primarily for the opportunity to loot. By mid-1991 the two largest militias in south-central Somalia, USC and SPM, began to splinter along clan and sub-clan lines; much of the heaviest fighting in the civil war was waged within rather than between the USC and SPM factions. Two rival, cross-clan factional coalitions—the Somali National Alliance (SNA), led by General Aideed, and the Group of 12, led by Ali Mahdi—briefly emerged in 1992, but were overwhelmed by the countervailing trend towards fractionalization and political fragmentation.[14] Fifteen factions—most with at least a modest armed wing—were represented in UN peace talks in March 1993.

Throughout most of the 1990s, factions dominated political representation in Somali national reconciliation talks, even though they enjoyed little support from Somali civil society. They were often disparaged as 'warlord' militias which were viewed as the main source of Somalia's crisis.[15] Because leadership over a recognized faction earned militia leaders a seat at the negotiating table, the number of factions in the country multiplied; by 1998, 27 factions were present at an Egyptian-sponsored peace conference. By 2000, the factions had largely ceased to exist as political or military units. They were replaced by a combination of other forms of VNSAs, ranging from self-styled local administrations to *sharia* court militias to private security forces.

The dramatic rise and fall of the role of the armed factions in the 1990s is one of the more intriguing puzzles of the Somali crisis. There are a number of

---

[13] Daniel Compagnon, 'Somali Armed Movements' in Christopher Clapham (ed.), *African Guerrillas*, Bloomington: Indiana University Press, 1998, pp. 73–90.

[14] Terrence Lyons and Ahmed Samatar, *Somalia: State Collapse, Multilateral Intervention, and Strategies for Political Reconstruction*, Washington DC: Brookings Institution, 1994.

[15] Ken Menkhaus, 'International Peacebuilding and the Dynamics of Local and National Peacebuilding in Somalia', in Walter Clarke and Jeffrey Herbst (eds), *Learning from Somalia: The Lessons of Armed Humanitarian Intervention*, Boulder: Westview Press, 1997, pp. 42–63.

partial explanations of their demise. First, the factions were victims of a broader process of political fragmentation along sub-clan lines in the late 1990s which tended to undermine any and all large, organized political units in the country. Second, factional leaders faced declining financial resources, as their clans and local businesspeople grew increasingly unwilling to contribute funds to militia leaders. Third, post-UNOSOM Somalia saw the rise of private security forces as well as local *sharia* court militias, which offered more respectable and less risky forms of paid employment than freelancing for a factional militia. The increased capacity of communities and businesses to protect themselves dramatically reduced opportunities for looting, which in essence deprived the factional militias of their main incentive to fight. One major development in 1999 was especially important in eroding the importance of the factional militias. In Mogadishu, an increasingly powerful group of businesspeople refused to pay 'taxes' to the factional militias at the seaports, and instead bought the militia out from under the feet of the militia commanders. Many of those gunmen were then integrated into *sharia* court militias in the capital.

In some instances, the dissolution of the armed factions coincided with the declining political fortunes of the faction leaders or warlords presiding over them. For instance, the top faction leaders in the heavily contested Jubba valley area—General Mohamed Hersi 'Morgan' (SPM), Col. Omar Jess (SPM/SNA), General Aden 'Gabio' (SPM), and Col. Omar Hashi (Somali National Front, of SNF)—either sought political asylum abroad or were reduced to second-tier status in Somali politics. In other cases, however, faction leaders adapted and built an alternative political-military base for themselves. Some faction leaders shifted their power base to formal regional administrations. The most successful example was Col. Abdullahi Yusuf, military commander of the SSDF, who assumed the role of President of the newly-formed autonomous state of Puntland in north-east Somalia in 1998. His SSDF militia was repackaged as the security sector of Puntland state. Yusuf then used Puntland as a platform to win the position of President of the Transitional Federal Government in 2004. To the south, several other clan militia commanders sought with less success to transform their power base from factional to regional administration. Some of these regional administrations actually provided modest levels of governance, others were little more than window-dressing. In the important port city of Kismayo, Col. Barre Hirale established the 'Jubba Valley Authority', formalizing control of the city by a splinter group of the defunct SNF. In the Bay and Bakool regions, the 'South-west Regional State' was created as a metamorphosis of the Rahanweyn Resistance Army, led by Col. Shatigaduud. And an SNA regional strongman, Sheikh Indha'adde, declared himself the 'governor' of Lower Shabelle Region.

These and other examples of militia and factional leaders restyling themselves as 'governors' and 'presidents' of regional states reflected the fact that the factions had earned a bad name in the 1990s, and that the international community was much more inclined to view regional administrations as more legitimate actors. The fact that these self-styled regional administrations were often little more than camouflage for continued militia occupation was not lost on local communities; the same militias continued to extort from the local population, only now the extortion was recast as taxation by warlords who had changed hats.

The capacity of Somali VNSAs to adapt their organizational names, leadership titles, and stationery to suit the needs of external actors illustrates how important external recognition was to the faction leaders, for whom the main prize to be won was a seat at international peace conferences and from there a seat in a declared government. Of the 15 factions convened for reconciliation talks by UNOSOM in 1993–95, all but one had English-language, not Somali names.[16] A shift in policy by the international community in the late 1990s towards engagement with regional and local polities—the so-called 'building block' approach to state-building in Somalia—coincided with efforts (described above) on the part of more astute militia leaders to maintain control over discrete pieces of territory and give themselves new hats as governors. The international community is generally unaware of the extent to which their preferences translate into adaptations by VNSAs in Somalia to recast themselves—at least superficially—to suit external needs. This phenomenon of 'rehatting' has occurred again in recent years with the rise of political Islam—some leaders have changed their titles from general to chairman to governor to sheikh but have never really changed from clan-based militia leaders. These 'extreme makeovers' are purely cosmetic and fool only inattentive foreigners.

While some warlords and militia leaders remade themselves into governors and mayors, others became businessmen, allowing them to generate an independent revenue flow to maintain sizeable militias under their command. One of the best examples of this was the Mogadishu-based militia leader

---

[16] One faction, the Somali Patriotic Movement, used the acronym SPM despite the fact that the letter P does not even exist in the Somali language.

Mohamed Afrah Qanyare, who served as a subordinate of General Aideed in the SNA before building his own sub-clan militia. He developed the lucrative Daynille airstrip in south Mogadishu, collecting landing fees from daily commercial flights into the city. In northern Mogadishu, the strongman Bashir Raghe generated profits as co-owner of the important El-Ma'an seaport complex and as a major exporter of charcoal.[17]

Because nearly all militia leaders engage in income-generating activities (some legal, others illegal), and because virtually all of the larger business groups in the country also employ large private security forces, it is difficult to disentangle these two categories of armed non-state actors in contemporary Somalia. Businesspeople and entrepreneurial militia leaders have come to resemble one another in some ways, despite having arrived at the same position via very different routes. The main difference is that most of the armed businesspeople have not sought to directly enter the political arena. Those businesspeople who have sought to parley their wealth and private security forces into direct political power—such as Mohamed Farah Aideed's former financial backer Osman Atto—have generally fared poorly, as discussed below.

An important lesson to be drawn from the rise and fall of the armed factions in the 1990s is that their superior ability to employ violence in pursuit of their interests failed to yield the results desired by the faction leaders. The lack of command and control over unpaid militias meant that the small groups of gunmen comprising the factional militias used violence in pursuit of more immediate and narrow goals—to secure war booty and extort payments at roadblocks in order to provide for their families. More than one young gunman in the early 1990s responded to UN efforts at demobilization and disarmament by arguing that 'my gun is my job'.[18] The chronic insecurity that their predatory behaviour visited on Somali society quickly undermined the factions' legitimacy in the eyes of local communities. A second lesson is that armed groups which are unable to pay wages to gunmen are much more vulnerable to disintegration. Finally, armed groups which find themselves in competition for recruits with more socially acceptable, less risky security forces—in the case of Somalia, private security forces or *sharia* court militias—are also likely to lose out.

---

[17] Andre Le Sage, 'Somalia: Sovereign Disguise for a Mogadishu Mafia', *Review of African Political Economy* Vol. 29, Issue 91, 2002, pp. 132–8.
[18] Author's fieldnotes, 1993.

*Sub-clan militias.* Virtually all Somali lineages have the capacity to quickly muster an irregular militia in defence of clan interests. When clan interests are threatened, elders are able to mobilize armed young men for short periods, drawing on a range of sources—pastoralists, private security guards, local police or *sharia* court security forces, and armed youth, including criminal elements. Command of sub-clan militias is typically enjoyed by an established militia leader, though the degree of actual control exercised over the irregular fighting forces is limited. Clan militiamen are paid infrequently and can return home or turn to criminal activity. Typically clan militias are two-tiered, with one set of gunmen maintaining status as permanent (if often unpaid) members of a standing militia while others are called on as needed but then return to other livelihoods. The clan's ability to mobilize a fighting force is essential for deterrence and occasional reprisal attacks. Warlords and political leaders rely heavily on their clan's militias. Not surprisingly, their relationship with clan elders is very complex; they rely on elders to mobilize forces even as militia leaders and elders compete for political leadership and sometimes have very different interests. Assessments which contrast 'illegitimate' warlords with 'legitimate' traditional authorities obscure the fact that clan elders are sometimes complicit with militia leaders in the use of violence to advance the lineage's interests. Some sub-clan militias are part of the complex insurgency against the TFG and Ethiopian occupation forces in Mogadishu and southern Somalia.

In the current fluid, post-Ethiopian-occupation environment in Somalia, exceptionally high levels of uncertainty and insecurity have created ideal circumstances for the clan-based militias to reassert a dominant role. Many of the militias which are now describing themselves as part of a moderate Sunni Islamist coalition (al-Sunna wal Jama'a, discussed below) are little more than clan militias.

*Armed gangs.* Small armed groups—termed 'gangs' here—are ubiquitous in Somalia, and form the most cohesive armed units in the country. Armed youths form small, tight circles to operate together to protect turf, extort protection money, engage in crime, operate roadblocks, or await opportunities to join a mobilized militia. The relationship between armed gangs and their clans is complex, as they are a source of crime but also, occasionally, a source of security. In Somalia, young gunmen are given a number of pejorative nicknames, including *mooryaan* and *jiri*.[19] Life as a gunman in armed groups is

---

[19] For one of the few close studies of Somali gunmen, see Roland Marchal, 'Les mooryaan

dangerous, especially at roadblocks, and the livelihood earned by freelance armed groups is reported to be not always good. The status of gunmen in Somalia has dropped considerably over the past decade, and it is considered somewhat shameful for a man to continue a life as a freelance gunman beyond the age of about 25; by then, most gunmen seek paid and respectable work as private security guards. Some armed gangs are reported to have been given contracts by insurgent groups to conduct ambushes on TFG and Ethiopian forces.

*Pirates.* Few other armed non-state actors have gained as much international attention in Somalia as the country's pirates. Piracy off the Somali coast is now an epidemic—there were 31 attacks in 2007, while in 2008 40 hijackings were carried out successfully and over 100 were attempted—earning the Somali coast the reputation as the most pirate-infested shipping lane in the world.[20] This has resulted in multiple resolutions by the UN Security Council authorizing international naval patrols off the Somali coast.[21] The pirates carrying out the actual attacks are small teams composed of a combination of gunmen, former fishermen, and usually at least one operative with more advanced nautical skills (typically an ex-coast guard member), who are equipped with speedboats, automatic weaponry, rocket propelled grenades, radios and global positioning system devices.[22] They typically work for warlords or powerful Somali political and financial figures, believed in some cases to include top individuals in regional and national administrations. They attack cargo ships, fishing vessels, and yachts; they board a ship, direct her to remote coves on Somalia's coast, and take the crew hostage.

Some Somalis have sought to portray the pirates as protectors of the Somali coastline from illegal foreign fishing, and it is true that illegal fishing has been a serious problem along the Somali coast. But the pirates are strictly focused

---

de Mogadiscio: formes de la violence dans un espace urbain en guerre', *Cahiers d'Etudes Africaines* Vol. 33, 1993, pp. 295–320.

[20] Mark Doyle, 'Somali piracy is worst in the world', BBC News (5 January 2006) http://news.bbc.co.uk/2/hi/africa/4584878.stm [accessed May 24 2008]; 'Somali Piracy Lawless, Lucrative', AP wire report (1 May 2008) http://www.national-anthems.net/forum/article/rec.travel.africa/69039 [accessed 24 May 2008]; 'Somali Piracy: Q and A', BBC News (9 January 2009) http://news.bbc.co.uk/2/hi/africa/7734985.stm; Roger Middleton, 'Piracy in Somalia', London: Chatham House Briefing Paper (October 2008).

[21] 'Piracy off the coast of Somalia.' http://www.imo.org/ [accessed 24 May 2008]

[22] Ken Menkhaus, 'Somalia: Dangerous Waters', *Survival* Vol. 51, No. 1, 2009.

on securing lucrative ransom payments for the captured ships and their crews. Ransoms have averaged between $500,000 and $1 million per ship in recent years, with several highly valuable ships reported to earn up to $3 million. This bonanza for Somali pirates may soon end, however, as their increasingly numerous and brazen attacks have prompted forceful external response. Several French military rescue operations have been launched since 2008, and in April 2009 the dramatic incident involving the pirating of the *Maersk Alabama* produced a prolonged stand-off with US naval vessels ending in the killing of three pirates and the arrest of a fourth. In response to a peak in piracy attacks in 2008–a year in which the pirates earned between $20 to $40 million in ransom and even managed to capture a Saudi supertanker, the *Sirius Star*—the UN Security Council passed several resolutions authorizing member states to enter Somali territorial waters and use 'all necessary means' to interdict and deter piracy. Over a dozen navies from countries as diverse as the US, China, Iran, India and Malaysia, as well as the European Union, are now patrolling the shipping lanes near Somalia in the Gulf of Aden and the Indian Ocean.[23]

It is estimated that about one thousand armed men are currently engaged as pirates. These individual pirates can do quite well—one reported earning $90,000 in a short period of time.[24] Successful pirates often retire after their first payment, leading to high turnover. But the lion's share of the ransoms is controlled by powerful political and business sponsors of the pirate groups. The December 2008 UN Monitoring Group report estimates that 20 per cent of the ransom goes to the financier of the pirate unit, and 30 per cent to 'sponsors' who handle underwriting of the costs of holding the ship, the negotiations, and payoffs to local officials.[25] This has produced a Mafia-like racket implicating top figures at the highest levels of Somali politics in the north-east coastal region of Puntland.[26] Puntland risks becoming a pirate version of a narco-state, though in recent months the administration there has made a serious effort to crack down on piracy.

*Private security forces.* The impressive growth of the Somali private sector since the mid-1990s—ranging from privately run seaports and airstrips

---

[23] International Crisis Group, *Somalia: To Move Beyond the Failed State*, Brussels: ICG Africa Report 147 (23 December 2008), p. 22; Menkhaus, 'Dangerous Waters.'

[24] 'Somali Piracy Lawless, Lucrative', as note 20.

[25] UN Security Council, *Report of the Monitoring Group*, paras 139–40.

[26] UN Security Council, *Report of the Monitoring Group*, paras. 107, 141–2.

through telecommunications and remittances companies to light industries like the Coca-Cola bottling factory in Mogadishu—has seen a parallel growth in sizeable private security companies owned and controlled by the business owners.[27] By the late 1990s, private Somali-owned security forces constituted some of the largest militia forces in Somalia.[28] Although their principal role is to protect the assets of the company or business owner, these security forces have at times been called into service for broader political purposes—in clashes with rival business groups, with warlords, and in a few cases against the Transitional Federal Government and Ethiopian forces occupying the capital. Because private security forces are regularly paid, they are more easily control-led and disciplined, and their patrols around business facilities can create a microclimate of security in a neighborhood that attracts small businesses and street vendors.[29] The strength of private security forces has translated into growing political and military clout for leading businesspeople, some of whom are simultaneously considered businessmen, warlords, and aspiring politicians. As a general rule, however, most Somali businesspeople are reluctant to lever-age their security forces for political ambitions, seeking to focus on their com-mercial activities. Those who have plunged into politics have had only mixed success.[30]

Few foreign companies currently operate in Somalia, for obvious reasons—high risk and low reward. One exception is foreign fishing trawlers, which enter Somali waters in pursuit of highly profitable tuna catches there. Somali waters are considered to hold some of the richest stocks of yellowfin tuna in the world, and according to maritime organizations, at any given time before 2007 there were hundreds of foreign trawlers illegally fishing Somali waters. Piracy has caused a major drop in that activity, leading to a significant drop in the worldwide catch of yellowfin tuna.[31] Although foreign trawlers have

---

[27] To date, there are no companies specializing in provision of private security in Somalia, as is common in neighbouring countries.

[28] At the time of completion of this study (February 2009), private international security companies were actively exploring business opportunities in Somalia, presumably in sup-port of proposed UN peacekeepers. If they enter the scene they will constitute a contro-versial new VNSA on the Somali scene.

[29] Author's interviews, Mogadishu, July 2004.

[30] The many businesspeople who have entered the arena of national politics in Somalia include the former TNG President Abdiqassim Salad Hassan; Osman Atto; the self-declared President and faction leader Ali Mahdi; and the former TNG Prime Minister Ali Khalif Galaydh.

[31] 'Somali pirates threaten Indian Ocean tuna industry', *Reuters* (22 January 2009) http://

armed themselves, they have not to date employed private security firms to protect them. However, foreign oil exploration companies, a new entrant, are hiring local armed guards.[32]

In addition, a number of international private security companies (PSCs) have had or are exploring contracts with local governments to provide coast guard services and training to build local coast guard capacity.[33] Several international firms, including UK-based HART, Canadian-based SOMCAN, and Saudi-based Al-Hababi, secured contracts to provide training and coast guard patrols to Puntland. The TFG signed contracts with an American-based firm, Top Cat, as well as the Northridge group, for coast guard services that never became operational.[34]

*Neighbourhood watch groups.* Neighbourhood watch groups, usually involving a combination of paid gunmen and armed residents who can be quickly mobilized if called out, have been a source of local security in Mogadishu since the early years of state collapse in 1991 and 1992. Some rural villages and towns have also seen variations on this theme. The nature of the relationship between community and gunmen varies. In some cases, gunmen have made a transition from looting villages to demanding a portion of the harvest in return for protection from other gangs, gradually becoming a part of the village's security rather than its principal source of insecurity. This particular arrangement constitutes an intriguing grey area between protection racket and nascent police force. One of the most important recent instances of a neighbourhood watch group was the deal struck in early 2008 between the new TFG Prime Minister Nuur Adde and the business community of Bakara Market, an area hit hard by insurgency and counter-insurgency violence, where TFG security forces had been accused of widespread looting.[35] The deal ceded authority for

---

www.flex-news-food.com/pages/21570/Fish/somali-pirates-threaten-indian-ocean-tuna-industry.html

[32] UN Security Council, *Report of the Monitoring Group*, paras. 100–1.

[33] Details on the most recent of these arrangements, in this case the French firm SECOPEX, are documented in the UN Security Council, *Report on the Monitoring Group*, paras. 97–9.

[34] For a recent, detailed analysis of international private security companies in Somalia and Somaliland, see Stig Hansen, 'Private Security and Local Politics in Somalia', *Review of African Political Economy* Vol. 35, No. 118, 2008, pp. 585–98.

[35] 'Somalia: private security forces begin patrolling Bakara Market', *InsideSomalia.org* (23 March 2008) http://insidesomalia.org/News/Business/Somalia-Private-Security-Force-Begins-Patrolling-Bakara-Market.html [accessed 25 May 2008].

policing the market neighbourhood to the private armed guards of the businessmen, with the understanding that if they kept the insurgents out, the TFG security forces would stay out as well. This type of hybrid, outsourced security arrangement—what Bruce Baker categorizes as 'state-approved civil guarding'—has considerable potential in Somalia and is discussed in more detail below.[36] However, businessmen who brokered the deal with the TFG Prime Minister report that their intent was not to form a sort of community policing structure, but rather to use the deal to form a private security company which would eventually expand its patrols beyond Bakara Market to other paying customers.[37] This 'commoditization of security' should come as no surprise to Somalis; insecurity has long generated profitable business opportunities in neighbouring Kenya and many other countries.

## Quasi-governmental armed groups

*Municipal and regional administrative security forces.* A number of formal subnational polities in Somalia—self-declared municipalities and regional governments—possess armed security forces in the form of police or defence forces which operate autonomously from declared national governments. These units blur the line between state and non-state armed groups in that the 'governments' they serve are of questionable legality and in a few cases are little more than warlord fiefdoms dressed up in the more palatable language of regional or district administrations. The militia of the 'Jubba Valley Authority' (JVA) led by Barre Hirale is one such example—the JVA is in reality little more than the occupation of the valuable port of Kismayo by a clan militia. The same was true of the Lower Shabelle Region security forces controlled by 'Governor' Sheikh Indha'adde or the militia of Johwar 'Mayor' Mohamed Dhere. By contrast, in other locations regional authorities have constituted more legitimate administrations, making it somewhat problematic to characterize their security forces as non-state in nature.

The actual size of the armed forces under the control of sub-national polities is not known, but the recent UN Monitoring Group report provides the best estimates yet.[38] The autonomous, non-secessionist state of Puntland's armed forces are believed to be in the range of 6,800 members, and are esti-

---

[36] Baker, 'Nonstate Providers of Everyday Security', p. 130.
[37] Interview by the author, July 2008.
[38] All data in this section on Puntland and Somaliland are derived from UN Security Council, 'Report of the Monitoring Group', paras 30–55.

mated to cost Puntland around $12.8 million (78 per cent of its total budget) per year. The largest portion of the Puntland security sector is the 5,000–man Darawiish, a paramilitary under the control of the Puntland President and his Minister of Security, which engages in a wide range of security operations. About 1,500 Darawiish were deployed to Mogadishu to support the Transitional Federal Government during the 2005–8 period when Abdullahi Yusuf (previously President of Puntland) served as TFG President.[39] The Darawiish have also been deployed to fight against the Somaliland military over the disputed areas of Sool and Sanaag. The Darawiish also support the Puntland police on internal security matters and cooperate closely with the Ethiopian National Defence Force (ENDF), from which they have received training. The Puntland Police force is much smaller, numbering 1,500, about half of whom have received training from the UN Development Programme. Puntland also has a Puntland Intelligence Service of undisclosed size and a 300–person Coast Guard.

From 1999 to 2005, the police and military of Puntland remained under the control of government authorities. When the Puntland President Abdullahi Yusuf won the position of President of the TFG in late 2004, however, he diverted much of the Puntland customs revenue to his 'national' government, depriving Puntland's officials of the ability to pay its security forces and run the administration. The result was the virtual collapse of the Puntland administration. The Darawiish and police resorted to extortion and looting, acting more like criminal gangs than law enforcement units. This plunged the region into the worst levels of insecurity it has experienced since the collapse of the Somali state in 1991. The recent (January 2009) selection of a new Puntland President, Abdirahman Mohamed 'Farole', and the December 2008 resignation of Abdullahi Yusuf as President of the TFG have raised hopes that the Puntland administration will regain control of its customs revenues and security forces. But even in the years when the Puntland administration had firm control over its security sector, it was often very difficult to distinguish between law enforcement and criminal activity there. A 2003 UN Panel of Experts report, commenting on training provided by a foreign security firm to the Puntland coast guard, warned of

---

[39] As of early 2009, some of the Puntland Darawiish are still in Mogadishu, despite the fact that the Mijerteen clan to which most belong lost power in the reconstituted TFG. They are there under the protection of local allied clans who view their continued role in the TFG as critical to the government's legitimacy.

a clear risk that 'coastguard' operations of the kind organized by the Puntland authorities could in fact provide legitimacy for sanctions-busting.... At the same time, the sale of licenses to foreign vessels in exchange for fishing rights has acquired the features of a large-scale protection racket, indistinguishable in most respects from common piracy.[40]

By contrast, Somaliland's security sector has remained under the close control of the government since the mid-1990s, so that one can justify treating those armed forces as VNSAs only by adhering to a very literal interpretation of the term (in that the secessionist Somaliland government remains unrecognized). Somaliland's security personnel are estimated at 15–16,000, including an army of 11,000 (of whom 6,000 are considered active), a police force of 3,000, and a prison officers corps of 1,540. The Somaliland government devotes $7.8 million, or half of its annual budget, to defence. It has successfully reduced the size and cost of its army over the years through demobilization and attrition.[41]

## Sharia courts and the sharia militias

Local, clan-based *sharia* courts began to arise in Mogadishu and towns in southern Somalia in 1995, and quickly became an important source of local public order. They have been closed down since the Ethiopian occupation and the expansion of the TFG's administration in December 2006, but are widely expected to return in some form in the near future. Each court possessed an armed security unit, known as the *sharia* police, which patrolled the streets and was called on to arrest criminals. Members of the *sharia* police were in most cases young gunmen attracted to the courts from warlord militias by the lure of a reliable salary and respectable job. With few exceptions, they were not a *mujahideen* force of committed Islamists.[42] But the courts were able to exercise a reasonable level of control over these units, in the process transforming them from a source of crime to a source of public order. Some but not all of these clan-based *sharia* court police were mobilized to fight the Alliance for the Restoration of Peace and Counter-Terrorism in 2006, and after the defeat of the Alliance many of its fighters were integrated into their clan's *sharia* court militia.

[40] UN Security Council, *Report of the Panel of Experts on Somalia Pursuant to Security Council Resolution 1474*, S/2003/1035 (4 November 2003), para.147.

[41] UN Security Council, *Report of the Monitoring Group*, paras 43–55.

[42] International Crisis Group, *Somalia: Combating Terrorism in a Failed State*, Brussels, May 2002.

## Contemporary armed insurgencies

Numerous armed groups sprang up in opposition to the Ethiopian occupation of parts of Somalia in 2007 and 2008. Collectively this collection of disparate militias is popularly known as the *muqaawama*. By late 2008 they controlled almost all of the territory of south-central Somalia from the southern border of Puntland at Galkayo to the Kenyan border.

*Shabaab* (also known as the *Harakat al-Shabaab al-Mujahidiin*). The *Shabaab* is the best known of a number of radical Islamist insurgencies that have arisen in Somalia since 2003. The decentralized cells which comprise the *Shabaab* militia are the most powerful set of VNSAs in Somalia today. *Al-Shabaab* is an overtly Jihadist movement which employs violent tactics ranging from assassinations to improvised explosive devices to conventional stand-off attacks. The *Shabaab* evolved out of two radical *sharia* courts in Mogadishu in the late 1990s, and subsequently grew into a dedicated, well-trained, multi-clan *mujahideen* force numbering about 400. They answered at that time to the Islamist hardliner Hassan Dahir Aweys, who held a top position in the Islamist umbrella group that eventually became known as the Islamic Courts Union, or ICU. When the ICU was ousted by Ethiopia's military occupation in December 2006, the ICU political leadership fled into exile, but the *Shabaab* regrouped inside Somalia, and soon began to operate as an autonomous force led by Aden Hashi 'Ayro. Tensions between the *Shabaab* and the opposition in exile (which came to be called the Alliance for the Re-liberation of Somalia, or ARS) grew into an open schism when the ex-ICU Islamist leadership joined in a coalition with non-Islamist Somalis in the ARS. Since 2007, the *Shabaab* and militias loyal to the ARS have clashed.

The *Shabaab* movement remains multi-clan in composition but over time power within it has shifted from the Haber Gedir clan, a powerful lineage in Mogadishu that opposed both the TFG and the Ethiopian occupation, to other clans. Clan tensions within the movement are increasingly serious. It is also split over leadership, tactics, and ideology. This was not a serious problem as long as Ethiopian forces occupied Somalia and Abdullahi Yusuf was TFG President—the *Shabaab* could define itself more by what it opposes than what it stands for. It enjoyed considerable passive support from the Somali public as the main source of armed resistance to Ethiopian occupation, and successfully conflated its Islamist agenda with Somali nationalist sentiment.

The *Shabaab* came into the public eye in 2003 and 2004 as perpetrators of a series of political assassinations of both foreign aid workers and Somali political and civic leaders. Targeted murders were not unknown in Somalia but the *Shabaab* took the tactic to new and shocking lengths. It succeeded in intimidating civic, clan, and political leaders to such an extent that few dared to publicly criticize the group. The *Shabaab* also desecrated an Italian colonial cemetery and established a mosque on it, earning a reputation as an extremely violent and radical movement. Internationally, the *Shabaab* gained attention when the US accused it of providing safe haven for a small number of East African al Qaeda (EAAQ) figures who were implicated in terrorist bombings in Kenya in 1998 and 2002. The refusal by Islamist and clan leaders to accept this accusation against the *Shabaab* heightened tensions between the US and the Islamists in 2005–6 and accelerated American efforts to work through local proxies to monitor and apprehend foreign terror suspects believed to be in Mogadishu.[43]

In their insurgency against the Ethiopians and the TFG, the *Shabaab* introduced a number of new tactics, many copied from the insurgency in Iraq, including widespread use of improvised explosive devices (IEDs) and occasional use of suicide bombers.[44] They also engaged in high-pressure recruitment in local schools (linked to threats against the families of recruits if they failed to join). They specifically used densely populated neighbourhoods as bases from which they launched mortar attacks, in an effort to bait Ethiopian forces to shell those areas indiscriminately, prompting further public outrage.

During late 2007 and into 2008, the *Shabaab*'s advances grew bolder. Initially the group seized towns for a brief period and then withdrew, but by early 2008 it began to hold territory, including the major port town of Kismayo near the Kenya border. The *Shabaab* initially demonstrated little capacity for or interest in governing; it typically handed over administration of 'liberated' towns to local clan authorities with whom it established a basic understanding. This was not surprising, given that the *Shabaab* had been strictly a militia with no capacity for or experience in politics. But that changed by mid-2008, when the group began to directly administer areas under its control. That produced a number of horrifying episodes, including the stoning of a young rape victim in Kismayo, that fuelled considerable anxiety in Somali communities and helped fuel local resistance to the *Shabaab* by late 2008. But by then the *Shabaab* and allied extremists had gained control over all of the territory from the Kenyan border to the outskirts of Mogadishu.

---

[43] International Crisis Group, *Counter-terrorism in Somalia: Losing Hearts and Minds?* ICG Africa Report no. 95, Brussels, 11 July 2005.

[44] Suicide is taboo in Somali culture and was virtually unknown in the country, though it is now becoming more common in the Somali diaspora. The introduction of suicide attacks is a dramatic break from the past.

In April 2008 the US government designated the *Shabaab* a terrorist group, and in May US forces launched a missile attack on a home in the remote town of Dusa Mareb which killed the *Shabaab* leader Aden Hashi 'Ayro. The *Shabaab* subsequently pledged to target all Americans and Westerners in Somalia and the region, as well as governments allied to the US. This has resulted in a bloodbath of assassinations, making Somalia the most dangerous place in the world for humanitarian workers in 2008 and leading to suspension of most humanitarian operations in the country. In a reflection of the growing splintering of the movement, not all *Shabaab* leaders embraced this policy. Indeed, one of the top leaders of the *Shabaab* since Ayro's death, Sheikh Robow, condemned attacks on national and international aid workers and is known to have provided security for aid convoys moving through his home regions. Robow followed that up, however, with threats against CARE, forcing that aid group to suspend operations.

At present, most observers concur that the *Shabaab* faces real difficulties. It no longer has the Ethiopians to fight, and the new TFG is led by a moderate Islamist, Sheikh Sharif. Local clan militias have successfully resisted *Shabaab* attempts to push into new territory in Mogadishu and in outlying areas. The Somali political leaders, including Islamists in the ARS, appear to have used the *Shabaab* to resist the Ethiopian occupation but now view the *Shabaab* as the main threat. Most of the *Shabaab*'s recruits since 2006 are not indoctrinated *mujahideen*, but simply young men and boys who were recruited under pressure or whose motives were more anti-Ethiopian than Jihadist. There is a real chance that the *Shabaab* hit its high water mark in late 2008 and will now face a lengthy period of retrenchment, co-optation, and marginalization. Even so, the *Shabaab* remains a very dangerous force in both Somalia and beyond. Its growing links to al Qa'ida are real, its capacity to indoctrinate suicide bombers was made evident in five synchronized terrorist bombings in Somaliland and Puntland in October 2008, and its ability to recruit from the large Somali diaspora is a source of major concern. The fact that one of the October suicide bombers was a Somali from Minneapolis raised fears that *Shabaab* could potentially engineer a terrorist attack well beyond its borders by using its diaspora members.[45]

*Other hardline Islamist armed groups.* Several other jihadist groups have emerged in Somalia since 2007. Jabhadda Islaamiga Soomaaliyeed, or JABISO, appeared on the scene in late December and is reported to be an

---

[45] For an excellent and more detailed breakdown of the *shabaab*'s sub-units and leadership, see UN Security Council, *Report of the Monitoring Group*, paras 71–86.

armed wing of al-Itisaam bil Kitaab al Sunna, a successor body to the once prominent Somali Islamist movement Al-Ittihad al-Islamiyya (AIAI). AIAI controlled several towns in Somalia for periods of time from 1991 to 1996 and had some links to al Qaeda, though the East Africa al Qaeda cell had considerable difficulty dealing with clan splits in the movement and with resistance on the part of some AIAI leaders to pursuing *jihad* against the United States.[46] AIAI was attacked and dispersed by Ethiopian forces in 1996, at which point AIAI opted to dissolve itself and exist as a loose network.[47]

Little is known about JABISO. It is believed to have several hundred fighters; it collaborates with the ARS but not with *Shabaab*, for ideological reasons. The UN Monitoring Group suggests that JABISO may have ties to the United Western Somali Liberation Front (UWSLF) in eastern Ethiopia, and, like the *Shabaab*, is likely to receive some support from Eritrea.[48]

Another radical Islamist armed group in southern Somalia is Ras Kamboni Mujahidiin, a group of Jihadist fighters based in the remote coastal areas of southernmost Somalia near the Kenyan border. This group, which is generally associated with the Ogaden clan, is linked to the hard-line leader Hassan Turki and has operational capacity both on the Kenyan side of the border and as far north as Mogadishu, where it has launched attacks on the Ethiopians and African Union peacekeepers (AMISOM). Turki cooperates with the *Shabaab*, has links to al Qaeda, and has been designated a terrorism suspect by the US government.[49]

A Jihadist group linked to the Marehan clan, also based in the Jubba region near the Kenyan border, is the Khalid bin Walid militia. It is more closely aligned with the ARS than with the *Shabaab*. Like the Ras Kamboni group, Khalid bin Walid forces took part in the successful takeover of Kismayo and have sought to play a role in Mogadishu.[50]

## Insurgencies now in government: the ARS

*Alliance for the Re-Liberation of Somalia (ARS).* The ARS was an umbrella opposition movement formed in Asmara, capital of Eritrea, in September

[46]Combating Terrorism Center, *Al Qaeda's (Mis)Adventures in the Horn of Africa*, West Point, NY: US Military Academy, 2007, pp. 29–46. http://www.ctc.usma.edu/aqII.asp.

[47] International Crisis Group, *Somalia's Islamists*, Brussels/Nairobi: ICG Africa Report no. 100 (12 December 2005).

[48] UN Security Council, *Report of the Monitoring Group*, paras 67–70.

[49] For more details, see ibid., paras 87–92.

[50] Ibid.

2007 and composed of Islamists from the former Islamic Courts Union, opposition parliamentarians who were expelled from the transitional parliament, and diaspora members. As a broad umbrella movement, the ARS represented a wide range of political viewpoints and was as a result better able to articulate what it was against—the Ethiopian military occupation of Somalia, and the TFG as it was then composed—rather than what it was for. Upon its formation, it was dismissed as irrelevant by the TFG, the *Shabaab*, and external actors like the Ethiopian and American governments, on the ground that it 'lacked a constituency' inside Somalia and exercised no control over any armed forces inside the country.

In 2008, the group split into two wings, the ARS-Djibouti (the moderate wing led by Sharif Hassan and Sheikh Sharif, know as the 'two Sharifs'), and the ARS-Asmara, a rejectionist group led by the hard-liner Hassan Dahir Aweys, who has been designated a terrorist suspect by the US government. The ARS leadership split over the decision by moderates in the group to agree to UN-sponsored peace talks with the TFG; hardliners opposed holding talks until their demand for full Ethiopian withdrawal from Somalia was met. Both wings of the ARS have built militia capacity inside Somalia, generally through deals struck with sympathetic clan militias who remain largely autonomous in terms of command and control. The ARS became a significant force in the anti-Ethiopian insurgency in 2008 with development of special units with heavy weapons, the best known of which is the *Jugta Culus* (Heavy Strike Force).[51] This has given both wings of the ARS new clout. But the highly decentralized nature of the militias, and the fact that they are mainly loyal to sub-clan interests in their local areas, mean that the ARS leadership cannot always proceed to action.

The moderate wing of the ARS reached an accord—the 'Djibouti Agreement'—with the moderate Prime Minister of the TFG in summer of 2008. That deal eventually produced an expanded unity parliament and the selection of a new President, Sheikh Sharif. At the time of this writing the new TFG has yet to select a Prime Minister or form a cabinet. The ARS-Djibouti has essentially become the new government, so that its militia—considered insurgents in the past, and terrorists by the old TFG—will now be considered a standing army, once it is integrated with the existing TFG military. For reasons noted below, this will be a very difficult task. Talks were held between militia commanders of the two wings of the ARS in late 2008 in Jalalaqsi,

[51] Ibid.

with the aim of affirming the unity of the ARS. Whether the two can actually reach an agreement to co-exist remains to be seen.

## Anti-Jihadist resistance groups

*Al Sunna wal Jama'a.* In response to the *Shabaab*'s dramatic success in capturing territory in southern Somalia, Ethiopia's post-intervention strategy has included providing backing to clan-based militias opposing the advance of Jihadist groups. These loose collections of militia have come to call themselves an Islamic front, Al-Sunna wal Jama'a, representing traditional Somali Sunni Muslims. In practice, al-Sunna is merely an exercise in rehatting and should not be confused with a genuine Islamist movement. 'A lot of militia groups and warlords are now trying to adapt to this new Islamist fashion, to reorganize themselves under the Islamist banner and crush the Shabaab', observed one Somali interviewed for a recent article in the *Washington Post*. 'I think they are just taking the label as a political opportunity.'[52] The most important aspect of these clan militias opposing the *Shabaab* is not what they call themselves, but the fact that they appear to be enjoying success, and are the most promising answer to the advance of the *Shabaab*.

## Transitional Federal Government paramilitaries

*TFG para-militaries.* Among the most problematic and complex VNSAs in Somalia today are the militia units which answer to a leader in the Transitional Federal Government and are therefore technically part of the TFG security forces, but which act autonomously from the TFG cabinet and are in reality clan-based para-militaries. Three units are or were especially important in this regard: the municipal security forces of the former Mogadishu Mayor Mohamed Dhere, the police force answering to the Chief of Police Abdi Hassan Awale 'Qeybdiid', and the security forces under the command of the National Security Services chief Mohamed Ali Warsame 'Darawiish'. Until his resignation, President Yusuf also commanded his own forces which answered directly to him. In the town of Baidoa, where until January 2009 the TFG maintained its parliament (the town was taken over by the *Shabaab* in January 2009), an additional paramilitary force, the Digle-Mirifle Liberation Army,

---

[52] Stephanie McCrummen, 'With Ethiopian pullout, Islamists rise again in Somalia', *Washington Post* 22 January 2009, p. A10 http://www.washingtonpost.com/wp-dyn/content/story/2009/01/21/ST2009012104112.html

was nominally integrated into the TFG security forces, and answered to the Governor of Bay region.

Estimating the number of security forces in the TFG has been very difficult because very many of the newly trained recruits promptly defect—with their weapons—to the armed insurgency or join criminal gangs. The UN Monitoring Group estimates the attrition rate at 80 per cent, and suggests that fewer than 3,000 may now be effective.[53] The TFG police force numbers 6,862, but has also seen defections.

These militias have been responsible for much of the predatory violence and crime directed against the Mogadishu population, mimicking the behaviour of warlord militias and armed gangs that plagued the capital up to 2006. They have also manned most of the armed checkpoints in and around the Mogadishu area, extorting money from vehicles and international aid convoys. Rival TFG paramilitary units have frequently engaged in armed clashes with one another over lucrative checkpoints. TFG ministers complain that these armed forces refuse to answer to their appropriate ministries and are a law unto themselves.[54] The inability of the TFG cabinet throughout 2007 and 2008 to control any armed forces rendered the cabinet extremely weak. In an extraordinary public acknowledgement of the loss of government control over these security forces, the Prime Minister in April 2008 demanded that they 'disarm' and hand over their weapons to the TFG.[55] The phenomenon of militia leaders taking on formal government titles of minister, mayor, and police chief but continuing to command their own paramilitaries and engage in predatory behaviour towards the civilian population is not unique to Somalia; it reinforces theories of predatory state structures and intentional de-institutionalization of states, developed by a number of social scientists in other conflict settings.[56] One of the major challenges facing the newly-reconstituted TFG under President Sheikh Sharif will be to bring these paramilitaries back under control.

## Assessment

*Political power and the ubiquity of violence as a tactic.* These case studies of VNSAs in Somalia reinforce the point that political power in the country

---

[53] UN Security Council, *Report of the Monitoring Group*, para 19.

[54] Author's interviews, Nairobi, March 2008.

[55] 'Somalia: Ethiopians Disarm Warlord', All-Africa.com, 11 May 2008 http://allafrica.com/stories/200805120009.html [accessed July 11 2008].

[56] See Will Reno, *Warlord States and African Politics*, Boulder: Lynne Rienner, 2000; and Andersen, Moller and Stepputat (eds) *Fragile States and Insecure People?*

today is closely linked to the ability to use or threaten to use violence. No political actor in Somalia is at present able to exercise 'soft power' of any consequence, unless it is twinned with an ability to mobilize armed violence as well. The most dramatic example of this is the TFG Prime Minister, Hassan Hussein Nuur Adde, and his cabinet.[57] Though they have been widely lauded as a voice of moderation, reconciliation, and good governance since replacing the previous Prime Minister and cabinet in late 2007, and though they enjoy considerable goodwill domestically and internationally, Nuur Adde and his government have been unable to translate that goodwill into political clout because of their complete lack of control over any armed forces. They are, in many respects, under house arrest, held hostage by elements within their own government. This point is also reinforced by the ARS, which in 2007 and 2008 quickly improved its political status and bargaining position in Somalia by making a concerted effort to build up a coalition of armed opposition forces willing to affiliate with the ARS. At the clan level, lineages such as the Digle-Mirifle which were marginalized politically in the 1990s have earned greater representation in Somali affairs since they gave themselves credible armed strength in the late 1990s. Finally, the case study of the *Shabaab* demonstrates that even a small group can enjoy magnified political importance if it is able to 'punch above its weight' in use of political violence. One of the great challenges of reconciliation and state-building in Somalia is creating greater political space for NSAs that do not command a capacity to employ violence but are critical to successful peace-building in the country. Civil society groups are at the top of this list.

Violence is not merely a tool used by leaders seeking power and groups seeking to control resources in Somalia. In the absence of a functioning state, households and communities rely heavily on the ability of clan or neighbourhood watch groups to threaten use of violence as a deterrent against attack or crimes by members of other lineages. Indeed, the threat of violence is an important source of conflict and crime prevention in Somalia. Like other forms of armed deterrence it tends to create a 'security dilemma', in which one clan's efforts to deter attack increase a neighbouring clan's sense of insecurity, producing the risk of a local arms race. But in Somalia this dynamic is at least partially offset by the constantly shifting nature of clan alliances, driven in no small part by a desire to maintain a rough balance of power to prevent any one clan from riding roughshod over others.

[57] Nuur Adde is likely to lose his post as Prime Minister as part of the formation of a new government, but his replacement had not been named at the time of writing (February 2009).

The threat of force each clan can muster in defence of its members provides an unspoken level of personal protection even to individuals who do not control or hire personal security. Professionals, journalists, and civil society leaders, for instance, are often able to take more openly critical positions against warlords and Islamists based on the expectation that their particular clan affiliation affords them protection. But this is a calculated risk, and one that has become much more dangerous in recent years thanks to the much more aggressive use of assassination and death threats on the part of both the *Shabaab* and the TFG.

*Rules and taboos governing the use of violence in contemporary Somalia.* There is a tendency in contemporary discussions of the Somali crisis to overstate the extent to which the 'rules of the game' regarding warfare and criminality have been transformed since 1991. Specifically, some observers portray 'traditional' armed violence in Somalia as bound by an extensive set of unwritten codes, all of which have been overwhelmed by the complete breakdown of social norms and taboos since the collapse of the state.[58] Likewise, armed criminality is said to have been transformed by the breakdown of customary law, or *xeer*, during the civil war, and the concomitant weakening of traditional elders' authority. There is truth to these claims—many taboos regarding use of violence in Somalia have been shattered in the past two decades, as is discussed below. But it is important not to romanticize Somalia's pre-colonial or post-colonial past. *Xeer* helped to deter levels of armed violence but did not prevent atrocities, and the Somali people's long history of migration and expansion is largely a story of conquest and displacement, not negotiation and co-existence. Likewise, some of the most egregious violation of social taboos regarding use of violence were committed by the government of Siyad Barre, which distinguished itself as one of the worst abusers of human rights in post-independence Africa.

Despite all this, there is a widespread sense among Somalis that long-standing rules regarding use of armed violence have been broken by VNSAs since 1991. Two periods of 'regime collapse' have been especially severe—first, the episode of uncontrolled, 'Mad Max' violence of 1988–92 (from the peak of civil war to the arrival of US-led UN peacekeepers in December 1992), and then in the period since 2003, which began with a 'dirty war' of political assassinations and was followed by unprecedented uses of violence in both

---

[58] One effort to revive traditional codes of conduct for war in Somalia was a publication by International Committee of the Red Cross, 'Spared by the Spear', Geneva, 1993.

the insurgency and counter-insurgency. In the period 1993–2003, there was a general trend toward reassertion of 'rules of the game' regarding use of violence.

The period of civil war in Somalia from 1988 to 1992 shattered many rules regarding the use of violence. The first violations were committed in 1988–89 by the Siyad Barre regime, which used mercenary pilots to flatten the country's second largest city, Hargeisa, and intentionally targeted fleeing civilians. This led to the deaths of as many as 50,000 northern Somalis and was characterized as genocidal by a US Congressional report.[59] In 1989–90, retreating regime forces engaged in scorched earth tactics in southern Somalia, looting the countryside and rendering populations there vulnerable to famine in 1991. Finally, that regime executed a large number of elders and political leaders from rival clans in 1989–90, in some cases in mass executions.[60] These egregious violations of human rights—aerial bombardments of cities, intentional targeting of fleeing civilians (and the tactic of collective punishment it reflected), scorched earth tactics, and group executions—were unprecedented in Somalia.[61] It is important to note that the wave of broken taboos regarding violence was initiated not by Somalia's many non-state actors, but by a dictatorial and uncontrolled state.

With the collapse of the state in January 1991, clan militias and gangs engaged in an orgy of uncontrolled violence. Initially the violence began with the ethnic cleansing of the capital. Members of clans associated with the Siyad Barre regime were especially targeted, as were members of weak minority clans unable to defend themselves. Acts of violence previously unheard of in Somalia—massacres of orphans, mass executions of clan elders, killing of pregnant women, and mutilation—became part of the cycle of violence and revenge attacks that defined much of the period. Rape of women from rival clans or weak social groups was especially endemic, and shattered long-standing taboos. Young men from weak social groups were forcibly conscripted as porters at gunpoint, becoming virtual slaves of militia groups. Repeated looting

[59] Robert Gersony, 'Why Somalis Flee: A Synthesis of Conflict Experience in Northern Somalia by Somali Refugees, Displaced Persons, and Others', *International Journal of Refugee Law*, Vol. 2, No. 1, 1990, pp. 4–55.

[60] Africa Watch, *Somalia: A Government at War with Its Own People*, London: Africa Watch, 1990.

[61] The Siyad Barre regime had executed ten dissident Muslim clerics in 1975, a move which shocked Somalis, and so the group executions of 1988–90 were not entirely unprecedented.

of communities caught in the shatter zone of the war, and then looting of international food relief, may or may not have been intentionally designed to produce famine, but they constituted another new and deadly form of violence in the country, contributing to an estimated 250,000 war- and famine-related deaths in Somalia in 1991–92. In Mogadishu, factional fighting introduced the tactic of indiscriminate bombardments of neighbourhoods (mainly by mortars and rocket propelled grenades), resulting in the destruction of much of the city centre and extensive casualties among civilians. General Aideed's faction introduced another new element into Somalia's warfare in his battle against UNOSOM forces in 1993, when he used women as human shields for his armed men. In what became emblematic of the breakdown of old regulations on the conduct of war, a T-shirt which read, in English, 'I am the Boss' was highly popular among Somalia's uncontrolled teenage gunmen.

Over the next ten years, teenage gunmen were no longer 'the Boss', as clan elders, *sharia* courts, and private security forces reduced gratuitous criminal violence in the urban areas. The main exception to this rule was the spike in highly lethal pastoral violence over access to pasture and wells; the widespread availability of semi-automatic weaponry, combined with growing pressures on rangeland, produced clan clashes resulting in death tolls as high as 50 to 100, a shocking increase compared with traditional clashes over land and water.

A new wave of violence began in 2003–4, with the aggressive use of political assassination by the *Shabaab*, producing a 'dirty war' between them and Ethiopian and US proxies in Somalia.[62] In response to the December 2006 Ethiopian occupation, the *Shabaab* and other insurgent groups embraced a range of new tactics which have broken taboos on the use of violence, including extensive use of roadside bombs (IEDs) and suicide bombings. Ethiopia contributed to the erosion of what few codes of conduct of warfare remained in Somalia by indiscriminate bombing of civilian areas where insurgents were based, including in one case use of white phosphorous bombs to empty an entire neighbourhood.[63]

Other forms of violence which had no precedent in Somalia also arose in the first decade of the new millennium. Piracy quickly became a lucrative

---

[62] International Crisis Group, *Counter-Terrorism in Somalia*, pp. 10–16.
[63] UN Monitoring Group, *Report of the Monitoring Group on Somalia Pursuant to UN Security Council Resolution 1724 (2006)*, S/2007/436, 27 June 2007, pp. 12–13 http://www.securitycouncilreport.org/atf/cf/%7B65BFCF9B-6D27–4E9C-8CD3–CF6E4FF96FF9%7D/SOMALIA%20S2007436.pdf [accessed July 11 2008]

epidemic on the Somali coast. And traffickers of migrants from the northeast coast of Somalia to Yemen began to adopt lethal practices of throwing passengers overboard when spotted by coastal patrols, resulting in hundreds of deaths. Collectively, all of these new and often deadly forms of violence have contributed to a strong sense that old norms and rules governing use of violence have been abandoned.

*Economic sustainability of violent non-state actors.* VNSAs have had to adopt new sources of funding over the past 17 years. In the early years of civil war, clan-based factional militias were able to sustain themselves through a combination of war booty (the way unpaid gunmen were recompensed in practice, and a windfall profit for warlords engaged in export of scrap metal) and fundraising by clan members in the diaspora. During UNOSOM's two and a half year intervention, fortunes were made by conducting business with the UN operation. Construction contracts, procurement, security, and property and vehicle rental were all big business surrounding an operation that cost an estimated $1.5 billion per year. Militia leaders were able to 'park' their gunmen as paid security guards for the UN and many NGOs in the country, and the more enterprising militia leaders switched into legitimate business. This shift from 'warlord to landlord' helped to create a new set of interests in public order and governance on the part of some individuals who had previously been conflict entrepreneurs, and contributed to the rise of a business class which helped to fund local governance and security arrangements upon the departure of UNOSOM in 1995.

In the late 1990s, factional militias' inability to secure a sustained flow of revenue was key to their gradual dissolution. Business leaders were unwilling to pay protection money to them, and bought militiamen out from under them; private security forces limited opportunities to loot; international aid agencies had greatly reduced their presence and were no longer a cash cow; and the diaspora grew weary of funding warlords.[64] Armed groups continued to man roadblocks to collect 'taxes' from vehicular traffic, but in general the opportunities to extort and loot to raise funds were considerably reduced.[65]

The VNSAs who replaced the factions from the late 1990s have a much wider range and arguably a more sustainable flow of revenue. Private business security forces are now part of the cost of doing business in Somalia and are

---

[64] Nonetheless, the diaspora still continues to play a role in funnelling funds to armed groups, as well as to the pirates.

[65] Menkhaus, 'Governance without Government.'

funded out of the profits from the businesses—unquestionably the most sustainable revenue flow of any VNSA. Militia leaders in possession of commercial assets—airstrips, beach-ports, and main commercial arteries—have seen their 'customs' collection interrupted by the Ethiopian occupation and efforts by the TFG to appropriate these assets, but are likely to regain control of these sources of revenue if the TFG fails. The *sharia* court militias have been disbanded by the TFG, but are also likely to be revived should the TFG fails, and will again be underwritten by businesspeople.

Clan militias continue to be funded principally by their clan members, mainly through fundraising by the clan elders. This is the most enduring type of support among all the VNSAs in Somalia, but it is episodic, driven by periodic security threats to the clan.

Armed insurgent groups—mainly the *Shabaab* and the ARS militias—receive financial and military support from Eritrea, in some cases provided by third party states in the Gulf.[66] Both the Islamic Courts Union (ICU) and the *Shabaab* have also received support from private sources in the Islamic world, including al Qaeda. Somali businesses and diaspora members have also contributed to Islamist militias. The *Shabaab*'s designation as a terrorist group by the US is likely to dry up contributions from fearful diaspora members. Perhaps unsurprisingly, given the extent of the war economy in Somalia, recent reports have alleged that the *Shabaab* and other armed insurgents are able to purchase arms from both African Union peacekeepers and Ethiopian forces, who are confiscating arms and then reselling them in the Mogadishu market.[67]

The VNSAs enjoying the most robust flow of revenue since 2007 are the paramilitaries within the TFG. But the sustainability of these revenue sources is very precarious. Until he was replaced, Mayor Mohamed Dhere's 'municipal' militia was funded by his control over the Mogadishu seaport and its customs revenue, a flow of income that the Prime Minister actively sought to wrest from him. The police were for a time earning salaries from international donors, but those salaries were suspended following serious allegations that the police were looting markets and assaulting civilians. Today, the police are earning a living mainly from the roadblocks they and other unpaid security forces are manning in the capital.

[66] UN Security Council, *Report of the Monitoring Group*, p. 9.
[67] Agence France Presse, 'UN accuses Uganda peacekeepers of arming Somali rebels', 23 May 2008 http://afp.google.com/article/ALeqM5j38l_J3FfV00Bep1bT_tXjLOQb4Q [accessed 11 July 2008]

The most important dimension to the question of economic sustainability of Somali VNSAs is that for many, the very sources of economic revenue which allow them to continue to operate would be threatened were a functional government established. This means that some of the VNSAs in Somalia today are seeking to use violence not in order to gain control of the state, but to block the establishment of a government. Assessing whose economic (and political) interests are threatened by state revival is a critical step in identifying spoilers in peace processes.

*Links between VNSAs and external actors.* As noted above, several of the most powerful VNSAs in Somalia today depend heavily on external sources of funds. In some respects this is inevitable, since the entire Somali economy is so heavily dependent on flows of funds from abroad, especially foreign aid and remittances from the diaspora. What is less obvious is how viable these VNSAs would be if they were cut off from external support. This is an especially important question in light of the fact that the armed conflicts which have devastated Mogadishu since 2006 have been, to a significant degree, proxy wars involving Ethiopia and Eritrea, with the US and Islamist patrons playing an important role as well. Ethiopia's support to President Yusuf and his TFG administration was essential to its creation and four-year survival, and both Ethiopia and the US have been important sources of support to armed groups within the TFG security sector. The ICU, ARS and *Shabaab* have all relied on Eritrea, some Gulf states, and private Islamist sources of funding.

Virtually all VNSAs in Somalia have sought, with varying degrees of success, to tap into the flow of international relief and development money entering the country. Some have created or infiltrated local charities to win contracts from international aid agencies. Others have 'captured' international NGOs operating in their territory, monopolizing an organization's vehicle and building rental and employment. Some of the more powerful militia leaders control transport companies and ports and earn considerable revenue from managing the movement of food relief. In a few cases, warlords with business operations have been known to intentionally incite insecurity and displacement in order to generate international food aid flows which provide them with new transport contracts.

Though heavily dependent on external backers and patrons for funds and weapons, VNSAs in Somalia are rarely if ever puppets of foreign actors. Instead they seek to manipulate outsiders—by professing commitment to a shared ideology or set of policy objectives—to win as much assistance from them as possible, all the while pursuing objectives that are often at variance with the interests of their patrons. Both the Somali state and non-state actors have been extraordinarily opportunistic with regard to foreign ideologies and interests that might earn external assistance. The Siyad Barre government, for instance, was famous for manipulating Somalia's geo-strategic importance to win foreign aid from the USSR (in the 1970s) and the West (in the 1980s), committing itself to 'scientific socialism' and then quickly rejecting it once the close ties with the USSR were broken in 1977. More recently, Somali militia leaders and politicians have scrambled to position themselves as 'anti-terrorist' to win favour from the US in the post-9/11 era. For its part, Somalia's opposition has emphasized its Islamist credentials in order to maximize access to revenue flows from the Islamic world, even as it accepts advisers and aid from avowedly secular Eritrea on the basis of the time-honoured principle of 'the enemy of my enemy is my friend'.

*Legitimacy of VNSAs in Somalia.* Contested legitimacy has been an enduring problem for most Somali actors, both violent and non-violent, during the period of prolonged state collapse. Some VNSAs have fared better than others on this score. As a general rule, their legitimacy waxes and wanes according to the extent to which they constitute a source of security or insecurity to some or all of the Somali public. Those which have been linked to efforts to provide security and governance—such as the *sharia* court militias and neighbourhood watch groups—have enjoyed relatively high levels of legitimacy in the public eye. Likewise, armed groups actively combating Ethiopian forces, such as the *Shabaab* and the ARS militia, legitimized themselves for much of the public by claiming to be a liberation movement and nationalist resistance to foreign occupation. Leaders of armed gangs, paramilitaries, and clan militias which are closely associated with crime, looting, or spoiling peace processes have very low legitimacy in the country.

Clan militias are the most complex of this group, in that they have very conflictual relations with their clan constituencies. On the one hand, on a day-to-day level they are a chronic source of crime and insecurity, and their leaders often take on many of the characteristics of warlords. Their own clansmen and elders complain about them and, in times of relative peace, often seek to weaken them. But at the same time the clan can ill afford to marginalize its militia leaders, because in times of heightened insecurity its members' security depends on the capacity of the militia to defend them. This gives militia leaders every incentive to stoke communal tensions, as that elevates their own importance as defenders of a clan.

Recent developments in Mogadishu have provided new insights into the problems and prospects of legitimacy of VNSAs in Somalia. First, the *Shabaab* has seen its fortunes rise and fall and rise again as it has assumed new roles in the Somali drama. Its initial move into Somali politics, in which it employed shocking levels of political violence, generated fear but not respect in Mogadishu. Its legitimacy rose with its impressive victory over the Alliance militias in 2006, which was perceived as a defeat of warlordism. The *Shabaab*'s equally shocking defeat at the hands of Ethiopian forces again undermined its standing with the public, but its revival as leader in the armed resistance to Ethiopian occupation has earned it greater levels of legitimacy among the Somali public than ever. With the Ethiopian withdrawal, the *Shabaab* again faces an ebb in its local support.

The experience of the TFG security forces provides a different set of lessons about legitimacy in Somalia. Because the paramilitary units answering to Mohamed Dhere, Qeybdiid, and Darwish successfully assumed formal roles in the TFG—even while remaining autonomous, predatory armed groups— they enjoyed valuable levels of external legitimacy from donors and the UN even as their domestic legitimacy remained very low.

*Community control over violence.* Efforts by community and civic leaders to control armed violence have been an enduring theme of the past 19 years of state collapse. Success in co-opting, containing and constraining VNSAs has varied from place to place and over time. The most successful communal efforts to control violence have occurred through a combination of factors. First, co-optation—in the form of provision of paid employment to gunmen under the control of a responsible third party (*sharia* court administration, private business, or local government)—has been the most consistently successful tactic; where gunmen have opportunities for more predictable, less violent, regularly paid, and respectable employment they have almost always taken that option. Second, communities which have managed to revive some form of local governance—often hybrid arrangements drawing on customary law, *sharia* law, and formal municipal administration—have been better able to deter violent crime by VNSAs. At times, communities have had some success in shaming VNSAs into better behaviour, as was evidenced in the extraordinary public mobilization against militia roadblocks in the summer of 2005 in Mogadishu.[68] Community-based efforts have not, however, been able to

[68] Menkhaus, 'Tragedy in Five Acts'.

deter broader communal and factional clashes over resources and power, and despite courageous initiatives by some civic leaders, they have proved easily intimidated and silenced by the threat of political assassination. Three categories of leadership which ought to have the clout to exercise some influence on VNSAs—clan elders, Muslim clerics, and business leaders—have in reality been relatively weak for that purpose. The result has been vacillation in security conditions and the autonomy of VNSAs; local communities will succeed for a time in pulling together arrangements to constrain armed violence, only to plunge into renewed levels of armed clashes and criminality. Some local communities in Somalia have endured several cycles of violence and relative peace over the past two decades. This reflects the fragile nature of community efforts to control violence and the actors predisposed to incite violence in pursuit of their interests.

## Conclusion

The effective revival of a functional central government in Somalia would help to reduce, if not eliminate, the ubiquity of violence on the part of the many armed groups operating in the country today. It would also reduce the extent to which political power is directly linked to the capacity to muster a credible threat of violence, eventually normalizing political life and rendering the threat of violence an unacceptable and illegal tactic in politics. Perhaps most important, an effective state would eliminate the need on the part of Somali households and communities to rely on a clan-based threat of force as a deterrent to crime.

Unfortunately, efforts to revive the Somali state have met with consistent failure, and prospects for success in the near future are not good. Even if a viable central government is set up, it will take years before it has the capacity to begin eliminating VNSAs' activities.

As it happens, it may not be necessary or even advisable to eliminate all VNSAs. As this chapter has sought to demonstrate, some of Somalia's panoply of VNSAs are providing security to communities and neighbourhoods and are viewed as legitimate, valued sources of public safety and order. They are an important part of the evolution of 'governance without government' in Somalia. The trajectory that state revival in the country will take is unknown, but one possibility is a mediated state arrangement in which a weak central government at least temporarily cedes authority for policing and security to legitimate local non-state actors. This is in fact already an informal practice in a number of weak states from Sudan to Afghanistan, and while it produces a number of problems, they may be more manageable problems than those associated with the current state of state collapse and insecurity in the country.

# 17

# Liberation Tigers of Tamil Eelam (LTTE)

## Failed Quest for a 'Homeland'

*Syed Rifaat Hussain*

Amongst the contemporary violent non-state actors, the Liberation Tigers of Tamil Eelam (LTTE) are one of the best known. From their emergence in the early 1970s, the LTTE waged a relentless armed insurgency in the north and east of Sri Lanka in pursuit of their goal to secure a homeland for the Tamil people, until their defeat in 2009. The LTTE-led armed Tamil insurgency, besides killing over 64,000 people, posed mortal dangers to the political independence, sovereignty and territorial integrity of the Sri Lankan state. This chapter focuses on the genesis and rise of the LTTE as a violent non-state actor, their tactical and strategic behaviour as an armed entity, and their ability to sustain themselves as a viable militant outfit. These issues are examined against the backdrop of the changing dynamics of ethnic conflict in Sri Lanka and the various failed attempts, including the 2002 ceasefire agreement, to end the deadly conflict. The analysis concludes by examining the prospects of the LTTE's survival as a banned entity which suffered military defeat in 2008–9.

## Introduction

Violent non-state actors (VNSAs) present several challenges to the authority of the state. First, some groups have developed capabilities to strike high-value targets across the globe through asymmetric means. The 9/11 attacks on the United States and the 7 July 2005 bombings in London epitomize this trend. The increased capacities of VNSAs have resulted from such factors as the interconnectedness and openness of modern societies which afford them global mobility and influence, easy availability of modern weaponry and explosives, enhanced opportunities to collect and transfer funds necessary for operations, and inherent difficulties faced by states in detecting and controlling their operations.[1] Second, by employing standard terrorist and insurgent tactics some VNSAs have tended to undermine prospects for regional peace and stability. For instance, the 2001/2 military confrontation between nuclear-armed India and Pakistan was provoked by a terrorist attack on the Indian parliament, which New Delhi believed had been perpetrated by a terrorist group backed by Islamabad. Third, VNSAs' activities pose mortal dangers to the internal stability and national cohesion of many developing states. Because of these challenges, the rise of armed groups has been described as a 'tier-one security problem'[2] facing the world today. Problems of state fragility and vulnerability facing developing countries have been greatly compounded by the activities of VNSAs.

The rise of VNSAs to global prominence is linked to the phenomena of failing states marked by 'weakened capacity, deeply divided societies, devastated economies, squandered resources, traumatized populations ... international organized crime and black market networks.'[3] How state failure promotes VNSAs is well depicted by Chester Crocker who notes that 'self-interested rulers...progressively corrupt the central organs of government', and they 'ally themselves with criminal networks to divide the spoils.' Consequently, the authority of the state is 'undermined...paving the way for illegal

---

[1] George P. Shultz and Coit Blacker, *Preventive Force: Issues for Discussion*, Stanford University Press, 2008, pp. 13–14. The enabling influence of globalization on terrorism is well noted by Tom Farer: 'For Al Qaeda and its ideological off-springs have arrived, not by chance, coincident with the integration of national economies into a global economic order vitally dependent on transportation and communications networks vulnerable to catastrophic attacks by militants able to access the very instrumentalities and technologies that have made integration possible.' Tom Farer, *Confronting Global Terrorism and American Neo-Conservatism: The Framework of a Liberal Grand Strategy*, New York: Oxford University Press, 2008, p. 2.

[2] Richard H. Shultz, Douglas Farah and Itamarah V. Lochard, *Armed Groups: A Tier-one Security Problem*, Colorado Springs: USAF Institute for National Security Studies, USAF Academy, 2004, p. 1.

[3] Monty Marshall and Ted Robert Gurr, *Peace and Conflict, 2003*, Maryland: University of Maryland Press, 2003, pp. 1 and 15.

operations.' In conjunction with these developments, 'state security services lose their monopoly on the instruments of violence, leading to a downward spiral of lawlessness.' And, 'when the state failure sets in, the balance of power shifts...in favour of armed entities [groups] outside the law' who 'find space in the vacuums left by declining or transitional states.'[4]

## The LTTE as a violent non-state armed group

Although terrorist groups form a distinct category of violent non-state actors, placing the LTTE in this distinct category is problematic. If terrorism is treated as a method, namely, politically motivated violence that deliberately targets civilians, then the LTTE are a problematic case of a terrorist organization, since LTTE violence has been primarily directed against the coercive capacities of the Sri Lankan state. Yet the LTTE have been guilty of enacting what Thomas Thornton calls 'enforcement' and 'agitational' terror.[5] 'Enforcement terror' denotes an insurgent organization's security system, the disciplining of its members, and the execution or punishment of alleged or real informers to deter them from cooperating with the regime. Agitational terror, by contrast, advances the organization's public agenda. Indeed, one could condemn terrorist methods without insisting that, whenever employed, they de-legitimate the group using them, converting it into an international outlaw. As noted by Ekaterina Stepanov, 'the fact that a group uses terrorist means in the name of a political goal does not necessarily delegitimize the goal itself.'[6] In practice, even Western countries have not consistently equated the tactic and its users. As pointed out by Tom Farer:

Over decades ... the United States looked the other way while the Irish Republican Army successfully solicited financial backing from ethnic-Irish communities in the United States. During the Central American war of the 1980s, the Reagan Administration continued its support for opponents of Nicaragua's leftist governments, the so-called 'Contras', despite their attack on the civilian population and did nothing to shut off financial support for right-wing paramilitary death squads in El Salvador.[7]

[4] Chester Crocker, 'Engaging Failing States', *Foreign Affairs*. Sept./Oct. 2003, pp. 34–5.
[5] Introduction in Marianne Heiberg, Brendan O' Leary and John Tirman (eds), *Terror, Insurgency, and the State: Ending Protracted Conflicts*, Philadelphia: University of Pennsylvania Press, 2007, p. 7
[6] Ekaterina Stepanova, 'Terrorism in Asymmetrical Conflict, Ideological and Structural Aspects', *SIPRI Research Report 23*, London, 2008, p. 12.
[7] Tom Farer, *Confronting Global Terrorism and American Neo-Conservatism: The Framework of a Liberal Grand Strategy*, New York: Oxford University Press, 2008, pp. 18–19.

However, the LTTE could easily be defined as a guerrilla movement. As will be argued below, the LTTE are clearly committed to changing the status quo and have used physical violence to pursue their declared aim of establishing a Tamil State (Eelam). The LTTE's motivation is predominantly political since, as an entity 'supposed to represent the grievances of the Tamil community', they have waged war on the Sinhala-dominated Sri Lankan state essentially as a 'parallel process of state-building primarily by military means.'[8]

The LTTE also set up a parallel civil administration within the territory under its control. They established structures such as a police force, law courts, postal services, banks, administrative offices, and a television and radio broadcasting station. The most prominent parts of the LTTE 'state structure' were the 'Tamil Eelam Judiciary' and the 'Tamil Eelam Police'. Formed in 1983 and with headquarters at Kilinochchi, the Tamil Eelam Police was reported to have several wings, including traffic, crime prevention, crime detection, information bureau, administration and a special force. LTTE cadres collected taxes; the 'Tigers' courts administered their version of justice and the entire law and order machinery was LTTE-controlled.

As part of their violent campaign the LTTE murdered government ministers, local politicians and moderate Tamil leaders. LTTE fighters attacked naval ships, oil tankers, the airport in the country's capital Colombo, and Sri Lanka's most sacred Buddhist relic, the Temple of the Tooth. They also attacked the Colombo World Trade Centre and the Central Bank, as well as the Joint Operations Command, the nerve centre of the Sri Lankan security forces. Unlike other suicide terrorists LTTE fighters did not deliberately target civilians, but they killed large numbers of them regardless. In the attack on the Central Bank in 1996, for example, ninety people were killed.[9]

The LTTE leader Vellupillai Prabhakaran justified armed struggle in the following words:

[I]t is the plight of the Tamil people that forced me to take up arms. I felt outraged at the inhuman atrocities perpetrated against an innocent people. The ruthless manner in which our people were murdered and colossal damage done to their property made me realize that we are subjected to a calculated program of genocide. I felt that the armed struggle is the only way to protect and liberate our people from a totalitarian Fascist State bent on destroying an entire race of people.[10]

---

[8] Jayadeva Uyangoda, *Ethnic Conflict in Sri Lanka: Changing Dynamics, Policy Studies 32*, Washington: East-West Centre, 2007, p. 42.

[9] Louise Richardson, *What Terrorists Want: Understanding the Terrorist Threat*, London: John Murray, 2006, pp. 138–9.

[10] Reporter, 1986. Vellupillai Pirapaharan's Interview, *The Week*, 3 March 1986.

The allegation of 'atrocious behavior' by the successive Sinhala-dominated governments as an underlying cause of the Tamil militancy is widely believed. For example, the deputy editor of the *Daily News*, T. Sabaratnum, in his three-volume study of the rise of LTTE, says the following:

The Tamil community has been subjected to a well thought out and carefully executed scheme of extermination. Through state-aided Sinhala colonization the extent of land under Tamil control was gradually eroded; through the disfranchisement of the Indian Tamils their numerical strength was severely reduced; through the enactment of the Sinhala Only policy they were rendered officially illiterate; through the enshrinement in the constitution of the unitary character of the state they were inextricably enslaved; and through repeated unleashing of state and mob violence they were denied the fundamental right of secure existence.[11]

While there may not be agreement on the precise number of suicide attacks carried out by the LTTE, there is little disagreement on the scale of such attacks. Robert Pape calculates that between 1987 and 2001 a total of 143 Tamil Tigers carried out 76 suicide attacks killing 901 people. According to *Jane's Intelligence Review* there were 168 LTTE suicide attacks in this period; Ricolfi estimates 191, while Sugeeswara Senadhira claims that the number of suicide missions carried out by the LTTE in the last two decades is more than 270.[12] The LTTE themselves claimed to have carried out 147 suicide operations during 1987–99 but they claimed responsibility publicly only for military attacks, not for their attacks on civilians, politicians or economic targets. The most important feature of these suicide attacks is the nationalistic fervour underpinning them: 'the LTTE's ideology is entirely secular one of national liberation. Their commitment is fuelled by hatred of the enemy and a desire to take revenge for their attacks, not by God.'[13]

Suicide terrorism has been one of the most potent weapons of the LTTE in their protracted armed conflict with the Sri Lankan state. Since their first suicide attack on 5 July 1987 when 'Captain Miller' drove a truck laden with explosives into a Sri Lanka army camp at Nelliady in Jaffna, blowing himself up, suicide attacks have been regularly used by the LTTE as 'an emphatic statement to the Sri Lankan government and the international community that the LTTE is a force to be reckoned with.'[14] Moreover, besides creating

---

[11] T. Sabaratnum, *Pirapaharan*. Downloaded 5 May 2008. Available at http://sangam.org/articles/view/?id=37/

[12] Sugeeswara Senadhira, 'Suicide Bombings: The Case of Sri Lanka', in *Security and Terrorism: Suicide Bombing Operations*, Vol. 5, 2007, p. 32.

[13] Ibid.

[14] Neloufer de Mel, *Militarizing Sri Lanka: Popular Culture, Memory and Narrative in the Armed Conflict*, New Delhi: Sage, 2007, p. 194.

panic and deep anxiety among ordinary citizens, a successful suicide attack also 'confirms the inefficacy of the administration, demoralizes law enforcers and boosts morale among the Tigers and their followers.'[15] According to one estimate as of 1 August 2006, the total deaths of members of the Black Tigers (the LTTE suicide wing), the Black Sea Tigers and the intelligence wing of the Black Tigers in suicide attacks amounted then to 316. The LTTE's own figure was 273. Of the suicide attacks, 23.73 per cent have been carried out by women.[16] The use of female suicide bombers is mainly due to operational considerations as 'females are not subject to the same kind of movement restrictions and body searches [as men]...and the layers of a woman's clothing can more easily disguise the bulky suicide belt which is more conspicuous under a man's shirt and trousers.'[17]

Despite having waged a wide variety of violence and warfare against the Sri Lankan state, the LTTE, unlike many other violent armed groups, also participated directly in several rounds of peace talks with the Sri Lankan government to end the ethnic conflict in Sri Lanka.[18] The LTTE's ability to wage peace along with war not only made it a unique violent armed group that carried 'guns' and 'ideas' simultaneously, but also raised the larger question of the role of norms in impacting its behaviour. Given the fact that non-state actors are becoming increasingly more responsible for effecting political outcomes, it is imperative for theories of norm socialization to be extended to violent non-state actors such as the LTTE, to see whether these groups are cognizant of normative and ethical arguments, or whether they operate in a moral vacuum.[19]

[15] Sugeeswara Senadhira, 'Suicide Bombings', p. 34
[16] Neloufer de Mel, *Militarizing Sri Lanka*, p. 194.
[17] Sugeeswara Senadhira, 'Suicide Bombings', p. 33.
[18] The LTTE participated in the following peace talks: 1985 Thimpu Talks, 1989–90 Premdasa-LTTE talks, 1994–95 Kumaratunga-LTTE talks, and the 2001–2 Cease Fire Agreement brokered by Norway. For an excellent analysis of internal and external factors which prompted the LTTE to come to the negotiating table for talks with the Sri Lankan government, see Pushpa Iyer, *Coming to the Table: Decisions and Decision-Making in a Non-State Armed Group, The Liberation Tigers of Tamil Eelam* (PhD Dissertation) Fairfax, Virginia, 2007.
[19] Theories of norm socialization based on constructivist philosophy hold that ideational forces are an important determinant of human behaviour. One of the important ways to detect the impact of norms on behaviour is to examine the discourse of norm breakers or violators. By examining shifts in rhetoric or discourse of the entities under observation, one can gain important clues to behaviour change. However, a significant limitation of the theories of norm socialization is their predominantly state-centric focus

There are at least two reasons which make the LTTE an apt case to study from the perspective of the impact of norms. First, the LTTE's long history of armed struggle spanning three decades ensures that there are sufficient grounds to test a long-term process like norm socialization. Secondly, focusing on the LTTE enables one to examine whether international norms have an effect on older terrorist groups and movements, and how far the fallout of 9/11 has added pressure on such groups to reexamine their strategies. A recent study found that the 'LTTE has consistently made arguments justifying their use of violence within the vocabulary and discursive contours of the international community, both before and after 9/11.'[20] This suggests that violent non-state actors are not impervious to the discourse and normative pressure emanating from the international community. Prabhakaran's speeches reveal an increasingly conscious effort to resist a collective identification with 'real terrorist' groups, and thus an acknowledgement of the basic norm against killing civilians.[21]

## Background to the conflict in Sri Lanka

Before analyzing the rise of the LTTE as a violent non-state actor, it is necessary to understand the dynamics of the ethnic conflict in Sri Lanka between the Sinhala majority and the Tamil minority. Even though the conflict in Sri Lanka is a complex, multi-actor, multi-level, multi-faceted and multi-causal phenomenon that defies a uniform description, there is no gainsaying that the ethnic enmity amongst the Sinhala, Tamil and Muslim communities functions as a structural cause of Sri Lanka's armed conflict. As pointed out by Neloufer de Mel:

[T]he ethnic category remains a significant paradigm in working out a negotiated settlement to the conflict that would involve devolution of power by region with linguistic autonomy. It shapes the civil-military balance, for there is a fine line between a

---

which leads them to ignore the important issue of the impact of norms on non-state actors, especially VNSAs. As a result the question of their socialization into norms remains understudied and under-theorized. For a good summary of the first wave of norm socialization literature see Martha Finnemore and Kathryn Sikking, 'International Norms Dynamics and Political Change', *International Organization*, 4, 1998, pp. 887–917.

[20] Deepa Prakash, 'Bombs and Bombast: Counter Terrorism Norms and Discourse of the LTTE', Unpublished paper, 2007, p. 6.

[21] Ibid.

highly ethnicized Sinhala army controlling Tamil militants in the name of public law and order, and a regulative state constitutive of Sinhala hegemony. The ethnic category over-determines many of the policies and strategies of the war so that while it may not be its sole animating factor, it is nevertheless pivotal within Sri Lanka's militarization in how it has pitted the Sinhala community against Tamils in mutually exclusive ways.[22]

Sri Lanka, known as Ceylon until 1972, is a multi-ethnic, multi-linguistic and multi-religious state with a population of about 20 million as of 2006. The people of the island are broadly divided into six categories: Sinhalese account for 74 per cent of the total population, Sri Lankan Tamils 12 per cent, Indian Plantation Tamils 5 per cent, Muslims 7 per cent, Burghers 1 per cent, and aboriginal tribes insignificant numbers.[23] On the basis of religion, the Sinhalese are either Buddhists or Christians, Tamils (both Sri Lankan and Plantation) are Hindus or Christians, and all Muslims follow the Islamic faith. Burghers are mostly Christians; and aborigines follow their native faith. Sinhalese mostly speak Sinhala, which belongs to the Indo-European group of languages with a mix of vocabulary and syntax of Dravidian languages. Tamils speak Tamil, a Dravidian language. Muslims speak Sinhala and Tamil, and Burghers speak English. The aborigines converse in native tribal languages. The majority Sinhalese began migrating to the island from North India around 500 BC and settled in the northeastern or dry zone. Buddhism came to the island in the third century BC and became an integral part of Sinhalese culture. The Sri Lankan Tamils, also known as Jaffna Tamils, trace their lineage to Tamil invasions from India of 300 AD. They live mainly in the northern and eastern districts. The Plantation Tamils, also known as Indian Tamils, trace their heritage to the colonial period when they migrated to Sri Lanka from the Indian province of Tamil Nadu to work on the tea plantations during British rule. The Indian Tamils are heavily concentrated in the highland districts. Since they lived on settlements separate from the Jaffna Tamils, the Indian Tamils did not assimilate into the greater Tamil society. This lack of integration resulted in both the Sinhalese and Jaffna Tamils viewing them as 'foreigners'. The third group, the Muslims, do not have a majority in any district but live as large minorities in two districts, Mannar and Ampari.

Sri Lanka gained independence on 4 February 1948 when the British, after ruling the Island since 1815, decided to transfer power to the Sri Lankan peo-

---

[22] Niloufer de Mel, *Militarising Sri Lanka*, pp. 32–3.
[23] N Manoharan, *Democratic Dilemma: Ethnic Violence and Human Rights in Sri Lanka*, New Delhi: Samskriti, 2008, p. 45.

ple by implementing the constitution drafted by the Second Royal Commission (popularly known as the Soulbury Commission). The leaders of the Tamils pleaded before that Commission for an equal share of power along with the Sinhalese majority. The Soulbury Commission tried to allay Tamil apprehensions by providing certain safeguards including the stipulation that the Parliament would not enact discriminatory legislation against a particular ethnic or religious minority to which all other groups were not simultaneously subjected.

Strains between the Tamil minority and the Sinhala majority first appeared over the status of Plantation Tamils who were rendered both stateless and voteless through three pieces of legislation passed by the post-independence government of Sri Lanka led by the United National Party (UNP). The All Ceylon Tamil Congress (ACTC), representing Sri Lankan Tamils, supported this legislative move which stripped nearly one million Plantation Tamils of their right to become citizens of Ceylon and sought their compulsory repatriation to India. The ACTS's anti-Tamil stance caused a split in the Congress, with S.J.V. Chelvanyakam forming the Federal Party (FP) which eclipsed the ACTC and became the dominant force claiming to represent the interests of the Tamil people.

The tensions between Tamil minority and Sinhala majority turned violent when the former launched *satyagraha* (peaceful non-cooperation) in June 1956 against the declaration of 'Sinhalese' as a sole official language by the charismatic Prime Minister S.W.R.D. Bandaranaike, whose Sri Lankan Freedom Party (SLFP) won the 1956 election by promising to make Sinhala the only official language, as against the existing two-language policy. The 'Sinhala Only Act' alienated the Tamils as this move was 'seen by the Tamils not only as a means of denying them opportunities of government employment but also as an instrument of cultural oppression and a denial of Tamil identity.'[24] Tamils, who had made up 60 per cent of the professionals employed by the state at independence (1948), fell to under 10 per cent by 1970. In the administrative service, the drop was from 30 per cent to fewer than 5 per cent during the same period, and most dramatically in the armed forces, Tamils went from 40 per cent to less than 1 per cent.[25] In riots in certain parts of Colombo and

[24] S.W.R. de A. Samarasinghe, 'The Dynamism of Separatism: The Case of Sri Lanka', in Ralph R. Premdas, S.W.R. de A. Samarasinghe and Alan B. Anderson (eds), *Secessionist Movements in Comparative Perspective*, London: Palgrave Macmillan, 1990, p. 51.
[25] Robert I. Rotberg, *Creating Peace in Sri Lanka: Civil War and Reconciliation*, Washington: Brookings Macmillan, 1999, p. 19.

Eastern Province, 150 people, mostly Tamils, died and thousands were injured. Extensive damage was done to the property and shops owned by the Tamils in these areas.

On 20 January 1956 the Tamil members of Parliament decided to form a United Front to pursue the following goals: (1) preserve their language and culture, (2) maintain the identity and freedom of the Tamil speaking people and (3) provide for their traditional home. They called upon the Tamils to struggle for the creation of a Tamil state which would offer to federate with the Sinhalese state on terms of complete equality if acceptable to both the nations, or elect to remain independent. The Federal Party's Convention held at Trincomalee on 18–19 August 1956 unanimously adopted a resolution which became a landmark in the Tamil struggle to secure equality of treatment for Tamil language and their rightful place in the Island's policy. The resolution made four key demands:

(1) Replacement of the present Constitution by a rational and democratic one based the federal principle and the establishment of one Tamil linguistic state, incorporating all geographically contiguous areas in which the Tamil-speaking people were numerically a majority.
(2) Restoration of the Tamil language to its rightful place, enjoying parity of status with the Sinhalese as the official language.
(3) Repeal of existing citizenship laws and enactment of fresh laws on the basis of a single test of residence; and
(4) Immediate cessation of colonizing of Tamil areas by Sinhalese.[26]

In a bid to accommodate Tamil sensibilities, Prime Minister Bandaranaike entered into an agreement with the Federal Party leader S.J.V. Chelvanyakam which assured that 'without infringing on the position of the Official Language Act, the language of administration in the Northern and Eastern provinces should be Tamil and any necessary provision should be made for the non-Tamil speaking minorities in the Northern and Eastern provinces.'[27] The Bandaranaike-Chelvanyakam Pact could not be implemented owing to pressure from the Sinhala-Buddhist forces which saw the agreement as whetting the Tamil appetite for separatism while eroding the gains of the Sinhala Only Act. The radical Tamils, on the other hand, dubbed the Pact as capitulation before the Sinhalese majority.

[26] Atvar Singh Bhasin, *India in Sri Lanka Between Lion and Tigers*, Colombo: Vijitha Yapa Publications, 2004, p. 28.
[27] Lionel Guruge (ed) *Sri Lanka's Ethnic Problem And Solutions*, Colombo: Centre for Policy Alternatives, 2006, p. 24

In 1959 a radical Buddhist monk assassinated Prime Minister Bandaranaike; this propelled his widow, Sirimavo, into politics. The following year, Sirimavo Bandaranaike was elected as the Prime Minister of Sri Lanka. Discrimination against the Tamil people continued unabated as her government passed an Act which made Sinhala the language of courts. The peaceful *satyagraha* protests organized by the Tamil political parties were brutally suppressed as the government responded to the unrest by declaring a state of emergency.

In 1965 an attempt was made to assuage the feelings of the Tamil community through the Senanayake-Chelvanayakam Pact. This Pact called for action to make Tamil the language of administration and record in the Northern and Eastern provinces. It sought to establish District Councils with power vested with the government to give directions in the national interest, and called for amendment of the land Development Ordinance to give priority to landless Tamil-speaking persons in the Northern and Eastern Provinces and Tamil-speaking persons in other part of the country. The measures contained in the Senanayake-Chelvanayakam Pact could not be implemented owing to a crusade launched by the Buddhist clergy with backing of the Sri Lanka Freedom Party.

The language issue continued to dominate Sri Lankan politics in the 1960s and early 1970s but now widened to include other Tamil grievances such as access to higher education, absence of economic opportunities, unequal land distribution, and agricultural settlements which Tamils described as 'colonization'.[28]

---

[28] The term 'colonization' refers to state-sponsored settlement schemes built around irrigation schemes that were perceived by the Tamils as an encroachment into the 'traditional homeland' in the North-East, aimed at changing the demographic composition. In rural Sri Lanka, land is a primary economic asset as well as an important basis of social and political mobilization. Since the state is the primary owner of land resources in the country, the political leadership of independent Sri Lanka identified land irrigation development in the sparsely populated Dry Zone and settlement of excess population from the rest of the country in newly developed colonization as major tasks to be attended to. The Tamils became increasingly concerned over the disproportionate benefits of such schemes being given to the majority ethnic group, and its adverse implications for ethnic balance and ethnic relations in the affected areas, as well as the safety of minority communities. For an excellent discussion of the land issue as driver of ethnic conflict in Sri Lanka see Shahul H. Hasbullah, P. Balasundarampillai and Kallinga Tudor Silva, *Addressing Root Causes of the Conflict: Land Problems in North East Sri Lanka*, Colombo: Vijitha Yapa Publications, 2005.

The passage of the 1972 Constitution further aggravated the widening ethnic divide because of the removal of minority safeguards in the preceding Soulbury Constitution and the pride of place accorded to Sinhala Buddhism. The 1972 Constitution stated that the Tamil Language Regulations 'shall not in any manner be interpreted as being a provision of the Constitution but shall be deemed to be subordinate legislation.' As noted by K.M. de Silva, 'the new balance of forces, of which the principal feature is the dominance of the Sinhalese and Buddhists in the Sri Lanka polity, was effectively consolidated... Indeed, the new Constitution accurately reflected the balance of forces.'[29] The 1972 Constitution also subjected the judiciary to the control of the legislature by eliminating appeals to the Privy Council on constitutional issues. This measure was a response to a Supreme Court finding against the 1956 Sinhala Only Act. For moderate Tamils 'it exemplified the futility of constitutional politics.'[30]

Disappointed and feeling frustrated that their non-violent tactics were not working to secure their right to be educated in their mother tongue, their right to represent their people in the legislature and also ensure their share of government, the Tamil leaders openly talked of secession. Various Tamil parties united to form the Tamil United Front (TUF) and began discussing the idea of a separate state of Tamil Eelam. The emergence of the TUF represented the coalescing of a Tamil response to the consistent transformation of a multi-racial, albeit unitary Sri Lankan state into an overtly Sinhalese-Buddhist one. Soon after the 1972 Constitution was adopted, the leader of the Federal Party, the precursor to the Tamil United Liberation Front (TULF), S.J.V. Chelvanayakam, resigned his seat in parliament in protest.[31] The electrocution of seven Tamil civilians attending the International Tamil Conference

---

[29] K.M. de Silva, *A History of Sri Lanka*, London: Hurst, 1981, p. 530.

[30] Brendan O' Duffy, 'LTTE: Majoritarianism, Self-Determination, and Military-to-Political Transition in Sri Lanka', in Marianne Heiberg, Brendan O' Leary and John Tirman (eds), *Terror, Insurgency, and the State: Ending Protracted Conflicts*, p. 260.

[31] S.J.V. Chelvanyakam won the Kanesanthruai by-election in February 1975, and after winning the elections made the following statement favouring separatism: 'We have for the last 25 years made every effort to secure our political rights on the basis of equality with the Sinhalese in a united Ceylon...It is a regrettable fact that successive Sinhalese governments have used the power that flows from independence to deny us our fundamental rights and reduce us to the position of a subject people...I wish to announce to my people and to the country that I consider the verdict at this election as a mandate that the Tamil Eelam nation should exercise the sovereignty already vested in the Tamil people to become free.' Quoted in Devanesan Nesiah, 'The Claim to Self-determination: a Sri Lankan Tamil Perspective', *Contemporary South Asia*, Vol. 10, 2001, p. 62

in Jaffna in 1974, attributed to firing and a baton charge by the police, further hastened the introduction of militancy into Tamil nationalist struggle.

The mounting feelings of estrangement nursed by the Tamil youth were further aggravated by the first Janatha Vimukti Peramuna or People's Liberation Front (JVP) armed insurrection[32] of 1971, which was ruthlessly crushed by the Sri Lankan government. Despite its failure, the JVP insurrection had a great demonstration impact on Tamil youth as it made them see armed struggle and violence as the answer to their problems of alienation, discrimination and unemployment.[33] Taking a cue from the success of the armed struggle of the Bengalis in East Pakistan which led to the birth of independent Bangladesh in December 1971, and reacting to the ultra-nationalist rhetoric by Tamil mainstream political parties which had now formed themselves into a joint front—the Tamil United Front (TUF)—young Tamils adopted a militant posture and began joining Tamil militant organizations in large numbers. In 1976 the Tamil United Liberation Front (TULF) succeeded the TUF, and at its first national convention held in Vaddukoddai it resolved 'that the restoration and reconstitution of the free sovereign secular socialist state of Tamil Eelam based on the right of self-determination inherent to every nation has become inevitable in order to safeguard the very existence of the Tamil nation in this country.'[34] The deepening alienation of the Tamil people stemming from the 'lack of any attempt to accommodate or even consider their views in the framing of the constitution was a major contributory factor to the emergence of the Vaddukoddai Resolution of 1976.'[35] The hardening of the Tamil

---

[32] The Janatha Vimukti Peramuna (JVP, or People's Liberation Front), a left-wing, mainly Sinhalese group headed by Rohana Wijeweera, launched in 1971 an armed insurrection to seize power in Colombo. Hundreds of JVP cadres, both boys and girls, attacked 93 police stations between 5 and 11 April but were able to capture only five, using mostly home-made weapons. The insurrection was brutally suppressed by the Sri Lankan government. More than 10,000 young people died as a result.

[33] As pointed out by Balasingham, persistent frustration led Tamil youth 'to abandon the Gandhian doctrine of ahimsa which they realized was irreconcilable with revolutionary political practice.... Confronted with a political vacuum and caught up in a revolutionary situation created by the concrete conditions of intolerable national oppression, the Tamil youth sought desperately to create a revolutionary political organization to advance the task of national liberation' Anton Balasingham, *Liberation Tigers and Tamil Eelam Freedom Struggle*, Madras: Political Committee of LTTE,1983, pp. 23–5.

[34] Apratim Mukarji, *Sri Lanka: A Dangerous Interlude*, Colombo: Vijitha Yapa Publications, 2005, p. 146.

[35] Devanesan Nesiah, 'The Claim to Self-determination: a Sri Lankan Tamil Perspective', *Contemporary South Asia*, Vol. 10, 2001, p. 62

position reflected a similar stance within the Sinhala community, which in 1977 brought to power the nationalist government of Junius Jayewardene at the head of a rejuvenated UNP.

In response to the TULF's Vaddukoddai Resolution, the Sri Lankan government invoked the Sixth Amendment which 'prohibited political parties and individuals from demanding or advocating a separate state for the Tamil-speaking people as a solution to the intractable ethnic conflict in Sri Lanka.'[36] This measure led the TULF to boycott parliament as it attempted to limit loss of support to nascent and more militant Tamil groups, including the LTTE.[37] In the aftermath of the 1977 general elections, more anti-Tamil riots occurred that 'served to increase the alienation of the Tamil people, which in turn led to a further increase in support for the secessionism.'[38]

## Founding and early history of the LTTE

The Liberation Tigers of the Tamil Eelam (LTTE) were founded by Vellupillai Prabhakaran on 5 March 1976, the day he conducted a successful bank robbery in Puttur. As a politically motivated youth who felt inspired by Napoleon Bonaparte, Alexander the Great and Indian Freedom Fighters, Prabhakaran at the age of 17 joined the Tamil Students League (TSL), founded by Kuttimani and Jagan in 1970.[39] In 1975, a faction of the TSL broke away and began calling itself the Tamil New Tigers (TNT). This splinter group comprised a handful of people led by Chetti Tanabalassingham, an ordinary criminal who 'taught Prabhakaran how to handle arms and explosives.'[40] On 27 July 1975 Prabhakaran assassinated Alfred Durayapa, former mayor of Jaffna. According to M.R. Narayan Swamy, 'It was Prabharkaran's first murder, and the first major assassination by Tamils. The assassination created a sensation in Sri Lanka. It also made Prabhakaran famous. His name soon acquired a halo and for the first time Jaffna youth began hearing about a secret group

[36] Brendan O' Duffy, 'LTTE: Majoritarianism, Self-Determination, and Military-to-Political Transition in Sri Lanka', p. 261.

[37] Ibid.

[38] Jagath P. Senaratne, 'Reflections on the Secessionist Insurrection in Sri Lanka: Consequences for Sri Lanka, and Lessons for the International Community', in Sridhar K. Khatri and Gerth W. Kueck (eds), *Terrorism in South Asia: Impact on Development and Democratic Process*, New Delhi, 2003, p. 256.

[39] Harkirat Singh, *Intervention in Sri Lanka: The IPKF Experience Retold*, Colombo: Vijitha Yapa Publications, 2006, pp. 21 and 151.

[40] Ibid. p. 151

which called itself the Tamil New Tigers.'[41] Prabhakaran, it was reported, killed Tanabalassingham to assume the leadership of TNT, and renamed the group as the Liberation Tigers of Tamil Eelam (LTTE) in May 1976. The immediate antecedents of the founding of the LTTE lay in the proliferation of many groups of Tamil militants who 'felt that peaceful political agitation by the old men had got nothing for the Tamils, and, it was the boys turn to secure rights for the Tamils.'[42] Even before the 1970s some elements within Tamil political parties had adopted a more militant course of action.

A clear indication of this trend away from constitutional path towards political militancy was the formation of an underground group, Pulip Padai (the Army of Tigers) in August 1961 at the historic Koenwaran temple in Trincomalee. Standing in its holy precincts facing the sea, Pulip Padai members took 'a solemn oath to fight for a Tamil homeland.'[43] In 1969, another informal group named the Tamil Liberation Organization (TLO) was formed, which included the future LTTE leader Prabhakaran amongst its founding members. The TLO pledged to plunge itself headlong into a violent struggle. The formation of the Tamil United Front (TUF) in 1972 led to the creation of the Tamil Elaingyar Peravai (Tamil Youth League) in January 1973. This split in 1975 with one group backing the TUF leadership while the other, calling itself Eelam Liberation Organization (ELO), committed itself to waging armed struggle. In February 1972 two well-known Tamil leaders, Chelvanayakam and Amritalingham, went to Madras in India, where they issued a statement that they 'would fight to establish a full independent state, and that they would need not only the support of the people of Tamil Nadu but the people of India.'[44]

The second half of the 1970s witnessed the expansion of militant outfits and intensification of armed militancy by Tamil youth. The Tamil Eelam Liberation Organization (TELO), People's Liberation Organization of Tamil Eelam (PLOTE), Eelam People's Revolutionary Front (EPRLF), Eelam Revolutionary Organization (EROS) and Liberation Tigers of Tamil Eelam (LTTE) all surfaced during this period. In 1977, a militant group called the Tamil Eelam Liberation Army (TELA) was set up along the lines of the Irish

---

[41] M.R. Narayan Swamy, *Tigers of Lanka: From Boys to Guerrillas*, Colombo: Vijitha Yapa Publications, 2004, p. 56.

[42] Shaheen Akhter, 'Ethnic Conflict in Sri Lanka: Domestic, Regional and International Linkages (1983–1993)' (Unpublished PhD Dissertation: Islamabad: Department of International Relations, Quaid-i-Azam University, 2007), p. 107

[43] M.R. Narayan Swamy, *Tigers of Lanka*, p. 24

[44] Harkirat Singh, *Intervention in Sri Lanka*, p. 20

Republican Army. The emergence of Tamil youth militancy, triggered by the adoption of the 1972 constitution and the 'pogroms of 1977, 1979, 1981 and 1983, and the consequent exit from parliament of the Tulf MPs'[45] created a situation in which the youth militants led by the LTTE were able to stake a claim to being the sole representatives of the Tamil people and assume the right to wage armed struggle on their behalf.

According to government figures, between 1976 and July 1983, 73 persons were slain by the Tiger underground militants, and from 1978 to 1983 the Tigers were responsible for more than 265 bombings, robberies, assaults and other criminal acts. Reacting to the armed struggle launched by the LTTE, the government of President Jayewardene banned the LTTE in 1978 and promulgated in 1979 the Prevention of Terrorism Act, which gave extraordinary powers to the police and army. In July 1979, President J.R. Jayewardene sent a brigade-strong Army contingent to Jaffna, and ordered its commander to 'wipe out terrorism' in six months. The anti-terrorism drive launched by Colombo reportedly led to extra-judicial killings and disappearances and forced many Tamil insurgents to seek sanctuary in South India. In December 1979, the contingent commander reported to President Jayewardene that 'the mission had been successfully completed.'[46]

Soon after its founding, the LTTE moved very quickly to establish its international linkages. In 1980, with the advent of Anton Balasingham's Marxist influence and a dispute with another leader, Prabhakaran left the LTTE and joined Tamil Eelam Liberation Organization (TEOL) for a while. On 27 November 1982, the first LTTE cadre to die in the conflict, 'Shanka', was killed in action, and that day was thereafter celebrated as the LTTE's 'Hero's Day'. On 15 July 1983 a LTTE cadre named 'Seelan' was injured and at his own request was shot dead by another to prevent his capture by the Army. A week later, the LTTE carried out an ambush of an Army Patrol in Jaffna in which 13 soldiers were killed. This LTTE attack sparked off the 'Black July' anti-Tamil riots in which hundreds of Tamil were killed and their business destroyed by Sinhalese mobs with the active connivance[47] of the Sri Lankan

---

[45] Devanesan Nesiah, 'The Claim to Self-determination', p. 64

[46] Jagath P. Senaratne, 'Reflections on the Secessionist Insurrection in Sri Lanka', p. 256.

[47] Commenting on the Sri Lankan government's role in the 1983 anti-Tamil riots, Neil Devotta writes: 'The 1983 riots thus saw every major institution in the country fail to live up to its obligations and responsibilities to protect its minority citizens; on the contrary, those institutions representing the state apparatus coalesced to attack the Tamils.' P. Sahadevan and Neil Devotta, *Politics of Conflict and Peace in Sri Lanka*, New Delhi: Manak, 2006, p. 21.

security forces. The Black July riots redounded to the LTTE's advantage as they 'opened a floodgate of young Tamils to various Tamil militant groups'[48] seeking revenge.

In 1984, Prabhakaran ordered all LTTE cadres to wear the cyanide vial and to use it rather than be captured. He wore one himself to institutionalize the 'cyanide culture' within the organization. During its formative phase, some of the high ranking LTTE leaders received training from Palestinian groups like Al Fatah (the military wing of PLO) and the Popular Front for the Liberation of Palestine (PFLP) in various training centres in the Middle East. It is widely believed that the 'use of suicide terrorist tactics, networking with Tamil diaspora for funds, propaganda and other services, arms transfers, and methods of motivating its cadres'[49] were techniques that the LTTE borrowed from their early training experience with the PLO.

## LTTE organization and military structure

Notwithstanding their claims to be a democratic organization, the LTTE, in reality, were an authoritarian and hierarchical organization controlled by Prabhakaran who enjoyed absolute power as their supreme leader. As noted by N. Manoharan: 'Prabhakaran has profoundly influenced the LTTE...as regards to its member's characteristic paranoia, fanatical bravery, relentless pursuit of vengeance, and disregard for human life.'[50] Prabhakaran's overarching influence was reflected in the pledge of allegiance made by LTTE cadres to the Eelam struggle and also specifically to Prabhakaran. He was both Chairman of the Central Committee of the LTTE and Commander-in-Chief of their military wing. Below him were a Deputy Commander and at least eight Special Commanders in charge of the Sea Tigers, Intelligence, Ordnance, the Black Tigers, Military Intelligence, Military Planning, the Women's Wing, and the Charles Anthony Brigade.[51] Each of the Northeast's eight districts was placed under an Area Commander who was accountable to Prabhakaran. Cadres of eight regional commands constituted political and military wings which were 'further sub-divided according to their specialized roles in several combat units in the military wing.'[52] Cadres did not receive any remuneration

[48] M.R. Narayan Swamy, *Tigers of Lanka*, p. 96.

[49] N. Manoharan, *Democratic Dilemma*, p. 83.

[50] N. Manoharan, *Counterterrorism Legislation in Sri Lanka, Policy Studies 28*, Washington: East-West Centre, 2006, p. 18.

[51] P. Sahadevan and Neil Devotta, *Politics of Conflict and Peace in Sri Lanka*, pp. 320-1

[52] Ibid., p. 321

and were ranked only posthumously on the basis of their service and the circumstances of their death.[53]

*The Sea Tigers.* The LTTE were the only militant organization in the world which had an effective naval arm—the Sea Tigers. The Sea Tigers unit was formed in 1984 and was later reorganized on a large scale as 'Sea Tigers of Liberation Tigers' with their own distinct emblem.[54] From their initial role as an arms smuggling mechanism for the LTTE, the Sea Tigers evolved into an offensive arm for the organization. Their principal aim was to undertake combat operations against the Sri Lankan Navy including suicide attacks. The Sea Tigers' fleet consisted of 15–m fibreglass boats of 250 horsepower mounted with light and heavy machine guns and grenade launchers. These boats were frequently rigged with explosives and they destroyed more than 30 Sri Lankan navy craft.[55] The emergence of the LTTE's sea power in 1991–92 posed a direct threat to the Sri Lankan forces, as 'the supplies of the army in the north were mostly sea oriented.'[56] In 1992, the Sri Lankan Navy came under increas-

---

[53] The Army can be further broken down into four main Brigades (known as Padaipirivu, with strength around 1,200 persons each) which are used for more conventional warfare. The Brigades consisted of the Charles Anthony Padaipirivu, the Jeyanthan Padaipirivu, the Vithusha Padaipirivu, and the Leopards Padaipirivu. The Charles Anthony Padaipirivu was considered the first conventional fighting formation of the LTTE. This unit, created 18 years ago, was responsible for Prabhakaran's safety, though it also participated heavily in major operations. It was composed of Tamils from the north known for their loyalty to him. The Jeyanthan Padaipirivu (created in 1993) employed both guerrilla attacks and conventional warfare. The Vithusha Padaipirivu, or Women's wing, was composed of the Malathy Brigade, the Sothiya Brigade, the Kutti Sri Mortar Brigade, the female portion of the Sea Tigers, and the members within the Black Tigers. The Malthay brigade was commanded by Col. Vithusha and acted as a regular fighting unit. The Sothiya Brigade was also a regular fighting unit. The Kutti Sri Mortar Brigade was the main artillery unit for the LTTE. The Leopard Brigade (also known as 'Chriithaigal') was known as the fiercest fighting unit within the LTTE; it included experienced cadres from other LTTE formations as well as youth from LTTE managed orphanages who were given extensive training. The Leopards were best known for spearheading the Katunayake air base attack in 2001 which nearly decimated the Sri Lankan Air Force. This information draws heavily upon Elizabeth Marsh, 'The Liberation Tigers of Tamil Eelam: Structure and Attacks' (Unpublished Paper), 2 Nov. 2006, pp. 3–4.

[54] Shaheen Akhter, 'Ethnic Conflict in Sri Lanka', p. 271.

[55] Channa Wickremesekra, 'Peace through Military Parity? The Tamil Tigers and the Government Forces in Sri Lanka', in Daniel P. Marson *et al.* (eds), *A Military History of India and South Asia: From the East India Company to the Nuclear Era*, Bloomington, 2007, p. 182

[56] Shaheen Akhter, 'Ethnic Conflict in Sri Lanka', p. 272.

ing pressure from the LTTE's sea-borne suicide attacks, sea mines and Sea Tiger commando raids conducted by Black Tigers. In May 1995, the Sea Tigers led a successful attack on the island of Mandathivu off the Jaffna peninsula, and in 1996 they played a vital role in attacking the coastal army base of Mullaitivu. They were responsible for the deaths of 19 Sri Lankan Navy personnel who were ambushed in a May 2006 naval engagement.

The Sea Tigers played an important role in making the seas unsafe for Sri Lankan naval traffic, and in crucial campaigns they acted as a deterrent against the landing of Sri Lankan forces. They also facilitated the LTTE's land operations by transporting troops to crucial battlefields. They took part in attacks on major bases also. The Sea Tigers had multiple classes of vessels, including an armour plated 'stealth' craft with a top speed of more than 35 knots, as well as a submersible commando vessel similar to a World War II Chariot and designed for special operations within naval bases and commercial ports.[57] Apart from their smaller attack craft, the Sea Tigers also possessed a number of larger merchant vessels used mainly for carrying weapons and other equipment for the Tigers.

*The Air Tigers.* The Air Tigers were a late addition to the growing military capabilities of the LTTE. They acquired an airstrip near Iranamadu, south of the LTTE's main base at Kilionchchi, in 2002. Two light aircraft were spotted at the airstrip by a military drone in January 2005. According to US intelligence sources one of the aircraft was a Czech-built Zlin Z 143. The LTTE pilots were thought to have been trained at flying clubs in France and the United Kingdom, and Tamil expatriates working with foreign airlines are reported to have helped the LTTE establish their air wing. The LTTE credits Colonel Shankar (alias Vythialingam Sornalingam), who worked as an aeronautical engineer with Air Canada, as the founder of its air wing.

The LTTE revealed their air capabilities with a bombing raid on the Sri Lankan Air Force's main base on 25 March 2007. The attack on the Katunayake Air Base killed three SLAF (Sri Lanka Air Force) personnel and injured another 16 and caused damage to two helicopters. The main target of the attack, the fixed-wing aircraft, escaped undamaged.[58] The day after the attack, the LTTE released photographs showing six members of their air wing with the LTTE leader Vellupillai Prabhakaran and a light aircraft that was identified as a Z 143. The photographs showed four improvised gravity bombs

---

[57] Channa Wickremesekra, 'Peace through Military Parity?'.
[58] 'The Tiger Air Force', *Jane's Terrorism and Insurgency Centre Briefing*, 29 March 2007.

attached to a Z 143 by a metal frame. These bombs were fairly large and were fin-stabilized. They were estimated to contain 25 kg of C4 explosive, according to Sri Lankan military sources quoted by *Jane's* sources.[59] On 24 April 2007 the LTTE carried out their second air raid when their planes bombed an army engineering unit in northern Sri Lanka which killed six soldiers and wounded 13.[60] On 22 October 2007, in a coordinated ground and air assault on the Sri Lanka Air Force (SLAF) base at Anuradhapura, the LTTE managed to destroy eight aircraft including one Mi-17 Hip-H, two Mi-24 assault helicopters, a BT-6 and a K-8 training aircraft, a King Air 200 reconnaissance aircraft and an Avro 748 transport aircraft.[61] Sri Lanka was forced to respond to these LTTE air attacks by upgrading its air defence capabilities and purchasing new MiG-29 combat aircraft and Mi-24 helicopter gunships from Russia.[62]

*The Black Tigers.* The Black Tigers, or 'Karum Puligal' in Tamil, were the elitist force of the LTTE. They were trained to hit high value targets through suicide attacks. Although the LTTE did not invent modern suicide bombing, they turned it into 'a vicious art form'.[63] Highlighting the importance of the Black Tigers for the LTTE cause, Prabhakaran stated: 'With perseverance and sacrifice, Tamil Eelam can be achieved in 100 years. But if we conduct Black Tiger operations, we can shorten the suffering of the people and achieve Tamil Eelam in a shorter period of time.'[64]

The Black Tigers had the ability to attack by land, sea, and air. The group pioneered the suicide jacket, a vest composed of several bombs for a suicide bomber to wear easily. They also pioneered the idea of hiding bombs inside the body. Victims of this group include a Sri Lankan President, the head of the Sri Lankan navy, a minister of National Security, an opposition leader, and a former Prime Minister of India, Rajiv Gandhi.[65]

---

[59] Ibid.

[60] Iqbal Athas, 'LTTE's second air attack kills six', *Jane's Defense Weekly*, 2 May 2007.

[61] Garth Jennings and Craig Caffrey, 'Sri Lankan Air force confirms loss of eight aircraft following the LTTE attack', *Jane's Defense Weekly*, 31 October 2007.

[62] Iqbal Athas, 'Sri Lanka bolsters air defences', *Jane's Defense Weekly*, 16 May 2007.

[63] Perry Alex, 'How Sri Lanka's Rebels Build a Suicide Bomber', *Time Magazine*, 12 May 2006 available at http://www.tamilnewsweb.com/14–05–6–PoliticsIsland.htm accessed on 20 June 2008.

[64] Rohan Gunaratna, 'The LTTE Suicide Terrorism', *Frontline*, 17, 2000.

[65] Perry, Alex, 'How Sri Lanka's Rebels Build a Suicide Bomber'.

An important organizational trait of the LTTE was that each branch of the service was divided by gender and had a secondary gender based leadership under the operational control of the respective unit/Wing leader, but under the administrative control of the Women's Wing leader.[66] Female emancipation seems to have been the primary driving force for women to join the LTTE.

## The LTTE's objectives and strategies

On 5 May 1976, Vellupillai Prabhakaran formed the Liberation Tigers of Tamil Eelam. Nine days later came the Vaddukoddai Resolution, which called for 'restoration and reconstitution of the Free Sovereign, Secular and Socialist State of Tamil Eelam based on the rights of self-determination inherent to every nation.'[67] The Vaddukoddai resolution was predicated on the notion that self-determination had become 'inevitable in order to safeguard the very existence of the Tamil Nation in this country.'[68] Imbibing the underlying philosophy of the Vaddukoddai resolution, the LTTE's primary goal has been the creation of a Tamil homeland for the Tamils of the northeast. According to Prabhakaran:

It is wrong to call our movement 'separatist'. We are fighting for independence based on the right to national self-determination of our people. Our struggle is for self-determination for the restoration of our sovereignty in our homeland. We are not fighting for a division or a separation of a country but rather, we are fighting to uphold the sacred right to live in freedom and dignity. In this sense, we are freedom fighters not terrorists.[69]

He further told Pratap, the Indian journalist who interviewed him: 'I named the movement 'Liberation Tigers since the Tiger Emblem had deep roots in the political history of Tamils, symbolizing Tamil patriotic resurgence. The tiger symbol also depicts the mode of our guerrilla warfare.'[70] From a modest beginning in the early 1970s, the LTTE came to have over 10,000

---

[66] A. Gunawardena, 'Suicide Terrorism: Is there a Counter? LTTE 'Black Tigers' - The Sri Lankan Experience' (M.Sc Dissertation, University of Leicester, 2003), p. 16.

[67] For the text of the Vaddukoddai Resolution see http://www. angam.org/FB_HIS_DOCS/Vauddukod.htm.

[68] Ibid.

[69] Anita Pratap, 'If Jayawardene was True Buddhist, I would not be carrying a gun: Prabhakaran Interview' *Sunday*, 11–17 March 1984.

[70] Ibid.

hardcore cadres. Its overarching aim was to establish a separate Tamil state (Eelam) through armed struggle.

The Tigers' strategy had four key components: preparing for war in peacetime, in line with the Maoist doctrine of retreat and recuperate; attempting to attain control over the Tamil struggle to gain legitimacy as the sole representative of Sri Lankan Tamils; subordinating the political struggle to the military one (as a strategic process the LTTE combined both war and politics, but the war option always prevailed over the political option); and combining guerrilla and conventional warfare tactics in battle.

The LTTE's armed struggle may be divided into six distinct phases. The first phase lasted from 1983 to 1987, the second from 1987 till 1990, the third from 1990 till 1994, the fourth from 1995 till 2002, the fifth from 2002 till 2007, the sixth and final phase from 2007 till May 2009 when the Sri Lankan armed forces managed to destroy and defeat the LTTE as a violent armed group by wresting control of the areas held by them and killing its top leadership including Prabharkran. Each of these phases entailed significant changes in the LTTE's tactics, concentration of military activities and targets, and the degree of its external support.

The first phase (1983–87) witnessed highly intense military confrontations between half a dozen insurgent groups and the Sri Lankan armed forces. During this phase the LTTE not only tried to develop themselves into a highly motivated fighting organization of 3–4,000 dedicated full-time cadres, but also established an independent arms procurement and supply network by drawing on the growing global diaspora of Sri Lankan Tamil expatriates and refugees. During this phase the LTTE received material and financial assistance from neighbouring India which 'due to its geo-strategic interests, stepped up political, military and financial support for the Sri Lankan Tamil militants after the 1983 ethnic riots.'[71] Between 1983 and 1987, the Indian intelligence agency, the Research and Analysis Wing (RAW), trained 'an estimated 1,200 Tamils in the use of automatic and semiautomatic weapons, self-loading rifles, 84 mm rocket launchers and heavy weapons, and in laying mines, map reading, guerrilla war, mountaineering, demolitions and anti-tank warfare.'[72] According to Rohan Gunaratna, a leading Sri Lankan expert on Tamil insurgency, by 1987 over 20,000 Sri Lankan Tamil insurgents were provided sanctuary, finance training and weapons either by the central Indian government or the state government of Tamil Nadu or by the insurgent

[71] Shaheen Akhter, 'Ethnic Conflict in Sri Lanka', p. 306.
[72] Ibid.

groups themselves.[73] According to a recent study, 'Tamil Nadu became a military academy for Tamil militants, where they learnt guerrilla tactics range from hit-and-run to frogman warfare.'[74] In addition to gaining guerrilla training and a modernized weapon arsenal, the LTTE were able to set up communication facilities and to move freely between India and Sri Lanka.[75] As a result of the massive support it received from New Delhi, by 1986–87 the LTTE 'clearly emerged as the dominant Tamil fighting force.'[76]

Drawing upon their superior dedication, organization, leadership and tactical skills, and partly because of their ruthless proficiency in killing rival groups, the LTTE managed to engage the Sri Lankan military decisively. Adopting an unconventional war strategy, the LTTE attempted to weaken the central government's authority and restrict the movement of its security forces by staging ambushes and mine attacks. Responding to the LTTE's attempts to take over the civil administration in the 'liberated areas' of the north and east, which was perceived as a 'unilateral declaration of independence', Colombo launched a massive military offensive along with the economic blockade. President Jayewardene declared that his government was determined to fight the militants until 'either they win or we win', and that his government would accept 'help from the devil himself, if necessary to fight terrorism' by Tamil militants.'[77]

During the second phase (1987–90) the main focus of the LTTE's armed struggle was to defeat the counterinsurgency operations launched by the 70,000–strong Indian peacekeeping forces which were invited by Colombo as part of the July 1987 Indo-Sri Lanka Peace Agreement (IPSA). Under the terms of the ISPA, the government of India assumed exclusive responsibility for monitoring and enforcing compliance with the agreement. 'If any military groups operating in Sri Lanka do not accept this framework of proposals for

---

[73] Rohan Gunaratna and Arabinda Acharya, 'India's Role in Ethnic Crisis in Sri Lanka', in M.B.I. Munshi (ed.), *The India Doctrine*, Dhaka: The Bangladesh Research Forum, 2006, pp. 270–1.

[74] Shaheen Akhter, 'Ethnic Conflict in Sri Lanka', p. 309.

[75] Rohan Gunaratna and Arabinda Acharya, 'India's Role in Ethnic Crisis in Sri Lanka', p. 271.

[76] Sumantra Bose, 'Flawed Mediation, Chaotic Implementation: The 1987 Indo-Sri Lanka Peace Agreement', in John Stedman, Donald Rothchild and Elizabeth M. Cousens (eds), *Ending Civil Wars: The Implementation of Peace Agreements*, Boulder: Lynne Rienner, 2003, p. 634.

[77] Quoted in Rohan Gunaratna and Arabinda Acharya, 'India's Role in Ethnic Crisis in Sri Lanka', p. 274.

a settlement', the agreement stated, India 'will take all necessary steps to ensure that Indian territory is not used for activities prejudicial to the unity, integrity and security of Sri Lanka.'[78] Concrete measures to this effect specified in the agreement and ancillary documents included collaboration between the Indian and Sri Lankan navies and coast guards to interdict guerrilla movements between Tamil Nadu and northern Sri Lanka, deportation by the Indian government of Sri Lankan citizens (on Indian soil) found to be engaging in terrorist activities or advocating secessionism, and even more remarkably, Indian provision of training facilities and military supplies for Sri Lankan security forces.

As for demobilizing and disarmament of combatants, the ISPA decreed that all Tamil guerrillas would have to surrender all weapons in their possession to specially designated Sri Lankan authorities within 72 hours of the signing of the ISPA. In return, the Sinhalese President would grant a general amnesty to all Tamil fighters and to all Tamil political prisoners in Sri Lankan jails and his government would 'make special efforts to rehabilitate militant youth with a view to bringing them back into the mainstream of national life.'[79] Finally, the Sri Lankan army and other security forces would revert to their pre-May offensive positions and be confined to their barracks for an unspecified time frame. How favourable the ISPA was for Colombo can easily be seen in the following remark made by President Junius Jayewardene: 'the major gain [of the government side from the ISPA] is that [Tamil] terrorism is over.... India is [now] willing to tackle this terrorist problem as an active partner with me...Earlier, they were training the terrorists.'[80]

Given the pro-Colombo bias of the ISPA, the LTTE's supreme leader, Prabhakaran, proclaimed that 'a working arrangement has to be made on the ground that will ensure the safety and security of the Tamils. Unless that working arrangement is established, the question of the LTTE disarming does not arise. It is better to fight and die than surrender the weapons in an insecure environment and die on a mass scale.'[81] After three months of an uneasy peace, Prabhakaran declared war on the Indian peace-keeping force. Defending its decision, the LTTE said that the 'Indo-Sri Lankan Accord fails to situate the essence and mode of our struggle as a liberation struggle, as a struggle

[78] Ibid., p. 641.
[79] Sumantra Bose, 'Flawed Mediation, Chaotic Implementation: The 1987 Indo-Sri Lanka Peace Agreement', p. 643.
[80] Ibid., p. 644.
[81] M.R. Narayan Swamy, *Tigers of Lanka*, p. 252.

for self-determination. Instead the Accord places our national struggle entirely on a fallacious promise reducing it to a simple problem of a discriminated minority group in a pluralistic social formation.'[82] The LTTE lost 711 of its members confronting the Indian forces, but membership in the Tiger movement more than tripled between 1987 and 1990, with almost 10,000 fighters mobilized by the time of the Indian withdrawal in March 1990. LTTE fighters moved rapidly to establish their control over the north and the east in the wake of the Indian pullout. By April 1990, the entire northeastern region came under LTTE administration. During this phase the LTTE also augmented their military capability as they 'surreptitiously received weapons and supplies to fight the Indian from their old enemy, the Sri Lankan armed forces, under orders from the Premadasa government ... and also captured large quantities of arms and ammunitions left by the Indians to their Tamil collaborator militias, who collapsed and disintegrated virtually without a fight as the Indian Peacekeeping Forces (IPKF) withdrew.'[83]

With the withdrawal of Indian troops there was a renewal of fighting between the LTTE and the Sri Lanka armed forces, initiating the third phase (1990–95) of conflict in which the LTTE engaged in a series of set-piece battles and hit-and-run operations to maintain their control over the north while ceding control of territories in the east to the government forces. The assassination of Rajiv Gandhi in May 1991 by an LTTE female suicide bomber led to an Indian ban on the LTTE as a terrorist organization. On 1 May 1993 an LTTE suicide squad assassinated Sri Lanka's President Premadasa. His slaying brought Chandrika Bandaranaike Kumaratunga to power. She pledged a new deal to the Tamils to end the ethnic conflict once and for all. In August 1994, she extended her 'hand of friendship' to the LTTE, and in a message to the nation declared that she 'would build a society without any discrimination where all the minority communities would enjoy equal rights as equal citizens.'[84] In 1994–95 the Chandrika government held four rounds of talks with the LTTE but these foundered on the rock of the latter's unwillingness to budge from their declared aim of the creation of Tamil Eelam.

In April 1995 the LTTE blew up two Sri Lankan navy gunboats in Trincomalee harbour, which marked the collapse of negotiations and the failure of

[82] Quoted in Rohan Gunaratna and Arabinda Acharya, 'India's Role in Ethnic Crisis in Sri Lanka', p. 275

[83] Sumantra Bose, 'Flawed Mediation, Chaotic Implementation: The 1987 Indo-Sri Lanka Peace Agreement', p. 653.

[84] Avta Singh Bhasin, *India in Sri Lanka*, p. 266

Chandrika's peace offensive and plunged the country into the fourth phase of armed conflict. Using the 100–day truce for 'fresh recruitments, training, re-grouping and planning',[85] the LTTE then intensified their military campaign against the Sri Lankan government by launching a four-pronged attack against the government troops stationed in Manditivu Island, which left 100 soldiers dead.[86] President Kumaratunga responded to the LTTE military offensive by stating, 'If peace cannot be achieved by peaceful means, we will resort to any means to restore it.'[87] Characterizing the LTTE as an 'impeccable enemy of the peace process', the government launched a series of military offensives—Operation Leap Forward, Operation Thunder Strike, and a three-pronged Operation codenamed 'Riviresa' (Sun Rise) which resulted in the government forces taking control of Jaffna in December 1995.[88] The loss of Jaffna, besides resulting in a large-scale dislocation of the LTTE's forces and equipment, forced the organization to shift its headquarters to Mullaitivu and Killionchchi.

With territorial gains as its key objective, the LTTE returned to long-drawn-out guerrilla warfare. In 1996, they repulsed an attack on the Mullaitivu military camps in an action that killed 1,400 Sri Lankan soldiers. From 1996 to 1999, the LTTE escalated suicide bombings which included a suicide attack on President Kumaratunga in December 1999. The other major suicide attacks were on the Central Bank in Colombo, the World Trade Centre, and the holy Buddhist temple of the Tooth Relic in Kandy. In April 2000, the LTTE captured the strategic Elephant Pass and positioned themselves to take the town of Jaffna and the air and naval bases at Palaley and Kaneksanthurai respectively.

In line with their strategy of talking peace from a position of strength, the LTTE declared a unilateral cease-fire on 24 December 2000 and renewed it every month until April 2001. The parliamentary elections held in October 2001 brought to power the United National Front led by Ranil Wickremasinghe. Consistent with his electoral pledge to hold peace talks with the LTTE, as Prime Minister Ranil Wickremasinghe proposed a ceasefire which was to be followed by a political solution to the ethnic problem. In February 2002 the LTTE and the Sri Lankan Government signed the Cease-fire Agreement (CFA) which was brokered by Norway. Valid for an 'indefinite period', the

---

[85] Shaheen Akhter, 'Ethnic Conflict in Sri Lanka', p. 454.
[86] Ibid.,
[87] Amit Baruah, 'Back to war: The Jaffna Offensive', *Frontline*, 28 July 1995.
[88] Shaheen Akhter, 'Ethnic Conflict in Sri Lanka', p. 454.

CFA called for a federal solution to the crisis in Sri Lanka with the creation of a semi-autonomous province under the control of the Tamil leadership. The CFA also had several important provisions relating to the cessation of military operations and confidence-building measures.

The conclusion of the CFA initiated the fifth phase of the ethnic war, characterized by deepening international engagement aimed at giving elusive peace a chance. Norway was named the facilitator and it was decided that that country, together with the other Nordic countries, should monitor the ceasefire through a committee of experts named the Sri Lanka Monitoring Mission (SLMM). Peace talks began in Phuket in Thailand on 16 September and additional rounds followed in Phuket, Norway and Berlin. The issues covered during these talks included: prisoners of war, child recruitment, disarmament of the LTTE, looking at federalism as an option, human rights violations, demining, continuing violence, and resettlement of Internally Displaced Persons. The six rounds of talks were marked by tensions over continuing incidents of violence, differences over key issues of de-escalation, and the removal of High Security Zones (HSZs). As a result of these talks, both sides agreed to the principle of a federal solution and the LTTE dropped their longstanding demand for a separate state.[89]

The accession to power in November 2005 of Mahinda Rajapaksa at the head of a Sinhalese coalition that promised to revisit the terms of the CFA between the government and the LTTE led to a marked escalation of armed violence on both sides and put the country on the warpath again. Having remained in force for over six years and having witnessed countless violations[90]

---

[89] On 31 October 2003 the LTTE put forward The Interim Self-Governing Authority (ISGA) proposal as a solution to end the war. The ISGA proposal suggested that an interim administration would be led by the LTTE, giving them powers over development, reconstruction, resettlement, raising and disbursing revenue, trade, foreign aid, natural resources, land issues and administrative structures. The government rejected the document and refused to use it as a base for further discussions.

[90] Violations of the ceasefire agreement included, among others, the non-disarmament of the paramilitary groups by the government, continued child recruitment by the LTTE, human rights violations such as abductions and harassment, and political killings. According to the SLMM website there were 4,173 violations up to the end of 2006. Of these the LTTE were responsible for 3,827 and the Government of Sri Lanka for 346 violations. Justifying Colombo's decision to abrogate the Ceasefire Agreement, the government's Defence spokesman Keheliya Rambukwella, claimed that the 'LTTE had violated the Ceasefire Agreement more than 10,000 times since it was signed in February 2002.' He went on to state that the 'the atrocities and terror tactics that the LTTE used on the civilians has not stopped. They made an agreement with the CFA, but underhand

of its key provisions by both sides, the CFA was unilaterally abrogated by the Sri Lankan government in January 2008.

The abandonment of the CFA marked Sri Lanka's plunge into a full-scale war, with Sri Lankan forces managing to drive out the LTTE from the east and going on the military offensive in the north. As a consequence of a military offensive launched by the government forces prior to the annulment of the CFA, over 1,000 LTTE cadres were killed including the former political wing head Parami Tamilselvan and Shanmuganathan Ravishankar, alias Charles, head of the LTTE's intelligence apparatus. According to data compiled by the Institute for Conflict Management, the LTTE lost 4,318 cadres after 1 January 2008, which was significantly more than the 3,345 cadres they lost over the whole of 2007 and 2,319 fatalities in 2006.[91] These enormous manpower losses, coupled with the harmful effects of the split caused by Col. Karuna's defection in March 2004 and the banning of the LTTE as a terrorist entity by many countries including the United States, the EU and the UK, raised doubts about the ability of the LTTE to survive as a cohesive military force and undermined their claim to be the sole representative of the Tamil people.

## Epilogue

The LTTE's unrelenting armed struggle for a homeland for the Tamil people over the past three decades witnessed many setbacks, but these reverses failed to dissuade its leadership and the 10,000 strong cadres from thinking and acting like a state. As perceptively noted by Jayadeva Uyangoda, 'In the LTTE thinking, war-making has fundamentally been a process of state-making for the Tamil nation.'[92] Caught in this 'quasi-state' trap, the LTTE found it impossible to forgo their claim to be treated as a political equal of the Sri Lankan State. This effort by the LTTE at potential state-making primarily through military means became an untenable proposition in face of the heavy military losses inflicted on them by the Sri Lankan armed forces in the last phase of the conflict.[93] The LTTE's state-making project suffered a

---

they continuously practiced violence and so we simply did not see the point in continuing the ceasefire.' Lanka Paranamanna, 'LTTE violate CFA 10,000 times: Rambukwella' *The Nation*, 6 Jan. 2008.

[91] Ajit Kumar Singh, 'Locked in Carnage', *South Asia Intelligence Review*, 49, 16 June 2008, p. 3.

[92] Jayadeva Uyangoda, 'Ethnic Conflict in Sri Lanka', p. 40.

[93] Apart from losing cadres in large numbers in battle against the Army's ground forces, the

huge setback with the virtual elimination of its presence from the Eastern Province and the evident erosion of some of the public support for its military campaigns.

Emboldened by the territorial gains made by the Sri Lankan armed forces in the east, the Army Chief Sarath Fonseka declared on 9 February 2008, 'LTTE leader V. Prabhakaran should realize that he cannot go ahead with his military campaign. They have no option other than to give up their struggle and enter the political mainstream.'[94] In the same vein, President Mahinda Rajapakse stated on 12 June 2008 that his government would not resume peace talks with the Tigers until the organization agreed to disarm.[95] The LTTE responded to these demands by saying that surrendering their arms would weaken the group's bargaining power and hence would be detrimental for any meaningful future talks.[96]

The elevation of the Thamil Makkal Viduthalai Pulikal (TVMP) leader Sivanesthurai Chandrakantham alias Pillayan to the position of Eastern Provincial Chief Minister, following the May 2008 Eastern Provincial Council elections that were boycotted by the LTTE and their allies, further weakened the LTTE position. The installation of the breakaway former LTTE leader as Chief Minister meant that the Sri Lankan government would not only maintain military control over the east but would also accelerate its effort to

---

LTTE suffered severe material damage inflicted by more than 50 air raids carried out by the Sri Lanka Air Force (SLAF) in 2008, which targeted the outfit's communication centres, training centres, and military bases often visited by senior leaders in the LTTE's last citadels in the Mullaitivu and Kilinochchi Districts. See Ajit Kumar Singh, 'LTTE: Rising Desperation', *South Asia Intelligence Review*, 43, 25 May 2008. p. 2. Available at http://satp.org/satporgtp/sair/Archives/6_43.htm#assessment1

[94] Ibid.

[95] 'When they are weak they call on the international community to arrange a ceasefire. During this period they train and rearm and then fight back. This time if they want to talk, they should disarm first', President Mahinda Rajapakse said. He went on to add: 'This man (Prabhakaran) and the three or four henchmen surrounding him are blood-thirsty killers. They have no feelings. It is very difficult to deal with them.' Quoted in Ajit Kumar Singh, 'Locke in Carnage', *South Asia Intelligence Review*, 49, 16 June 2008, p. 3.

[96] Reacting to the Sri Lankan government's calls to surrender its weapons, the LTTE political leader, Balasingham Nadesan, said: 'Any approach that disturbs the balance of power and parity of status [between the government and rebels] are counter-productive to the peace process... the balance of power and the parity of status are very crucial for any meaningful negotiations.' Quoted in 'Sri Lankan President questions Tamil rebel's commitment to ceasefire', *Jane's Terrorism and Insurgency Centre*, 18 June 2008.

weaken the LTTE's administrative grip over the areas under their control. By devolving powers over police and land to the Eastern Provincial Council for the first time ever, the Sri Lankan government not only made it easier for the TVMP to reinvent and legitimize itself as a 'democratic force' but also gave it the opportunity to transform its armed units into a legitimate police force and thereby also 'reassure the Tamil people that their fear of government sponsored Sinhalese settlements in the north and east will be less likely in the future.'[97] The empowering of the TVMP, the arch-rival of the LTTE, essentially meant that the latter would come under increasing political pressure by the Tamil community to dilute their demand for a separate Tamil state and negotiate for a greater power and rights for the Tamil people. Yet deviating from their state-making project was not an option for the LTTE. Faced with this existential challenge, they continued to wage armed struggle even when it became quite evident that this had become a losing strategy. This failure to change course ultimately led to the LTTE's undoing.

In early November 2008, the Sri Lankan armed forces captured Pooneryn, the LTTE's military headquarters located on the North-Western coast. Addressing the nation following the fall of Pooneryn, President Mahinda Rajapakse called on the LTTE leader Prabhakaran to 'immediately lay down' arms and 'come to the negotiation table.'[98] Pooneryn's strategic location enabled the Sri Lankan armed forces to position themselves for a final assault against Kilinochchi town and Mullaitivu. On 17 November 2008, Sri Lankan troops captured the strategically important town of Mankulam, and on 2 January they overran Kilinochchi Town, the *de facto* capital of the projected Tamil Eelam. Three days later, the 59th Division of the Sri Lankan armed forces captured Mullaitivu Town, the LTTE's military capital as well as the strongest Sea Tiger base.

These rapid military advances by the Sri Lankan Army prompted the Army chief, Lieutenant General Sarath Fonseka, to declare that the war was '95 per cent' over. In an interview broadcast on 6 January 2009, General Fonseka told the Independent Television Network that 'the LTTE not only lost 95 per cent of the land it held but also lost within the last one year 8,000 terrorists.' The following day, Colombo announced its decision to proscribe the LTTE, describing them 'as one of the most dangerous and deadly extremist outfits in

---

[97] Jehan Perera, 'Pillayan success may pave the way for future LTTE entry', *Daily Mirror*, 20 May 2008. A9.

[98] Ajit Kumar Singh, 'Relentless Assault', *South Asian Intelligence Review*, Vol. 7, No. 20, November 2008. p. 3

the world, which had 'inspired' networks worldwide, including Al Qaeda in Iraq.'[99]

The escalating war in the North created a situation of 'humanitarian disaster' as the LTTE began using the substantial civilian population trapped in Mullaitivu as human shields. With civilian casualties mounting, the United Nations and other international agencies, as well as a number of foreign governments, issued urgent calls for a 'humanitarian ceasefire from 'both sides'. The demand for a 'humanitarian pause' was rejected outright by Colombo which claimed that it was following a 'Zero Civilian Casualty Policy'.[100] Faced with the prospect of a military defeat, the LTTE made an offer of a ceasefire on 31 March which was rejected by Colombo. Vowing to finish off the LTTE, President Rajapakse declared, 'We will not cave into pressures from any international quarters locally and internationally and will not stop until the war was completely over.'[101]

On 5 April 2009 the Sri Lankan security forces captured the entire Puthukkudiyiruppu region, the LTTE's last stronghold, and ended the long siege of the last square kilometre held by the LTTE. More than 420 LTTE cadres including some of its top commanders were killed in the battle. On 20 April the Sri Lankan troops captured a three-kilometre-long LTTE-built earth bund in the Putumattalan and Ampelavanpokkanai areas of the NFZ in Mullaitivu District, and enabled over 40,000 civilians trapped in the area to escape the battle zone. In a nationally televised speech, President Mahinda Rajapakse described the exodus of Tamil civilians from the NFZ as the 'largest-ever hostage rescue mission in history' and urged the LTTE to surrender within next 24 hours.[102] Cornered into a 'tiny patch of jungle about the size of a football field' in their shrinking stronghold at Vellamullaivaikkal, a hamlet on the northeast coast of the island, the LTTE, on 17 May 2009, announced their decision to lay down their arms and admitted defeat.[103] Vowing to recapture 'every inch of land', the Sri Lankan Army went ahead and blew up bunkers in which the LTTE leaders had been holed up. More than one hundred senior

---

[99] Ibid.

[100] Ajit Kumar Singh, 'No Humanitarian Pause', *South Asian Intelligence Review*, Vol. 7, No. 39 (April 2009), p. 4

[101] Ibid.

[102] Emily Wax, 'Sri Lanka sets deadline for rebel surrender', *Washington Post*, 21 April 2009.

[103] Emily Wax, 'Sri Lankan rebels admit defeat, vow to drop guns', *Washington Post*, 18 May 2009,

leaders perished in the conflagration. Those killed included the LTTE chief Velupillai Prabhakaran, the Sea Tigers' chief Soosai and the LTTE intelligence unit chief Pottu Amman.[104] The victory of the Sri Lankan Armed forces over the LTTE brought an end to the most violent phase of the struggle of the Tamil people to pursue their dream of a Tamil Eelam.

---

[104] G.H. Peiris, 'End of the Eelam War', *South Asian Intelligence Review*, Vol. 7, No. 45, 18 May 2009.

# 18

# Private Military Firms

## The Profit Side of VNSAs

*P.W. Singer*

On 19 March 2003, US forces invaded Iraq. It was a defining moment for the Middle East, as well as for US foreign policy, causing repercussions for the region, and for America's standing in the world, that are likely to last for years if not decades. But the Iraq war was also important in another way. When the future histories of the war are written, they will have to talk about the role of a new actor in war and world politics, not discussed in past histories.

The Iraq war was a defining moment for the new category of violent non-state actors (VNSAs) known as private military firms. While the overall industry of private firms providing military services is little over a decade old, it exploded in size and scope after the Iraq invasion, almost as if the industry was put on steroids. In turn, it soon became clear that the growth of this new VNSA had gone too far, too fast, creating a series of difficult dilemmas and negative results both for the situation in Iraq and for world order beyond.

This chapter will explore the private military industry, discussing its background and dynamics, its role in what is the 'crucial case' example of Iraq, and a series of policy dilemmas that this unique new VNSA brings for international security and governance.[1]

[1] H. Eckstein, 'Case Studies and Theory in Political Science.' In F.I. Greenstein and N.W.

## What is the private military industry?

Privatized military firms (PMFs) are business providers of professional services intricately linked to warfare; in other words, the corporate evolution of the age-old practice of mercenaries. As opposed to individual 'dogs of war', as mercenaries were known in the past, PMFs are corporate bodies that can offer a wider range of services, ranging from conducting tactical combat operations and strategic planning to logistics support and technical assistance.

While novel in its sector, the rise of this industry simply repeats a broader shift from the primacy of manufacturing to services that has taken place in other industries, and reflects the increasing importance of outsourcing in global business practices. But what is distinct about PMFs is that they represent a profound development in the manner that security itself is both conceived and realized. With the rise of this industry, clients can now access capabilities that extend across the entire spectrum of formerly state-monopolized military activities, simply by writing a cheque.

The private military industry emerged at the start of the 1990s, driven by three dynamics—the end of the Cold War, transformations in the character of warfare that have blurred the lines between soldier and civilian, and the rise of privatization. First, with the end of global bipolar confrontation, professional armies have been downsized, while there has been an increase in global instability, creating both supply and demand. Secondly, while warfare in the developing world has become messier—heightening the demand for capable professional military services—the most advanced militaries are increasingly reliant on off-the-shelf commercial technology, often maintained and operated by private firms. Lastly, there has been an ideological trend towards governmental privatization, with many of the state's former commanding heights—schools, prisons, policing—turned over to the marketplace. This created a new space and demand for the establishment of the privatized military industry. It is important to note that few changes appear to loom in the near future to counter any of these forces.

Not all military firms are alike, nor do they offer the exact same services. The industry is just as diverse as the general outsourcing trade. The private military industry is divided into three basic business sectors:

1) Military provider firms, commonly known as 'private military companies' or 'PMCs' (also sometimes self-described as 'PSCs' or 'private security firms'),

Polsby (eds), *Handbook of Political Science. Political Science: Scope and Theory*, Vol. 7, Reading, MA: Addison-Wesley, 1975, pp. 94–137.

offer direct, tactical military assistance to clients, including serving in combat roles.

2) Military consulting firms draw on retired officers and NCOs to provide strategic advisory services and training for clients looking to transform their organizations.

3) Military support firms provide logistics, intelligence, and maintenance services to armed forces. In an era of downsizing, this allows soldiers to concentrate their own energies on combat and also reduces politically sensitive reserve call-ups.

While even the world's most powerful military has become increasingly reliant on this industry (the Pentagon has made over 3,000 contracts with PMFs over the last decade), it is important to stress that the industry and its clientele are not just an American phenomenon.[2] Private military activities have operated in over 50 nations, on every continent but Antarctica.[3] For example, EU militaries are greatly dependent on such firms in external deployments, as their publics have not been willing to support needed investment in such areas as military transport and support. Thus, European peacekeepers in Afghanistan rely on contracted air transport from a Ukrainian firm that flies former Soviet jets. The contract is worth more than $100 million. Likewise the British military, perhaps repeating the mistakes made by the US, has begun to contract out its logistics to the KBR-Halliburton firm.

## PMFs' role in Iraq

Estimates of the number of contract personnel in Iraq vary widely. In 2006, the United States Central Command estimated the number to be around 100,000 (such a perfectly round figure raises some questions). In the same year, the Director of the Private Security Company Association of Iraq estimated that 181 private security companies were working in Iraq with 'just over 48,000 employees'. In 2007, an internal Department of Defence census of the industry found that almost 180,000 private contractors were under employment in Iraq (compared with a total of 160,000 US troops at the time). Even this figure was thought by officials to be a low estimate, since a number of the biggest companies, as well as many firms

[2] International Consortium of Investigative Journalists, 'Making a Killing', The Center for Public Integrity Report, 28 October 2002.
[3] P.W. Singer, *Corporate Warriors*, Ithaca, NY: Cornell University Press, 2003, chapter 1.

employed by the Department of State or other agencies or NGOs, were not included in the census.[4]

So, after almost five years, no one had an exact head count of contractors in Iraq. Part of the confusion lies in the way that different observers categorize the industry in various ways. For example, the lower estimates tend only to count armed military provider types (or, as they sought to be called in Iraq, 'private security'), while the higher counts tend to include the entire industry of companies providing military services, but also sometimes lump in contractors carrying out non-military functions, such as reconstruction.

While we may not know the exact number, what we do know is that even the lowest estimates place the number of contractors at a significant percentage of the US military presence, and perhaps even more numerous those directly part of the state military. We thus know it is certainly well over the size of any US Army division and, even more, well over the sum of all the troops that other nations have sent to Iraq combined (today numbering roughly 12,000 and in steep decline owing to withdrawal plans). So, for all President Bush's talk of building a 'Coalition of the Willing', the reality is that the Iraq war has seen the creation of something new: a 'Coalition of the Billing'.

With these greater numbers come greater costs. By one count, as of July 2007, over 1,000 contractors have been killed in Iraq, and another 13,000 wounded (again the data are patchy here, the only reliable source being insurance claims made by contractors' employers and then reported to the US Department of Labor).[5] Since the 'Surge' started in January 2007 (this was the second wave of increased troop deployments, focused on the civil war), these numbers have accelerated; contractors have been killed at a rate of nine a week. These figures mean that again, the private military industry has suffered more losses in Iraq than the rest of the coalition of allied nations combined. The losses are also far more than any single US Army division has experienced.

It is important to note that these VNSAs, paid for by the taxpayer (either directly via the US government, or indirectly via companies employed by the US government doing things like reconstruction, which in turn hire PMFs), come from all over the world. In addition to Iraqi and United States citizens, contractors working in Iraq also include citizens from at least 30 other coun-

[4] T. Christian Miller, 'Contractors outnumber troops in Iraq', *Los Angeles Times*, 4 July 2007, p. 1.
[5] Bernd Debusmann, 'In outsourced U.S. wars, contractor deaths top 1,000', *Reuters*, 3 July 2007.

tries, some of whom were hired in violation of their home state laws. Indeed, a special investigation report by the *Chicago Tribune*, an article which won the Polk Award for best international reporting, revealed how some subcontractors used deception and coercion to recruit such '3rd party nationals' to work at US bases in Iraq.[6]

These personnel numbers translate into immense financial figures as well. The Senate Armed Services Committee estimated that reliance on contract employees has 'grown dramatically' over the last few years, reaching $151 billion in 2006 (again, this figure probably uses a wide definition of contractor services and includes overall Pentagon operations, not just in Iraq).[7] For example, the largest contract in the war has been with Halliburton-KBR. Continuing its work with the LOGCAP programme, it provided the Iraq mission's logistics, as well as the efforts to restore the Iraqi oil system, which was originally included under Pentagon contracting (many claim without proper competition). By the summer of 2007, the contract value for just this one company's work in Iraq was reported to be worth as much as $20.1 billion.[8]

To put this into context, the amount paid to Halliburton-KBR for just that period is roughly three times what the US government paid to fight the entire 1991 Gulf War. When putting other wars into current dollar amounts, the US government paid Halliburton about $7 billion more than it cost the United States to fight the American Revolution (1775–83), the War of 1812 (1812–15), the Mexican-American War (1846–48), and the Spanish American War (1898) combined. Even more interesting, the $2.2 billion that the US Army has claimed Halliburton overcharged is almost double the amount that it cost the US to fight the Mexican-American War, in current dollars: a war that won the US Arizona, New Mexico, and California.[9] Having made $2.7 billion in profits in 2006, the firm announced in 2007 that it would be relocating to the United Arab Emirates, where it would not have to pay US taxes or worry about an extradition treaty with the United States.

While many people focus on the booming numbers, even more important to the discussion of the industry are the roles that private soldiers have performed, each critical to the success or failure of the operation. In addition to

---

[6] Cam Simpson and Aamer Madhani, 'U.S. cash fuels human trade', *Chicago Tribune*, 9 October 2005.
[7] William Matthews, 'JCS Nominee is Warned: Crack Down on Contractors.' *Defense News*, 6 August, 2007, p. 14.
[8] Matt Kelley, 'Largest Iraq Contract Rife With Errors', *USA Today*, 17 July 2007.
[9] Ibid., p. 20.

war-gaming and field training before the invasion, private military employees handled logistics and support during the war's buildup. (For the armchair generals who sometimes downgrade the military importance of logistics, General Omar Bradley perhaps put it best, 'Amateurs talk about strategy. Professionals talk about logistics.') The massive US complex at Camp Doha in Kuwait, which served as the launch-pad for the invasion, was built by, operated by, and even guarded by an armed private contractor force.

During the invasion of Iraq, private military employees served these and a variety of critical roles, from handling the logistics and support for troops as they advanced into Iraq to maintaining, fuelling, and arming many of the most sophisticated weapons systems like the F-117 stealth fighter, the Apache attack helicopter, the F-15 fighter, and the U-2 reconnaissance aircraft. They even helped operate highly technical combat systems like the Global Hawk UAV and the air defence systems in the Patriot missile batteries and on board numerous US Navy ships.

But it was in the ensuing occupation period that the firms' roles would expand even further. While President Bush declared 'Mission Accomplished' at his infamous 1 May 2003 aircraft carrier landing press event, violence in Iraq escalated over the next years. As the mission grew more difficult, private military firms began to be used as a stopgap, in lieu of sending more US troops to compensate for the lack of significant allied support.

Private military personnel from all three business sectors played key roles. Military support firms provided logistics and other forms of technical support and assistance; military consulting firms provided the training of the post-Saddam police, paramilitary, and army, as well as training in other analytic roles, including the military intelligence realm that would later prove so controversial; and military provider firms multiplied on the ground. They provided convoy escort and protection of key bases, offices, and facilities from rebel attack. Even the top US official in Iraq, the Coalition Provisional Authority head Paul Bremer, was guarded by a private military contingent from the Blackwater firm, replete with three privately-crewed armed helicopters that were the same model that US Special Operations forces used. In short, the Iraq operation could not have been carried out without private military support.

At same time, the darkest episodes of the Iraq war all involved privatized military firms. These included the allegations of over-billing and other forms of war profiteering that have swirled around Dick Cheney's old Brown & Root-Halliburton firm, the tragedy of four employees of the Blackwater military provider firm being killed and mutilated on video at Fallujah and the subsequent battles that engulfed the area in 2004, the ensuing Abu Ghraib prison abuse scandal—where private military employees were reported by US Army investigators to have been an integral part of the pattern of abuse—and, of course, the 2007 Nisour Square shootings in Baghdad, in which Blackwater contractors were accused of killing as many as 17 Iraqi civilians.

## Why use corporate warriors?

While people often discuss the issue of private military firms in terms of economics, suggesting that hiring them must be because of financial cost savings, the reality is that this new VNSA is utilized because of political cost savings. The Iraq war illustrates this.

History will debate much about the Iraq war and its motivations and miscalculations. But consensus has already started to build that insufficient US forces were sent for the mission expected of them because of a failure of leadership, or rather pure hubris on the part of civilian leadership in the US, especially President Bush, Vice President Cheney, and Secretary of Defence Rumsfeld and their so-called 'neoconservative' cheerleaders. Indeed, a few months before the 2003 invasion, Rumsfeld publicly excoriated one of his senior military advisors, Army General Eric Shinseki, for even suggesting that the operation might not be a 'cakewalk' as some were predicting, and that additional US troops would be needed after the initial fight. As with Cassandra in the tales of the Trojan War, Shinseki's warnings were first ignored and then, too late, proved true.

Even worse, the planning for the Iraq operation only focused on the invasion itself and there were no realistic plans or structures in place for what would come after it. This was the height of folly. It ignores a most basic lesson of Carl von Clausewitz, one of the thinkers most cited at military academies; Clausewitz wrote that in war, one should ensure 'Not to take the first step without considering the last.'[10]

As the military and the Bush Administration wrestled with the policy dilemmas presented by this lack of planning, the new VNSA of private military contractors seemingly provided an attractive answer to many of their problems. The key difference from prior wars in the modern era is that this alternative had not existed previously.

---

[10] Carl von Clausewitz, *On War*, ed. and trans. Michael Howard and Peter Paret, Princeton University Press, 1984, p. 584.

It is sometimes easier to understand this by looking at the issue in reverse. If a core problem that US forces faced was that of insufficient troops, there were several potential answers, but each of them was considered politically unpalatable. The first would have been not to invade the country, and instead focus on the actual group that had attacked the US on 9/11, Al Qaeda, which had been based in Afghanistan, not Iraq.[11] Indeed, if most Americans had been informed that the operation would require hundreds of thousands of troops, leave thousands of them dead, cost literally hundreds of billions, and last for years, all the while targeting a foe that was not linked to 9/11, they probably would have demurred. But that was not the way the public debate went in 2003; driven by calculated misuse of intelligence reports, the debate focused more on weapons of mass destruction that turned out not to exist.

With the decision made to invade Iraq, one answer to the problem of insufficient forces would have been for the Bush Administration to send more regular forces, beyond the original 135,000 planned. However, this would have involved publicly admitting that it, and most particularly Secretary Rumsfeld, had been wrong in their planning. Plus, such an expanded force would have been an incredible burden on regular state military forces already stretched thin by the war in Iraq, Afghanistan, as well as broader global commitments.

Another option would have been a full-scale call-up of the National Guard and Reserves, as originally envisioned for such major wars in what was called the 'Abrams Doctrine'.[12] However, to do so would have prompted a massive outcry amongst the public (as now the war's effect would have been felt deeper at home), exactly the last thing the Administration wanted as it headed into what was a tight 2004 Presidential campaign.

Some proposed persuading other allies to send their troops in, much as NATO allies and other interested members of the UN had sent troops to Bosnia and Kosovo, to help spread the burden. However, this would have involved tough compromises, such as granting the UN or NATO command

---

[11] P.W. Singer, 'Iraq Can Wait till Phase 1 Done', *Baltimore Sun*, 19 March 2002.

[12] When the US military shifted to an all-volunteer, professional force in the wake of the Vietnam War, military leaders set up a series of organizational 'tripwires' to preserve the tie between the nation's foreign policy decisions and local communities. Led by then Army Chief of Staff General Creighton Abrams (1972–74), they wanted to ensure that the military would not go to war without the sufficient backing and involvement of the nation. Timothy Sullivan, *The Abrams Doctrine: Is It Enduring and Viable in the 21st Century*, US Army War College Research Paper, 2005.

of the forces in Iraq, in which the Bush Administration simply had no interest. In addition, much of the world vehemently opposed the invasion, which often seemed to delight the Bush Administration in the run up to the war (recall the whole 'Old Europe' and 'freedom fries' silliness). So, the likelihood of NATO or the UN sending troops was always minimal.

By comparison, the private military industry was an answer to these problems, and importantly an answer that had not existed for policymakers in the past. It offered the potential backstop of additional forces, but at no political cost. That is, there was no outcry whenever contractors were called up and deployed. While the gradual death toll among American troops threatened to slowly wear down the President's approval ratings, contractor casualties were not counted in official death tolls and had no impact on those ratings. Hence, even losses by these non-state actors were looked at by policymakers as almost a 'positive externality', to use an economic term. That is, the public usually did not even hear about them, and when they did, they created far less blowback on the government.

From what we can see from tracing the contracts, the decision to employ contractors in Iraq did not come in one single, grand conspiratorial meeting (as many opponents of Vice President Cheney often assume), but rather through an ever expanding series of decisions at multiple levels. Time and again, a need would crop up (be it truck drivers for fuel convoys or guards for civilian leaders) that the military either did not want to divert limited forces to, or could not meet with the troops on hand. Private military contractors would then be hired. So a good predictor of political action was actually the economic maxim known as 'Say's Law', a theory that explains how supply helps fuel greater demand. Once one service had been carried out in one sector, and it was proven that this VNSA could be useful, the market soon expanded to other sectors and across the system.

## Public security issues, private military dilemmas

The mix of the profit motive with the fog of war that takes place with this new type of VNSA has brought a series of challenges for governance and world order into the field.

1) *Military contractual dilemmas.* First, when it comes to military responsibilities, the incentives of private companies to make a profit may not always be in line with the client's interests or those of the public good. While in an

421

ideal world there would be good competition, management and oversight, producing cost and qualitative efficiencies, government contracting is not always set up to ensure this. Thus, the general concerns with any contracting handover (overcharging, over billing hours, providing insufficiently trained personnel, quality assurance issues, etc.) cross over into the military realm with this kind of VNSA.

This has been at the centre of the war-profiteering allegations made against such firms as Kellog Brown & Root-Halliburton and Custer-Battles. These firms were operating under 'cost-plus' contracts ripe for abuse, with the examples in Iraq ranging from selling overpriced petrol to charging for services not actually rendered (such as billing for meals that were not cooked for the troops or convoys shipping 'sailboat fuel', as Halliburton truck drivers laughingly termed charging the government for moving empty pallets from site to site).[13] Custer Battles, a PMF startup once featured on the front page of the *Wall Street Journal*, as its revenue had grown by a factor of 100 through Iraq contracts, has since been accused of running a Ponzi-like structure of subsidiaries and false charges. Overall, according to testimony before the House Committee on Oversight and Government and Reform, the Defense Contract Audit Agency has identified more than $10 billion in unsupported or questionable costs from battlefield contractors—and it has barely scratched the surface.

Such corruption does not just represent lost state funds; it represents lost opportunities for use of those funds to actually support the public mission. The situation got so bad that the Special Inspector General for Iraq Reconstruction (SIGIR) dubbed corruption as the 'second insurgency' in Iraq.[14]

More important than lost taxpayer dollars is the question of lost control. Even though they are doing military jobs, contractors are ultimately non-state actors that fall outside the state's military chain of command. Two levels of decision are injected into a military operation. The first is at the unit/corporate level. A company has the choice of what contracts to take and when to depart or 'suspend' operations because it thinks the physical or profit risks are too dangerous relative to the rewards. These business decisions can bolster forces when business is profitable, but also put the military at the industry's mercy. PMFs lie outside national military controls and structures, so clients

---

[13] Kathleen Schalch, 'KBR drivers say they risked their lives to pad profits', National Public Radio, *Morning Edition*, 8 June 2004

[14] Matt Kelley, 'Record cases in contract probe; Crackdown aims at 'second insurgency'', *USA Today*, 15 August 2007.

must worry about how they can replace such services if things go awry or the firm or its employees refuse to carry out orders in the midst of a crisis. During the summer of 2003, the upsurge of violence in April 2004, and a wave of contractor kidnappings in July 2004, US forces in Iraq faced a subsequent surge of firms delaying, 'suspending', or ending operations. Their concern for their private personnel and assets was valued as more important than the public mission; as a result there were stresses on supplies such as fuel and ammunition, and troops' welfare, even forcing troops onto food rations. Retired Army Major General Barry McCaffery testified to Congress in 2007 about his worries that these were just warning signs of the worries that should come with turning over so much of the system to private firms: 'Under conditions of great danger such as open warfare... they will discontinue operations. Our logistics system is a house of cards.'[15]

This issue came to the fore again in September 2007. A convoy guarded by Blackwater contractors was reported attacked in Baghdad and a raging gunfight ensued. As many as 17 civilians were killed in the crossfire and another 13 wounded. The firm members described their actions as self-defence, while the Iraqi government described them as a 'crime' and claimed that the firm had 'opened fire randomly'. The Iraqi government, which was already quite angry with the firm after a series of earlier incidents—including the alleged shooting of one of its personnel by a drunken Blackwater contractor on Christmas Eve 2006 and several armed standoffs between Iraqi police and Blackwater contractors—then announced that the firm's licence to operate in Iraq was revoked and that it would be banned from the country.

There were two problems: Blackwater, which was one of the biggest PMFs operating in Iraq at the time, actually had no licence with the Iraqi Interior Ministry for it to revoke (which illustrated the complete lack of controls and mismanagement within this space), and kicking out the company would leave the US State Department in Iraq without security in the middle of a war zone. It was a classic case of over-outsourcing. The US government's diplomatic security force had been hollowed out, at the same time that the need for it had expanded (note: a consortium of companies led by Blackwater had received a $1 billion contract to do the global State Department diplomatic security job the year before, so it was never a lack of money that was the cause of the hollowing out). The embassy was so reliant on the company that it had no

---

[15] 'Testimony of General Barry R. McCaffrey (USA, Ret.), Adjunct Professor of International Relations, United States Military Academy, Before The House Armed Services Committee', *PRNewswire-USNewswire*, 31 July 2007.

back-up plan for what to do without it. Within hours of the Iraqis' announcement, Secretary of State Condoleezza Rice had to call the Iraqi Prime Minister to ask him to allow the firm to stay, hampering other US efforts to pressure the very same government for action on political reform.

Likewise, PMFs have another new level of decision at the soldier/individual employee level. Whereas a soldier has no legal discretion once he or she enlists or is drafted, an individual employee decides who he or she wants to work for, where, when, and for what price. Even when deployed, they still have the choice on when to stay or leave (if they get a better job offer from a competing firm, think the mission and/or their superiors are not worth it, or simply are tired of the job, want to see their family, etc.). As in all industries there are mixed results. Some PMF employees have endured greater risks and dangers than their military equivalents, including battles in Iraq during which PMFs rescued coalition forces, rather than the other way around. A particular battle in Najaf was widely reported: Blackwater employees helped protect a CPA (Coalition Provisional Authority) headquarters and rescue a wounded US Marine while fighting off hundreds of attackers, all the while using firm helicopters for supply and support. At the same time, though, turnover within many firms is quite high and flights home are often full of PMFers who have decided it is time to leave with their bank accounts full and their heads still on their shoulders. An added complication is that many firms hire employees that have never worked together, or bring in third party nationals (in Iraq, the PMF nationalities range from Americans and British to less-well-paid Salvadoreans, Fijians and Serbs). Thus cost savings can come at the price of lesser bonds of group loyalty or patriotism, showing how gains in one area can harm another.

2) *The open military market.* The private military market is global, but it is also effectively unregulated. There are insufficient controls over who can work for these new corporate VNSAs and who these corporate VNSAs can work for. The discretion in recruiting, screening, and hiring for public military roles has been largely left to private firms, with mixed results. PMF employees have ranged from distinguished and decorated veterans to bad apples that do not best represent the public interest. In Iraq, this problem was magnified by the gold rush effect, where many of the firms that entered the market were entirely new to the business or else escalated in size in a manner reminiscent of the height of the Internet boom.

On the skills side, many PMF employees represent the peak of the military profession. For example, there are a great number of recently retired 'tier one'

US Special Forces operators (arguably among the best soldiers in the world) in Iraq, as well as more ex-British SAS troops than serve in the current SAS force. At the same time, however, the rush for profits and mass numbers brought in a lesser crop of skills, with potential grave consequences. For example, US Army investigators of the Abu Ghraib prison abuse found that 'Approximately 35% of the contract interrogators lacked formal military training as interrogators.'[16]

On the human rights side, the vast majority of PMF employees are honourable men and women. However, many firms have had minimal or insufficient screening, sometimes hiring individuals with questionable backgrounds later proving embarrassing for the wider public mission. Darker examples in Iraq range from the hiring of an ex-British Army soldier who had earlier been jailed for working with Irish terrorists to another firm bringing in an ex-South African apartheid regime soldier who had admitted to firebombing the houses of over 60 political activists back home.

The problem of clientele mirrors that of employee recruitment, with corporate best practices in great variance, and often in contradiction. For example, as more complex emergencies overwhelm the collective international capacity to respond effectively, the emerging private military marketplace has stepped forward to offer humanitarian organizations a new means to enhance their capacities without turning to traditional state military assistance. This is the option being quietly chosen by many humanitarian clients.

Indeed, one limited study found that humanitarians have contracted PMFs in war zones such as Afghanistan, Bosnia, the Democratic Republic of Congo, East Timor, Haiti, Iraq, Kosovo, Mozambique, Sierra Leone, Somalia, and Sudan. In total, the study found more than 40 contracts between PMFs and humanitarian actors (and it was by no means a comprehensive survey).[17] The firms have gone to work for the full gamut of humanitarian actor types, including privately funded NGOs (both secular and religious), state agencies, and international agencies. How things have changed is illustrated by one non-governmental humanitarian organization that hired a PMF in Iraq to

[16] Major General George Fay and Lieutenant General Anthony Jones, US Army 'Investigation of Intelligence Activities at Abu Ghraib', 2004. Available at http://news.findlaw.com/hdocs/docs/dod/fay82504rpt.pdf.

[17] P.W. Singer, 'Humanitarian Principles, Private Military Agents: Some Implications of the Privatized Military Industry for the Humanitarian Community' in Humanitarian Policy Group, *Resetting the Rules of Engagement: Trends and Issues in Military—Humanitarian Relations*. February 2006. download at: http://www.brookings.edu/views/articles/singer20060307.htm

protect its facilities and staff; the humanitarian group even had its own sniper teams, which killed several insurgents.

The problem is that, although the privatized military industry may open up possibilities, its use in such a way also poses fundamental questions about the very future of the humanitarian ethic of neutrality. It also raises simple problems of practical implementation. Despite the huge amount of hiring, the research found only three humanitarian agencies that had formal documents on how their workers should relate to PMFs and their staff, and only one organization that had detailed oversight guidance for its PMF employees, such as instructions on rules of engagement. However, even that organization had difficulty implementing the guidelines, given the lack of expertise within its country teams.

These sorts of challenges are tough enough when companies are working for what most would describe as 'the good guys'. But it is an even more difficult issue to decide who are the good guys, especially when the private interest becomes part of the equation. States are not inherently 'good' or 'evil', nor are VNSAs. The 2005 'rent a coup' episode in Equatorial Guinea, involving a well known PMF, illustrates the problem of teasing out exactly what is the right or moral thing to do in the absence of external guidance or rules. On the one hand, the firm and its private funders (allegedly including several well known public figures in the United Kingdom) were convicted of plotting the violent toppling of a government, for reasons of profit.[18] On the other hand, the would-be 'victim', the state of Equatorial Guinea was run by President Teodoro Obiang, who took power following a coup, after which his predecessor, Francisco Macías Nguema, was executed by firing squad, and who presides over one of the most authoritarian regimes on the continent. Raising more questions about equity is that today, many of the PMFers who took part in the planned coup are in jail, while the alleged funders of it are not.

3) *Public policy through private means.* The private military industry provides the new possibility of seeking public policy ends through private, non-state, military means. This allows governments to carry out actions that generally would not gain legislative or public approval. This can be an advantage in meeting unrecognized or unsupported strategic needs, but can disconnect the public from its own foreign policies.

The increased use of contractors in Colombia is an illustration of this trend on the covert operations side. But, as the stark public division over the Iraq

[18] For further on this episode, please see Robert Young Pelton, *Licensed to Kill*, New York: Crown, 2006.

war illustrates, this can be worrisome even for overt, discretionary operations. The problem is that the goals of contractors can contrast with the goals of the mission overall. In Iraq, for example, the research shows that while PMFs carried out a variety of important roles, the overall effect of their operations proved to be a hindrance rather than a help to the counter-insurgency efforts of coalition forces.

Not all contractors are 'cowboys' or 'mercenaries' as they are often described. But their 'job', as the Blackwater CEO Eric Prince put it, is a different one from the broader 'mission'. In their focus only on the contract, they drive convoys up the wrong side of the road, ram civilian vehicles, toss smoke bombs, and fire weaponry as warnings, all as standard practices. As one contractor described, 'Our mission is to protect the principal at all costs. If that means pissing off the Iraqis, too bad.'[19]

They have also weakened American efforts in the 'war of ideas' both inside Iraq and beyond. As one Iraqi official explained, even before the recent shootings, 'They are part of the reason for all the hatred that is directed at Americans, because people don't know them as Blackwater, they know them only as Americans. They are planting hatred, because of these irresponsible acts.'[20] In turn, the abuses committed by contractors have been covered extensively across the wider Muslim world, and this has had an effect on the US government. For example, after the 2007 Blackwater shootings, every single media outlet in the Middle East reported on the episode, focusing on how the US could hire such '...arrogant trigger-happy guns for hire, mercenaries by any other name', as the UAE-based *Gulf News* put it.[21] The Al Jazeera satellite news channel reported on the US hired contractors as 'An army that seeks fame, fortune, and thrill, away from all considerations and ethics of military honour.... The employees are known for their roughness. They are famous for shooting indiscriminately at vehicles or pedestrians who get close to their convoys.'[22] In the newspaper *Al-Sharq Al-Awsat* Fahmy Howeydi, one of the more influential commentators in the entire Arab world, compared Blackwater 'mercenaries' to Al Qaeda, coming to Iraq's chaos to seek their fortunes.

[19] Steve Fainaru, 'Where military rules don't apply.' *washingtonpost.com*, 20 September 2007, http://www.washingtonpost.com/wp-dyn/content/article/2007/09/19/AR2007 091902503_pf.html.

[20] Fainaru, 'Where military rules don't apply.'

[21] 'Guns for hire in troubled waters.' *Gulf News*, 18 September 2007, http://www.gulfnews. com/opinion/editorial_opinion/region/10154563.html.

[22] BBC Monitoring International Reports, 'Al-Jazeera TV highlights Blackwater incident in Iraq', 18 September 2007.

The use of contractors also promoted a double standard towards Iraqi civilian institutions that undermines efforts to build up these very same institutions, another key lesson of counterinsurgency. As one Iraqi said of Blackwater, 'They are more powerful than the government. No one can try them. Where is the government in this?'[23] That he was an Iraqi Army soldier encapsulates the problem of how a VNSA can undermine respect for the state.

Finally, contractors have forced policymakers to jettison strategies designed to win the counterinsurgency on multiple occasions, before they even had a chance to succeed. The US Marine plan for counterinsurgency in the 'Sunni Triangle' of Iraq in 2004 was never implemented, because of uncoordinated contractor decisions. This helped turn Fallujah into a rallying point of the insurgency. More recently, US government leaders planned to pressure the Iraqi government to necessary action on the political benchmarks of the 'surge'; instead, they had to request Iraqi help and understanding in cleaning up the aftermath of the 2007 Blackwater shootings in Baghdad.

This has created a growing tension between private contractors and American military units and how they coordinate their activities (or not). This was heightened by the fact that contractors often earned twice as much as US soldiers or more, even though that same taxpayer is the source of the money for both. In June 2006, the Government Accountability Office reported that 'private security providers continue to enter the battle space without coordinating with the U.S. military, putting both the military and security providers at a greater risk for injury.'[24]

As a result, US military officers frequently expressed their frustrations over sharing the battlefield with such private forces operating under their own rules and agendas, and concern about the consequences for their own operations. For example, Brigadier General Karl Horst, deputy commander of the US 3rd Infantry Division (responsible for the Baghdad area) tellingly put it, 'These guys run loose in this country and do stupid stuff. There's no authority over them, so you can't come down on them hard when they escalate force. They shoot people, and someone else has to deal with the aftermath.'[25]

---

[23] Sabrina Tavernise and James Glanz, 'Iraqi report says Blackwater guards fired first' *New York Times*, 19 September 2007, http://www.nytimes.com/2007/09/19/world/middleeast/19blackwater.html

[24] Government Accountability Office (GAO), *Rebuilding Iraq: Actions Still Needed to Improve the Use of Private Security Providers*, GAO-06–865T 13 June 2006, available at: http://www.gao.gov/docdblite/details.php?rptno=GAO-06–865T

[25] As quoted in 'Contractors in Spotlight as Shootings Add Up', *Charlotte Observer*, 11 September 2005, 6a.

More broadly, outsourcing as a means of undercutting transparency in foreign policy raises deeper concerns, including concerns for the long-term health of democracies. As Arthur S. Miller once wrote, 'Democratic government is *responsible* government—which means *accountable* government—and the essential problem in contracting out is that responsibility and accountability are greatly diminished.'

4) *PMFs and the legal grey area.* Like many other VNSAs, PMFs have also introduced dilemmas on the legal side, as much of law is a state centred system.

Private military firms and their employees are integral, inherent parts of military operations. But, at the end of the day, they are not part of the military. This means that the old legal codes, which seek to create a sharp delineation between civilians and soldiers, are not readily useful. One cannot describe PMF employees as simply accompanying the force like the sutlers of old (the merchants and camp followers who sold their wares to troops in the field, up to the 1800s), when they are carrying and using weapons, interrogating prisoners, loading bombs, and fulfilling other mission-critical roles. This leaves a disturbing legal vacuum. As one military law analyst noted: 'Legally speaking, they [military contractors] fall into the same grey area as the unlawful combatants detained at Guantánamo Bay.'[26]

On the contractor side, the lack of clarity means that if they are captured, it is up to their adversaries to define their status. An illustrative example is the case of the three American employees of *California Microwave Systems*, whose plane crashed in rebel held territory in Colombia in 2003. These three crewmen have been held since, with their Geneva rights as POWs not upheld by either the rebels or their own US government clients, and the executives of the firm that hired them washing their hands of the matter.

Such difficulties also play out on the side of accountability. It is often unclear which authorities are to investigate, prosecute, and punish crimes committed by PMFs and/or their employees, and how, when and where. While the military has established legal structures that constitute the court martial system, the legal status of contractors in war zones is murky. How a business organization and its corporate chain of command are held accountable is even further removed from the present system. As one military lawyer succinctly described, 'There is a dearth of doctrine, procedure, and policy.'

[26] Philip Carter, 'Hired Guns', *Slate*, 9 April 2004, http://www.slate.com/id/2098571.

Indeed, the owner and employees of a circus face more legal inspection and accountability than those of a private military firm.

Although private military firms and their employees are now integral parts of many military operations, they tend to fall through the cracks of legal codes, which sharply distinguish civilians from soldiers. Private military contractors are not exactly civilians, given that they often carry and use weapons, interrogate prisoners, load bombs, and fulfil other critical military roles. Yet they are not quite soldiers, either, in that they are not part of the service or in the chain of command of military forces, and might not even be of the same nationality.

International law does not define the status of contractors (they do not fit the international mercenary definition) and lacks the actual means to enforce itself without the state. This defers the problem to the state level. Normally, an individual's crimes fall under the local nation's laws. But PMFs typically operate in failed state zones; indeed, the absence or weakness of the local state government is usually why they are there.

Within Iraq, for example, this legal problem was further complicated by a little known memo known as Order 17. In one of the many decisions that will lead history to judge the Coalition Provisional Authority (CPA) as one of the more inept governing organizations in modern times, two days before the CPA dissolved itself it issued an order that could be interpreted as giving foreign contractors immunity from Iraqi law. While the legal standing of this order is questionable now, the interpretation of it held. Contractors saw themselves as above the law and the record seemed to back them up. In the three years that followed that CPA order, not one contractor operating in Iraq was prosecuted or convicted for any crime involving an Iraqi victim or any kind of conduct in the battle space.

The lack of international or local state capability forces the question of accountability back to the home state of the contractor. But because the acts were committed abroad, the application of home state law is problematic. Some states have effective laws, but no means to enforce them abroad, such as South Africa and Nepal, which have legally prohibited their citizens from working for PMFs to no avail, while most states have certain aspects of laws, but large gaps in them, such as the US.

The US, for example, has two key laws that might be applied to contractors it has hired working abroad. These entail the extra-territorial application of civilian law in the Military Extra-territorial Jurisdiction Act (or MEJA, originally passed in 2000) and the Uniform Code of Military Justice (UCMJ, with the definition of civilians falling under the jurisdiction of military law expanded from times of declared war to contingency operations in the autumn of 2006).[27]

The reality is that they are almost never actually used. MEJA says that a civilian working for the Pentagon or Pentagon contractor can be prosecuted back in the US if they commit a felony abroad. But it was originally designed for family abuse cases among those living in military bases, not for the conduct of contractors in a battle zone. Its scope has not included contractors working for other agencies or organizations than the Pentagon, nor is civilian law set up to decide issues in war (as opposed to normal civilian felonies), such as what constitutes a violation of the rules of engagement. Indeed, the only applications of MEJA in the last four years in Iraq were against a KBR contractor who had attempted to rape an American army reservist while she was sleeping inside a trailer in the Green Zone, and against another contractor who tried to bring child pornography with him back to the US. In turn, while the UCMJ legal change happened in the autumn of 2006, the Pentagon is yet to issue a guidance paper on how and upon whom US military officers should use it in the field. Without the instructions from above, its effect has been like a tree falling in the forest with no one there. Is it real or not, if no one hears it fall?

That the law rarely goes into action on contractor issues certainly has not helped the sense of legal controls over this new VNSA. Not only did this vacuum help impel contractors towards more aggressive actions; it completely invalidated the message that American political advisers were trying to push to their Iraqi counterparts of the necessity of establishing the 'rule of law' as a way of ending the insurgency. Finally, the contractors' seeming freedom from justice was considered a particular affront. 'The Iraqis despised them, because they were untouchable', said Matthew Degn, former senior American adviser to the Interior Ministry. 'They were above the law.'[28]

For example, it was reported that 100 per cent of the translators and up to 50 per cent of the interrogators at the Abu Ghraib prison were private contractors from the Titan and CACI firms respectively. The US Army found that contractors were present in 36 per cent of abuse incidents that its investigators were able to identify and cited six particular employees as being

---

[27] Peter W. Singer, 'Frequently Asked Questions on the UCMJ Change and its Applicability to Private Military Contractors.' January 12 (2007), http://www.brookings.edu/views/op-ed/psinger/20070112.htm.

[28] Fainaru, 'Where Military Rules Don't Apply.'

potentially culpable in the abuses.[29] However, while the enlisted US Army soldiers involved in the Abu Ghraib abuse, who were cited in the reports, were properly court martialled for their crimes, not one of the private contractors named in the Army investigation reports has yet been charged, prosecuted, or punished, the US Army feeling that it did not even have jurisdiction to do so if it wanted.

In another incident in 2005, armed contractors from the Zapata firm were detained by US forces, who claimed they saw the private soldiers indiscriminately firing not only at Iraqi civilians, but also at US Marines. Again, they were not charged, as the legal issues could not be squared.[30]

Other cases included the Aegis 'trophy video', in which contractors set video of them shooting at civilians to Elvis Presley's song *Runaway Train* and put it on the Internet; the alleged joyride shootings of Iraqi civilians by a Triple Canopy supervisor (which became the subject of a lawsuit after the two employees, who claim to have witnessed the shootings, lost their jobs); and a reported shooting on Christmas Eve 2006, where a Blackwater employee allegedly got drunk while inside the Green Zone in Baghdad, got into an argument with a guard of the Iraqi Vice President, and then shot him dead.[31] In none of these cases was anyone charged, prosecuted, or punished.

Indeed, more than 100,000 private military contractors who are in Iraq have been deployed there for almost five years, and yet not one has been prosecuted or punished for any crime of conduct on the battlefield. While this shows a huge disparity with the dozens of US and allied soldiers that have been prosecuted for crimes large and small in Iraq (as every force has its bad apples), perhaps a more illustrative point of comparison is with civilian life. The town of Westport, Connecticut, has roughly the same per capita income (over $70,000 a year) as the PMF population in Iraq. But even this comfortable suburb has a crime rate of above 28 per 1,000 citizens, as compared with the 0 per 1,000 rate with PMFs. Thus, private military industry shows an

---

[29] Major General George Fay and Lieutenant General Anthony Jones, US Army 'Investigation of Intelligence Activities at Abu Ghraib', 2004. Available http://news.findlaw.com/hdocs/docs/dod/fay82504rpt.pdf.

[30] David Phinney, 'Marines Jail Contractors in Iraq', CorpWatch.com, 7 June 2005.

[31] Robert Young Pelton, 'Blackwater Contractor Kills Vice President's: Green Zone Shooting Just One of Many Industry 'Dirty Secrets' Iraqslogger.com, 8 February 2007; 'In Iraq, a private realm of intelligence-gathering', *Washington Post*, 1 July 2007. Sean Raymont, '"Trophy" video exposes private security contractors shooting up Iraqi drivers', Telegraph, 26 Nov. 2005; Tom Jackman, 'U.S. contractor fired on Iraqi vehicles for sport, suit alleges', *Washington Post*, 17 November 2006; A20.

astonishing contrast with either military or civilian equivalents. We can only conclude that with PMFs, we have stumbled upon the perfect 'Stepford Village' in Iraq, where human nature has been overcome, in the midst of a war zone; or else that we have a clear combination of an absence of law and absence of political will to deal with this VNSA when it comes to the law.[32]

5) *Private questions for the public military*. Finally, the extensive use of private contractors in public military roles raises a series of long-term questions for the military itself. The military has long seen itself as a unique profession, set apart from the rest of civilian society as it is held accountable for the safety and security of that society. In turn, the military profession was integral to the rise of the state. As Tilly wrote, 'War made the state and the state made war.'[33]

The introduction of PMFs and their recruiting from within the military, to take on military roles, brings a new dynamic into this realm. PMFs signify the morphing of this once unique professional identity onto the regular civilian marketplace, and at the same time the loss of many of the public roles that the state's military had once monopolized.

Thus, soldiers tend to have a mixed attitude about PMFs. On one hand, they feel deeply overstretched and overburdened in today's security environment. While deployed on a range of global missions and now enmeshed in Iraq, the US military is actually 35 per cent smaller than it was at the height of the Cold War; the British military is as small as its been since the Napoleonic wars. PMFs are thus filling a gap in the force structure that soldiers recognize and worry about. Additionally, PMFs offer the potential for many soldiers to have a second career that still keeps them within an occupational field they know and love.

However, there are also brewing concerns within the military about what this industry will mean for the health of the profession, as well as general resentment over firms and individuals using the training and human investment that the military provided for personal and organizational profit.

---

[32] For further on this, please see P.W. Singer, 'Frequently Asked Questions on the UCMJ Change and its Applicability to Private Military Contractors', 12 January 2007, available at http://pwsinger.com/commentary_070112.html; Congressional Research Service, 'Private Security Contractors in Iraq: Background, Legal Status, and Other Issues', updated 21 June 2007: available at: http://www.fas.org/sgp/crs/natsec/RL32419.pdf

[33] Charles Tilly, 'Reflections on the History of European State-Making', in Charles Tilly (ed.), *The Formation of National States in Western Europe*, Princeton University Press, 1975, p. 42.

Soldiers also look at many of the roles taken over by firms—from training to technical support—and worry whether the loss of these professional skills and functions will hamstring the military in the future.

A particular problem area that Iraq has brought to the fore is how an expanding PMF marketplace has the potential to hurt the state military's retention of talented soldiers. Soldiers in the PMF industry can make anywhere from twice to ten times what they make in the regular military. In Iraq, the rates have grown astronomically, with former Special Forces troops garnering as much as $1,000 a day.

While soldiers have always had competing job options in the civilian marketplace, such as Air Force pilots leaving to fly airliners, the PMF industry is significantly different. PMFs keep the individual within the military, and thus public, sphere. More important, the PMF industry is directly competitive. It not only draws its employees from the military, it does so to fill military roles, thus shrinking the military's purview. The overall process is thus brilliant from a business standpoint and self-defeating from the military's perspective. PMFs use public funds to recruit on the basis of higher pay and then charge back the military at a higher rate, all for the human capital investment that the military originally paid for.

The issue has become pointed for Special Forces units, as they have the most skills (from the longest human capital training investment) and, in turn, are the most marketable for the firms to their clients. Elite force commanders in Australia, New Zealand, Britain and the United States have all expressed deep concern. One US Special Forces officer described the issue of retention among his most experienced (10 years plus) troops, so integral to unit cohesion, as 'at a tipping point'. The policy responses in these states have been insufficient. Some foreign militaries now allow their troopers to take a year's leave of absence, in the hope that they will make their quick money and return, rather than be lost to the market for ever; the US military created a special working group to 'explore' the issue.

## The policy response

The private military market has expanded at a breakneck business pace, while government has yet to even recognize its responsibilities as the public regulator or even as a non-gullible client. The outcome is a distortion of the free market that would shock Adam Smith, an interface between business and government that would awe the Founding Fathers, and a shift in the military-industrial complex that must have President Eisenhower rolling in his grave.

Without change it is a recipe for bad policy, and bad business. It is first essential to lift the veil of secrecy that surrounds the industry. While the obvious focus would seem to be on covert operations, transparency is actually more needed on the Enron-like accounting. Far too many of the public numbers on the PMF industry are baseline figures or estimates.

Thus, the client in this case must exercise its rights by undertaking a comprehensive survey to finally figure out the full scope of what it has outsourced and what the results have been. This is the only way to learn the right lessons and maximize results. The government should also require that all current and future contracts involving non-classified activities be releasable for public scrutiny, like other government documents. Each contract should also have 'contractor visibility' measures, which would list the number of employees to carry out the functions and what they are being paid, thus limiting obscene abuses. Legislatures must resist corporate donors and lobbyists and instead support the military in an effort to bring some transparency and accompanying financial sense to the matter.

Secondly, the military must take a step back and figure out just what roles and functions are in our best national security interests to privatize and what are not. We are now starting to see this debate within the US military as to whether some roles and functions should not have been outsourced in the first place and whether a rollback is needed. This will continue as more of the Iraq-generation field officers advance in the ranks. For example, US Army Colonel Peter Mansoor is one of the most influential military thinkers on counter-insurgency. In 2007, he told *Jane's Defense Weekly* that the US military needs to take

...a real hard look at security contractors on future battlefields and figure out a way to get a handle on them so that they can be better integrated—if we're going to allow them to be used in the first place...if they push traffic off the roads or if they shoot up a car that looks suspicious, whatever it may be, they may be operating within their contract—to the detriment of the mission, which is to bring the people over to your side. I would much rather see basically all armed entities in a counter-insurgency operation fall under a military chain of command.[34]

Similarly, US CENTCOM commander Admiral James Fallon noted, private contractors should not be seen as a 'surrogate army' of the State Department or any other agency whose workers they protect. 'My instinct is that it's easier and better if they were in uniform and were working for me.'[35]

---

[34] As quoted on Nathan Hodge, 'Revised US Law Spotlights Role of Contractors on Battlefield.' *Jane's Defense Weekly*, 10 January 2007, p. 10.
[35] Mike Baker, 'Cowboy' Aggression Works for Blackwater.' *AP*, 25 September 2007.

This debate must continue and expand to include the many PMF clients beyond the US military. A general lesson of privatization, from cities privatizing garbage collection to Cisco outsourcing its router production, is that outsourcing can be greatly beneficial, up to the point where it begins to challenge core functions. This equally holds for any military. The old military doctrine on contracting had been that if a function was 'mission-critical' or 'emergency essential' (that is, effecting the success or failure of the operation), then it should be kept within the force. It also held that civilians should be armed only under extraordinary circumstances, for their self-protection, certainly not deployed in roles that mandated it as a functional requirement. We must either return to respecting these older, well thought out standards or create new ones. The present ad-hoc process yields only inferior results.

The third lesson is self evident, but equally ignored: privatize something if it will save you money or raise quality; if not, then don't. All too often, we outsource first and do not even bother to ask questions later.

Privatization can be greatly beneficial. But too frequently the hoped-for gains are directly undermined by misunderstanding the underlying assumptions of the theory. That something is private does not mean it is inherently better, quicker, or cheaper. Rather, it is through leveraging free-market mechanisms that one potentially gets better private results. If there is competition on the open market to get the best price, if the firm is able to specialize and build redundancies, if the client is able to provide oversight and management to guard their own interests, and if the firm is properly motivated through the terms of the contract and a fear of being fired, then success can be achieved. Instead, the government often forgets these simple lessons and gets not the best of privatization, but the worst of monopolization.

Tapping simple business expertise will thus aid the government to become a better client. When it comes to assessing the costs and benefits, a smart client runs its own numbers. Sadly, a number of PMF contracts simply began when a firm came in claiming that it would save the state money and no one examined it for themselves (neither then nor afterwards).

Good competition will yield better quality and price. By comparison, some 40 per cent of US Defence Department contracting is non-competed, with more than $300 billion non-competed over last five years. For example, in the contracting with the CACI firm at Abu Ghraib prison, US Army investigators not only found that an employee of the firm may have helped write the work order, but that the hire of interrogators was simply added to a contract dating to 1998, for computer services!

One of the great challenges in overseeing this new VNSA is that while the amount of contracting with such non-state actors has boomed, the number of governmental contract officers (the 'eyes and ears' of the government, who do monitoring and oversight) has shrunk. By one count, the number of Pentagon defence services contracts is up by 78 per cent since the late 1990s, while the number of officials tasked with overseeing them is *down* by over 40 per cent.[36] In turn, many who hire these VNSAs, such as humanitarian and other non-state groups, have no trained contracting officers for the job.

The contract structure is also greatly important. The 'cost plus' arrangement has become a needless default and is utilized in far too many situations with PMFs. In effect, this structure rewards companies with higher profits the more they spend. When combined with lax or absent oversight, it is ripe for abuse and inefficiency, besides running counter to everything Adam Smith wrote about free markets.

To have a successful outsourcing experience, we must let the markets work for us when dealing with corporate VNSAs, rather than doing our utmost to take away any market advantage. The potential punishment of being fired or the cost of having a terrible reputation allows the marketplace in other business realms to be self-correcting. However, these usual sanction mechanisms have too often been short-circuited. For example, in 2007, the Pentagon awarded the new Logistics Civilian Augmentation Program (LOGCAP), potentially worth up to $150 billion, to Halliburton-Kellogg Brown and Root (KBR), DynCorp, and Fluor. Yet the government has also cited those three companies for 29 cases of serious misconduct in the last decade of contracting (the category includes 'false claims against the government, violations of the Anti-Kickback Act, fraud, conspiracy to launder money...').[37] When a client so defangs itself, it sends a terrible signal not only to such firms, but also to their would-be competitors, as well as to the men and women who are supposed to be doing the oversight and investigation.

Finally, action must be taken on the issue of legal accountability. This is not only important for the task of regulating the private military industry and the individuals within it, but also in our responsibility to our public military. To pay contractors more than soldiers is one thing; to give them a legal free pass on top of that is unconscionable.

[36] Renae Merle, 'Government short of contracting officers: officials struggle to keep pace with rapidly increasing defense spending', *Washington Post*, 5 July 2007, P. E8.
[37] Roxana Tiron, 'Watchdog group: Government awards contracts despite firms' misconduct', *The Hill*, 19 July 2007.

Loopholes must be filled and new laws developed to cover the variety of legal and jurisdictional dilemmas. A key requisite is to extend legal clarity to the questions of who can work for the firms, who the firms can work for, and what bodies and codes will investigate, prosecute, and punish any wrongdoing and in what domains.

As this is a transnational industry, there is a need for international involvement. Proposals range from updating the international anti-mercenary laws to creating a UN body that sanctions and regulates PMFs. However, any movement on the international front will take years, while the PMF industry is in the here and now. This means that each state that has an involvement with the industry, either as client or as home base, and thus has an imperative need to develop and amend laws relevant to PMFs. It may sound like an extreme burden, but dealing with the legal challenges of new industries is what ensures a living law, as states have had to do so with the rise of telecommunications or the Internet.

In an ideal arrangement, states will coordinate their efforts and attempt to involve regional bodies to maximize coverage and ease the path to international standards. For example, the discussions of regulation set to begin in the United Kingdom would do well to pursue coordination with other EU states, and the same could be worked out in other regional settings. The US similarly should communicate on this issue with its friends and allies, to bring laws into alignment.

## Conclusions

The forces that drove the growth of the private military industry seem set in place. Recalling the Internet comparison, while the Iraq private military 'bubble' will ultimately burst when that conflict simmers down at some point, the overall industry is here to stay for at least the next decades.

Despite this, the governments of the world remain woefully uninformed and ill-equipped to deal with the industry, as either client or regulator. The strength of systems of democracy and capitalism is that they are supposed to be self-correcting and self-improving. When it comes to the private military world, though, our governments seems to be repeatedly ignoring not just the basic lessons of better business, but also those of smart public policy.

So, oddly enough, the emergence of private military industry often brings us to some deep questions. When thinking about such private military firms doing jobs once held by soldiers, many evoke the memory of President Eisenhower and his fears of a 'military industrial complex'.

Yet the guidance of the very first American conservatives may be more helpful. The authors of the *Federalist Papers*, who helped guide the writing of the US Constitution—John Jay, Alexander Hamilton, and James Madison—warned about the role of any private interests not responsive to the general interests of a broadly defined citizenry. The plan that the Founding Fathers had for government in the new United States sought to make officials responsive to the general interests of this citizenry. In turn, they also set up internal controls designed to check the ambitions of those holding power within government. Their worry was that, when private interests move into the public realm and public influence on public policy is stifled, governments tend to make policies that do not match the public interest. The issue of private military firms should be weighed in this balance of public and private today.

PMFs may be corporate actors, but they are VNSAs participating in war all the same. In the end, we must always remember that the stakes in warfare are far higher than in other corporate realms. In this most essential public sphere, both national and international security are at stake, as well as people's lives. Clemenceau in World War I declared that 'War is far too important to be left to the generals.' The same holds true for the CEOs.

# 19

# Non-State Actors in Conflict

## A Challenge for Policy and for Law

*Alyson J.K. Bailes and Daniel Nord*

## Introduction and context

The problem of non-state actors was not invented on 11 September 2001, but the events of that day propelled it to the centre of international policy debate. The shocking demonstration of the power of a small, transnational, non-state group also drew attention back to the non-Westphalian[1] features of most twenty-first century armed conflicts, and to the way that civil wars in weak states both feed upon and breed international crime, smuggling, predatory business behaviour and terrorism.

At the conceptual level, two related premises started to be treated as axioms, at least by most English-speaking analysts: that non-state actors are undermining the modern state's fundamental attribute of a monopoly of the (legitimate) use of force; and that no traditional method of strategy or diplomacy can be used to deter, discipline or negotiate with. Both points have some force, but the problem lies in the impact on strategy and policy when the two propositions are merged. The US Administration of George W. Bush famously concluded after 9/11 that the only methods to use against hostile non-state

---

[1] The word 'Westphalian', referring back to the Treaty of Westphalia 1648, is commonly used to describe an international system based upon sovereign nation-states and focusing its efforts for security on their interactions.

actors, with their sponsors and abettors, were ostracism, coercion and elimination typical of all-out war. It sought to apply a strategy of military counterforce, treating the new enemy in some ways like the Cold War Soviet bloc—monolithic, ideology-driven—but adopting a military strategy based on preemption and maximum force superiority rather than deterrence, containment or balance. At the same time, the Administration declined to have its choices limited by either national or international laws if these seemed to it to favour the enemy's freedoms more than they protected the good. The USA's National Security Strategy document of September 2002 explicitly rejected 'legalistic' solutions for the challenges posed by terrorism and possible proliferation of mass-destruction techniques, just as it favoured ad hoc coalitions over fixed institutional frameworks.[2]

In the years since the US-led invasions of Afghanistan and Iraq (in 2001 and 2003, respectively) there has been time for the contradictions of this new strategy to be exposed in their turn. Coercion, especially by military force, has not proved an efficient way of defeating—or even demoralizing—hostile non-state actors, or transforming the habitats where they thrive. Voices inside and outside the United States have also warned that actions against states or individuals that sidestep or directly violate the laws and conventions of international behaviour are essentially self-defeating. Without law, ill-intentioned actors are encouraged to claim the same freedom for unconstrained pursuit of their own interests that the world's greatest democracy has claimed. Without law, it is harder to define in the first place who are the 'good' and 'bad', or what precise rules the terrorists or WMD developers and smugglers are breaking. Without law, what safeguard is there for the majority of states and citizens who have continued all along to behave as they ought?

The USA's own policies have highlighted the contradictions of an approach that downplays law both as a guide and as a tool. Washington has itself sought to tackle transnational non-state menaces by promoting new laws or the equivalent in the UN Security Council[3] and elsewhere, for example in the International Maritime Organization for port and harbour safety and container security. Even if occasional use of such methods could be explained as

---

[2] 'The National Security Strategy of the United States of America', published 17 Sep. 2002, URL http://www.whitehouse.gov/nsc/nss.pdf.

[3] See especially UNSCR 1373 of Sep. 2001 on global measures against terrorist financing and UNSCR 1540 of Apr. 2004 on unlawful trafficking and possession of WMD (all UNSCR texts are at at http://www.un.org/Docs/sc.ref).

a utilitarian choice, the chances of their working depend *inter alia* on respect for the legal authority of the institutions concerned and are not improved by other US actions calling that authority in question. Again, President Bush in his second term emphasized democracy building as a guarantor of good international behaviour; and in most definitions, democracy is inseparable from the rule of law.

At the end of the twenty-first century's first decade, it has thus become clearer that the security policy community cannot evade the challenge to which this chapter is addressed. How exactly do non-state actors of all kinds threaten the rule of national and international law, and what responses might best combine effectiveness with sustainability and legitimacy? While focused specifically on armed conflicts, this volume has shown how many different types of such actors may come into question: internal and external, sub-state and trans-state, groups and individuals, politically and commercially motivated, 'bad' and 'good'. Many such players are also complicit in non-conflict-related security problems—chronic low-level terrorism and criminal violence, illegal possession and transfer of Weapons of Mass Destruction (WMD), the general challenges of money-laundering, smuggling and trafficking, cyber-crimes and cyber-sabotage.

In the following sections this concluding chapter will recapitulate the main challenges posed by non-state actors in conflict and relate them specifically to the rule and enforcement of national or international law. It will then examine two sets of possible responses: (a) those aiming to provide (re-provide) appropriate and enforceable laws in the national context, and (b) those aiming to define, prevent and punish offences through the medium of international law. In practice these two modes are less distinct because many modern solutions require national enactment/enforcement of an internationally defined obligation or norm. A final section rehearses the lessons emerging and briefly relates them to non-conflict-related aspects of the non-state challenge.

## Defining the challenge

*What is a conflict?* For the purpose of most chapters in this volume, defining 'armed conflict' is not an issue—the situations in Iraq, Afghanistan, Somalia or Sudan can only be described that way. More precise definition is usually a headache for those analysts who seek to document and compare deaths, costs and other damage and need to draw dividing lines for that purpose between conflict and other forms of armed violence.[4] However, when focusing on the role of law as such, it is important to note a different set of formal and international-legal issues that apply.

International humanitarian law (IHL), also known as the Laws of War or *jus in bello*, only applies (as a *lex specialis*, a specialized branch of law) in a situation of an armed conflict. Thus in any given case of violence including violence of non-state actors (NSAs), definitions do have a role in deciding what types of law are relevant. Interestingly, the drafters of the Geneva Conventions[5]—which are still the core of the IHL *acquis*—purposely avoided giving any definition of 'armed conflict' in the text. The idea was that judgements on applicability should be based on fact and not risk being turned into a legal technicality. Since 1949, however, legal definitions for armed conflicts have multiplied, the most widely quoted being provided by the International Criminal Tribunal for the former Yugoslavia (ICTY) in the Tadić case submitted to it in 1994. The Court ruled that such a conflict exists 'whenever there is a resort to armed force between States or protracted armed violence between governmental authorities and organised armed groups or between such groups within a State.'

This definition makes clear that both international and internal clashes may be considered as armed conflict, but gives no guidance on how much armed force and violence is necessary. For IHL purposes, counting deaths alone is not enough. A brief incident at sea or a border clash between armed forces can result in many deaths without constituting an armed conflict as understood by IHL. Legal scholars have argued that such a conflict must involve more than isolated challenges and must extend over a certain time: on this view, a single terrorist attack or act of rebel sabotage does not make a 'conflict'. With regard to territorial application of IHL, the Tadić case definition states that it is applicable 'in the whole territory of the warring States or, in the case of internal conflicts, the whole territory under control of a party, whether or not actual combat takes place there.' Thus, since the intensity of fighting in the Helmand Province of southern Afghanistan certainly is of the magnitude of an armed conflict, humanitarian law is also applicable in the far quieter north of the country.

---

[4] For a well-established statistical approach see the Uppsala Conflict Data Base, http://www.ucdp.uu.se.

[5] These four Conventions were negotiated in April-August 1949 and cover the treatment of wounded, sick or shipwrecked members of the forces, POWs, and protection of civilians.

In short, IHL as a *lex specialis* replaces some already existing legal norms during an armed conflict, and the practical implications of this will be pursued below. In new types of conflict violence where the technical criteria for applying IHL may not be met, remedies can and should be found in other legal systems such as human rights law and/or national legal systems.

*Who are the actors?* In the class of armed conflicts as a whole, many sorts of non-state actors are involved and they can be categorized in several ways. The first distinction to make is between those originating inside or outside the conflict locality:

Internal non-state actors include organized armed groups of various kinds, terrorist groups/networks, actors using arms or other illegal force for non-political motives (such as bandits, kidnappers, looters), legal and illegal actors in the private business sphere including local defence/security service providers and arms traders, non-governmental organizations, citizens' groups and other organized communities such as churches or self-conscious ethnic communities.

External non-state actors include groups related to the conflict parties (combatants and refugees who have been driven out, sympathizer groups linked for example by ethnicity, exiles and diasporas), international terrorist groups/networks, smugglers and other war suppliers including traders in 'conflict commodities,'[6] traffickers in other contraband and in human beings, transnational criminal networks, private military and security companies based abroad, 'normal' foreign businesses owning property or trading or investing in the country, international media, international NGOs and charities, and individual aid volunteers.

International organizations, which play many roles in conflicts from military and civilian 'peace missions' through political mediation and advice to provision of humanitarian aid and economic assistance, are not states but do not exactly fit the non-state definition either. Few have any supranational powers or are able to act as legal entities distinct from the states that compose them, above all in the defence and security field. Still, some of their actions—such as aid from the European Union's rapid humanitarian intervention fund, ECHO, or UN food aid—have a 'de-nationalized' and de-politicized flavour not unlike international NGOs; while the implication of the UN's or NATO's or the EU's sending of troops is clearly different from that of a nation inter-

---

[6] Diamonds are the best-known case of goods traded directly to finance VNSA activities, but the range may include drugs (Afghanistan, Colombia) and high-value minerals or oil, for example.

vening under the Westphalian system. For present purposes it may be best to sidestep definitions and simply note that these actors can have an important impact on the non-state dimension of conflicts outside their members' territory. They always intend and normally manage to reduce problems caused by VNSAs, but their very entry to the scene may also complicate or even aggravate certain non-state dynamics.[7]

Fig. 19.1 A Simple Categorization of Violent Non-State Actors[8]

| | Seeking change | Pro or anti-status quo | Profit motive |
|---|---|---|---|
| Armed rebels | YES | ANTI | (secondary) |
| Pro-government militias/'death squads' | NO | PRO | (instrumental) |
| Warlords/clan chiefs | NO | PRO | (secondary) |
| Terrorists | YES | ANTI | (instrumental) |
| Criminals, gangs | NO | (indifferent) | YES |
| PMCs/PSCs | NO* | (indifferent)* | YES |

* These are the *instrinsic* qualities of PMCs/PSCs, given that their services are in principle available to all: but once hired they of course adhere to the side that pays them.

Most ways of classifying internal VNSAs in conflict are based on factors such as motivation, stance regarding the established power or status quo, and degree of organization. A simple example of such an analysis, covering the actors mainly addressed in this chapter, is in Figure 19.1. Actors are less often categorized as 'legal' or 'illegal' because these terms, strictly, can only refer to the formal chain of authorization, which says little about their true nature and impact. A militia or private military company employed by the state is appointed by a technically legal authority, but may use just as much excessive and illegal violence as its anti-state counterpart. Some fully 'legal' transactions, such as arms sales to a government party, can have nefarious end-results for security, order and human rights. In reality, the net impact of each grouping for good or ill, and the judgement on whether it shifts the situation more towards law or lawlessness, is a function of many factors whose combination differs in different conflicts over space and time. Actions clearly designed to

[7] There have been cases of individuals on peacekeeping missions trafficking in weapons, and buying drugs or prostitutes. See also the next sub-section.
[8] The table is adapted from Ulrich Schneckener, 'Armed Non-state Actors and the Monopoly of Force', in *Revisiting the State Monopoly on the Legitimate Use of Force*, DCAF Policy Paper 24, Geneva 2007, text at http://www.dcaf.ch/publications/.

break down order in a 'strong state' or developed-country environment could represent an attempt to establish order in the power vacuum and/or abusive setting of a weak or mismanaged polity. They could be widely viewed as legitimate democratic protest when occurring in a dictatorial or 'hermit' state, or when the international majority sees them as part of a justified effort for national self-determination.[9]

## Patterns and phases of violence

Other important differences in the roles and impact of VNSAs reflect the changing phases of conflict (or cycles in long-standing crises like the one between Israel and the Palestinians). Early in a conflict, all sides are likely to have predominantly political motives—even if these are strengthened by economic, social, ethnic or confessional grievances. The state authority, trading on its own legitimacy, may at first hold back from using tit-for-tat 'terror tactics' or non-state proxies. Later, as resources are exhausted, order is weakened and more external players are drawn in for good or ill, the likelihood grows that rebel groups will experiment with terrorism; that they and any existing terrorists will start using violence also to fund themselves;[10] that local leaders or 'warlords' will take up arms to protect their own fiefs; that the state will be tempted to sponsor its own vigilantes or 'death squads'; and that openings will be created for international terrorists, arms traffickers, criminals and smugglers, and private military companies on both sides. Reacting especially to the mounting human distress, well-intentioned external NSAs like charitable and humanitarian NGOs, and would-be mediators, will also be drawn in.

An important turning point comes as and when the international community decides to intervene: but the changes may not all be for the good. International sanctions, often imposed as a first stage, create openings for smugglers and other criminal elements to operate for profit and to assist illegal transfers from sympathizing states. Actual military intervention can spread violence and disorder as a result of rebels being driven to new areas or across frontiers, new refugee flows, and/or pressure on the targeted party to shift towards more

---

[9] These points underline why there is a major difference between *legality* and *legitimacy*, above all in conflicts that spring from earlier state abuses or neglect, and also why legitimacy has no single or simple definition. On that issue see particularly Chapter 1 in this volume and the literature on conflicts in the Middle East.

[10] This feature is strongly developed in some Latin American conflicts, like that in Colombia.

extreme and 'asymmetrical' methods including terrorism. When a peace deal is in prospect it is not uncommon for each side to stage a surge of violence so as to come to the table with more assets in hand, while extremist factions may splinter out of the groups that agree to negotiate, and 'spoiler' groups can arise to carry on or expand violence outside the negotiating framework. As for 'benign' NSAs, foreign NGO and charity representatives may still be very active during the phase of pacification and initial rebuilding, and tricky issues arise when national or institutional 'peacebuilders' seek to harness them within a civil-military framework as part of the overall restoration of order.[11] Under current thinking, local NGOs and civil society groups are also likely to be assigned important tasks in peace-building or even become primary engines of reform. Private military and security companies are increasingly often employed to work on demobilization of combatants, defence restructuring/ retraining and Security Sector Reform (SSR) generally; while economic reconstruction and rebuilding work can draw in a wider range of legitimate business interests.

If seen as a single arc from the point of view of law and law enforcement, these phases move from a status quo where legal authority exists but may be ineffective or abusive; through a phase of increasing lawlessness and confusion as some parties compete to wield the legal authority and many others profit from evading it; to a process of normalization in which violence ebbs and a single legal authority emerges again with a purely national, international or (quite often) mixed character. VNSAs are in their heyday in the middle phase but remain very important in the closing stage both as targets for remedial activity and as potential lawless spoilers. 'Benign' NSAs from home and abroad become most important in this last phase and may, indeed, be built into the new status quo on a continuing basis. The challenges for and applications of the law in greater detail for each phase will be examined below.

*What exactly is the problem and is law the answer?* The general challenges posed by VNSAs throughout this conflict sequence are related both to the internal and international rule of law:

---

[11] This issue has arisen in the Provincial Reconstruction Teams (PRTs) set up by ISAF troop contributing countries in Afghanistan, but there is similar unease over US government attempts to tighten control over NGOs receiving funds for reconstruction or democratization work elsewhere. The NGOs' worry is that confusing military and humanitarian roles can blur their own principles of impartiality and independence and in practical terms, expose them more often to attack by anti-intervention elements.

(i) they commit offences against all kinds of laws, including those relating to arms and the use of violence but also provisions on human rights and, often, civil law provisions in areas like property, trade and taxation;

(ii) their actions further weaken the internal law-making and law-enforcing authority within their territory, public respect for and trust in the law, and—at least in some cases—the credibility of and respect for international standards of law and the institutions that represent them;

(iii) as non-state (and often trans-state) actors, they are inherently difficult to target and discipline using national and international laws in the field of war-fare and weaponry that were originally designed to apply to states. If, as discussed above, this leads even actors from democratic states to question law's value as a tool and a defence, the copy-cat spiral of lawlessness may do much deeper and longer-lasting damage than anything that the VNSAs could have inflicted directly.

It may seem obvious that reasserting and restoring the rule of law, and where necessary adapting it to new targets, is the answer to this set of challenges: indeed, that is what the rest of this chapter is about. It is hard to frame this as a scientific conclusion, however, because so few studies have focused on exactly how different VNSAs impact upon the law, and how different law-related responses have performed in reducing the damage. Many policy makers recently, not only in the USA, have preferred to try direct and physical ways of re-establishing 'order' and an official monopoly of force. Others have focused on changing violent actors' minds and motivation or at least weaning away their followers, a method which sometimes bypasses the law in favour of political and economic incentives (including amnesties)—though it can also involve new legal rights and constitutional protection for the aggrieved parties.

One robust argument for using the law as, at least, part of the remedy after violence is quelled is that whoever is left in charge ought to respect the law themselves. Replacing chaos with autocracy, especially a partial, corrupt and non-accountable autocracy, is the quickest way to trigger the conflict cycle again. Equally, putting people in charge who are nice but unable to assert their monopoly of force, or leaving the line of legal inheritance unclear among a mixed group of 'successors', means that the conflict has not really been ended at all. Law is thus a convincing answer if it can apply to the rulers as to the ruled, and is combined with the power to enforce it. This in turn depends not only on the capacity of the appointed authorities but also—given that the general desire is to minimize the use of force—on the level of popular readiness to obey the new system without coercion, and on a good 'fit' between the structure and content of law and justice and the given post-conflict environment. Thus the legitimacy of the new status quo rests not only on the quality of the law itself, or formal observance of its letter, but depends just as critically on the political, constitutional, economic and societal processes that accompany it.

In the next sections, the law-related options available within such a framework are explored under two headings:

(a) ways of 're-legalizing' the situation within the state (or conflict zone) by rebuilding the rule of law and the means of its enforcement and bringing as many actors within the law as possible;
(b) ways of 'internationalizing' the legal order by applying and enforcing various kinds of international legal provisions.

Both methods can be used by both internal and external actors, and in practice any managed transition out of conflict needs both. If all goes well, (a) should predominate over time as normality returns and the local authorities can execute their own international obligations.

While a major aim of the whole process is to minimize the power of and risk from violent NSAs, the legitimacy and effectiveness of solutions depend on working *with* the right kinds of non-state actors at home and abroad. International and national NGOs are important movers on humanitarian law and human rights monitoring, civil society groups and media can play a key role in 'guarding the guardians' of law, while businesses must respect the law and also develop their self-regulation to get a grip on corruption, smuggling and technology leakage. Businesses, civil society networks, the media and cultural figures help to keep a recovering post-conflict society in touch with the outside world and can channel expectations, ideas and best practices that also assist in tackling new problems as they arise. Last but not least, closer integration in multilateral groupings has been an important part of post-conflict recovery strategies for states in Europe and, in a more traditional inter-governmental setting, in the South-east Asian (ASEAN) and the African sub-regions.

This scheme of analysis leaves out the question of legality and legitimacy of international intervention itself. It is of course an issue of real concern, not just in the case of forceful interventions, but even in relation to major political, economic and humanitarian inputs that are not *ipso facto* guaranteed to be impartial, law-building and productive of peace. Apart from the limits of space, however, the main argument for not dwelling on it here is that even when this type of intervention is part of the problem, it is not a non-state problem. The interveners are themselves states (or multi-state organizations) and remain so when engaging with non-state targets.[12] It cannot be over-stressed, however, that if an intervention designed to curb VNSAs is itself seen as unlawful or illegitimate or both (in nature and/or execution), it will make it far harder—for both practical and moral reasons—to apply the legal techniques in classes (a) and (b) above with any hope of lasting success.[13]

## Aspects and phases of 're-legalization' within the nation

*Towards a settlement.* The attempt to repair internal breakdown of law starts during the conflict, and its simplest form is the reassertion of control and authority by one of the parties. A government force that is still on the road to military victory can signal progress by, *inter alia*, imprisoning and trying people whom it charges with conflict-related crimes including incitement, looting, profiteering and theft as well as armed insurrection. Either governmental or non-governmental forces can mark their control of territories by starting to deliver state-like services including welfare, schooling etc.,[14] but also police forces, prisons and courts for civil offences. Foreign NSAs that have been colluding with the opposing factions, including extractive industries or traffickers in 'conflict commodities' as well as military and security companies,[15] can be expelled, brought to justice, or forced to 'legalize' themselves by concluding agreements with the (re-)conquering authorities. All such steps clearly help to rebuild a legal order: but so long as they reflect the self-assertion of one party based on its military success, there is no guarantee of the quality of the law they will establish—especially in terms of universality and impartiality—and even less, of the results in terms of natural justice.

[12] Interveners' objectives and methods are sometimes also heavily influenced by non-state 'advisers', for instance from émigré and oppositional circles, from NGOs and investigative media, and of course from private business.

[13] For a forthright discussion of criteria for intervention see Gareth Evans and Mohamed Sahnoun, 'The Responsibility to Protect', *Foreign Affairs*, Nov./Dec. 2002.

[14] This has been a prominent aspect of Hamas' and Hezbollah's profile but is not a strong point for the Taliban, for example.

[15] The question of how to establish legal discipline and answerability over PMCs/PSCs is far too complex to cover here, but see (in addition to Chapter 18 of this volume) Caroline Holmqvist, 'Private Security Companies: the Case for Regulation', SIPRI Policy Paper No 9 of Jan. 2005, text available at http://www.sipri.org.

Today, however, it is rather unusual for a conflict to run its course without some international engagement. In an intermediate scenario, the latter may take the form of supporting one side that is deemed more legitimate, and doing only the minimum needed to seal its success. In this case the picture just drawn of reassertion of authority will largely hold good, but with the difference that the winners must also try to satisfy the expectations of their sponsors. Whether that leads to more genuine law-building and law-abiding climate depends very much on the sponsors themselves. There have been and still are several cases where the intervener, for largely selfish reasons, encourages the rule of a 'strong man', or of a particular faction and ideology, rather than promoting pluralistic politics or the rule of impartial law—which may indeed be alien to his own practice.

In a more 'advanced' scenario, a relatively altruistic, often institution-based international force intervenes to make and/or keep peace and takes temporary control of at least part of the conflict-ridden territory. Such control always has implications for law and order because of the way it reduces VNSAs' freedom of play (in principle, on all sides); starts to renew the normal disciplines of society; and renews at least some orderly contact with the outside world (transport, delivery of goods, media access, etc.). Any international force and even any coalition of more than brief duration will need to have its own legal protocols regulating (among others) its rules of engagement, military discipline, 'status of forces' and so forth.[16] It may or may not make its own forces answerable to the local justice system,[17] but in any case it is responsible for ensuring that they respect relevant international laws and standards. Its mandate may or may not include helping in the identification and capture of individuals to be tried later for war crimes, and perhaps collecting evidence against them.[18]

---

[16] A Status of Forces Agreement (SOFA) covers such matters as the treatment of visiting forces under customs law and local civil or criminal jurisdiction. NATO and the UN have developed standard SOFAs for their operations.

[17] This aspect has been controversial in Iraq where the USA has come under criticism, and faced problems itself, as a result of exempting not only its own forces but also non-state contractees (including PMCs/PSCs) from any but its own jurisdiction. During 2008 US/Iraqi negotiations on a new SOFA for US forces have also become hung up on this issue.

[18] Since NATO forces were first deployed in the Former Yugoslavia in the 1990s, there has been a long-running debate over whether and how these forces should help in tracking down war criminals.

This traditional type of peace-keeping or peace-making intervention does not, however, necessarily imply an attempt to make or enforce local law. It is a catalytic input designed to (re-)create the conditions where others can safely and effectively start doing those things, either on the basis of the status quo ante or through a process of new creation and reform. In the interests of the latter, peace missions often include, or even consist entirely of, the import of foreign personnel to (re)train and (re-)equip the local armed forces, police, border guards, intelligence services, prison workers, judicial personnel and so forth: but their mandates usually avoid the trainers directly exercising the functions they are training for, or provide for them to work side-by-side with the locals.[19] (More on this below, in the post-conflict context.)

For examples of interveners exercising more direct and distinct legal functions it is necessary to look to two other, more 'intrusive' models of intervention that have been repeated in recent years: the formal designation of the foreign interveners as an occupying force—which has been the status of US and British forces in Iraq under UNSC Resolution 1483 of 22 May 2003;[20] and the establishment of an international administrative authority, as in Kosovo since the UN civilian mission UNMIK was created by UNSCR 1244 in June 1999.[21] Under both these models, an external—national, plurinational or international—authority fills the legal vacuum directly, at least in the fields seen as vital for suppressing violence, reasserting order, and providing a legal framework for the intervener's own operations.[22] It can do this in two different ways: defining, administering and enforcing the law through its own personnel (including foreign policemen acting in 'executive' mode);[23] and/or appointing local personnel for the job while keeping the authority to regulate

---

[19] Both the UN and the EU have carried out several missions where their contribution consisted entirely of police training; the EU has also designed missions focused on reform of law and justice (Georgia) and border monitoring (Moldova/Ukraine, Gaza Strip).

[20] This Resolution also recognized the US- and UK-established Coalition Provisional Authority as taking over normal government duties.

[21] A shorter-lived example was UNMISET in East Timor, established in 2005 by UNSCR 1410.

[22] Other priority tasks can be creating a legal framework for new elections and constitution-making; enactments on individual and group rights; and pressing economic matters such as the status of debts and claims, handling of state property, trade and customs regulations, aviation agreements etc.

[23] On this see Renata Dwan (ed.), 'Executive Policing: Enforcing the Law in Peace Operations', *SIPRI Research Report no. 16*, London: Oxford University Press, 2002.

and monitor their actions. These approaches are commonly combined with the kind of training and restructuring programmes mentioned above, which should eventually 'localize' the execution of, and then full responsibility for, crucial security- and law-related functions.

Under all these scenarios the question arises of what law is being enforced. In the simplest case the pre-conflict law of the local state can still be applied, but there are obvious difficulties about foreign personnel having to interpret and enforce it. So long as insecure conditions call for the military to take on enforcement roles, they are likely to be short of relevant experience, and even paramilitary and police personnel who are trained for this function may struggle in an alien environment. A headache in many multinational police or justice-focused missions is that the participants from different nations have widely varying legal traditions and experience.[24]

Most often, however, the law itself is not a given because local and international plans for a lasting settlement include revising some or all parts of it, from large constitutional features down to individual matters like gender rights. Doing this through channels and processes that are themselves legal takes time—for instance, waiting for the convocation of a new parliament—and so there is often a gap to be filled by provisional ordinances issued by the occupying authority/international administration, by an internationally recognized provisional government, or by some combination. When foreigners do (or guide) the drafting, they must decide whether to follow an available international norm (for example, a UN document), or the intervener's own law, or a good model available in the same region, or something *sui generis*. The obvious issues (in the present context) are whether the chosen model will correctly identify and 'grip' the VNSA challenges of the given territory; whether it gains support and understanding from the local actors (including benign NSAs) whose help it needs; and whether it facilitates transition to the 'normal', fully 'localized' phase.

*During and after a settlement.* The process of making peace—which may have several stages from ceasefire through creation of a negotiating framework to promulgation of a full settlement—is the keystone in the arc of re-legalization as defined above. It determines not only the new legal order in the territory but also who its recognized 'owners' are. Those who join an agreement and undertake to implement it are thereby coming within the law, regardless of

---

[24] These variations include some important and visible features such as whether police should be armed or not.

former status. They gain local/international recognition and protection—often including explicit amnesty—either as part of the new central authority or as legally recognized non-governmental actors (opposition parties, provincial/tribal leaders, social and religious movements etc). The price they pay typically includes renouncing unlawful/unauthorized violence, respect for the law generally and for others' rights, and compliance with basic international obligations. Some or all of these may be subject to international monitoring. When, as so often recently, the end of the conflict entails creation of more than one sovereign state on the territory of the old one, the settlement must also address the relations between the new entities.

For those who are inside this process it is the single most powerful way of 'migrating' out of VNSA status into a fully legal order. Often in twentieth century decolonization people became internationally respected national leaders after indulging in outright terrorist behaviour—and still more, armed violence—in the pre-independence conflict. When the transformation is less complete and successful, it can be because of something in the new leaders' own behaviour (including both disrespect for the law and incompetence); poor design and incompleteness of the agreement itself; failure to achieve the necessary minimum of physical control before starting to rebuild; and/or deliberate sabotage by 'spoiler' and 'splinter' groups, perhaps abetted by powers abroad.[25] A crucial judgement is about whom to bring into the settlement and whom to leave out, and historical experience suggests that excluding too many former VNSAs—even when there are strong legal and moral grounds for it—makes a new order both more contentious and more fragile from the start.

Recognition of these problems has prompted new international thinking in recent years on how to bolster the main design of a peace-building process with measures specifically aimed at mastering VNSA problems. Three main elements are relevant to most locations and will ideally be combined and coordinated, drawing on outside help initially but aiming for full 'localization' within a finite period:

(1) *Legalization of the military*: the aim here is to end up with a single set of armed forces under government control, able to defend the country (possibly

---

[25] For many detailed examples of conflict persistence due to proliferation of parties, incomplete settlements, 'spoilers' etc., see Renata Dwan and Micaela Gustavsson, 'Major Armed Conflicts', in *SIPRI Yearbook 2004: Armaments, Disarmament and International Security*, Oxford 2004. Text available at http://www.sipri.org/contents/conflict/SIPRI%20 Yearbook%202004/document_view.

in alliance with neighbours) and behaving lawfully themselves. This normally entails a Disarmament, Demobilization and Reintegration (DDR) programme to return excess combatants (of all kinds) to civil life, often linked with an amnesty for the rank-and-file and/or rewards for surrendering weapons. DDR can go wrong when enough civilian jobs cannot be found, disarmament is not thorough (because illegal arms trafficking continues, because some groups escape abroad, or for other reasons), payments to ex-soldiers are given in a way that encourages further disorder,[26] groups like child and women soldiers are ignored or their special requirements overlooked, and so forth.[27] It is also an incomplete solution if measures are not taken at the same time to build up the legitimate army, because the gap will be filled either by partisan militias (consider what happened in Iraq) or by PMCs/PSCs, or by obliging foreign peacekeepers to stay for too long.

(2) *General security sector reform (SSR):*[28] this encompasses the definition of a new defence concept and military establishment but also much more: adequate provision for border control and customs, paramilitary (if relevant) and police forces, intelligence services, appropriate laws on security-related behaviour (including the carrying of weapons and the regulation of association and protest) and a court system to execute them, prisons, international agreements on aspects closely related to effective justice like extradition, an export control regime for weapons and other strategic items, and measures to carry out universally or locally relevant international obligations, for example on non-proliferation, money-laundering, or illegal migration. In the present context a key task of SSR is to define what roles, if any, NSAs will henceforth legitimately play in the security process and how any behaviour beyond those limits will be punished. For example, at least in the Western understanding,[29] SSR should include checks and balances such as parliamentary oversight and transparency aimed at 'guarding the guardians', where there are roles also for academics and NGOs.

---

[26] For example, giving money for guns has led to people smuggling in more guns to get more money, or the ex-soldiers have just squandered the cash.

[27] Several such cases arising during UN missions are dissected in Heiner Hänggi and Vincenza Scherrer (eds), *Security Sector Reform and UN Integrated Missions: Experience from Burundi, the Democratic Republic of Congo, Haiti, and Kosovo*, Geneva Centre for Democratic Control of Armed Forces (DCAF), 2007.

[28] For a rich quarry of material on SSR see the five yearbooks (2003–7) of DCAF (see note 27), all downloadable at http://www.dcaf.ch/publications/kms/series_yearbooks.cfm?nav1=5&nav2=5.

[29] See e.g. Philipp Fluri and David Spence (eds), *The European Union and Security Sector Reform*, London: John Harper Publishing. 2008.

(3) *Post-conflict justice*:[30] the best-known purpose of this is to punish war crimes and other mass atrocities (on all sides) as a way both of reasserting the rule of law and deterring repetitions, but it also embraces 'truth and reconciliation' processes aiming at confession and catharsis more than punishment, and possibly the handling of damages and compensation, restitution of property, and so forth. War crimes as such may be handled by special national courts, by referral to the International Criminal Court (ICC), or by a 'mixed' model combining local and foreign judges. The choice of methods is a delicate matter on which it is prudent to defer to local feeling and circumstances: for instance, methods focused on atonement are less suited to situations with wrongdoing on all sides, and where state fracture has occurred the criminal process quickly takes on diplomatic overtones that can aggravate rather than reduce post-conflict frictions. Processes should be designed to 'catch' as many types of non-state actor as possible: a radio station owner has already been punished for messages of hate in Rwanda, and it is highly desirable (if difficult) to include private company personnel.

Local needs may call for other particular efforts, for instance to combat local and/or international terrorism that persists independently of, or as a mutation of, earlier armed violence. Minimizing terrorist damage to the population is genuinely a test of a new government's grip and legitimacy; but there are pitfalls if the whole SSR process becomes skewed towards tough anti-terrorist measures, or the new state is pushed too far this way by its outside backers—with a risk in both cases of neglecting other important aspects of internal security and undue damage to civil rights.[31] Reasserting central authority in matters of economic regulation, trade, customs, taxation and property rights becomes more crucial when non-state economic actors, local and external, have been heavily implicated in violence and/or trafficking. If the state has an arms industry or produces sensitive strategic materials, early action is needed to establish and enforce export controls designed to include non-state actors—and so on. All this said, it is worth repeating that the most

[30] See Annika Hansen and Sharon Wiharta, *The Transition to a Just Order: Establishing Local Ownership after Conflict, A Practitioner's Guide*, FBA Handbook no. 2, Stockholm: Folke Bernadotte Academy, 2007; and by the same authors, *The Transition to a Just Order: Establishing Local Ownership after Conflict, A Policy Report*, FBA Research Report no. 4, Stockholm: Folke Bernadotte Academy, 2007.

[31] Ekaterina Stepanova, *Anti-terrorism and Peace-Building During and after Conflict*, SIPRI Policy Paper No. 2 of 2003, text at http://www.sipri.org/contents/conflict/Publications1.html.

important keys to success in all such tasks are linked to the basic legitimacy and authority (not just legality) of the new regime, which in turn rest on many political, economic, social or cultural factors and perhaps, these days, almost as much on external as on domestic choices.

## 'Internationalization' of legal remedies

Applying international laws within conflict situations can serve numerous purposes: to guide and standardize action by the authorities (including during an SSR phase), to facilitate international cooperation where the negative phenomena spread beyond national territories, to protect against abuses by the 'winners', and—in cases where enforcement is possible outside national borders—to make up for the powerlessness or unwillingness of national legal authorities to grasp the relevant problems. Most of the examples following here are about how such approaches can be used against VNSAs, but some refer also to protecting the rights of non-state players.

As discussed above, the precise applicability of various kinds of international law depends first of all on the legal classification of a situation where VNSAs are active. If it meets the legal criteria for definition as an armed conflict, then international humanitarian law (IHL) is applicable to all parties. If not, then international laws of human rights will be applicable to define mainly what can be done by the state and those acting under its direct authorization. The third relevant system is international criminal law, since some VNSA actions such as drug trafficking, piracy, or attacks on internationally protected persons or property will either fall under universal jurisdiction or be subject to specific agreements for inter-state cooperation.

*Conflicts between states.* In international armed conflict (a war between two or more states), which is very rare today, VNSAs in a legal sense have only a marginal role to play. They will probably not be able to qualify for the status of combatant, since they will not be part of the armed forces nor meet the criteria set up in the 1949 Third Geneva Convention or the first Additional Protocol negotiated to that Convention in 1977[32] of responsible leadership, having a fixed distinctive sign recognizable at a distance,[33] carrying arms openly, and carrying out operations in accordance with the laws and customs

---

[32] Additional Protocols 1 and 2 cover respectively the protection of victims of international, and of non-international, armed conflicts.

[33] Not needed for Additional Protocol 1.

of war. The two possible exceptions could be rebels/insurgents fighting against an occupying power, and a pro-government militia fighting on behalf of its government against the armed forces of the other state. If VNSAs do not qualify for the status of combatants they should be defined as civilians, which makes it illegal for them to directly participate in the armed operations—and they can be punished for this.

The case of Private Military Companies comes up again in this context. PMCs deliver services either to private firms or under governmental contract, to the armed forces for example. In the former case they will be designated as civilians—even if they do 'harder' security jobs such as guarding a civilian facility or person against attacks—but will of course have the universal right to use force in self-defence if under attack. If they go beyond this in their operations and take active part in the conflict, they lose all protection as civilians, can be actively targeted, and can also be charged under the law.

The status of PMCs contracted by the armed forces depends on what they are doing. If they perform unarmed support tasks such as cleaning services, vehicle repair or providing food, they can fall under the legal category of 'civilians accompanying the armed forces'. As civilians they cannot be legally targeted—though they may suffer collateral damage if located close to a military target—but they still have the right to prisoner-of-war (POW) status if captured. If their work involves directly supporting and taking part in the military operation, for example by providing armed escorts for military logistical convoys or guarding military installations, then they should either be integrated into the armed forces or in other ways meet the criteria set in the Third Geneva Convention—something that has rarely happened in practice.

When looking at recent problems in Iraq, it is fair to note that most of the work done by PMCs for the US military has been of the first, clearly civilian kind. However, some PMCs have also worked at collecting and analyzing intelligence for military commanders, which could be viewed as a kind of direct participation in the hostilities and thus not suitable for civilians. It is arguably in such scenarios, where PMC personnel become involved in the actual hostilities but are not nationals of the commissioning state and are not included in its armed forces, that they come closest to the technical definition of a 'mercenary'.[34]

---

[34] It is notorious that international laws penalizing mercenarism have been almost impossible to apply, because (without going into details) the criteria in the legal definition of a mercenary in article 47 of Additional Protocol 1–which in any case applies only to an international armed conflict—are set so high that it is very hard to 'make them stick' on

*'Laws of war' in an internal conflict.* It is safe to say, however, that the overwhelming majority of VNSA conflict roles are played out in the context of an internal armed conflict. A striking difference here from an international armed conflict concerns the status of the parties. When Common Article 3 of the 1949 Geneva Conventions was written in the late 1940s, and again during the preparation of Additional Protocol 2 (1977),[35] the drafters took the view that the anti-state party in an internal armed conflict (insurgents, rebels, etc.) was illegal and should not be recognized. Hence, while there are norms on basic humanitarian protection for victims of the conflict (civilians, wounded, prisoners), the definitions of combatants and POWs—who have certain rights regardless of the side they fight on—do not exist. Without such special status, persons on the rebel side may in principle be prosecuted under national law for the very fact of participating in the armed conflict.

This situation is of course a disincentive when trying to attract rebels/insurgents to abide by the laws of war themselves, or to negotiate a peace agreement, and it helps reinforce the remark made in the last section (apropos of amnesties and 'inclusive' settlements) that sometimes bypassing the law is the price of a positive NSA solution. As an example, Colombia in the 1990s decided that captured rebels would still in effect enjoy a POW status and should not be prosecuted just for fighting. However, this was an exception and the general rule is one of a marked legal asymmetry between fighters connected or not connected with the state authorities. Members of a pro-government militia also technically lack combatant status, but there is little risk they will be brought to court by the government for taking part in hostilities. They can however open themselves to prosecution—as is true of all VNSAs—if they commit war crimes such as directly targeting civilians, murder, torture, rape and plunder. Since these crimes are under so-called universal jurisdiction, all states can prosecute and deliver sentence for them, as can an international tribunal such as the International Criminal Court (provided it has jurisdiction in the given time and place).[36] If these crimes are committed by persons meeting the definition of terrorists they can also be prosecuted in that connection.

---

any individual. There is a saying that if someone is shot for being a mercenary, then his lawyer should be shot with him for incompetence, and reading article 47 one can understand this.

[35] See note 32.

[36] See http://untreaty.un.org/ for information on the ICC and other international tribunals.

With regard to rules on means of warfare—weapons and techniques—in an internal armed conflict, it is generally agreed that under humanitarian law the rules which the state has signed up to internationally are applicable to its territory and also binding for non-state actors in the same territory. This means that all parties in such a conflict should refrain from using weapons banned under customary international law, such as dum-dum bullets and chemical and biological weapons, and others banned by specific treaties the state is party to, such as incendiary weapons, landmines and booby-traps (covered by the Convention on certain Conventional Weapons, CCW)[37] or anti-personnel mines (under the Ottawa Convention).[38]

An interesting recent development in this context is the effort to get non-state actors to 'sign on' to international norms on weapons. The NGO Geneva Call[39] has persuaded VNSAs in places such as Burma/Myanmar, India and Iran to declare that they will no longer use mines in their operations and accept external monitoring to ensure that this undertaking is not violated. Geneva Call aims to gradually broaden the efforts to more VNSAs and more aspects of humanitarian law. This is a helpful and important way of addressing the reality of non-state roles in present-day conflicts, but—as noted—the legal non-recognition of such actors in internal conflicts remains a stumbling-block to engaging them fully.

*Human rights law.* The second set of relevant international legal norms concerns human rights, which traditionally protect the individual or the group against the state. These norms set the framework for national legislation and decisions, and a state may be called on to defend its actions before monitoring organs such as commissions, committees and courts of international and regional organizations. If a state faces a public emergency threatening its existence it may derogate some (not all) of the rights; but this must take place in accordance with certain procedures and other states' parties to the human rights treaties must be informed. Thus, there are human rights norms applicable both in times of civil emergency and during an armed conflict.

[37] Full title: Convention on Prohibitions or Restrictions on the Use of Certain Conventional Weapons which may be deemed to be Excessively Injurious or have Indiscriminate Effects, opened for signature 1981.

[38] Also known (for short) as the APM Convention, opened for signature 1997.

[39] See http://www.genevacall.org and, for a more general discussion, 'Engaging Non-state Armed Groups', *UNIDIR Disarmament Forum* no 1/2008, Geneva May 2008 (http://www.unidir.org).

On the traditional view that human rights are defences against state interference, abuses by VNSAs could not be so classified and would have to be treated instead under—for instance—criminal law (as below). However there are cases from Latin America where states have been seen as responsible for the actions of pro-government militias (death squads), the argument being that the state, by unleashing them, has failed in its duty to ensure the security of the individual.[40] In the last few years there has also been an increasing effort by some legal scholars to argue that human rights belong to everybody and should also be respected by everybody. Under this argument it would be possible for other VNSAs besides pro-government militias to be considered in violation of human rights norms, and moving in that direction could be seen as an adjustment to the modern realities of conflict along the same lines as the developments discussed above in IHL. However, at present this appears to be more an argument for new law than a plausible interpretation of the old.

*International criminal law.* Crimes committed during conflict that invoke international criminal law can be divided into crimes that come under universal jurisdiction, which all states under customary international law can prosecute and sentence for, wherever they occur; crimes that are 'internationalized' by a treaty whereby states agrees to cooperate, criminalize the act and either prosecute or extradite if another state demands this; and crimes where the state may prosecute and sentence on account of some connection to the state.

Crimes under universal jurisdiction that may be committed by VNSAs include some already mentioned—war crimes and piracy—to which genocide[41] and crimes against humanity may now be added. The legal criteria for establishing intent to commit genocide are problematic and will be no easier to apply to VNSA activities. However, the category of 'crimes against humanity' is easier to make stick, and since it is now also applicable in times of peace, or when IHL does not apply, it can be used to penalize widespread and systematic violations of human rights so long as these can be shown to be part of a overall plan.

With regard to terrorism, there are 13 international legal conventions describing different types of terrorism (including hijacking, bombing of planes

---

[40] In principle the same case could be made about government use of a PMC that results in (avoidable) damage to human rights.

[41] Outlawed by a UN Convention adopted in December 1948.

or ships, attacking diplomats, financing of terrorism), and states party to the treaties have agreed to cooperate and criminalize these actions, and either prosecute or extradite the offenders.[42] UNSC Resolution 1373, mentioned above, instructs all states to criminalize and prevent certain terrorism-related activities and to ratify the existing international legal frameworks. International drug trafficking has since 1988 come under a similar international legal framework whereby states will cooperate and prosecute or extradite offenders.[43] An interesting feature of this convention is the mechanisms for exchanging information, and for seeking permission from a flag state to conduct a search and visit on a ship. More recently, states seeking to put the Proliferation Security Initiative (PSI)[44] on a more secure legal footing have promoted an international maritime convention allowing ship searches and visits under certain conditions in order to find WMD and WMD-related technologies in transit.

As noted above, UNSC Resolution 1540 already establishes general standards for prohibiting non-authorized ownership of WMD and WMD-related dual-use goods, and these norms are designed to be enforced above all against possible non-state offenders. In current negotiations at the UN on a universal Arms Trade Treaty (ATT), one of the most debated points has been whether the norms states are asked to observe should include a blanket prohibition on arms transfers to non-state end-users.[45] For the future, similar proposals may be expected regarding other transnational offences likely to occur in conflict conditions, such as human trafficking.

## Final reflections

The lesson of this chapter is that where lawlessness and weak or absent law have been part of a non-state problem—as they almost always are—many of the *prima facie* remedies involve using and applying or creating new kinds of

---

[42] See http://untreaty.un.org/English/Terrorism.asp.

[43] UN Convention on Narcotic Drugs and Psychotropic Substances, see http://unodc.un.or.th/convention/

[44] The PSI was launched by the USA in 2003 to organize inter-state cooperation in various shipping- and transport-related parts of the WMD anti-proliferation effort, but was deliberately not law-based or institutionalized. See Christer Ahlström, 'The Proliferation Security Initiative: International Law Aspects of the Statement of Interdiction Principles', in *SIPRI Yearbook 2005*, Oxford: Oxford University Press, 2005.

[45] Paul Holtom and Siemon T Wezeman, 'Towards an Arms Trade Treaty', *SIPRI Yearbook 2007*, Oxford: Oxford University Press, 2007.

law in response. For this to work in practice, the law must be accompanied by authority, legitimacy, maximum public consent, and capacity to enforce. Correct political choices and behaviour can achieve much in this context but there is no escape from the need also to apply—perhaps considerable—material resources.

Resource gaps as much as local incompatibilities explain why international intervention and support become features of almost all contemporary conflicts. External 'pump-priming' is one way to secure the rapid material changes that are often needed, most obviously to stop the killing and humanitarian distress, but also to tip the resource balance back towards the central authority from the many who will have profited from a 'war economy'. To avoid fresh distortions and abuse, it is clearly desirable that funding for the key elements of security, political and legal transformation should be channelled through an international organization or, at least, transparently coordinated among national donors. Even the best-intentioned aid givers can hamper rebuilding when they tie diverging sets of norms and conditions to their contributions, or employ too few safeguards against malpractice and corruption. However, perhaps the single most important thing that interveners can do is to create the conditions for the fastest and most effective possible 'localization' of those central functions most intimately linked to sovereignty—including the monopoly of force. Lack of local 'ownership' in SSR and in rebuilding generally has increasingly often been diagnosed as a reason for local state and non-state actors alike continuing to indulge in violence (since they do not pay for the consequences) or, conversely, becoming aid-dependent and over-passive in addressing their own problems.[46]

At the same time, in the twenty-first century rebuilding a state must mean fitting it to survive in and play a part in the ongoing process of globalization. Since so many aspects of the VNSA challenge—arms trafficking, criminal finance, illegal migration and certain kinds of terrorism—are linked with transnational processes and often subject to international law as well, a new/restored legal authority should be encouraged to find solutions from global best practice rather than reinventing the wheel. External partners, when designing legal solutions for a state's unique internal problems, often forget to offer it what could be relatively easy 'fixes' for meeting its external obligations on issues like WMD proliferation, money-laundering or epidemic reporting. (From now on, assistance in building a climate change policy must be added

---

[46] See Hansen and Wiharta, as note 30 above.

to the checklist!) A successful internationalizing strategy will also mobilize the kinds of well-intentioned NSAs—businesspeople, networked NGOs, academics or even Internet users—who, as already noted, can often help (re-) build healthy external ties.

A problem that cannot be ignored, given the stress that has been placed above on political, psychological and cultural conditions for solving the VNSA challenge, is that the outer world itself is divided along regional, cultural and other lines on what it regards as good internal and external security behaviour. If Western interveners try to impose their own undiluted model on a recovering state in another region, it may not only fail to take root but also set the nation at odds with its neighbours. The West should learn the lesson of its own twentieth century experience, when success in mastering both inter- and intra-state conflicts came most easily to nations embraced by regional organizations—NATO and the EU. Similar stories exist outside Europe in South-East Asia (integration of Vietnam, Laos, Cambodia and potentially Burma) and in Africa, especially the Southern sub-region. While intervention dominated by close neighbours and coloured by their interests also has its pitfalls, it is still a good general rule that organizations and other outside interveners should look first for useful models on the control of VNSA problems—both national and transnational—in the target country's near neighbours.

Overall, if following the paths of law is rarely easy (or cheap), a law-based and law-friendly approach can claim two major advantages in post-twentieth century conditions. First, an individually applicable law can reach down and out to problematic non-state actors, including 'unknown unknown' threats, in ways that physical coercive action (or executive action more generally) never can. Secondly, the international or harmonized aspect of law is one of the better answers to the quandary of respecting national specificity, ownership and sovereignty while building defences against both transnational threats and state aggression. The compromise lies in letting an international standard define the parameters over which no state—not even the mightiest—has discretion, while the recognized state authority keeps the right to enforce the standard within its own jurisdiction and to find its own answers for any aspects not so defined.

As mentioned at the start of this text, the roles of non-state actors in security are not limited to conflict and armed violence. In fields like transport security, critical infrastructure protection, accident and emergency response, energy security and environmental security—but also the production of medicinal drugs for epidemics—the processes of privatization and globalization have left the private business sector often standing in society's front line of defence. Business operators also become part of the problem when they collude with criminals and terrorists, or carry on illicit dealing in the various brands of dangerous goods.[47] NGOs and civil society networks are well known as positive influences in security (monitoring the authorities or playing humanitarian functions themselves), but the methods of non-state association can also be used for conspiratorial purposes and the encouragement of hate crimes. Computer hackers and cyber-saboteurs can bring most security-relevant functions of civilized society to a halt. If legal methods have a role to play, even in conflict settings where law often faces its greatest handicaps, they are *a fortiori* indispensable for regulating, guiding and where necessary bringing to book all the corporate, group and individual actions involved in these different 'peace-time' dimensions. One reason for stressing this point at the close is that the better the law can do its job vis-à-vis non-state actors generally, the less risk there should be of conflicts breaking out in the first place, and the less chance of an escalation in inhumanity and destructiveness when they do.

[47] On these aspects see Alyson JK Bailes, 'A "New Deal" between State and Market', in *Denationalization of Defence: Convergence and Divesity*, Øyvind Østerud and Janne H Matláry (eds.), Aldershot: Ashgate, 2007; and for more on the issue, see Alan Bryden and Marina Caparini (eds.), *Private Actors and Security Governance*, DCAF yearbook 2006.

# INDEX